LAROUSSE
PARIS

I am to be taken back home
as a souvenir of your stay
at les Rives de Notre-Dame.

Paris, December 2002

Editorial director
Marie-Pierre Levallois

Senior editors
Édith Ybert, Anne Luthaud

Proofreading
Annick Valade, Chantal Barbot,
Henri Goldszal, Françoise Mousnier,
Julien Ringuet

Art director
Emmanuel Chaspoul
with
Olivier Caldéron,
Martine Debrais, Delphine Jacquot

Graphic design
Daniel Leprince

Picture researchers
Nathalie Bocher-Lenoir,
Nane Dujour, Nanon Gardin

Production manager
Annie Botrel

Maps
Édigraphie

Index
Marie-Thérèse Ménager

English translation
Translate-A-Book, Oxford, England

Consultant
Martyn Back

Written by

Béatrice de Andia
DÉLÉGUÉE GÉNÉRALE À L'ACTION ARTISTIQUE DE LA VILLE DE PARIS

Myriam Bacha
DOCTORAL STUDENT IN ARCHITECTURAL HISTORY

Prof. Jean-Luc Chassel
UNIVERSITÉ PARIS X-NANTERRE

Xavier Chaumette
FASHION HISTORIAN, LECTURER AT PARSON'S SCHOOL, PARIS
AND FIDM LOS ANGELES

Thérèse de Cherisey
JOURNALIST AND SOCIOLOGIST, WRITER OF GUIDEBOOKS AND CD-ROMS

Bertrand Dreyfuss,
HISTORIAN OF PARIS, WRITER OF GUIDEBOOKS

Nanon Gardin
PICTURE RESEARCHER, ARCHIVIST

Marie Girault
ART HISTORIAN AND JOURNALIST

Renée Grimaud
WRITER OF GUIDEBOOKS AND ART BOOKS

Loïc Jacob,
DOCTORAL STUDENT AT UNIVERSITÉ PARIS X-NANTERRE

Georgina Letourmy
DOCTORAL STUDENT IN ART HISTORY

Marie-Thérèse Ménager
GEOGRAPHER

Françoise Monnin
ART HISTORIAN AND JOURNALIST

Denis Montagnon
ART HISTORIAN, WRITER OF GUIDEBOOKS ON PARIS AND ART BOOKS

Rafaël Pic
CHIEF EDITOR OF MUSÉART, WRITER OF BOOKS ON PARIS

Pierre Pinon
ARCHITECT AND HISTORIAN, RESEARCH DIRECTOR AT CNRS

Dr Simon Texier
LECTURER AT UNIVERSITÉ PARIS IV-SORBONNE

Claudine Zuzinec
ART HISTORIAN

with
Thérèse de Cherisey, Rupert Hasterok, Dominique Van Egroo

Acknowledgements

Mairie de Paris/Bibliothèque historique de la Ville de Paris/Cité de la Musique LA VILLETTE/Comédie-Française/Groupe hospitalier Bichat-Claude Bernard/Groupe hospitalier Lariboisière-Fernand-Widal/Groupe hospitalier Necker-Enfants malades/Groupe hospitalier Pitié-Salpêtrière/Hôpital des Quinze-Vingts/Hôpital européen Georges-Pompidou/Hôpital Saint-Antoine/Hôpital Saint-Joseph/Hôpital Saint-Louis/Hôpital Tenon/Institut Curie/Institut du Monde Arabe/Musée Dapper/Marché du livre ancien et d'occasion/Musée Carnavalet/Moulin Rouge/Office du tourisme de la Ville de Paris/Olympia/Studio 28/Service des cimetières/Théâtre de la Bastille/Théâtre des Bouffes du nord/Théâtre des Bouffes-Parisiens/Théâtre de la Cartoucherie de Vincennes/Théâtre Marigny/Théâtre Silvia Monfort/Théâtre du Vieux-Colombier

AND

Monsieur Charelet, CIMETIÈRE DU PÈRE-LACHAISE/Nathalie Darzac, SERVICE COMMUNICATION INSTITUT DE FRANCE/Philippe François, RESPONSABLE DES DROITS D'AUTEUR AFFÉRANT À LA GRANDE ARCHE DE LA DÉFENSE/M. Habert, CHEF DU SERVICE COMMERCIAL, SOCIÉTÉ NOUVELLE D'EXPLOITATION DE LA TOUR EIFFEL/Mademoiselle Hayette, CENTRE SOCIO-CULTUREL DE LA RUE DE TANGER (19e)/Joël Huthwohl, BIBLIOTHÈQUE-MUSÉE DE LA COMÉDIE-FRANÇAISE/Josette Martinage, DOCUMENTALISTE À LA DIRECTION DE LA COMMUNICATION DE LA SNCF/Jean-Charles Petitpierre et Aurélia Keilany, SERVICE COMMUNICATION PARCS ET JARDINS DE LA MAIRIE DE PARIS/Monsieur Rais, DIRECTEUR DES AFFAIRES CULTURELLES DE LA GRANDE MOSQUÉE DE PARIS (Ve)/Bertrand Roger, cinémas MK2/Barbara Schlanger, ASSISTANTE DU GRAND RABBIN NATIONAL DE LA SYNAGOGUE DE LA VICTOIRE/Blanche Gardin et Nicolas Deconinck/Veronique Martin-Letournou et Marie Deschamps

Exclusive distribuor for Canada : Messageries ADP, 1751 Richardson, Montreal (Quebec)

ISBN 2-03-585012-6
Larousse, Paris

LAROUSSE
PARIS

With the support of

ACTION ARTISTIQUE

City of Paris

LAROUSSE

21 RUE DU MONTPARNASSE 75283 PARIS CEDEX 06

CONTENTS

FOREWORD

Victor Hugo said: «Paris is the anvil of fame», adding that « When Paris is ill, the whole world has a headache.»

Sacha Guitry wrote: « Being a Parisian is not about being born in Paris, but being reborn there; it's not about being in the city, but being part of it; it's not about living in Paris but making a living from Paris - for this is a city that brings both life and death. Being from Paris is like belonging to a club: Parisians are elected to life membership, and this is both a privilege and a responsibility. When Paris has done you the honor of admitting you, you must be at her beck and call, devoted to her every whim. Loving Paris makes us proud, for it becomes so necessary that we begin to believe that we may be of some use to her».

Paris is a mysterious and magical city, full of light and secrets. Here, the past takes youth by the hand and reveals its frivolous and tragic history.

The streets of Paris are alive with children smiling, women weeping , mothers calling, men rebelling...but they are also filled with songs, with stolen kisses on park benches, with lovers embracing in doorways. The greatest writers, poets, painters and photographers have immortalized the places where old memories live on. Some are preserved intact, others have been damaged over the passing years, but the soul of the city, like the swooping swallows in the 'faubourgs', still flutters in the gray-blue sky of the capital. Then suddenly the colours change, turning from pink to gray, from crimson to deep blue, and the clouds gently caress the Eiffel Tower before scudding off towards La Défense.

When I was a child in Algeria I used to listen to the radio: a Parisian station broadcasting advertisements and popular songs by Tino Rossi, Maurice Chevalier, Lucienne Boyer and Charles Trenet. I got the impression that in Paris nobody ever did any work, that people spent their time singing and dancing. Paris was a city of pleasure. Some years later, one November, I arrived at the Gare de l'Est and saw that the truth was very different : life in Paris was thankless, hard, cruel, but also full of charm and beauty. The Metro quickly became my friend, with its unique smell, its squealing train wheels, its slamming doors, its dusty, white-tiled walls, and its huge posters advertising the best shows in town.

In Paris there are gardens, trees, vast squares and tiny courtyards, proud, plush residential buildings, modern apartments with gawdy terraces, flower-covered balconies, rows of restaurants, bistrots smelling of coffee and wine, and cosy «bars-tabacs» where the regulars come to shoot the breeze. Montmartre has its Sacré-Cœur, the Arc de Triomphe stands proudly at the top of the Champs-Élysées, the most beautiful avenue in the world, and the Eiffel Tower, so unpopular when it was first built, has become the world's fiancée. The Opera and the Palais-Royal vie with each other in terms of elegance; Belleville and the Buttes-Chaumont jealously guard the remnants of the century; the place des Vosges remains aloof while the bateaux-mouches glide past the île Saint-Louis, Notre-Dame and the Conciergerie. We can stroll along the Seine with its riverside booksellers, daydream on the place de Furstenberg, amble through the Parc Montsouris or the streets of Pigalle, but Paris wasn't built in a day and to know her and love her as she deserves takes many hours of idle wandering.

This book, with its wealth of pictures, its historical accounts written by specialists and artists, and its rare photographs selected with great care and sensitivity, takes you into the heart of a city that is a symbol of both the human spirit and of freedom: the Tuileries Gardens, the Louvre, the marvels of the Orsay Museum...these treasures are open to all.

Taxi drivers are the barometers of daily life. They drive up and down the avenues grumbling, smiling, and listening to the radio. The little Sunday markets remind us of the provinces; Paris is made up of separate districts whose church bells ring out the passing hours.

In Paris, this proud metropolis convinced of its own greatness, being in love is a necessity. The city loves to offer up her treasures: her most beautiful evenings, her deepest nights. She is proud of the Concorde and the Bastille – she is never well-behaved, and her pride can sometimes turn to fury.

Paris is brave and generous. She loves her people, and they love her back. The great Parisian screen actress Arletty once said to me « My first mirror is the Seine ». She lived near the pont Mirabeau.

Jean-Claude BRIALY

PARIS
10 places to visit

PARIS THROUGH THE AGES

When the remains of wooden dugout canoes were discovered on the river bank at Bercy, it was realized that the history of Paris went back to the Neolithic period. Recently excavated sites are scattered along the banks of the Seine and its tributaries, along the river beds and cutoffs. The large number of these sites is an indication of how long it took to select the right place to build the future city of Paris.

Ile de la Cité: Gallo-Roman Lutetia

Given the task of conquering Gaul, Julius Caesar soon grasped the strategic and economic advantages of the Paris Basin, the place where east-west rivers were crossed by north-south land routes. From his account of the campaign, we know that Gallic people of the Parisii tribe had settled on one of the islands in the Seine. Their town, known as Lutetia, consisted of huts surrounded by fortified ramparts, and was only accessible by water. To land there, the Romans moved upstream, seized some boats on the River Marne, and then came downriver to the town, which they burnt down in 52 BC.

Caesar's army set up camp on the south bank of the Seine. They built a temple on top of the hill overlooking the river, and below it a forum; on the south side of the promontory they built an amphitheater (to the east) and splendid thermal baths (to the west). Houses appeared on the slopes of the hill, some facing south and with marvelous views. There was no wall around this settlement. The Pax Romana held the barbarians beyond its borders. The Ile de la Cité was occupied by adminis-trative buildings, and connected to the banks by two bridges firmly fixed to stone pillars. The main road ran south to Orléans and north to Saint-Denis and Belgium. Villas (like those discovered in Belleville) were built on the ring of hills overlooking Paris. The best-known temple, dedicated to the god Mars, was on the Butte Montmartre.

Paris never stopped growing from the time of the Roman invasion up to the Capetian era (942-1328). Recent archeological digs, undertaken by the Commission for Old Paris in the Latin Quarter and close to Notre-Dame, have uncovered much about Gallo-Roman Paris: it had narrow lanes, some of the houses were richly decorated with frescos and niches for lights, and were built above channels carrying water and heating. From the time of the first invasions, some of the population withdrew to the island, which was fortified by its first city wall. The Left Bank was gradually abandoned. Julian the Apostate, the Roman military governor, lived in the Lutetia garrison for three years; he had a palace on the Left Bank, and it was there in 360 that he learned he had been made Roman Emperor. The retreat to the Ile de la Cité became a necessity a century later, when the Huns arrived at the gates of Paris. Attila's troops were defeated by the Romans and the Visigoths in a battle near Châlons-sur-Marne in 451. Legend has it that a young woman from the provinces, the future Saint Geneviève, protected the people of Paris by preventing them from fleeing and making sure they received food. Today the remains of the saint are preserved in the middle of a crypt on the Hill of Sainte-Geneviève.

Early Middle Ages: Paris becomes Christian

In 481, Clovis, the founder of the Merovingian Dynasty, made Paris the center of his kingdom. His successors did not live there

1

2

much, but between them built two large basilicas: Saint-Etienne on the Ile de la Cité, and Saint-Martin-des-Champs to the north. The Carolingians moved away from Paris, which lost its importance. Times were hard. Invasion followed invasion, and damaging raids were common. In 885, the Normans, or Vikings, sailed up the Seine toward Burgundy, burning and pillaging as they went. They laid siege to Paris, which held out for 18 months. The forts guarding the Grand Pont and the Petit Pont went up in flames. Despite a terrible winter - the invaders used the iced-up river to reach its ramparts - the Normans did not manage to capture the Cité. In order to proceed upstream, they had to skirt round it, carrying their boats along the banks of a cutoff as far as Bercy and the Marne. Paris was defended and saved by Gozlin, its bishop, and by Charles III the Fat, king of France. Their palaces stood near the Cathedral of Saint-Etienne.

Royal capital of the Capetians

Peace gradually returned after the year 1000. The inhabitants of Paris cautiously settled on the edges of both banks. The churches of the Cité built chapels there which quickly became independent parishes. Monasteries were built around the impressive remains of Lutetia: Saint-Germain-des-Prés, Saint-Victor, and Saint-Marcel. They invited colleges from other countries to settle in the area. Gradually, the Latin Quarter grew up on the Left Bank; its university was founded by Robert de Sorbon in the middle of the 13th century.

The development of the Right Bank took a very different route. The land was flat, covered in marshes, and hemmed in by a cutoff from the Seine. This part of Paris became known as the Town, as compared to the Cité on the island, and the University

on the Left Bank. On the northern banks of the Seine, the Town swarmed with life. It was organized around the harbors built on either side of the Place de Grève. The harbors were controlled by the guilds, and specialized in such trades as timber, corn, fish, meat, and hay. The water-sellers directed and coordinated traffic on the river.

The Town became prosperous, and spread out alongside the waterways and highways. In the 9th century, the first Capetian kings, who succeeded the Carolingians, built a wall on the Right Bank to protect the suburbs and outlying areas; this ran in an arc from Saint-Gervais to Châtelet. As the Town grew richer and expanded at the end of the 12th century, King Philippe-Auguste had to build a third concentric wall. This one bore his name and curved out from the Porte Saint-Antoine to the Porte Saint-Martin and the Porte Saint-Denis, and back to the Seine. It enclosed Saint-Germain-l'Auxerrois, the two bridges and the forts guarding them. The Louvre fortress was built outside the walls to protect Paris from invasion along the river. On the Left Bank, the University district was surrounded by fortifications. These ran in a semicircle from Porte Saint-Bernard to the Tour de Nesle via the Porte Saint-Jacques and the Porte Saint-Michel. Once the city's safety was assured, churches and palaces grew up along the river banks, and on the island work was stepped up on the construction of Notre-Dame, which Abbot Suger had begun in 1163. The cathedral, with its fine slender vaults, wonderful sculptures and stained-glass windows, became one of the centers of Christianity.

In the middle of the 13th century, King Saint Louis built the

1. The "Three Dignitaries" map of Paris attributed to Braun (about 1530)
This is one of the seven known maps of Paris dating from the Ancien Régime. Here you can see the wall of Philippe-Auguste and the larger one built by Charles V, which reflects the growth of the city in the 15th century, especially on the Right Bank, the principal area for trades and craft workers.

2. *View of Paris and Arrival of Louis II of Anjou* (miniature from the *Chronicles of Jehan Froissart*, 15th century)
At the beginning of the 15th century, Paris was flourishing thanks to the wise policies of Charles V. Behind the recently built ramparts are, from left to right: the Temple, the Abbey of Saint-Martin-des-Champs, the Church of Saint-Jacques-de-la-Boucherie, Notre-Dame, and the Sainte-Chapelle, with, hidden behind the Porte Saint-Denis, the Abbey of Saint-Germain-des-Prés.

3. First seal of the Guild of Water-sellers (1210)
From the 12th century, the town council of Paris used a boat on its seal and coat of arms, and the motto "Fluctuat nec mergitur" (It sails and does not sink) acknowledging the powerful Guild of Boatmen, which controlled and co-ordinated trade on the river between Paris and Mantes before it took on wider municipal responsibilities.

Sainte-Chapelle and set up his Parliament in the middle of the royal palace in the Cité. The Town, which was expanding all the time, was divided into sections by two major north-south roads. To the east was Rue Saint-Martin, which connected with Rue Saint-Jacques on the Left Bank, and to the west Rue Saint-Denis, which continued across the river along Rue de la Harpe. The two were joined by fragile bridges consisting of stone pillars and a timber roadway; each of these had two rows of houses on them. Prosperity continued under Philip the Fair, who at the beginning of the 14th century encouraged the development of a new class of people: the bourgeoisie. Some 50 patrician families of financiers and successful merchants built substantial fortunes. Their houses rivaled those of the princes and feudal grandees. At that time, Paris had about 210,000 inhabitants and for several years was the largest city in Europe.

The Hundred Years' War and urban development under Charles V

The Hundred Years' War, and the epidemics which followed it, were the darkest hours in the history of Paris. Under the first Valois monarchs (14th to 16th century), invasions from England came as far as the gates of the capital. The people living in the suburbs were terrified and moved back into the city. They found refuge in houses emptied by the Black Death which, in 1349, had killed off half the population. After the defeat of John II the Good, the French king, at Poitiers and his imprisonment in London, Paris rebelled. Etienne Marcel, the influential and powerful provost of the merchants of Paris from 1355 and 1358, fueled the people's discontent. In an attempt to overthrow the Valois, he tried to replace them with the King of Navarre. With the support of a bourgeois group, Marcel set about establishing a Free Town, governed like those of Florence and Venice, Bruges and Ghent. However, lacking both money and an army, he had to appeal to English mercenaries. When the people of Paris discovered he was betraying them, they rebelled, expelling the King of Navarre and throwing the remains of Etienne Marcel, assassinated by a supporter of the young King Charles V, from the top of the city wall.

The royal armies were skilfully led by Constable du Guesclin, and reconquered most of the kingdom. The monarch's authority was reinforced when he located his administrative institutions in Paris, which then became the permanent center of government. Life at court was cultivated and elegant, attracting the greatest writers, philosophers, and artists in Europe. Once he had secured the safety of Paris by building a fourth defensive wall, which doubled the city's size, Charles V launched a major building program. He restored the Palais de la Cité, the Louvre, the Hôtel Saint-Pol (his favorite residence), and most of all Vincennes, whose nine towers overlooked a game forest and embodied the medieval vision of an ideal city. He was well versed in literature, and had the authors of Classical Greece and Rome translated into French. In the Falconry Tower at the Louvre, he kept his collections of magnificent illuminated manuscripts and gold artifacts. He was a lover of nature, and used plant designs to decorate buildings, sculptures and paintings, tapestries, and objets d'art. Around his palace he laid out gardens; the one at Saint-Pol had a menagerie with lions, aviaries with rare birds, and deer left free to roam.

During the Regency of his son Charles VI - whose madness soon became apparent - power was weakened and divided between rival princes. The people rebelled several times, and even killed each other during the civil war which set the Armagnacs against the Burgundians.

The English took advantage of the chaos. After their victory at Agincourt in 1415, they forced the French to sign the Treaty of Troyes which handed them the crown of France and a large part of the kingdom. The Lancastrians quickly seized Paris, and the young Henry V was crowned in Notre-Dame. His uncle, the Duke of Bedford, reigned over the capital for nearly 20 years. The fate of Paris looked grim. Joan of Arc failed to take Paris. Thanks to her, Charles VII was crowned in Rheims, but set up his court on the banks of the Loire. Only in 1436 did he reconquer Paris and his kingdom.

Paris neglected: the Wars of Religion

The kingdom emerged strongly from its long crisis, and enjoyed an artistic rebirth. François I (1515-47) attracted Leonardo da Vinci to Amboise, and at Fontainebleau he commissioned frescos from Primaticcio. But Paris remained medieval at a time when Tours and Blois flourished under the influence of the Italian Renaissance. The great churches built at that time reveal the cultural climate: Saint-Germain-l'Auxerrois and Saint-Gervais, Saint-Eustache and Saint-Etienne-du-Mont were all a blend of the Gothic and Renaissance styles.

In the 16th century, the reigns of the last Valois kings were nonetheless marked by a number of improvements. King Henri II of France and his sons transformed the Louvre, where Pierre Lescot and Jacques Androuet built the Cour Carrée. The queen, Catherine de Médicis, commissioned Philibert de l'Orme to build the Tuileries Palace and Gardens.

1. *Murder of Etienne Marcel* (Simon and Jean Maillart, 15th century)
Following the defeat at Poitiers and the imprisonment of King John II the Good in London, the merchants' provost Etienne Marcel tried to replace the Valois dynasty with the princes of Navarre and establish a regime in Paris on the model of the Free Towns of Italy and Flanders. However, he was rejected by his family and the loyalists, and his body was thrown from the top of the city walls.

2. View of Paris, the Ile de la Cité and the death of King Clothaire (miniature by Jean Fouquet in *The Chronicles of Saint Denis*, 15th century)
In the reign of Charles V, several talented artists illustrated works commissioned by the nobility. After the Limbourg brothers' work for the Duc de Berry, Jean Fouquet was chosen by the powerful Abbey of Saint-Denis to illustrate the history of the kings of France, which he portrayed in a 15th-century setting. Shown here are the Ile de la Cité with the Palais-Royal and the King's Garden.

3. *Portrayal of the Magnificent Celebrations at the Tournament held in the Place Royale on April 5, 6, and 7, 1612* (Claude Chastillon)
The Place Royale (now the Place des Vosges), built by Henri IV, was the first city square in Paris, opened on the occasion of the betrothal of Louis XIII and Anne of Austria.

However, the political situation deteriorated when the royal princes tried to exploit problems caused by the Reformation. In May, 1588, the Catholic League headed by Henri de Guise seized Paris during the Days of the Barricades. In the name of their faith, their supporters drove Henri III out of Paris and sealed off the city. In his search for a resolution, the Catholic Henri III formed an alliance with his Protestant cousin, the King of Navarre. Together they surrounded the capital in the summer of 1589. But their siege was in vain. Despite famine, destruction, and epidemics, the people of Paris held firm. Refusing to side with the monarchy, they assassinated Henri III who, before his death, recognized the King of Navarre, the future Henri IV, as his legitimate successor.

The great achievements of Henri IV and Marie de Médicis

"Paris is worth a mass," said King Henri IV when he entered the capital in 1594, and found nothing but ruins and desolation. This left the first of the Bourbon kings free to build and improve the city until it reflected his dynastic vision. First he rebuilt the seats of power. Along the Seine, he linked the Louvre to the Tuileries with a 980 ft (300 m) gallery. Around the Cité he built riverside roads, built the Pont Marchand and, more importantly, the Pont-Neuf which joined the two banks. In the space at the western tip of the island, he had a triangular square built by Métezeau, the Place Dauphine, flanked by brick and stone houses. On the Left Bank, he opened the Rue Dauphine in line with the Pont-Neuf. This was the first new road: it was 26 ft (8 m) wide and it sliced mercilessly through the maze of narrow lanes lined with tall houses. On the Right Bank, beyond the Hôtel de Ville, which he partly rebuilt, he created new districts in the old Marais. On the site of the Tournelles gardens, he laid out the Place Royale (now the Place des Vosges). The financiers supporting the king bought mansions around the central garden, their even lines broken on the north and south sides by the King's Pavilion and the Queen's Pavilion. Princely and aristocratic mansions were built in the surrounding area, such as the Hôtel de Diane de France (which became the History Library of the City of Paris), the Hôtel de Ligneris (which became the Musée Carnavalet), and the Hôtel de Sully (now headquarters of the Center for National Monuments). The Marais was

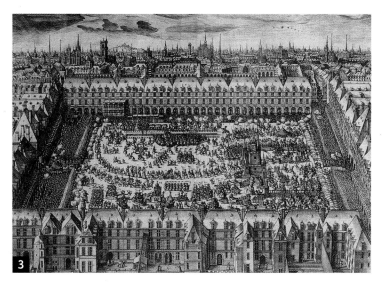

divided into lots and became fashionable. Along Rue des Francs-Bourgeois, Rue du Temple, Rue des Archives, and Rue François-Miron, mansions such as the Hôtel de Beauvais appeared (the future annex of the Administrative Tribunal), built by Lepautre, and the Hôtel Aubert de Fontenay, known as the Hôtel Salé (now the Picasso Museum), built by Bourlier. Although plans were abandoned to build the Place de France, with a semicircle of mansions for State dignitaries, the Jesuits worked wonders at the Church of Saint-Paul; they brought together people from high society, such as the Marquise de Sévigné, and successfully acquired the services of great preachers, such as Bossuet and Massillon.

In 1610, following the assassination of Henri IV, his widow, Marie de Médicis, became Regent. Her name is associated with three great building achievements: the Cours de la Reine, the Ile Saint-Louis, and the Palais de Luxembourg. The first of these, with its monumental gate in the form of a triumphal arch, is an esplanade beside the river. It was the preserve of the court, its aristocrats and their carriages, and was the equivalent for western Paris of Le Mail in the east. The latter was laid out by Henri IV beside the Seine near the Arsenal, and was a tree-lined walk where military people and local inhabitants could meet and take a stroll. Across the water from there lay two virtually uninhabited islands, the Ile Notre-Dame and the Ile aux Vaches. Joining these together as the Ile Saint-Louis, and developing it successfully was Marie de Médicis' second major project. Riverside roads were built to support the unstable banks of the Seine. A grid of streets was laid out, dominated by a church which bore the name of Saint-Louis, the greatest of the Capetian kings. The developers paid for two bridges joining the two arms of the Seine. The Pont Marie was quickly completed, while Le Vau's Pont de la Tournelle suffered many trials and tribulations. The lots on the island were bought up by wealthy financiers and the top ranks of the nobility. Splendid mansions were built, such as the Hôtel Lauzun, the Hôtel Lambert, and the Hôtel Bretonvilliers, well known for their picture galleries. The Ile Saint-Louis was soon nicknamed "The Island of

Palaces." The Palais du Luxembourg was the Regent's third great project. Marie de Médicis wanted to build herself a retreat and leave the Louvre free for her son Louis XIII and his young wife, Anne of Austria. The latter had magnificent apartments built there which today house the collections of Egyptian Antiquities. Salomon de Brosse was commissioned to build the Palais du Luxembourg and its gardens, basing them on the Palazzo Pitti in Florence and the Boboli Gardens. Its reception rooms were richly decorated and its galleries decorated with a series of paintings by Rubens, which portrayed events in the life of the Queen.

The "great" Paris of Louis XIV

The Grand Siècle, the great century which reached its height during the first 30 years of Louis XIV's reign, opened with the building of the Collège des Quatre Nations, which Cardinal Mazarin commissioned Le Vau to design. This fine domed building was to be linked to the Louvre by a bridge, the Pont de la Paix, which, at the beginning of the 19th century, was finally built under the name of the Pont des Arts. The building of the eastern façade of the Louvre produced a confrontation between French and Italian styles. Bernini came to Paris to put forward his design. But the Sun King preferred that of his architect, Perrault, which was more Classical and less Baroque. The new style, as defined by Le Brun, followed the lead of François Mansart, whose dome at Val-de-Grâce founded a school of architecture and whose baldachin, recalling the one in Saint Peter's, Rome, was much appreciated by Bernini, who considered it one of the masterpieces of Paris.

Under the influence of Colbert, who wanted to keep

Louis XIV in his capital, Paris was smartened up. Now spared the threat of invasion, its ramparts were destroyed. The fortifications built by the last Valois kings were pulled down and replaced by tree-lined walks overlooking the surrounding countryside. The Sun Gates - the Porte Saint-Denis and the Porte Saint-Martin, built by Blondel and Bullet, and also the Porte Saint-Bernard and the Porte Saint-Antoine - marked the main entrances to Paris with triumphal arches. In line with a policy which he applied to all industries, Colbert refused to allow manufactured goods to be imported, and so he founded the Gobelins and Faubourg Saint-Antoine factories, which made marvelous tapestries and crystal of the finest quality. In 1685, as a way of celebrating the reign of the Great King, Jules Hardouin-Mansart designed two royal squares: one, the Place des Victoires, was round, and the other, the Place Vendôme, was octagonal. Both served as magnificent settings for statues of Louis XIV, which were put up in the middle of the squares. However, the most moving legacy of the Sun King was the homage he paid to his armies, and particularly to the soldiers wounded while fighting for France. At the end of the Esplanade, the Hôtel des Invalides looks out majestically over the Seine. Its grid-pattern of buildings and courtyards, dominated by a dome designed by Jules Hardouin-Mansart as the sovereign's tomb, embodies the majesty of French Classicism and recalls the plan of the Escorial, near Madrid, built by the Sun King's grandfather, Philip II of Spain.

When Louis XIV withdrew to Versailles, the nobility left the Marais to settle on land between the Luxembourg and the Invalides; this belonged to the University and the Abbey of Saint-Germain-des-Prés, which the king linked to the Louvre by building the Pont Royal, designed by J-A Gabriel. The Faubourg Saint-Germain, now studded with magnificent mansions set between courtyard and garden, became the stronghold of the leading aristocrats. Its buildings symbolized a refined lifestyle carried on discreetly behind impressive porches. Saint-Sulpice, the parish church of this noble suburb, was designed in the taste of the day by the Italian architect Servandoni.

At the same time, the Faubourg Saint-Honoré, the financial district, was built on the Right Bank. Around the Hôtel d'Evreux and the Hôtel de Charost, along the Rue du Roule, magnificent mansions were built outside the city walls with gardens running down to those of the Champs-Elysées.

The Rococo style prevailed in the palaces, mansions, and churches of the Regency. Furniture made in the Faubourg Saint-Antoine, where André Charles Boulle was a leading figure, was covered in tortoiseshell encrusted with gilded bronze. In the churches, the altars were lavishly regilded. The chancel of Notre-Dame was reworked by Jules Hardouin-Mansart. Mansions were elaborately paneled in white and gold. Fashions changed at a brisk rate: after the rocaille look came the country style, then the passion for Chinese and Turkish things, and various other excesses. Under the influence of the Encyclopedists, private chapels disappeared, replaced by music rooms laid out in the middle of apartments, and literary salons flourished.

The major building schemes of Louis XV

In the middle of the 18th century, no doubt under the influence of the enlightened Marquise de Pompadour, King Louis XV decided to involve himself in the building plans for Paris. He undertook three major projects. One benefited the Army, another the Church, and the third the Town. He pacified the clergy by building two splendid churches, designed like Roman temples: Sainte-Geneviève (the future Panthéon) on the Left Bank, designed by Soufflot, and on the Right Bank the Madeleine, designed by Contant d'Ivry, although this was not completed until the July Monarchy, by Pierre Vignon and Jean-Jacques Huvé. To please the Army, the École Militaire (J-A Gabriel's masterpiece) was built at the gates of the capital on the

1. Henri IV entering Notre-Dame (engraving by Philippoteaux and Trichon)
Henri de Navarre was recognized by King Henri III as his legitimate successor, and in 1589 he took the name of Henri IV, but was only accepted by a minority of French people. After conquering the Holy League at Arques (1589) and Ivry (1590), he rejected Protestantism, was crowned at Chartres and entered Paris in 1594, after its people had withdrawn their resistance to him. Here he is seen on his white horse, greeting the crowd as they acclaim him.

2. The Hôtel de Ville and the Place de Grève (painting by Raguenet, 1757)
On the site of the old House of Pillars, François I commissioned Boccador to design the Hôtel de Ville, backing on to the Church of Saint-Jean. The City Hall building stands proudly on the Place de Grève, where celebrations and executions were held, as well as markets and harbor activities, with boats unloading directly onto the square.

3. Tournament given by Louis XIV in the courtyard of the Palais des Tuileries on June 5, 1662 (French School, 17th century)
Between the Louvre and the Tuileries Palace, built by Catherine de Médicis, was a densely populated district which gradually disappeared. Henri IV built a gallery alongside the river, and his grandson, Louis XIV, cleared the area around the main palace. At that time he organized lavish celebrations, such as the tournament on June 5, 1662.

road to Versailles with, to its front, the Champ de Mars dedicated to military training and horseriding. Finally, to please the municipal authorities, a royal square was planned with an equestrian statue of Louis XV in the role of the Pacifier as its centerpiece; this was designed by Bouchardon and carried out by Jean-Baptiste Pigalle. The Place Louis-XV (now the Place de la Concorde) was located in the west of Paris, between the Tuileries Garden and the gardens of the Champs-Elysées, with views of the river and the Faubourg Saint-Germain on the opposite bank. The ditches around its perimeter contained sunken gardens. The main entry points were decorated by pillars supporting the Marly Horses, sculpted by Nicolas Coustou and Antoine Coysevox, which added a bucolic air to the square. After the excavations at Pompeii and Herculaneum, architecture shed its decorative excesses in favor of a more rigorous style modeled on Antiquity. Not far from the Luxembourg Palace, the residence of the Comte de Provence, Charles de Wailly was commissioned by the Count to build the Odéon in a semicircular square. The fashion for columns was widely adopted on façades and in courtyards. They decorated the entrances to the Hôtel de Soubise (now the National Archives) and the Hôtel de Salm (now the headquarters of the Legion of Honor), and more importantly the École Militaire and the Palais-Royal.

This was the age when theatrical performances were in fashion, and actresses were treated like royalty. Famous dancers, such as Mlles Guimard and Colombes, had their benefactors build them Palladian-style mansions surrounded by gardens. Great lords as well as upstarts commissioned country houses for themselves: these were Neoclassical pavilions, revised and updated in the English style, which despite their modest size contained every imaginable comfort and refinement. The green belt which surrounded Paris in 1789 contained almost 150 follies, the largest and most picturesque of which – and the only ones to survive today - were those in the parks at Monceau and Bagatelle. These gardens were commissioned by the Duc de Chartres and the Comte d'Artois. Full of surprise elements, they were influenced by the Encyclopedists and J-J Rousseau and offered fantastic, dreamlike vistas: Egyptian pyramids, Turkish tents, and Chinese pagodas conveyed the delights of other exotic cultures;

temples of love and atmospheric tombs symbolized the happiest and saddest moments in life.

Most of the follies were built close to the capital, where the sixth city wall was constructed. This was the most grandiose and ephemeral scheme of the Ancien Régime. The wall of the Farmers-General was designed by Claude-Nicolas Ledoux; work began in 1784. The wall contained 55 monumental gates. These Greek-style structures were both round and square, elegant and massive, impressive and amusing; they stood at the administrative and fiscal boundaries of the city and served as tollhouses. They were part of a plan to rationalize and improve living conditions on the outskirts of Paris, but they were rejected by people living in the suburbs, and were attacked and in many cases pulled down in the early weeks of the Revolution.

Revolution and Empire

Following the storming of the Bastille on July 14, 1789, the people of Paris, exasperated by their miserable treatment, took to the streets, attacked the symbols of monarchy and the Church, ransacking palaces and churches. Many monastic buildings were destroyed at that time. The Constituent Assembly and the Convention nationalized church property and seized the assets of foreigners. To provide meeting places for national representatives, semicircular rooms were built for members of the Convention (Palais des Tuileries, by Gisors), the Five Hundred (Palais Bourbon, by Gisors), and the Senators (Palais du Luxembourg, by Chalgrin). A statue of Liberty was put up beside the guillotine on the Place de la Révolution (formerly Place Louis-XV) to celebrate the values of the new régime. In the name of culture, museums were opened to show the collections of Lenoir and Vaucanson. To improve public health, large ceme-

teries were laid out beyond the city walls. On the slopes of a wooded hill in Belleville, in the park of Père Lachaise, Hittorff designed a great burial garden. Once more the capital was transformed.

Napoléon Bonaparte had the Denon Gallery built at the Louvre to show off the treasure he had brought back from his Italian campaigns. When he became Emperor in 1804, he ordered the Arc de Triomphe de l'Étoile to be built on Chaillot Hill, in full view of the Louvre, to the glory of his Grande Armée. On the heights of Passy (now the Trocadéro), he had a palace built for his son, the King of Rome. For the people of Paris, who suffered badly from a lack of water, he had a network of 12 fountains built, the best known of which is at Châtelet, with its palm tree and Egyptian sphinxes. To improve the flow of traffic in the city, where the roads were narrow and twisting, he planned a long arcaded street: the Rue de Rivoli. Shopping streets sprang up beside the blocks where people lived. They offered a range of fashion and fancy goods, alongside theaters and panoramas, and crowds of people flocked to them.

Paris in the 19th century: the Grands Boulevards and the suburbs

Under the Restoration and the July monarchy, the fashion was for all things English. Immigrants from London introduced not only the British style of town square, which was adapted for use in Paris, but also the art of horseriding, a taste for tea, pastries, English-style newspapers, clubs, and horseracing. The Nouvelle Athènes, in the 9th *arrondissement*, became the center of fashion. Writers, artists, and painters had their salons and studios there. The Grands Boulevards became the setting for major public events. Strollers, aristocrats, and theater people wandered there beneath the trees. Everyone who wanted to be seen went there: society women and demimondaines, dandies, and seamstresses. People hurried to its 150 or so theaters, circuses, and cabarets. The Grands Boulevards are 2.5 miles (4 km) long: working-class in the east, and elegant in the west. Their sparkle and liveliness were quite unlike the calmer dignity of the Faubourgs Saint-Germain and Saint-Honoré, which had become aristocratic neighborhoods. Their narrow, quiet streets gave no hint of the luxurious apartments and huge private gardens. To the north of the Rue Saint-Martin and the Rue Saint-Denis, the Faubourg Poissonnière revealed an opulence which had started at the end of the Ancien Régime. Close to where the financiers and businessmen lived, Brongniart was commissioned to build a Greek temple: the Bourse (stock exchange), a veritable palace of money. Further east, the Faubourg Saint-Antoine was livelier and more creative, but also had revolutionary instincts. Around the studios of its famous cabinetmakers lived swarms of hard-working people. These craftsmen had been making furniture for two centuries, producing unique pieces for the royal court and selected customers: chairs and commodes, tables and desks which were masterpieces of technique and fine design. Meanwhile, the buildings in the central districts had deteriorated, because they had not been properly maintained when their owners fled Paris during the Revolution, and because many were now too densely populated, a trend that only increased in the Industrial Revolution.

Paris consolidates

As always happens, successive régimes pay tribute to their past heroes. In the Restoration, an Expiatory Temple was built at the place where Louis XVI and Marie-Antoinette were buried. At one end of the Pont de la Concorde, the Palais Bourbon was given a Neo-Greek façade to match that of the Madeleine, which was still being built. To improve the traffic flow, the ditches around the Place de la Révolution, now Place de la Concorde, were filled in. In the center of the square, Louis-Philippe put up the Obelisk of Luxor, a present from the Viceroy of Egypt, Mehemet Ali, to Charles X.

On the Place de la Bastille, close to where the riots of the Three Glorious Days took place (July 27, 28, and 29, 1830), a column was built bearing the Spirit of Liberty. Louis-Philippe also reconstructed the Hôtel de Ville and started to restore several Gothic buildings, including Notre-Dame and Sainte-Chapelle.

1. *Customs barrier at La Villette* (Swebach, about 1822)
Near the end of the Ancien Régime, the Farmers-General built a wall around the city. The 35 tollhouses were variously designed by Ledoux as Neoclassical temples, or as round, square, and octagonal buildings. Part of their function was to decorate the outskirts of the city, but there was widespread discontent, and some of the buildings were burnt down on July 12 and 13, 1789.

2. *The celebration of the Supreme Being at the Champ de Mars* (Pierre-Antoine Demachy, 1723-1807)
During the Revolution, the Champ de Mars was used for grand parades. After the Federation's celebrations on July 14, 1790, when Talleyrand conducted mass in front of Louis XVI and Queen Marie-Antoinette, a huge crowd watched the celebrations of the Supreme Being, organized by Robespierre. The State's principal bodies paraded past a Liberty column dressed in Antique-style costumes designed by David, the Convention's official painter.

3. *The return of the Emperor's ashes* (Jung)
Between Ledoux's tollhouses on top of Chaillot Hill, Napoléon I built a triumphal arch dedicated to his armies, which was completed during the July monarchy. The Prince de Joinvile, son of Louis-Philippe, brought the Emperor's ashes there after his death on Saint Helena.

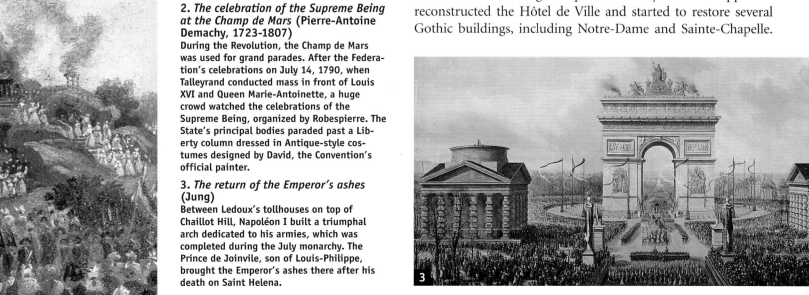

1

At the same time, he built two large libraries: the Bibliothèque Sainte-Geneviève and the Bibliothèque Nationale. Between 1840 and 1845, he surrounded Paris with a massive wall (the seventh) with external bastions. Finally, on the edge of the built city, he granted large tracts of land to the railroad companies, who set about building a network of tracks across the whole of France to its borders. Terminal buildings were also constructed, the predecessors of the Gare du Nord and the Gare de l'Est, the Gare Saint-Lazare and the Gare Montparnasse, not to mention the Gare d'Austerlitz and the Gare de Lyon.

Major transformations under Haussmann

Napoléon III (1852-71) was still under the influence of English culture when he made Paris a model city. Each day, in his office in the Tuileries, the Emperor met Prefect Haussmann. The latter joined the Louvre to the Tuileries and launched a huge program to regenerate the city. His aim was to improve safety, public health, and the traffic flow by building broad avenues radiating out from the center, and concentric tree-lined boulevards to link up with the outer districts. Haussmann redesigned the Ile de la Cité and the market at Les Halles, the "heart and belly" of Paris. To cater for the influx of country people drawn by the bright lights of the city, he brought outlying suburbs into the city and created 20 *arrondissements*, which acquired their own administrative and educational infrastructures.

Assisted by the geologist Belgrand, Baron Haussmann built underground networks to remove waste water, and supply fresh water and gas (soon followed by electricity) to every story. He employed engineer Alphand to develop green areas in the city: English-style squares (such as the Square de Trévise), French-style gardens (the Gardens of the Champs-Elysées), shady parks (Monceau, Montsouris to the south, and the Buttes-Chaumont in the old quarries to the east). Most significantly, he adapted two former forests, the Bois de Vincennes to the east, and the Bois de Boulogne to the west. Soon, bourgeois apartment buildings in the so-called Haussmann style took their place on the airy avenues and boulevards. Following the lead of financiers such as the Pereire brothers, the 17th *arrondissement* blossomed with stone houses for the well-to-do, with finely worked balconies and other decorations. Around the Palais Garnier, the Second Empire's most lavish building, the Opéra district grew up, its richly decorated façades housing banks, insurance companies, and grand tourist hotels.

Gradually, the city's center of gravity shifted westward. The classes became segregated: to the west were the rich, to the east the poor. Along the Champs-Elysées and the Avenue de l'Impératrice (Avenue Foch), many magnificent mansions appeared. Horseriders and carriage drivers headed toward the Bois de Boulogne. On the other side of town, immigrants and workers occupied the eastern districts, in a crescent running round from the 18th *arrondissement* to the 14th. This included the eastern hollow of the Paris Basin and the semicircle of hills

dominated by the Butte Montmartre and Sacré-Coeur, built between 1873 and 1929. The city became densely populated with three million inhabitants. Open spaces were rare apart from the banks of the Seine between the Pont de la Concorde and the Pont d'Iéna. This became the site for a series of World Fairs. Inspired by the Crystal Palace in London, they exhibited the latest advances in technology in huge galleries, and turned Paris into an international showplace for the arts, science, and progress. The most spectacular buildings constructed for these exhibitions included the following: in 1867 and 1878, the Palais des Sciences (built on the site of the future Grand Palais and the Petit Palais); the Palais de Chaillot and, facing it, the Eiffel Tower, 984 ft (300 m) high (1889); the Grand Palais and the Petit Palais (1900); and the Palais de Tokyo and the Palais du Trocadéro by Carlu (1937).

Reconstruction after the Commune

The suppression of the Rebellion of the Commune in 1871 shattered the working-class suburbs of Paris; the population of the capital changed. Under the Third Republic, Paris inherited a rich patrimony: the events of the Commune and the fires of 1871 meant that several symbolic buildings had to be rebuilt along the Seine. The Tuileries and the Hôtel de Ville, the Cour des Comtes and the Palais de la Légion d'Honneur had gone up in smoke. In addition, the universities had to be rebuilt, particularly the Sorbonne, where Napoléon III had laid the foundation stone. This was followed by the transformation of the Latin Quarter under the leadership of Jules Ferry, who built new university faculties and Grandes Écoles. In the 15th *arrondissement*, the Institut Pasteur acquired an excellent site. The Seine became the principal axis, with the newly built museums to the west and the main buildings of the capital - the Cathedral, the Palais de Justice, and the Hôtel de Ville - to the east. Between the two, when the railroads were at their peak, the Gare d'Orsay was built opposite the Louvre.

Paris in the Belle Époque

The Belle Époque was a time of frivolity and dancing, but it was also a creative period. In painting, Impressionism was followed by the École de Paris

2

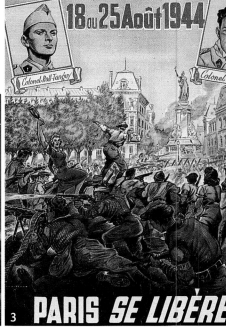

3 PARIS *SE LIBÈRE*

and Surrealism, which spread throughout Europe and attracted artists from all over the world to Montparnasse. In architecture, after the lively Art Nouveau style favored by Hector Guimard, came the pared-down Modernist style prevalent in the 1930s. Winners of the Grand Prix de Rome and former students of the École des Beaux-Arts designed most of the official buildings: ministries, museums, high schools, and mansions of the 8th and 16th *arrondissements*. The Perret brothers designed the Théâtre des Champs-Elysées and the Museum of Public Works (now the Economic and Social Council building). Laprade built the Museum of African Arts at the Porte Dorée, and Mallet-Stevens the street which bears his name. Le Corbusier designed the La Roche et Jeanneret house in Rue du Docteur-Blanche.

Contemporary Paris

After World War II, there was a housing crisis in the capital. Many overcrowded apartments and houses had become dilapidated. During the 1950s, these blocks were condemned and gradually replaced by large developments such as the Front de Seine (15th), the great towers of the 13th, and by office blocks. During the presidency of Georges Pompidou, the roads running along the Right Bank were turned into an urban highway, and the Pompidou Center was built.

In 1975, Paris became a *département* of France. The election of a mayor in 1975 brought new impetus to town planning. The move to the west, with the creation of Beaugrenelle and its towers beside the Seine, was counterbalanced by improvements to the eastern district of Bercy, with the Palais Omnisports and the Ministry of Finance; opposite these, the Seine Rive-Gauche

district was built, and the new National Library. To the northeast of the capital, a former urban railroad was converted into the Promenade Plantée: a green corridor. The banks of the Canal Saint-Martin and the Canal Saint-Denis were redeveloped. In place of the old factories came parks, some of them very large, such as the Parc André-Citroën, the Parc de Bercy, the Parc de la Butte du Chapeau-Rouge, and the Parc de la Villette. Some 200 small gardens were laid out to decorate squares and crossroads. A further 150 new fountains were added to the 150 old ones supplying water in the city center.

From the 1980s, Paris acquired several new major buildings. Most of the important projects were part of an improvements program begun by President François Mitterrand. Some were designed to adapt buildings to new functions, such as the rebuilding of the Louvre. Others were gigantic new projects, such as the Cité des Sciences et de l'Industrie (1982-5), the Opéra-Bastille (1984-9), the Grande Arche at La Défense (1985-9), the Pyramid by Ieoh Ming Pei for the Louvre (1989), and the Bibliothèque Nationale de France, completed between 1990 and 1995.

The start of a new millennium has brought a new-found energy to the capital, both in terms of major building projects and the new developments in eastern Paris. All share the same Postmodern desire for originality, expressed in the forms used and the technical skills which challenge both time and space. The shapes of buildings change according to the time of day and the light. At night, Paris turns into another world, when its bridges and monuments are illuminated, as engineers exert their understanding of electricity to sculpt, blend, and regenerate the products of twenty centuries of architecture.

1. The arms of the City of Paris
The arms of Paris are crowned by towers and ramparts - recalling the city walls - supported by a knight, symbolizing the spirit of defense, and a civilian with one foot resting on the Constitution, and surrounded by flags, alluding to victories. Over the centuries, the central image has remained unchanged: beneath a band of fleur-de-lis is the boat of the Guild of Boatmen, which "sails and does not sink."

2. Baron Haussmann (daguerrotype by D F Millet, about 1850)
In 1850, Napoléon III and Haussmann decided to build wide streets to improve both traffic flow and troop movements. Prefect Haussmann transformed Paris into a modern city with boulevards and avenues lined with stone apartment buildings, bordered by trees, and adorned with squares, parks, and splendid buildings, such as the Opéra.

3. Paris is Liberated, August 18-25, 1944 (poster issued by the Communist Resistance)
After the dark years of the Occupation, the joy of Liberation burst out everywhere. General Leclerc's 2nd Armored Division paraded through the city's main streets to the cheers of a jubilant crowd.

4. Building the French National Library in 1994
In the 1990s, the east of Paris was improved and large cultural projects were built there. The Place de la Bastille was given a people's opera house, and the French National Library was built in the 13th *arrondissement*.

PARIS
in history

Wall of Thiers

ST-OUEN

LES BATIGNOLLES

NEUILLY

Wall of the Farmers-General

LES TERNES

Fg MONTMARTRE

Fg RICHELIEU

Fg ST-HONORÉ

PASSY

AUTEUIL

Fg ST-GERMAIN

Wall of the Farmers-General

GRENELLE

Fg ST-MICHEL

POINT DU JOUR

ISSY

Fg ST-JACQUES

VAUGIRARD

PETIT MONTROUGE

VANVES

Wall of Thiers

MONTROUGE

Wall of Philippe-Auguste (1215)

Wall of Charles V (1420)

Wall of the Farmers-General (1785

Wall of Thiers (1846)

Paris today

Fg ST-DENIS Former suburbs of Paris

ISSY Communes included within the Wall of Thiers

LIGNANCOURT

ONTMARTRE

LA CHAPELLE

LA VILLETTE

Fg ST-LAURENT

Fg ST-LAZARE

ST-DENIS

Fg ST-MARTIN

BELLEVILLE

Wall of the Farmers-General

Fg DU TEMPLE

Wall of Charles V

MÉNILMONTANT

Wall of Philippe-Auguste

Wall of Thiers

CHARONNE

Fg ST-ANTOINE

FONTARABIE

PETIT-CHARONNE

Fg ST-VICTOR

ST-MANDÉ

Fg ST-MARCEAU

BERCY

LA GRANDE PINTE

LES DEUX MOULINS

LA GARE

IVRY

LA GLACIÈRE

LA MAISON BLANCHE

NTILLY

1 km

A Tour
of
10 Districts

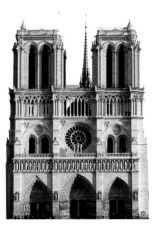

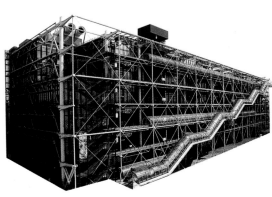

NOTRE-DAME
and surrounding area

Notre-Dame

Ile de la Cité to
Ile Saint-Louis

Latin Quarter

Panthéon district

Around the Jardin des Plantes

Aerial view of Notre-Dame
The Cathedral of Notre-Dame stands at the
prow of the Ile de la Cité. This island, the
historical and geographical center of the city,
was transformed by Haussmann who wanted
to built an administrative complex there. The
neighboring Ile Saint-Louis has retained its
17th-century mansions. Across the Seine to
the south, the Latin Quarter has been the
focal point for colleges and universities since
the Middle Ages.

Notre-Dame

Notre-Dame is one one of the most important Gothic churches in Europe, by virtue of its age and architectural quality. It stands at the heart of the history of Paris and France, the capital's principal church and seat of a bishopric, later raised to an archbishopric in 1622. While its spectacular medieval art has inspired the imagination of artists for centuries, it is also one of the country's greatest Catholic centers.

A masterpiece of Gothic architecture

◆ A model of harmony

The vast forecourt of Notre-Dame was enlarged in the 19th century, providing a more open view of the façade which until then was hemmed in by houses. The pale stone was recently restored, making the sculptures stand out well, even though we tend to forget that in the Middle Ages they were polychrome. Many were destroyed in the Revolution and remade in the 19th century. However, the beauty of Notre-Dame also stems from the harmony of its architecture, which, while retaining some of the heaviness of the Romanesque period, also reveals the boldness and lightness of the Gothic. The harmonious proportions of the main façade's two towers and galleries are most striking. The rose window, almost 33 ft (10 m) in dia-meter and symbolizing divine infinity, is set in a square, representing the earth, and subtly reminds the viewer of the mystery of "God made man." The nave is 360 ft (110 m) long and 108 ft (33 m) high, and makes its

impact through its great size and the solemn procession of its pillars.

◆ The long building process

The middle of the 12th century was a period of great piety, but also one of economic boom and creative freedom which saw the development of cathedrals such as Sens, Noyon, and Laon. At Saint-Denis in 1140, Abbé Suger started to rebuild his church on a grand scale which anticipated the Gothic style. This was the prevailing mood when, around 1163, Bishop Maurice de Sully and the chapter decided to build a cathedral dedicated to Notre-Dame on the Ile de la Cité, on a site which had been dedicated to worship since the Gallo-Roman era, and where two churches presently stood, Saint-Etienne and Notre-Dame. The foundation stone was laid in the presence of

Pope Alexander III on April 23, 1163. The plan, drawn up by an unknown architect, envisioned replacing the two old churches with a single, vast building.

The king and the congregation all contributed to the building, the rich through gifts and the poor with their labor. The choir was consecrated by 1182, the nave completed in 1196, and the façade and its towers were finished between 1200 and 1250. Even though building continued into the 14th century, Notre-Dame displays a unity of style rare in such long-term projects. It was a masterful statement of Early Gothic.

In the 13th century, however, it was felt that not enough light was coming into the church. The tall windows were enlarged, which meant supporting the vaults on large flying buttresses. From 1258, architects

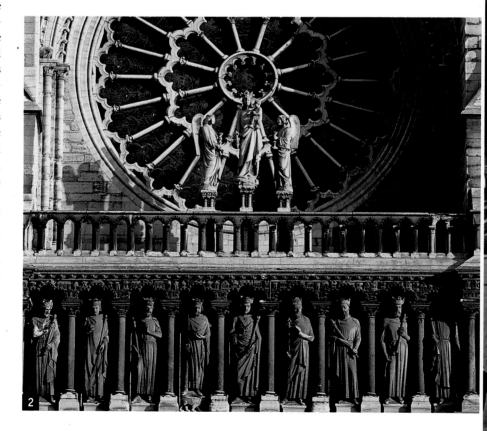

Jean de Chelles then Pierre de Montreuil enlarged the transept, lighting it with huge rose windows. Finally, the chapels radiating from the chevet were built, and lit with huge windows, which meant that work on the site continued until about 1320.

◆ *Sculptures on the portals*

The sculptures at Notre-Dame were partly destroyed during the Revolution. The great portals on the façade were extensively rebuilt in the 19th century. On the left-hand portal is the story of the Virgin Mary, and on the center the Last Judgment. On the right, the Sainte-Anne portal includes a tympanum with a Virgin in Majesty dating from the 1140s. The niches in the gallery above the portals contain 28 statues of the

1. Portal of the Virgin Mary
The façade's North Portal contains a group of sculptures dedicated to the Virgin Mary, the cathedral's sacred patroness. Damaged in the Revolution and restored by Viollet-le-Duc, the sculptures lost the colors they had in the Middle Ages.

2. Gallery of the Kings
Above the portals, the niches of this long gallery contain statues of the 28 kings of Judea, ancestors of the Virgin Mary and Christ. They were confused for a long time with the kings of France, and were destroyed in the Revolution, then remade under Viollet-le-Duc.

3. Façade of Notre-Dame
The façade was completed in the middle of the 13th century, a remarkable example of Gothic symmetry. There are some variations, however: the South Tower is narrower than the North, and the North Portal has a gable above it, its decorations sculpted in the shape of a triangle.

4. Gargoyles on the North Tower
Notre-Dame's gargoyles were added by Viollet-le-Duc to express a Romantic vision of the Middle Ages popular in the 19th century. Fixed to the tops of the towers, these fantasy animals, or creatures of the devil, are outlets for rainwater from the gutters.

Hall of Fame

Eugène Viollet-le-Duc (1814-1879)

is the man who restored Notre-Dame. In 1843, he was commissioned to restore Vézelay, one of the most beautiful Norman abbeys but so dilapidated that "trees were growing" through its stones. He was then only 26, but had already acquired an encyclopedic knowledge of medieval architecture through research and travel. His restorations, based on meticulous research, saved many medieval buildings such as the Château de Pierrefonds, Notre-Dame Cathedral, and the city of Carcassonne. However, his desire to "restore" vanished elements, even those which had never been completed, aroused lively comment and accusations of pastiche. ■

kings of Judea, the ancestors of Christ. In 1793, Revolutionaries mistook them for the kings of France and broke off their heads. Those you see today were remade to designs by Viollet-le-Duc in the 19th century. However, thanks to a sensational discovery in 1977, the original heads, though mutilated, are today on show at the National Museum of the Middle Ages. The portals of the transept (the Cloister Portal on the north side, the Saint-Etienne Portal to the south) are fairly well preserved and reflect the richness of sculpture in the second half of the 13th century.

◆ Stained glass and furnishings

Notre-Dame still has three large 13th-century stained-glass windows: the rose windows on the façade and transepts. The North Window is the best preserved, and shows the Virgin carrying the Infant Jesus and sur-

rounded by 80 biblical characters. In the course of time, the cathedral has been richly furnished, notably with a series of "Mays," the paintings offered to the Virgin Mary each year, on May 1, by the Guild of Goldsmiths. Some of these 76 paintings have disappeared, while others are in museums. The most important, particularly those by Le Brun and Le Sueur, still adorn the chapels. The cathedral also has a fine 14th-century statue of the Virgin. At the end of the choir is a *Pietà*, sculpted by Guillaume Coustou, flanked by a statue of Louis XIII, by the same artist, and one of Louis XIV by Coysevox. This group was commissioned by Louis XIV, following a vow made by his father, Louis XIII, to dedicate France to the Virgin Mary if he could only be granted an heir. His wish was fulfilled after 23 years of marriage.

From the restorations of Viollet-le-Duc to today

At the beginning of the 19th century, Notre-Dame was in a pitiful state,

with mutilated statues, stones dislodged, and the spire missing. The damage had been caused both by man and the weather. A restoration program was launched, and in 1843 Lassus and Viollet-le-Duc were put in charge. The latter carried out the building work, pulling down various 17th- and 18th-century additions and replacing many elements that had disappeared. He also built a much taller spire than the original and added a number of statues, notably the gargoyles and fantastic animals. Even today, work goes on to protect the building from pollution eroding the stone, and to repair damage from the storm of 1999. Many worn-out stones have been replaced. However, great concern is now being voiced about the authenticity of such restorations.

Notre-Dame in history

Notre-Dame has been the scene of important events in the history of France. Beneath its vaults in 1302, Philip the Fair called a major meet-

1 **2**

ing of ecclesiastics, noblemen, and citizens to assert the temporal independence of the kingdom with respect to the papacy. And while the royal coronations were traditionally held in Rheims Cathedral, Henry VI of England was crowned king of France at Notre-Dame in the middle of the Hundred Years' War (1430). In the Revolution, the cathedral became the Temple of Reason, then of the Supreme Being, before being returned to Catholic worship. Napoléon was crowned Emperor in Notre-Dame in 1804.

Many other official ceremonies have taken place there, sometimes to plead for divine leniency in times of misfortune, sometimes to thank God for France's victories, notably the Liberation service on August 26, 1944. Notre-Dame is also the main place for state funerals. On November 12, 1970, the official ceremony for the death of General de Gaulle was attended by many foreign heads of state as well as the world's media.

Notre-Dame and the arts

In the Middle Ages, the forecourt staged performances of religious "mystery plays," including one written in the 13th century by the poet Ruteboeuf. The so-called "Notre-Dame" music school had developed the polyphonic style by the 12th century. The great late 19th-century organ, Cavaillé-Coll's masterpiece, has more than 6,000 pipes. Many scores have been composed for this instrument, which is one of the largest in the world.

The cathedral features in many paintings, and made literary fame in Victor Hugo's *Notre-Dame de Paris*. Published in 1831, this novel's portrayal of a dark and tormented Middle Ages has inspired many interpretations, from Jean Delanoy's film of 1956, with Anthony Quinn and Gina Lollobrigida, to the musical drama by Luc Plamondon and Richard Cocciane which has attracted thousands of spectators since 1999.

A place of worship

The splendor of the architecture and the crowds of tourists should not obscure the building's spiritual purpose. A flagstone marks the spot where, in 1886, writer Paul Claudel

had the vision leading to his conversion. The Sunday services and celebrations attract many believers, as do the lectures in Lent, each year given by one or two famous preachers.

Facts & Figures	
Length : 430 ft (131 m)	
Width : 157 ft (48 m)	
Area : 59,202 sq ft (5,500 sq m)	
Height beneath vaults : 115 ft (35 m)	
Height of towers : 226 ft (69 m)	
Number of steps in North tower : 387	
Height of spire including weather vane : 315 ft (96 m)	
Weight of spire (wood and copper) : 827 tons (750 t)	
Diameter of North and South transept windows : 43 ft (13 m)	
Weight of great bell (South Tower) : 14 tons (13 t) with a clapper of 1,100 lb (500 kg)	
Date when bell was cast : 1686	

1. Notre-Dame from Quai de la Tournelle
The two arms of the Seine divide beneath the impressive bulk of the cathedral, standing in the east of Ile de la Cité. Large flying buttresses balance the thrust of the vaults, and support the enlarged choir windows.

2. Rose window in south of transept
The rose windows in the transept are 43 ft (13 m) in diameter and masterpieces of medieval stained glass. This window's radiating imagery is dedicated to Christ surrounded by saints and angels. The North window depicts the Virgin and Child, surrounded by biblical characters.

3. Choir and nave of Notre-Dame
Built between 1163 and 1196, the choir and nave are a major example of Early Gothic architecture. The weight of the ogival vaults rests on impressive columns at the lower level. The tall windows were enlarged in the 13th century, but the first span of the nave, left, is from the original structure.

4. Mid-Lent at Notre Dame
The cathedral forecourt was considerably enlarged by Haussmann's plan, and in the 20th century was the scene for various popular celebrations. At the mid-Lent parade in 1936, the cooks' float was a sight to behold.

Ile de la Cité to Ile Saint-Louis

Sainte-Chapelle, the Conciergerie, and Notre-Dame give an idea of the power and influence of the Ile de la Cité in the Middle Ages. This island, the cradle of the City of Paris, lost its political power in the 14th century, but is still the hub of judicial and religious power. Although its medieval buildings and alleys have almost completely disappeared, the Ile de la Cité is still a very attractive area with its delightful Place Dauphine, leafy squares, flower market, and quaysides.

The island's long history

The Ile de la Cité was occupied by a Gallic tribe, the Parisii, from the 3rd century BC, then in the Roman period became the political and administrative center of an open city. It was gradually fortified against flooding, and filled up with houses and public buildings. Once it had its own wall, it looked like a real city. In the 6th century, Clovis and his son, Childebert I, established their royal palace there, the seat of their kingdom, and an early cathedral. Though at first only a simple dwelling, the old royal palace was completely rebuilt over the centuries to contain the kingdom's seat of power and its high court of justice.

Palais de Justice

The Palais de Justice occupies the site of the old medieval royal palace, evidence of the remarkable continuity of power in the Ile de la Cité. Despite the extent of subsequent building work, several older buildings remain intact, notably Sainte-Chapelle and the Conciergerie.

The Palais de Justice (main law courts) is something of a monumental labyrinth, a legal beehive used daily by three kinds of people: magistrates and clerks of the court; police and the accused; and lawyers and litigants. When there are big trials, the courts are always in the national news. Hordes of tourists, unaware of all this activity, between Sainte-Chapelle and the Conciergerie, while access to the legendary "Quai des Orfèvres," headquarters of the Judicial Police, is tightly controlled while they carry on their inquiries, and feed the imagination of novelists and moviegoers.

◆ Sainte-Chapelle

Saint-Louis had Sainte-Chapelle built in record time (1246-8) to contain the Crown of Thorns and other relics of Christ which had been brought from Constantinople. Although threatened with destruction in the Revolution, it recovered its splendor, and most notably its spire, after being restored by Viollet-le-Duc in the 19th century.

Sainte-Chapelle marks the high point of Gothic architecture. Its lower chapel, open to people of lesser rank, served as a base for the upper chapel, set aside in those days for the royal family and their entourage. The latter has huge stained-glass windows, separated by slender shafts which are supported by massive buttresses. The soaring vaults emphasize the building's lightness and luminosity.

◆ Law courts and the Conciergerie

The Grand-Salle, built by Philip the Fair, redesigned in 1622, and restored after 1871, is today the "Salle des Pas-Perdus," the center point of the Palais de Justice. Similarly, the present principal civil courtroom began as the Capetian palace. This was the seat of the Revolutionary tribunal which condemned thousands of people to the scaffold, including Marie-Antoinette, and shut them up in cells in the Conciergerie. The latter retains various aspects of the medieval palace: the Salle des Gardes and the Salle des Gens d'Armes; the clock tower, the city's first public clock (1371); and, on the quayside, the Tour de César, the Tour d'Argent, and the Tour Bonbec, which was completely restored after a fire in 1935.

The Cour du Mai, the main entrance on Boulevard du Palais, has elegant gilded railings and dates from Louis XVI. Most of the other rooms and legal chambers were laid out

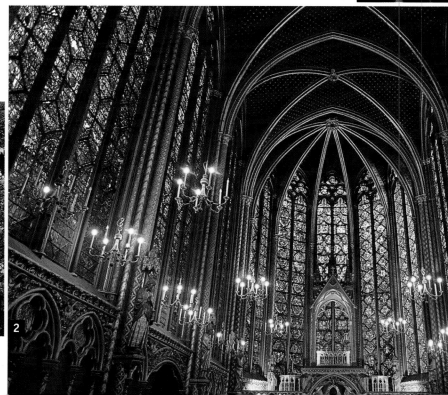

between 1840 and 1914, after being partly burnt down in 1871 during the Commune.

Pont Neuf and Place Dauphine

◆ *The oldest bridge in Paris*

The Pont Neuf was the first bridge to span the Seine all the way across. Work began in 1578 and was not completed until 1603 after Henri IV had added his impetus to the project.

Instead of being lined by houses, as was common at the time, the bridge was only used for traffic and, another innovation, provided with sidewalks. Semi-circular lookout points above each pillar gave new views of the Seine and were sur-mounted by shops, freestanding to begin with, then fixed from 1775 to 1854. The imposing equestrian statue of Henri IV that stands in the middle of the bridge dates from 1818 and replaced the original ver-sion, which was destroyed in 1792. It was partly cast in bronze from the statue of Napoléon on the Vendôme column, and its cornices are deco-rated with a total of 384 grotesque masks.

The Pont Neuf is the oldest bridge in Paris and also the most famous. Pissarro and Derain painted it, the American artist Christo "wrapped" it for two weeks in 1985, and, more recently, it featured in Léo Carax's film, *The Lovers of Pont-Neuf.*

◆ *The second royal square*

Place Dauphine is a delightful, shady square, flanked by restaurants, tea rooms, and highly prized apartment buildings, and frequented by lawyers and lovers of old Paris. This square, which now gives on to the rear of the Palais de Justice, was built in 1608 by Henri IV. It was the second royal square, after the present Place des Vosges. Named in honor of the

1. Kenzo's floral Pont Neuf
The Pont Neuf is the oldest bridge in Paris, spanning the Seine for four centuries. In recent years, it has had various artistic treatments, being wrapped by Christo and bedecked with flowers by Kenzo.

2. Sainte-Chapelle
Set in the middle of the Palais de la Cité, the Sainte-Chapelle was built by Saint Louis in the 13th century to accommodate the Crown of Thorns and other relics of Christ. It is a marvel of Gothic architecture, with magnificent stained glass held in place by the slenderest of shafts.

3. Conciergerie
Protected by its towers, the Conciergerie still contains much of the medieval palace. In its very early days, it was used as a prison. During the Terror of 1793-4, thousands of suspects waited in its cells for the summary judgments of the Revolutionary Tribunal. Many, like Marie-Antoinette, were condemned to death and sent to the guillotine.

4. Place Dauphine
Built in 1608 to the west of the palace, Place Dauphine has lost its original perfect unity as well as the third side of its triangle. Its brick and stone façades do have a special charm, though, and lovers of old Paris are very fond of it.

5. The "Vert-Galant"
Nicknamed the "vigorous gallant" for his amorous adventures, Henri IV was France's most popular king. He commissioned both his bronze equestrian statue on Pont Neuf, and Place Dauphine. The statue was remade in 1818.

Dauphin, the future Louis XIII, Place Dauphine was located on the King's Garden, at the tip of the island. Shaped like an isosceles triangle, its three sides were flanked by 32 identical houses of brick and white stone. Up to the end of the 17th century, magnificent parties were held there. In the following centuries, houses were raised in height, demolished, and new ones built, destroying its uniformity. In 1871, during the Commune, when the fire at the Palais de Justice reached the base of its triangle, people feared the worst. Although restoration work has helped to preserve Place Dauphine's charm, there are only two 17th-century houses left: the two symmetrical buildings opposite the equestrian statue of Henri IV.

Impact of Haussmann

In the 19th century, Haussmann adopted a policy of cleaning up and restructuring the Ile de la Cité. He built straight streets aligned with the bridges and destroyed everything which seemed a threat to health and safety. Several churches, the medieval Hôpital-Dieu, the Hospice des Enfants Trouvés (dating from 1747), and dwellings between the palace and the cathedral had to be sacrificed. Only one area, beside Rue du Cloître-Notre-Dame, still conveys an idea of how the streets around the cathedral looked in the Middle Ages. What the Cité lost in character, it gained in perspectives and green spaces.

◆ Looking for old remains

After this building program, the area of the forecourt in front of Notre-Dame was quadrupled and the island acquired massive, functional new buildings: the Hôtel-Dieu and Prefecture of Police. Recent excavations beneath the forecourt have led to an "archeological crypt" being built, where you can see remains of the wall from the Late Roman Empire and the Merovingian cathedral. On the forecourt, lines of white stones recall the city as it was before Haussmann. A bronze plaque with the arms of Paris marks the point from which all road distances in France are measured.

◆ The Cité's four squares

To the south of the forecourt, Square Charlemagne has a statue of the emperor which was erected in the 19th century. Between Notre-Dame and the Seine, Square Jean XXIII has replaced the bishop's palace, wrecked during riots in 1830. The square contains the last elm trees in Paris, and was created to provide a view of the cathedral. Square de l'Ile-de-France, at the eastern tip of the island, stands on a former islet and now contains the moving Memorial to French Martyrs of the Deportation (1962). At the other end of the island, Square du Vert-Galant is shady and refreshing in summer, attracting fishermen, vagrants, and dreamers who come to contemplate the pretty view of the river, the Louvre, and the Institut de France.

◆ Flower market

In contrast to the black robes of the lawyers and the austere feel of the public buildings, the flower market offers exhilarating scents and colors. Parisians buy palms and fig trees there to give their apartments a tropical look, or geraniums and rose bushes to decorate their balconies. On Sundays, there is a bird market.

Ile Saint-Louis

Lying to the east of Ile de la Cité, the Ile aux Vaches and Ile Notre-Dame were only inhabited after they had been joined together and connected to the right bank by the Pont Marie in 1614. The plan for this new settle-

ment was simple: a central street with side streets at right angles to it, and a road running around the edge of the island which still provide a marvelous walk.

The new island, and its main street, took the name of the Church of Saint-Louis, built from 1664 to designs by Le Vau, and richly deco-

rated. The elite classes quickly adopted this new district. Overlooking the river, they built some remarkable mansions, notably the Hôtels Lauzun and Lambert.

The Ile Saint-Louis has retained almost all its 17th-century dwellings. Some were formerly occupied by famous people, such as President Georges Pompidou and actress Michèle Morgan; and others still are, for example the mansions of the Rothschild family. However, perhaps the island's most famous institution of all is Berthillon's ice-cream parlor, which for decades has kept Parisians flocking there for its chestnut or sour cherry bombes glacées.

1. Flower market
The Cité's flower market in Place Louis-Lépine is popular with Parisians. A profusion of green plants and bouquets brightens the severe setting, between the Hôtel-Dieu, the Commercial Court and the Prefecture of Police. On Sundays, there is a bird market.

2. Booksellers near Notre-Dame
These booksellers ply one of the oldest trades in Paris, operating from pitches on the quays which they rent from the city authorities. Their "boxes" contain an inexhaustible supply of second-hand and sometimes antiquarian books, prints and reproductions of paintings, postcards and souvenirs.

3. Picnic at the tip of Ile Saint-Louis
The banks of Ile Saint-Louis provide one of the most enjoyable walks in Paris. Walkers can stroll by the old mansions on the riverside, maybe take a quick snack or, on sunny days, try sunbathing by the water.

4. Rue Saint-Louis-en-l'Ile
This busy street is the island's main axis and runs all the way along it. Many of its historic façades have been preserved. At No 51, the gateway of the Hôtel de Chenizot (c 1730) is crowned by a faun's head and two fantastic animals supporting a richly worked iron balcony.

5. Pont Sully
In the 19th century, the town planners improved the city's traffic flow by building a number of new bridges. The Pont Sully (1876) links the two banks of the Seine via Ile Saint-Louis. At the eastern tip of the island, it passes a pleasant square with broad views upstream toward the Arsenal and Austerlitz.

Latin Quarter

This part of the Left Bank, occupied by the University and the book industry since the Middle Ages, is called Latin because that was once the language of scholars. The name might equally have been inspired by its Gallo-Roman past, still visible at the Roman baths of Cluny. Every day, tens of thousands of students and tourists crowd its boulevards and narrow streets. Exotic cafés and restaurants jostle with bookstores and publishing houses, stores selling comic books and second-hand records, and cinemas. Place Saint-Michel, overlooked by Davioud's impressive fountain of 1860, is a lively meeting place at the start of the "Boul' Mich'," the Boulevard Saint-Michel, which the humorist Ferdinand Lope said he wanted to extend all the way to the sea.

The intellectuals' district

Within a radius of several hundred yards from the Sorbonne are three of the most reputable high schools in France: Henri-IV, Louis-le-Grand, and Saint-Louis. A little further off is the Collège de France, where the greatest scholars of the day teach. On the hill of Sainte-Geneviève, five minutes away on foot, are the Law faculty, the École Normale Supérieure, and, near the Seine, the Jussieu faculty. The Latin Quarter is still an intellectual focal point, with a tradition going back to the Middle Ages.

◆ Birth of the University

At the beginning of the 12th century, several teachers settled on the Left Bank of the Seine. The fame of these independent teachers and the range of disciplines they taught attracted a crowd of students from all over Europe. Gradually, a "University of Teachers and Students" took shape, asserting its wish to be autonomous even though the Cathedral School was alone entitled to award teaching diplomas. The new body was officially recognized by King Philippe-Auguste and the Pope between 1200 and 1215. Paris, like Bologna, thus became an intellectual capital of Western Christianity.

The students of the day were grouped by country of origin, and paid their teachers privately. The four faculties (Liberal Arts, Theology, Canon Law, and Medicine) did not have their own premises, and lessons were sometimes given in the street. Rue du Fouarre owes its name to the bundles of straw the students sat on.

◆ The colleges and the Sorbonne

Many colleges founded by religious orders (the Bernardins and Cordeliers, for example) or by benefactors (such as the Queen of Navarre and the Bishop of Beauvais), still remembered in certain street names, accepted young monks and poor students, and also provided teaching rooms. A king's chaplain, Robert de Sorbon, opened a college in 1257 that quickly acquired a reputation for the quality of its theological teaching. This was the start of the Sorbonne, today the seat of the Education Offices of Paris and several universities of international repute. The Sorbonne's great domed chapel was built from 1635 to 1642 by Le Mercier at the instigation of Cardinal de Richelieu, and is a masterpiece of Classical architecture. Other buildings date from the reconstruction of 1855-1901. Some lecture rooms were given a theatrical-style decoration, in particular the Great Amphitheater painted with an allegorical fresco by

Puvis de Chavannes. At first the Collège de France, founded in 1530 by François I, specialized in the "Three Languages" (Greek, Latin, and Hebrew) before gradually extending its scope to all disciplines. Since then, very eminent scholars have given free public courses there. In 2001, you could hear Pierre-Gilles de Genne, Nobel Prize winner for Physics, on "Mosses," or philosopher Anne Fagot-Largeault on "The ethics of research in the Life and Health Sciences."

◆ *Publishers and bookstores*

As the cradle of the University, the Latin Quarter is also the home of the book industry. The name of Rue de la Parcheminerie (Parchment) preserves the memory of the medieval copyists and illuminators. The first printing works in France was founded in 1469 under the auspices of the University, and the Printers' Guild was firmly entrenched in the district throughout the Ancien Régime. Many publishers, such as Odile Jacob, still have their offices there, beside the huge bookstores.

◆ *Student protests*

In the Middle Ages, the University's internal squabbles sparked frequent riots. The indiscipline of the students often aroused protests from the bourgeoisie and brought crackdowns from the authorities. Some lawbreakers tried to pass themselves off as students to escape lay justice, whose penalties were harsher.

The University was weakened intellectually under the Ancien Régime, suppressed in the Revolution, and then reorganized according to Imperial standards. In the 20th century, the spirit of anti-authoritari-

1. Foundation stone of the Sorbonne
The old College of Theology, founded by a royal chaplain, Robert de Sorbon, became the seat of the University and was rebuilt from 1885. The foundation stone was solemnly laid before the teaching body in their gowns.

2. Amphitheater at the Sorbonne
The Great Amphitheater can hold more than 2,000 people. It is used for concerts and special events, as well as for lectures and university ceremonies.

3. May, 1968, Rue Gay-Lussac
In May, 1968, the rebellion in the Latin Quarter shook the whole of French society. The students occupied the Sorbonne, and barricades were raised around it. In the

violent confrontations with the police, cobblestones were torn up from the streets and used as missiles.

4. Place de la Sorbonne
This impressive 17th-century chapel built by Cardinal de Richelieu is seen to best advantage from the square, a shady open space recently embellished with a pool. Along its sides are bookstores and cafés where students meet between lectures.

5. Shakespeare & Co bookstore
This famous bookstore at 37 Rue de la Bucherie is a meeting-place for lovers of English language and literature.

anism returned, coming to a dramatic climax in the events of May, 1968, when a political, social, and cultural protest movement sparked a student revolt. Student discontent broke out at Nanterre University in the suburbs, then quickly spread to the Latin Quarter. Barricades went up everywhere, and torn-up paving stones were used as missiles. At the Sorbonne, which the students occupied night and day, they and other young revolutionaries dreamed of a more democratic, freer, more creative, and more brilliant world. The protest movement came to an end in June.

Boulevards and side-streets

The Boulevards Saint-Michel and Saint-Germain were laid out in the 19th century. Today they are lined with clothing stores, bookstores, and fast-food outlets. Meanwhile, the picturesque side-streets have their own specific character. Their names recall old trades or a nearby college. Sometimes, an unusual shop sign has been adopted as the street name: the Rue du Chat qui Pêche (the fishing cat), for example, the narrowest in Paris, or the Rue de la Harpe (harp). Masses of restaurants, mainly Greek, make these streets especially lively; there is also the Caveau de la Huchette, one of the first jazz clubs, and a little theater which since 1957 has continuosly staged two plays by Ionesco, *The Lesson*, and *The Bald Prima-Donna*.

Church of Saint-Julien-le-Pauvre

You would think you were in an old village: the shady square with its 400-year-old locust tree, a small church, a tiny cobbled square, and a well. Saint-Julien-le-Pauvre, one of the oldest churches in Paris, has been the Melchite (Greek Catholic) church since 1889. Inside is a beautiful screen (ikonostasis) made in Damascus in 1901. At the turn of the 12th and 13th centuries, the monks of Longpont built a priory there in an archaic Gothic style. Being so close to the University, the church had a ready congregation of teachers and students. Albertus Magnus, Saint Thomas Aquinas, Dante, and Petrarch came here to meditate.

Church of Saint-Séverin

The oldest parish in the Latin quarter is now considered the most progressive in Paris. The building was reconstructed between 1230 and the 16th century, gradually increasing in width although the street layout prevented it from growing in length. The Classical 17th-century decoration of the choir and, in 1837, the addition to the façade of the Gothic portal from an old church in the Cité, Saint-Pierre-aux-Boeufs, has given the building a composite character. Flamboyant Gothic is the predominant note, especially in the design of the vaults and pillars in the ambulatory behind the choir, and in the bell tower's tall spire. The 15th- and 16th-century stained glass, and the great organ, a splendid instru-

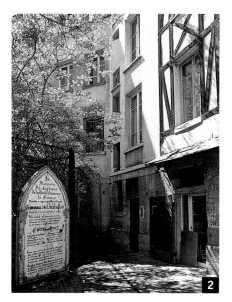

ment from the Louis XV period, add further to its opulence.

National Museum of the Middle Ages

This extraordinary complex includes the remains of the ancient baths, the Gothic mansion of the Abbots of Cluny, and a unique collection of medieval art. Since September, 2000, a medieval-style garden has been laid out around the buildings.

◆ Gallo-Roman baths

These public baths, rare remains of the Gallo-Roman city, were probably built by the Guild of Boatmen of Lutetia at the beginning of the 3rd century. The surviving elements include the site of a gymnasium, the hot and tepid baths, and the vaulted ceiling of the huge frigidarium (cold baths).

◆ Hôtel de Cluny

The Hôtel de Cluny was built in 1485-98 for the Abbots of Cluny, a powerful Burgundian monastery, and is an early example of a dwelling set between courtyard and garden. A large galleried wing, reached via a fine staircase tower, housed the apartments, while the small arcaded wing connected with the outbuildings. It is one of the few manorial residences from this period to have survived in Paris, its evident concern for luxury and comfort conveyed by the sculpted decoration of the doors, windows, and fireplaces, and the abundance of secondary staircases.

◆ The museum

It was here that Alexandre du Sommerard, a passionate art lover, kept his collections. These were bought by the State in 1842, and have since been enlarged to show the diversity and refinement of medieval art. The most famous work is undoubtedly the *Dame à la Licorne* ("Lady with the Unicorn"). It was commissioned from a studio in the Netherlands by the powerful Le Viste family, and consists of six tapestries, five of them each illustrating one of the senses. While specialists are still trying fully to decipher their symbolic meaning, the elegance of the lady playing the organ (Hearing), and another select-

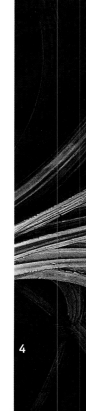

ing a delicacy from a box (Taste), and the fine lines of the unicorns, rabbits, birds, monkeys, and flowers convey an entrancing dreamworld. The museum also contains the 21 sculpted heads from the Gallery of the Kings of Judea at Notre-Dame, which were rediscovered in 1977.

1. Saint-Michel fountain
This impressive, theatrically decorated fountain, built in 1860, overlooks Place Saint-Michel at the start of the "Boul' Mich'." Young people from all over the world meet here before going to look round the district.

2. Caveau des Oubliettes
This cellar at No 1 *bis* Rue Saint-Julien-le-Pauvre puts on jazz and blues nights, and also contains a museum, the Historic House of Old French Song.

3. *The Lady with the Unicorn*
The six tapestries of the *Dame à la Licorne* series, a jewel of late 15th-century art, are in the National Museum of the Middle Ages. Here, in a delightful setting dotted with small animals, a finely dressed young woman offers a mirror to the fabulous unicorn, so illustrating one of the five senses: Sight.

4. Church of Saint-Séverin
Fine examples of Flamboyant Gothic architecture adorn this parish church, the oldest in the Latin Quarter. In the ambulatory behind the choir, the sprays of ribs supporting the vaults flow down into slender cabled columns like the branches of a palm tree.

5. Musée de Cluny
This luxurious 15th-century dwelling was built by the Abbots of Cluny on the site of the ancient baths destroyed in the 4th century, though three rooms have survived. It contains the National Museum of the Middle Ages, which has recently been embellished with a reconstruction of a medieval garden.

Panthéon district

The Panthéon bestrides the top of the hill of Sainte-Geneviève. It is an enormous building, 361 ft (110 m) long and 272 ft (83 m) high, and was designed by Soufflot in the 18th century. It overlooks a broad square surrounded by other impressive buildings: a church, a lycée, a library, the local town hall, and the Law faculty. Its great size stands in contrast to the narrow neighboring streets, which are often steep and lined with stores, like the Rue Mouffetard and Rue de la Montagne-Sainte-Geneviève, and to the delightful little squares like the Place de l'Estrapade and the more touristy Place le la Contrescarpe.

Sainte Geneviève, patron saint of Paris

Geneviève was born in about 420 to a rich family in Nanterre, and is remembered in Paris as a devout woman who, in 451, resisted the Huns, and, in 475, saved the city from famine. On her death, in about 502, King Clovis had her buried in the Church of Saints-Pierre-et-Paul, which he had commissioned on top of the hill overlooking the Ile de la Cité so that he could be buried there with his wife, Clotilde. Very soon after, Geneviève was declared a saint. The church became an abbey, and both it and the hill were given her name. Her remains were burned and thrown in the Seine in the Revolution, but her statue, built in 1928 on the Pont de la Tournelle, still watches over Paris.

The Panthéon, formerly the Church of Sainte-Geneviève

When he was seriously ill, Louis XV made a vow to build a new church to house the shrine of Sainte-Geneviève if he survived. He did, and was as good as his word. The architect Soufflot was commissioned in 1756 to carry out the building. Steeped in the culture of the Ancients, he designed a gigantic church in the shape of a Greek cross, surmounted by a majestic dome. Work was halted after the architect's death in 1780, and not properly resumed until 1791. The Revolu-

tionary parliament then changed the building's function, deciding instead to create a pantheon: a temple dedicated to great men. It commissioned Quatremère de Quincy to repair various faults, cracks having already appeared, and make the building look like a mausoleum.

◆ A necropolis for the Republic

Restored as a place of worship between 1806 and 1831, then again from 1852, the building became a lay temple once and for all to house the ashes of Victor Hugo in 1855. Sixty-one people are now buried in the Panthéon, including the writers Voltaire and Zola; Victor Schœlcher, who in 1848 abolished slavery in the French colonies; and Jean Moulin, the great Resistance leader in World War II. On April 20, 1995, Marie Curie became the first woman to be honored by this Republican temple, its pediment inscribed with the words: "To the Great Men, from their Grateful Country."

Church of Saint-Etienne-du-Mont

The Church of Saint-Etienne-du-Mont owes its fame to its rood-

screen, and to the worship of Sainte-Geneviève, whose shrine it has housed since the Revolution. It was built from 1492, but not completed until 1626. It thus displays a transitional style between Flamboyant Gothic and the spirit of the Renaissance, especially in the composition of the façade and its elegant roodscreen.

Around Rue Mouffetard

Fondly known as "La Mouffe," the Rue Mouffetard and its neighboring streets make up a very lively "village." Around the top end, "La Mouffe" is crammed with restaurants from all over the world: Spanish, Caribbean, Italian, Greek, Mexican, and even French. The lower part is a riot of color at market time. In the middle is the Contrescarpe: a small, shady square surrounded by cafés, once the resort of writers Rabelais, Ronsard, and Du Bellay, who used to meet in a tavern there in the 16th century. The district's liveliness goes back to when Rue Mouffetard was the last part of the road to Italy inside Philippe-Auguste's city wall. It was very busy, encouraging merchants and craftsmen to settle there, with the added bonus of having the Abbey of Sainte-Geneviève nearby.

Val-de-Grâce

The Val-de-Grâce contains a highly reputable military hospital, and a church that is one of the most remarkable examples of 17th-century architecture in Paris, and one of the best preserved. Located at the foot of the hill of Sainte-Geneviève, the Abbey of Val-de-Grâce was built in 1621 at the instigation of the devout Anne of Austria, who often prayed there. Here too she vowed to build a church if Heaven would grant her an heir. In 1638, after finally giving birth to the future Louis XIV, she commissioned François Mansart to carry out the building. The church was begun in 1645, and completed to his plans after his death. It is crowned by a magnificent cupola decorated with a vast tiered fresco by Mignard, featuring some 200 figures on clouds. The canopy, with its twisted columns, is like that of Saint Peter's

in Rome. The convent beside the church was completed in 1665. Its buildings were closed down in 1789, then handed over to the Army Medical Service and modernized in 1950. The new military hospital in the gardens dates from 1979.

1. Accordion player, Rue Mouffetard
The accordion is the traditional instrument of popular dance halls and songs about old Paris. You can still hear its familiar melodies in the streets of "La Mouffe."

2. Rue Mouffetard market
With its many boutiques and restaurants selling exotic dishes, Rue Mouffetard has been a shopping street since the Middle Ages. It also has one of the Left Bank's principal markets.

3. The Panthéon
In the Revolution, the Abbey Church of Sainte-Geneviève became a "pantheon." Some of France's most illustrious names are buried in its crypt. The pediment of this Republican temple is inscribed: "To the Great Men, from their Grateful Country."

4. Roodscreen, Saint-Etienne-du-Mont
The roodscreen closing off the choir at Saint-Etienne-du-Mont (1545) is one of the rare surviving examples in France. Its elegant decoration reflects the transition from Flamboyant Gothic to Renaissance style.

5. The Panthéon from the Luxembourg Garden
Soufflot's dome for the Panthéon caused considerable debate in the 18th century. At 272 ft (83 m), it is not the tallest in Paris, but its imposing bulk, standing on the hill of Sainte-Geneviève, is visible over much of the Left Bank.

6. Church of Val-de-Grâce
This church is one of the finest 17th-century architectural creations in Paris. It was built to plans by Mansart at the request of Queen Anne of Austria. The cupola is decorated with a fresco, a masterpiece by Mignard.

Around the Jardin des Plantes

H ere you can see diamonds and orangutans, dinosaur skeletons and living microscopic animals, a museum where the ceiling changes from day to night, and butterflies of every imaginable color. The Jardin des Plantes is an enjoyable place to walk and a scientific observatory. Around it are a tremendous variety of different places, from the Arènes de Lutèce, a Gallo-Roman amphitheater, to the Institute of the Arab World, with its ultramodern architecture. The district first grew up around a very old church dedicated to Saint Marcel (5th century), a bishop who gave his name to a medieval market town.

Arènes de Lutèce

It is a long time since this amphitheater was used by gladiators. Today it is more of a curiosity for tourists, a place for local children to play, and for games of pétanque. It was built in the 1st century, then badly damaged in the Barbarian invasions of the 3rd century, and vanished into the undergrowth. Its ruins were only discovered in 1869. These were partly excavated in 1883, in a project vigorously supported by Victor Hugo, and were completely laid bare in 1918. Their partial restoration (six sections of terrace out of 35) does not reflect the initial size of a stadium which, located outside the city on the eastern slope of the hill of Sainte-Geneviève, could hold 10,000 spectators.

Jardin des Plantes

The pathways of this botanical garden attract lots of people, as do its new Grande Galerie and the tropical glasshouses.

◆ Collecting and classifying

The Jardin des Plantes started from Henri IV's plan, completed by Louis XIII, to create a "royal garden for medicinal plants." It opened to the public in 1640, and consisted of a small building housing collections of "all things rare in nature." In 1809, its collection of specimens from the world's animal, vegetable, and mineral kingdoms covered an area of 3,600 sq yd (3,000 sq m). Plant hunting had developed a great deal in the 18th century; Buffon was a particularly influential figure, helping to build the institute into a real scientific forum. In the 20th century, the "total researcher," Théodore Monod, was one of the most distinguished of all traveler-collectors.

◆ Museum of Natural History and the Ménagerie

The museum, started in 1793 by Bernardin de Saint-Pierre, set out to combine its scientific approach with helping a mass audience to learn about the living world. To this end, a Ménagerie was started in 1794, attracting and captivating ordinary people. For six months, in 1827, more than 600,000 visitors enthused over the giraffe, the first ever seen in France, which had been presented to Charles X by Egypt. In the Museum, a large selection of stuffed animals,

ject. The building, designed by Jean Nouvel, acts as a bridge between civilizations. While the north façade echoes old Paris, the Moorish treatment of the south façade is an elegant, modern reinterpretation of Arab architecture and decorative art.

The Mosque

The Mosque was built in 1922-6 to honor Muslims killed in World War I. With its 108 ft (33 m) minaret, the Mosque is primarily a place for prayer and teaching. However, it is open to the public and provides a restful environment with a hammam, a pretty patio with a fountain, and colorful, finely decorated rooms where you can have couscous, mint tea, and pastries.

skeletons, and animal pictures were hung on the walls or from the ceilings, creating a weird atmosphere. Even though the systems of classification were increasingly refined, by 1965 the main Zoology Gallery was looking like a real Noah's Ark, and was closed for the next 30 years.

◆ Grande Galerie de l'Evolution

When the main gallery reopened in 1994, it had been completely reorganized. Instead of showing rows of specimens from the whole collection, the museum uses just a selection to illustrate the evolution of life. Its aim is to show the diversity of present-day species, to explain the evolution of living organisms in Earth's history, and help people to think about how man has influenced evolution through environmental changes. There are interactive sites, recordings of animal cries, and lighting effects that change the ceiling/sky from day to night, all of which bring the scene to life and add a touch of mystery.

◆ Elsewhere in the Gardens

The Jardin des Plantes has many other attractions: a botanical garden with more than 2,600 varieties, a menagerie, a micro-zoo where you can see microscopic species, a green maze, rare and valuable trees (some planted by Buffon), and tropical glasshouses. Three galleries house thousands of specimens: giant crystals, precious stones, fossil rocks, dinosaur skeletons, and amazingly colored insects.

Institute of the Arab World

This institute was opened in 1987. Its aim is to promote exchanges between France and the 20 Arab countries associated with the pro-

1. Arènes de Lutèce
The amphitheater is a pleasant small park with a past going back to ancient times. Rediscovered in 1869, the old sports stadium's terraces could hold 10,000 spectators.

2. Glasshouse in Jardin des Plantes
Ever since it was founded by kings of France in the 17th century, the Jardin des Plantes has collected and tended thousands of plants in its glasshouses.

3. Gallery of Evolution
The Grande Galerie, opened in 1994, shows the story of life on Earth since the earliest times. The museum's vast collection of stuffed animals is displayed together with special sound and visual effects.

4. Institute of the Arab World
Architect Jean Nouvel's south façade merges the most up-to-date technology with traditional Moorish art. Thousands of geometrically arranged metal apertures open and close according to the light conditions.

5. Hammam at the Paris Mosque
The Mosque opened in 1926, and is primarily a place of worship, but also provides an insight into life in a Muslim country, with a traditional hammam offering steam baths and massages.

CHURCH OF SAINT-GERMAIN-DES-PRÉS
and surrounding area

Church of
Saint-Germain-des-Prés

Saint-Germain to Passerelle
des Arts

Montparnasse to Cité
Universitaire

The Odéon and Luxembourg
district

Aerial view of Saint-Germain-des-Prés
The streets surrounding the church reflect the
historic layout of the Abbey of Saint-Germain-
des-Prés, but the broad streets created by
Haussmann have changed the district's
appearance. The section of Boulevard Saint-
Germain running beside the church was built
in 1866, when several old streets vanished.
Rue de Rennes, which intersects it almost at a
right angle, is also from the 19th century. A
curious fact: the numbering of this street
begins with Nos 41 and 44, the plan to extend
it to the river having been later abandoned.

Church of Saint-Germain-des-Prés

Its bell tower, begun at the dawn of the year 1000, is the symbol of this district. The Church of Saint-Germain-des-Prés was founded in the 6th century and rebuilt in the Middle Ages to become the heart of a monastic empire and a brilliant intellectual center. Today it is one of the largest Romanesque buildings in Paris. Though damaged in the Revolution, it was restored in the 19th century.

Remains of a famous monastic community

You need a lot of imagination to summon up the huge monastic complex which before the Revolution extended over the whole district. Today only the church and bishop's palace remain, made of stone and brick in the Henri IV style. The fortified perimeter followed the lines of Boulevard Saint-Germain (then Rue Taranne), Rue Saint-Benoît, Rue Jacob (then Rue du Colombier), and Rue de l'Echaudé. The refectory and the large Lady Chapel, a design by Pierre de Montreuil that was compared with Sainte-Chapelle, were lost in 1802 when Rue de l'Abbaye was built. The Great Cloister adjoining the church was replaced by a square containing some pieces of the Lady Chapel. The stables were in the delightful Place de Furstemberg, while Rue Bonaparte now covers the Great Garden.

The Merovingian basilica

The history of this establishment goes back to 542, when Childebert, son of Clovis, returned from his Spanish campaigns with the relics of Saint Vincent. To provide them with a dignified resting place, Germain, Bishop of Paris, persuaded the king to build a basilica and a monastery. The Basilica of Sainte-Croix-et-Saint-Vincent was consecrated in 558, and so richly decorated (with a gilded ceiling and a roof in gilded bronze) that it came to be nicknamed Saint-Germain-the-Golden. In time, the basilica officially adopted the name of the bishop who consecrated it and was buried there in 576. Almost nothing remains of this first basilica, where a number of Merovingian kings were buried, from Childebert to Dagobert. It was attacked several times by the Normans, and burnt to ashes in 855.

A Romanesque jewel with a Gothic choir

Once they had recovered from this blow, the abbots set about rebuilding the church, which was essentially the building you see today. Construction of the bell tower began in 990. Its massive appearance and stout buttresses reflect the defensive concerns of an age when the bell tower might also have to serve as a keep. The Chapelle Saint-Symphorien, in which traces of frescos from the 1290s can be seen, was built a few years later, like the interior with its three naves (mid-11th century). The historiated capitals, some of which have been preserved at the Musée de Cluny, are among the most remarkable in Romanesque sculpture. The present vaulted nave was rebuilt in the Gothic style in the 17th century, but the Flamboyant choir, blessed in 1163 by Pope Alexander III, is authentic Gothic. Supported by magnificent flying buttresses and crowned with a halo of chapels radiating from it, this choir inspired the builders of Notre-Dame.

Great moments at the abbey

The Benedictine Abbey owned meadows and vineyards, was surrounded by fortified walls, and with the University shared control of the Pré-aux-Clercs, the wasteland which ran down to the river. The abbots, though, looked far beyond the river, founding monasteries as far away as Italy and Bohemia. For centuries, the Abbey was an important intellectual center that made itself felt all over Europe with, in the 17th century,

Hall of Fame
Childebert (495-558)

It was Childebert, third son of Clovis, who founded the Abbey of Saint-Germain. While on a military expedition to Spain, he was unimpressed by the inhabitants of Saragossa who tried to stand up to him by parading with the tunic of Saint Vincent. Childebert seized the tunic, which, together with a golden cross, became the main elements of the treasure that the basilica was built to contain. This very Christian king not only paid for the church's magnificent decoration, but then, not content with providing mere material gifts, granted the monks rights of ownership over the waters of the Seine, with fishing rights and powers of justice. On his death, Childebert wished to be laid to rest in the basilica with his wife Ultrogothe, thus inaugurating the main burial vault, along with Saint-Denis, of the Merovingian kings. ■

learned monks such as Mabillon, Félibien, and Montfaucon. Meanwhile, the Saint-Germain Fair, which took place just outside in Rue de Buci, filled its coffers nicely, attracting merchants from Flanders, Germany, and Italy, and a host of customers.

Revolution and upheaval

Then came decline. In March, 1762, a fire ravaged the Fair, and it never recovered. The Revolution applied the final blow. The monks were expelled in 1791. A fire destroyed the precious library. The church became a store for saltpeter, which steadily eroded the walls and the last remaining statues.

Great restoration programs of the 19th century

In 1802, the church was finally restored for worship. In 1822, however, the architect E H Godde, who was in charge of its restoration, had to demolish the upper story of the two towers flanking the choir, which were in danger of collapsing. A vast program to decorate the interior was commissioned from artists such as Flandrin, for the nave and choir, and

Heim, for the grisaille paintings in the Lady Chapel. These great 19th-century restorations, with their polychrome paintings, helped to give the church its present appearance.

Facts & Figures	
CHURCH OF SAINT-GERMAIN-DES-PRÉS	
Length: 213 ft (65 m)	
Width: 69 ft (21 m)	
Height: 62 ft (19 m)	
THE FIRST ABBEY	
Consecrated in 558, destroyed in 885	
Five kings were buried there: Childebert, Childéric II, Dagobert, Chilpéric I, Clotaire II	
THE NEW ABBEY	
Bell tower: begun in 990	
Nave: begun about 1025-30	
Choir: begun in 1144, consecrated by the Pope in 1163	
Vault of nave: rebuilt in 17th century in style of choir	
Chapelle Saint-Symphorien: 11th century	
Paintings in choir and nave: 19th century	

1. Capital in the ambulatory
While the heads of the Biblical kings framing the porch were hammered off in the Revolution, the capitals, some of them decorated with figures in the Romanesque tradition, have mostly survived to our own times. The originals are in the Musée de Cluny.

2. Nave of the church
A popular venue for concerts, the nave acquired its Gothic appearance relatively late (17th century). The murals by Hippolyte Flandrin date from restorations carried out in the 19th century.

3. Terrace of the Deux-Magots, c 1960
Clients of the Café des Deux-Magots have included Jean Giraudoux, André Breton, Henri Matisse, Jean-Paul Sartre, and Simone de Beauvoir. Diderot, who lived at the same address, was not able to enjoy its famous chocolate, as the café only opened a century after his death, in 1873. Like its neighbor, the Flore, the Café des Deux-Magots has been classified as a historic monument.

4. Church organ
The organ at Saint-Germain-des-Prés dates from the second half of the 17th century and came from the vanished Abbey of Saint-Victor, which was on the site of the present Jussieu faculty building.

Saint-Germain to Passerelle des Arts

The name Saint-Germain-des-Prés has a universal resonance. Its fame stems mostly from the time when the district was frequented by writers Jean-Paul Sartre and Simone de Beauvoir, poet Jacques Prévert, singer Juliette Gréco, and writer and musician Boris Vian. Its cultural life flourishes still, sustained by its many publishers, bookstores, galleries, and art schools, and even cafés that award prizes for literature. However, the district's middle-class population has been on the increase since the 1970s, with an invasion of luxury businesses around the ancient abbey.

A place for having fun and for thinking

◆ Where existentialists gathered

After World War II, the streets beside the 1,000-year-old church became the focus of partying and existentialism. Sartre, who was staying at the Hôtel de la Louisiane, Rue de Seine, made the Café de Flore in Boulevard Saint-Germain his daily headquarters. There he kept open house at a table near the stove, persuading the owner to provide him with a personal telephone line. The author of *La Nausée* was actually doing no more than continuing a well-entrenched literary tradition. Those very same benches had previously accommodated Maurras and the followers of Action Française, then Jacques Prévert and his cronies in the October Group. A few yards from the Flore, facing the bell tower, is the equally famous Café des Deux-Magots. It still has the two Chinese statuettes which gave it its name when, in 1873, it was a fabric store specializing in cloth by the meter. Since 1933, it has awarded a prize for literature, with Raymond Queneau the first winner.

◆ From the Lipp to the jazz clubs

Opposite, on the other side of the boulevard, is the Alsatian Brasserie Lipp, named for its founder, Anatole Lipp. It too has a prize for literature, the Prix Cazes, founded in 1934. A favorite with writers and politicians, an early Lipp regular was Alfred Jarry, who arrived by bicycle and, it is said, started his meals with the dessert. Others were Léon-Paul Fargue, the restless poet of the streets, whose father produced the ceramics decorating the walls, and Antoine de Saint-Exupéry. Other literary landmarks worth mentioning are two bookstores, La Hune and Le Divan. The latter opened in 1921 opposite the abbey, and attracted fans of Stendhal. Its replacement in 1998 by a Dior boutique underlines the changing character of the district: luxury is overtaking literature.

The partying tradition, which during the Liberation had shaken local God-fearing citizens, has also been somewhat stifled. Le Tabou, in Rue Dauphine, was the most popular of the cellars where musicians like Mouloudji, Juliette Gréco, Miles Davis, and Claude Luter got together, along with writers (Camus, Vailland, Claude Mauriac, and Boris Vian) and artists and actors (Roger Blin and Jean-Louis Barrault), to celebrate their new-found liberty with a blast of bebop or boogie-woogie.

A very commercial district

◆ Luxury, frenzy, charm

As well as Dior, a number of the deluxe trades traditionally encamped on the Right Bank have been trying since the 1990s to secure a foothold in Saint-Germain-des-Prés. In 1995, the luggage-maker Vuitton set up behind acres of plate glass opposite the abbey. In 1996, a gleaming marble boutique selling Cartier jewelry replaced a famous record dealer in the square, just next to a new Lanvin boutique. In 1998, Armani established an "emporio" on the site of the Publicis-Saint-Germain, a drugstore which had only been there since 1965 but had added life to the area until late at night.

To the south of the square, all the streets going toward Sèvres-Babylone, Montparnasse, and Saint-Sulpice are lined with boutiques selling ready-made clothes, shoes, fine leather goods, jewels, perfume, and household linen. Some are luxurious, like the jeweller Boucheron in Rue des Saints-Pères, and all are very busy. During sales, the district goes crazy. To the north of the square, toward the Seine, fashion gives way to boutiques for interior decorating and furnishing fabrics, engravings and old books, and a profusion of art galleries, especially near Rue de Seine

and Rue des Beaux-Arts, and the "antique dealers' block" on the riverside and neighboring streets.

◆ Buci, the queen of markets

The festive, crowded atmosphere still to be found at the Buci market is a far cry from the street as it was eight centuries ago. At the time of Philippe-Auguste's city wall, one of the main gates for entering the capital was at the crossing of the present Rue Saint-André-des-Arts and Rue André-Mazet. Beyond lay the city, guarded by sergeants of the watch. On this side was the kingdom of traders, dealers, and mountebanks. In Rue de Buci, people bought and sold things, eating on the street along with the fruit and vegetable sellers, or in a

5

more comfortable setting such as the Restaurant Landelle, favored by the cream of the 18th century's intelligentsia and free-thinkers. Today, foreigners and locals still enjoy sitting on the café terraces, which are heated in winter, to sip a glass and observe the passing throng and the colorful stalls of the lively market, or maybe do some shopping themselves in one of the stores selling fine foods and delicacies.

1. Terrace of the Deux-Magots
The café and its terrace, with its splendid view over the square, continue to attract crowds of customers on the trail of its famous literary figures.

2. Brasserie Lipp
Lipp opened in 1871, and has long been a favorite with politicians, including Georges Pompidou and François Mitterrand.

3. Buci market
Formerly one of the Left Bank's main streets, Rue de Buci is now a market street crammed with colorful stalls.

4. Place Furstemberg
Created to provide the Abbey with an exit onto Rue du Colombier (now Rue Jacob), the street was widened at its center to make a delightful tiny square, and formerly housed the abbey stables. It is named for Egon de Fürstenberg, abbot of Saint-Germain at the end of the 17th century.

5. Duke Ellington and Boris Vian
After World War II, the cellars and jazz clubs of Saint-Germain flourished. The great American musicians loved coming here to sow the seeds of bebop, and were welcomed by brilliant artists such as Boris Vian, author of *A Manual of Saint-Germain-des-Prés*.

4

Riches of bygone days

◆ Havens of peace and quiet streets

Close to the shopping streets, where you can sometimes hardly get through the crowds, there are some very quiet streets and squares. The Place de Furstemberg, shaded by paulownias, is the most delightful of these havens of peace. The painter Delacroix (1798-1863) moved into one of the houses in 1857 to deal with his final commission to paint the frescos in the Church of Saint-Sulpice; the house is now his museum. Strolling on toward the Seine, you detect an aristocratic atmosphere in Rue Dauphine. It is almost 33 ft (10 m) wide, and in the 17th century was one of the capital's most beautiful streets and the first to be equipped with street lamps, on the eve of the Revolution. Together with Rue Christine, it was the result of a successful property development carried out in the reign of Henri IV. This happened immediately after the opening of Pont Neuf, and was made possible through the sale of lands and houses belonging to the Grands-Augustins monastery.

It certainly makes a contrast with Rue de Nevers, a narrow street, hemmed in by buildings, which has not been altered since the 13th century. You can easily imagine its pavements made slippery by rain and streams of refuse thrown from the windows. The situation had hardly improved at the beginning of the 20th century, when Pierre Curie was run over and killed there by a coachman unable to control his horses.

◆ The Mint and the Institut

Two state-controlled establishments stand majestically on Quai de Conti: the Hôtel des Monnaies (the Mint) and the Institut de France. The former was built in 1771-7 by Antoine, a young architect unknown at the time. Its linear sobriety and harmony of scale make it the first major building in the Louis XVI style.

Inside, the coin museum tells the story of coinage and the evolution of the art of medalmaking.

The Institut de France contains five academies, including the Académie Française, in the former Collège des Quatre-Nations. This was founded by Cardinal Mazarin who, in his will of 1661, stated his wish to spend his fortune on the education of noblemen from remote provinces. The building's pure lines and semi-circular façade were designed by Louis Le Vau in 1662. It stands in harmony with the Louvre, where the architect designed the King's Apartments; facing each other, the two make a fine pair. The main courtyard leads on one side to the Mazarin Library, the cardinal's personal library, which was opened to scholars in 1643. On the other side is the former Mazarin Chapel, beneath the dome of which the solemn sessions of the Académie Française have taken place since 1806.

4

◆ **On Pont des Arts**

This footbridge built in 1803 was the first cast-iron bridge in France, its design inspired by English wooden bridges. Its name stems from the way it links the Institut with the Palace of the Arts, ie the Louvre. It is for pedestrians only and is lined with benches and decorated with tubs of flowers, giving strollers a splendid view of the Seine: upstream to the Ile de la Cité

5

and Notre Dame, downstream to the Louvre and Musée d'Orsay.

◆ **Ecole des Beaux-Arts**

The Ecole des Beaux-Arts is in the former 17th-century Monastery of the Petits-Augustins, of which the main surviving elements are the Chapel and the Cloister, which became the Cour du Mûrier. Here in 1795, Alexandre Lenoir established the Museum of French Monuments to hide fragments of architecture and decorations from Revolutionary vandals, including the porch of the Château de Gaillon (since returned to its original site) and the front of the Château d'Anet. In 1816, the former monastery was allocated to the École des Beaux-Arts and its buildings remodeled over almost half a century by architect Félix Duban.

1. Hôtel des Monnaies
No coins of the realm have been minted here for a quarter of a century, though the Hôtel des Monnaies continues to make medals, and in a museum display tells the story of the metal franc piece.

2. École des Beaux-Arts
The École des Beaux-Arts is descended from the Royal Academy of Painting founded by Le Brun under Louis XIV. It was set up in 1816 in its present home, the disused Monastery of the Petits-Augustins.

3. Institut de France
The marble interiors of the Collège des Quatre-Nations, designed by Le Vau, bear the stamp of the Grand Siècle. After serving as a college for young noblemen from France's new provinces, it was given by Napoléon to the Institut and the Académie Française.

4. Passerelle des Arts
At the beginning of the 19th century, this was a real engineering feat, the first cast-iron bridge in France. Time and repeated buffeting from the wake of passing barges proved fatal. It had to be rebuilt in 1982, and the number of arches reduced from nine to seven.

5. Mazarin Library
The Institut is a splendid setting for France's first public library, created at the wish of Mazarin after his death (1661).

The Odéon and Luxembourg district

The Carrefour de l'Odéon is busy throughout the year and until late at night. People traditionally gather beneath the statue of Danton in the middle of the square: musicians, tap-dancers, shaven-headed Buddhists shaking handbells, or demonstrators chanting slogans through their megaphones. With two Métro lines stopping here, it is an ideal place to meet before going to the Théâtre de l'Odéon or one of the many cinemas and restaurants in the district.

Actors and theaters

At No 14 Rue de l'Ancienne Comédie, a Minerva sculpted by Etienne Le Hongre is one of the last traces of the Hôtel des Comédiens du Roy, built by François d'Orbay in 1688. The actors' presence gladdened the heart of Francesco Procopio dei Coltelli, a Sicilian who moved into premises across the road in 1684 and was one of the first to serve the new beverage which became madly popular: coffee. In his shop, Le Procope, which is still there today, the Encyclopedists Voltaire, Rousseau, and Diderot, and revolutionary thinkers Marat and Camille Desmoulins talked for hours on end.

In 1770, the auditorium of the Comédiens du Roy collapsed in ruins. A new theater was built on the site of the Prince de Condé's former mansion, which the King had bought and given to the people. In 1767, the Marquis de Marigny commissioned Peyre and Wailly to built the Théâtre Français, but it was not opened until 1783. Its colonnaded front and side wings (now gone) are a good example of the French Classical style. In 1797, the Revolutionaries renamed it the Odéon. Though twice destroyed by fire, in 1799 and 1818, it was rebuilt each time. Today, under the official name of Théâtre de l'Europe, it often hosts companies from abroad, whose shows are subtitled.

Revolutionaries and surgeons

The statue of Danton (1759-94), a reminder of the Revolution, was built at the Carrefour de l'Odéon in 1891, on the site of Danton's house. Just opposite is an arcade, the Cour du Commerce Saint-André, leading to the delightful Cour de Rohan, containing a mansion from 1636. Here in 1791, in a setting so redolent of Old Paris with its uneven cobblestones and store signs, Doctors Guillotin and Louis tried out their deadly invention, the guillotine, on a number of hapless sheep. Here, too, Marat set up the printer's known as The People's Friend. Camille Desmoulins (No 2 Place de l'Odéon) and Hébert (lodging in Rue du Tournon) were near neighbors. Several of these Revolutionaries gathered at the Club des Cordeliers, which met nearby at the former Cordelier monastery, founded in the 13th century. The refectory still exists, a rare example of the Flamboyant Gothic for Paris, and holds interesting temporary exhibitions. Opposite is the former Royal Academy of Surgeons, built between 1776 and 1786, now housing a museum of medicine. Further along is the charming Hôtel de la Confrérie des Chirurgiens, built at the end of the 17th century and now occupied by the Institute of Modern Languages.

The publishers' district

At the beginning of the 19th century, Louis Hachette founded his

nal location. Its foundation goes back to the 12th century, but the church you see today was begun in 1646 and not completed until the eve of the Revolution. Its main façade was designed by Servandoni in 1732 (and redesigned after 1770). The North Tower was built in 1780 by Chalgrin, and the South Tower was never finished. The church is one of the biggest in Paris: 361 ft (110 m) long and 108 ft (33 m) high (239 ft/73 m for the North Tower). The great conches presented as fonts to François I by the Republic of Venice are still in place, as are *The Assumption* painted by Lemoyne in 1731 and the frescos completed by Delacroix in 1861. The organ, rebuilt by Aristide Cavaillé-Coll in 1862, is one of the most impressive in Paris, with nearly 6,500 pipes.

bookshop on Boulevard Saint-Michel. A few years later, Pierre Larousse opened offices in Rue Pierre Sarrazin.

In the second half of the 19th century, Alfred Valette and his wife Rachilde revived the old *Mercure de France* in Rue de Condé, attracting a swarm of Symbolist writers. Ernest Flammarion started modestly by selling unsold stocks beneath the arcades of the Théâtre de l'Odéon. Then, as he became successful, he settled in Rue Racine, where his firm still operates a century later.

José Corti, the famous publisher specialising in literature and the social sciences, Belin, Herscher, and many others have offices in the Odéon district and nearby.

Around Saint-Sulpice

For a long time the Church of Saint-Sulpice had a famous seminary next to it, and was a center for stores selling religious items. The seminary was closed down in 1906 and replaced by a tax office. The rosary and crucifix merchants held out for longer, but since the 1970s have given way to luxury boutiques such as Christian Lacroix, Yves Saint-Laurent, and Annick Goutal. Only one religious bookshop seems to be still flourishing.

◆ The well-preserved church

Saint-Sulpice is one of those rare churches in Paris not to have suffered too much in the Revolution. Its architecture was left intact and many of its works of art are in their origi-

1. Shakespeare and Company
This bookstore, today on the banks of the Seine opposite Notre-Dame, was founded in 1922 at No 12 Rue de l'Odéon by Sylvia Beech, first publisher of Joyce's *Ulysses*.

2. Théâtre de l'Europe
The former Théâtre de l'Odéon, where Sarah Bernhardt made her debut and Jean-Louis Barrault staged his famous productions, today specializes in works by foreign companies.

3. Cordeliers monastery
The Cordeliers monastery is a Franciscan foundation which later housed meetings of the Revolutionary club of the same name, formed by Danton. Now only the 13th-century refectory remains, used for exhibitions.

4. Saint-Sulpice
On the forecourt, in front of Servandoni's façade, the name of the Fountain of the Four Cardinal Points is a pun on the four ecclesiastics portrayed (none of whom was a cardinal).

5. Boutiques at Saint-Sulpice
Liturgical stores are in decline in the district, giving way to the onslaught of fashion boutiques.

◆ Poetry on the square

The church's forecourt is embellished with a fountain by Visconti (1848) portraying four bishops: Massillon, Fléchier, Bossuet, and Fénelon. For some years, a very popular flea market and poetry market have been held on Place Saint-Sulpice in spring. The typically Parisian Café de la Mairie in the square was where author Georges Pérec sat when he was writing his diary of observations on the local scene, while Christian Vincent filmed several scenes there for *La Discrète*.

The Luxembourg Palace: from the Queen to the Senators

◆ Palace of a Florentine queen

The Luxembourg palace, now home to the Sénat (French Upper House) was built at the beginning of the 17th century for Marie de Médicis. Wishing to get away from the Louvre after the assassination of her husband Henri IV, the Queen bought the Duke of Luxembourg's mansion (the present Petit-Luxembourg, residence of the President of the Sénat) and nearby plots, and had a palace

and garden built in the spirit of the Palazzo Pitti in Florence, where she spent her childhood. The first stone was laid in 1615. The architect, Salomon de Brosse, designed a majestic palace ushering in French Classicism on a grand scale with its unified and balanced style. The Florentine influence comes through mainly in the use of rustication to break up the façades' monotony and create a more "cheerful" atmosphere. The interior decoration was based on the opulent colors of gold and azure, made with lapis lazuli. Some remains of this scheme were retained in 1816 in the Salle du Livre d'Or. The most magnificent part of the palace is a gallery which the Queen commissioned Rubens to decorate: 24 canvasses recounting the life of Marie de Médicis with prolific use of symbols and allegories.

◆ Seat of the Upper House

In the Revolution, the palace was turned into a prison, then in 1799 handed over to the Sénat, which has sat there ever since, except during wars and revolutions. In the 19th century, the architect Gisors brought his 102 ft (31 m) façade forward by building two identical pavilions on the garden front. In the 1970s, architect Christian Langlois was commissioned to dig out space round the

palace and main courtyard to make parking spaces, reception rooms, audio-visual control rooms, and offices opening onto patios. Since then, the Sénat complex has expanded continually toward Saint-Sulpice via old or recently-built blocks linked to the palace by footbridges and underground tunnels.

◆ The Luxembourg museums

In 1750, France's first public museum of painting opened in the gallery of the Luxembourg Palace, showing about 100 masterpieces from the king's cabinet. Closed in 1780, it reopened in 1818 under the name Musée Royal du Luxembourg, and was devoted to living artists. In 1886, it left the palace for a purpose-built home overlooking Rue de Vaugirard. Then, in 1937 the museum of living artists was transferred to the Palais de Tokyo. Since 1973, the Musée du Luxembourg has put on temporary exhibitions chosen by the Sénat and the Minister of Culture. In 2000, the exhibition of landscapes photographed from the air by Yann Arthus-Bertrand was so successful that it was later shown for several months outside the garden railings.

◆ The "Luco"

Students happily call it the "Luco" without knowing that in the Gallo-Roman period a suburb of Lutetia,

known as Lucotitius, ran as far as the site of the Luxembourg Garden. The main survivor of Marie de Médicis' Italian-style garden of grottos, fountains, and green borders are the Fontaine Médicis and the geometric plantations of trees in staggered rows. The Luxembourg was enlarged in the Revolution by the annexing of the Carthusian monastery, then shrunk by Haussmann when Rue Auguste Comte was driven through it, but its orchard preserves some memory of the nursery-tending monks. It has offered free propagation courses since 1809. Next to it, a beekeeping school produces several hundred pounds of honey each year. The Luxembourg Garden attracts many students from the nearby universities as well as local children and retired people, drawn by its many

statues; courts for tennis, real tennis, and bowling; playgrounds for children; the carousel loved by the poet Rilke; the puppet theater; and benches hidden beneath shady trees. To the south, after Davioud's fine railings, the park leads to the Marco Polo and Cavelier de la Salle Gardens, and Carpeaux's famous sculpture, *The Four Quarters of the World*.

1. Café de la Mairie
This café has an excellent view of the Church of Saint-Sulpice and the square.

2. Time off in the Luxembourg Garden
The Garden fascinated Romantic writers, who loved to wander through the trees in the southern part; today it is a favorite with students and joggers.

3. Garden front of the Sénat
Seat of the French Upper House since 1799, the Luxembourg Palace was financed by Marie de Médicis, who wanted to recreate the architecture of her childhood dwelling, the Palazzo Pitti in Florence.

4. Luxembourg Garden
In the Revolution, the Luxembourg Garden was swelled by the Carthusian monastery to almost 124 acres (50 ha), but property schemes in the Second Empire reduced its area by half.

5. Nursery garden
The Luxembourg's nursery belonged formally to the nearby Carthusian monastery, which was annexed in the Revolution.

6. The Luxembourg's Orangery
The Orangery was built in the Second Empire, and its Museum of Living Artists was France's first public gallery.

Montparnasse to Cité Universitaire

I ts name, taken from Mount Parnassus, the Greek mountain dedicated to poets and muses, was given to it in the 17th century by students who went there to recite poems on a small hill close to the present Montparnasse-Raspail intersection. It was a prescient choice, as Montparnasse became the crucible of the 20th century's great artistic movements. Nowhere more so than in this area – except for a time in Montmartre – did people write, paint, sculpt, and draw with such brilliance. World War II brought all this to an end. In the 1970s, pressures of town planning, as symbolized by the Montparnasse Tower, drove the penniless artists away. Those with a little money, and bourgeois bohemians too, can still find studios and houses to rent in its peaceful narrow streets. Montparnasse is a lively district from morning to night, filled with cafés and cinemas, theaters and Breton crêperies.

The golden age of bohemia

By the end of the 19th century, Montparnasse was attracting artists and intellectuals with its rural atmosphere, little houses, and the famous Bal Bullier, which opened in 1847. It was mostly in the years 1910-20, however, that the district saw a great influx of painters (Modigliani, Utrillo, Soutine, Braque, Chagall, and Picasso), sculptors (Bourdelle and Zadkine), and poets (Paul Fort, Max Jacob, Apollinaire, and Blaise Cendrars). Russian political exiles also settled there (Lenin and Trotsky), and many American writers (eg Hemmingway and Henry Miller). They

talked for hours in the new cafés, whose owners often accepted paintings or drawings in payment: La Closerie des Lilas, Le Dôme, La Rotonde (now gone), Le Select (the first café in Montparnasse to stay open all night), and La Coupole. In the 1930s, Picasso, Kandinsky, Max Ernst, Giacometti, and Miró met at Atelier 17, a four-storied studio building at No 17 Rue Campagne-Première, while Modigliani worked at No 3. The building at No 21 Avenue du Maine, where around 1910 the Russian painter Marie Vassilieva created an "artists' canteen," now contains the Chemin de Montparnasse: a small museum documenting the district's finest hours and showing the work of foreign artists who have come there to live. The studios of Bourdelle and Zadkine have also been turned into museums, and recall the time when the two sculptors worked there.

Beneath the Tower

People may paint at Montparnasse, but they sing there as well. Since the second half of the 19th century, Rue de la Gaîté has had the biggest concentration of theaters and concert-cafés in Paris. The legendary Folies-Bobino, where Mayol and Fréhel performed, has become a hotel, but the Gaîté-Montparnasse, the Théâtre Montparnasse, and the Comédie-Italienne seem to have resisted pressure from the sex-shops since 1980. Rue d'Odessa and Rue du Départ have a number of crêperies, the Gare Montparnasse being the point of arrival for migrating Bretons to Paris. The old station was in the news in 1895 when the Granville express was derailed, and the locomotive careened onto the boulevard. The station was demolished in the 1960s, and rebuilt as part of the huge Maine-Montparnasse development scheme. Next to it stands the 686 ft (209 m)-tall Montparnasse Tower, built in 1973, while the Jardin Atlantique was built 59 ft (18 m) over the tracks. Nearby, the Place de Catalogne has a striking collection of Neo-Classical buildings by Ricardo Bofill and a pool in the shape of a

massive, dark disk, which its designer, Shamai Haber, has called *The Crucible of Time.*

A famous cemetery

When it was built in 1824, the Montparnasse cemetery, then called the Cimitière du Midi, was outside Paris. Today it still has its windmill, one of the last in the city. Although one of the smallest cemeteries in Paris, many artists and intellectuals are buried there, including composer Saint-Saëns, sculptor Bourdelle, painter Soutine, actress Jean Seberg, and singer Serge Gainsbourg. A cenotaph was built for poet Charles Baudelaire, and the tomb of Brancusi is decorated with one of his sculptures, *The Kiss.* Writers Jean-Paul Sartre and Simone de Beauvoir share the same tomb.

Around the Lion of Belfort

In the middle of Place Denfert-Rochereau sits the Lion of Belfort. This major junction on the route of Parisian demonstrations was one of the first to greet the arrival of

1. La Coupole, c 1930
La Coupole opened in 1927 and quickly became a favorite with Parisian bohemia. Here Lenin, Modigliani, Pascin, Man Ray, and Cocteau came to sit on the terrace, or inside beneath the 16 pillars decorated by local artists.

2. Gare Montparnasse
The district's transformation from 1961 meant building a new station set back from the original site, which reached as far as the present Place du 18-Juin.

3. The Tower and Place du 18-Juin
The Montparnasse Tower was built between 1969 and 1972 on foundations sunk 197 ft (60 m) into the limestone to avoid the Métro. It is 686 ft (209 m) tall, 105 ft (32 m) wide, and weighs 132,250 tons (120,000 t). From its top floor, open to the public, there are spectacular views of Paris.

4. The Lion of Belfort
This replica of the lion made in Belfort by sculptor Auguste Bartholdi commemorates the courage of the people in the Siege of 1870-1, and is an essential stage in major protest marches.

5. The Observatory
One of the world's oldest observatories still in use, it stands precisely on the Paris meridian, which is modeled inside the building. Its treasures include Arago's telescope and various optical instruments made by Foucault, Le Verrier, and their peers.

Leclerc's Second Armored Division in August, 1944. In the fever of the May, 1968 riots, students attacked and seized the Lion. South-west of the square are two symmetrical pavilions built by Claude Nicolas Ledoux in 1787. They were part of the wall of the Farmers-General, which ringed Paris, and formed the Enfer tax gate. Next to one of them is the entrance to the Catacombs.

On Boulevard Raspail, the Cartier Foundation has a collection of international contemporary art. The glass and steel building was designed by Jean Nouvel (1994), architect of the Institute of the Arab World.

Near Avenue Denfert-Rochereau is one of the world's oldest observatories, built in 1661 on the orders of Louis XIV and Colbert.

The Avenue du Général-Leclerc leads to the market in Rue Daguerre.

Avenue René Coty runs down to Parc Montsouris, a delightfully undulating park flanked by charming cul-de-sacs. In one of these is the villa where Henry Miller wrote *Tropic of Cancer*. Beyond is the Cité Universitaire: 100 acres (40 ha) of parkland where students from more than a hundred countries live in housing which often reflects the architecture of their homeland.

THE POMPIDOU CENTER

and surrounding area

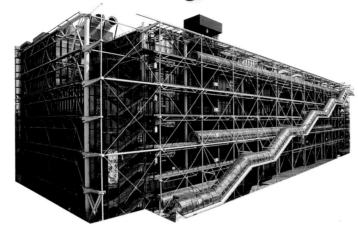

The Pompidou Center

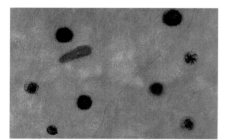

National Museum
of Modern Art

The Marais

Beaubourg district
and Les Halles

Châtelet and Hôtel de Ville

Aerial view of the Pompidou Center
The Pompidou Center is a great center of
attraction for Parisians and visitors alike. It
stands in the heart of Paris, at the point
where the 1st, 2nd, 3rd, and 4th
arrondissements meet, and a few yards
from the line of the *cardo*, the main axis
of Roman Lutetia. To the west, Les Halles,
the "belly of Paris," where the whole city
came for its provisions, was destroyed
in 1971 to make way for bars, art
galleries, and fashion boutiques.
To the east is the Marais district
with its splendid mansions.

The Pompidou Center

It's a gasworks, a ship in dock, a cultural supermarket ... the Pompidou Center, its massive glass and steel framework covered in yellow, red, blue, and white pipes, has been called all sorts of things. For all that, it is still a symbol of modernity. The building is an outstanding piece of late 20th-century French architecture and houses the world's largest museum of modern art after MOMA in New York. It also has a library, an institute for acoustic and musical research, bookstores, a design boutique, and a fashionable restaurant.

A cultural center for Paris

"I passionately want Paris to have a cultural center which will be both a museum and a creative center." In 1969, when President of France Georges Pompidou (1911-74) made this declaration, he can little have suspected that, thanks to him, 30 years later some 25,000 people would come every day to this, the world's most famous cultural center. Art lovers come for an exhibition of Picasso's sculptures or an avant-garde installation; students to research a documentary film on the Ivory Coast or to do their course work; and tourists come to visit the museum or just to photograph the city from the top story.

The center's concept was inspired by the "Houses of Culture" started by minister André Malraux (1901-76), and involved bringing together in the same place works of art, books, music, cinema, audiovisual research, performances, and artistic events of every kind. It would be a one-stop place available to all, its architecture embodying a spirit of openness and modernity.

"Show the inner workings"

The competition for the project was launched the same year. Two years later, the jury had 681 responses to look at. Under the presidency of Jean Prouvé, a specialist in metal structures, they declared Italian Renzo Piano and Englishman Richard Rogers the winners. The two had conceived an enormous transparent cube. "A building which will not be a monument but a celebration, a big urban toy," wrote R Piano. The project was unbelievably empty, its five stories amounting to five flat spaces, free of any walls or internal structures. Its partition walls were in fact movable panels. The essential service equipment was put outside the building, covered by enormous colored tubes. The water pipes were green, the air pipes blue, those for electricity yellow, and those for human traffic (basically, the escalators) were red. We must, said the Italian architect, "put the inside outside, and show the inner workings." The transparent walls were simple screens supported by 14 gantries, each bearing girders weighing 80 tons (73 t).

From wasteland to piazza

The chosen site was that of an old village called Beau Bourg, which became a district of Paris under Philippe-Auguste. A merchant district in the 17th and 18th centuries, then heavily populated, the area gradually deteriorated. In 1930, it had 240 hotels, essentially devoted to prostitution. It was classified as a "No 1 condemned block" and pulled down from 1932. In 1972, it was reduced to a wasteland, and turned into a parking lot. This is where, in 1977, the Pompidou Center was inaugurated with two exhibitions: one on Marcel Duchamp and the other on the theme of Paris-New York. A pedestrian-only square, the "piazza," slopes gently down to the main entrance. Very quickly, this was invaded by street performers, visitors, and curious onlookers. Inside the Center, at street level, a covered "forum" extends the square in the direction of Rue Renard behind the building, providing a reception area where people can work out how to get to the various activities on offer.

Hall of Fame
Architect Renzo Piano.
"At the beginning, building the Pompidou Center was more a kind of rude gesture," recalls Renzo Piano, one of the building's two architects. "We had a lot of fun. I was even mildly surprised that they paid us for putting up such a challenge to the classic institutional building." Ever since 1964, when he graduated in Milan, this architect has had fun. At the beginning of his career, he was influenced by Jean Prouvé and dreamt up functional but poetic machines, rather than buildings. Winning the Pritzker Prize, the world's top award in his special area, Piano has designed many museums in Switzerland, the Netherlands, United States, and New Caledonia, as well as offices, housing, bridges, and airports. ∎

Below ground level are the performance spaces, and on the ground floor is the CCI (Center of Industrial Creation), a bookstore, cinemas, and information desks. Above, the most-visited areas are on the various stories: the library (BPI), the National Museum of Modern Art (MNAM), and rooms for temporary exhibitions. The IRCAM (Institute for Acoustic and Musical Research and Coordination) is located 52 ft (16 m) underground beneath the adjoining Place Saint-Merry. To reach it, you have to leave the Center and take an elevator.

Big changes in 2000

"Beaubourg full to the brim" was the headline in *Le Monde* in 1984. The building, designed to take 5,000 visitors a day, had been getting five times that number since it opened. It was overused, rusting, and needed a rapid refit. Most of the access doors had to be closed for reasons of security; blind walls built to hang works of modern art; and the carpet, which crowds of people had started sitting on from day one, replaced with a less fragile wooden floor.

1. The outside escalator
Like a lighted snake, the Center's escalator is mounted on the façade and enclosed in a transparent Plexiglass tunnel. Designed to take 5,000 visitors a day, it has to deal with 25,000. Since the latest renovations, access is reserved for visitors to the museum and exhibitions.

2. Façade of Pompidou Center
Once this aquarium of a cultural center opened, architects could think of nothing but transparency. The new *Grands Projets* in Paris, from the Cartier Foundation to the new National Library and the Pyramid at the Louvre, all followed this trend.

3. "The gasworks"
Green pipes for water, blue ones for air, yellow for electricity, and red for human traffic: as architect Renzo Piano put it, they had to "put the inside outside, and show the inner workings."

4. The ground floor
The galleries in the entrance hall are the only ones to have kept their transparency since the renovations of 2000. On the upper floors, screen walls now protect works of art on show.

5. Restaurant Georges
Architects Dominique Jacob and Brendan MacFarlane designed aluminum shells to decorate the top-story restaurant built when the Center was renovated in 2000.

In 1997, the Center closed. Its renovation lasted more than two years. Architect Renzo Piano was again brought in, but it was his colleague Jean-François Bodin who redesigned the library, the museum rooms and those for big exhibitions. He also added a sixth story, which gained several hundred square feet of space. An elegant, all-aluminum restaurant was built on the roof terrace by two young designers, Jakob and MacFarlane. Now it is a place which, everyone agrees, is more comfortable, better suited to its holdings of thousands of books and works of art, but less fun. Pompidou's dream has become reality.

Facts & Figures

The Pompidou Center in statistics
Framework : 16,500 tons (15,000 t) of Krupp steel
Size : 492 ft (150 m) x 164 ft (50 m) x 164 ft (50 m)
Area : 753,480 sq ft (70,000 sq m) arranged over 6 stories
Number of employees : about 1,200
Museum attendance : 850,000 people a year up to 1996 (60% French including 35% Parisians, 25% from other European countries)
Museum collections : about 45,000 works including 1,400 on permanent exhibition

National Museum of Modern Art

The Pompidou Center is itself so fascinating that most visitors are happy just to go around it. They travel up the long escalator to admire the panoramic view of the city through its transparent walls, and other views from the terraces. They forget that the fourth and fifth levels contain the biggest collection of modern and contemporary art in Europe! Here you can discover Western art since 1905, with countless masterpieces by painters, sculptors, architects, designers, photographers, video makers, and installation artists. The collection, which in the beginning favored French art, is now much more open to international movements, largely thanks to the German art historian Werner Spies, who was its director from 1997 to 2000.

The museum that reinvents itself

◆ A stream of new acquisitions

When the Pompidou Center project was approved, Paris had two major national collections of modern art: the Museum of Modern Art, created in 1937 and ten years later installed in the Palais de Tokyo under the leadership of art historian Jean Cassou; and the National Center of Contemporary Art, inaugurated in 1967 at Rue Berryer. The former was made up of two collections: those of the Musée du Luxembourg (founded in 1818 by King Louis XVIII) and the Jeu de Paume (opened in 1922 to show foreign art). The combined collection grew rapidly from donations, such as those by collectors Paul Rosenberg and Eva Gourgaud, and artists such as Sonia Delaunay and sculptor Constantin Brancusi. Since 1977, donations have grown apace, the most spectacular coming from the widows of painter Kandinsky and writer Michel Leiris, the heir of Picasso's famous dealer, Daniel-Henri Kahnweiler. Purchases also multiplied after 1982, when Minister of Culture Jack Lang doubled the museum's budget.

Today, the collections include some 45,000 works, with some 5,000 paintings, 2,200 sculptures, 17,000 drawings, 13,000 photographs, 380 installations, 850 videos and multimedia works, and 750 films by artists.

◆ Evolving architecture

The National Museum of Modern Art (MNAM) is "a much more reliable and flexible tool than other such museums," said architect R Piano at the project's outset. Twenty-five years later, he also took on some of the renovations.

The museum emerged even bigger than before, with 150,700 sq ft (14,000 sq m) given over to the collection instead of 107,600 sq ft (10,000 sq m). On each level is a long gallery equipped with large cubic areas, separated from each other by corridors containing smaller works – especially drawings and photographs. The museum now has 75 main rooms, with white walls and wooden floors.

Chronological and thematic collections

Since the Pompidou Center reopened in 2000, the Museum of Modern Art, combined with the Center of Industrial Creation, keeps about 1,400 works from its collections permanently on show; these include the fields of photography, design, and architecture. The quota given to contemporary art has increased: one-third of the area is

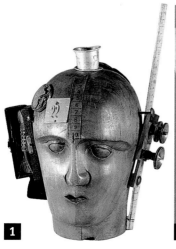

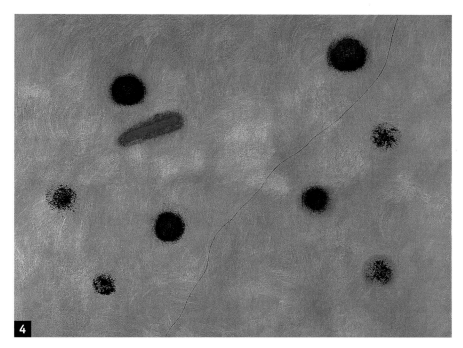

4

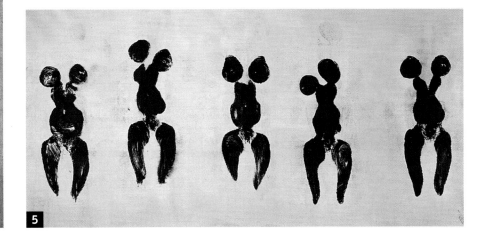

5

◆ *Surrealism makes its mark*

The next section is more playful, showing the work of the Dada group and their successors, the Surrealists. The former dealt mainly in the art of provocation: Marcel Duchamp expressed his criticism of modern society in *Bicycle Wheel* (1913) by presenting a ready-made object, mounted on a stool and turning in the void, as a work of art. The Surrealists introduced "dream paintings": Chirico, Dali, and Magritte explored

6

taken up by works from the last ten years. The historical and modern collections, from 1905 to 1960, are shown on Level 5; the contemporary collections, from 1960 to the present day, on Level 4. Within the chronological display, thematic connections are pointed out which reveal influences and allow comparisons to be made.

◆ *Modern masters*

To discover the National Museum of Modern Art, you first have to immerse yourself in color. The Fauves group, formed in 1905, make the first rooms a riot of reds, oranges, blues, and other pure colors, often laid as flat tints. The barely sketched shapes and surprising points of view of Derain, Marquet, Matisse, and Dufy are entirely seductive.

Then come the Cubists, who revolutionized form with their careful

analyses of space, and restructured shapes into geometric structures. The display of masks and fetishes, recently donated by the Derain and Magnelli families, underlines the influence of African art on the Cubists. Thus we see connections between a Baoulé statuette from the Ivory Coast and Picasso's *Female Bust* (1907), a study for *Les Demoiselles d'Avignon*. Around these are hung canvasses in the earth colors of Braque, Juan Gris, and Léger. An entire room is devoted to collages and assemblages by Braque and Picasso.

In the same period, an Expressionist movement started, having powerful-graphic qualities and using contrasting and unusual tones to heighten expressive intensity. Its representatives were Russian (Chagall, Larionov, and Gontcharova), German (Kirchner and Nolde), and Czech (Kupka).

---

1. *The Spirit of Our Times or Mechanical Head* **(Raoul Hausmann)**
This work was created by the German Dadaist Raoul Hausmann in 1919. Cubism and Dadaism launched the technique of bringing together various objects in one three-dimensional work.

2. *Sheet Music and Guitar* **(Picasso)**
This 1912 collage is one of the first Picasso made. With his friend Braque, he was one of the pioneers of this technique.

3. *Luxury I* **(Henri Matisse)**
In 1907, Matisse (1869-1954) painted the first of his canvasses entitled *Luxury*. It reveals all the typical elements of Fauvism: simplified forms, bright colors, and foreshortened perspective.

4. *Blue I* **(Joan Miró)**
In 1969, Miró (1893-1983) painted three large blue canvasses which the National Museum of Modern Art has recently acquired.

5. *Anthropometry of the Blue Period* **(Yves Klein)**
In 1960, Klein (1928-62) completed this "anthropometry" of prints taken from nude female bodies coated with paint.

6. *Inquisitive Children* **(Karel Appel)**
The Cobra group (from COpenhagen, BRussels, Amsterdam), to which the Dutchman Appel belonged, were fired by spontaneity and the expressive power of color, as in this picture painted in 1948.

the unconscious, their works using free association of ideas and forms to represent dreams, fantasies, and visions.

The close links between Surrealism and popular and primitive art are demonstrated by showing the desk of writer André Breton. Alongside it is a display of Aboriginal paintings, Pre-Columbian pottery, carved Inuit ivories, semi-precious stones, shields, mirrors, shells, mounted butterflies, and Katchina dolls from Arizona – in all, some 2,000 objects. Miró, Max Ernst, André Masson, Roberto Massa, and Wilfredo Lam are shown, and one room demonstrates the influence of the European Surrealists on American painters Arshile Gorky and Jackson Pollock. Starting from a line guided by the unconscious, they arrive at the primacy of gesture.

◆ Abstract and figurative

Many adjoining rooms illustrate the evolution toward abstract art and the return to figurative modes. We see the beginnings of abstraction from 1908 with Kandinsky, whose violently colored works became increasingly simplified; the sensitive geometry of Klee and Malevitch; the simple lines and primary colors of Mondrian and Theo Van Doesburg; the vibrant color of Robert and Sonia Delaunay; the search for a new space, both mental and physical, in the perforated canvasses of Lucio Fontana; the monochrome paintings of Yves Klein in deep ultramarine (a color that became the artist's trademark); the return to realism in the inter-war years with Fautrier and Picasso; and the human figure, still present in Bonnard's work (he has 11 paintings in the collection, from 1947 onward), and, in a more tragic vein, in those of Francis Bacon and Giacometti.

◆ The contemporary collections

The major movements of the 1960s and 1970s each have their own room. One shows American Pop Art, or "capitalist realism," which for Robert Rauschenberg was inspired by the imagery of advertising, for Roy Lichtenstein by strip cartoons, and for Andy Warhol by newspapers. The other shows the "New Realism,"

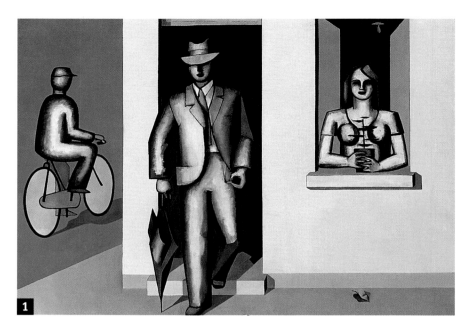

which elevated everyday objects to works of art: the accumulations of Arman, Christo's wrap-ups, and Niki de Saint-Phalle's polyester "babes" covered in various objects and entitled *Crucifixion*. Here too are optical and kinetic art with Joseph Albers, Adam, Vasarely, and others.

Some rooms are devoted to a specific artist, such as Jacques Monory, whose figurative painting is inspired by thrillers and Hollywood films, and Christian Boltanski and his "fictitious autobiography." Other rooms contain an environment you go into, such as Dubuffet's *Winter Garden* (1968-70), a kind of polyester cavern, a closed and unstable world that poses questions about time and

space. There are mobiles (Rauschenberg), relics (Messager), and imprints (Penone) of many different shapes and forms. Some are difficult to classify, but there are explanatory texts in each room and, in the main aisle, you can sit beside sound points and hear artists' voices explaining their processes.

Sculpture

Picasso's bronze *Petite Fille Sautant à la Corde* (1950) welcomes visitors at the top of the museum's staircase, and a great deal of space has been given over to sculpture. A whole room is allocated to the large bronze *Le Capricorne* (1948) by the Surrealist Max Ernst, and a monumental animated work by Tinguely, *Requiem*

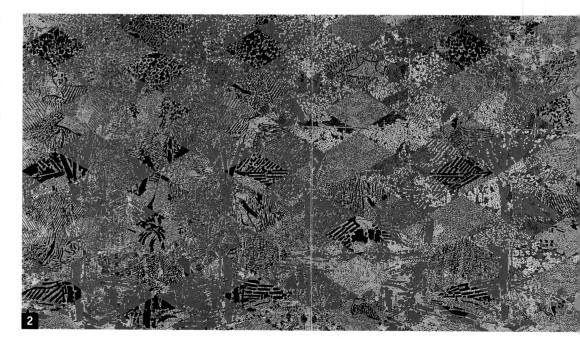

for a Dead Leaf, stands at the entrance to the contemporary collections. On Level 5, three terraces have been specially designed for sculptures. *Morning* (1944) by Laurens and Braque's *Woman Bathing* (1947) stand out against the sky with, in the background, the Tour Saint-Jacques and Notre-Dame. Behind bronzes by Miró and Max Ernst, and a stabile by Calder, you can see the Sacré-Coeur and Montmartre.

◆ Brancusi's sculpture studio

When he died in 1957, the famous Rumanian sculptor Constantin Brancusi left his studio to the State, on condition that it was preserved in its original condition. This is a total work of art, comprising 294 finished and unfinished works, equipment, clothing, work benches, a fireplace, and even some marble dust and wood shavings. In 1977, it was installed in the piazza in front of the

Pompidou Center in a purpose-built structure. After it was damaged by floods, Brancusi's studio was closed from 1990 to 1997. Now, completely transformed by Renzo Piano, it is open once more.

Selective exhibits on architecture and design

About 200 of the pieces on show relate to architecture and design. This part of the collection was begun in 1991, and consists of 400 models, 2,000 drawings and 1,800 objects, which occupy five of the museum's rooms, interposed between the rooms for paintings, sculptures, and other works. The first recalls the years 1920 to 1940, the Bauhaus school in Germany and the international venture, the Union des Arts Modernes. Another covers the 1960s, with its utopian visions and the plastic revolution. Priority is given to prototypes and the relation between creativity and industry. The large number of industrial donations, for example by Braun, Calor, IBM, and Moulinex, has made it possible to assemble typical settings which delight people who remember those times. How many visitors are left dreaming in front of the 1954 Vespa, perhaps thinking of Audrey Hepburn in the film *Roman Holiday*.

Photography and video

When the Pompidou Center opened, the collection consisted only of two Surrealist photographs and

1,700 negatives from the sculptor Brancusi's collection. Since then, purchasing priority has been given to this most typical 20th-century activity. The inter-war period is emphasized, concentrating on such figures as Brassaï and Moholy-Nagy. Donations have also been forthcoming, for example from the families of Kertész (1977) and Man Ray (1994). The video image is also well represented at the Pompidou Center with, for example, the American Dan Graham's *Present Continuous Past(s)* (1974): an installation in which the visitor is filmed and recorded in a place surrounded by mirrors, with an interval between the moment he sees himself and when the filmed image returns to him. Finally, in a room called "New Media," visitors can consult videos, CD-ROMs, and sound recordings.

1. Au Cycliste (Jean Hélion)
This 1939 canvas, with its schematic figures and bright colors, marks the return of painting to figurative art.

2. Cassone VI (François Rouan)
In Rome in 1980, Rouan (born in 1943) sought a balance between the abstract and the figurative. In *Cassone VI*, he painted fragments of motifs and enclosed them in a series of lozenges.

3. Requiem for a Dead Leaf (Tinguely)
This mobile, completed by Tinguely (1925-91) in 1957, stands at the entrance to the museum's contemporary collections. The artist has created many Dadaist-inspired machines.

4. Salon de l'Élysée (Yaacov Agam)
Typical of the 1970s, this room which Agam (born in 1928) conceived in 1974 for the antichamber of the Elysée Palace (where Georges Pompidou then lived) is wholly kinetic.

5. Woman Standing II (Giacometti)
This spindly sculpture by Giacometti, with its uneven surface, is part of a series of standing female nudes. It was modeled in plaster then forged in bronze in 1959-60. His isolated characters are often compared with those of existentialist literature.

Beaubourg district and Les Halles

Once the Beau Bourg was joined to the capital by the wall built around it by Philippe-Auguste, it became something of a mercantile district. Today's stores reflect those times, as does the complex at Les Halles, built where the king had located his market. For a long time, too, it was inhabited by monks, around the Church of Saint-Merri, and men of the law around Châtelet and its prison. In the Middle Ages the area was completely built up, then in the Second Empire it had major thoroughfares driven through it from all sides. Now it was more than ever devoted to business, with little respect for its old houses, which became more and more shabby and were replaced by dubious hotels and stalls for tourists. Here and there, in their vaulted cellars built on three levels, some of their past spirit has resurfaced. A number of art galleries have now moved in there.

Around the Church of Saint-Merri

◆ Church and business

Although by the 12th century the district's main street was the present Rue Beaubourg, the first community grew up around the Church of Saint-Merri, between Rue Saint-Martin and Rue du Temple. The merchants who set up there specialized in clothing, carpentry, and making barrels and handcarts. Today still, the clicking of sewing machines and the traffic jams caused by delivery vehicles indicate the presence of wholesale luggage makers, milliners, and hosiers.

The church has a reputation for friendliness, and is much used, as it has been since 700, when Saint Médéric was buried there. It was rebuilt in the 13th century, then again in the 16th, in a Flamboyant Gothic style, and underwent further Baroque embellishments in the 17th century, in line with the fashion of the day, like the mansions around it.

◆ A surprising fountain

Between the chevet of the church and the Pompidou Center, an extraordinary, animated, rainbow-colored fountain brings a carnival atmosphere to this historic part of the district. Called *Homage to Stravinsky*, it was completed in 1983 by Jean Tinguely and Niki de Saint-Phalle at the request of composer Pierre Boulez, director of the IRCAM, which was built beneath this square.

◆ One of the city's oldest streets

Rue Saint-Martin, which runs in front of the church, doubled as the Roman road from Senlis to Orléans. Pilgrims used it to go to Tours and the tomb of Saint Martin, and many troubadours went with them. Here the poet Gérard de Nerval (1808-55) was born; he hanged himself in a nearby street. Along its narrow cobbled way are some fine ironwork and grotesque figures, and one or two courtyard interiors hint at past splendors.

◆ Rue Quincampoix

In the parallel street, some of the houses contain art galleries, the old vaulted cellars having been turned into exhibition rooms (see, for example, Galerie Koralewski at No 92). A few carriage entrances and pieces of ironwork, and some painted ceilings, glimpsed through tall windows, are reminders that grand mansions were built here in the 17th and 18th centuries, such as the Hôtel de Belfort and the bank of the famous Scots financier John Law.

Before the latter went bankrupt, he was so successful that he could not go out in the street without speculators crowding around him. Nearby, the Théâtre Molière, built in 1791, has recently been revived as a House of Poetry.

◆ Second Empire additions

Under Napoléon III, Rue Rambuteau and Boulevard Sébastopol were built, making it possible to travel quickly from the south to the north of Paris. The wide boulevard ran in a straight line from Place du Châtelet to the future Gare de l'Est, separating the Beaubourg area from Les Halles market.

Les Halles

◆ The market by the cemetery

In 1183, the king ordered a market to be built near the Cimetière des Innocents. Food supplies arrived by river, and were unloaded on quays nearby. In 1786, the cemetery had to be removed to make way for the living and their provisions. The bones of two million corpses were transferred to the Catacombs. Today, only the *Fontaine des Innocents*, a fountain sculpted in 1549 by Jean Goujon and partly modified in 1788 by Pajou, provides a reminder of the enormous graveyard.

◆ Baltard's pavilions

When he rebuilt the market halls in 1851, Victor Baltard designed two

iron pavilions. Napoléon III complained: "Iron, nothing but iron." Then, in 1969, Les Halles was so short of space that it had to move to the outskirts, to Rungis. The Baltard pavilions were demolished (one was preserved and reassembled at Nogent-sur-Marne), which stirred up a general outcry. The whole district was destroyed, leaving a gaping hole whose future was argued about for a long time.

◆ Forum des Halles

In 1979, architects Claude Vasconi and Georges Pencreac'h finally built the Forum des Halles, a shopping complex on four underground levels. A rectangular square provides a lighting well. While the new glass and steel structures lack the elegance of the old ones, something of the spirit of Baltard still lingers there. People do not buy carrots and coal there any more, but clothes and CDs. In 1985, also underground, a new covered square was built, along with a swimming pool and a tropical conservatory.

◆ Gardens of Les Halles

On the surface is a paved 12 acre (5 ha) garden. It has 20,000 shrubs, 600 trees, clematis, Virginia creeper and wistaria climbing on trellises, bowers designed by François-Xavier Lalanne, 11 fountains, and a flower garden linking Les Halles station, the Bourse de Commerce, and the Church of Saint-Eustache.

Around the gardens

◆ Bourse de Commerce

At the end of the garden stands the superb metal dome of the former Corn Exchange (1768). Beside it is a column, built at the end of the 15th century, and comprising the last remains of the palace which Catherine de Médicis had built there.

◆ Church of Saint-Eustache and Montorgueil market

Just to one side is the Church of Saint-Eustache (1532-1637), its plan and balanced vaults echoing those of Notre-Dame. It has a magnificent organ with 8,000 pipes. Berlioz and Liszt played there, Molière was baptised there, and Colbert was buried in a tomb sculpted by Coysevox and Tuby. Having survived the Revolution, when it was turned into a Temple of Agriculture, it suffered a bad fire in 1840 and was restored by Baltard. Today, the Church of Saint-Eustache welcomes visitors curious to see its collection of old paintings. On the way out, they can do some shopping in the Montorgueil district, which has had a lively market since the Middle Ages.

---

1. At the café in 1900
Restaurants and bistros were always in plentiful supply around Les Halles market. Workers went there to restore their strength, and the middle classes liked eating and drinking in their company.

2. Forum des Halles
The steel arches of the Forum des Halles, built in 1979, echo the arches of the nearby Church of Saint-Eustache (background right) and the dome of the Bourse de Commerce (background left).

3. Écoute (Henri de Miller)
Placed on the forecourt of the Church of Saint-Eustache is *Listen*, a giant head which Henri de Miller carved from Burgundy sandstone in 1986, and which children often climb on. The stones of the forecourt repeat the ear motif.

4. Stravinsky fountain
Since 1983, this fountain conceived by Niki de Saint-Phalle and Jean Tinguely has been spouting jets of water from its fantastic figures and metal mobiles.

5. Fontaine des Innocents
On a more academic note, the Fontaine des Innocents (16th-18th centuries) is all that remains of the vast cemetery which stood there from the beginning of the Middle Ages. Now in the center of a pedestrian square, it has become a favorite meeting place for Parisians.

Châtelet and Hôtel de Ville

Flanked by two theaters and various cafés, Place du Châtelet is one of the great nocturnal meeting places and an ideal spot for a drink before or after a show, a film, or dinner in a restaurant. This is where the city's main streets meet, as well as its two main Métro lines. Place de l'Hôtel de Ville is also very busy, with nearby Rue de Rivoli and its many stores. There is always something going on there: a carousel all year round, a skating rink in winter, giant screens showing World Cup football matches, etc. But few visitors to these squares realize that they are walking on the foundations of the city's great fortress, and on the old Place de Grève, where so many people were executed.

Place du Châtelet

◆ The old fortress

Place du Châtelet takes its name from the Grand Châtelet which Louis VII had built in 1154 to control the Grand Pont from the Right Bank. This stone fortress replaced a wooden tower built two centuries earlier to protect the inhabitants of the Ile de la Cité from Viking invaders. After Philippe-Auguste's wall was built, the Châtelet lost its military function but remained the seat of the Provost of Paris, responsible to the king for administering the capital. It also housed the highest court and a prison (where the poor inmates huddled at the bottom of damp cells while noblemen shut up in the Bastille could order themselves fine meals). Despite suffering damage, the overcrowded fortress remained standing until 1806, when it was pulled down to improve connections between the two banks of the Seine.

◆ The two theaters

In the middle of the square stands the Fontaine de la Victoire, otherwise known as the Palm Fountain, built in 1806 to celebrate the victories of Napoléon I. It was formerly a dozen yards to the east, but was moved in 1858 when the square was redesigned by Baron Haussmann.

The two symmetrical theaters were built in 1862 to plans by Davioud. Their Renaissance-inspired façades are similar, but differ both in their dimensions and decoration. The 3,000-seat Théâtre du Châtelet was originally intended for spectacular shows and music. Renamed the Théâtre Musical de Paris, it was modernized in 1989. Its curtain was decorated by G Garouste, its loggia by V Adami, and the foyer by François Morellet. Opposite, the former Théâtre Sarah-Bernhardt bore the actress's name for a long time, after she hired it in 1898 to appear in her favorite roles: *L'Aiglon*, *La Dame aux Camélias*, and *Tosca*. It was completely modernized in 1968 and renamed the Théâtre de la Ville.

◆ The solitary tower

Beside this theater, and strangely isolated in its own beautiful square, is a finely sculpted 16th-century Gothic tower. This is the Tour Saint-Jacques, last remains of the Church of Saint-Jacques-de-la-Boucherie which stood on the route of pilgrims to Santiago de Compostela and was demolished in 1797. The church's name shows how many butchers lived in this district during the Renaissance, and how powerful they were. Together with the goldsmiths (recalled in the nearby Rue and Quai des Orfèvres) and the bankers, they occupied the area around the Hôtel de Ville. Other trades active in the district were the *mégissiers* (tanners), who gave their name to the Quai de la Mégisserie. This riverside street is today occupied by plant and animal merchants.

Hôtel de Ville

◆ Water-sellers lead the way to city government

The first municipal institutions and the arms of Paris originated in the Middle Ages with the guild of boatmen and water-sellers. This powerful guild had navigation rights in the area around the capital. The merchants' provost, who was their head, and the aldermen, the officials who assisted him, were elected by a so-called "citizens' assembly." From the 12th century, this provostship of merchants had responsibilities not only for commercial matters, but municipal ones too. It was in effect a

kind of de facto town council. In the 13th century, its seal was still a large boat loaded with goods, the "seal of the water-sellers in Paris." In the course of the centuries the boat became a seagoing ship on choppy waves, surmounted by fleur-de-lis. In the 17th century, when Paris wanted a coat of arms, it took this motif. In the 19th century, a Latin motto was added: *Fluctuat nec mergitur* (It floats and does not founder).

◆ From "citizens' parlor" to city hall

The seat of the municipal office was called the "citizens' parlor." In the 13th century, it stood beside the Seine near the Grand Châtelet. In 1357, merchants' provost Etienne Marcel moved it to the Maison aux Piliers which he had bought on Place de Grève. This was really the birth of the Hôtel de Ville (even though that name only dates from the 16th century), which still stands on the same spot today. The Maison aux Piliers was first enlarged, then demolished and replaced by a real palace. Its construction began in 1533 to plans by the Italian Boccador, and was not finished until 1628. New blocks were added from 1836 to 1850 without touching the 16th/17th-century façade, which overlooks the square. In 1871, however, the Communards set it on fire and burnt it to ashes. The present building, with its 108 statued niches, its great spiral staircases, and its mirrored galleries, is a reconstruction carried out between 1874 and 1882 to plans by Théodore Ballu and Edouard Deperthes. The reconstruction of the façade is exact, while the rest is in the same style as the old building.

◆ The former Place de Grève

Place de l'Hôtel-de-Ville is fringed by fountains by François-Xavier Lalanne and has been pedestrianized for several years. Until 1830 it was called Place de Grève, and its present size dates from works carried out by Haussmann. In the Middle Ages, it was a small square which sloped gently down to the Seine and the Port de Grève, one of the largest

docksides in Paris. When the city's administrators moved into the Maison aux Piliers, it became the setting for all kinds of great events: celebrations, revolts, and public executions. Ravaillac, assassin of Henri IV, was violently executed there, and the famous poisoners and alleged witches La Voisin and La Brinvilliers were burnt. It was also the place where day laborers came in search of work, whence the expression to be *en grève*, later modified to mean "on strike."

1. Théâtre de la Ville
Though originally intended for theatrical performances, this 1862 building now often features contemporary dance.

2. Sarah Bernhardt
Sarah Bernhardt, a famous actress at the end of the 19th century, hired the theater from 1898 to 1922 and had it redecorated at her own expense. One of its rooms now has a small museum dedicated to her. In 1968, it was renamed Théâtre de la Ville.

3. Tour Saint-Jacques
This is all that remains of the medieval Church of Saint-Jacques-de-le-Boucherie. The building, which stood on the pilgrims' way to Santiago de Compostela, was demolished in 1797.

4. Forecourt of Hôtel de Ville
The present Hôtel de Ville (City Hall) was rebuilt between 1874 and 1882 on the site of the old building, destroyed by fire in the Commune. All kinds of activities take place here, with a skating rink, a giant screen showing films, or a stage for singers at the Music Festival.

5. Place de Grève
Up to 1830, Place de l'Hôtel-de-Ville was called Place de Grève. Here, before the seat of the city's administrators, celebrations and riots took place, as well as public executions like that of Ravaillac, assassin of Henri IV.

6. Fountain in Place du Châtelet
The Egyptian-inspired Fontaine de la Victoire was built in 1806 in the middle of Place du Châtelet as a tribute to the victorious campaigns of Napoléon I.

The Marais

It means "the Marshes," after the marshes that caused the Seine to flood in the Middle Ages. Today, in this part of Paris once loved by kings of France, you will find galleries for contemporary art and the city's favorite gay bars. On the north side, the district is given over to commerce, with Asian jewelers, Yugoslav clothes makers, and businesses run by 'pieds noirs' (French people originally from Algeria). To the south it is more residential and luxurious, a reflection of its splendid past. You only have to look up: everywhere around the famous Place des Vosges, the former Place Royale, the stonework proclaims the greatness of France's 17th-century architects. At that time, the nobility built magnificent mansions here. Although somewhat damaged in the Revolution, these buildings have been transformed into museums, libraries, and cultural centers.

Birth of the Marais

◆ Monks and medieval knights

In the Middle Ages, only a few churches stood on the recently dried-out marshes, surrounded by sheep and market gardens. In 1139, the Knights Templar (a military and religious order founded at the time of the First Crusade) settled there. Their enclosure, surrounded by a fortified wall, ran between the present Rues du Temple, de Bretagne, de Picardie, and Béranger, forming a free town which gave refuge to people hiding from the taxman or the law. Later, all the buildings in this enclosure were demolished: the church in 1796, the keep in 1808, after serving as a prison for Louis XVI and his family, and the Palais du Grand Prieur in 1853 to make way for Square du Temple. Nothing now remains of the Knights Templar's little empire. However, several other religious communities did follow them into the Marais from the beginning of the 13th century, for example the monasteries of the Blancs-Manteaux and Sainte-Croix-de-la-Bretonnerie.

◆ Jewish settlers

Toward the end of the 12th century, a Jewish community settled in the Marais. It grew considerably in the 19th century as refugees arrived from Central Europe, and again in the 20th century with repatriated Jews from North Africa. Now, centered on Rue des Rosiers, the district bears many signs of Jewish occupation, with signs in Hebrew, Jewish bookstores, stores selling religious objects and kosher food, restaurants serving Jewish specialities, and synagogues – including one built by H Guimard (Rue Pavée) and another with an internal metal framework designed by G Eiffel (Rue des Tournelles).

◆ Royal residences

In the middle of the 13th century, the brother of Saint Louis, Charles d'Anjou, King of Sicily, built himself a residence near the present Rue de Sévigné (he himself is commemorated only in another street name, Rue du Roi-de-Sicile). In the following century, Charles V built a new enclosure which followed the present lines of Boulevards Beaumarchais, des Filles-du-Calvaire, and du Temple. This development fixed the boundaries of the present district. The King left his Palais de la Cité and moved into the Hôtel Saint-Paul and neighboring houses. The new residence was twice as large as the Louvre (but today is only recorded in street signs), and encouraged prelates and great lords to build mansions nearby. Then, under Charles VII, the Court moved into the Hôtel des Tournelles, until Henri II died there during a tournament in 1559. His widow, Catherine de Médicis, decided to leave the district, but the noblemen were already used to living there, and continued to build mansions, notably the Hôtel Carnavalet and Hôtel d'Angoulême.

The district's finest treasure

◆ Place des Vosges

The abandoned Hôtel des Tournelles was used as a horse market and to stage several famous duels. In 1605, Henri IV had the idea of building a square on the site, surrounded by a silk factory and craft workshops. The houses around it were to be built in brick and stone in the same style, with three stories, roofs in the form of truncated pyramids, and a street-level arcade. The factory was destroyed two years later and replaced by identical buildings. The result was so successful that in the

end the nobility took over the 36 dwellings.

Place Royale (the present Place des Vosges) was opened in 1612, two years after the death of Henri IV, on the occasion of the marriage of Louis XIII to Anne of Austria, and of her sister, Elisabeth of France, to the future Philip IV of Spain. In 1639, an equestrian statue of Louis XIII was erected in the middle of the square.

◆ *The golden age: the 17th century*

The building of Place Royale gave new impetus to the Marais. Its golden age lasted through the 17th century up to the beginning of the 18th. Everywhere, people built magnificent mansions with splendid courtyards and gardens. They were designed by the best architects of the day: Androuet du Cerceau, Le Vau, Lepautre, Le Muet, Mansart, Boffrand, and others, and decorated by the painters Vouet, Le Brun, Mignard, Boucher, Natoire, and Van Loo.

In addition to the aristocracy, half of the city's financiers lived in the Marais in the 17th century, as well as one out of three magistrates at the beginning of the next century. In the salon of Mme de Sévigné and at the house of Scarron and his wife, the future Mme de Maintenon, they talked of literature and art. At the Hôtel de Montmor, where the philosopher and scholar Gassendi lived, they discussed the sciences. They went to the Church of Saint-Louis-des-Jésuites to hear the sermons of Father Bourdaloue and the music of Marc-Antoine Charpentier. The Comédiens du Marais troupe moved to Rue Vieille-du-Temple from 1634. A property developer called Claude Charlot improved and built many streets in the district, and even installed a market, the Enfants-Rouges, the name coming from the orphans living in the nearby hospital.

The 18th century brought new splendor with the Hôtels de Rohan and de Soubise, the façades of the Hôtels d'Albret and de Sandreville, and the Hôtel Hallwyll (rebuilt in 1765 by C N Ledoux, this is the only surviving mansion designed by this visionary architect, a lover of Antique forms). Fashion then swung to the new suburbs of Saint-Germain and Saint-Honoré. The Marais, deserted by the affluent, lapsed into decline.

The Marais, a thriving museum

◆ *Decline and rebirth*

The Marais was abandoned, sacked, and pillaged in the Revolution, and taken over by craftsmen, small businesses, warehouses, and schools. The stonework deteriorated, walls turned

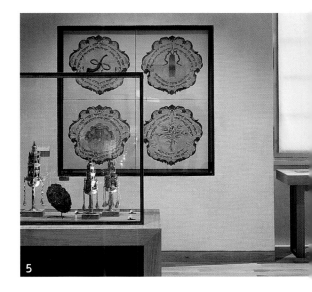

1, 2. Around Rue des Rosiers
There had been a Jewish community in the Marais since the Middle Ages, but its population soared in the 19th century as refugees arrived from Central Europe. Here strollers will discover restaurants specializing in Central European and Middle Eastern dishes as well as kosher products and books in Hebrew.

3. Place des Vosges
Place Royale was opened in 1612 on the occasion of Louis XIII's marriage to Anne of Austria, and was inhabited by the nobility and wealthy financiers for two centuries. Renamed Place de l'Invisibilité in the Revolution, in 1800 it took its present name.

---

4. Hôtel de Sully
This mansion was built in 1624 for a rich financier in an ostentatious Renaissance style, and has kept its historic façades with sculptures depicting the elements and the seasons. It was acquired by the State in 1953 and has been superbly restored. It now houses the National Office of Historic Monuments.

5. Museum of the Art and History of Judaism
This museum in the 17th-century Hôtel de Saint-Aignan, Rue du Temple, is constantly growing from private donations. It puts on thematic exhibitions and retrospectives of painters of the Ecole de Paris.

black, and the interiors grew cluttered with fittings – not to mention what was destroyed. Certainly, some mansions were saved, like the Hôtel d'Aumont, bought by the City in 1932 for use as a civil service court, and the Hôtel de Sens (1474-1519), which, much restored from 1936, became the Forney Library. As for the rest, the Marais sank into oblivion. Not until 1962, and Malraux's law defining conservation areas, could any renovation begin. That same year, the launch of the Marais Festival also drew attention to the state of the district when it put on shows in its most beautiful locations. Since then, the mansions have been restored one after the other, and have recovered their brilliance. Often, though, their doors remain shut to protect owners who have bought magnificent apartments there. Others may be visited, however, and it is still a pleasure to wander around Place des Vosges, the churches, and the streets themselves, before taking a break in the square by Sainte-Catherine's market or strolling around the lively Jewish district.

◆ Around Place des Vosges

The arcades of Place des Vosges buzz with trendy restaurants, antique dealers, art galleries, and boutiques. Two central blocks, slightly taller than the others, are the King's and Queen's Pavilions. In the south-east corner, the former Hôtel de Rohan-Guéménée, where Victor Hugo lived, now houses his museum, featuring his drawings, photographs, and interesting pieces of furniture which he decorated. Further along, a passage leads to the Hôtel de Sully,

today occupied by the National Monuments Center. Built from 1624, it is profusely decorated with Renaissance-style sculptures, some of which represent the Four Seasons and others the Four Elements.

◆ Musée Carnavalet

This museum devoted to the history of Paris is in the Hôtel Carnavalet, a Renaissance building dating from 1548, decorated with sculptures by Jean Goujon and redesigned in 1655 by François Mansart. The Marquis de Sévigné loved this mansion, living there from 1677 to 1696. The museum moved there in 1866 and later, finding itself short of space, in 1989 annexed the neighboring Hôtel Le Peletier de Saint-Fargeau (1686-90). It now has 140 rooms

showing the history of the capital from its origins to the present day, including old decorations from apartments in Place des Vosges and Neolithic canoes found in the 1990s during excavations at Bercy.

◆ Picasso Museum

The museum's charm stems from the juxtaposition of the artist's works, so audacious and varied, and the harmony of a superb 17th-century dwelling, the Hôtel Salé (1656-9). This dialogue of styles and ages recurs in the new interior designs of the mansion, some of the decorations, center lights, and furniture having been commissioned from Diego Giacometti, brother of sculptor Alberto. The majestic main staircase, by the Marsy brothers, leads to a chronological, sometimes thematic, display of works that remained with Picasso all his life, for example the

Still Life with Cane Chair, and *Pan's Flute*. There are paintings, collages, relief tableaux, ceramics and almost all his one-off sculptures. There is an exceptional collection of drawings. In all, the museum contains more than 3,500 works.

◆ Museums galore

Many mansions in the Marais have been converted into museums. The Hôtel de Saint-Aignan (c 1650) was adapted in 1998 for the Museum of the Art and History of Judaism. The Hôtel de Guénégaud, built by François Mansart around 1650 and reworked in the 18th century, houses the Museum of Hunting and Nature. The Musée Cognacq-Jay in the Hôtel Donon (late 16th century) has a fine display of 18th-century art and furniture, bequeathed by the founders of the Samaritaine department stores. The Museum of the History of France is in the Hôtel de Soubise, with its extraordinary Louis XV Rococo interior designed by Germain Boffrand in 1735-9. The European House of Photography is in the Hôtel Hénault de Cantobre (18th century). The Hôtel de Rohan displays apartments dating from 1750. It is a long list, not to mention the mansions converted into libraries or cultural centers, such as the Hôtel de Lamoignon (1584-1612), which has become the History Library of the City of Paris.

◆ Musée des Arts et Métiers

On the edge of the Marais, in the former Abbey of Saint-Martin-des-Champs, the Musée des Arts et Métiers was completely restructured in 2000. It shows the great technological inventions from the 16th century to modern times in the fields of physics, optics, engineering, telecommunications and so on; automata from the end of the 18th century; and collections of clocks.

◆ Churches of the Marais

Saint-Paul-Saint-Louis (1627-41) is the largest church in the Marais. Formerly known as Saint-Louis-des-Jésuites, it was a Jesuit training center (its monastery buildings have become the Lycée Charlemagne). As a mark of its power, it was modeled on the Church of Gesù in Rome and sur-

mounted with the largest dome in Paris at that time. Many of the church's treasures are today in the Louvre or at Chantilly, but it still has a masterpiece by Delacroix: *Christ in the Olive Garden* (1827). Saint-Gervais-Saint-Protais is one of the small churches built in the earliest period of the Marais (6th century). Rebuilt several times, its Gothic structure is masked by an impressive Classical façade built in 1621 by Clément Métezeau. In the 17th century, the local aristocracy went there to hear Couperin play the organ. The church has kept its 16th-century stained glass, 17th-century paintings, and painted paneling.

1, 2. Musée Carnavalet
This 16th/17th-century mansion contains sections of apartments from Place des Vosges decorated by Le Vau and Le Brun. The building was redesigned by Mansart and became the 17th-century residence of the Marquise de Sévigné. In 1866, it was turned into a municipal museum showing the city's history.

3. Boutique in the Marais
Some of the Marais' traditional businesses (for example bakers and butchers) have been converted into fashion boutiques.

4, 5. Picasso Museum
The Picasso Museum has been in the Hôtel Salé (17th century) since 1985, and shows the collection as donated by the painter's heirs on his death in 1973, a total of 3,516 works, regularly supplemented by acquisitions and donations. The vestibule contains sculptures by the finest artists from the Château de Versailles, and the museum houses a fascinating collection of Picasso's works.

6. Conservatoire des Arts et Métiers
This is an industrial training school, and its museum tells the story of technology in the setting of the former Abbey of Saint-Martin-des-Champs, which was converted to its present use in 1793.

THE LOUVRE
and surrounding area

The Pyramid and the Louvre

The Louvre Museum and its collections

Toward the Place Vendôme

Toward the Tuileries

Aerial view of the Louvre
Since the Pyramid was built, the Louvre has attracted five to six million visitors a year, about twice as many as ten years previously. The works at the Grand Louvre have not just renewed and enlarged this marvelous palace-cum-museum, but in their wake have revived the whole surrounding area: a district brimming with gardens, museums, churches, quiet and magnificent squares, luxury stores, arcades and hidden *passages*.

The Pyramid and the Louvre

It has specially treated panes of glass to keep it transparent. Set in a steel frame, they are like the facets of a cut diamond. The Louvre Pyramid stands in the middle of the Cour Napoléon, the main courtyard of Paris's largest palace, reflecting the sky and the clouds, the spray from the fountains, and the lights of evening. It adds a dramatic contemporary flourish to the landscape of the new Grand Louvre, a massive building and restoration project begun in 1981, and extending as far as the Tuileries Gardens.

The Pyramid and the Cour Napoléon

◆ A transparent symbol

The Pyramid is 80 ft (21.64 m) high and 112 ft (34.2 m) wide, and immediately recognizable. Its symbolic shape, recalling the pyramids of Egypt, was designed by architect Ieoh Ming Pei to mark the entrance to the Louvre Museum. The materials he used needed to be restrained and in harmony with the historic setting of the palace. The black granite around the base and the steel of the frame recalls the color of the lead roofs. The glass reflects the sky and, says Pei, "does not compete with the stone." From inside, you can clearly see the sculptures decorating the buildings around the Cour Napoléon.

◆ The play of light, sky, and stone

This modern glass and steel building in the heart of the Louvre caused much controversy when it was first planned. More than two years of arguing delayed the project. Today, though, few remember the Cour Napoléon as it was before the Pyramid: stonework blackened by pollution, stunted shrubs, and vehicles parked everywhere. When it was inaugurated on March 30, 1989, the Pyramid and the three small pyramids surrounding it brought the once gloomy Cour Napoléon back to life. The restored façades and sculptures were returned to their original ocher color. The ground was paved with black granite and sandstone. Water bubbled and spouted from seven triangular fountains. The water, like the glass, Pei explained, "changes with the light and the sky." He added, "At Versailles, Le Nôtre, who was a great spatial designer, also played with air and water to create an illusion. I have tried to get back to that tradition of French architecture in the Grand Siècle." In tribute to that splendid age, a statue of Louis XIV in the manner of Bernini sits in the middle of the courtyard to mark the end of the vista extending through the Carrousel to the Champs-Elysées, Arc de Triomphe, and La Défense. No one now chooses to recall that Louis XIV did not like this statue and had it changed by Girardon into a Roman general and retitled *Marcus Curtius Escaping the Flames of Hell*, which explains the flames under the horse and the plumed helmet in place of the royal wig!

The Grand Louvre

◆ The Pyramid: tip of the iceberg

The Pyramid is only a tiny part of the gigantic renovation scheme for the Louvre and the surrounding area. This had doubled the museum's permanent exhibition area from 333,684 sq ft (31,000 sq m) in 1984 to 645,840 sq ft (60,000 sq m) when work finished in 2001. The reception and public service areas are 13 times bigger and the scientific, technical, and administrative departments are five times bigger. The palace's façades have been restored, the Museum of Decorative Arts given a new look, and a parking lot built for 80 buses and 600 automobiles. In addition, there is a shopping arcade, the "Carrousel du Louvre," a research laboratory for the Museums of France, an amphitheater for the École du Louvre, and space for fashion shows. The Tuileries Gardens have been completely restored, and a new foot-

Facts & Figures

THE PYRAMID

Weight :	105 tons (95 t) of steel and 116 tons (105 t) of frames in glazed aluminum
Number of panes :	675

THE COUR NAPOLÉON

Area :	301,392 sq ft (28,000 sq m)
Surface lighting :	74 black lamp posts, 17 bollards
Façade lighting :	3,280 linear ft (1,000 m) of lighting
Roof and building lights :	200 floodlights
Number of statues of famous men :	86
Number of granite or sandstone paving slabs :	650,000
Number of pumps supplying the fountains :	50

IN THE MUSEUM

Exhibition area :	644,333 sq ft (59,860 sq m) including 190,523 sq ft (17,700 sq m) in Richelieu wing
Reception area :	240,037 sq ft (22,300 sq m) including 182,988 sq ft (17,000 sq m) in Napoléon Hall
Service areas :	830,981 sq ft (77,200 sq m)

4

1. Constructing the Pyramid

The building of the Pyramid symbolized the whole reworking of the Grand Louvre. Started in 1981, the project first enlarged and modernized the museum, then extended to the whole surrounding area.

2, 3. The Pyramid

Since its opening in 1989, the Pyramid has marked the entrance to the museum, in the heart of the palace. In his concern to retain the courtyard's harmonious appearance, Pei used simple shapes based on the triangle, and unobtrusive materials: the glass and water do not conflict with the original stonework.

4. Staircase in the Pyramid

A spiral staircase leads to the Napoléon Hall, which connects with all the wings of the museum. Here, beneath the transparent roof, is the reception area with information desks, ticket offices, a bookshop, etc.

3

HALL OF FAME

Ieoh Ming Pei is the man who built the Pyramid. Before the Grand Louvre project, Pei established a solid international reputation designing banks, control towers, and art galleries with clean, geometric lines. In the US, in particular, he designed the Kennedy Library in Boston, the National Gallery of Art's new East Building in Washington, DC, and the Boston Museum of Fine Arts. Born in China in 1917, he studied architecture in the US at Massachusetts Institute of Technology before studying under Gropius at Harvard. His study project there was "An Oriental Art Museum in Shanghai." Gropius said of this work that Pei showed his talent for combining a modern concept with fundamentally traditional materials. ∎

bridge, the Passerelle de Solférino, has been built across the Seine.

◆ The challenge

How could an 800-year-old palace be transformed into a modern museum opening onto the heart of the city? That was the challenge set by President of the Republic François Mitterrand in 1981 when he announced the Grand Louvre project, a proposal that would turn the whole of the Louvre into a museum and consign 5,000 officials from the Ministry of Finance, currently in the Richelieu wing (one-third of the complex), to new premises at Bercy. The chief aims were to provide better public facilities, improve the way the works were exhibited and increase the number on show (many were then being held in storage). In addition to the space needed to show the collections, as much space again would be needed for related activities: storage facilities, conservation laboratories, restaurants, an auditorium, conference rooms, a reception area, toilets, etc.

◆ Pei's key concepts

The first major step in the museum's modernization fell to the Chinese-American architect Ieoh Ming Pei. Until then, the museum, dating from 1793, had occupied one wing about 875 yd (800 m) long beside the river; this had been designed for royal use and contained enormous staircases. For the new museum to work, it needed a more compact design. Together with the Richelieu wing, it would occupy a U-shaped area. Pei developed his architectural plan around two key concepts. Firstly, the entrance had to be in the center of the complex, in the middle of the Cour Napoléon. Secondly, digging under the Cour Napoléon would create the space needed for a reception area and various other services without spoiling the palace. This was where the pyramid idea came from. From the outside, it "gives the new entrance a surface presence" while being the most economic shape in terms of space. From the inside, visitors can "enjoy an excellent view of the wings of the Louvre and their sculptural decorations. They are in a well-lit space and do not feel cut off from the urban landscape. These are optimal conditions for feeling that they are in an historic place," wrote the architect.

The Louvre, a historic palace

From the end of the 17th century, almost all the crowned heads of France lived at the Louvre. Some 20 rulers and as many architects and decorators have contributed to the château-turned-palace. The construction of the Pyramid continues a long tradition of renewal at the palace.

◆ The medieval fortress

Around 1200, to strengthen Paris's defenses against the invading English, King Philippe-Auguste built a fortress to the west of the city's ramparts, in the place known as "Louvre." Its keep, the "Great Tower," was the symbolic center of the kingdom, standing 98 ft (30 m) high with a diameter of 49 ft (15 m). After the castle had lost its defensive role,

Charles V (1364-1380) redesigned it as a royal residence. He had the architect Raymond du Temple build new living quarters and put a library in the keep. The archeological excavations made during the Grand Louvre project brought to light remains of the medieval castle. Today, beneath the Cour Carrée, you can see the ditches of the fortress, the base of the keep, the Salle Saint-Louis (13th century) and, at the entrance to the Galerie du Carrousel, the enclosure built by Charles V.

◆ The Renaissance palace

The Louvre was abandoned for a century and a half by kings who preferred living in the Loire Valley, but was then radically transformed in the Renaissance. François I pulled down the "Great Tower" in 1528, and in 1546 decided to build a luxurious residence on the old foundations. He commissioned architect Pierre Lescot, the work continuing during the reigns of Henri II and Charles IX. The façades, pierced by large windows, were ornately sculpted by Jean Goujon, who also decorated the Salle des Cariatides.

◆ The "Grand Plan"

Soon after his arrival in Paris in 1594, Henri IV devised his "Grand Plan" to link the Louvre to the Tuileries, the palace built by Catherine de Médicis, and quadruple the size of the courtyard by demolishing the old fortress. He saw the first stage carried out: the Grande Galerie or "Riverside Gallery." Louis XIII and Louis XIV carried the plan further. Under them, architects Le Mercier then Le Vau built the Cour Carrée, enlarging the old Renaissance square. To the east, facing the city, architect Perrault designed a colonnaded façade. Poussin, then Romanelli and Le Brun decorated the galleries and the Queen's chamber. The Louvre's Golden Age came to an end when Louis XIV decided to rule from Versailles. Napoléon I and Napoléon III completed the "Grand Plan" by adding the north wing and the buildings on the north and south sides of the Cour Napoléon. In 1871, at the time of the Commune, part of the gigantic palace was destroyed when the Tuileries were set on fire.

1. Cour Carrée, Lescot wing
The oldest part of this Renaissance masterpiece is the west wing, built by P Lescot and decorated by J Goujon, while the clock pavilion and the other part of the wing were built by Lemercier from 1624. Le Vau completed the buildings in the Cour Carrée after 1660.

2. Cour Carrée in 1862
In this room, which had been completely restored a dozen years previously, the museum's masterpieces are crammed together on the walls, as was the fashion at the time. As early as the 17th century, exhibitions were held there periodically, and these became known as "Salons."

3. Pavillon de Flore
The Pavillon de Flore was part of the Château des Tuileries. It was completed in 1610, at the same time as the Grande Galerie. Napoléon had it pulled down, then built a larger wing adorned with Imperial symbols and a graceful statue of Flora, sculpted by Carpeaux.

4. Salle des Cariatides
This surviving element of the Renaissance palace was recast under Napoléon III. It takes its name from the monumental female figures (caryatids) sculpted by Jean Goujon in 1550 to support the musicians' gallery.

5. Marly and Puget courtyards
Two vast courtyards were glassed in by Pei to provide a light and spacious area for large-scale French sculptures such as the *Marly Horses* by Coustou.

The Louvre Museum and its collections

On November 18, 1993, the Louvre Museum celebrated a double event: its bicentenary and the opening of the Richelieu wing, providing 231,426 sq ft (21,500 sq m) of new exhibition space. As museum director Pierre Rosenberg explained, the Louvre "has the unique good fortune to bring together a royal gallery from the Ancien Régime (like the great museums of Florence, Madrid, and Vienna) and collections patiently acquired during the 19th and 20th centuries (like those of museums in Berlin, London, and New York)."

◆ Metamorphosis of an old museum

The Louvre Museum was founded on July 27, 1793, by decree of the first revolutionary government body. Named the Central Arts Museum, it showed the royal collections in the Grande Galerie. Earlier, after Louis XIV had gone to Versailles, the Academies moved into the Louvre to exhibit more than 400 pieces from the royal collection. Henri IV was the first to house his collection of antique and contemporary works in the Grande Galerie. Later, artists came to live at the Louvre, and from the end of the 17th century a big exhibition of contemporary paintings and sculptures was held every two years in the Salon Carré. The palace has a long tradition of acquiring works of art, especially under Vivant Denon, who became director-general of the museum in 1802, with substantial gains accruing from Napoléon's victories. As the collections grew, the museum gradually took over more and more space from the palace. The wing incorporating the Pavillon de Flore was opened to the public in 1968. Even so, the palace had never really been reorganized as a museum. Now this has been done. Between 1990 and 2000, all the collections were moved to new or renovated galleries: a total of some 34,000 works that provide a coherent picture of Ancient civilizations and Western Art from the Middle Ages to the middle of the 19th century. In addition, temporary exhibitions feature works from the Louvre alongside works from other museums. Some focus on one artist (Pisanello in 1996, Denon in 1999, and Primaticcio in 2004), others on an artistic movement ("16th-Century Drawings from Bologna" in 2001, "Artistic Life under the Ramses" in 2002), and still others on different eras ("Egyptomania" in 1994, "After Antiquity" in 2000).

Antiquities

◆ Oriental antiquities

The Department of Oriental Antiquities was founded in 1881 and shows works from a vast geographical area extending from the Mediterranean to the Indus, where civilizations and cultures go as far back as 6000 BC. The Story of the Flood, the Song of Songs, and many themes from Greek and Roman mythology come from this part of the world. This is where the first cities appeared, governed by political, military, and religious administrations. Writing started around 3300 BC in Uruk, Mesopotamia, between the Tigris and the Euphrates. The roots of our civilization go back there. The Louvre's collections are closely linked to developments in archeological research, and are divided into three main geographical and cultural areas: Mesopotamia (including, in particular, the civilizations of Sumeria, Babylon, Assyria, and Ana-

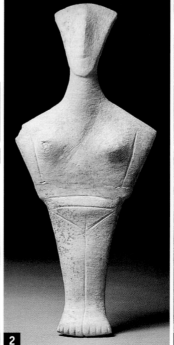

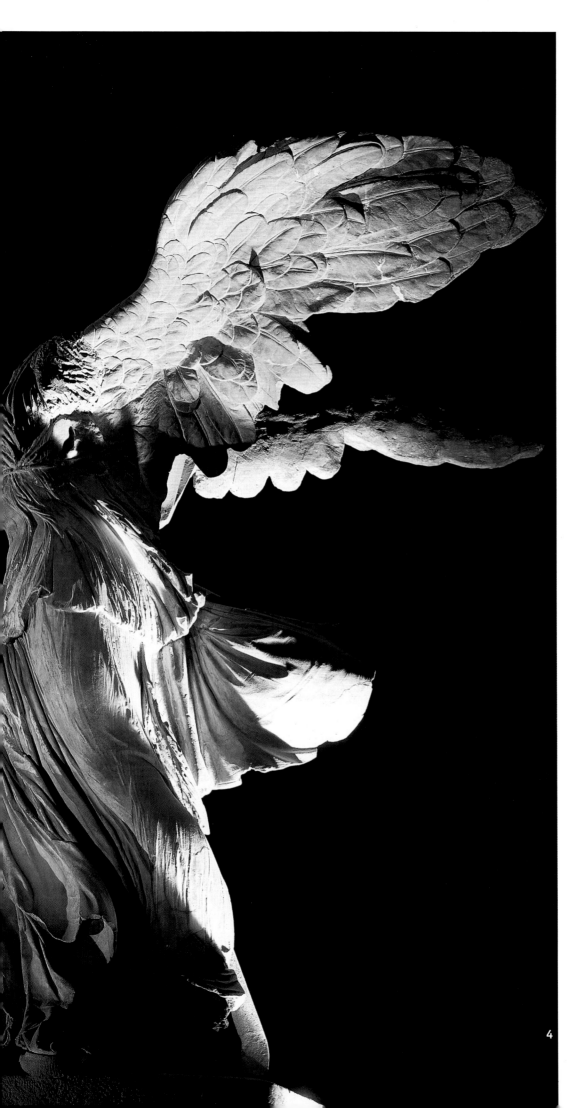

tolia), Iran, and the Levant (the eastern coast of the Mediterranean and Cyprus).

◆ *Egyptian antiquities*

This department has a whole range of Egyptian masterpieces, including the *Scribe Accroupi*, a scribe seated cross-legged (2600-2350 BC), the graceful *Porteuse d'Offrandes*, a young girl carrying offerings (2000-1800 BC), the great sphinx found at Tanis (c 1898-1866 BC), the huge bust of Amenophis IV, who called himself Akhnaton (c 1365-1349 BC), the tomb fragment in painted limestone featuring the goddess Hathor protecting Seti I (c 1300 BC), the

1. Winged Assyrian bulls
These bulls with men's heads guarded the palace gate of Sargon II of Assyria (721-705 BC) at Khorsabad. The city, today in northern Iraq, was discovered in 1843 by French consul P E Botta, who sent the finest sculptures to the Louvre.

2. Female statuette from the Cyclades
This statuette with "crossed arms" is typical of the marble figurines sculpted in the Cyclades group of Greek islands in the Bronze Age (3200-2000 BC).

3. The goddess Hathor and King Seti I
This bas-relief painted in the 13th century BC comes from the tomb of Seti I in the Valley of the Kings. It was brought from Egypt by Champollion, who persuaded King Charles X to found a Museum of Egyptology at the Louvre.

4. *The Winged Victory of Samothrace*
Found on the island of Samothrace, this statue (c 190 BC) commemorates a naval victory. Together with the *Venus de Milo* it is one of the most famous works of Antiquity.

5. The "Eagle of Suger" Vase
Abbot Suger had this Ancient porphyry vase (1147 BC) turned into a liturgical vessel. It is one of the treasures of the Royal Abbey of Saint-Denis.

bronze statue of the god Horus (1069-664 BC), and the sarcophagus of Chancellor Imeneminet (8th century BC). The department was founded in 1826 by Jean-François Champollion, the man who deciphered the hieroglyphs, and since 1997 has been organized on thematic lines: writing and scribes, housing and furniture, costume and finery, music and games, the tombs, etc. It is easier for visitors to understand the daily life and customs of people living in the Nile Valley in ancient times when they can look at displays of everyday objects: weapons, tools, containers, furniture, toiletries, clothes, musical instruments, etc.

◆ Greek, Etruscan, and Roman antiquities

Based on the royal collection of antiquities, begun in the reign of François I and subsequently enlarged thanks to archeological finds, national conquests, and constant acquisitions, this department covers every period in the history of Greek, Etruscan, and Roman art from the Neolithic Period (4th century BC) to the 6th century AD. Its marvelous sculptures include the Cycladic idol from the island of Karos (2700-2400 BC), fragments from the Parthenon frieze (5th century BC), the *Winged Victory of Samothrace* (c 190 BC), the *Venus de Milo* (c 100 BC), the fine sarcophagus of a couple from a great Etruscan family (late 6th century BC), and busts of Roman emperors. In addition, there are ceramics, gold and silver plate, ivories, glassware, jewels, mosaics, and frescos.

Paintings

Mona Lisa, the world's most famous painting, has done much to boost

the Louvre's fame. It is one of the museum's 6,000 European paintings from the end of the 13th century to the middle of the 19th. It is also one of the Louvre's original works, acquired by François I for his "cabinet of paintings" at Fontainebleau. This collection, considerably added to by Louis XIV, formed the basis of the Central Arts Museum in 1793. Since then, the department has grown steadily, especially from donations and purchases which, for example, in 1989-99 added 159 paintings.

◆ French painting

Two-thirds of the paintings in the Louvre's collection are from the French school, from the earliest portraits, such as *Portrait of King Jean the Good* (c 1360) and *Portrait of King Charles VII* (c 1445) by Jean Fouquet, up to the Barbizon school. One of the oldest masterpieces is the *Pietà de Villeneuve-lès-Avignon* (c 1460), attributed to Enguerrand Quarton. Among the Mannerist paintings of the Fontainebleau school are the elegant *Diana the Huntress* (c 1550) and the titillating

Gabrielle d'Estrées with her sister. There are learned allegories by Simon Vouet (1590-1649) and portraits by Philippe de Champagne (1602-74), while in their use of chiaroscuro in both religious and popular works Georges de la Tour (1593-1674) and the Le Nain brothers (c 1600-77) reveal the influence of Caravaggio. In terms of Louis XIV's favorite painters, the Louvre has 39 by Poussin, the great Classical master, ten by Claude Gallée (known as Le Lorrain), whose studies of light have led people to see him as one of the forerunners of Impressionism, and almost all of Le Brun's output, in particular his vast canvases on the history of Alexander. Not to mention Hyacinthe Rigaud, whose magnificent portrait of Louis XIV in his coronation robes (1701) so delighted the court at Versailles that they kept it rather than giving it to the King of Spain, for whom it was intended. Louis XV, on the other hand, had no part in the museum's collection of sensitive, poetic, spicy, and light-hearted 18th-century pictures. This was rather the work of a 19th-century collector, La Caze, who

bequeathed eight canvases by Watteau, including his *Pierrot*, 13 by Chardin, and nine by Fragonard. These charming pictures were followed by more austere works revealing a taste for Antiquity and history painting, such as David's *Oath of the Horatii* and *Coronation of Napoléon I*. Théodore Géricault's *Raft of the Medusa*, shown at the Salon in 1819, announced the arrival of Romanticism. Delacroix brought brilliance of color and movement in *Liberty Leading the People* (1830) and *Scenes from the Massacres at Chios* (1824). In an opposite vein, Ingres impressed with his clarity of form and purity of line in *Portrait of Monsieur Bertin* (1832) and *The Turkish Bath* (1862). From 1830, there was a renewed taste for nature and landscape, as demonstrated by Camille Corot (more than 130 of his works are in the Louvre) and painters of the Barbizon school such as Théodore Rousseau.

◆ *Italian painting*

The Italian school is the best represented of the foreign schools at the Louvre. François I acquired several works by Leonardo da Vinci,

Raphaël, Titian, and other contemporary masters. Later, Louis XIV took over ready-made collections such as those of Mazarin and the banker Jabach, which include works by Raphaël and Titian. Seizures during the Revolution and under Napoléon, and further acquisitions in the 19th and 20th centuries, completed the royal collections, though these were notably lacking in earlier painters. Today the Louvre has an

outstanding selection of Renaissance works, including paintings by Leonardo da Vinci (*Mona Lisa, The Virgin of the Rocks, The Virgin, The Child and St Anne*, and *La Belle Ferronière*), Raphaël (*La Belle Jardinière, Portrait of Baldassare Castiglione*, and *The Holy Family of François I*), Titian (*Man with a Glove, Pastoral Concert*, and *The Entombment*), Veronese (*La Belle Nani* and *Marriage at Cana*, a huge canvas, recently restored), and Mantegna, court painter at Mantua (*St Sebastian, The Calvary*, and a series of paintings for Isabella d'Este's study in the Gonzaga Palace), Carpaccio (*St Stephen Preaching at Jerusalem*), Ghirlandaio (the moving *Portrait of an Old Man and his Grandson*), Piero de la Francesca (*Sigismondo Malatesta*), and Antonello de Messine (a superb *Condottiere*). The museum also has masterpieces by painters from the

---

1. *The Battle of San Romano* (Uccello)
The *Battle of San Romano* (c 1450-55) was painted for the Médicis. There are three separate scenes; the other two are in Florence and London. Uccello's use of rhythmic rows of lances and geometric stylization were part of his innovative technique.

2. *Mona Lisa* (Leonardo da Vinci)
Leonardo was so fond of this picture (c 1503-6) that he took it with him when François I invited him to France in 1516. On his death in 1519, it was placed in the king's "cabinet of paintings." Leonardo's genius, the work's

perfection, and the mystery surrounding the model's identity have made it the world's most famous painting.

3. *The Marriage at Cana* (Veronese)
This masterpiece of decorative Venetian painting (1563) was commissioned from Veronese for the refectory of the monastery of San Giorgio Maggiore.

4. *Pierrot*, formerly known as *Gilles* (Watteau)
This *Pierrot* (c 1718-19) is full of mystery: a simple-looking, dreamy figure standing alone on a stage, possibly at the Théâtre de la Foire. We do not know who Watteau painted it for, nor who the model was.

5. *The Raft of the Medusa* (Géricault)
Inspired by a true story, this work was shown at the Salon of 1819 and marked the beginning of French Romantic painting with its spirit and dramatic intensity.

13th to the 15th centuries, such as Cimabue (*Madonna of the Angels*, c 1270), Fra Angelico (*The Coronation of the Virgin*, 1430-5) and Paolo Uccello (*The Battle of San Romano*, 1437). The 17th/18th-century collection has been considerably enlarged in recent years and is especially rich in works by Caravaggio (*Death of the Virgin*, *The Fortune Teller*), and a series of ten paintings of Venetian festivities by Guardi, and Tiepolo father (*The Last Supper*) and son (*Carnival Scene*).

◆ Spanish painting

The Louvre has 80 Spanish paintings, from the Gothic artists of Catalonia and Castile to Goya, El Greco, and the great names of the "Golden Century" (Zurburan, Ribera, Velasquez, and Murillo). Among the major works are El Greco's *Christ on the Cross* (c 1580), Ribera's *Club-footed Boy* (1642), Murillo's B*eggar Boy* (1650), and several portraits by Goya including the splendid *Portrait of the Marquesa de la Solana* (c 1791-4).

◆ Northern Europe

Although it is not as strong as the Italian collection, the Louvre's

North European schools include the major Flemish, Dutch, and German painters from the 14th to the 16th centuries. Among them are Jan van Eyck's *Virgin of Autun* (c 1435), a strongly hieratic composition against a jewel-like background landscape, *The Moneylender and his Wife* (1514), a fascinating genre scene by Quentin Metsys, Hieronymus Bosch's almost Surrealist *Ship of Fools* (c 1490-1500), and Vermeer's serene and luminous *The Lacemaker* (1664) and *The Astronomer* (1668). The German pictures feature a fine *Portrait of the Artist* by Dürer, a delicate *Venus in a Landscape* by Lucas Cranach, and the portrait of *Erasmus* by Holbein the Younger. Rubens has his own section with a series of 24 canvases on *The Life of Marie de Médicis* which display lively groupings from mythology with iridescent skin and brilliant silk costumes. Two rooms devoted to Rembrandt show moving self-portraits, biblical scenes such as the famous *Pilgrims at Emmaüs*, the impressive still life *The Skinned Ox*, and one of his rare nudes, *Bathsheba at her Toilet*, for which his second companion, Hendrickje Stoffels, was the model. The English school is thinly represented at the Louvre, although there are some fine portraits by Reynolds and Gainsborough, and a few landcapes by Constable and Turner.

Sculpture

Ever since the large open-air statues were put in place beneath the great

windows of the Marly and Puget courts, all the sculptures at the Louvre seem to be attracting more notice. These courts make a marvelous setting in which to admire the Baroque power of Puget's *Milon of Crotona* (1682), which formerly stood at the head of the Allée Royale at Versailles, and the spirit of the equestrian groups that once decorated the Château de Marly: *Fame and Mercury* (1706) and Guillaume Coustou's *Marly Horses*. The French sculptures are displayed in chronological order in the rooms around the two courts, and give a very full account of its evolution from Romanesque and Gothic works, which have come from churches, to the lions and tigers of Antoine-Louis Barye, the great animal sculptor of the 19th century, via the wonderful nymphs of Jean Goujon from the Fontaine des Innocents (1547-9), and Falconet's graceful *Woman Bathing* (1757). The most famous of the foreign sculptures include *The Nymph of Fontainebleau* (1542-3) by Benvenuto Cellini, with its typically

etiolated form, and two works by Michelangelo, designed for the tomb of Pope Julius II.

Other departments

As well as its antiquities, paintings and sculptures, the Louvre contains two other departments of similar merit. The Graphic Arts section is based on Louis XIV's collection of drawings and includes works by Leonardo da Vinci, Primaticcio, Dürer, and Rembrandt, which, in view of their frailty, are only shown in temporary exhibitions. The Objets d'Art collection contains furniture, tapestries, ivories, gold objects, jewelry, glass, faience, and small bronzes from late Antiquity to the 19th century. Among them are treasures from the Abbey of Saint-Denis and the Sainte-Chapelle,

tapestries from the "Maximilian's Hunts" series (Brussels, 1528-33), Louis XIV furniture by the great cabinetmaker Charles Boulle, crown jewels, etc. In 2000, the Louvre also acquired works from Africa, Oceania, Asia, and the Americas. They offer a taste of the Musée des Arts Premiers, which is due to open on Quai Branly.

6

1. *The Moneylender and his Wife* (Metsys)
This 1514 picture is one of the earliest examples of genre painting in the Low Countries, though the seriousness of the characters and the scales, symbolizing the last judgment, also give it a moralizing dimension. The mirror with its reflection of a man reading is a motif often used by Van Eyck, who no doubt gave Metsys the idea.

2. *The Lacemaker* (Vermeer)
Along with *The Astronomer* or *The Geographer*, this painting from 1664 is one of the Louvre's two canvases by this master of light and color, who only painted some 40 pictures in his life.

3. *Bathsheba at her Toilet* (Rembrandt)
The Louvre has a dozen Rembrandts – portraits, self-portraits, and biblical scenes – but this is one of his rare nudes, painted in 1654. Rembrandt's model for Bathsheba was Hendrickje Stoffels, his second companion.

4. *Portrait of the Marquesa de la Solana* (Goya)
The Louvre's Spanish collection is limited but representative, its several masterpieces including this highly subtle portrait.

5. *The Slave,* known as *The Rebel* (Michelangelo)
Michelangelo carved this statue, and another known as *The Dying Slave*, also at the Louvre, between 1513 and 1515 for the tomb of Pope Julius II. When they were finally not used for the tomb, the artist gave them to his friend Roberto Strozzi, who in turn presented them to Henri II of France.

6. The *Marly Horses* (Coustou)
This equestrian group and its companion, both now in the Louvre, were commissioned by Louis XV for the watering place in the park at Marly. They are a tribute to wild nature and to man's ability to tame it.

Toward the Tuileries

In 1981, when the Grand Louvre project was approved, the intention was only to enlarge and restructure the Louvre Museum. The neighboring Tuileries were not involved. Then, however, as the underground shopping arcades and parking lots were designed, and archeological digs revealed their marvelous finds, the area around the Carrousel was completely disrupted. It was time to think again. Now the final phase of works at the Grand Louvre has meant redesigning the Carrousel area and the Tuileries, building the Solférino Footbridge to link with the Musée d'Orsay, which opened in 1986, and renovating the museums facing the gardens: the Musée des Arts Décoratifs and the Orangerie.

A hundred-acre garden in the heart of Paris

Once the Avenue du Général-Lemonnier had been placed underground, the gardens of the Carrousel and Tuileries formed an unbroken unit of more than 99 acres (40 ha) extending from the Louvre at one end to Concorde and the Champs-Elysées at the other. The aim was both to restore them to their past glory and to link them to contemporary developments.

◆ The palace that disappeared

Between the Tuileries Garden and the old Carrousel courtyard stood a château that Catherine de Médicis commissioned Philibert Delorme to build in 1563. Several kings carried on the work, which was completed under the Empire. Then in 1871 three soldiers of the Commune set fire to it. After much debate, the ruined palace was demolished, and only the two wings were restored.

◆ Italian style, formalized by Le Nôtre

True to her Florentine origins, Catherine de Médicis attached great value to the garden in front of her château. On land previously used for making tiles, she had an Italian-style garden laid out, decorated with fountains, a maze, and a grotto adorned with glazed earthenware by Bernard Palissy. Devastated by civil wars, the garden took on a more Classical appearance under Claude Mollet, Henri IV's gardener. Then André Le Nôtre, working for Louis XIV, completely redesigned it to harmonize with the château, which the architects Louis Le Vau and François d'Orbay had just completed. A straight grand avenue opened the perspective, with ornate parterres, terraces, steps, and an iron ramp for horses; pools and groves; and statues in wooded bowers. The Tuileries Garden was a forerunner of Versailles. In the course of time, it lost its rigorous layout, but was continually adorned with new statues.

◆ The Carrousel

In 1662, to celebrate the birth of the Dauphin, Louis XIV gave a great tournament or 'carrousel' in the Tuileries courtyard, which became known as the Cour du Carrousel. Napoléon I had a triumphal arch built there to mark his Grande Armée's victory at Austerlitz. This was modeled on the Arch of Septimus Severus in Rome. Its bas-reliefs tell the story of the 1805 campaign. It is surmounted by a chariot drawn by the Horses of Saint Mark and two figures representing Fame. When

the château was demolished, the carroussel site was redesigned as a garden.

◆ The renovated gardens

In 1991, the complete renovation of the gardens was begun. The triumphal arch now forms a majestic entrance, with lines of clipped yew trees radiating from it and "expanding the space" as far as the Tuileries terrace. The groves of the Great Covert (the wooded part of the garden) have been restored. The two semi-circular marble benches, made in 1799, have been turned into

romantic pools planted with water iris and populated by ducks. Between 1998 and 2000, more than 40 contemporary works (by Giacometti, Dubuffet, Louise Bourgeois, Henry Moore, Roy Lichtenstein, etc) have appeared in the gardens, making the Tuileries a wonderful museum of statuary from ancient times to the 20th century.

From one musuem to the next

Right beside the Louvre are five other museums, three in the Marsan wing and pavilion and two in the Tuileries Garden.

◆ Museums of the Central Union of Decorative Arts

Here you can find a French bedroom from the end of the Middle Ages, a study from the 1530s, and a gallery of retables. In its Middle Ages to Renaissance department, the Musée des Arts Decoratifs takes a more lively approach than simply laying out period pieces in chronological order. Next to it since 1982, the Musée de la Publicité has a collection of more than 100,000 old and new

posters and 20,000 film posters. Also in this wing since 1997 is the Musée de la Mode et du Textile with its exhibitions on textiles and fashion.

◆ Museums in the garden

The National Gallery of the Jeu de Paume, in the former real-tennis court, puts on contemporary art exhibitions such as Arman in 1998 and Morellet in 2000. Its counterpart, the Musée de l'Orangerie, is housed in an 1892 building and features Monet's *Water Lilies* and the wonderful Walter-Guillaume collection of works from Impressionism to 1930. It is currently closed for restoration until at least 2002.

1. The River (Maillol)
The gardens of the Carrousel and the Tuileries contain more than 60 20th-century sculptures. Most were moved there in 1999-2000, but those by Aristide Maillol arrived as early as 1964.

2. Round pond in the Tuileries
This pond on the east side of the garden is only half the size of the octagonal pond near Concorde. The two ponds nevertheless appear to be the same size.

3. Carrousel garden
When they were commisssioned in 1990 to design the Carrousel garden, Jacques and Peter Wirtz revived the art of topiary (clipped trees), designing yew hedges which radiate from the foot of the arch.

4. The Carrousel Arc de Triomphe
Built by Napoléon I as a tribute to his army, the Carrousel's triumphal arch consists of eight marble columns surmounted by statues representing soldiers of the Empire.

5. Sailing boats in the Tuileries
Apart from the eternal pleasure of sailing boats on the round pond, the Tuileries also has playgrounds for children.

6. Dubuffet at the Jeu de Paume
Since the Impressionist paintings went to the Musée d'Orsay, the Jeu de Paume has been devoted to temporary exhibitions: from Dubuffet in 1991 to Picasso Erotique in 2001.

Toward the Place Vendôme

The districts close to the Louvre are a mixture of very different places: government offices and banks in their own gilt-paneled mansions, fashionable boutiques with minimalist window displays, ultramodern market halls and ancient studios for milliners and textile workers, majestic royal squares from the time of Louis XIV and arcades from the beginning of

the 19th century, palaces and former convents, and Irish pubs and Japanese restaurants – all variously populated by tourists, actors and architects, designers and office workers. To the east of Avenue de l'Opéra, on the Palais Royal side, the streets are narrower, with many arcades and lots of different activities, while toward Place Vendôme everything is much more lavish and uniform. But the border between the two is not always clear.

In the Louvre's shadow

◆ Place du Louvre

The spacious esplanade between the Louvre and Saint-Germain l'Auxerrois offers good views of Perrault's monumental colonnade on one side and the fine Flamboyant Gothic porch of the church on the other. For a long time, however, private mansions and other buildings blocked the view and separated the palace of the French kings from the parish church where they often went to hear Mass. The square dates from Haussmann's time, when he commissioned Jacques-Ignace Hittorff to build the Neo-Gothic town hall (now that of the first *arrondissement*) which stands beside the church. The belfry (1862) has an 83-bell carillon that rings four times a day, followed by a late 18th-century air (*The Tambourin* by Rameau, *The Reapers* by Couperin or *It's raining, shepherdess* by Fabre d'Eglantine).

◆ Saint-Germain l'Auxerrois: the royal parish church

Built on the site of an old Merovingian sanctuary, Saint-Germain d'Auxerrois was built in several stages, notably in the 13th century (choir, portal, and Chapel of the Vir-

gin) and 15th century (porch, nave, aisles, and chevet). Its bell, Marie, pealed out on August 24, 1572, to announce the Massacre of St Bartholomew's Day. The church has lost almost all its rich Ancien Régime furnishings except for the splendid churchwardens' pew designed in 1684 by Le Brun, and some windows.

◆ Oratoire du Louvre

Between Rue Saint-Honoré and Rue de Rivoli, the Temple of the Oratory, allocated to Protestant worship since 1811, was the Chapel Royal from the time of Louis XIII to Louis XV. The court often came to hear great preachers such as Massillon and Malebranche. The church was founded by the Oratorians in 1621 and built by Métezeau and Le Mercier, the royal architect commissioned to work on the Louvre in 1624. His portal was not completed until the 18th century.

◆ Rue de Rivoli

The Rue de Rivoli provides a covered pedestrian arcade from the Louvre to Concorde. Running parallel to the very old, and narrow, Rue Saint-Honoré, it was built in 1802 by Napoléon I to ease the city's east-west traffic flow. The buildings on

this "triumphal way" beside the Tuileries and the Louvre had to be all alike, with an arcade at ground level and three upper stories, the top one set in a curved roof. As well as elegant boutiques and souvenir stores, the arcades of the Rue de Rivoli contain several luxury hotels, such as the Meurice, inaugurated in 1907, Angelina's tea rooms, founded in 1903, the oldest English bookshop in Paris, Calignagni, and the Louvre des Antiquaires which houses 250 antique dealers in an area of 107,640 sq ft (10,000 sq m).

Palais Royal

The Palais Royal is occupied by the Ministry of Culture, the Council of State, and the Constitutional Council. In its galleries and gardens, people stroll quietly about or just browse in the elegant boutiques selling old dresses by great couturiers, medals and little lead soldiers, brocaded waistcoats, perfumes of amber and iris, and aprons for well-heeled gardeners.

◆ From Cardinal's Palace to Palais Royal

The large maritime trophies in the Galerie des Proues (its wall facing the courtyard with the columns designed by Buren), and a balcony supported by lions' heads overlooking Rue de Valois, are all that remain of the Cardinal's Palace, built here by Richelieu to be closer to the king, then living in the Louvre. It became the Palais Royal in 1643 when Anne of Austria moved in with the young Louis XIV; later it was granted to the Orléans family until 1848.

◆ Grandeur and levity

The palace was constantly reshaped in the 18th century, being variously renovated or rebuilt as a result of fires. In 1781, to bring in funds, the extravagant Duc d'Orléans, the future Philippe-Egalité, divided one-third of the garden into plots and commissioned architect Victor Louis to build rental blocks around the perimeter, with arcades at

ground level to be let as shops. In 1784, short of money to finish the operation, Philippe had wooden shacks built to protect the foundations, and let these out for business. Nicknamed the "Tartars' Camp," it quickly became "the meeting place for every crook, swindler, rogue, and villain at large in the capital." The temporary buildings lasted for about 50 years. Loose morals and freedom of thought went hand in hand in this princely domain, which the police were barred from entering. During the Revolution, it was one of the hotbeds of dissent in Paris. Under the Consulate and the

1. The Women's Club (M Lix)
This sketch from life shows a meeting of the Club des Femmes in the church of St Germain-l'Auxerrois at the time of the Commune.

2. Oratory of the Louvre
The Oratory church was made over to Protestant worship in 1811. It was founded in 1621 by the congregation of the Oratory, then Louis XIII decided to make it the Louvre's chapel, and ordered its axis to be changed to align with that of the palace.

3. La Samaritaine
The Samaritaine department stores, built between 1910 and 1928, are fine examples of commercial architecture at the beginning of the 20th century, with their iron frames and huge windows. The Toupary Restaurant on the sixth story has wonderful views over the river and the city.

4. Arcades of Rue de Rivoli
The Rue de Rivoli is lined from Palais Royal to Place de la Concorde with buildings sharing similar arcaded façades and containing souvenir stores and elegant businesses.

5. Place des Pyramides
The statue of Joan of Arc, sculpted by Frémiet in 1874, sparkles at the center of Place des Pyramides. The square was built in 1802, its name a reminder of Bonaparte's victory in Egypt in 1798.

6. Palais Royal in the 18th century
Built between 1781 and 1784, the arcades of Palais Royal were immediately thronged with people. Artists, writers, politicians, ruined gamblers, high-class ladies, and women of lesser virtue paraded beneath the arcades and in the garden, which the police were barred from entering.

Empire, the Palais Royal was more popular than ever. People came for the cafés, restaurants, gambling houses, boutiques ... and the "young ladies." Then, in 1814, the future Louis-Philippe recovered the palace of his forefathers. He commissioned Fontaine to complete the Victor Louis plan and gave the buildings their present appearance. The Galerie d'Orléans replaced the wooden structures. The women and the places of ill repute were banned. Today the businesses are elegant, the inhabitants people of distinction and senior officials.

◆ Imprint of the 20th century

The Palais Royal remained a quiet, empty backwater until, in 1986, a series of black and white columns were planted in the Cour d'Honneur, strange drum-like shapes by Daniel Buren which aroused passionate debate and encouraged people to rediscover its charm. Our age is also leaving its mark, just as previous generations have done. New additions are the Pol Bury fountains in the Galerie d'Orléans, the *Tribute to Malraux* sculpture by Jean-Michel Alberola in the Passage des Fontaines, and several adjustments to the garden layout.

◆ The theaters

The Comédie Française is attached to the west side of the Palais Royal. Philippe d'Orléans commissioned Victor Louis to rebuild the auditorium space after the 1763 fire at the Salle du Petit Cardinal, on the corner of Rue Saint-Honoré and the present Rue de Valois. All that now remains of Louis's theater, after several bouts of rebuilding and restora-

tion, is the façade on Rue de Richelieu. The Théâtre du Palais Royal, on the corner of Rue Montpensier, was also designed by Victor Louis and rebuilt by Louis Regnier de Guerchy in 1830. Its most glorious days were under the directorship of Marguerite Brunet, known as *La Montansier*, who acquired it in 1790.

Impact of the 17th and 19th centuries

The maze of streets around the Palais Royal contains impressive features from the 17th century, the period when Mazarin, Colbert, Lully, and many bankers moved into the district; and some astonishing 19th-century buildings such as the great reading room of the National Library and numerous shopping arcades.

◆ Place des Victoires

This lovely square, dating from the 17th century with a central equestrian statue of Louis XIV, is today surrounded by elegant fashion boutiques. In his own day, Louis XIV appeared there not on a horse but on foot, and the square was much more beautiful. In 1679, Marshal of France La Feuillade wished to show his

admiration for the king, who had just signed the Treaty of Nijmegen, so he commissioned the sculptor Desjardins to design a statue of Louis XIV, standing in coronation robes, crowned by Victory, and crushing a three-headed monster that represented the conquered nations of the Triple Alliance. Some years later, in 1685, the courtier-marshal asked Hardouin-Mansart to build Place des Victoires as a setting for the king's statue. This was the first of the royal squares dedicated to Louis XIV. It was circular, something new at the time, and completely surrounded by symmetrically designed façades. The royal statue was destroyed in the Revolution and replaced under Louis XVIII by this

equestrian statue by Bosio. The rigorous plan of the circus has suffered from alterations to its buildings and from Rue Etienne-Marcel being driven through it in 1883.

◆ Church of Notre-Dame des Victoires

The church was built between 1629 and 1740, and owes its name to the victories of Louis XIII, particularly at La Rochelle. It was part of the Convent of the Augustinian Hermits, destroyed in the Revolution. Since 1836, it has become a place of pilgrimage, and contains a vast number of ex-voto tablets. In the choir, seven paintings by Carl Van Loo depict the life of St Augustine and the pledge of Louis XIII at the Siege of La Rochelle. Carried out between 1746 and 1755, they are a rare example of a pre-Revolutionary decorative scheme to have originated in a church.

◆ Bibliothèque Nationale

Since the introduction of copyright libraries in 1537, making it obligatory to hold one copy of all printed matter, the Royal Library, then the National Library, has continued to expand, its latest move being the opening of the BNF-Tolbiac. As

1. Buildings beside the Palais Royal garden
Among the few people fortunate enough to live in the buildings surrounding this leafy enclave have been Colette, Cocteau, and Jacques Grange, decorator of the Hôtel Costes, Rue Saint-Honoré, and the Ladurée pâtisserie on the Champs-Elysées.

2. Beneath the arcades in Palais Royal
Today the arcades in Palais Royal are populated by quiet officials and shoppers drawn by the elegant boutiques.

3. The Buren columns
Two hundred and sixty columns in black granite and white marble, some of them sunk in trenches with a thin stream of water: these drum-like shapes by Daniel Buren caused a scandal when they were put up in the Palais Royal courtyard in 1986.

4. National Library
The reading room was built by Labrouste in 1863, and is remarkable in many ways: for the free use of ironwork in the structure, the slimness of its cast-iron columns, the lightness of its cupolas covered in white porcelain plaques set between friezes, and the softness of the overhead lighting.

5. Place des Victoires
This was the first royal square dedicated to Louis XIV. It was commissioned from J H-Mansart by a courtier, and still has great charm, surrounded by elegant boutiques.

early as 1724, Colbert had to transfer part of the king's library to Rue Vivienne for want of space at the Louvre. In the 17th century it took over various mansions, including the old Hôtel Mazarin. Further expansions followed in the 18th and 19th centuries, and now it extends over a huge rectangle between Rues de Richelieu, Colbert, des Petits-Champs, and Vivienne, not to mention its annexes on Square Louvois and in Passage Colbert. The remains of the Hôtel Mazarin are its most remarkable heritage, along with the magnificent reading room built by Labrouste in 1863. One wing of the wonderfully decorated Hôtel has survived. This was built by François Mansart in 1644 and contains two galleries, one above the other. The upper one, the Galerie Mazarine, has retained its wall paintings by Romanelli and Grimaldi, while the lower, the Galerie Mansart, has been spoiled. Labrouste's reading room, the former reading room for printed material, remains a model of 19th-century architecture, with its slender columns and metal arches supporting nine domes covered with ceramics, each lit by a circular window. Since 1998 and the transfer of printed matter and periodicals to Tolbiac, the Richelieu site holds just the special collections: manuscripts, prints and photographs, maps and plans, music, coins, medals, and antiquities.

◆ The 19th-century galleries and passages

A number of glass-roofed arcades were built in the 1820s: Passage Choiseul, and Galerie Colbert, Galerie Vivienne, Galerie Véro-Dodat. They did well out of the lively scene then going on at Palais Royal. Customers could stroll round these shopping arcades without worrying about the rain or the horses at a time when there were no sidewalks. Much renovated today, they still house a few old businesses, but most are now fashion boutiques. The Galerie Colbert, however, was rebuilt in its original style in 1985, and houses departments of the National Library and the National Institute for the History of Art.

◆ The Stock Exchange

In 1808, Napoléon I ordered the building of an "Imperial Stock Exchange Palace," built by Alexandre Brogniart in the style of an ancient temple. Today it is little more than a museum, now that shares are traded by computer rather than by auction. The dealing rooms are much quieter nowadays, and are now to be found in various places around the Stock Exchange itself.

Along Rue Saint-Honoré

Rue Saint-Honoré is a major east-west street, one of the most important in Paris before Rue de Rivoli was built. Today, as in the past, the social level of its inhabitants rises gradually as you go from east to west.

◆ Saint-Roch

Non-worshippers too come to this church for its concerts and to look at the paintings and sculptures. Saint-Roch was begun in 1653 to designs by Le Mercier. In 1705, Jules Hardouin-Mansart extended the nave into the Lady Chapel, though the new vault could not be added until the banker John Law provided the money in 1719, and the façade was only completed in 1739 to a design by Robert Cotte. The church is often associated with artists and writers, and Pierre Corneille, Pierre Mignard, André Le Nôtre, and Diderot were buried here.

◆ **Place du Marché Saint-Honoré**

This square was built close to Rue Saint-Honoré in 1807, and has many restaurants and fashion boutiques. In the center is a large glass hall built by the Catalan architect Ricardo Bofill in 1997, and containing the offices of the BNP-Paribas bank.

◆ **Church of the Assumption**

This former monastery chapel was built in 1776 to plans by Charles Errard, and is the parish church of the Polish community in Paris. On Sundays, they flock here to meet up in the square.

The lap of luxury

Place Vendôme and neighboring streets, especially Rues de la Paix, de Castiglione, and Saint-Honoré, are the preserve of wealth and luxury: the home of banks, the Sultan of Brunei, couture houses, luxury hotels, and jewellers. The square's renovation in 1992 has only added to its harmonious charms.

◆ **Place Vendôme**

The idea of the square was put forward by a group of speculators, then taken up by Louvois in 1685. In the king's name, the superintendent of buildings bought the Hôtel de Vendôme and the neighboring Capuchin monastery, and commissioned Hardouin-Mansart to build a square in their place. It was to be the setting for an equestrian statue of Louis XIV, dressed in Antique style, sculpted by François Girardon. The statue was inaugurated in 1699, and the square, at first called Place Vendôme in memory of the old mansion, then Place des Conquêtes (after the other royal square, the Place des Victoires), was named Place Louis-le-Grand. After the king had sold the land to the city, many wealthy financiers moved into the mansions behind Mansart's façades around the square, with its distinctive canted corners.

◆ **The Vendôme column**

The king's statue was destroyed in the Revolution, and the square renamed. In 1806, Napoléon had Rue de la Paix built and put up the Vendôme column as a tribute to his soldiers' victory at Austerlitz. It was designed by Gondoin and Lepère, and forged with metal from the Austrians' guns; the spiralling reliefs, the work of Etienne Bergeret, tell the story of the 1805 campaign. The figure on top is a statue of Napoléon I as Caesar, by Chaudet. The statue was to change with successive regimes: in 1814, Napoléon was replaced by Henri IV, then under Louis XVIII, by a fleur-de-lys. In Napoléon III's reign, a copy of the Napoléon I statue was restored there, but in 1871, under the Commune, the whole column was toppled. The painter Courbet was responsible for this enterprise. In 1873, he was forced to restore both column and statue at his own expense.

5 Cartier

1. Passage des Panoramas
The district has a number of covered arcades typical of the 19th century. They are frequently renovated, and contain old businesses as well as fashionable boutiques.

2. Place de la Bourse
In 1808, Napoléon decided to build an "Imperial Stock Exchange Palace" in the style of a great monument to Antiquity. To make room for it, the former convent of the Filles-Saint-Thomas was immediately demolished. The Bourse was not opened until 1826.

3. Lady Chapel, Church of Saint-Roch
The Lady Chapel is like a rotunda, and almost as big as a church. It was built by Mansart in 1710 thanks to a lottery win. Its grandiose decoration portrays the mystery of the Incarnation and the Redemption.

4. Place Vendôme
Napoléon looks down on the majestic square from the top of this column, decorated with bas-reliefs telling the story of the Austerlitz campaign. Today it is a moneyed, deluxe square with jewelers, banks, and the legendary Ritz Hotel with its memories of Proust and Princess Diana.

5. A window at Cartier's
The windows of Cartier, Van Clef & Arpels, Mauboussin, Boucheron, and Chaumet glitter with diamonds in Place Vendôme and along Rue de la Paix. A sign of the times is Tati Or, now in business on Cartier's doorstep.

THE OPÉRA
and surrounding area

Garnier's Opera House

The Grands Boulevards

From the Madeleine
to Monceau

Aerial view of the Opéra
The Opera House was part of a grand
19th-century town-planning scheme
to build a new district. The opening
of the new Avenue de l'Opéra
not only provided a view of
the new building, but above all
established a link between the modern
districts of the capital (the 8th and
17th *arrondissements*) then being built
and the old districts of Palais–Royal,
which were separated by the
Grands Boulevards.

Garnier's Opera House

"National Academy of Music." Those are the words inscribed in gold letters on the pediment of Charles Garnier's Opéra. This building and the Eiffel Tower are unusual in that they both feature the architect's name. Garnier's Opéra is a complete work of art, the most spectacular building of the Second Empire, crowned by Apollo holding aloft his golden lyre.

"The style I use is my own" (Charles Garnier)

◆ "It's Napoléon III style"

Napoléon III decided in 1858 to build a new Opera House for Paris. The competition attracted 171 entrants, including Viollet-le-Duc, the Empress's favorite. But the jury voted unanimously for the young Charles Garnier. The foundation stone was laid in 1862. Building work lasted 13 years, and the "Garnier Palace" was inaugurated on January 5, 1875. An army of 71 sculptors, and dozens of painters, mosaicists, artists, and craftsmen of every kind, followed the orders of their "general," Charles Garnier, who, in his Opéra, achieved a synthesis of all the plastic arts under the aegis of architecture. Empress Eugénie was apparently disdainful:

"What sort of style is that? It's not a style at all! It's neither Greek, nor Louis XVI, nor even Louis XV!" Garnier replied, "No, those styles have had their day ... this is Napoléon III! And you are complaining!"

◆ A splendid sense of order

Like opera itself, Garnier wanted his building to address the mind and the senses at the same time. His architecture is Classical, based on order and rhythm. For the second story, he was inspired by the Louvre Colonnade by Claude Perrault (1668); for the ground level he took inspiration from the Royal Wardrobe (now the Navy Ministry) on Place de la Concorde, the work of Jacques-Ange Gabriel (1768) – two archetypes of French Classicism.

◆ A rational, clear plan

Garnier adopted a simple, logical plan, but was innovative in the way he juxtaposed the various components so that their external architecture reflected their function. The loggia indicates where the public foyers are located. The central dome corresponds to the cupola in the auditorium. The massive, square structure, which culminates above the dome, contains the stage and its huge machinery. The two semi-circular pavilions flanking the side façades are the entrances for, on one side, the season-ticket holders, and on the other, guests of honor.

◆ A riot of color

The architect used a rich palette of techniques and materials: wrought iron, bronze, repoussé brass, electroplating, gilding, and mosaics. He used marble in profusion from many different sources: peach-tree marble with tints of flesh-pink, white, and pale green, green Swedish marble, cherry-red and red Languedoc marble, red Finnish porphyry, deep-blue marble, black Dinant marble, etc.

◆ *Lyrical decorations*

Beginning with the exterior, a profusion of statues provide an invitation to music and dance. Eight groups of figures embellish the doors in the main façade: Harmony, framed by Poetry and Music; Instrumental Music with seven figures, one a woman playing the viol and another

1. The Opéra Garnier
This massive building stands at the end of Avenue de l'Opéra. Some find it rather clumsy, others sometimes compare it to a big cake topped with pistachio icing.

2. Roof of the Opéra Garnier
The large gray-green dome, with Apollo above it, overlooks the broad south terrace, and crowns the auditorium. An unusual feature of the terrace is the beehives, honey from which is sold in the Opéra's boutique.

3. *The Dance* (Jean-Baptiste Carpeaux)
This is the Opéra's most famous sculptural group. From its first showing in 1869, its sensuality enraged many people, who saw it as an assault on modesty. The present copy by Paul Belmondo dates from the 1960s.

4. Restoring the figure of *Fame*
To celebrate the new millennium, the whole of the Opéra Garnier's exterior was restored. Its gilded surfaces gleam like new.

5. Chagall's ceiling
When he painted this ceiling in 1964, Chagall was inspired by nine famous operas and ballets, including Mozart's *Magic Flute* and Wagner's *Tristan and Isolde*.

Hall of Fame
Charles Garnier (1825-98)

The architect Charles Garnier was born in the working-class district of Mouffetard, the son of a blacksmith and a lacemaker. A brilliant pupil, he was soon noticed and entered the studio of Hippolyte Lebas, the architect of Notre-Dame-de-Lorette (1836). In 1848, he made his name by winning the Grand Prix de Rome. He worked on a project for the Conservatoire des Arts et Métiers which seemed fairly orthodox, then left for Italy to visit Rome and Florence. There he gradually found his style. A stay in Greece completed his education. He became architect to the City of Paris, and had few private clients. In Paris, apart from the Opéra, he completed a panorama theater for the Champs-Elysées, the present Théâtre Marigny, and the Cercle de la Librairie building, in Boulevard Saint-Germain, today the École du Patrimoine. He also built the casinos at Monte Carlo and Vittel. ■

the double flute, while two children personify the Sound of Spring Water and the Sound of the Wind; the Idyll; the Cantata; the Song; Drama; Dance, shown by nine figures; and Lyrical Drama, in which Vengeance with spread wings tramples on the traitor wounded by the gladiator. The most remarkable and best-known is *The Dance*, by sculptor Jean-Baptiste Carpeaux. He provoked a scandal, an "outrage to modesty," for creating such a sensual work. Today this sculpture is housed in the Musée d'Orsay, and has been replaced by a replica by sculptor Paul Belmondo.

The building is adorned with effigies in stone and gilded bronze, busts and medallions of composers grouped around Mozart, masks inspired by Greek theater, groups of children, allegories of architecture and industry, painting and sculpture ... all the way up to the sculptures of Harmony and Poetry, surmounted by A Millet's famous *Apollo*, flanked by two winged horses.

◆ Rich interior decorations

The decorations are even more sumptuous in the interior, with allegorical paintings, colored marbles and granites, mosaics shimmering with gold, and women torchbearers. Two statues in bicolored marble sit enthroned as caryatids at the entrance to the auditorium. Facing them is the Great Staircase, which turns twice on itself, and was built from 33 different marbles. It leads to the huge foyer, richly decorated with paintings by Paul Baudry and mosaics by Salviati, which opens onto the exterior loggia.

The auditorium is in red and gold, the de rigueur colors of the day, but seats barely 2,000 spectators, which is not many given the building's size. Spatial priority was given to the huge stage, its enormous machinery, and to the staircases, foyers, and vestibules where the rituals of society were enacted. In 1964, the old ceiling was covered by a new one, painted by Chagall and depicting nine operas and ballets.

1

2

Great days at the Opéra

On March 22, 1880, Giuseppe Verdi came in person to direct *Aïda*. The closing years of the 19th century belonged to Wagner with the first production of *Lohengrin* in 1891. June 7, 1910, saw the Paris première of the Ballets Russes. Vaslav Nijinsky and Ida Rubinstein danced Rimsky-

Korsakov's *Scheherazade*. The corps de ballet's leading dancers – George Balanchine, Serge Lifar, Rudolf Nureyev, Noella Pontois, and Marie-Claude Petragalla – were the true stars of the Palais Garnier, more so than the singers.

On June 6, 1964, and February 19, 1965, Maria Callas triumphed in Bellini's *Norma* and Puccini's *Tosca*. On April 7, 1973, Gundula Janowitz delighted the audience in *The Marriage of Figaro*, directed by Giorgio Strehler.

Rolf Liebermann's time as administrator (1973-80) was seen as a new "golden age" at the Opéra. In 1983, the production of Messiaen's *St Francis of Assisi* was the Opéra's second venture into contemporary music, following *Lulu* by Alban Berg in 1979. In 2000, couturier Christian Lacroix

designed the costumes for *Joyaux*, Balanchine's famous ballet first performed in 1967. Since the opening of the Opéra Bastille, the Palais Garnier has specialized mainly in dance productions.

Facts & Figures

Statistics for the Opéra
Dimensions : 567 ft (173 m), long, 410 ft (125 m) wide, 269 ft (82 m) high
Area : more than 108,504 sq ft (11,000 sq m)
Number of doors in 1875 : 2,531
Number of keys in 1875 : 7,593
Main foyer : 177 ft (54 m) long, 43 ft (13 m) wide, 59 ft (18 m) high
Number of steps : 6,136, inc 1,000 in marble
Stage : 89 ft (27 m) deep, 157 ft (48 m) wide
Number of employees : more than 1,000
Corps de ballet (2000-2001 season) : 12 star dancers, 12 solo dancers, 40 supporting dancers, 34 coryphées, 51 quadrilles

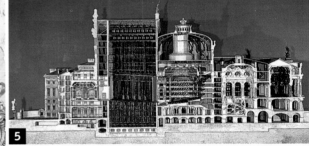

1. Sylvie Guillem in *Juliette*
Sylvie Guillem was the leading dancer of the corps de ballet directed by Nureyev for only a short time (1984-9), but made a great impression. She spent the main part of her career with the Royal Ballet in London.

2. The Great Gallery at the Opéra
Many different types of marble give the decorations an especially opulent look. Here the series of double Corinthian columns surrounding the gallery are made of pink marble to match the banisters of the main staircase.

3. Maria Callas in *Norma*
Maria Callas had a great triumph in Bellini's *Norma*, directed by Zefirelli in June, 1964, and May, 1965. In the last performance, on May 29, the singer fainted and the performance was stopped.

4. The auditorium
The auditorium, a symphony in red and gold, can hold only 2,000 people. All the boxes in the gallery have two parts: one for enjoying the performance, the other, at the back, so that members of the audience can talk to each other.

5. Cross-section of the Opéra Garnier
The auditorium occupies only one-third of the total area. The largest interior space is taken up by the set machinery behind the artists' foyer, and by the dancers' rehearsal rooms.

The Grands Boulevards

"J'" aime flâner sur les Grands Boulevards," sang Yves Montand in the 1960s (I love strolling on the Grands Boulevards). For him these boulevards, "the vibrant heart of Paris," with their crowds, their stalls, bazaars, and noisy street vendors – places which recall "pleasant moments in history." Long renowned for their liveliness, they have a long history which goes back to the 17th century.

Historically, the Grands Boulevards run from the Bastille to the Madeleine. However, in the course of time, the expression has come to mean the boulevards from Place de la République to the Madeleine: the Boulevards Saint-Martin, Saint-Denis, de Bonne-Nouvelle, Poissonnière, Montmartre, des Italiens, des Capucines, and de la Madeleine. The Boulevard Haussmann is a younger relation, built in the 19th century.

A promenade on the site of the ramparts

◆ Louis XIV's plan

In 1670, Louis XIV decided to demolish the ramparts protecting the capital to the north and east, from Porte Saint-Antoine to Porte Saint-Honoré, and replace them with boulevards. The word *boulevard* comes from the Dutch *bolwerck*, and originally meant the flat top of a rampart. This meaning was now extended to refer to a new kind of long promenades bordered by a double row of trees on each side. The boulevards were 118 ft (36 m) wide, with a 66 ft (20 m) roadway in the middle, and separated from the city by a street running alongside them. On the outer, suburban side, they were flanked by a small ditch, beyond which it was forbidden to build for at least 197 ft (60 m), and then not too high, so that views of the countryside should be preserved.

◆ Creeping expansion of the city

During the 18th century, these visionary promenades, set apart from the city, were gradually absorbed into the urban environment. The roads running alongside the promenade disappeared. Houses grew closer together. The ban on building at the base of the boulevard was respected, however, as can still be seen in one of the old mansions whose façade stands well back from the roadway: Hôtel de Montholon, Boulevard Poissonnière, built in 1785.

By the end of the 18th century, from Porte Saint-Denis to the Madeleine, the Grands Boulevards were lined on the city side with private mansions. Their main entrances gave onto parallel streets, like Rue des Petits-Champs. The financial aristocracy gathered in this area, and, in Faubourg Saint-Honoré to the west, built the magnificent private mansions which today give this exclusive district its special character.

◆ Haussmann imposes order

When Haussmann became Prefect of the Seine in the Second Empire, the Grands Boulevards were already a symbol of urban modernity, and universally fashionable. The "sulphurous baron" wanted to give them a more ordered shape: he laid down building lines for new developments, turned the roadway into a real thoroughfare, and installed street furniture on the sidewalks: street lamps, newspaper kiosks, and fountains.

History on the Boulevards

Until the Revolution, the Grands Boulevards were mainly for strolling, or taking a walk with the family. There was still a "country" atmosphere. Then, on July 12, 1789, two days before the fall of the Bastille, the Grands Boulevards "entered politics." That day, rumors ran through the city that Necker, Louis XVI's Minister of Finance, had been dismissed. To demonstrate their feelings, the people of Faubourg Saint-Antoine marched for the first time along the Grands Boulevards on their way to Place Louis-XV (Place de la Concorde). Going past the Théâtre de la Porte-Saint-Martin, the angry mob attacked the aristocrats gathered there for a performance.

Conversely, after the fall of Robespierre in 1794, the present Boulevard des Italiens and the area round it became the main place for aristocrats to get together. At the time it was called "Little Koblenz" after the German town to which many of them had emigrated at the same time as Louis XVI's brothers. Under the Restoration, it was called Boulevard de Gand in memory of Louis XVIII's exile to Ghent during the Hundred Days. During the Three Glorious Days (July 27-9, 1830), the Grands Boulevards featured once more in the history of people's politics. The King's troop positioned its rearguard on the boulevards, and fighting broke out at the Porte Saint-Denis and Porte Saint-Martin. In February, 1848, the first bloody confrontations took place on Boulevard des Capucines between the people and the National Guard.

Since World War II, the Grands Boulevards have become an important venue for voicing political opposition. Up to 1968, one in four of Paris's demonstrations involved a procession from the Madeleine to the République.

The hub of *La vie parisienne*

In the 19th century, first the theaters moved onto the boulevards, followed by the Opéra, and restaurants and cafés frequented by society people: Frascati, which doubled as a café and gaming room, Tortoni, Café Riche, La Maison Dorée, Café Hardy, and Café Anglais. The Café de la Paix, on Place de l'Opéra, is the only survivor from this period. Its interior decorations were designed by Garnier, architect of the Opéra. The heyday of the grands boulevards lasted until World War I, and though they are still quite lively today the atmosphere is not the same.

Until the Second Empire, the atmosphere was more aristocratic and middle-class to the west, from Boulevard des Capucines to Rue Montmartre. This was the stamping ground of the "dandies". To the east,

from Boulevard Saint-Martin to Boulevard du Temple, it was markedly more working-class. The Boulevard du Temple was called "the boulevard of crime" after the popular melodramas which were staged there and people flocked to see. It partly disappeared in 1862, when Haussmann built the vast Place de la République. Impressionist painters

---

1. Café de la Paix
This last survivor of Paris's 19th-century cafés was designed by Armand, architect of the Grand Hôtel, in 1863. Its decoration, with mirrors, stucco columns with composite capitals, and tall ceilings peopled with mythological figures, is the work of Garnier.

2. Avenue de l'Opéra around 1900
Opened in 1876, this avenue forged a link between the old districts of Palais–Royal and the new ones being built behind Place de l'Opéra.

3. *Boulevard des Capucines* (J. Béraud)
Jean Béraud specialized in painting the boulevards. This view shows the scene in front of the Théâtre du Vaudeville, on the corner of Rue de la Chaussée d'Antin, in 1889. Bourgeois men and women dressed in black mingle with red-trousered soldiers. The street furniture of kiosks and Morris columns was added by Haussmann.

4. Façade, Boulevard des Italiens
From the 1830s the Boulevard des Italiens, built over the former ditches of Louis XIII's wall, became one of the great meeting places of Parisian society. In 1850, Haussmann instigated the construction of massive buildings with colonnaded façades, caryatids, and large windows.

5. Rex cinema
Constructed between 1930 and 1932, and now housing the largest cinema in Paris, this building, along with the Trois Quartiers, marked a radical and sudden break with the Haussmann-style architecture of the boulevards. Its topmost element, a Babylonian ziggurat celebrating the art of Cinema, is the epitome of modernism.

of the day – Monet, Renoir, Caillebotte, Pissarro, Degas, and Toulouse-Lautrec – immortalized the crowds of passers-by, the cafés, the stages of the theaters, the Opéra, and the circus. They were fascinated by these broad, leafy thoroughfares and the new ones then being built, like Avenue de l'Opéra in 1878. Many of their dealers opened galleries around the Grands Boulevards and the auction rooms in Rue Drouot.

◆ Boulevard theater

The story of the boulevard theaters really began after 1830 with romantic dramas by Victor Hugo, Alexandre Dumas, Alfred de Vigny, and George Sand. They made a great impression with the new range of plays they presented. The place which today best symbolizes this period is the Théâtre des Variétés, Boulevard Montmartre. Built in 1807, it presented Frédérick Lemaître's triumph in *Kean* by Alexandre Dumas in 1836 and, from 1849, Henri Murger's great success, *La Vie Bohème*. In the Second Empire, the singer Hortense Schneider had the whole of Paris rushing to see *La Belle Hélène* and other comic operas by Jacques Offenbach. Revived today by actor Jean-Paul Belmondo, it continues the great tradition of boulevard theater. Nearby on Boulevard Poissonnière, the Théâtre des

Nouveautés is a kindred spirit.

The Théâtre du Gymnase, opened in 1820 on Boulevard de Bonne-Nouvelle, saw the début of the great tragic actress Rachel. Revived in 1962 by Marie Bell, it enjoyed a renaissance until the actress died in 1985. Since then, it has been turned into a music hall, specializing in one-man or one-woman shows. The well-known stand-up comic Coluche became famous after making his debut at this café-theater.

The oldest theater on the Grands Boulevards is the Théâtre de la Porte-Saint-Martin, built by

The Folies-Bergère, near Boulevard Poissonnière, has specialized since 1918 in spectacular reviews, and had its moments of glory with stars such as Josephine Baker, Mistinguett, and Maurice Chevalier. Today, along with the Lido and the Crazy Horse in the Champs-Elysées, they still still promote the image of "gay Paree" to the world.

◆ *The magic of the cinema*

The many multiplex cinemas are an important feature of the lively atmo-

Marie-Antoinette in 1781 to house the Opéra after the theater in the Palais Royal burnt down. Later, it was one of the theaters to enjoy success with great romantic dramas like *La Tour de Nesle* and *Lucretia Borgia*. After being razed to the ground during the Commune, it was rebuilt in 1873, and really made its name in December, 1897, with the triumph of *Cyrano de Bergerac*. In the 1970s, the success of the musicals *Hair* and *Starmania* brought it a new lease of life. Its neighbor, the Théâtre de la Renaissance, built in 1872, was bought by Henri Varna in 1942, and he revitalized it with a repertory of plays and operettas. Its greatest success was *Who's Afraid of Virginia Woolf?*

◆ *All singing, all dancing*

While some theaters put on the occasional operetta, others specialize in song and dance. The leading light here is, of course, the Opéra Garnier, its pediment bearing the inscription "National Academy of Music." There is also the Opéra Comique, known as the "Salle Favart" after a famous 18th-century singer. Rebuilt in 1898 after a fire, it stands on the site of a theater built in 1783 for the Italian players for whom the nearby boulevard is named.

The temple of music-hall is the Olympia on the Boulevard des Capucines, where in 1954 Bruno Coquatrix converted an old cinema that became the No 1 venue for popular singers. Its best-known stars are Gilbert Becaud, Charles Aznavour, and Johnny Halliday. Charles Trenet gave his farewell concert there in 1999. The other music halls in the area, such as the ABC and the Concert Mayol, disappeared in the 1970s. In the 1960s the Golf-Drouot saw pop singers like Richard Anthony and Sylvie Vartan rise to fame.

1. Sales time at the Galeries, 1900
This view of women hurrying to the opening of the Sales in the Belle Epoque recalls the 1960-70s slogan: "There's always something happening at the Galeries Lafayette."

2. Brel at the Olympia in 1966
It was at the Olympia, in the fall of 1966, that Jacques Brel said goodbye to the French stage and music hall before retiring to the Marquesas Islands. That year he wrote his most famous song, *Amsterdam*.

3. Galeries Lafayette
On September 1, 1895, Théophile Bader opened a knicknacks and fashion accessories store on the corner of Rue Lafayette and Rue d'Antin. The business prospered, and Bader extended his store into the blocks on Boulevard Haussmann. The Great Hall, with its famous glass cupola and iron structure, was inaugurated in 1912.

4. Store sign for Au Printemps
The flowery style of the Printemps sign reflects the blossoming of Art Nouveau during the Belle Epoque. The store's present buildings were built after a fire in 1881.

5. Crédit Lyonnais building
Founded in Lyons in 1863 by Henri Germain, this bank opened its Paris offices in 1869 on Boulevard des Italiens. The building recently suffered a fire, but the façade was preserved.

sphere of the Grands Boulevards. They are part of a long tradition, for the first public showing of the Lumière brothers' *Cinématographe* took place in December, 1895, in the Salon Indien of the Grand Café, Boulevard des Capucines. At No 35 on the same boulevard, the famous Nadar had his photographic studio, to which everyone flocked to have their portrait taken. The first Talkie, *The Jazz Singer*, had an exclusive showing at the old Cinéma Auber, Boulevard des Italiens, today a department store. Until the 1950s, only the cinemas of the Grands Boulevards and Champs-Elysées held exclusive screenings. The Rex cinema on Boulevard Poissonnière was built in 1932 on the model of big, glamorous American cinemas, and caused a sensation with its architecture in reinforced concrete, its gigantic auditorium with a ceiling glittering with stars, and its immense screen. It is still a monument to the art of Cinema, and runs visits behind the scenes and to the projection room.

Center of the newspaper industry

In 1832, Louis Havas set up his press agency in Rue du Louvre. In 1989, the newspaper *Le Monde*, which succeeded *Le Temps* after World War II, left Rue des Italiens for the Left Bank. Between those two dates, for more than 150 years, the heart of the newspaper industry was located between the Richelieu-Drouot intersection and Boulevard de Bonne-Nouvelle. Here were the offices of *Le Galois*, *Le Temps*, *Le Figaro*, *Le Siècle*, *Le Petit Parisien*, *Le Matin*, and many others. The journalists were regulars at various boulevard cafés such as Le Napolitan in Boulevard des Capucines (today a Hippopotamus restaurant), where at the end of the 19th century the gossip columnists who were the inspiration for "boule-

vard wit" used to gather. Le Madrid, founded around 1860 in Boulevard Montmartre, was more politically minded. Here, various opponents of the regime came together: the Republican lawyer Gambetta, the journalist Rochefort from *La Lanterne*, and the writers Vallès and Baudelaire. On the corner of Rue du Faubourg-Montmartre, Le Brébant, opened in 1865, was the favorite meeting-place of the Goncourt brothers, who organized their famous "Spartan dinners" attended by the critic Sainte-Beuve, which were followed by the "Raw Beef dinners" where guests included Zola, Daudet, Bourget, and Mirbeau.

The last building in this district to be designed as a newspaper office is 100 Rue Réamur, occupied by *L'Intransigeant* in 1932. *France-Soir* followed it, before moving away recently, like many others. But the press still has some representatives around the Grands Boulevards, with *Le Figaro* in Rue du Louvre, and *L'Agence France-Presse* in Place de la Bourse.

The Grands Magasins and the bazaars

Most typical of Parisian life today is perhaps the area around the Grands Magasins. There, an assortment of people hurry towards Le Printemps and Les Galeries Lafayette, and the neighboring streets lined with boutiques. The first two big department stores on the boulevards opened about ten years after Bon Marché, designed by Aristide Boucicaut, set

up on the Left Bank. Le Printemps, founded on Boulevard Haussmann in 1865 by Jaluzot, is still doing great business, like its neighbor the Galeries Lafayette, created in 1896 by Théophile Bader. After a fire in 1881, Le Printemps was rebuilt by Paul Sédille, and it was renovated in 1904. The architect was inspired by the work of Eiffel, and used metal for both the framework and as part of the decorations. With its marvelous iron and glass cupola, Le Printemps impressed itself on its age as the prototype not only of the department store, but also of the modern industrial building. In the 19th century, big bazaars developed beside the

Grands Magasins, some examples of which can still be found in Boulevard Poissonnière.

"There are so many things to see"

The stalls that Yves Montand sang about have disappeared, but on the Grands Boulevards, and all around, there are still a lot of things to see: the exhibitions and auctions at the Drouot salerooms; the splendid architecture of banks such as the Crédit Lyonnais (1878) with its iron frame and stone decorations; the BNP at La Maison Dorée, designed in 1839 in a Neo-Renaissance style; and the Société Générale, with its remarkable hall and staircase dating from 1900.

◆ Workshops in the Sentier district

Between Rue Montmartre, the old newspaper district, and Rue Saint-Denis, which is still dominated by prostitution, the Sentier has been the center of the rag trade since the Middle Ages. There, successive generations of immigrants have made and sold textiles: Armenians, Turks, Jews from Central Europe and North Africa, Pakistanis, and Chinese – all living side by side in this district.

◆ The old covered Passages

The district's many covered arcades – so fashionable in the 1840s, are an important part of its character – Passage du Grand-Cerf, Passage Bas-four, and Passage du Caire. Some have become a little grim, while others have been restored and recovered their 19th-century charm. This is particularly true of Passage des Princes, at No 5 Boulevard des Italiens, and Passage des Panoramas, 11 Boulevard Montmartre, today famous for its stamp dealers, while Passage Jouffroy contains the Musée Grévin, which opened in 1882. This is a waxworks which is continually increasing its collection and now features soccer players Barthez and Zidane, singers Madonna and Michael Jackson, actors Charlie Chaplin and Marilyn Monroe, etc.

◆ Gare Saint-Lazare: a million passengers a day

The Gare Saint-Lazare was built from 1837, and was continually

enlarged for the rest of the century. Originally, it was for well-off travelers going on vacation or coming to visit Paris, which accounts for the magnificence of its glass and steel halls, allegorical statues, and rich decoration; also the luxury hotel in front of it, the Grand Hôtel Terminus, today the Concorde-Saint-Lazare. The station's function has changed since Monet painted it. Today, people commute in here from the outlying areas. Of the 115 million travelers using Saint-Lazare each year, 95% come from the suburbs, which probably makes it the world's largest station serving the suburbs.

---

1. Cirque d'Hiver
The Winter Circus opened in the Second Empire and is now, since the closure of the Medrano in Pigalle, the last permanent circus in Paris. It has been run by Bouglione family for generations. Its polygonal structure is unique in this city.

2. Demonstration over Algeria
The boulevards have been a favorite route for popular marches since 1789. The Revolution of 1848 actually broke out on Boulevard des Capucines.

3. *The Time for Everyone* (Arman)
This is one of two sculptures by Arman which have decorated the courtyards of Gare Saint-Lazare since 1985. The other one, called *La Consigne à Vie*, features a pile of suitcases.

4. Théâtre de la Porte-Saint-Martin
This old theater is famous for two legendary productions: *Cyrano de Bergerac* in 1897, and the pop musical *Hair* in 1970.

5. Place de la République
Built in 1860, this square brought about the demolition of the most notorious part of the "boulevard of crime," where in 1830-40 the greatest melodramas of the 19th century were performed in the theater. In 1958, the meeting to celebrate the founding of the Fifth Republic took place here.

6. Porte Saint-Martin
This gateway in the shape of a triumphal arch was built in 1674 to mark Louis XIV's victories in the Dutch War. When Napoléon returned from Austerlitz in January, 1806, he entered Paris through this gate.

From Madeleine to Monceau

Not far from the Gare Saint-Lazare and the busy Grands Magasins, the Madeleine district is a haven of peace. Even so, there is plenty of commercial activity around the church, built like an Antique temple. Along Faubourg Saint-Honoré, there is still the occasional 18th-century mansion, for example the Elysée Palace and the buildings occupied by the British and United States Embassies. On the Parc Monceau side, you come to an elegant district with typical 19th-century buildings including impressive offices, opulent apartments, and old private mansions, some of which are now museums.

The land of luxury

Close to the Grands Magasins, another kind of business sprang up around the Madeleine and Faubourg Saint-Honoré: deluxe restaurants from the 1900s (Maxim's, 1899; Lucas-Carton, 1904); a delectable pâtisserie (Ladurée); ultra-smart, sometimes exotic grocers (Hédiard and Fauchon); tableware stores (Baccarat and Lalique for crystal, silverware at Christofle, porcelain at Bernardaud); shoe stores (Weston and Charles Jourdan); hairdressers (Carita); and all the greats of *haute couture*: Lanvin, Saint-Laurent, Lagerfeld, Ferraud, Versace, Cardin,

etc. Not forgetting the famous saddlers, Hermès, with its dazzling window displays offering ostrich-skin bags and silver bracelets, silk scarves and linen tablecloths, fine porcelain services and made-to-measure rawhide boots. On Boulevard des Capucines, Old England, founded in 1860, sells tweeds and cashmeres. Older still, from 1827, the department store Les Trois Quartiers is now home to a collection of boutiques.

Two churches, two styles

◆ *La Madeleine*

From the outside, the Sainte-Marie-Madeleine church is a Greek temple. It almost did not become a church. It stands at the end of the northward axis leading from the Place de la Concorde, and in many respects the two places share the same turbulent history. Although its building was approved under Louis XV (1759), it was not completed until Louis-Philippe's reign (1842). After the Revolution, the building, then under construction, came close to being earmarked for use as the Stock Exchange or Commercial Court. In 1806, Napoléon decided to make it an Antique temple glorifying the Grande Armée, and architect Vignon was appointed. After the Restoration, Louis XVIII opted for a religious function, and so the Madeleine became a church in the shape of a Latin cross contained within a Greek temple. It was consecrated in 1842,

and established itself as a society church on October 20, 1849, when Frederick Chopin's funeral took place there. All of Romantic Paris was there, as it was for the funeral of singer Charles Trenet in 2001.

◆ *Saint-Augustin*

Visible from the Madeleine, the Church of Saint-Augustin's curious Romanesque-Byzantine architecture is a central feature of Boulevard Malesherbes. It was built between 1860 and 1870 by Baltard, the cast-iron specialist who designed Les Halles, is topped by a dome embellished by a sort of lantern, and has four domed corner turrets. The façade contains a rose window and three arcades decorated by Jouffroy. A statue of Joan of Arc looks over the forecourt.

From the death of the King to the triumph of the Republic

◆ Square Louis XVI

This quiet square on the corner of Boulevard Haussmann and Rue Pasquier was the Madeleine cemetery where the people guillotined on Place de la Révolution (now Place de la Concorde) were buried, among them Louis XVI and Marie-Antoinette. Here stands the expiatory chapel, a small Neo-Classical building which Louis XVIII had built in 1815-26 by Fontaine to commemorate the royal family.

◆ Elysée Palace

In 1718, a private mansion was built for the Comte d'Evreux which in 1873 became the official residence of Presidents of the Republic. In 1753, the Marquise de Pompadour bought it and enlarged it. On her death in 1764, the royal favorite left it to her lover, Louis XV. After serving various functions, the mansion was sold to the financier Beaujon, who decorated it further. In 1786, it came into the hands of the Duchesse de Bourbon, who called it the Elysée-Bourbon. In the Revolution, it became a gaming house and the gardens were used for parties.

From 1805, Prince Murat, Napoléon I's brother-in-law, made some more alterations and then gave it to the Emperor, who spent little time there except at the end of his reign. After he left it in April, 1814, he returned for the Hundred Days, in the spring of 1815, and abdicated there on June 22. In memory of his uncle, Prince-President Louis Napoléon Bonaparte decided to move into the house. Here he plotted his *coup d'état* on December 2, 1851. Once he was Emperor, Napoléon III rarely lived at the Elysée, but organized various major building programs.

For more than a century, the Elysée remained almost unchanged until President Pompidou arrived in 1969. Under his orders, the private apartments were decorated with modern works by Ernst, Giacometti, Delaunay, Matisse, and Hartung. Pierre Paulin and other eminent designers brought in new furniture. After a return to the 18th-century style under Valéry Giscard d'Estaing, in 1981, the Elysée went back to modern art with François Mitterrand. A group by Arman, paying tribute to the French Revolution, was set up in the vestibule. Philippe Starck and Jean-Michel Wilmotte decorated the private apartments.

◆ Monceau: its park and museums

The Parc Monceau bears few traces of its original design by Carmontelle in 1773, having been redesigned in the 19th century by Alphand. One or two *fabriques* have survived (items of garden architecture designed to surprise the visitor), including the *naumachia*, an oval pool surrounded by a colonnade. There is also the Chartres rotunda, an old customs house built by Ledoux which was part of the enclosure of the Farmers-General.

The mansions bordering the park form a unique Second Empire group, while the whole of the "plaine Monceau" is typical of 19th century architecture. Three collectors of the

period have left museums laid out in the houses where they lived. The Nissim-de-Camondo Museum contains 18th-century works in a mansion built in the style of the Trianon at Versailles. The Jacquemart-André Museum retains the atmosphere of a luxurious private mansion of the Second Empire. It was built in 1869-75 by the architect Parent for the banker Edouard André, and houses the collection which he and his wife, the portrait-painter Nélie Jacquemart, assembled there. Its treasures include works from the Italian Renaissance and the 18th century in France, as well as a group of frescos.

---

1. Church of the Madeleine
This Greek temple concealing a church in the form of a Latin cross is a sanctuary to the glory of Mary Magdalen. Christ on the Cross makes only a discreet appearance. Since the funeral of Frederick Chopin, this has become the artists' church.

2. Window at Weston
Despite its very British name, the Weston brand is French. Over the years, it has become *the* deluxe shoemaker for men. In Paris, people refer to "My Westons" and each year dash to the sales there.

3. Store front of Hédiard
This luxury grocer's on Place de la Madeleine competes for top place with Fauchon. Both have become brand names.

4. Fashion boutique
Paris is the world capital of fashion in general and of *haute couture* in particular. The latter's practitioners divide themselves between Faubourg Saint-Honoré and the Champs-Elysées district.

5. Elysée Palace
This private mansion, built in 1718, was occupied from 1753 by Mme de Pompadour, the favorite of Louis XV. Under the Empire, it became the residence of Prince Murat, then Napoléon. Since 1873, it has been the official residence of Presidents of the Republic.

6. Garden party at the Elysée Palace
For 20 years now, on July 14 each year, the Republic's senior officials and "stars" of the moment are invited to take *petits-fours* and Champagne in the Presidential gardens.

THE EIFFEL TOWER
and surrounding area

The Eiffel Tower

Champ de Mars
and Invalides

Around Trocadéro

From the Rodin
to the Orsay Museum

Orsay station and Museum

Aerial view of the Eiffel Tower
The "Old Iron Lady" is more than a hundred
years old, and dominates the Paris skyline.
Beneath her, the Champ de Mars and the
Invalides have staged Universal Exhibitions
and live cheek by jowl with other exhibition
sites: the Trocadéro Gardens (1878 and 1937),
the Palais de Chaillot, the Palais de Tokyo
(1937), the Grand Palais, the Petit Palais,
and Pont Alexandre III (1900).
All around, the opulent apartment buildings
of western Paris unfold in a massive
geometric pattern, the legacy of
Haussmann's great urban plan.

The Eiffel Tower

To mark the year 2000, the Eiffel Tower was set ablaze with fireworks. This showpiece of the 1889 Universal Exhibition, criticized by Maupassant as "that tall, thin pyramid of iron ladders," was scheduled to be pulled down, but then became a huge radio mast and has survived the years to be the world's favorite symbol of Paris.

1

A landmark monument

More than ever, the Eiffel Tower deserves its name as the "sentinel of Paris," equipped as it is with a powerful bright-white beam which sweeps the city every night. In the course of the 20th century, its outlines were highlighted many times before it was transformed, in 1984, into a tree of light through the magic of 352 sodium bulbs. Its astonishing iron frame, panoramic views, boutiques, and two restaurants – not to mention the light shows re-enacting Thomas Edison's meeting with Gustave Eiffel, and others showing how the tower was built – make it the most visited building in Paris.

Crowned by aerials

The Eiffel Tower is not only a building for tourists: on top of it are more than 110 transmission antennae of every kind, relaying programs for some six TV channels and 30 radio stations. These have also added to its original height: from 984 ft (300 m) it went up to 1,045 ft (318.7 m) in 1957, and in 2000 reached 1,063 ft (324 m). More important still, its role as a transmitter saved it from demolition.

The 1,000-foot tower

As early as 1832, the English engineer Richard Trevithick dreamed of reaching for the sky with a building 1,000 ft (300 m) tall. In that same year, Gustave Eiffel was born. Before the Eiffel Tower, only two buildings had even managed 558 ft (170 m): the Washington Monument, and the Mole Antonelliana in Turin—and they were made of stone. In May, 1884, Eiffel learned that the government wanted to celebrate the centenary of the French Revolution with an inspirational monument. His engineers, Emile Nouguier and Maurice Koechlin, designed a 984 ft (300 m) mast "consisting of four metal, latticework beams as the feet, which then came together and rose to the top, bound together at regular intervals by metal tie-beams." Initially, Eiffel was not interested, and it needed an architect, Stephen Sauvestre, to make him change his mind by designing an architectural cladding with, notably, four decorative arches binding the four pillars beneath the first platform. Eiffel patented the work in the names of his three associates, bought the rights from them, and put his sole name to the Tower.

Ahead of the competition

In 1886, when the *Journal Officiel* published its program for the competition to design the Universal

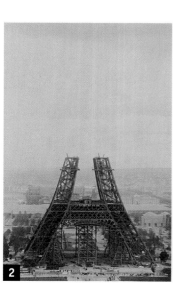

2

1. Structural detail
The Eiffel Tower's frame consists of 18,000 pieces of iron joined by 2.5 million rivets. The openwork structure gives it a semblance of lightness, though in fact this is to keep it stable in even the stormiest weather.

2. Stages of construction
It took five months to build the concrete foundations on which the pillars stand. The metal part was then raised in 21 months. Work began on January 28, 1887, and was completed on March 31, 1889. This record speed was achieved thanks to the prefabricated nature of the structure, still rare at the time, and to the intensive work rate of the men, who labored seven days a week.

3. Renovating the Tower
Although "she" never seems to change, the "Old Iron Lady" has had several facelifts. The color of her paintwork has changed six times, her structure has been reinforced and lightened, and new levels and platforms have been installed.

4. Site of the 1937 Exhibition
Built for the Universal Exhibition of 1887, the Eiffel Tower was to be demolished later. Here it still is, overlooking the site of the 1937 Exhibition, its survival justified by the permanent radio station which crowns it.

Hall of Fame

Engineer Gustave Eiffel
(1832-1923).
He was the man with the genius not only to design a 984 ft (300 m) tower, but to build it successfully and, best of all, have it bear his name. Born in 1832, he was an average student at the École Centrale, but found himself, at the age of 26, responsible for building a railroad bridge over the Garonne at Bordeaux. In 1867, he set up his own company, specializing in metal or metal-frame buildings, including several bridges, a church, a synagogue, a jetty, and a railroad. Although they completed several spectacular projects, such as the Maria-Pia Bridge in Porto and the Garabit Viaduct in the Cantal region, the Eiffel company would not have outstripped its competitors if its founder had not shown a strong flair for publicity by building "his" Tower. Eiffel also designed the skeleton for the Statue of Liberty which, before it arrived in New York, dominated the rooftops of Paris while it was being assembled.
The Panama Scandal destroyed the career of this great industrial leader, and he later turned his efforts toward research, notably in the field of air resistance. ◼

grant of 1.5 million francs, and secured the exploitation rights for 20 years, and any profits accruing.

A model building site

Digging began on January 28, 1887. They had to go down 36 ft (11 m) to find a stable gravel bed. Once the foundations were completed, they started raising the tower. Hydraulic jacks beneath each leg enabled them to regulate the angles of inclination and make sure the first platform was horizontal. The pillars rose at a slant, and were only supported by scaffolding when they had reached 85 ft (26 m). The iron sections were rolled in the mills at Pompey, drilled in factories at Levallois-Perret, transported to the site, and assembled by hot riveting. It was one of the first sites to use this prefabricated process. They worked intensely hard, seven days a week. Two threatened strikes were quickly

suppressed. On March 31, 1889, the tower was completed and the French tricolor was hoisted above it.

A financial success

The tower was a financial success. It had two million visitors during the Exhibition, earning Eiffel 6,509,901 francs, against construction costs of 7,457,000 francs plus 1 million in running costs. The difference was quickly made up after the Universal Exhibition, and soon the venture was making a handsome profit.

Saved by the airwaves

In 1893, Eiffel was condemned for his part in the Panama Scandal, gave up running his businesses, and went back to research. His main concern was to prove the tower's usefulness and get his lease renewed. There were a series of meteorological and aerodynamic experiments, then wireless telegra-

Exhibition site, the 1,000-foot tower was listed as part of it, which faced the other contestants with a *fait accompli*. Nevertheless, 107 projects were submitted. G Eiffel won the contract easily. He built the tower at his own expense, helped only by a

2

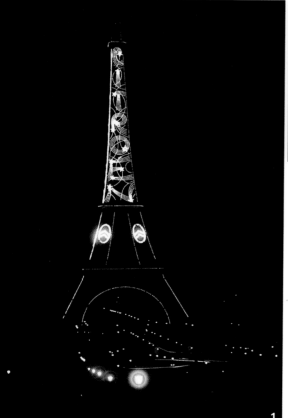

1

1. Citroën advertising in 1925
In 1889, the Tower was lit by 90,000 gaslights, a beacon, and two projectors whose beams swept the Exhibition pavilions. In 1900, 3,200 incandescent electric lamps were used. From July 14, 1925, André Citroën sponsored lighting until 1936, when the Citroën company withdrew on grounds of expense. The Tower was nicknamed "Widow Citroën."

2. Illuminations for the 1937 Exhibition
In 1937, André Granet, G Eiffel's grandson, designed illuminations for the Universal Exhibition. In 1958, powerful projectors were placed in trenches, their beams crossing at the top of the Tower. In October, 1984, 352 sodium bulbs were installed, some within the girders.

3. Millennium celebrations
The end of the millennium was celebrated with a giant illuminated board counting down the days from April 5, 1997. A circular beacon was mounted on top of the Tower, and in the night, 20,000 bulbs lit up the girders for several minutes at the start of each hour.

4. Fireworks for 2000
The firework display on New Year's Eve was directed by Yves Pépin and Christophe Berthonneau.

5. Illuminations for J-M Jarre concert
In May, 1989, J-M Jarre produced a *Son et Lumière* show at the foot of the Tower: "Lighting of the Eiffel Tower—Copyright Société Nouvelle d'Exploitation de la Tour Eiffel—Designed by Pierre Bideau."

3

4

5

phy arrived to save his masterpiece after they ran a pioneering radio link in 1898 between the Eiffel Tower and the Panthéon. The Army then used the tower as a long-distance communications ant-ennae, extending its range from 248 miles (400 km) in 1904 to 1,860 miles (3,000 km) in 1906, and reaching the United States in 1908. A permanent radio station was installed in 1906, followed by television in 1935. Three years later, it was transmitting regularly. The concession was renewed, and extended in phases until December 31, 1979.

Latest renovations

In 1980, the City of Paris took over the management of the tower and started a huge restoration program. The structure was reinforced and lightened by 1,481 tons (1,340 t), which had been added over the years. The old spiral staircase to the top was replaced and auctioned off in sections, and the elevators were modernized. The entrances were renovated, a gourmet restaurant and meeting rooms were built, and a range of exhibitions and events were organized. Visitor numbers, which had stabilized at around three million, exceeded six million in 1998. Foreigners now recognize the tower as the symbol of tomorrow's Europe.

Facts & Figures

The concept : 1,700 overall plans, 3,628 detailed plans involving 40 people for two years on the 18,038 pieces of the giant metal structure, held together by 2,500,000 rivets

Construction time : two years, two months and five days with 150 workers at the Levallois-Perret factory and about 150 on site

Weight : 11,053 tons (10,000 t) distributed over its four pillars at no more than 22 lbs/in (4 kg/cm), the equivalent of a chair bearing a man of 176 lbs (80 kg)

Number of steps to the top : 1,665 via the east pillar

Painting : 66 tons (66 t) to repaint the tower every seven years

Number of visitors : 1889: 1,968,287; 1900: 1,024,887; 1999: 6,368,534; the 100 millionth visitor, a woman, was celebrated on September 9, 1983

111

Champ de Mars and Invalides

The Champ de Mars is flanked by broad, leafy avenues and quiet streets with old apartment buildings, some enjoying excellent views over the Esplanade des Invalides. It is a spacious and mainly residential district, with its private, church-funded, and bilingual schools; embassies; offices and middle-class inhabitants. The liveliest areas center on its few shopping streets, such as Rue Cler and Rue Saint-Dominique. There are some interesting Art Nouveau developments, notably at 29 Avenue Rapp (by Jules Lavirotte), but the main areas for tourists are the Invalides, the Espace Eiffel-Branly with its shows and exhibitions, and, above all of course, the Eiffel Tower.

École Militaire

This military academy was created in 1751, on the edict of Louis XV, to train 500 cadets recruited from the penniless nobility, and is the work of Jacques-Ange Gabriel. The architect, also responsible for Place Louis XV (today Place de la Concorde), designed a fine Classical block with a pedimented central pavilion, surmounted by a quadrangular dome, which now looks across the Champ de Mars to the Eiffel Tower.

The École Militaire belongs to the Army, and was once the center of France's equestrian tradition.

The Champ de Mars

When Louis XV decided to build the École Militaire on the Grenelle plain, it was still open country. The huge space running up to the Seine was then used as a practice ground for military maneuvers, but the fashion at the end of the Ancien Régime for English thoroughbred horses meant it also served as a racecourse from 1780. Racing resumed in 1833 while the course at Longchamp was being laid out in the Bois de Boulogne (this opened in 1857).

The Champ de Mars also provides a vast and splendid setting for big public events, initially with celebrations of the Revolution.

Subsequently, the Universal Exhibitions were located there. After the 1900 Exhibition, the City of Paris was short of funds and sold part of the land. Two long strips of residential buildings were put up on each side of the Champ de Mars, and the remaining land was turned into gardens between 1908 and 1928. Even in its reduced state, the Champ de Mars still covers 52 acres (21 ha), giving the city a massive green space and setting off the Eiffel Tower to great effect.

Large-scale public events are still staged at the Champ de Mars. Recently, these have included the celebration of the Tower's centenary on June 17, 1989, with several hundred thousand spectators; the Three Tenors concert (Carreras, Domingo, and Pavarotti) on July 10, 1998; the celebration of the end of the soccer World Cup with a concert by Jean-Michel Jarre on July 14, 1998; the dawn of the Second Millennium on December 31, 1999; and a big Johnny Halliday concert on June 10, 2000.

Unesco

The headquarters of Unesco (United Nations Organization for Education, Science, and Culture) is a vast Y-shaped building. Its concave façade runs smoothly around the half-moon of Place Fontenoy, facing the back of the École Militaire. It was set up in 1945 to promote peace and human rights, and today has 188 member states. The building's architecture is suitably international, having been designed by the American Marcel Breuer, the Italian Pier Luigi Nervi, and the Frenchman Bernard Zehrfuss. As well as the formal beauty of its monumental architecture (and that of the neighboring conference building) and the humanitarian and cultural activities available to the public (exhibitions, conferences, concerts, shows), the Unesco headquarters also has an excellent collection of art from the second half of the 20th century with, for example, sculptures by Calder and Moore on the esplanade.

Hôtel des Invalides and Saint-Louis-des-Invalides

The Hôtel des Invalides was created by Louis XIV as a home for wounded and disabled soldiers. Building began in 1671 under Libéral Bruant (architect of the Salpêtrière Hospital), continued in

1677 by Jules Hardouin-Mansart, and was completed by Robert de Cotte in 1750. This huge rectangular building, standing on a 31 acre (12.5 ha) plot, accommodated 3,000 Pensioners in 1710, and is one of the finest examples of architecture from the age of Louis XIV. The north façade spreads out before the wonderful perspective of the Esplanade des Invalides, which continues over Pont Alexandre III to the Grand and Petit Palais. The central part, arched like a monumental gateway, is very splendid, with an unbelievable number of trophies depicting weapons and military symbols adorning its cornices.

Its great masterpiece is the domed Church of Saint-Louis, which, regilded for the fifth time for the Bicentenary of the Revolution, now shines out over Paris. It was built as an extension of the so-called Soldiers' Church, its design inspired by a plan by François Mansart, uncle of Jules Hardouin-Mansart, for a Bourbon chapel at Saint-Denis. The dome took on a new function when it received the tomb of Emperor Napoléon I, whose ashes were solemnly brought to Paris from Saint Helena in 1840. Carefully restored since the 1960s, the Invalides houses three museums: the Army Museum, the Museum of the Order of the Liberation, and the Museum of Relief Models.

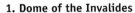

1. Dome of the Invalides
The dome of the Church of Saint-Louis-des-Invalides is a majestic masterpiece of Classical elegance, built by Jules Hardouin-Mansart between 1679 and 1706. More than 26 lbs (12 kg) of gold leaf were used to regild the dome for the Bicentenary of the French Revolution.

2. Concert on July 10, 1998
On July 10, 1998, the Three Tenors (Carreras, Domingo, and Pavarotti) gave an open-air concert on the Champ de Mars.

3. Façade of the Invalides
Libéral Bruant, one of the great architects in the age of Louis XIV, designed the long (640 ft/195 m) façade of the Hôtel des Invalides, with its very pure lines enlivened by trophies and arms decorating its cornice, and a great arched gateway. At the center of this monumental gate is an equestrian bas-relief of Louis XIV, flanked by Prudence and Justice.

4. Napoleon's tomb
Beneath the church's double dome, an enormous tomb holds the ashes of Emperor Napoléon I, brought here from Saint Helena in 1840. Around it are Pradier's 12 colossal statues representing Victories (1843-52).

5. Unesco Palace
The headquarters of Unesco (United Nations Organisation for Education, Science, and Culture) was built between 1955 and 1958 by three architects of different nationalities: Marcel Breuer, an American of Hungarian origin; the Italian Pier-Luigi Nervi; and Frenchman Bernard Zehrfuss.

6. The Wall of Peace
The Wall of Peace on the Champ de Mars was inspired by the Wailing Wall in Jerusalem. Visitors can leave messages of peace in specially designed holes in the structure.

Around Trocadéro

Facing the Eiffel Tower on the Right Bank is Chaillot Hill, topped by a great 1930s palace housing museums, a theater, and other cultural centers. Out on the esplanade, rollerbladers and skateboarders use the space to practice their skills, while others, especially in summer, seem to mistake the great fountain for the seaside, stripping off for a dip and drying themselves in the sun on the lawns.

On top of the hill

Although its slope is fairly steep, Chaillot Hill is today much less of a hill than it was. Originally, it sloped down to Étoile from Passy Cemetery (a small cemetery behind Place du Trocadéro where Debussy and Manet are buried). It was leveled off in 1867 to make room for pavilions built for the Universal Exhibition. Then, in 1878, Gabriel Davioud built a huge exhibition palace with a 10,000-seater concert hall. The palace then housed the Museums of Comparative Sculpture and Ethnography, ancestors of the museums that are now in the Palais de Chaillot. Although Parisians did not like its Moorish style, the Palais de Trocadéro survived until 1935, before being demolished to make way for the present palace.

Palais de Chaillot

The Palais de Chaillot was built by architects Carlu, Boileau, and Azéma for the 1937 Exhibition. It consists of two wings, each 640 ft (195 m) long, built over the foundations of the old palace but twice as wide. In the center, two monumental pavilions enclose a forecourt 180 ft (55 m) long, with spectacular views of the Eiffel Tower and overlooking gardens reached by two immense flights of steps. The esplanade has been dedicated since 1987 to the Rights of Man and is a regular rallying point for demonstrations in defense of worthy causes.

◆ Theater and cinema

Beneath the forecourt of the Trocadéro is the Théâtre de Chaillot with its nine huge rectangular bays overlooking the garden terraces. The theater enjoyed a golden phase in the 1950s, with the bare sets of Jean Vilar, and actors such as Gérard Philippe and Jeanne Moreau. In the 1990s, Jérôme Savary staged his more whimsical shows there.

Another famous institution was the Cinémathèque Française, founded in 1936 by Henri Langlois, and his Cinema Museum. The latter was a victim of the fire which swept through the Paris wing in 1997. It is due to reopen at Bercy. The Palais de Chaillot contains another place for art and experiment, the Salle Firmin Gémier, and

three museums, which today are being drastically modified. They are the Maritime Museum and the Museum of Mankind in the Passy wing; and in the Paris wing, the Museum of French Monuments.

◆ Maritime Museum

In 1827, the Duc d'Angoulême, eldest son of Charles X, created the Musée Dauphin, today the Maritime Museum, starting with a collection of model ships put together in 1748 to instruct shipbuilding engineers. Its holdings were enlarged with paintings taken from the Louvre and Versailles collections, and boats and artillery pieces found in various arsenals. The museum was located at the Louvre after the Revolution, and moved to the Palais de Chaillot in 1938. Other important items include the model of the *Soleil Royal*, a ship built in 1669, a ceremonial barge built for Napoléon I in 1811, and Joseph Vernet's series of paintings of the harbors of France. Now being renovated until about 2004, the Museum is still open to the public for exhibitions.

1. Paris World Fair of 1937
During the Fair, visitors could take this little train to go from place to place. Here it passes the Palais de Chaillot, designed for the occasion by architects Carlu, Boileau, and Azéma. The palace's curving wings partly straddle the foundations of the Trocadéro Palace, built for the 1878 Exhibition.

2. Trocadéro Gardens
Vast steps and gently sloping lawns lead from the Palais de Chaillot to two English-style gardens extending to either side of the great Warsaw (or Trocadéro) fountains. These shady gardens make a pleasant contrast with the stern lines of the palace.

3. Colonnade of the Palais de Tokyo
A tall colonnade in white stone binds the two wings of the Palais de Tokyo, one of them housing the Museum of Modern Art of the City of Paris. The building was designed by architects Dondel, Viard, Aubert, and Dastugue for the 1937 Exhibition. Ornate sculptures decorate the patio, depicting the muses and tales from mythology.

4. Museum cafeteria
There are so many museums in the district that visitors find taking a break most welcome, especially when the cafeteria's great windows offer such fine views of the sculptures, gardens, and the Eiffel Tower.

5. Museum of French Monuments
Same-size casts and models give a wonderful insight into the world of French monuments. Visitors can compare the evolution of styles and subjects period by period and region by region. The idea for this museum, founded in 1879, came from Viollet-le-Duc, who restored Notre-Dame Cathedral.

◆ Museum of French Monuments

Based on an idea by Viollet-le-Duc, the Museum of Comparative Sculpture opened to the public in 1882 in the Palais du Trocadéro, and was then completely revised to concentrate on French monuments for its reopening in the Palais de Chaillot in 1937. This museum shows casts, models, and reproductions of murals. It includes the Romanesque porch of the Church of Saint-Pierre-de-Moissac and the Gothic porch of Chartres Cathedral, the Renaissance decoration of the Fontaine des Innocents in Paris, and the figure known as "La Marseillaise," carved in the 19th century for the Arc de Triomphe. The museum is about to merge with the French Architectural Institute to form the "Cité de l'Architecture et du Patrimoine." Once it has been renovated and enlarged, it will include plaster collections and models as well as contemporary pieces. It will also have an exhibition space and a multimedia library devoted to contemporary architecture.

◆ Museum of Mankind

The Museum of Mankind was created in 1938, and brings together the collections of the Trocadéro's former Museum of Ethnography and the anthropological galleries of the Museum of Natural History. Its aims were didactic: to trace the evolution of the human race since its beginnings via a mixture of art, sculpture, models, costumes, and artifacts. However, once its most beautiful pieces have gone to the new "Musée

des Arts Premiers" currently being built at Quai Branly, it will have to rethink its mission.

◆ Trocadéro gardens

The sloping Trocadéro gardens cover an area of 25 acres (10 ha) and considerably enhance the Palace's appeal. Although there are wooded areas on either side, the central part is designed around pools and fountains, with sprays and jets spurting 165 ft (50 m) high, driven by 20 side cannons. It also has a wonderful display of 1930s sculpture. The beauty and freshness of the gardens make them a favorite place for Parisians and visitors to stroll in summer.

Musée Guimet

The National Museum of Asian Arts is named for its creator, an industrialist and collector from Lyons called Emile Guimet. Back from an expedition to China in 1876, Guimet had a museum built in Lyons to house the collections he had brought with him. In 1886, he gave these to the State, but wanted them to be shown in Paris, so he built a new museum, a slightly enlarged version of the one in Lyons.

In 1935, it took over the Trocadéro's Indo-Chinese collections, and in 1945 the Louvre's Far Eastern works, and is now one of the most beautiful museums devoted to the arts of Asia. It owes much to the dynamism of French archeological expeditions to the East, bringing back such marvelous finds as the Begram Treasure (Afghanistan), a fine example of the

wealth of commercial exchanges between East and West in the first half of the 20th century. Formerly too cramped for space, the Musée Guimet reopened in January, 2001, after five years of renovation by architect H Gaudin. Only the circular entrance has been kept, with its upper library decorated with cariatids. The rest of the building was completely gutted, and reorganized round an inner courtyard. As one enters, the first thing one notices is the zigzag staircase spiralling upwards like something from a Piranesi drawing. In the galleries, brushed steel, gray Tunisian stone, and Brazilian woods set off the collections, now displayed in a more coherent and complete manner. Thus a gigantic *naga* (a spirit with a human bust and a snake's body) from the Giant's Causeway at Angkor has been brought up from the cellars to lead the way to the Khmer sculptures, the richest collection known outside Cambodia, with their gods with half-closed eyes and graceful *apsaras* (celestial dancers). About one-third of the pieces on

show are new exhibits, drawn either from the reserve collections, new acquisitions, or the many recent donations, such as the *thang-ka* and Nepalese and Tibetan bronzes from the Fournier Collection acquired in 1989, and the Indian textiles, jewels, and *objets d'art* from the Riboud donations of 1999 and 2000.

Palais de Tokyo

Like the Palais de Chaillot, the two buildings making up the Palais de Tokyo were built for the Universal Exhibition of 1937. Since 1879, the museum in the Luxembourg Orangerie had been devoted to living artists, but when it ran out of space, it seemed a good idea to mark the occasion of the Exhibition by building a new National Museum of Modern Art in two facing palaces, one to house the contemporary art collections of the City of Paris, then in the Petit Palais, and the other the State collection. In the 1934 competition, 128 proposals were submitted, including those of T Garnier, Le Corbusier, and Mallet-Stevens. The winner was the Classical-looking design of architects Dondel, Viard, Aubert, and Dastugue. The two palaces, the municipal and the national, face each other around a patio opening onto the quayside, tied together by a double colonnade, which creates an impression of symmetry despite the uneven ground. The patio's rich sculptural decora-

tions are dominated by A Bourdelle's *France*, erected in 1948 to commemorate the Free French volunteers. The exhibition areas are very well lit, both from above and the side, thanks to the comb-like cutouts in the rear façades. Unfortunately, the heralded "confrontation" of the two collections hardly took place. The advent of war delayed the transfer of the City's collections, and the museum could only show temporary exhibitions before it opened in 1961. Then the national collections were moved to the Centre Georges Pompidou, inaugurated in 1977, and the Palais de l'Etat, after being used as a staging post prior to the opening of the Musée d'Orsay, then as the Centre de l'Image (with a film school, the Femis, and the National Photographic Center) now awaits a new role. Meanwhile the Musée de la Ville has prospered from a dynamic exhibitions policy (Mark Rothko, Fauvism in Europe), to the detriment of its permanent collections, which are rarely on show.

1. The Trocadéro fountains
The pools and fountains at the Trocadéro are laid out on several levels. They enliven the huge perspective opening out from Place du Trocadéro as far as the École Militaire, via the Seine, Eiffel Tower, and Champ de Mars.

2. Dufy's *Electric Fairy*
Raoul Dufy's *La Fée Électricité* is one of the spectacular works in the National Museum of Modern Art of the City of Paris. This huge painting, which decorated the hall of the Pavilion of Light at the 1937 Exhibition, celebrates the use of electricity in the modern world and all those who contributed to its discovery—in all, 110 people from all periods.

3. Auguste Perret's staircase
The most original, and the best suited to its function, of the new museums built for the 1937 Exhibition was without doubt the Museum of Public Works, built by Auguste Perret at the corner of Avenues d'Iéna and Wilson. Today it is occupied by the Economic and Social Council.

4. Buddha meditating (Musée Guimet)
This Khmer buddha is one of the Asian art treasures of the Musée Guimet, which opened on Place d'Iéna in 1888.

From the Rodin to the Orsay Museum

Hidden behind tall gates in the Faubourg Saint-Germain district are about a hundred of the 300 private mansions built in the 18th century. Some still belong to old families, and others have been subdivided into luxury apartments, but most are now occupied by ministries, offices, and embassies. The Faubourg Saint-Germain is also full of fashion boutiques and antique dealers, especially around Rue du Bac, many of which have taken over the premises of older, specialist stores.

1

The discreet charm of the Faubourg

The hundred or so beautiful mansions, which today are the Faubourg's most charming feature, were built in the 18th century. Then, the old aristocracy spurned the Marais, which had become too cramped and enclosed, for Paris's western districts, which were on the road to Versailles and, since the building of Pont Royal in 1685, very close to the Louvre and Tuileries. The old country roads extending around Paris—Rue Saint-Dominique, Rue de Grenelle, and Rue de Varenne—were the reason the land was divided into long strips going from one street to the next. These narrow lots determined the very characteristic plan of Paris's mansions, located "between courtyard and garden," with the courtyard generally on the north side so that the sun would shine on the garden façade. Except on Heritage days, these mansions are seldom accessible to the public unless they contain a museum or a restaurant, such as

the Musée Rodin, the Musée Maillol, and Latin America House, where they often put out tables in the park in fine weather. The Dutch Institute, in the old Hôtel Turgot in Rue de Lille, organizes concerts, conferences, and exhibitions.

Rodin Museum

Museums in houses where artists lived always have a special character. The Hôtel Biron, where Auguste Rodin lived, combines a beautiful setting and lovely gardens with a fascinating display of sculptures. The mansion was built in 1728-30 by Jean Aubert to designs by Jacques-Ange Gabriel, and is one of the most beautiful in the Faubourg Saint-Germain. Its elegant Rococo decoration and vast garden make it seem like a château. The Dames du Sacré-Coeur lived there in the 19th century, then in 1908 it acquired new tenants, among them A Rodin (1840-1917), who managed to convince the State to buy the house when he took it over. In return, the artist donated his sculptures, drawings, archives, and private collections to the State in 1916. The Musée Rodin was opened in 1919, and houses the permanent collection, including the famous *The Kiss*, as well as works by other artists (Monet, Renoir, and Van Gogh)

from Rodin's private collection. The chapel, built for the Sisters in 1875, houses temporary exhibitions such as one on Balzac in 1998, and another on Rodin's pupil and unhappy lover, Camille Claudel, in 1991. One room is devoted permanently to her, and features *The Wave* and *L'Age Mûr* (*Maturity*), and reveals how the two artists influenced each other. The courtyard and seven acre (three ha) park, which became a sculpture garden in 1993, are a wonderful place to walk, surrounded by the artist's monumental bronzes of *The Burghers of Calais*, *The Gates of Hell*, *The Thinker*, *Balzac*, and other works, including fragments of Antique statues collected by Rodin.

Maillol Museum

At 57-59 Rue de Grenelle, Edme Bouchardson's beautiful Four Seasons fountain (1739-46), installed to supply the district with water, marks the entrance to the Musée Maillol. Its origins go back to 1934, when the Catalan sculptor Aristide Maillol, then more than 70, met Dina Vierny, a young Russian immigrant from Odessa. She was only 15, but Maillol saw in her his ideal of absolute beauty. Dina Vierny became his sole model and muse for ten years,

2

then, on his death in 1944, his heiress, both in the material and spiritual senses.

She was completely devoted to his memory, and in 1964 gave the State 18 of Maillol's statues, which André Malraux, Minister of Culture, placed in the Tuileries Garden. Seeking to set up a museum dedicated to Maillol, she bought up, one by one, the apartments on the site of a convent (the Couvent des Récollettes, dating from the 17th century), where Alfred de Musset had once lived.

Helped by the architect Pierre Devinoy, she finally succeeded in opening "her" museum, just a few months after the 50th anniversary of Maillol's death. All aspects of the sculptor's work are on show, including his lesser-known ceramics and tapestries. The image of the beautiful Russian woman is everywhere, in sculptures, drawings, and paintings by Maillol, and also in works by Henri Matisse and Pierre Bonnard. This very personal museum also contains the private collection of Dina Vierny, a former art gallery owner and passionate collector. Here you can see her special love for the Surrealists, Russian artists, and naïve pieces signed by Marcel Duchamp, Wassily Kandinsky, Serge Poliakoff, Yankilevski, Camille Bombois, and others. The exhibitions also reflect her personality, and make this an especially charming museum to visit.

Church of Saint-Thomas Acquinas

Concealed between the main thoroughfares of Boulevard Saint-Ger-

main and Rue du Bac is the peaceful Place Saint-Thomas-d'Aquin. The church, formerly attached to a Dominican monastery, was begun in 1682 to plans by P Bullet. The monks' choir, behind the main altar, was built in the following century, as was the façade, which dates from 1765-69. It represents a continuation of the austere Classical style used by Robert de Cotte at the Church of Saint-Roch. The interior has many 18th and 19th-century paintings.

1. Hôtel de Salm
Facing the Musée d'Orsay on Rue de Lille is the elegant Hôtel de Salm (1782-7), which today contains the headquarters and museum of the Order of the Légion d'Honneur.

2. *The Burghers of Calais* (Rodin)
Sculpted by Rodin in 1889, the figures are "slowly processing to their deaths" and commemorate the six Calais dignitaries who, in 1347, sacrificed themselves to hand over the keys of their city to the king of England.

3. *The Thinker* (Rodin)
Rodin carved his *Thinker* in 1880-82 for *The Gates of Hell*. The sculpture was then enlarged and placed in front of the Panthéon in 1906. At the time, it was often seen as a socialist symbol. In 1922, it was taken back to the Rodin Museum.

4. Auguste Rodin in his studio
In 1908, when the poet Rilke, then his secretary, discovered the Hôtel Biron for Rodin, the sculptor was 68. For some 30 years he had been working in a studio in Rue de l'Université, and had a larger studio in his villa at Meudon, near Paris, where he had lived since 1893.

5. *Desire* (Aristide Maillol)
The draughtsman, sculptor, and artist Aristide Maillol (1861-1944) is best known for his sculptures in a Classical vein, almost all of them female nudes.

6. The Fountain of the Four Seasons
The fountain in Rue de Grenelle, representing Paris, the Seine and the Marne, is an 18th-century masterpiece, wholly the work of Edme Bouchardson.

Orsay station and Museum

The Musée d'Orsay covers Arts of the Western World from 1848 to 1914, and is located in a former railroad station dating from 1900. This much is generally known, but few people realize that when the station was built, the painter Edouard Detaille jokingly said that it looked like a palace of fine art. He added that the Palais des Beaux Arts (now the Grand Palais) looked like a station, and suggested to Victor Laloux, architect of the Gare d'Orsay, that he swap them around, if it was not too late! The painter's wishes have been partly granted today, as the former Gare d'Orsay was turned into a museum in 1986.

Gare d'Orsay

In 1897, the Orléans Railroad Company wanted to move its terminus to a more central and elegant location than the dull Saint-Marcel district where the Gare d'Austerlitz stood. Its gaze fell on the ruins of the Cour des Comtes, which the Communards had burned down in 1871, and on the neighboring barracks. The two lots were admirably situated, opposite the Tuileries Garden and on the edge of Faubourg Saint-Germain. To reach them, they had to extend the tracks from Austerlitz via a cutting, and then a tunnel, along the Seine. The company organized a competition, and in 1898 chose Victor Laloux's plan for a station with a hotel above it. Laloux had won the Grand Prix de Rome for architecture in 1878, and had built the façade of the station in Tours for the same company.

The prospect of the Universal Exhibition opening in spring 1900 lent impetus to the work. The task of laying 3,989 yd (3,650 m) of track and of building the station involved 300 workers by day and 80 at night.

The first trains were running by the end of May, 1900.

◆ A deluxe station

Only long-distance trains used the Gare d'Orsay. The coaches were unhitched at Austerlitz and hauled over the final leg by an electric locomotive. The passengers then alighted in a monumental station looking more like a spa building than a place for heavy machinery. The lack of smoke made it possible to decorate the roof with luxurious cream-colored plaster coffers. All the latest equipment was put to use: sloping ramps, service elevators, baggage handling counters, and elevators for the passengers. Metal surfaces, being thought too industrial, were avoided as far as possible, and sheet-metal structures were decorated with ornamental cast-iron coatings to make them look more elegant. A heavy stone façade covered the outside of the building.

◆ Soon out of date

Thirty years later, the station was seen as unsuitable for increased traffic and longer trains. Its main tracks were closed in 1939, and its huge superstructure was rendered useless. In 1961, the national railroad company decided to sell the building and keep just a few tracks which, now linked to the Gare des Invalides, form part of the suburban train system, the RER. A competition was then launched to replace the station with a combined conference center and hotel. Le Corbusier took part in the competition, which was won by architects Gillet and Coulon. But there were delays in starting the work, and then the demolition of Baltard's market halls at Les Halles in 1971 caused such a wave of protest that it was decided to preserve the Gare d'Orsay. In 1973, it was listed as a historic monument, and in 1978 it was classified.

◆ From station to museum

At the same time, the Museums of France board was looking for some-

where to put its collections of Impressionist painting, now too numerous for the Jeu de Paume. The d'Orsay site was ideal, opposite the Tuileries and between the Louvre and Orangerie Museums. The decision to devote the station and its hotel to the art of the second half of the 19th century, and the early years of the 20th, was taken by President Giscard d'Estaing. There was still an awkward problem to resolve: how to get the necessary space without harming the original setting. A limited competition was organized between six teams of architects. The winners were Colbec, Bardon, and Philippon, who proposed having visitors move along the length of the building, and closing off all access to the quayside. The Milanese architect Gae Aulenti was commissioned in 1980 to design the interior. Work began at the site in 1978, and the museum opened to the public on December 9, 1986.

1. Wall detail
The Gare d'Orsay was built between 1897 and 1900 by the Orléans Railroad Company, which wanted to have a terminus in the heart of the city rather than in the outer district where the Gare d'Austerlitz was. It was built on the site of the old Cour des Comtes, burned down by the Communards in 1871.

2. The former railroad station
This luxurious station was designed exclusively for visitors, so it was decided to conceal its metal components beneath a richly decorated stone façade. Similarly, the deluxe hotel attached to the station masked off the iron gables of the main hall.

3. From station to museum
Rail traffic at Orsay ceased in 1939. The station faced an uncertain future and was threatened with demolition, but in 1973 the idea of using it as an art museum won approval. The Musée d'Orsay was inaugurated in 1986, preserving the stonework, iron structures, and stucco decorations of Victor Laloux's original building.

4. The sculpture court
In the former Arrivals Hall, the center aisle displays sculpture from 1850 to 1870.

5. *The Dance* (Jean-Baptiste Carpeaux)
This group was designed in 1869 for Garnier's Opera House, and caused a scandal when it was unveiled. The press saw it as a bacchanale "reeking of vice and stinking of wine."

121

The museum's collections

The Musée d'Orsay is a place where many different artistic forms are brought together, not just the great innovative styles of the day such as Impressionism and Art Nouveau, but also official and academic art, long relegated to the reserve collections. The museum not only houses painting, sculpture, graphic arts, and *objets d'art*, but also furniture, architecture, photography, and their relationships with literature and music. It includes not only French art, but also European and Western art. The collections, originally based on works from the Louvre, Jeu de Paume, and National Museum of Modern Art, are constantly being enlarged, thanks to acquisitions, donations, and legacies. Some pictures of enormous value have arrived since the museum opened in 1986: *The Origins of the World* by Gustave Courbet, in 1995; *Berthe Morisot with a Bouquet of Violets* by Edouard Manet, in 1998; and *Portrait of Gustave Geffroy* by Paul Cézanne, in 2000.

◆ A "sculpture garden"

Visits begin along a "street" that runs beneath the former main hall, reached by a few steps which go down to about the level of the old railroad tracks. From this splendidly vaulted area, there is a gradual ascent via a series of walkways flanked by ramps. Sculptures are displayed on either side: Barye's *Lion*, Rude's *Napoleon Reawakening to Immortality*, and Charles Cordier's poly-

chrome *Negro from the Sudan*. Under the excellent lighting of the great nave, the groupings recall the sculpture gardens that were very fashionable in the 19th century. At the far end are wonderfully mobile groups by Jean-Baptiste Carpeaux: *The Dance*, a relief for the Opera House, and *The Four Quarters of the World* from the Observatory Fountain.

◆ The great masters of French painting

The neighboring rooms, like those located beneath the roof, which also benefit from natural light, are devoted to the great masters of French painting. Although Ingres and Delacroix are not very well represented, because their most important canvases date from before 1850 and have remained at the Louvre, here at the d'Orsay you can find Millet's *The Gleaners*, Corot's *The Studio*, and Courbet's *Burial at Ornans* and *The Studio*. However, what makes the museum such a success is the collection of Impressionist paintings, one of the richest in the world. They include: Manet's *Olympia*, Degas's *Absinth* and his bronze *Little Dancer, Fourteen Years*

Old, Renoir's *Bal du Moulin de la Galette*, Van Gogh's *Church at Auvers-sur-Oise* and *Self Portrait*, Cézanne's *The Card Players,* and Degas's *Dancer with Bouquet Waving on the Stage* and *The Tub.*

◆ Art in all its forms

Objets d'art and furniture occupy an important place, with the Third

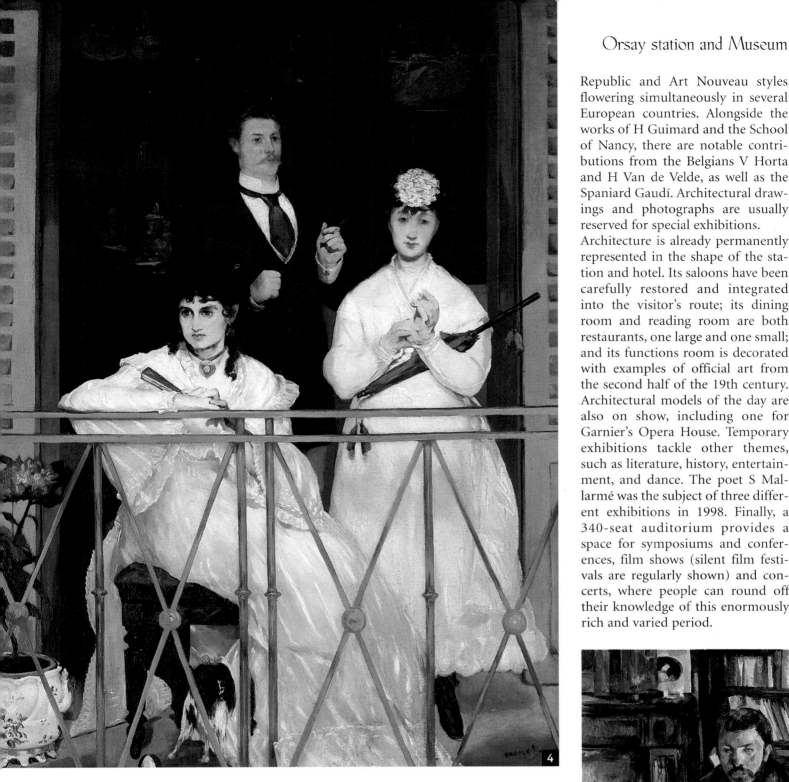

Republic and Art Nouveau styles flowering simultaneously in several European countries. Alongside the works of H Guimard and the School of Nancy, there are notable contributions from the Belgians V Horta and H Van de Velde, as well as the Spaniard Gaudí. Architectural drawings and photographs are usually reserved for special exhibitions. Architecture is already permanently represented in the shape of the station and hotel. Its saloons have been carefully restored and integrated into the visitor's route; its dining room and reading room are both restaurants, one large and one small; and its functions room is decorated with examples of official art from the second half of the 19th century. Architectural models of the day are also on show, including one for Garnier's Opera House. Temporary exhibitions tackle other themes, such as literature, history, entertainment, and dance. The poet S Mallarmé was the subject of three different exhibitions in 1998. Finally, a 340-seat auditorium provides a space for symposiums and conferences, film shows (silent film festivals are regularly shown) and concerts, where people can round off their knowledge of this enormously rich and varied period.

1. Paneling from the Hôtel de Béar
This Art Nouveau paneling in elm, ash, and oak, encrusted with mother-of-pearl, was designed and made by Jean Dampt between 1900 and 1906.

2. *Wild Poppies* (Monet)
Monet painted this work in 1873 during his so-called "Argenteuil" period, characterized by the great freshness of his painting. He used free touches of color to evoke the vibrant atmosphere of a summer's day seen through a hazy image of people and flowers.

3. *Garden at l'Etang-la-Ville* (Vuillard)
Like Bonnard, Vuillard was a member of the Nabis group, founded in 1888. Influenced by Gauguin, its "prophets" advocated a new art inspired by "medieval stained glass, Japanese prints, and Egyptian painting."

4. *The Balcony* (Manet)
Manet was influenced by Velasquez and Goya, and in this 1863 work takes up a theme dear to the latter. But he disconcerted critics of the day with the dreamy looks of his subjects, and the contrast between the delicate white muslins and the violence of the green of the balcony and shutters. The woman in the foreground, who was to marry his brother, is the painter Berthe Morisot.

5. *Gustave Geffroy* (Cézanne)
This 1895 canvas is one of the museum's most recent acquisitions. After the third Impressionist exhibition of 1877, Georges Rivière wrote, "The artist most attacked and ill-treated by the press and public in the last 15 years is Cézanne." However, Cézanne was to have a profound influence on French painting, opening the way to Fauvism and Cubism.

THE ARC DE TRIOMPHE

and surrounding area

The Arc de Triomphe

The Champs–Elysées district

The 16th *arrondissement*

Place de la Concorde

Aerial view of the Arc de Triomphe
Place Charles-de-Gaulle is one of the busiest junctions in Paris. It stands at the meeting point of three *arrondissements*: the 8th, 16th, and 17th. Designed by J-I Hittorff at the instigation of Baron Haussmann, it consists of 12 avenues radiating from the Arc de Triomphe into districts renowned for luxurious living and high culture. From its position at the top of the Champs-Elysées, the Arc de Triomphe has magnificent panoramic views over the surrounding districts, all the way from La Défense to Place de la Concorde.

The Arc de Triomphe

The Arc de Triomphe is one of the city's landmark monuments. It stands almost 164 ft (50 m) high in one of the best-known and most-visited districts, and provides magnificent all-round views highlighting not just the star-shaped circus at its feet but also the long vista which runs from the Louvre to the Grande Arche at La Défense. Its physically central position, and weighty symbolism, make it a natural assembly point for popular rallies and national ceremonies.

Thirty years in the making

Napoleon I wanted to build four triumphal arches to symbolize his victories. Only two were actually built: the Carroussel, near the Louvre, and the Arc de Triomphe in the Place de l'Etoile (today Place Charles-de-Gaulle). The latter was dedicated to the Grande Armée and took a long time to build. Work began on the Emperor's birthday on August 15, 1806, and was completed 30 years later. The death of its first architect, J-F Chalgrin, the return of the Bourbon monarchs to power, as well as disagreement about the design considerably delayed pro-gress. In 1830, J-N Huyot built the great entablature, the ogival arch designed to support the upper pavement and the coffered vaults of the main arch. The monument was inaugurated on July 29, 1836.

Sculptures and bas-reliefs

The passage of time and changes of régime also affected the purpose of the monument. In 1833, it was decided that the sculptures and bas-reliefs should glorify not only the armies of the Empire but also those of the Republic. Each pillar features a sculptural group 39 ft (12 m) high. On the Champs-Elysées side are *The Departure of the Volunteers of 1792,* or *The Marseillaise,* by F Rude, on the right, and *The Triumph of 1810,* by J-P Cortot, on the left. On the other side are *The Resistance of 1814,* on the left, and *The Peace of 1815,* on the right, both by A Etex. Above these and on the sides of the arch are six large bas-reliefs in panels.

To rouse national feelings still further, the arches of the monument were engraved with the names of 150 Imperial and Republican victories, and 664 officers. On the ground in the center of the arch is a bronze plaque with the star of the Legion of Honor, an order founded by Napoleon in 1802; the Emperor's eagle is set in the medallion.

A focus for ceremonies

With its highly symbolic architecture, the Arc de Triomphe provides the setting for large-scale national mem-orial ceremonies. Although Napoleon never saw the completed arch, his coffin, on its return from Saint Helena, was carried through the Arc de Triomphe on December 15, 1840, on its way to his tomb at the Invalides.

In 1877, the remains of Thiers, who had inaugurated the arch in 1836, were also brought there. On the night of May 30, 1885, the arch served as a cha-pel of rest for the body of Victor Hugo before his ashes were taken to the Panthéon. Since May 28, 1921, the central arch has contained the Tomb of the Unknown Soldier, a simple mem-orial stone bearing a flame which is relit every day in memory of World War I.

Place de l'Etoile and the Marshals' mansions

When the Arc de Triomphe was built, Place de l'Etoile was an uneven shape, and since 1785 had marked the bound-ary of Paris with two customs houses built by Claude-Nicolas Ledoux; these were destroyed when the neighboring communes were brought into the city.

126

The Arc de Triomphe

Facts & Figures

Architects :	J-F. Chalgrin, L. Goust, J-N. Huyot, A. Blouet
Height :	163 ft 6 in (49.546 m)
Width :	147 ft (44.82 m)
Depth :	73 ft (22.21 m)
Depth of foundations :	27 ft (8.37 m)
Dimensions of main arch :	Height, 96 ft 6 in (29.42 m); Width, 48 ft (14.6 m)
Stones used :	Château-Landon stone for the building, Chérence stone for the sculptures
Area of stones used :	394,985 sq ft (36,695 sq m)
Area of wood used :	107,640 sq ft (10,000 sq m)
Amount of iron, cast-iron and lead used :	141 t (128,000 kg)
Total weight :	49,200 t (50,000 tonnes)
Cost :	9,348,910.60 francs

The present design, adopted by Haussmann, dates from 1854 and consists of a circus 394 ft (120 m) in diameter with 12 avenues branching from it at regular intervals. The façades were designed by Hittorff and built by C Rohault de Fleury.

1. Renovation of the Arc de Triomphe
The Arc de Triomphe was restored between 1988 and 1990. At that time it was covered with a sheet in the French colors, and concrete was injected to strengthen the foundations.

2. The Arc de Triomphe illuminated
Facing down the Champs-Elysées, the Arc de Triomphe is lit with special care. The tricolor flag marks the Tomb of the Unknown Soldier.

3. *La Marseillaise*
On the arch's right-hand pillar, the group sculpted by F Rude shows *The Departure of the Volunteers of 1792*. The volunteers from Marseilles brought their song to Paris, and this became the *Marseillaise*.

4. The Unknown Soldier
The soldier buried beneath the Arc de Triomphe was chosen from thousands of bodies at Verdun in 1920. Eight coffins were displayed in a chapel of rest, and Government minister A Maginot assigned a soldier to place carnations on one of them. This man became the symbol of the nation. His remains were buried at a solemn ceremony on January 28, 1921. A plaque states: "Here lies a French soldier who died for his country – 1914-1918." Since 1923, tribute is paid to him on November 11 each year.

The Champs–Elysées district

The Champs-Elysées district is one of the most lively and dynamic in Paris, a successful blend of glamour, tourism, and business. Its many boutiques attract strolling Parisians, office workers, and foreign visitors. At night, its restaurants, cafés, cinemas, and shows are a paradise for night owls.

Avenue des Champs-Elysées

In Greek mythology, the Elysian Fields (in French, Les Champs-Elysées) were the resting-place for the souls of the just. The Champs-Elysées in Paris is 2,055 yds (1,880 m) long and runs from Place de la Concorde to Place Charles-de-Gaulle. It was built in 1667 by Le Nôtre for Colbert, in order to open up a vista between the Tuileries and Saint-Germain-en-Laye. Le Nôtre laid out a tree-lined promenade from Place Louis XV (today Place de la Concorde) to the Rond-Point des Champs-Elysées. Beyond that, the roadway remained a country lane. In 1835, the architect J-I Hittorff was commissioned to install lighting and build fountains, a panorama

theater (a trompe l'oeil painting on the interior wall of a rotunda), and a summer circus. In 1858, Haussmann asked A Alphand to convert the promenade into a real garden equipped with attractions. The avenue then became a residential area for wealthy people who built themselves magnificent private mansions. The main survivors of that period are the four fountains and the Le Doyen and Laurent restaurants (by Hittorff), the Théâtre du Rond-Point and the Théâtre Marigny (the former summer circus), two former panorama theaters, the Le Hon-Sabatier mansion (at No 15), and, at No 25-27, the Hôtel de la Païva, present headquarters of the Traveler's Club. This relatively late development of

the avenue, beginning in the Second Empire and continuing to the present day, gives it its particularly opulent and eclectic atmosphere.

◆ *The city's showcase*

At the beginning of the 20th century, as vacant lots grew rarer, houses gave way to more commercial buildings such as the House of Guerlain at No 68, built by Charles Mewès in 1913, with its distinctive metal-framed bow window. Deluxe hotels began to appear: the Elysée Palace in 1899 and the Claridge in 1912. Because the Grand Palais was nearby, where the Motor Show had been held since 1901, and the headquarters of the Auto-mobile Club of France were in Place de la Concorde, automobile manufact-urers such as Renault, Cit-roën, Mercedes, and Hotchkiss were encouraged to build showrooms on the Champs-Elysées. Other com-mer-cial companies also moved in: the Crédit Commercial de France bought and converted the Elysée-Palace Hotel in 1922, and the archi-tect André Arfvidson built the premises of the First National City Bank at No 52-60 in 1931 (now the Virgin Megastore). Twelve arcades are now in place to cater for the increasing number of boutiques.

As a Mecca for tourists, the Champs-Elysées attracts both visitors and residents. People like to be seen there, stroll about, and enjoy themselves. High-class restaurants such as Le

Doyen and Fouquet's, cinemas, theaters, and shows such as the *Lido* offer a hundred ways to relax.

The Avenue des Champs-Elysées is a legendary name with an impressive place in history. The avenue's associations with royalty explain why Louis XVI was brought here from Varennes on June 25, 1791. Here too, on August 26, 1944, General De Gaulle paid homage at the Tomb of the Unknown Soldier and led a grand parade down the avenue.

1. Avenue des Champs-Elysées
This lively avenue is a meeting-place for tourists, walkers, and business people. The big commercial showrooms, boutiques, famous restaurants, and show theaters all contribute to its enviable status as "the most beautiful avenue in the world."

2. Exhibition at the Rond-Point
The lower part of the avenue between Place de la Concorde and the Rond-Point now stages open-air exhibitions, like this one by the sculptor Botero in 1993.

3. The Liberation of Paris in 1944
On August 26, 1944, the day after the city was liberated, General de Gaulle paid tribute to the Unknown Soldier and drove down the Champs-Elysées in triumph before thousands of onlookers.

4. The great harvest of 1990
On June 24, 1990, young farmers publicized the agriculture business by turning the Champs-Elysées into a giant cornfield which was then harvested.

5. The Guerlain building
Built in 1913 by C Mewès for the perfumer Guerlain, it is very typical of the architecture of its day. The bow window combines the techniques of metalwork with a decorative style close to Art Nouveau.

The Bicentenary of the Revolution was celebrated here in 1989 with a grand procession, organized by Jean-Paul Goude, and the Harvest Festival on June 24, 1990. Every year, great annual events take place here: the military parade on July 14, a national holiday, and the finish of the Tour de France cycle race.

◆ A timely update

By the end of the 1980s, it had to be admitted that the Champs-Elysées had fallen victim to its own success and lost its glamour. There were still plenty of banks and airline offices, but cut-price stores had been replacing the high-class boutiques and covering the old façades with gaudy

signs, café terraces were spreading everywhere, and vehicles were clogging the service roads.

In 1990, therefore, the City of Paris started a "Champs-Elysées Initiative" aimed at raising the tone once more. Underground parking lots were built so that pedestrians could use the service roads, the sidewalks were renewed, rows of new trees were plant-ed, and signage and café terraces became subject to new regulations. To round off the project, architect Jean-Michel Willmotte and industrialist Jean-Claude Decaux introduced new street furniture. Traffic lights, street lamps, bus shelters, benches, news-paper kiosks, and Morris columns fitted with telephone booths now blend more harmoniously with their surroundings.

The avenue has recovered its attractiveness as a place to walk.

Avenue Montaigne

Luxury rules in Avenue Montaigne, from the Drouot-Montaigne sale-room, where precious objects and valuable paintings send auction bids rocketing, to the opulent apartments belonging for the most part to rich Iranians, Lebanese and South Americans.

This broad leafy avenue derives much of its glamour from its fashion houses and theater. As early as 1923, the great *couturière* Madeleine Vionnet moved into No 50. Balenciaga followed in 1937, Jacques Fath in 1940, and Christian Dior in 1947. Today's occupants include Ungaro (No 2), Lacroix (No 26), Dior (still at No 30), Chanel (No 42), Mugler (No 49), and Scherrer (No 51).

At the bottom of the avenue, the Théâtre des Champs Elysées catered for a wide audience. Designed by Roger Bouvard, Henry Van de Velde, and then Auguste Perret, who built it between 1911 and 1913, it is an Art Deco masterpiece. The large reliefs on the façade are by Antoine Bourdelle. The auditorium is covered by a dome painted by Maurice Denis, and the central lighting is by René Lalique.

The Grand Palais

The creation of the Grand Palais, designed for the Universal Exhibi-

tion of 1900, was a contentious affair. When the project was announced in 1895, it attracted a wave of protests: it meant the destruction of the Palais de l'Industrie, built for the Universal Exhibition of 1855, and threatened to spoil the gardens by the Champs-Elysées. A competition was nonethe-less launched on April 22, 1896, to build a palace dedicated to the fine arts, which would put on art exhibitions, concerts, and the equest-rian competition, which was then held in the Palais de l'Industrie.

The palace would stand on an avenue linking the Champs-Elysées and the new Gare des Invalides (today the RER station and Air France terminal) via the Pont Alexandre III, also being built for the Universal Exhibition. The competition stip-ulated an H-shaped plan covering a large area that could be used in its entirety for big events or divided into smaller sections. It was also to be designed to blend in with the existing buildings around it.

No entry answered all the requirements, and the commission was eventually given to three architects: H Deglane, A Louvet, and A Thomas. A fourth, C Girault, was made res-ponsible for coordinating the works. The foundations were started in spring 1897, and the building was inaugurated when the exhibition opened in 1900.

The Grand Palais has a façade in free-

now in progress and should be completed in about 2003.

The Petit Palais

The Petit Palais, standing on the other side of Avenue Winston Churchill, has not had such a controversial history. Architect C Girault's plan was unan-imously approved, and once the Universal Exhibition of 1900 was over the building acquired the City of Paris' collection of works of art from Antiquity to the beginning of the 20th century.

Its colonnaded façade matches that

of the Grand Palais. Behind it, the building is arranged around a semicircular garden. A hundred years after it was built, it suffers from a severe lack of space, which forces its keepers to reduce the permanent collections in favor of temporary shows of, for example, Cartier jewels or works by Tiepolo, which attract a much larger public. This building too is being fully renovated.

stone that tones in with the Invalides, visible across the river, while the vast canopied roof provides wonderful lighting for its art exhibitions.

When the building opened, it showed the Contemporary and Centennial Exhibitions of Art. Since 1901, it has presented the Salon shows of the Société des Artistes Français and the Société Nationale des Beaux-Arts, the Automobile Show up to 1961, and the Air Show between 1909 and 1952. In 1937, the Palais de la Découverte (Science Museum) moved into the area by Avenue Franklin D Roosevelt.

Since 1971, the National Galleries of the Grand Palais have occupied the central part of the building and put on big shows such as Toulouse-Lautrec (1992), Cézanne (1996), and Egyptian Art in the Age of the Pyramids (1999-2000). The Biennial Antique Dealers show and the International Contemporary Art Fair take place in the central nave.

Since 1993, however, much of the building has been closed. After a bolt fell out of the glass roof, a survey of the building revealed that the foundations and metal frame were in poor condition. Some people called for the building to be demolished, but a restoration program is

---

1. Couturier Christian Dior
The House of Dior has been at No 30 Avenue Montaigne since 1947, and is one of the many fashion houses to have given the avenue its reputation since the 1920s.

2. Entrance to the Petit Palais
The main entrance is richly decorated with sculptures and fine ironwork. To the right of the steps, a sculpture by Ferrary represents the Seine and its tributaries.

3. Glass roof of the Grand Palais
In 1993, during an exhibition called "Design: Mirror of the Century," a rivet came away from the glass roof. Because of the risks involved, it was announced that the palace, built for the Universal Exhibition of 1900, would be demolished. Since then work has been put in hand to strengthen and restore it. The nave now has a protective net. The National Galleries of the Grand Palais and the

Palais de la Découverte have meanwhile remained open to the public.

4. Petit Palais
Built by Charles Girault from 1897 for the Universal Exhibition of 1900, the Petit Palais is a companion to the Grand Palais on the other side of Avenue Winston-Churchill. It houses the City of Paris' collections of works of art, comprising sculptures, paintings, and art objects from Antiquity to the beginning of the 20th century. It also stages temporary exhibitions. A restoration program has been in progress since February, 2001.

5. Théâtre des Champs-Elysées
Located at No 15 Avenue Montaigne, this theater was inaugurated in 1913 and became a great attraction. Its distinctive Art Deco style is the work of the Perret brothers and sculptor A Bourdelle. Josephine Baker's *Revue Nègre* premiered there in 1925. Since its renovation in 1986-87, it has been the home of Montaigne-Drouot auction house.

Place de la Concorde

The square was given its present name in 1795 to symbolize the reconciliation of the French people. It was originally called Place Louis XV and built to accommodate an equestrian statue of the king, then renamed Place de la Révolution in 1792, when the guillotine was set up there. At the beginning of the 19th century, it was redesigned and an obelisk brought from Egypt was erected. Although this historic square is part of a Unesco-listed world heritage site, it has been increasingly spoilt by excessive traffic and use as a parking lot. Now its monuments are being restored, and there is a renovation plan aimed at restoring its best features.

A square for a statue

In 1753, Louis XV set aside the land between the Tuileries and the Champs-Elysées for an equestrian statue of himself. The royal architect, J-A Gabriel, was commissioned to design a square to contain it. Inauguration of the statue, begun by E Bouchardon and completed by J-B Pigalle, took place on June 20, 1763. The square surrounding it was finished in 1772. It is a vast rectangle with canted corners containing pavilions, surrounded by a balustrade and isolated by ditches to form a kind of island with views over the Seine, Tuileries Gardens, and the Champs-Elysées. Only on the north side is it closed, by two large buildings with identical façades designed by J-A Gabriel.

In 1792, Place Louis XV was renamed Place de la Révolution, and the statue of the king was toppled

and replaced by Lemot's statue of Liberty in stone and plaster, which remained there until 1800. The guillotine at the end of the Tuileries sliced off 1,119 heads including those of Louis XVI (on January 21, 1793), Marie-Antoinette, Danton, and Robespierre.

Concorde's obelisk

Renamed Place de la Concorde in 1795 by the Directoire, the square was extensively reorganized in the 1830s. Louis-Philippe decided to put up a strictly non-political monument: one of the two obelisks that Mehemet Ali, Viceroy of Egypt, had presented to France in 1831. Transporting this 75 ft (23 m)-high, 230-t monument in pink granite by sea and river to Paris proved to be an extraordinary advent-ure. Finally, on October 25, 1836, the obelisk from the entrance of Rameses II's temple in Thebes (now Luxor) was set in the middle of the square. The base, telling the epic story of the obelisk's voyage from Egypt, was designed by J-I Hittorff, who was responsible for renovating the square. On each side of the obelisk he placed two fountains, the Fountain of the Seas and the Fountain of the Rivers, statues symbolising great French cities above each of the eight pav-ilions surrounding the square, and memorial columns on the balustrade running along the edge of the ditches (which were filled in 1854). The columns fulfill a double role: their rostrums (a word applied also to the rams of old war galleys) symbolize the arms of the city of Paris and the naval genius of France, while at the same time they support lamps to light the square.

Restoration and a new look

Since the 1980s, the square's statues, columns, and fountains have been extensively restored. They have recovered the brightness that J-I Hittorff wanted them to have: "The flesh of the statues are a Florentine bronze color (deep bronze), the drapery a Venetian bronze (green), and the accessories and ornaments are gilded." The obelisk has been completely restored and decorated with a pyramidion in gilded bronze like the original. Better still, more than three-quarters of the square is to be pedestrianized, and the ditches and lawn borders partly restored to provide a continuous promenade from the Louvre to the top of the Champs-Elysées.

Behind the twin façades

With their terraced roofs, corner pavilions and colonnades, the twin façades closing the north side of the square recall the Louvre colonnade by C Perrault facing Saint-Germain l'Auxerrois. The façades were built by J-A Gabriel between 1766 and 1775, and today house the Navy Ministry,

on the east side, and the Automobile Club and Hôtel de Crillon on the other. The Navy has been there since 1789 (formerly it was the Royal furniture depository); it was dec-orated by architect J Gondouin and refurbished under the Second Empire. The Automobile Club and Hôtel de Crillon did not arrive until early in the 20th century. Their premises are in two former private mansions built behind Gabriel's façade for the king's secretary, Rouillé de l'Estang, and the Duc d'Aumont (bought in 1788 by the Comte de Crillon). The Hôtel de Crillon is the flagship of the French group Concorde-Taittinger; its guests inc-lude celebrities such as Harrison Ford and Madonna, as well as foreign heads of state and their delegations.

Across the bridge: the Assemblée Nationale

The Pont de la Concorde leads straight to the French Parliament building. It was first planned under Louis XV, but built between 1788 and 1791, partly with stone from the Bastille "so that people could still trample on the old fortress." This center of democracy, whose colonnaded façade approached by 30 steps matches the Church of the Madeleine across the river, was originally two princely dwellings built in 1730 for the Duchesse de Bourbon, daughter of Louis XIV, and her lover, the Marquis de Lassay, and then confiscated by the nation in 1791.

The Hôtel de Lassay, now the residence of the President of the Assemblée, has kept its original appearance

fairly well, although the Palais Bourbon, where the Deputies sit, has been radically altered. The original mansion, which looked like the Grand Trianon, was "enveloped" by a new building, begun in 1806 by architect B Poyet, to give the river frontage "a noble and religious style." The Assemblée complex extends well beyond the Palais Bourbon, with underground galleries leading to neighboring buildings and providing each Deputy with a private office. In all, some 3,000 people work in an area with a floor surface of 180,400 sq ft (55,000 sq m).

1. Entering the Hôtel Crillon
The hotel's luxurious looks and wonderful position on Paris' largest square make it the most glamourous in the capital. Heads of state and stars of show business stay there in magnificent suites.

2. Place de la Concorde
The two large fountains next to the obelisk were designed by J-I Hittorff and built between 1836 and 1846. One represents sailing by river, the other sailing by sea.

3. The obelisk
In 1831, Mehemet Ali, Viceroy of Egypt, presented Louis-Philippe with this obelisk which today stands in Place de la Concorde. It came from the Temple of Rameses II at Thebes, and a special barge, the *Luxor*, was built to ship it to France. The voyage to Toulon took about two years, and the obelisk was not finally put up here until 1836. In the 1990s,

it was restored to its former glory with a gilded pyramidion.

4. Pediment of the Palais Bourbon
The façade of the Palais Bourbon, seat of the French Parliament, echoes that of the Church of the Madeleine on the far side of Place de la Concorde. The pediment was sculpted by Cortot between 1838 and 1841. France stands in the center, between Strength and Justice, symbolizing the legislative process.

5. Benches of the Assemblée Nationale
Deputies elected for six years by universal suffrage sit in this room. Their job is to assess new laws, debate issues and vote on them. Laws must be finally approved by the Sénat, the Upper House.

The 16th arrondissement

I ts location in the west of Paris, on the road to Versailles, made the 16th *arrondissement* the favorite district for the aristocracy who, from the 17th century, built châteaux and residences there. None has survived, but in due course the area was filled with private mansions, villas, and apartments. It has lost none of its old elegance, and is one of the city's most conservative districts.

West of Etoile

Avenue de la Grande Armée is a continuation of Le Nôtre's axis running from the Louvre Palace. Somewhat lacking in charm, it is lined with office blocks and showrooms selling automobiles and motorbikes. It continues to Porte Maillot, dominated by the Palais des Congrès, a huge 1970s building completely remodeled in the 1990s by C de Portzamparc, architect of the Cité de la Musique. Avenue Foch, leading to the Bois de Boulogne, has a very different look. Originally Avenue de l'Impératrice (renamed Foch in 1929), its imperial layout was Haussmann's idea. It is 394 ft (120 m) wide, the broadest street in Paris. Vast lawns separate the roadway from the service roads and the apartment buildings. When it opened in 1854, it attracted a swarm of aristocrats, but time and property speculation have prevailed over their magnificent private mansions. The most famous, the Palais Rose, was demolished in 1969. This smaller copy of the Grand Trianon at Versailles was built for Comte Boni de Castellane by P-E Sanson in 1896-1902. In front of No 90, the entrance to Porte Dauphine Métro station is one of the very few to have kept their 1902 Art Nouveau entrance by H Guimard.

Villages of the 16th

The three villages of Chaillot, Passy, and Auteuil which form the 16th *arrondissement* became part of the city in 1860, but each has retained its special character. Chaillot is full of offices, administrative buildings, embassies, and cultural centers. Its larger buildings, typically 1930s in style, include the Palais du Conseil Economique et Social in Place d'Iéna, the Palais de Tokyo, and Palais de Chaillot which contains several museums. Nearby are the Musée Guimet with its Far Eastern Art collection, and the Musée Galliera, a smaller 19th-century palace devoted to fashion.

The Passy district, around the Rue de Passy, is more intimate. A busy business center by day, it becomes quiet and residential in the evening. It also has several small museums, such as the Musée Balzac and Musée Marmottan. The latter has a large number of works by Claude Monet, including *Impression, Soleil Levant*, medieval illuminated manuscripts, and a fine First Empire collection.

Despite its population growth, Auteuil has kept its charming rural character thanks to 19th-century private developers who built picturesque villas enclosed by greenery, such as the Boileau hamlet (1838) and Villa de Montmorency (1852).

In the architectural vanguard

This wealthy outer *arrondissement* contains several innovative buildings by major architects.

Art Nouveau pioneer H Guimard put up some 27 buildings in the 16th, of which about 20 survive today. In 1910, at 25 *bis* Rue Franklin, the Perret brothers built one of the first concrete apartment buildings, faced with ceramic slabs.

In 1924-1925, Le Corbusier built the Villa Jeanneret and Villa La Roche in Square du Docteur Blanche, home since 1968 of the Le Corbusier Foundation, which looks after the famous architect's heritage. On the banks of the Seine looms the impressive outline of the circular Radio-France building, 525 ft (160 m) in diameter, built by architect B Henry between 1955 and 1963. The beehive layout of the interior contains offices, production, recording, and television studios, an auditorium, and a museum of communications. The archives are in the central tower.

Bois de Boulogne

This remnant of the Rouvray Forest which surrounded the original Gallo-Roman settlement known as Lutetia was given its present name in 1469. The 2,087 acre (845 ha) park you see today is the result of radical changes made in the Second Empire. Directed by Haussmann, A Alphand and the landscape architect Barillet-Deschamps removed several roads and laid out more winding pathways. Because of a mistake made when measuring ground levels, the lake originally planned had to be split into two parts joined by a large waterfall.

The park's many attractions include Longchamp racecourse (1857), the zoological gardens (1860), the Auteuil racecourse (1873) and the greenhouses of the municipal nurseries (1898-1901).

The varied landscape (forest, English garden, waterfall) draws all kinds of people to the Bois de Boulogne. By day you can see people exercising and strolling about, but when darkness falls the park becomes the haunt of prostitutes, transvestites, and other creatures of the night.

Following the great storm of December, 1999, which destroyed 395 acres (160 ha) of trees, a program was launched to restore the Bois de Boulogne to its original state as conceived by A Alphand in the Second Empire.

1. Porte Dauphine Métro station
At the foot of Avenue Foch, the Porte Dauphine Métro station entrance is one the very few designed by H Guimard to have kept its enameled ironwork and glass canopy shaped like a dragonfly's wings.

2. Longchamp racecourse
(E Manet, Louvre)
Longchamp racecourse was opened in 1857 in the heart of the Bois de Boulogne to replace the one in Champ de Mars. It became a meeting-place for horseracing fans and society people, especially on glamourous occasions such as the Prix de l'Arc de Triomphe.

3. Teatime at Bagatelle, 1906
In the 18th century, a folly was built in the Bois de Boulogne for Comte d'Artois, and in the 19th century it became a place where high-society people came to relax.

4. Avenue Foch
A symbol of Second Empire prosperity, Avenue Foch was opened in 1854. It has a combination of private mansions and more recently built apartments.

5. Musée Galliera
Built by L Guinain between 1878 and 1894 for the Duchesse de Galliera, this metal-framed building is the work of G Eiffel's company. Since 1977, it has been the Museum of Fashion of the City of Paris.

6. Greenhouses at Auteuil
This unusual group of greenhouses was built from 1895 to 1898 by the engineers Schwartz and Meurer to plans by J-C Formigé. They stand at No 3 Avenue de la Porte d'Auteuil in the Louis XV nurseries and contain wonderful tropical plants.

SACRÉ-COEUR
and surrounding area

The Basilica of Sacré-Coeur

The Butte Montmartre

Beneath the Butte

Aerial view of Sacré-Coeur
This symbol of Paris was designed in 1874 by
Paul Abadie and overlooks the capital from
the top of the Butte, or hill, of Montmartre.
The basilica is an unmistakable landmark,
familiar to all, its shape sometimes likened
to a sumptuous wedding cake, its worldwide
fame sustained by a constant barrage of
postcards, keyrings, scarves, and other
items bearing its image.
Each year, millions of tourists come to visit
the Sacré-Coeur, enjoying all-round views of
up to 30 miles (50 km) and exploring the
lanes and picturesque flights of steps
on the hill.

The Basilica of Sacré-Coeur

The bright-white basilica sits on top of the hill, crowned by a mass of domes and tall, slender campaniles. Along with the Eiffel Tower and Notre-Dame, it is one of the emblems of Paris. Each year, more than six million tourists climb the hill to visit this center of prayer and pilgrimage. Its conception at the end of the 19th century was part of one of the most extraordinary periods of upheaval in the city's history.

Saving both nation and church

The splendors and euphoria of the Second Empire ended in a series of dramas. In the dreadful year of 1870, the army fell at Sedan, abandoning Alsace-Lorraine. Napoleon III was taken prisoner, and the Prussians surrounded Paris.

France looked on helplessly as Rome was annexed by Italy. The nation, the church ... everything seemed to be collapsing.

The country was gripped by a major political, social and moral crisis. The bloody episode of the Paris Commune in May 1871, in which 30,000 were slaughtered, only deepened the crisis. People wondered if all these misfortunes were not the sins of previous years coming home to roost. Religious believers begged the Sacred Heart of Jesus to grant them national redemption. In the hope that their prayers would be answered, Alexandre Legentil, a Parisian businessman living in exile in Poitiers, promised to build a church on the site of the Opera House, for him a "symbol of decadence."

The national vow

Legentil's promise soon became widely known, and in 1872 was backed by the Archbishop of Paris, Monseigneur Gilbert. A committee to carry out the "national vow" was formed the same year, and tried to get a law passed declaring state approval for the new church, so they could acquire the site. The question caused stormy debates in Parliament. Georges Clemenceau and Emile Zola were especially hostile to the plan which, in their view, was aimed merely at expiating the crimes of the Commune. Nonetheless, on July 24, 1873, Parliament decided by a majority vote to grant state approval.

The site finally chosen was Montmartre. The top of the hill was an unbuilt area and had the further advantage of being high up and very visible. The "Martyrs' Mount" was also associated with Saint Denis, first bishop of Paris, who was beheaded there.

1 | 2

138

The Basilica of Sacré-Coeur

The competition of 1874

The public competition organised in 1874 to choose an architect specified that the church would be dedicated to pilgrimages. Provision should therefore be made for "side aisles running the length of the nave and around the sanctuary" and numerous chapels to accommodate large processions and say several masses at the same time.

Despite the importance of the commission, only 78 plans were submitted (a hundred less than for the Opera House competition). Leading names in French architecture abstained: Viollet-le-Duc was opposed to the project, while others claimed lack of interest (knowing that the Archbishop was keen to choose his own winner). First prize went to Paul Abadie by 12 votes to five. It was his first domed church, designed in a Romanesque-Byzantine style rather than Neo-Gothic, the so-called national style of the second half of the 19th century, which was no longer in favor.

A long and difficult operation

Construction of the basilica began on June 16, 1875, but it was not inaugurated until October 16, 1919. The work took much longer and cost much more than had been estimated. Building such a large structure on a hilltop pitted with gypsum quarries was a great challenge. To ensure stability, the foundations had to be dug more than 110 ft (33 m) deep. The national subscription underwriting

1. *Christ Giving His Blessing* (pediment)
This sculpture of Christ on the pediment of Sacré-Coeur was carved by Georges Thomas around 1890, and is typical of the official Neo-Baroque style of the day.

2. The basilica and the square
At the top of the Butte Montmartre, Sacré-Coeur overlooks Square Willette, a beautiful landscaped garden laid out in the 1930s to plans by Jean-Camille Formigé. The square stands on the hillside with steps on one side; on the left is the funicular railway station.

3. Eclectic architecture
The 1874 competition was a victory for the Romanesque-Byzantine style in France. After the quarrel between the advocates of Neo-Gothic, led by Viollet-le-Duc, and the supporters of eclecticism, it marked a great renewal of interest in churches with oriental domes. Many architects were inspired to follow its example.

the work remained open for almost 50 years. After Abadie died in 1884, he was to be succeeded by five architects. Louis-Jean Hulot was the last; he completed the tower and the basilica's ornamental sculpture.

Eclectic architecture

Abadie wrote this about Sacré-Coeur: "I have sought inspiration from our beloved monuments at Charente and Périgord, but I have not copied any of them. It will have the blood of its fathers, but neither their look nor their form." Many elements of the basilica's architecture are in fact inspired by the Romanesque period, but the architect successfully brought together the various styles. Unfortunately, his successors mis-represented his original plan, chiefly by exaggerating the height of the domes, which helps to give the building its tiered, wedding cake appearance and makes the interior very dark. Being built in chalky Château-Landon stone, it tends to go even whiter after winds or rain. It stands on a crypt which is bigger than the main building. Following on from the porch and the narthex, the nave has a square plan, leading to the choir surrounded by seven chapels and crowned by a massive dome.

Richly decorated interior

The basilica's decoration was planned from the beginning, but not carried out until the beginning of the 20th century. Outstanding among its many exterior sculptures are those of Saint Louis and Joan of Arc by Hippolyte Lefebvre. Inside, the most impressive features are the mosaics, mainly by Henry Pinta, Luc-Olivier

FACTS & FIGURES
SACRÉ-COEUR IN STATISTICS

Duration of the national subscription : 50 years	
Number of donors : 10 million people from all over France	
Cost of a stone carved with the donor's initials : 300 francs	
Cost of the building : 40 million francs	
Architects : Paul Abadie, succeded by Honoré Daumet, Charles Laisné, Henri Rauline, Lucien Magne, Louis-Jean Hulot	
Number of foundation piles : 83	
Depth of the foundations : 110 ft (33 m)	
Length of the building : 280 ft (85 m)	
Width of the building : 115 ft (35 m)	
Height of the dome : 273 ft (83.33 m)	
Interior measurements of the dome : height, 180 ft (55 m); diameter, 53 ft (16 m)	
Height of the campanile : 276 ft (84 m), or more than 690 ft (210 m) counting the height of the hill above sea level	
Area covered by mosaics : 1558 sq ft (475 sq m)	
Weight of La Savoyarde, the great bell : 19 t, the biggest in France	

Merson, Marcel Imbs, and Henri-Marcel Magne. Two bravura pieces are *The Assumption* (in the dome) and *The Triumph of the Sacred Heart* (in the apse apse of the nave). The windows, completed between 1903 and 1921, were destroyed by bombing in 1944 and replaced from 1946 by works by Théodore G Hanssen and Jacques Le Chevallier.

A focus for prayer and pilgrims

When it was consecrated in 1919, the Church of Sacré-Coeur was named a basilica, which for Christians means a place dedicated primarily to the reception of pilgrims. Every year since then, it has been visited by thousands of pilgrims from all over France and throughout the world, be it for large-scale celebrations or a few minutes of silent prayer. People make their devotions in a virtually unbroken stream. At night, when the basilica is closed, the faithful wait in turn, for an hour or more, in silent adoration before the Holy Sacrament. On the first Friday evening of the month, there is an open Night of Adoration when people may come and pray at any time they choose.

1. *St George Slaying the Dragon*
This bronze sculpture, between the bell tower and the largest dome, was sculpted by Sicard and cast at the famous Monduit foundry, which also worked with Viollet-le-Duc.

2. Building the basilica
Although impressive, the basilica conceals almost half its structure below ground. The Montmartre sub-soil had been weakened by gypsum quarrying, and the foundations had to be more than 110 ft (33 m) deep. A vast crypt was dug out beneath the nave.

3. Communicants in May, 1939
As well as a sight for tourists, the basilica is also a focal point in France for pilgrimages. Every year, almost two million Christians come to worship the Sacred Heart of Jesus. At Easter, there is a large procession from the foot of the hill to the church.

4. *The Triumph of the Sacred Heart*
The mosaic in the apse of the nave, by Henri-Marcel Magne and Luc-Olivier Merson, shows the Sacred Heart of Jesus being glorified by the Catholic Church of France. This part of the church is lavishly decorated with murals.

141

The Butte Montmartre

Tourists on the hunt for a real village atmosphere in a well-conserved area are often happy just to visit Place du Tertre and a few surrounding streets. However, the real attractions of the Butte are to be found a little further away. Montmartre's rich character lies in its diverse history, its inhabitants, and its architecture. The hill, which became part of central Paris in 1860, has always attracted mystics and been a strategic fortress, as well as providing the setting for the most astonishing artistic innovations of the 19th century. Apart from the basilica, its buildings are fairly modest. To appreciate the real style of the place, you have to stroll around its steep lanes and tiny shaded squares. Its attractions include interestingly designed studios, a shaded walk, an Art Nouveau window, a pink house painted by Utrillo, and a wonderful view from the top of a flight of steps.

The sacred hill

◆ From Mercury to Jesus

This hill, dominated by the 19th-century basilica dedicated to the Sacred Heart of Jesus, was already a sacred place in Roman times. At that time it was dedicated to the cult of Mercury, the god of merchants, thieves, and travelers. By the 6th century there was a small settlement with a chapel and cemetery. In the 9th century, in memory of the early Christians mar-

tyred there, the best-known being Saint Denis, first bishop of Paris (3rd century), it was called the Mount of Martyrs, whence its present-day name, Montmartre. In 1096, the monks of Saint-Martin des Champs founded the first abbey on the Butte. This became an influential convent for nuns when the Benedictines took it over in 1134 at the instigation of the king. The Church of Saint-Pierre is the only site remaining from this royal abbey. Other religious founda-

tions located nearby are the Carmelite convent of Montmartre, founded in 1928, where today some 20 nuns live in seclusion, and the Benedictine Priory whose nuns help welcome pilgrims to the basilica.

◆ Church of Saint-Pierre

The Church of Saint-Pierre was built in the second half of the 12th century and substantially altered in later years; its façade dates from 1755. In the Revolution (1794) it was renamed the Temple of Reason before being reinstated as a place of worship the following year. Later it served as a station for Chappe's telegraph, and a special tower was built above the choir. With its semi-circular and ogival vaults, Saint-Pierre-de-Montmartre is rich in late Romanesque, pre-Gothic architecture. Though threatened with demolition, it was eventually restored by Louis Savageot between 1899 and 1905. Two modern features are the windows by Max Ingrand (1954) and the carved bronze doors by Tommasi Gismondi (1980).

◆ The Cimetière du Calvaire

To the left of the square in front of the church, an iron gate opens onto the Cimetière du Calvaire, a classified monument. It was built for the parishioners of Montmartre at the

end of the 17th century, and has long been a burial place. Sarcophagi dating from the late Roman Empire and the Merovingian period have been discovered. Only open on All Saints' Day (November 1), this is the smallest and oldest cemetery in Paris.

From guns to folklore

◆ *A rebellious tradition*

The strategically important heights of the Butte were occupied by the future Henri IV in 1590, by Russian Cossacks in 1814 and by the English in 1815. Montmartre acquired a reputation for rebelliousness. After being declared a "free commune" in 1790, the Butte saw the first bloody episode of the Paris Commune. On March 18, 1871, when the army was ordered by Thiers to capture the 171 cannons assembled on the Butte by the National Guard in opposition to the armistice, the mob intervened. Communards captured Generals

1. Place du Tertre
Once a village square with a Town Hall, the square today is a must-see venue for tourists, many of whom cannot resist having their portraits drawn.

2. Slow race, Rue Lepic
There have always been eccentric events on the Butte. At the beginning of the 20th century they had "slow races," the object being to move as slowly as possible up Rue Lepic and be the last to arrive in Place du Tertre. Spectators helped the competitors to slow down.

3. Steps on Rue des Saules
Crossing the Butte is all about going up one lot of steps and down another. Like Rue Mont-Cenis, Rue des Saules leads from the heart of the Butte down to the Town Hall of the 18th *arrondissement*.

4. Harvest, Montmartre-style
The grape harvest in Montmartre takes place each year. The vines were planted in 1929 on the corner of Rues des Saules and Saint-Vincent by local inhabitants anxious to stop new apartments being built on the site. Harvest-time is accompanied by a grand procession in costume.

143

Lecomte and Thomas and shot them. This ignited a trail of violence that spread through Paris.

Place du Tertre

◆ *A Mecca for tourists*

Before it moved to Place des Abbesses, Montmartre's first town hall was located in Place du Tertre, with Georges Clemenceau one of its first occupants. This square is now the center of tourism in Montmartre, visited by nearly four million people a year.

You can quite often find Rue Saint-Rustique completely deserted, while the whole of Rue Norvins is packed with people going to and from the Place du Tertre and Rue Lepic. The painters took over the square almost a century ago and make most of their money from the tourist hordes.

◆ *Almost a stage set*

In many ways, Montmartre looks quite like a stage set. Take the vineyard on Rue des Saules. It was planted by a committee anxious to prevent the famous architect Henri Savage from building a terrace of apartments. They acquired the land and turned it into a green space.

By planting these vines, even on a

north slope, they were also reviving the memory of a very old tradition of wine-growing on the Butte. Ever since, each harvest has been accompanied by a procession in costume led by the mayor of the "free commune" of Montmartre, and several hundred liters of wine are auctioned.

Belle Epoque and bohemian life

The Moulin de la Galette, in Rue Girardon, and the Lapin Agile

cabaret in Rue des Saules have played an important part in the Montmartre legend. The old windmill is no longer open to the public, but you can still watch an evening's cabaret at the Lapin Agile.

◆ *Moulin de la Galette*

The Moulin de la Galette (the windmill also called Blute-Fin) was at the height of its popularity in the Second Empire and Third Republic, and was immortalized in 1894 by Renoir

in a painting that now hangs in the Musée d'Orsay. It all started when the miller, a man called Debray, had the idea of opening a dance hall and serving hot pancakes. People rushed there to drink and dance beneath the trees and the great wooden sails. Today, from Rue Lepic, you can still see the tops of the trees and two windmills.

◆ Le Lapin Agile

Montmartre's oldest cabaret has hardly changed since the time when Van Gogh, Picasso, and Renoir went there. It was bought in 1902 by the cabaret singer Aristide Bruant and then taken over by Frédéric Gérard, known as Frédé. Here stars such as Pierre Brasseur, Annie Girardot, Georges Brassens, and Claude Nougaro performed. Today, too,

young singers come to try their luck. The cabaret's sign, a rabbit escaping the stew pot, was designed around 1900 by the humorist André Gill when it was no more than a modest restaurant with a reputation for sauté of rabbit. The sign gave it its new name, the Lapin à Gill ("Gill's Rabbit"), which soon became the "Lapin Agile."

◆ Artists in Montmartre

Around 1900, Montmartre became a magnet for penniless artists in search of picturesque settings. Painters, writers and musicians enjoyed a bohemian existence, as recounted by Francis Carco and Roland Dorgelès in From Montmartre to the Latin Quarter (1927) and In the Heyday of the Butte (1963). As early as the 1930s, however, people started complaining about the transformation of Montmartre into a folksy tourist village.

◆ The Bateau Lavoir

The studios of the Bateau Lavoir or "Floating Laundry" stand on Place Emile-Goudeau, a pretty little tree-shaded square with a drinking fountain, formerly called Place Ravignan. Although destroyed by fire in 1970, they were rebuilt and still provide space for artists. At the beginning of the 20th century they were simple

wooden studios, with no electricity and a communal standpipe. This was where Georges Braque, Juan Gris, Adameo Modigliani and Picasso painted some of their most famous works.

Avenue Junot: a modern intruder

◆ The avenue by the Château

Avenue Junot dates from 1910, and brought modern planning to the edge of the village. This 490 yd (450 m)–long thoroughfare was part of a massive road-building project, typical of the Haussmann period, aimed at relieving the area round Sacré-Coeur. Parts of the streets of old Montmartre (Rues Girardon, du Mont-Cenis, des Saules, and de l'Abreuvoir) were to be demolished but, fortunately, the scheme was not completed. The waste ground, overgrown with wild grasses and covered with shacks, disappeared when Rue Caulaincourt was laid out, but the legendary Château des Brouillards, the beautiful 18th-century white mansion where Gérard de Nerval lived, is still the stuff of dreams for lovers walking past it.

◆ Palaces for artists

Avenue Junot was soon filled with private mansions and artists' studios. These broke with the boh-

---

1. Moulin de la Galette
Of the 30 windmills that stood on the Butte in the 19th century, only two have survived: Moulin de la Galette, also called Blute-Fin, and Moulin Radet. Today they stand inside an enclosure that once housed a famous dance hall, the Moulin de la Galette, painted by Auguste Renoir in 1894.

2. Place Emile-Goudeau
Strolling from one square to the next is one of the pleasures of Montmartre. As well as the small hotel once called the Hôtel de l'Europe, Place Emile-Goudeau, formerly Place Ravignan, is home to the Bateau-Lavoir. Many artists lived in this studio complex, and it was here that Picasso painted his famous Demoiselles d'Avignon in 1907.

3. Toulouse-Lautrec
As he chronicled the night life and cabaret scene in Montmartre, Toulouse-Lautrec made a legend of La Goulue, chief dancer at the Moulin Rouge.

4. Lapin Agile
This little restaurant in Rue des Saules took its name from the humorist André Gill who drew its sign. The Lapin à Gill quickly became the "Lapin Agile." Many artists were regulars at this night spot, once known as the Cabaret des Assassins.

emian tradition of the rudimentary studio, and reflected a new luxurious lifestyle. Francisque Poulbot, who painted everyday life on the Butte, lived there, and a little further on, at No 36, is architect Adolphe Thiers' residence for artists with its refined lines and big windows. From the main door, you can glimpse the richness of its interior decoration.

At No 22 Rue Simon-Dereure, a pretty bas-relief adorns the entrance to the former villa-studio of the sculptor Louis-Aimé Lejeune, another building by Adolphe Thiers, who also designed the "Montmartre for Artists" complex at 187-189 Rue Ordener.

◆ A Dada house

At No 15 Avenue Junot is the house of the Dada writer Tristan Tzara, designed by Viennese architect Adolf Loos in 1924. This is the most remarkable house on the street, its sober façade contrasting abruptly with its rich interior. Set on a large stone base, the second story consists of a smooth wall with a large loggia set into it. The full measure of Loos'

talent can be seen in the way he organized the interior space into a series of different levels, making each room highly functional and giving it a strong individual identity.

Place des Abbesses

◆ Art Nouveau Métro entrance

On the southern slopes of the Butte, Place des Abbesses is the center of a lively area full of shops, cafés, and restaurants. Here the fashionable world rubs shoulders amiably with the village spirit of old Montmartre. In the square, the Art Nouveau Métro entrance is the work of Hector Guimard. It used to be at Hôtel de Ville station before it was brought here in 1970. This and the one at Porte Dauphine are the only two in Paris to have kept their glasswork.

◆ Paris' first modern church

The Church of Saint-Jean-l'Evangeliste, also known as Saint-Jean de Montmartre (1894-1904), is Paris's first modern church. Abbot Sobeaux commissioned it from Anatole de Baudot, a disciple of Viollet-le-Duc, to compensate for the lack of space at Saint-Pierre.

It is made of brick and reinforced concrete (a system patented by the engineer Paul Cottancin), its façade clad in glazed sandstone, and exudes an extraordinary impression of lightness.

With its columns 82 ft (25 m) high and 18 in (50 cm) wide, and vaulting no wider than 3 in (7 cm), it was feared that it would collapse, and building was halted for a time. Although the construction method was new, the architect's taste for the Gothic is clear to see. The interior was decorated from 1913, and includes frescos in the choir by Alfred Plauzeau and Art Nouveau windows in the nave by Jac-Galland from drawings by Pascal Blanchard.

---

1. Château des Brouillards
Made famous by Gérard de Nerval, this mansion also once belonged to Pierre-Auguste Renoir and his son Pierre, the actor. Through the window, Pierre wrote, "You could see Mont Valérien and the hills of Meudon, Argenteuil, and Saint-Cloud, and the plain of Gennevilliers. In clear weather, you could see the Basilica of Saint-Denis. We were truly in heaven."

2. The Tristan Tzara house
The Tzara house, designed for an avant-garde writer by an avant-garde architect, is Adolf Loos's only building in Paris. The façade's strong, sober lines set it apart from the private mansions and Art Deco artist's studios in the vicinity.

3. Villa Léandre
This villa at 23 *bis* Avenue Junot stands in a cul-de-sac next to small apartment buildings. It was built in 1926, and ten years later took the name of the Montmartre humanist Charles Léandre.

◆ Théâtre des Abbesses

It is rare to find a contemporary building in Montmartre, but the Théâtre des Abbesses, annexed to the Théâtre de la Ville, was built in 1996. It has a distinctive red-painted pediment and its Neo-Classical façade is a mark of architect Charles Vandenhove's respect for the local architecture. Inside, the controversial painted decorations by Olivier Debré are the dominant feature. Everything about this atypical work is aimed at creating a total spectacle.

Museums and Curiosities

◆ Intimate museums

Montmartre has several small museums, some of which may only be visited by appointment. One such is Erik Satie's "cupboard", the tiny room where the composer of the *Gymnopédies* lived. The Museum of Montmartre, at the end of a garden in Rue Cortot, relates the history of the Butte. It occupies a small 17th-century manor house which belonged to an actor in Molière's troupe. At the beginning of the 20th century, part of the house was divided into artists' studios and the artists Dufy and Suzanne Valadon, and the latter's son, Maurice Utrillo, lived there.

The Espace Montmartre-Salvador Dali provides a theatrical setting for sculptures, engravings and distorted images (anamorphoses) by the Surrealist artist.

◆ A jumble of curiosities

On the Butte you can stumble across all kinds of curious things. Rue de l'Armée-d'Orient is one of those quiet places whose many charms are seldom explored. The "Jewish court-

---

4. Entrance to Abbesses Métro station
This wonderful entrance, designed by Hector Guimard, came from the station at Hôtel de Ville. Along with the Church of Saint-Jean de Montmartre, built in brick and reinforced conrete by A de Baudot, this Art Nouveau masterpiece gives Place des Abbesses a strong 1900s atmosphere.

5. Théâtre des Abbesses
Designed in 1996 by the Belgian architect C Vandenhove, this small theater combines the intriguing look of a Neo-Classical temple with a red façade that echoes the bricks of Saint-Jean de Montmartre. Standing at the end of a courtyard, the theater is sympathetically flanked by an apartment building with fluted columns.

yard" at 40 Rue Durantin, with its central staircase, is an exceptional piece of 19th-century Restoration-period architecture. In the Impasse Marie-Blanche there is a house, built in the Troubadour style in the 19th century, that echoes some of the decorative elements at the Hôtel de Charles de l'Escalopier (1835), which

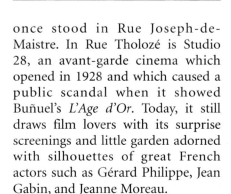

once stood in Rue Joseph-de-Maistre. In Rue Tholozé is Studio 28, an avant-garde cinema which opened in 1928 and which caused a public scandal when it showed Buñuel's *L'Age d'Or*. Today, it still draws film lovers with its surprise screenings and little garden adorned with silhouettes of great French actors such as Gérard Philippe, Jean Gabin, and Jeanne Moreau.

Beneath the Butte

The areas around the Butte vary greatly in atmosphere, some geared to tourists, the others more typically Parisian. On the east side, narrow bazaar-like streets are lined with shops bursting with brightly colored fabrics and braids; to the west is a vast, quiet cemetery where some of the tombs are as ornate as works of art.

Just behind the broad boulevards and the night spots, which buzz with life after dark, are some very peaceful private enclaves with fine 19th-century buildings and charming small museums. Almost everywhere you can find reminders of legendary figures: famous Belle Epoque dancers from the Moulin Rouge such as La Goulue and Jane Avril, or Romantic artists and writers of the Nouvelle Athènes group such as Gustave Moreau and Georges Sand.

Montmartre cemetery

◆ A museum of tomb sculpture

Montmartre cemetery occupies the largest green space in the 18th *arrondissement*, being prominently located to the west of the Butte and covering 30 acres (12 ha). It was laid out in 1798 under the Directoire and has seen many changes. A random walk along its pathways reveals a large number of works of art, architecture, and sculpture. The numerous sculptures include the recumbent figure of Godefroy Cavaignac, carved by François Rude, the bust of Castagnary by Auguste Rodin, and the Art Nouveau tomb of Emile Zola, whose ashes were later transferred to the Panthéon.

◆ Famous occupants

Many famous people are buried in this cemetery, some of whom had a great influence on life in Montmartre. They include the writers Vigny, Stendhal, and Sacha Guitry, painters Greuze and Fragonard, composer Berlioz, and La Goulue, star of the Moulin Rouge who was painted by Toulouse-Lautrec. Among the more recent arrivals are the singer Dalida, film-maker François Truffaut and author-composer Michel Berger.

From Place Saint-Pierre to the Goutte d'Or

Place Saint-Pierre is a very lively place, a mixture of visitors to Sacré-Coeur Parisians and people from the Ile-de-France who come to Saint-Pierre market to buy fabrics from the extraordinary range on display.

◆ Halle Saint-Pierre and the Museum of Naïve Art

To the east of the square, the Halle Saint-Pierre was built as a covered market in 1868 and has retained its typical Second Empire style: a cast-iron structure with brick and mill-stone infill. It was renovated in 1986, and now houses the Musée en Herbe (children's museum), and the Max Fourny Museum of Naïve Art which has a fascinating collection of paintings and sculptures, and stages interesting temporary exhibitions.

◆ The old Dufayel department stores

A short distance away, along the Rue Andrea-del-Sarte, you can see the sculptures by Falguière and Dalou on the impressive façade of the old Dufayel department stores. This vast retail enterprise was built in 1895 in metal and freestone by Gustave Rives, and at the time was on a par with the *grands magasins* on Boulevard Haussmann. Only the façades have been preserved.

◆ The Goutte d'Or

The Goutte d'Or district was described by Emile Zola in *L'Assom-moir*, and celebrated in song by Aristide Bruant. It has since undergone enormous changes but has retained the exotic exuberance for which it has been renowned for 50 years. The Villa Poissonnière, built in 1840, is a haven of greenery (access via No 42 Rue de la Goutte-d'Or). Further north, the Church of Saint-Bernard, built by Lucien Magne (1861), is the only church in Paris inspired by the 15th-century Late Gothic style.

Entertainments at the foot of the hill

Beneath Sacré-Coeur and the splendid Square Willette, laid out between 1880 and 1932 to plans by Jean-Camille Formigé, is a lively entertainment district that goes back to the 19th century.

◆ Théâtre de l'Atelier

The Théâtre de l'Atelier is a modest building in a small shady square which has an almost provincial charm. It was designed in 1822 by Louis-Pierre Haudebourt and has become a real institution. In the 1920s, the actor-director Charles Dullin staged highly innovative pieces there, with scenery designed by Picasso. His successors have continued its intimate tradition, putting on both a classical repertoire and contemporary plays.

◆ The Elysée-Montmartre and the Trianon

The Boulevard de Rochechouart is the departure point for tours of Montmartre and is intensely busy at night. The Elysée-Montmartre started life at the beginning of the 19th century and reached the height

of its fame in the 1880s with the performances by La Goulue and Valentin the Rubber Man. Its beautiful façade, dominated by the plaster figure of a female dancer, leads into an auditorium which, after a period as a venue for wrestling and boxing matches, is now devoted to present-day music. From 1902, the Trianon (the former Théâtre Victor Hugo, converted to a cinema in 1936) has occupied part of the Elysée-Montmartre's premises. A fine example of fin-de-siècle architecture, it now puts on a varied program of concerts, films, and theme nights.

◆ La Cigale

In *Montmartre: the pleasure and the crime*, Louis Chevalier, the historian of life in Paris, declared the superiority of the Boulevard du Rochechouart over the Boulevard du Clichy. The former was at once popular and cultivated, the latter lived only for pure pleasure. La Cigale is part of both these worlds. In 1887, it replaced the famous Boule Noire, one of the oldest variety venues in Montmartre. Here, in the interwar years, the revue star Mistinguett rose to fame. The present façade, a sober white wall pierced with portholes, is from 1928. The auditorium was renovated by Philippe Starck at the end of the 1980s.

"Montmartre: the pleasure and the crime"

◆ The Moulin Rouge

The Moulin Rouge has been rebuilt or transformed several times since it opened in 1889. It symbolizes the party spirit, or even the debauchery, of the area around Place Pigalle. The lithographs of Toulouse-Lautrec

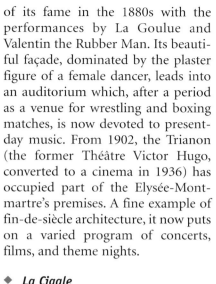

3

4

1. Montmartre cemetery
Built in 1798 and enlarged in 1847 before returning to its original size, this monumental cemetery has witnessed many local changes. In 1888, the viaduct on Rue Caulaincourt was built above the tombs to link the Butte and Place de Clichy.

2. Marché Saint-Pierre
Facing the hall of the same name, Saint-Pierre market is housed in a modern development in Rue Charles-Nodier. Here, Parisians and suburbanites come to buy every imaginable kind of fabric, arranged on various floors. Along with the Tati stores on Boulevard de Rochechouart, Saint-Pierre market is one of the most convivial and socially integrated places in Lower Montmartre.

3. Moulin Rouge
Built in 1889, the most famous review theater in Paris was first rebuilt in 1903 by E Niermans, in an Art Nouveau style. Then in 1925 it was again restyled, this time by A Thiers, who built the artists' studios in Avenue Junot. Only the scarlet windmill, which has overlooked Boulevard de Clichy since the Belle Epoque, has never changed.

4. Museum of Naïve Art
In 1986, the collection of Naïve Art was brought to the Halle Saint-Pierre, which had been renovated by C Charpentier and J Valentin. The former covered market was built in 1868 by a pupil of V Baltard.

immortalized its legendary stars: Jane Avril and La Goulue, the leading *revue* dancers of the Belle Epoque. Crowned by Adolphe Willette's red-painted windmill, it still puts on its famous shows.

◆ Museum of Eroticism

Famous as a center of the sex business, the Boulevard de Clichy has for some years also had a museum wholly devoted to the subject. On its façade, reproductions of works of art lure the passing trade; inside, they display the history of the pleasures of the flesh.

Cul-de-sacs, villas, and secret alleyways

A stone's throw from the bright lights, sex shops and ceaseless din of the Boulevard de Clichy lies another world, a calm and secret place of lanes and alleyways bordered by gardens, picturesque studios, villas, and well-to-do apartments.

◆ Cité Véron, Cité du Midi

Going into the Cité Véron or the Cité du Midi, you can find houses, studios, theaters and former public baths which are full of character. In the 1930s, Cité Véron was the haunt of Pigalle's petty criminals. Jacques Prévert lived there for 20 years, and there too Boris Vian composed his most famous song: *The Deserter*.

◆ Villa des Platanes

The Villa des Platanes is less picturesque but more spectacular, with an extraordinary Italianate porch. At the end of the courtyard stand two

magnificent apartment buildings with monumental staircases and sculptures. This very unusual development was built in 1895 by Edmond Deloeuvre, a local architect who lived in the vicinity of Boulevard de Clichy.

◆ Avenue Frochot

A long time ago, this deluxe private avenue closed off its access to Place Pigalle. Entrance, for residents only, is today via Rue Victor Massé. The street is lined with magnificent mansions in the Gothic and Neo-Classical styles, dating from the 1830s. Alexandre Dumas the Elder, the painter Pierre-Auguste Renoir, and his son Jean, the film director, as well as Toulouse-Lautrec, have lived in this haven. Several show business stars still live there today.

◆ Art Deco stained-glass window

To the left of the entrance to Avenue Frochot (2 Rue Frochot) is an impressively large stained-glass window. Set in fine 1920s wrought iron-work, it depicts waves in a rough sea. This Art Deco work was designed in about 1929 by Akenauer in American industrial glass. The window illuminates a gaming room: the roulette wheel is placed in the centre of the stage of a former theater in the round. This was built in 1954 at the instigation of André Villiers, an apostle of intimate theater who wanted all the spectators to be the same distance from the actors.

◆ Cité Malesherbes

The Cité Malesberbes also leads off Rue Victor Massé. Built in the 1850s, it is lined with private mansions, each having its own garden. The most distinctive of these was built in 1858 by Anatole Jal for the painter Jollivet. The artist decorated it with enameled painted panels, mainly red, which give the façade its unusual appearance.

Romantic Paris and Nouvelle Athènes

In the 9th *arrondissement*, the area around Place Saint-Georges owes its elegant looks to several developments dating from the beginning of the 19th century. At that time, many artists moved into this quiet, leafy

district, which seemed to encourage creative activities, and which they called Nouvelle Athènes (New Athens).

◆ Place Saint-Georges and Place Gustave Toudouze

The lovely Place Saint-Georges was built in 1824 as a circus around a fountain and a monument dedicated to the illustrator Gavarni. At No 27, the mansion of Adolphe Thiers is now a library, and at No 28 the richly decorated Renaissance-style building is the former Hôtel de la Païva. Nearby, Place Gustave Toudouze has a more irregular shape, but is quiet and shady, surrounded by cafés and restaurants.

◆ Museum of Romantic Life

This delightful evocation of Romantic Paris is hidden away in Rue Chaptal at the end of a cobbled courtyard, in the Restoration-period house (19th century) where the painter Ary Scheffer played host to the greatest artists of his day: Ingres, Delacroix, Liszt, Lamartine, and above all Frédéric Chopin and his mistress George Sand. Today it is the Museum of Romantic Life.

◆ Gustave Moreau Museum

No less stimulating is the studio of painter Gustave Moreau, since transformed into a museum according to

his wishes. Here on two floors of a mansion in Rue de la Rochefoucauld, a large collection of works by the Symbolist painter is displayed on the walls and in old cabinets. Everything remains intact, clothed in the magic of Gustave Moreau's paintings.

◆ A cluster of theaters and cabarets

The area at the foot of the Butte is an important center for the Romantic movement and also, since the end of the 19th century, a mecca for theater and cabaret. Venues include the Théâtre de l'Oeuvre, Comédie de Paris, Théâtre Saint-Georges, Casino de Paris, and many more.

◆ Two 19th-century churches

South of Nouvelle Athènes, two churches embody the renewal of religious art in the 19th century. Notre-Dame-de-Lorette (1823 – 36) is lavishly decorated. For the build-

ing, architect L-H Lebas chose a very sober style inspired by Romanesque Christian basilicas; for its decoration, he called on painters from the Ingres studio (Roger, Orsel, and Picot), whose art combines simplicity of design and magnificent color. Thirty years later (1861–7), Sainte-Trinité was built at the end of Rue de la Chaussée d'Antin. The architect T Ballu wanted to express the bourgeois character of the district by using a Renaissance style. The façade, with its high bell tower, is rich in decorative details; the majestic interior contains one of the best organ cases in Paris.

1. Place Saint-Georges
This circus was laid out in 1824. Its dominant feature is a splendid building designed in 1840 by E Renaud. Typical of the Neo-Renaissance style fashionable under the July monarchy, it was briefly home to the famous Marquise de Païva (1851–2).

2. Entrance to Avenue Frochot
The mixture of building styles does not impair the charm of this private avenue built under the July monarchy by Judge C Picot. To the left of the entrance is one of the most spectacular Art Deco windows in Paris.

3. Façade of Villa des Platanes
For the façade of this 1895 apartment building at 58–60 Boulevard de Clichy, architect E Deloeuvre built a bow window, a design imported from England.

4. Place Pigalle
Like Place Blanche and Place Clichy, this square was laid out following the destruction of the wall of the "farmers-general" by Prefect Haussmann in 1860. Since the beginning of the 20th century, this crossroads between the Butte and Lower Montmartre has been the center of Paris night life, packed with fashionable bars as well as sex shows and prostitutes.

5. Museum of Romantic Life
This Neo-Classical house at the end of a lane off Rue Chaptal, formerly owned by the painter Ary Scheffer, contains a delightful evocation of the years between 1830 and 1850. There are mementos of George Sand, a statue of Chopin, and a reconstruction of the studio of the painter, a friend of King Louis-Philippe.

THE BASTILLE
and surrounding area

Spirit of the Bastille

Around the Bastille

From Nation to Belleville

The New East

Vincennes

Aerial view of the Place de la Bastille
This bird's eye view clearly shows the
different aspects of the surrounding districts.
On one side are Haussmann's apartment
buildings and straight boulevards, on the
other a marina and a less formal area with a
more provincial atmosphere, in which the
modernity of the Opera House is not
intrusive.

Spirit of the Bastille

The name Bastille alone is enough to summon thoughts of revolution, liberty, equality, and fraternity. We think immediately of July 14, 1789, the day the people captured the prison, a symbol of royal despotism, of which only minute traces remain. We think less readily of the revolutions of 1830 and 1848, uprisings led by working–class people. And yet, it is they who are remembered in the July Column, where the Spirit of the Bastille holds aloft the torch of Liberty.

The July Column

◆ The Spirit of Liberty

The Spirit stands with one foot on the earth's globe, the other poised for flight as its wings start to beat. In one hand it grasps the broken chains of slavery, in the other the torch of Liberty. The Spirit of Liberty, or "Spirit of the Bastille," was sculpted by Dumont and stands on a column 170 ft (51.5 m) high. It is dedicated "To the glory of French citizens who took up arms and fought for the defense of public liberty in the memorable days of July 27, 28, 29, 1830."

◆ The 504 victims

Inaugurated in 1840, this bronze column, designed by the architects Jean-Antoine Alavoine and Joseph-Louis Duc, was inspired by Trajan's Column in Rome. The names of the 504 victims of the "Three Glorious Days" of revolution are engraved on its shaft. At the four corners of its white marble pedestal stand bronze figures of the Gallic cockerel. There are also lion's heads, Leo being the sign of the zodiac for the month of July, and sculptures of the coat of arms of Paris.

◆ Tombs of the insurgents

Originally, the insurgents of 1830 were laid to rest in converted vaults beneath the pedestal. The victims of the 1848 revolution were buried beside them. But in 1871 the Communards, intending to destroy the Column, set fire to a boat they had moored directly below it on the Saint-Martin canal. While the shaft of the Column held firm, flames ravaged the tombs, reducing the skeletons to ashes.

From fortress to prison

◆ Porte Saint-Antoine

The July Column stands on the site of the Porte Saint-Antoine, a gateway built in the 14th century to defend the easternmost entrance to Paris. This gate marked the boundary between city and countryside, and everyone had to pass through it to reach the royal residences of the East, Vincennes in particular. The sovereigns entered their "gentle city" along this road, as did the ambassadors of foreign countries. But it was also the route for enemy invasions. Its strategic position led King Charles V to convert what was an advance post into a fortress.

1 **2**

◆ The Fortress of Saint-Antoine

The first stone of the fortress was laid in 1370, the last 12 years later. Its architecture was inspired by military works in southern France, whence its name *bastide* (fortress) which, as pronounced by Parisians, became *bastille*. Eight towers rose over the fortress and there were four entrance gates. Cannons were ranged along the walls to increase its defenses. During the Fronde, which set the nobility against the young King Louis XIV, the Duchesse de Montpensier ordered the cannon to be fired from the towers of the Bastille at the King's troops gathered in the Faubourg Saint-Antoine.

◆ A legendary prison

As the city grew beyond its ramparts, the Bastille progressively lost its defensive role, and from the time of Louis XI it became a prison. Just a *lettre de cachet*, a letter under the King's seal, was enough to have someone imprisoned. The reasons varied, but the most usual ones were resistance to royal authority or improper behavior. Voltaire, the Chevalier de Latude, and the Marquis de Sade were sent to the Bastille, as were other young men from high society said to have dishonored their families or rank through their behav-

1. Place de la Bastille
The Place de la Bastille has become a fashionable district, and the surrounding area is full of cafés, shops, and restaurants. On the square itself, skateboarders and roller skaters put on their own show.

2. The Spirit of Liberty
An allegory of Liberty, the statue on the July Column symbolizes the revolutionary spirit of Parisians. With one foot on the terrestrial globe, the Spirit brandishes the torch of Liberty in one hand and the broken chains of slavery in the other. The gilded bronze figure by Dumont is 11.5 ft (3.5 m) high.

3. Base of the Column
The July Column stands on a rectangular marble base bearing an historic inscription. The dates (July 27, 28, 29) commemorate the three-day uprising of July 1830, known as the "Three Glorious Days." The Gallic cockerel stands at all four corners.

4. Bastille Opera House
The architecture of the Bastille Opera House was designed to be in keeping with other elements in the square. The curving façade of the building echoes the cylindrical shape of the July Column, here reflected in its tinted windows. The maximum height of the Opera House matches that of the Column: 170 ft (51.5 m) exactly.

Hall of Fame

Marquis de Sade

The Marquis de Sade was imprisoned at the Bastille from 1784 to 1789. The Bastille's high-ranking prisoners enjoyed certain creature comforts. The Marquis de Sade was allowed to use his own furniture and china. He was regularly in touch with the outside world, issuing instructions through his wife who twice a month supplied him with cooked fruit, jams, and cakes. For an agreed sum, paid in cash, the Marquis was served at table by the Governor's butler. He dictated his own menus, each meal beginning with soup, followed by meat, then a cream dessert, and finally cooked apples or pears.

The Arsenal Library, Bastille Archives, MSS 12455 and 12456 ■

ior. Of all those detained, the most mysterious was the Man in the Iron Mask. Even today no one knows who was concealed behind this mask (which was really made of velvet). It may have been Louis XIV's twin brother, financial superintendant Fouquet, or someone else close to the seat of power.

◆ Royal archives

The Bastille was soon also used to store the royal archives. On the eve of the Revolution, the presence of forbidden books and records of important royal affairs, such as the poison scandal of 1675, or the Affair of the Queen's Necklace in 1785, helped to feed the rumor mill: both posed a danger to the throne.

Symbol of the Revolution

◆ *The storming of the Bastille*

On July 14, 1789, the Parisian mob attacked the Bastille. The fortress held only seven prisoners, but it was still the symbol of the King's arbitrary power. Its governor, Launay, was killed, as were the Swiss guards posted there to defend him. The "conquerors of the Bastille," born in the Faubourg Saint-Antoine, became the first heroes of the Revolution. The Bastille was taken in less than four hours, ransacked, and the seven prisoners freed and carried out in triumph. Secret records, archives, and censored publications were thrown into the moat.

Only a few months later the bastion that had resisted all onslaughts for the previous 520 years was razed to the ground. Some of its stones were used to build models of the prison, and others to build the Pont Louis XVI, today the Pont de la Concorde.

◆ *The elephant fountain*

With the Bastille flattened, the First Empire came up with plans to build a fountain in the shape of an elephant, one of the emblems of Napoleon I. In 1815, a rough model in wood, brick, and stone, designed by the architect Alavoine, was put up next to the present-day Opera House. Other monumental projects followed as the square was redeveloped, all aimed at winning back this symbolic place for Paris and its inhabitants. This was where, in *Les Misérables*, Victor Hugo lodged Gavroche, his Paris street urchin who became a hero of the Revolution, dying on the barricades in 1832.

◆ *From one revolution to the next*

The square was central to the revolutions that shook Paris during the 19th century. The riots in July, 1830, the "Three Glorious Days," brought about the fall of Charles X. Many insurgents died in the fighting, and once Louis-Philippe, the "Citizen King," was raised to the throne, he ordered a commemorative column to be erected to the French citizens who died to defend freedom. Inau-

1. Celebrations of July 14, 1790
On July 14, 1790, one year after the Bastille was torn down, a ball was held on the site of the ruins, with decorative arches recreating the shape of the fortress. This celebration, like others held all over Paris, ended a day of festivities to commemorate the 1789 Revolution.

2. Demolition of the Bastille
On July 15, 1789, and without any authorization, nearly 700 workers under a contractor called Palloy set out to demolish the prison. Although most of the work was done by November, 1789, it was not completely finished until April, 1791.

3. Celebrations of July 14, 1936
The Place de la Bastille has kept its strong symbolic powers since 1789. Understandably, it was an important rallying point in 1936 during the big workers' strikes that took place in France and elsewhere in Europe. Today, it is still a popular venue for concerts, sports events, and demonstrations.

4. Elephant fountain
In 1810, to celebrate the construction of the Ourq canals, it was decided to build a monumental fountain on the square. The favored design was an elephant blowing water through its trunk. A stone model was put up, but only lasted a few years.

1

2

gurated in 1840, the July Column was built on the base that had been intended for the elephant fountain. In 1848 there was another uprising against royal authority. Workers and artisans died in their thousands on the Place de la Bastille and in the streets around the Faubourg Saint-Antoine. Their remains joined those of their brothers under the July Column, but in 1871 the Communards reduced their bones to ashes.

◆ On the trail of the Bastille

Apart from the symbolism of the word "Bastille," little remains of the old fortress-prison. In Square Galli, by Pont de Sully, some large blocks of stone lie almost unnoticed among the flowerbeds. These are remains from the Tour de la Liberté, discovered in 1899 at the top of Rue Saint-Antoine and brought here. Otherwise, there is little to see apart from the plan of the Bastille on a marble plaque at No 3 in the square, and the line of cobblestones marking the site of the fortress.

Facts & Figures	
THE COLUMN	
Height : 170 ft (51.5 m)	
Number of steps : 240	
Number of victims' names engraved on shaft : 504	
Weight : 174 t	
THE PRISON	
Dimensions : 223 x 121 ft (68 x 37 m) x 79 ft (24 m) high	
First stone laid : 1370	
Last stone laid : 1382	
Destroyed : July 14–November, 1789	
Number of cells : about 50	
First person imprisoned : Hugues Aubriot	
Number of prisoners when the Bastille fell : 7	

3 **4**

Around the Bastille

From the 1980s onward, the creative avant-garde and the most fashionable meeting-places have moved toward the east side of Paris. First they took over the Marais, then they spread to the Place de la Bastille and the streets to the east, such as Rue de Lappe, Rue de la Roquette, and Rue du Faubourg Saint-Antoine. This old district of craftsmen and workers, with its revolutionary traditions, has been gradually transformed by an influx of architects' offices, artists' studios, galleries, shops, bars, and fashionable restaurants. A large number of young people come to work and play around the Bastille, making some of its streets intensely busy by day and full of life and color in the evening.

Major developments

◆ The Bastille Opera House

The creation of the Bastille Opera House, inaugurated on July 13, 1989, has played an important role in driving the cultural and economic regeneration of eastern Paris. This monumental building by the Canadian architect Carlos Ott was designed to be a new temple of opera, both more modern and more popular than Garnier's Opera House. The great auditorium seats 2,700 people and the multipurpose hall, 600 to 1,500. Acoustic quality was the supreme consideration, dictating the way space and materials were used; stone and wood predominate, particularly oak and pearwood.

◆ Promenade Plantée

From the rear of the Bastille Opera House to the edge of the Bois de Vincennes, the Promenade Plantée, or tree-lined esplanade, has replaced the old Bastille-Vincennes railroad. More than 2.5 miles (4 km) long, it runs along the top of the old viaduct before returning to street level and entering a cutting.

This regeneration work was begun in the wake of building the Bastille Opera House, and involved replacing the ballast and rails with gardens and ponds designed by architect Philippe Mathieux and landscape gardener Jacques Vergely. Running along the viaduct, where it overlooks the street and the traffic by some 33 ft (10 m), the new esplanade offers a rare view of the city and the surrounding rooftops and terraces. It is a great place to enjoy the sun, free from the roar of the traffic below. Then the esplanade strides over the Jardin de Reuilly, and returns to street level in the Allée Vivaldi until it reaches the Reuilly Tunnel. There, next to the pedestrian walkway and still on the site of the old railroad land, is a track for rollerskating and skateboard enthusiasts. The Tunnel itself is enhanced by rockeries and waterfalls. The Promenade Plantée continues through a cutting before returning to street level. Here the pedestrian footpath runs alongside a one-way track for cyclists and rollerskaters heading toward the Bois de Vincennes.

◆ Viaduc des Arts

Beneath the Promenade Plantée, the viaduct's 60-odd arches were renovated by architects Patrick Berger and Jean-Michel Wilmotte to house workshops and arts and crafts shops, and several cafés. Behind the glazed frontages, artisans can be seen at work: restorers of tapestries, silverware, architectural models and antique linen, glass engravers, cabinetmakers, potters, and even stringed instrument makers.

The Viaduc des Arts is almost 1 mile (1.5 km) long, and forms a kind of extension to the nearby Faubourg Saint-Antoine. After Rue Rambouillet the atmosphere changes: instead of craft studios, there are shops selling computers or toys. Here the viaduct comes to an end.

◆ Port de l'Arsenal

With its 176 berths, the Arsenal basin is a real boating harbor in the middle of Paris. Where the Seine and the Canal Saint-Martin meet (the latter covered by the Boulevard Richard-Lenoir from the Place de la Bastille up to the Rue du Faubourg-du-Temple), pleasure boats and some barges can sail up to the Bassin de la Villette and the Canal de l'Ourcq in the north of the city. Mostly, it is place where Parisians and tourists like to relax and enjoy a change of scenery, strolling from the Bastille down to the harbor through the gardens laid out along the banks.

A picturesque district

Behind the Bastille, on either side of the Rue du Faubourg Saint-Antoine, is a labyrinth of streets, alleys, and courtyards, where all the trades related to furniture-making once grouped together, alongside bars, dance halls, and brothels. It was a district where people worked hard and played hard. Nowadays, trendy South American- and Asian-style restaurants are gradually replacing the pleasure spots once owned by people from the Auvergne. Furniture shops with their gleaming gilt have given way to art galleries and fashion boutiques; the passages are flourishing and being converted to private apartments; the courtyards have been smartened up by young Internet companies, and the Bastille is still one of the most lively districts in Paris.

◆ Rue de Lappe

Lined with bars, restaurants, and nightclubs, the little Rue de Lappe carries on some of the Bastille's traditions from the time when it was called the "Bastoche." In the 19th century it was crowded with dance halls, where the upper classes came to slum it among the "Apaches", the hooligans of the day. Scrap merchants from the Auvergne, who had migrated to the city, opened the first dance halls, converting their warehouses and workshops into improvised dance halls. Striking up on their flutes or musettes, a kind of bagpipe, they pulled in the dancers.

Gradually, these dance halls became permanent features. The arrival of increasing numbers of Italians in the 20th century brought further changes. Their instrument, the accordion, took over from the musette. The most famous *bal musette*, the "Balajo" ("Jo's dance hall"), was founded in 1936 and still attracts crowds of night owls. Inaugurated by Mistinguett, it was host to many great figures of cinema, song, and sport, such as Jean Gabin, Edith Piaf, and Marcel Cerdan.

◆ Rue de la Roquette

The Rue de Charonne and Rue de la Roquette both contain lively

---

1. Viaduc des Arts
The arches of this old railroad viaduct are now filled with boutiques and restoration workshops. The glass-fronted arcades opening onto Avenue Daumesnil reveal the workings of many little-known trades and also sell contemporary designs.

2. The Promenade Plantée
This is a "green corridor" laid out in a varied series of carefully cultivated plots and wild gardens, with unexpected views of the city. Here people can stroll for almost 2 miles (3 km), free of any traffic. The promenade follows the old railroad line, which until the middle of the 20th century connected the Gare de la Bastille with Vincennes.

3. Bastille Opera House
The Opéra-Bastille was designed by the Canadian architect Carlos Ott. The main stage in the largest hall can seat 2,700 people, and is surrounded by five secondary stages, which can be used for rapid scene changes.

4. Arsenal basin
Sheltered from the urban helter-skelter of Place de la Bastille, the Arsenal basin gives Parisians a real haven of peace and quiet. Its harbor is used by commercial and pleasure craft. A garden runs along one of its banks from Place de la Bastille to the Pont Morland.

5. Chapelle des Lombards
This nightspot in Rue de Lappe is surrounded by cafés, restaurants and discos. Known for its Afro music, it continues the tradition of popular dance halls in this lively district.

ing of the royal abbey of Saint-Antoine-des-Champs attracted large numbers of people seeking protection at the convent. In the 15th century, the king granted the nuns of the abbey a privilege exempting the Faubourg's artisans from the restrictive authority of the guilds. As a consequence, many more craft workers rapidly settled to the east of the Bastille. Furniture was their chief product, mainly because it was easy to transport wood along the Seine to supply the workshops. Virtually the whole population worked together: cabinetmakers, varnishers, marquetry designers, casemakers, upholsterers, bronzers, gilders, and so on. In the 19th century, the growth of the furniture trade brought changes to both production and sales methods. Machines were increasingly used, and workshops became specialized. Buildings were purpose-built for use as workshops: the ground and second stories had large windows fixed to cast-iron frames, while the upper floors were residential. Today, because of foreign competition, there are fewer artisans, but those that remain are guardians of a "craft memory," the trustees of skills handed down over the years and respected worldwide.

◆ **Courtyards and alleyways**

By all working together, these trades formed a very special urban fabric. A maze of courtyards and passages draws the visitor into the heart of an

unassuming but surprising world. First to attract the eye are the carriage entrances on the Rue du Faubourg leading into the little islands of calm where artisans ply their trade. Then there are the closely-set windows on the different floors, indicating the presence of workshops. These cobbled ways have a provincial charm of their own, linking various side streets away from the main roads. The Passage l'homme on the Rue de Charonne hides away almost secretively. The Passage du Chantier on the Rue du Faubourg has a different feel, with its many manufacturers' stores. The bright signboards, the carpets outside the doors, and the bustling sales assistants all contribute to its unusual atmosphere.

◆ **From the abbey to the hospital**

Founded in 1795 on the site of the old royal abbey of Saint-Antoine-des-Champs, the Saint Antoine hospital consists mainly of buildings dating from the 19th century, like the arches at the entrance. André Wogensky, who had worked with Le Corbusier, was responsible for others built in the 1960s. Of the abbey, nothing has survived from the 12th century. The Clock pavilion, opposite the hospital entrance, was rebuilt in the 1770s before the Revolution forced the nuns to leave, and one of the fountains, built in 1719 on the orders of Louis XV, stands opposite the hospital entrance.

passages, courtyards, shops, and bistros, and the latter also has a public garden, something rare in this district of few green spaces. The two symmetrical pavilions marking the entrance to the Square Marcel Rajman are remains from the old Petite Roquette prison, which stood around the garden until 1970. This prison, built in 1836, was for children and young delinquents. To rehabilitate them, the authorities relied less on the virtues of imprisonment and more on setting an example. The Petite Roquette was right next door to the Grande Roquette prison, a place reserved for prisoners awaiting transfer and those condemned to death. The guillotine was set up in front of the two pavilions, equally close to both prisons, to serve as a warning. The five stones used to wedge the wooden parts of the guillotine – and which gave the prison the nickname of "the abbey of the five stones" – still stand opposite the Rue de la Croix-Faubin.

◆ **Rue du Faubourg Saint-Antoine**

In contrast with the great Haussmann boulevards, the Rue du Faubourg Saint-Antoine has retained its architectural diversity, reflecting both the styles of the past and the importance of the furniture trade in the area. As the principal axis of eastern Paris, it had earlier been the main road east to the countryside and the royal residence at Vincennes. From the 12th century onward, the found-

◆ *The Aligre market*
Every morning except Monday, the Aligre district becomes extremely lively. Food sellers and bric-a-brac dealers crowd the square, and for a few hours turn it into a kind of souk. The rest of the time, specialist traders such as greengrocers, butchers, fishmongers, and cheese-sellers operate from a single building.

1. The Balajo
In 1935, Georges France (nicknamed Jojo) bought the Café Au Vrai de Vrai and renamed it Bal à Jo. This dance hall has become a real staple of Bastille life, a favorite of celebrities such as Jean Gabin and Edith Piaf. Today's young trendsetters still come to dance here alongside the regulars.

2. Courtyard at 13 Rue Titon
This courtyard façade with its many windows is typical of the Faubourg Saint-Antoine. Here in these studios people can work for long periods in natural light. Many artisans have been replaced by residents in search of a quiet neighborhood, and many workshops have become art galleries and fashion boutiques.

3. Rue du Faubourg Saint-Antoine
Famed for its furniture-making, this district has a network of courtyards and alleyways filled with craft workshops, like this *passage* with its manufacturers' shops.

4. Aligre market
At this picturesque market they sell both food and bric-a-brac, the dealers and customers huddled around piled-up displays of natural produce and more exotic goods.

From Nation to Belleville

The Place de la Nation is the easternmost of the principal squares in Paris. It stands almost straight in line with the Louvre, Place de la Concorde and Etoile. This was where Louis XIV triumphantly entered the city in 1660 with his young wife, Marie-Thérèse. Later, it witnessed the dark hours of the guillotine before becoming now, like the Place de la Bastille and the Place de la République, the rallying point for all kinds of demonstrations. The Avenue Philippe-Auguste, which runs away north, leads to Père-Lachaise cemetery, a resting-place for the deceased and a popular park for the living, and continues up to the old villages of Ménilmontant and Belleville.

The Nation district

◆ Place de la Nation

This square was called the Place du Trône in the 17th century, and a large triumphal arch was put up to honor the entry into the city of Louis XIV and Marie-Thérèse.
In the Revolution it was renamed the Place du Trône-Renversé (Square of the Overturned Throne). Around 1,300 victims were guillotined there in less than a month and a half. It returned to its earlier name of Place du Trône in 1805 and finally became Place de la Nation in 1880. The old name survives today in the short Avenue du Trône, the Passage du Trône, and the nearby Rue des Colonnes du Trône. Here too was the Foire du Trône, the fair held there from the 19th century to 1965, when it moved to the Pelouse de Reuilly in the Bois de Vincennes.

◆ The Triumph of the Republic

In the middle of the Place de la Nation is *Le Triomphe de la République*. Sculpted by Jules Dalou and inaugurated in 1899, this bronze group, 36 ft (11 m) high, symbolizes the victory of France and the values of the Republic: Liberty, Justice, Labor, and Law.

◆ Columns and pavilions

The tollhouses still standing by the Cours de Vincennes are survivals from the time of the "farmers-general" (1697-1789), and were built under Louis XVI by Claude-Nicolas Ledoux. The two columns, 98.5 ft (30 m) high, were crowned in the 19th century by statues of St Louis, by Antoine Etex, and of Philippe-Auguste, by Alexandre Dumont. The former represents justice, the other military power, and both were designed to promote the unification of France and the concept of nationhood.

◆ Picpus cemetery

When the guillotine was set up on the present Place de la Nation, its victims were thrown into communal graves dug in the nearby gardens of Picpus convent. In the 19th century, families of the victims bought up the land, and established a community of nuns to pray for the dead. Among the victims were such famous people as La Fayette, Chateaubriand, and André Chénier. The cemetery can be visited, and the list of those executed, some 1,300 in total, can be seen in the convent chapel.

Père-Lachaise cemetery

When it was built in 1804, this cemetery stood on the outskirts of Paris on the site of an old Jesuit house. In the 17th century its Superior, Père La Chaise, was confessor to Louis XIV. Given the task of developing the site, Brongniart, architect of the Stock Exchange, aimed to make not only a burial place but also a garden.

To increase its attractiveness as a cemetery, the tombs of Abélard and Héloïse, La Fontaine, and Molière were transferred there.

◆ A place for walks and memories

With its 110 acres (44 ha) and 5,300 trees, the Père-Lachaise cemetery attracts more than two million visitors a year, drawn by the charm of its romantic pathways and the beauty of its 19th-century tombs. Among the many famous people buried there (alongside many more who remain anonymous) are writers Marcel Proust and Oscar Wilde, composer Georges Bizet, archeologist Champollion, and Doors singer Jim Morrison. One of the most visited tombs is that of Allan Kardec, founder of Spiritism.

◆ The Wall of the Federalists

Dedicated to the memory of the 147 Communards executed on May 27, 1871, the Wall of the Federalists (Mur des Fédérés) is one of the cemetery's main places for contemplation and pilgrimage. This final tragic episode in the bloody week of May 21–28 brought the uprisings to an end and confirmed the victory of the ruling powers. The insurgents, who had taken refuge in the pathways of the cemetery, were shot against this wall by troops of the Thiers government. A further 1,800 Communards were buried beside them.

Belleville and Ménilmontant

Perched upon hills, these old villages became part of the capital in 1860. A century later, when people thought the only way to renovate a district was to demolish it and put up rows of apartment blocks, these communities suffered a great deal. Since then, the inhabitants have joined together to try to preserve what remains of the spirit of the place. Instead of outright destruction, they campaigned for the rehabilitation of run-down housing, dilapidated workshops, and disused factories. As a result, amid the over-regimented high-rise blocks you can still find a few hidden gardens, flights of steps, and cobbled alleys lined with small houses.

◆ Parc de Belleville

Flights of steps and gently sloping, winding paths guide the visitor through the Parc de Belleville, covering more than 10 acres (4 ha) with a rise and fall of 82 ft (25 m). Designed by François Debulois and Paul Brichet, it symbolizes the history of the district with its few acres of vines (Pinot Meunier and Chardonnay varieties), and its fountains and grottos recalling earlier springs and gypsum quarries.

◆ The Apaches

Life in these two villages took on another dimension with the construction in the mid-19th century of fortifications to protect the capital. Here on the fringes of the city, rival gangs of young thugs, nicknamed "Apaches" by the press, settled their feuds. Some notorious figures emerged from this criminal group, their reputations becoming inflated over the years, like that of Amélie Hélie. Nicknamed "Casque d'Or," she was brought to the screen by Simone Signoret in a memorable 1952 film (Casque d'Or/Golden Marie), directed by Jean Becker. The spirit of rebellion was especially strong at the time of the Paris Commune in 1871. Belleville rose up and its inhabitants joined in the fight, many sacrificing their lives.

◆ Cabarets and masquerades

Belleville and Ménilmontant were the favored places for dance halls and cabarets. Every year, on the eve of Lent, young people paraded down from here to the Tuileries. This descente de la Courtille, or "parade from the Pleasure Gardens," lasted until the beginning of the 19th century, and brought together people from all walks of life for a few hours of wild release.

---

1. Place de la Nation
The former Place du Trône reveals a blend of republican and royal themes. The statues of Philippe-Auguste and Saint Louis crown the columns of the old wall of the "farmers-general", their backs turned to Dalou's sculpture of Le Triomphe de la République.

2. Mayday demonstration
Like the Bastille and the République, the Nation is an obligatory port-of-call for all political demonstrations, especially Mayday processions celebrating Labor.

3. Place Edouard Renard
Close to the Museum of African and Oceanian Arts at Porte Dorée, this scuplture of France the Civiliser by Léon Driver, a pupil of Rodin, recalls the country's colonial past.

4. Père-Lachaise cemetery
This most famous of Parisian cemeteries – Molière, Balzac, Chopin, and Oscar Wilde are all buried here – is a good place to walk and admire the splendid mausoleums and countless statues.

5. Parc de Belleville
There are fine views from the terraces of this park laid out on the hillside at Belleville. Here you can really appreciate how hilly the city is.

The New East

S everal landmark buildings in the city's New East have sprung up on either side of the Seine, stimulating a significant transformation of that part of the city. The all-sports stadium at Bercy, the Palais Omnisports, opened in 1982, the Ministry of Economy and Finance in 1989, the National Library in 1996. Work is still in progress, and controversies have yet to be resolved over how some areas should be developed, especially on the Left Bank, but the basic policy of realignment toward the east of Paris, supported by the state and the city since the 1970s and 1980s, has already borne fruit. The opening in 1998 of the Météor Métro line, linking the National Library to the Madeleine via Bercy and the Gare de Lyon, has strengthened this development.

Gare de Lyon

◆ The Campanile

When the Gare de Lyon was built between 1895 and 1902, its campanile, or clock tower, was one of the tallest in the world. Today it looks very small amid the huge buildings and office towers that surround it, though there is a good view of it from the new Pont Charles de Gaulle, which since 1996 has linked the Gare d'Austerlitz and the Gare de Lyon.

The Gare de Lyon was built to cater for the increase in traffic at the end of the 19th century, and with the upcoming Universal Exhibition of 1900 was designed as a showpiece. Its architect, Marius Toudoire, and

sculptors set out to promote the grandeur of France. The façade of allegorical sculptures in the form of young female nudes glorifies the power of the nation, paying special tribute to Electricity and Mechanics. This 1900 façade is now protected as a historic monument, as is the metal hall by the engineer-architect Denis.

◆ Le Train Bleu

Another classified monument is the Train Bleu. This famous restaurant, situated on the second story of the station, was built in 1900 to publicize the Paris-Lyon-Mediterranean train company. Its name came from the blue express train which served the Côte d'Azur from 1922. It consists of two rooms, the Grande Salle and the Salle Dorée, and two lounges, one Tunisian and the other Algerian. The paintings decorating the walls and ceiling extol the attractions of the cities served by the train. More than 30 artists were involved in this project, each chosen to represent their native city. The ceilings were commissioned from leading artists of the time such as Dubufe, Flameng, Maignan, and Saint-Pierre. In time the Train Bleu became a legendary place, patronised by famous artists such as Colette and Salvador Dali. Louise de Vilmorin wrote in *La Lettre dans un Taxi* (1957): "There is no finer restaurant in Paris than the one at the Gare de Lyon."

The new Bercy

In a state of upheaval since the 1970s, the area between the Gare de Lyon and Porte de Bercy has almost completed a transformation that will make it the city's eastern counterpart to La Défense in the west. It has become an important business center with office blocks, administrative buildings, and exhibition halls. It is also a residential and recreational area with a park, hotels, shops, restaurants, theaters, the Palais Omnisports and a multiplex cinema, not to mention the Maison du Cinéma due to be housed in an astonishing building designed by American architect Frank Gehry.

◆ Ministry of Economy and Finance

This huge horizontal block stands side-on to the Seine, forming an arch over the quayside and its surging traffic, its end pier planted in the river itself.

Boats can travel rapidly from the Ministry to the Chamber of Deputies, and there is a circular helipad on the roof. It is an impressive building, overlooking the Seine at the Quai de la Rapée, and was designed for efficiency. An enormous space was needed to bring together all the services of the Ministry of Economy and Finance, part of which had been occupying a wing of the Louvre. Rapid access to the center of Paris was also essential, especially for ministers. Inaugurated in 1989, it was designed by two

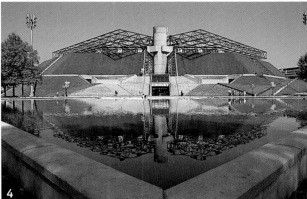

architects, Paul Chemetov and Borja Huidobro, who were also responsible for the renovation of the Grande Galerie de l'Evolution in the Jardin des Plantes. A series of buildings with side-wings are set around courtyards and gardens, and sculptures break up the rigid lines of the whole. The interior is lavishly decorated with contemporary paintings and tapestries, enhanced by mosaic marble floors. With its 5,500 civil servants, 2.5 million sq ft (225,000 sq m) of space and all the various services gathered there, including a crèche, post office, shops, etc, the buildings of the Ministry of Finance form a "city within a city."

◆ Palais Omnisports de Paris-Bercy (POPB)

This truncated, grass-covered pyramid is something of a surprise. Inaugurated in 1983, it is the work of three architects: Pierre Parat, Michel Andrault, and Aydin Guvan. Its

1. Train Bleu
This famous restaurant decorated with Belle Epoque paintings owes its name to the deluxe train which from the 1920s ferried the famous down to the Mediterranean.

2. Jardin Huet, Bercy
In this city park overlooked by new apartments, flower beds, rose gardens and orchards have been laid out alongside spacious lawns, a belvedere, and a maze. It was designed by the architects Ferrand, Feugas, Roy, and Huet, and the landscape gardener Lecaisne.

3. Ministry of Finance
Overlooking the Seine, the building consists of a huge arch spanning the Quai de la Rapée. Until 1812, this was where taxes were collected at the city gates.

4. Palais Omnisports Paris-Bercy
The city's largest indoor hall sits beneath a metal framework supported by four concrete pillars, its sides covered with grass. Operas and concerts are held here, as well as sports events.

innovative character stems not only from its shape but also from the technical miracle of its steel skeleton resting on four concrete pillars, the concept of Jean Prouve. The POPB gives the city a massive, modular show space, which can be rearranged to accommodate from 3,500 to 17,000 spectators for rock concerts, performances by the Spanish Riding School of Vienna, cycle racing, surfing competitions or some 20 other types of sports event.

◆ Parc de Bercy

The wine warehouses at Bercy have been replaced by a 35-acre (14-ha) park. Some aspects of the original site have been preserved: the hundred-year-old plane and chestnut trees are still there, as are the cobbled paths for carrying the wine from the banks of the Seine, and a few buildings and romantic ruins. The first part of the park, on the POPB side, has been called "the meadow" after its great lawn set aside for leisure and recreation. The second part, the "garden of memory," recalls the history of the place with its plants laid out like vineyards. The third part, the "romantic garden," is embellished with a canal, a small lake, and a soothing array of greenery.

◆ "Bercy Village"

Some typical old wine warehouses have been classified as historic monuments, notably the Cour Saint-Emilion and the L'Heureux warehouses. In keeping with the way the district has evolved, many of the buildings today house hi-tech businesses, while cafés and restaurants help to create a welcoming atmosphere in the heart of "Bercy Village." They have been renovated out of respect for their past, and as a means of reintroducing the wine and food industries to the area. A museum of wines and gastronomy has opened in the L'Heureux warehouses and Bercy pavilions. These warehouses also contain the mar-

velous Musée des Arts Forains (Fairground Art Museum), with its antique merry-go-rounds and wooden horses, puppets, rifle ranges, and music saloons with slot machines, while a Venetian exhibit can be visited in another warehouse.

◆ The Bercy footbridge

The Bercy-Tolbiac footbridge will link the Left and Right banks of the Seine, an area which has been expanding for the last 20 years. Designed by Dietmar Feichtinger, it will consist of two structures: a main bridge, flanked on each side by a walkway to provide pedestrians with an exceptional view over Paris and the Seine.

Around the National Library

The most spectacular center of Paris' New East, the French National Library (BNF), was completed in 1995. Some apartments have already been built nearby, and a group of art galleries will open in Rue Louise Weiss to help bring life to the district. Development of the Left Bank is still far from complete. This is a gigantic city planning project involving an area of more than 250 acres (100 ha), of which about 74 acres (30 ha) are built above the rail tracks serving the Gare d'Austerlitz. Plans are still ongoing. The original project envisaged pulling down several old buildings, but this move was strongly contested and had to be modified. This is why the refriger-

ated warehouses, which have become squats for artists, may now be preserved, and the former flourmills known as the Grands Moulins de Paris may become the home of a new university.

◆ The National Library of France

Designed by Dominique Perrault, the Bibliothèque Nationale de France (BNF), or François Mitterand Library, was opened in 1995. The four towers of this "temple to culture" rise up from a stepped platform like open books. The conservation and administration services, located high above the reading rooms, enjoy an unrestricted view over the Seine and the entire city. Readers, on the other hand, have to go down to the center of the complex. The reading rooms on the first floor are open to the public, while those on the garden level are reserved for researchers. These rooms are very comfortable and well-designed, and have excellent lighting. Views of the garden from the corridors help to dispel the tedium of lengthy walks from one room to another.

◆ The "Fridge" and the artists' squats

"le Frigo" was an ice factory and refrigerated warehouse in the first half of the 20th century, and was due to be knocked down to make way for new buildings. Since the 1980s, however, 250 artists have moved in, breathing new life into

5

the industrial building. An Italian artist has even redesigned and decorated one apartment in an illusionist style derived from theater sets. Here, trompe l'oeil and pasteboard have created a world which has no connection with the original structure. Such has been the level of protest against demolition, it is likely the "Frigo" will be preserved.

---

1. Bercy wine warehouses in 1929
The old complex of wine warehouses at Bercy has been replaced by a 35-acre (14-ha) park. The plane trees and chestnuts have been preserved, along with several of the original buildings.

2. The Great Steps, National Library
This grand flight of steps linking the new library to the square above has been criticized for its exotic wood cladding, which gets slippery in wet weather. The square is like the bridge of a ship, with splendid views over the Seine and eastern Paris.

3. National Library (BNF)
The library's four book towers were designed by D Renault and surround a magnificent garden carpeted with ferns and mosses and planted with mature umbrella pines.

4. Reading room
The reading rooms at the BNF are well-equipped with screens for viewing written or audiovisual documents.

5. Le Frigo (The Fridge)
This abandoned industrial complex was occupied in the 1980s by young, unknown artists. Today it has become a center of artistic creativity, staging exhibitions and shows.

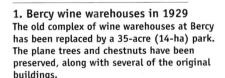

4

The Bastille and surrounding area

Vincennes

With its lakes, racetrack, floral gardens, and zoo, the Bois de Vincennes is now part of Paris, while the city of Vincennes remains in the adjoining *département* of Val de Marne. These two cities have associations going back to the Ancien Régime. From the 12th century, Vincennes became a royal residence, partly because of the nearby forest. The kings loved hunting and often set up house in places where they could enjoy their favorite sport. After it was abandoned as a royal residence, the château was occupied by the famous Vincennes Royal Porcelain Factory. Following the Revolution, the army took it over, and the forest became fields for maneuvers. It was not until Napoleon III came to power that they were turned into an English-style park, and the château was restored.

Château de Vincennes

◆ From fortress to château

In the 11th century, the Crown bought the hunting forest of Vincennes from the Abbey of Saint Maur. Philippe Auguste had the forest enclosed and built a manor house. Saint-Louis added a chapel, which was completed under François I.

From the 14th century, the Valois family transformed the manor into a huge fortress with a curtain wall spiked with towers. In the 17th century, the keep became a prison and Le Vau built two majestic wings for royal occupation. Louis XIV stayed there in 1660 with his young wife Marie-Thérèse.

◆ An underrated monument

Despite having suffered from wars and destruction arising from its military use, the Château de Vincennes has kept its proud appearance. It is well worth a visit to see the rectangular curtain wall and towers, including the 180 ft (54 m) Tour du Village, the superb keep, a masterpiece of 14th-century military architecture, the royal chapel with Renaissance windows, and the beautiful Cour d'Honneur bordered by the Classical architecture of the royal wings.

Bois de Vincennes

The hunting grounds of kings, this former forest also has associations with Saint Louis, who dispensed justice there beneath an oak tree. Under Louis XV, the woods were opened to the public. In the 19th century, it became a military training ground. In 1860, however, Napoleon III assigned the Bois de Vincennes to the City of Paris so it could be made into a park, an eastern counterpart of the Bois de Boulogne. Commissioned to lay it out in the English style popular at the time, Alphand dug out small valleys and lakes. Later, the park gradually acquired a racecourse, a zoo, a flower garden, and many other facilities that make it so enjoyable today.

◆ Parc Floral

Created in 1969, the Parc Floral is landscaped with streams, ponds, and contemporary sculpture and has an exceptional collection of nearly 100,000 plants in its 84 acres (34 ha). The Valley of Flowers, their colors straight from a painter's palette, the Garden of the Four Seasons, and the Iris Garden offer an abundance of scents and vistas. Assorted pavilions and patios offer bonsai and wildlife exhibits, including a butterfly house. Large floral displays are organized every year, with tulips in spring and dahlias in summer. Beyond the glassy waters of the Miroir d'Eau is a bandstand where jazz and classical concerts are held in summer.

◆ Vincennes cartridge factory

The army's old cartridge factory (Cartoucherie) became a prison during the Algerian war, and was later abandoned. Since the 1970s, it has been used by theater groups, its first tenant being Ariane Mnouchkine's famous Théâtre du Soleil.

◆ The Racecourse

Founded in 1863 and renovated in 1980 by Philippe Morin and Thierry Mostini, Vincennes Racecourse is best known for its 6,560-ft (2,000-m) trotting track and for the Prix d'Amérique, the famous race held there every year. Nearby, a riding club and pony club instruct both accomplished riders and beginners.

◆ The Paris Farm

This has an orchard and kitchen garden to show city children how fruit and vegetables are grown, and a sta-

ble and farmyard to help them learn all about life down on the farm. There are informative exhibits on activities such as milking, butter making, sheep shearing and wool spinning.

◆ The Zoo

The Zoo at Vincennes covers a 37-acre (15-ha) site and has a collection of more than 1,000 animals including a giant panda, okapi, sloths, and king penguins. One of its inhabitants, an elephant, was recently in the news when an analysis of its genes revealed that it did not belong to either of the two known species, the Asian and African, but was from a third, previously unknown species. The Vincennes Rock is 213 ft (65 m) high and was restored in 1997. Sheep gambol on its slopes, and there is an exceptional view over Paris from the top.

◆ The Buddhist Institute

On the banks of Lac Daumesnil, the Togo and Cameroon pavilion built for the Colonial Exhibition of 1931 is now a place of worship for the Buddhist community in Paris. In 1985, a Tibetan temple was built nearby.

Museum of African and Oceanian Arts

Also built for the Colonial Exhibition of 1931, this impressive building is an important example of Thirties architecture and decorative style. The huge bas-relief on the façade, sculpted by Janniot, praises the contribution made by the civilizations of Asia, Africa, Oceania, and the West Indies to metropolitan life. For the interior decoration, frescoes and furniture, the architects Jaussely and

Laprade called on the greatest names of the period, such as Pierre Ducos de la Haille and Emile Ruhlmann. It was André Malraux, then Minister of Culture, who created this museum dedicated to African and Oceanian arts. In the basement, a large aquarium contains many tropical species. The current plan is to move the collections to join those of the Musée de l'Homme (now at the Trocadéro) in a new museum scheduled for Quai Branly.

5

---

1. Château de Vincennes
Standing at the gates of the capital, the château has been modified several times since the Middle Ages and each stage of its enlargement and restoration can be traced. One of its defining elements is the keep, built in the 14th century.

2. Lac Daumesnil
This 19th-century lake was designed in the same romantic spirit as English-style gardens of the 18th century. On one of its islands is a small round temple, built above artificial grottos.

3. Vincennes Zoo
The zoo dates from 1934 and features an innovative system of ditches and railings to convey the impression that the animals can move around almost freely.

4. Feeding the elephant seal
This marine mammal's feeding times always attract visitors, especially children.

5. The Buddhist Institute
This pavilion was designed by H Boileau and L Carrière to represent Togo and Cameroon at the Colonial Exhibition of 1931. From 1933 to 1971, it contained an industrial museum, and since 1977 it has been a place of worship for the Buddhist community. Inside is a fine 33 ft (10 m)-high gilded Buddha by the sculptor Mozes.

4

LA VILLETTE
and surrounding area

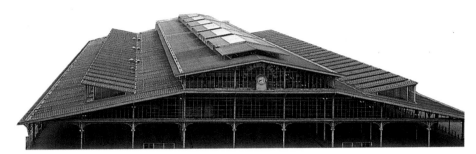

The Great Hall

Parc de la Villette

La Villette canal basin

Around Canal Saint-Martin

The Buttes-Chaumont

Aerial view of La Villette
The Parc de la Villette, standing on one of Paris's largest industrial sites, is today home to several cultural institutions. In the foreground, the Cité de la Musique looks out over the Fontaine aux Lions. The Great Hall stands in the center, surrounded by themed gardens. On the opposite bank of the Ourcq Canal, the Géode fronts the impressive Cité des Sciences et de l'Industrie. Here at the heart of a district undergoing a complete transformation, La Villette symbolizes the renaissance of East Paris.

The Great Hall

With its vast iron nave measuring 215,000 sq ft (20,000 sq m), the Great Hall lived through the old industrial past and has since undergone a successful architectural conversion. Built in 1867 and classified as a historic monument in 1979, this old hall is today an essential feature of the Parc de la Villette, a 124 acre (50 ha) park laid out in 1985 and devoted to leisure and culture.

A masterpiece of 19th-century iron architecture

The present Great Hall is the former central cattle hall of La Villette's Abattoir and Cattle Market, opened in 1867. It was the finest building in a huge complex built by Louis-Adolphe Janvier (1818-78) and Jules de Mérindol under the direction of Victor Baltard, director of works for Paris. Ten years after the demolition of Baltard's Les Halles, the preservation of this masterpiece of iron architecture, and its respectful conversion, was a momentous event.

The Great Hall is almost 820 ft (250 m) long and built entirely of iron and cast-iron. Use of cast iron as a building material reached its heyday in the 19th century. It was the ideal material for simple, large-scale structures such as this, made from identical components that could be mass-produced. The skeleton consists of a huge latticework of iron trusses resting on rows of tall columns forming nine aisles of equal dimensions. Its unencumbered floor space allowed complete freedom of movement. Above the upper floor, the hall has large glazed openings, fitted with shutters, which lit the side aisles; the central aisle was lit by a roof lantern.

Born in the "City of Blood"

Baron Haussmann, Prefect of the Seine, was much concerned about modernization and public health, and in November, 1858, he proposed building a cattle market and a huge abattoir in one and the same place. Until then, Paris had been supplied with meat via five abattoirs, set up in 1810 in outlying districts. La Villette had both rail tracks and canals, and was an ideal site for the new establishment. The "City of Blood" was opened in 1867. It reached its Golden Age at the turn of the 20th century and would leave its mark on the district for a long time: offal collectors, slaughtermen, and wholesale butchers gave the area its distinctive character, and even today several local restaurants maintain its tradition for serving prime meat.

End of the butchers

In the 1950s, the abattoirs proved inadequate for the latest methods of food production. In 1958, the public authorities built gigantic, ultra-modern buildings on part of the original site. La Villette was declared a "Market in the National Interest," and opened in 1969. It was the biggest abattoir in Europe. Even before it was finished, it became clear that it was much too big, particularly since the freezer industry could now transport meat by refrigerated truck and the animals could be slaughtered closer to where they were raised. The abattoir closed its gates, once and for all, on March 14, 1974. It was a bitter reversal, and a massive financial loss.

Rejuvenating the area

In 1982, architects Bernard Reichen and Philippe Robert were commissioned to transform the old cattle hall. These two architects had worked together since the 1970s, and had become specialists in the conversion of industrial buildings. They had made a distinguished contribution to the La Mouche abattoirs in Lyons, the famous Tony Garnier building, and at the Menier chocolate factories at Noisiel. Their success in this area has been

achieved by finding the right mix between preserving national monuments and creating contemporary buildings. Here too, at La Villette, they responded successfully to the problem of integrating contemporary elements into a classified building, mindful of the need for continuity in the process.

Conversion to a multi-purpose hall

The general shape of the hall, the logic behind its construction, and its architectural details have been preserved. The materials used are modern versions of those employed in the 19th century: steel, glass, stone, and wood. Optimal use has been made of the space, lighting, and acoustics in creating the new multi-purpose arena. The building had to be sealed, for reasons of comfort and safety. Priority was given to creating a modular space: side balconies, special decks, and movable metal gangways mean that this versatile space can be used for a wide variety of events. The architects have clearly achieved their double aim of reviving an existing site and creating a new use for it. The Great Hall opened to the public in 1985.

The park's nerve-center

Since it opened, the Great Hall has drawn a great variety of audiences and staged all manner of events, including an annual jazz festival, theater productions by famous directors such as Patrice Chéreau, concerts featuring big names like Léo Férré, and forums and conferences on a range of subjects. There have also been several memorable exhibitions in its short life. Exhibitions on subjects as diverse as cinema (1987), funfairs (1996), and gardens (1998) were all very original shows, perfectly in keeping with the spirit and design of the place. For the past 15 years, the Great Hall has played a pioneering role in terms of its cultural policy.

FACTS & FIGURES

THE GREAT HALL (FORMER CATTLE HALL)	
Length : 790 ft (241 m)	
Width : 282 ft (86 m)	
Height to ridge : 62 ft (19m)	
Total area : 223,135 sq ft (20,730 sq m)	
Maximum capacity of cultural center : 15,900 people	
Formerly, maximum capacity of market/abattoir : 6,490 cattle, 37,690 sheep, 3,960 pigs and veal calves	
Lifespan of market/abattoir : 107 years (1867-1974)	
Opening of cultural center : 1985	

1. Great Hall and fountain
Designed in 1811 by Pierre-Simon Girard, engineer of the Canal de l'Ourcq, the Fontaine aux Lions was then on the Place de la République. It was moved to La Villette in 1867.

2. Abattoir days
Along with those at Vaugirard, La Villette's abattoirs supplied Paris with its meat until the 1970s. Although considerably enlarged, they became obsolete and were closed in 1974.

3. Walkway flanking the Great Hall
From the park entrance to the footbridge over the Canal de l'Ourcq, this long walkway with its undulating canopy protects visitors and guides them through the park. Here you can see one of the follies (red kiosk) designed by the park's master of works, architect Bernard Tschumi.

4. Detail of girders
Its fine structure of iron arches and girders makes the Great Hall one of the most remarkable surviving examples of industrial architecture in Paris.

5. Interior of the Great Hall
The work of the Great Hall's original architects (Janvier, Mérindol, and Baltard) has been scrupulously preserved in the renovation by Reichen and Robert. Here you can see the only part of the building which has not been enclosed.

Parc de la Villette

In 1982, François Mitterrand decided there should be a big cultural project on the site of the old abattoirs at La Villette. In the heart of a 124 acre (50 ha) park, the multi-purpose Great Hall would be joined by a museum of science and technology, an academy of music, and concert halls. This grand presidential project was an important landmark in the history of urban life in Paris. Devoted to industry since the 19th century, north-eastern Paris would now become one of the capital's cultural beacons. The whole regeneration project cost about one billion francs.

A city park

◆ The garden city

The Parc de la Villette was laid out from 1986, and has quite transformed the appearance and atmosphere of the whole district. A principal element in the program to regenerate the eastern part of Paris, funded jointly by the City and the State, its design gave rise to a major international competition, won in 1983 by the Swiss architect Bernard Tschumi. A new kind of park was coming into being at that time: the urban park, where architecture and landscape were of equal importance. The site was exceptional but limited, being divided in two by the Canal de l'Ourcq, and Tschumi unified the disparate buildings with a simple and rigorous plan.

◆ Themed gardens

The park invites exploration, and harbors many surprises. A cobbled promenade (made from the abattoir's cobblestones) winds for almost 2 miles (3 km) through no less than 11 themed gardens designed by famous visual and landscape artists. A stroll through the gardens is an absorbing experience. The bamboo garden is located 20 ft (6 m) below the level of the park: you walk through its foliage on strips of black and white pebbles, designed by Daniel Buren, while a concrete cylinder emits strange electro-acoustic music. There are mirror gardens, dunes, fog zones, and things designed to startle you. The way plants and non-living features are combined to create different effects marks an extraordinary step forward in the arts of landscaping.

Beside a path, pieces of giant bicycles are planted in the ground, the work of sculptor Claes Oldenburg.

◆ Follies and walkways

Bernard Tschumi's follies, made of concrete covered in red metal, stand out from the greenery and are scattered 130 yd (120 m) apart all over the park. Some are purely decorative, others contain workshops for children, an information center, a snack bar, and even a concert room (the Trabendo, formerly Hot Brass). The architect responded to the determining presence of the Canal de l'Ourcq by designing two elevated walkways: the Galerie de l'Ourcq runs parallel to the water for 660 yd (600 m), while the Galerie de la Villette crosses over it to link up Porte de Pantin and Porte de La Villette at either end of the park; each of these has a Métro station. Some of the follies can be reached directly from these walkways.

◆ The meadows

The park has two large lawns on either side of the canal: the Circle and Triangle meadows. Surrounded by plane trees, they are places to relax which local people love to use. Football players have taken over part of the ground, which means the lawns are continually having to be relaid! The Triangle meadow also has a famous open-air film festival each summer, an event that attracts audiences from all over Paris.

◆ *Living in the park*

There are so many things to do in the park that you could almost live there! Every season the events and attractions include dances, concerts, a circus, a funfair, and an equestrian center. The Théâtre Paris-Villette, which opened in 1985, and the Maison de La Villette, the information and exhibition center, respect the area's old identity while mainly favoring contemporary works. Both were set up in former abattoir buildings. The multicultural Pavillon Paul Delouvrier, designed by Oscar Tusquets, has put on some spectacular events including Navajo Indian sand paintings (1996), and chants and rituals of the Australian Aborigines (1997).

1. The Dragon Garden
This huge slide is just the tongue of the dragon, a gigantic sculpture 262 ft (80 m) long located in the north of the park. With the Géode in the background, the dragon slide is a popular attraction for young and old alike.

2. Bicycle handlebars
This handlebar fragment is one of several bits of buried bicycle, the work of American artist Claes Oldenburg. These scaled-up versions of a pedal, wheel, and handlebar all add to the fun of the park.

3. Lamp post
The Parc de la Villette is dotted with all kinds of innovative furniture. The lamp posts, seats, and trashcans were designed by Philippe Starck.

4. The Acrobatics Garden
The Jardin des Voltiges takes its name from its gymnastics appararatus and the exercises which can be performed there. It also features a novel sound experiment with two cupolas, several yards apart, from which people can hear each other perfectly, even while speaking softly. The garden is connected by walkway to ten others, all designed around botanical or educational themes.

5. Stairway
The Canal de l'Ourcq, which divides the park in two, is where the two walkways crossing the park intersect. Here visitors use stairways and elevators to transfer from one to the other.

A massive science museum

◆ Cité des Sciences: a European leader

The watchword of the people who designed La Villette was to be innovative but preserve its remarkable heritage. This was a real challenge for the architect of the future Cité des Sciences et de l'Industrie, inaugurated on March 13, 1986, to coincide with the passing of Halley's Comet. Adrien Fainsbilder had to reuse the main saleroom building for the abattoirs (which had never been finished). Now the the largest establishment devoted to popular science in Europe, it has an area of 1,076,400 sq ft (100,000 sq m) surrounded by moats 43 ft (13 m) deep. The design has three principal features: the water that surrounds it, the plants growing in its bioclimatic glasshouses (a technical feat carried out by British engineer Peter Rice), and the light that falls from rotating domes and illuminates the museum space.

◆ A hive of activity

Since it opened, the Cité des Sciences has had several hundred thousand visitors a year from all over the world. "Explora," the permanent exhibition, uses games, etc, to explain inventions that have changed our daily lives, and shows what is going on in scientific research. Temporary exhibitions are also organized by the Cité. The one in 1995, on packaging, was very successful. "Cité for Children" and "Techno Cité" are some of the many teaching activities on offer for groups and individuals.

◆ The Géode and Cinaxe

After a trip through the holds of the *Argonaute*, a submarine from Toulon now in front of Cité des Sciences, the Géode is the next port of call. This is one of the unmissable places in Parc de la Villette, an impressive concrete sphere covered in triangles of polished steel (6,433 in all) containing a semi-circular screen with an area of 10,764 sq ft (1,000 sq m). Sensation-seekers lean back in their chairs and can feel really absorbed in the show. Cinaxe, to the west of the Cité, is even more dizzying: the whole auditorium actually moves, to give the spectator an even more realistic impression of what it's like to be a racing driver or an astronaut.

Cité de la Musique: the architecture of sound

◆ The splendid entrance

While the Cité des Sciences dominates the north side of the park, the main features of the south side are the two buildings making up the Cité de la Musique. Their fairly unobtrusive lines were designed by Christian de Portzamparc between 1984 and 1995 in a style blending both the monumental and the fragmentary. Located at the edge of the park, the Cité de la Musique boldly marks the entrance to it and looks out toward the Great Hall and the Fontaine aux Lions. The fountain was designed in 1810 by Pierre-Simon Girard, the engineer who built the Canal de l'Ourcq, and was originally set on what is now Place de la République, before being moved to La Villette in 1869 as a drinking trough for cattle. It was splendidly renovated in 1993.

◆ The Conservatoire Supérieur de Musique

This academy has replaced the old Paris Conservatoire de Musique in

1 **2**

Rue Madrid, whose premises had become increasingly inadequate. Behind its impressive white façade, its walls curved to limit sound emissions, it has 150 classrooms and studios, accommodation for the students, a dance department, and rehearsal and concert rooms. The great organ room is underground, lit by a truncated cone in the middle of a patio.

◆ Music Museum, café and concert hall

Facing the Conservatoire, the east wing of the Cité de la Musique is V-shaped.

At the front is the Café de la Musique, decorated by Elisabeth de Portzamparc, which provides a meeting place for musicians and visitors.

The entrance to the building incorporates one of the park's follies, and leads to the great concert hall, an oval space surrounded by a long corridor. The hall has a modular design and uses the most up-to-date acoustic techniques.

On the upper floors, the Music Museum has an extraordinary collection of instruments from many different countries. Earphones are available for visitors to learn more about the pieces on show. Each day, a musician gives a talk and plays his favorite instrument.

◆ The Zénith

Music is everywhere at La Villette: in the Cité, the Great Hall, the gardens, and the park too, where sax players and drummers like to play. The Zénith is actually one of the city's major concert halls. Originally designed by Philippe Chaix and Jean-Paul Morel as a temporary building, its metal frame is covered by silvered canvas to provide a modular space able to take 6,400 people. Since the first concert, given by Renaud in January, 1984, all the great names in popular music have performed at the Zénith. The concrete tower, which formerly supplied feed to the abattoir stables, now supports a red airplane, the Zénith's symbol.

1. The Great Concert Hall
This highly successful, oval-shaped concert hall is in the eastern wing of the Cité. The modular space can be adapted for different-sized groups, from a symphony orchestra to a chamber quartet.

2. Cité des Sciences
The world's largest science museum is designed to enable young and old to explore a raft of scientific inventions using playful experiments and more serious methods.

3. The Géode
The Géode is the only building of its kind in the world. With its 6,433 triangles of polished steel, its architecture was inspired by the work of the American engineer Richard Buckminster Fuller.

4. The Zénith
Designed as a concert hall which could be quickly erected and dismantled, the Zénith has become one of the key venues for music in Paris. Now a permanent structure, it has spawned several smaller versions in other French cities.

5, 6. Cité de la Musique
Behind its spotless façades, this complex by Christian de Portzamparc reveals a very subtle structure with a highly colored decorative scheme.

La Villette canal basin

A new urban center

◆ The Rotunda at La Villette

The first scheme in the district plan was the restoration of Place de la Bataille de Stalingrad and the former Saint-Martin Rotunda. This was the most magnificent of the customs houses in the wall of the Farmers-General, built on the eve of the Revolution for purposes of tax-collecting rather than defense. The Rotunda was designed by C-N Ledoux in an extremely sober style, inspired by Andrea Palladio's Villa Rotunda near Vicenza. It was spared from destruction when the Métro bypassed it on an elevated track, but was still isolated by the surrounding traffic lanes. On the Bassin de la Villette side, the area around it has been opened up by a square, designed by Bernard Huet in 1988.

◆ Rejuvenating the canal basin

The canal basin, linking the Canal de l'Ourcq and Canal St Martin, was laid out to align with the Rotunda. From its opening in 1821, it attracted gentlemen who came there in winter to skate. Subsequently, the industrial development of La Villette turned it into a gigantic transit center. Many of the buildings which cluttered the place have been destroyed. At the beginning of the 20th century it was an infamous place, but now it is a water sports center, with a tournament taking place each year. Its banks have been paved and planted to provide a promenade leading to the Parc de la Villette.

◆ Alive with contemporary architecture

Next to the Quais de la Loire and de la Seine, new buildings have appeared since 1985, all for housing except the Sté André headquarters (1991). Built by Stanislas Fiszer, its impressive scale forming a counterweight to Ledoux's Rotunda. Other buildings by Edith Girard, Yves Lion, and Dominique Perrault are very different in style, but all are designed to provide the best views over the canal basin and Rotunda.

Sensitive renovation

◆ From warehouse to cinema

La Villette owes much of its charm to its preserved and renovated buildings. For some years, the warehouses on Quai de la Seine have contained cinemas and a restaurant. These initiatives have not only been an aesthetic success, they also make the canal an ideal place to meet and relax.

◆ The Magasins Généraux

The fate of the old Magasins Généraux was more chaotic. This was one of two warehouses built in 1853; during the Commune it was set on fire, then rebuilt, and again went down in flames in 1989. After years of waiting, it is now planned to use it for a glass making school. The other building has long been occupied by artists' studios, and should soon be renovated. The dock warehouses at Pont de Flandre have recently been converted into offices on either side of a rebuilt harbor basin. This pool is now purely ornamental, but once was an unloading point for cargo.

The regeneration of the area around the canal basin happened at the same time as the park was being laid out. In a few years, this old industrial site has become a big attraction in Paris's New East.

4

Around Rue de Flandre

A new district has been built at La Villette canal basin; around its buildings from the early industrial era stand fine pieces of contemporary architecture.

5

◆ *Lifting bridge on Rue de la Crimée*

Walking from the canal basin to Parc de la Villette, you come to the lifting bridge on Rue de la Crimée. It was built in 1866 to replace a swing bridge and to let the barges through more quickly. The roadway still rises several times a day. Traffic is brought to a halt when this happens, but pedestrians can use a footbridge leading them, for example, to the Church of Saint-Jacques-Saint-Christophe, built in 1844 for the old commune of La Villette.

◆ *Les Orgues de Flandre*

A few yards from there, on Avenue de Flandre, small 19th-century apartment buildings are flanked by new developments such as the Orgues de Flandre (Flanders Organs), designed in 1980 by Martin van Treeck. Instead of building simple towers, the architect grouped a diverse range of blocks around a large garden: some are like American skyscrapers, and others, with terraces of varied height, look like organ pipes. Rue de Flandre, once the main road to Belgium, has now become a very lively, well-landscaped, and attractive avenue with a broad mix of inhabitants.

1. Ledoux's Rotunda
Built by Ledoux on the eve of the Revolution, the building served as a customs house. The architect was inspired by Andrea Palladio's Villa Rotunda near Vicenza, but wanted to give it a palatial magnificence. This is why its offices were plundered on July 13, 1789.

2. The Magasins Généraux
The first modern warehouses on La Villette canal basin were built in 1853 by the engineer Emile Vuignier, who was influenced by the dockside developments in Liverpool, then the most successful in Europe.

3. The Orgues de Flandres
This impressive housing development by Martin van Treeck breaks with building styles of the 1970s, and takes its name from the very varied heights of the blocks, which look like organ pipes.

4. La Villette canal basin
Today the basin is completely given over to leisure, especially water sports. Linking the Canal de l'Ourcq and Canal Saint-Martin, it was until recently an abandoned industrial site. A promenade along the banks leads to the Parc de la Villette.

5. Lifting bridge on Rue de la Crimée
This is the original version of the bridge built in 1886 and is a fine example of the complete renovation of Paris's canals at the end of the 19th century. Basins, locks, quayside walls, and footbridges were all replaced to modernize the network.

Around Canal Saint-Martin

A few barges still navigate the locks on Canal Saint-Martin, but most of the traffic on this stretch of waterway is for tourists. Coming from the Arsenal basin, the boats travel up the canal to Parc de la Villette, final stage in their trip through eastern Paris. For a long time there were threats to cover the canal completely over (or even to build a freeway there), but it is still as picturesque as ever.

A legendary canal

◆ From the Seine to the Seine

The Canal Saint-Martin forms a network with the Canal de l'Ourcq and Canal Saint-Denis. When Napoléon I was First Consul, he wanted to build it to bypass the center of Paris and join the Upper Seine with the Lower (at Saint-Denis), to supply the capital with goods and drinking water from the River Ourcq, north-east of Paris. The Emperor was also hatching plans to improve eastern Paris. In fact, the canals have contributed greatly to the development of the surrounding districts, but the industrial site at La Villette, built to be close to the railroad, harmed trading on the Canal Saint-Martin, and its warehouses were quickly demolished.

◆ Famous faces

On the banks of Canal Saint-Martin, boatmen, stevedores, and lock-keepers mingled with a suburban population famed for their cheeky humor. This working-class neighborhood became a legendary setting for many tales, and some famous films. Marcel Carné's *Hôtel du Nord* (1938), adapted from a novel by Eugène Dabit, has passed into posterity thanks to the performances of Louis Jouvet and Arletty. Actually, the film was shot in the studios at Billancourt: the canal, locks, and quayside were completely rebuilt by designer Alexandre Trauner. The hotel was destroyed, but its replacement still displays the old, evocative name.

A land of intersections

◆ Gare de l'Est and Gare du Nord

Rue des Récollets leads from the waterside to a district very different from that surrounding the canal. Between Gare de l'Est and Gare du Nord is a part of Paris that is continually on the move. The two stations are only a few hundred yards apart, and both of them are served by major thoroughfares: Boulevard Magenta, Boulevard de Strasbourg, and Rue La Fayette. The Gare de l'Est was built in 1852, and played an important part in the economic development of La Villette; when the station's resources became too overstretched, it was expanded between 1924 and 1931. The Gare du Nord, designed by J-I Hittorff, was given a new boost when the Eurostar service opened in 1994, putting London only three hours from Paris.

◆ Place Franz-Liszt

Place Franz-Liszt is a small square on the Rue La Fayette. It was laid out in the 1820s to provide a junction for several streets; at the same time, it was the setting for the new Church of Saint-Vincent-de-Paul, built by Lepère and Hittorff (1824-44). This Romanesque-style building on lands of the former Saint-Lazare priory was the subject of a scandal in its day. The façade was decorated with plaques of Volvic lava, enameled and colorfully painted by the artist Jules Jollivet. These were deemed inappropriate by the Archbishop of Paris, and were taken down a year after they were completed (1861).

Fine old buildings

Despite the dominance of 19th-century architecture, the Canal Saint-Martin has still retained several old buildings which have deeply influenced its history and landscape.

◆ Hôpital Saint-Louis

At the beginning of the 17th century, King Henri IV had a hospital for plague victims built outside the city limits. Built in brick and stone by Claude Vellefaux and Claude Chastillon, it consisted of four blocks and a chapel arranged around a square courtyard. It soon fell into disuse, but was completely preserved. Its presence did not suit the engineers of the Canal Saint-Martin,

who had to make a detour to the west. It was restored to use as a hospital in the 20th century, and has been considerably enlarged.

◆ Couvent des Récollets

Also near the canal, this old monastery is today in ruins, and for a long time has been uncertainly awaiting rehabilitation. It was built three years before the Hôpital Saint-Louis (1604), became a hospice for old men in 1794, then a military hospital, a school of architecture, and finally an artists' squat and scene of notorious parties! After a long debate (led by, amongst others, two musicians from the

popular French rock band Les Rita Mitsouko), the city decided to enlarge the Villemin Gardens bordering the monastery as far as the canal.

◆ Church of Saint-Laurent

Facing the monastery, the Church of Saint-Laurent reveals an interesting mixture of styles. In the 17th century, a magnificent Lady Chapel was added to the 15th-century Gothic building. The Baroque façade was replaced in the 19th century by a then-fashionable Flamboyant Gothic version. On the tympanum is *The Last Judgment* in enameled lava, by the brothers Balze (1870).

1. Hôpital Saint-Louis
Along with Place des Vosges and Place Dauphine, the Hôpital Saint-Louis is one of the finest examples of "brick and stone" architecture from the time of Henri IV.

2. Gare du Nord
This 1866 masterpiece by Hittorff replaced the first station serving Belgium, built in 1846.

3, 6. Canal Saint-Martin
The canal was conceived by Napoléon as a way of modernizing Paris, but was quickly seen as an obstruction to traffic. Its existence was long under threat, but now it has become a favorite place for walkers.

4. Church of Saint-Laurent
The blend of Gothic and Classic styles does not detract from the appeal of this church, located between Rue du Faubourg-Saint-Martin and Boulevard de Magenta. Its stained glass dates from the 1950s.

5. Hôtel du Nord
This modest hotel on the canal was the main setting for Marcel Carné's famous film of the same name, and has become a nostalgic treasure. It embodies working-class Paris and the quick-fire humor which the popular screen actress Arletty so splendidly portrayed.

The Buttes-Chaumont

When the Buttes-Chaumont park was laid out on the Calvus Mons (Bald Mount) in 1863, it added an important dimension to the history of East Paris. As at La Villette 120 years later, the whole landscape was completely changed. The old America quarries, whose stone was shipped across the Atlantic, now lay abandoned, and Haussmann, Prefect of Paris, decided to build one of Paris's most beautiful

out is best seen from a 213 ft (65 m) long suspension bridge, rebuilt in 1971, while the source of the name "Bridge of Suicides" hardly needs explaining (it has long been covered by wire netting).

◆ An architectural park

Architect Gabriel Davioud, best known for his Town Hall of the 19th *arrondissement* opposite the park, was largely responsible for its present

◆ La Mouzaïa

South of the square and Rue de Bellevue, a series of lanes known as "villas" make up the La Mouzaïa estate. Its Villas des Fleurs, des Lilas, and de la Renaissance were all designed in the 1890s on similar lines: on either side of the lane, tiny gardens front modest detached houses. Originally built for workers, they are now much sought after for their charm and quiet location.

◆ The Danube hamlet

In the middle of these villas is a hamlet: the Hameau du Danube. Here, 28 houses stand beside a private, Y-shaped lane. They were built in 1924 by architects Georges Gonnot and Eugène Albenque in a very individual style: a happy marriage of canopies, pergolas, and decorative brickwork in a lush green setting.

parks on the site. He commissioned it from Jean-Charles-Adolphe Alphand, head of Parks and Gardens, and the city's gardener-in-chief, Pierre Barillet-Deschamps. Their vast task was quickly completed in 1867, and the park was inaugurated on April 1 to coincide with the Universal Exhibition being held in Paris.

Parc des Buttes-Chaumont

◆ Hilly terrain

Alphand exploited the hilly terrain, and the deep excavation sites, to give the park the almost wild appearance of mountain country. Winding paths run around a lake with gushing waterfalls and streams. From the Etretat Cliff (the Hollow Needle) to the Tivoli Gardens (Temple of Sybil), the park is full of references to other places, which is typical of a Haussmann-era park. The hilly lay-

outlines. At each of the six entrances, he built picturesque lodges in polychrome brick, decorated with faience and medallions bearing the city's arms. He also designed a café-restaurant and two brasseries in the style of Italian country villas, and the delightful Greek temple at the top of the park (reached by climbing some 200 steps). From here you can see the whole of northern Paris, from the Orgues de Flandre to Sacré-Coeur. Here too, you can watch for migrating swifts.

Around Place Rhin-et-Danube

Although heavily modernized in the 20th century, the Buttes-Chaumont district has retained some fine urban features from previous times, with its cul-de-sacs and detached houses. Mostly, these are to be found around Place Rhin-et-Danube.

◆ From Miguel-Hidalgo to Edgar Poe

Rue Miguel-Hidalgo is less rural, but its houses are still interesting. Some are very modern, with roof terraces, white-painted walls, and plain façades. Before leaving Rue de Mouzaïa, take a look at the little Church of Saint-François-d'Assise, built by Paul and Augustin Courcoux (1926). Here, the architects were inspired by Italian Romanesque churches, particularly in the bell tower, with its decorative brickwork.

Quite close to Buttes-Chaumont, but on the other side of Place Rhin-et-Danube, a small estate perched on a hill around Rue Edgar-Poe is worth a visit. At its western end, overlooking Paris, is an astonishing house on piles, built by Jean Welz in 1930, and recently renovated.

◆ Along Boulevard Sérurier

Although long neglected, the fringes of the 19th *arrondissement* have recently come into their own. The Square de la Butte-du-Chapeau-Rouge, designed by Léon Azéma in 1939 on the site of some old fortifications, has broad lawns and fine architectural elements, and overlooks the plain to the north-east of

Paris. Not much visited because it is so far out, it has lately acquired two buildings by contemporary architects: the Robert-Debré Pediatric Hospital (Pierre Riboulet, 1988), a vast, curved slab covered in white tiles, and the Archives de Paris (Henri and Bruno Gaudin, 1991), two impressive blocks fronted by a glazed reading room.

1. Parc des Buttes-Chaumont
Along with the Parc Montsouris, the Buttes-Chaumont (1867) is one of the largest public gardens built in the Second Empire. From 2001, it is being completely renovated.

2. Hôpital Robert Debré
The construction of this hospital in 1988 brought life back to the whole district, and the Church of Notre-Dame-de-Fatima-Marie-Médiatrice, completed in the 1950s and soon abandoned, reopened its doors.

3. La Mouzaïa
On the fringes of Haussmann's Paris, near Place de Rhin-et-Danube, La Mouzaïa is a collection of lanes laid out in parallel groups and known as Villas. These are lined with houses, all with their own garden, which, though small, are much prized by their owners.

4, 5. La Butte du Chapeau-Rouge
This park was laid out on the site of old city fortifications, built around 1840, and pulled down after 1919. On a sloping site, Léon Azéma, architect for the City of Paris, built one of its most beautiful modern parks in 1939. Here are all the elements of a 1930s garden, when a Classical look was being revived.

6. Archives de Paris
Since 1991, this fine building by Henri and Bruno Gaudin has been open for readers researching the history of Paris, and lovers of genealogy who flock here to find their ancestors. An excellent addition to Boulevard Sérurier, it symbolizes the regeneration of East Paris.

LA DÉFENSE
Beyond the city walls,

The Grande Arche

The CNIT and Esplanade

Aerial view of the Grande Arche
It took almost 30 years to complete
the La Défense district. This "French
Manhattan" covers more than 1,852 acres
(750 ha) and is one of the biggest paved
areas in the world. Dominated by the
Grande Arche, the third grand monument
on the axis formed by the Louvre
and the Arc de Triomphe, this showcase
of modern architectural styles has one
of the best views of Paris.
Nearly 100,000 people use
it each day.

The Grande Arche

The Grande Arche de la Défense, a gigantic cube in white marble, is today's version of a triumphal arch. It is the last great monument on the grand perspective that begins at the Louvre. Since it was inaugurated at the time of the Bicentenary of the French Revolution, it has become one of the most visited buildings in France. After 20 years of controversy and false starts, Paris at last provided its business district with a worthy monumental gateway.

Finishing off the great perspective

In 1640, under Louis XIV, Le Nôtre planted avenues of trees in the gardens of the Louvre Palace. Since then, the perspective he created has been constantly extended by prestigious buildings: the Carrousel Arch, Tuileries Garden, the obelisk in Place de la Concorde, the Champs-Elysées, and finally the Arc de Triomphe. Under the Second Empire, the perspective was further extended beyond Avenue de la Grande Armée. At the far end, Napoléon III erected a statue of Bonaparte on the "Rond-Point de l'Empéreur." After the war of 1870, the Emperor's statue was replaced by "The Defense of Paris," a monument celebrating the heroes of the Siege of Paris, which later lent its name to the new district of La Défense. In 1950, it was decided to build a business center there, something which the city lacked. The architects took into account the view from the Louvre, but were unsure how to finish the historic perspective. From 1969, numerous projects were put forward, but none was found to be satisfactory. Finally, in 1983, the Grande Arche won everyone over with its beauty and clean lines.

A difficult birth

The Grande Arche started out as a freehand sketch by a Danish architect unknown in France, Johan Otto Von Spreckelsen. However, from the 419 projects submitted, the simplicity of this scooped-out cube, like "a window on the world," convinced both the competition jury and the President of the Republic, F Mitterrand, who gave his approval. Its construction was nevertheless blighted by disagreements and controversy. In the next four years, there were frequent clashes of opinion between the architect and those in charge of operations, reversals in French political life, and confrontations between public and private interests; and many changes were made to the schedule. The architect said he had to examine five or six different sets of plans. This is no doubt why, to general amazement, he suddenly withdrew from the project on July 31, 1986, and left it to Paul Andreu, his French opposite number, to complete the work. Despite all these difficulties, the Grande Arche, described by Spreckelsen as "a triumphal arch for mankind," was inaugurated as planned on July 14, 1989, the Bicentenary of the French Revolution.

An exceptional structure

Hovering at the center of the building, in a space said to be big enough to hold Notre-Dame Cathedral, are what the architect called "clouds." These white fiberglass sails, stretched between the two pillars, provide the

Facts & Figures	
Width (north-south) : 351 ft (106.9 m)	
Depth (east—west) : 367 ft (112 m)	
Height : 364 ft (110.9 m)	
Total weight : 330,624 tons (300,000 t) (or three times the Eiffel Tower)	
Total area : 2,368,080 sq ft (220,000 sq m)	
Carrara marble slabs covering the walls : 34,000	
Building time : four years	
Wind speed : 25 mph (40 km/h) at the base, 62 mph (100 km/h) near the top	
Speed of elevators : 5.2 ft (1.6 m) per second, 1,560 people per hour	
The challenge : The concrete beams needed to build the upper part have a span of 230 ft (70 m) and weigh 2,755 tons (2,500 t), and had to be cast directly 394 ft (120 m) above ground	

The Grande Arche

colossal building with a scale and underline its purity. The structure supporting the panoramic elevators has been left visible, linking the base and the roof of the building like a ladder linking earth and sky. The Arche stands slightly out of line with the buildings on the Esplanade. The architect had to do this for technical reasons, and turned them to his advantage. Positioned thus, the building reveals the beveled contours of its walls, and this has the effect of making it appear less rigid. One of this triumphal arch's peculiarities is that people work inside it. As well as the offices occupying 36 stories of the pillars, the base contains a Documents Room devoted to European affairs, while in the roof there is the Human Rights Foundation and its exhibitions, a restaurant, and an open-air viewing platform with one of the finest views of Paris.

1. Building the Grande Arche
From 1969, many projects were submitted for the last great building on the Louvre perspective. On May 25, 1983, the Danish architect Johan Otto von Spreckelsen was declared the winner. The Grande Arche was inaugurated on July 14, 1989.

2. The west façade
Spreckelsen's genius was to have imagined a double-sided "cube." To the west, the Arche looks toward the Village Valmy and the Triangle de l'Arche, two recent districts at La Défense. Beyond the sculptures by Takis, a wooden footbridge passing over a rock garden leads off the square.

3. The "clouds" at the Grande Arche
Hovering like clouds between earth and sky, the sails stretched between the two pillars of the building reduce the power of the wind, which visitors always find surprising. The view outward embraces all of La Défense and extends to the Louvre and beyond.

3

The CNIT and the Esplanade

Construction in 1958 of the CNIT building, the National Center for Industry and Technology, launched what became the new district of La Défense. It was originally built for a Universal Exhibition, and was inaugurated by General de Gaulle in 1959, soon becoming an emblem of the quality of French architecture and technology. André Malraux called it a modern-day "cathedral." The modernity of the CNIT building made it a leader among professional exhibition sites for 30 years. In 1989 it was renovated and reopened at the same time as the Grande Arche, and for the 100,000 people working at La Défense it is the real core of their city.

From "Flower Show" to new technologies

The CNIT building was a real technological feat, born of the partnership of three architects, all Grand Prix de Rome winners, who at the time were called the "Three Wise Men": Robert Camelot, Jean de Mailly, and Bernard Zehrfuss. The building's exceptional character stems from its thoroughly avant-garde design. It consists of a shell of mesh-reinforced concrete, 715 ft (218 m) at the sides, resting on only three points of support.

Work began in mid-June, 1956, under the direction of engineer Nicolas Esquillan. It took 27 months of work and nearly 500 workers and engineers to complete the triangular building, in area as big as Place de la Concorde. In the 1960s, the CNIT had its finest years, with events including the "Flower Show." Exhibitions followed each other regularly, covering such diverse subjects as machine tools, advertising, and do-it-yourself. Until 1974, no exhibition had less than a million visitors.

Thirty years after it was built, the CNIT was renovated by architects Michel Andrault and Pierre Parat. The interior was completely redesigned, and the original façade, which had been classified as a historic monument like the roof, was restored to its original state. When it was turned into the Center for New Industries and Technologies, the CNIT became an international business center for 60 countries, a congress center, and a European forum for IT and communications. It also has a hotel and nearly 200 boutiques. About 10,000 people use it each day.

The Esplanade

The Esplanade at La Défense is as long as the Champs-Elysées, and forms a continuation of the great Parisian avenue. It begins at the Seine at Pont de Neuilly and rises in a gentle slope to the Grande Arche. All the footbridges and squares at La

Défense converge on the Esplanade, which is the backbone of La Défense. The district has 29,592,000 sq ft (3,000,000 sq m) of office space as well as acres of greenery, a panoramic cinema, many large-scale sculptures, and a range of cafés and restaurants. When it was built, the architects took the view that it should be a city without automobiles. The pedestrian is king, and it is not unusual to go around a corner and find a group of *pétanque* players. In 1964, a development plan was produced covering a huge area straddling the communes of Puteaux, Nanterre, and Courbevoie. The top of the hill at La Défense is 72 ft (22 m) higher than the level of the Seine. It was here that the planners decided to build a vast artificial plateau totalling 99 acres (40 ha). The site became a tremendous testing ground for town planners and architects, each set to outdo the other. Towers soared upward by the dozen, reaching ever higher. The other side of this vertical city is La Défense's underground world of technical departments, parking garages, railroads, road networks, and commercial centers. Wherever one stands at La Défense, there are spectacular views of the various different levels. Some of the skyscrapers have sets of steps built up the outside, like the stepped ramparts of medieval fortresses. Going up the Esplanade is like going back in time. Although the Esso Tower, the district's first, has vanished and been replaced by the "Coeur Défense" (an impressive, brand-new office complex), the "Nobel Tower," which in 1966 was the district's first real skyscraper, is still recognizable. Not so Tower CB16, built in 1969 and completely changed in the course of recent renovation. La Défense is in perpetual flux and, on the Saint-Germain-en-Laye side, the Grande Arche looks out on an immense landscape of the future.

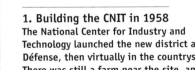

1. Building the CNIT in 1958
The National Center for Industry and Technology launched the new district at La Défense, then virtually in the countryside. There was still a farm near the site, and cows and sheep on the Nanterre plain.

2. "La Défense de Paris"
The 19th-century jury preferred this bronze allegory by sculptor Louis-Ernest Barrias to an Auguste Rodin design. Its polystyrene replica stood at La Défense while it was being built, then was burnt in a schoolboy prank. The original was placed on its plinth in 1983, a hundred years after its inauguration.

3. The CNIT and the Bull Tower
After the CNIT was turned into an international business center, large companies like Bull, the French IT giant, moved to La Défense.

4. The PB6 Tower
Designed by Ieoh Ming Pei, architect of the Louvre Pyramid, this skyscraper with its concave façade, like the fore-edge of a book, was a real technological challenge: 492 ft (150 m) high on a base of only 102 ft (31 m).

5. Sculpture by Bernar Venet
The fragile balance and interlaced form of Bernar Venet's *Indeterminate Double Line* (1988) is an important feature of the Michelet district. The sculpture is one of 70 works of art at La Défense, which is a real open-air museum.

6. Interior of the CNIT
Not to touch the famous mesh-reinforced concrete roof, measuring 715 ft (218 m) at its sides, was not the least of the challenges facing the architects responsible for renovating this modern-day "cathedral." Despite the interior's huge size, it is surprisingly well lit.

VERSAILLES
Beyond the city walls

The Château de Versailles

Parc de Versailles
and the Trianons

Aerial view of Versailles
Versailles was born of the ambitions
of an all-powerful king, the genius of the
artists he surrounded himself with, and the
labor of hundreds of thousands of men.
It is not only the symbol of power, courtly
splendor, and pleasures enjoyed under the
Ancien Régime. It is also a hymn to the
mastery of nature which binds us
incessantly to its seasons, to the elements,
to the stars, and even to the gods. All this
is reflected in the palace's terraces and
views, its marbles and clipped trees, its
ornamental pools, its statues, and
hidden bowers.

The Château de Versailles

The vast Palace of Versailles is a masterpiece of symmetry whose every perspective is a delight to the eye. As one approaches the Palace from the Place des Armes, the stone and pink brick of the walls, the high roofs of bluish slate, and the irregular wings enclosing three separate courtyards all provide a very striking picture. From the park, the long stone façade and the flat Italianate roof adorned with balustrades, trophies and vases give an impression of openness and unity.

Building in stages

The contrast between the two façades of this palace-cum-museum cannot be understood without some knowledge of how it was built. At the heart of the palace, on the town side, in the so-called Marble Courtyard, the simple hunting lodge Louis XIV inherited from his father is preserved almost intact. On the garden side, however, it is a different story: Louis XIV concealed the original building within a gigantic stone envelope designed to reflect his power as he transferred the seat of government to Versailles. The château was not finished during the Sun King's reign, and was later transformed under Louis XV and Louis XVI.

◆ The "little house of cards"

When the future Louis XIII went hunting at Versailles with his father, Henri IV, it was a land of woods, heath, and pastures, dotted with pools. Once he was king, he built a modest house there in 1623. He liked the place so much that, no longer content just to spend the night there after hunting, he had Philibert Le Roy extend it in 1631. But it was still only a "little house of cards," as Saint-Simon put it. Then, in 1661, at the age of 23, Louis XIV became king. He too took an interest

in this small château of brick, stone, and slate, so fashionable at the beginning of the century. He called in the architect Louis Le Vau, the gardener Le Nôtre, and the decorator Charles Le Brun. He replaced the outbuildings with two new wings, and added a large iron balcony and other embellishments. These initial works, carried out between 1661 and 1668, did not radically alter the old château, whose buildings still stand round the Cour de Marbre. In the gardens, he organized magnificent festivities, to which he invited the whole court. The most famous of these, called "The Pleasures of the Enchanted Island," took place in May, 1664.

◆ The "new château"

In 1668, after throwing another magnificent party in the gardens, "The Great Royal Entertainment," Louis XIV decided to enlarge his château to match his great prestige. He was, though, still fond of the old

château of his youth, and did not want to demolish it. Le Vau built a new extension, the so-called "envelope" into which he integrated the original château on the garden side, and which was to contain the *Grands Appartements*. Following Le Vau's death, further extensions and modifications continued for decades, but Versailles still retained the contrast between its buildings on the courtyards, with their typical Ile-de-France brick and slate style, and the garden façades inspired by Italian palaces.

◆ The royal residence

Louis XIV had harbored a distrust of Paris since the "Fronde," the rebellion he had experienced at the age of ten. On May 6, 1682, he moved himself and his government to Versailles. Apart from the Regency period, the royal family was to live at Versailles for a hundred years. In 1678, an enlargement program was launched under the direction of Jules

The Château de Versailles

Hardouin-Mansart and Charles Le Brun. Thousands of workers were employed—masons, sculptors, carpenters, painters, cabinetmakers, upholsterers, gilders, and laborers. The buildings trebled in area. The château's characteristic architectural and decorative style now came into its own—a style that would influence all of France, and Europe too. Decoration of the Hall of Mirrors and its two Salons, symbolizing the monarch's absolute power, was completed in 1684. To accommodate his Court, its staff and his large family, Louis XIV continually added new buildings: the South Wing (1678-82) and North Wing (1685-9) leading out from the main body of the château, the Orangery, the Stables, the Grand Commun, the Trianon ... The final building of his reign was the Royal Chapel, begun in 1699 by

4

---

1. Lake with *La Seine* (Le Hongre)
Two vast ornamental pools, decorated with reclining bronze statues, reflect the château's garden façade and emphasize its horizontal lines. These masterpieces of 17th-century statuary are allegories symbolizing the rivers of France.

2. Garden façade with *The Vase of Peace*
The marble vases on the corners of the terrace are *The Vase of Peace,* by Tuby, and *The Vase of War,* by Coysevox. They refer to great events in Louis XIV's reign, their decoration reflecting that of the Salons of War and Peace located above them.

3. Garden façade, detail
A balustrade bristling with trophies and firepots breaks up the flat Italianate roof. The façade, whose varying depth makes it even more pleasing to the eye, is surmounted by statues of the 12 months of the year, and Apollo and Diana, symbolizing the rhythms of earthly life.

4. Cour de Marbre
The old château surrounding the Cour de Marbre was built by Louis XIII. Louis XIV decorated it with statues, columns, and other adornments.

Jules Hardouin-Mansart and finished by Robert de Cotte in 1710. Also at that time, a new town was built next to the palace, radiating toward it. This was Versailles, the first of the great modern capitals, forerunner of cities such as Washington, DC and Brasilia.

◆ The grand rebuilding project

On the death of Louis XIV in 1715, the Court abandoned Versailles for the whole of the Regency. It returned in 1722 with Louis XV and stayed until the Revolution. The palace again underwent major modifications. The *Appartement des Bains* and the Ambassadors' staircase were destroyed, and the apartments of the King, the Queen, and the Royal Family were redesigned to make them more comfortable and intimate. J-A

Gabriel, who directed the new works, also built the Petit Trianon (1762-4) and the Royal Opera (1768-70).

From the Kings to the Republic

Versailles today offers two images: some 120 rooms are as they were in the former royal residence, and about as many again make up the Museum of the History of France created by Louis-Philippe.

◆ A major history museum

At the close of the Ancien Régime, Versailles exemplified all the finest things that French arts and crafts had produced in the 17th and 18th centuries. But the Revolution stripped the palace of many of its treasures. The château was "preserved and maintained at the expense of the Republic for the pleasure of the people and to form institutions useful to agriculture and the arts." Under the Empire, it became an imperial residence. Napoléon had it restored. In 1830, it was threatened with destruction. To "save" it, Louis-Philippe decided at his own expense to turn it into a museum dedicated to "all the glories of France." He brought in more than 6,000 paintings and 2,000 sculptures.

◆ The restorations

In 1870, the château became the Prussian staff headquarters. The German Empire was proclaimed in the Hall of Mirrors. As for the former royal residence, it was not until the 20th century that programs

1 **2**

FACTS & FIGURES	
THE CHÂTEAU	
Area of roofs : 27 acres (11 ha)	
Windows : 2,153	
Rooms : 700	
Staircases : 67	
Restorers of works of art : 18 (cabinetmakers, gilders, upholsterers, etc)	
THE PARK	
Area : almost 2,000 acres (800 ha) Petit Parc : 185 acres (75 ha), Grand parc : 1,650 acres (670 ha)	
Trees : 200,000	
Flowers planted each year : 210,000	
Gardeners : 48	
THE GRAND CANAL	
Area : 57 acres (23 ha)	
Perimeter : 3.5 miles (5.6 km)	
THE FOUNTAINS	
Fountains : 55	
Water jets : 620	
Water consumption : 127,138 cu ft (3,600 cu m) per hour at full capacity	
Hydraulic engineers : 8	

could be started to restore the exterior and interior decorations, thanks to the generosity of certain patrons. After the Opera in 1957, the Queen's Bedroom and the Hall of Mirrors in 1976, and the King's Bedroom in 1980, the latest major restorations have been to the clock in the Cour de Marbre, the Cabinet of Dispatches—where the kings received couriers and spies—and the ceiling of the Hercules Salon. The Royal Opera and the Chapel are now used for plays, ballets, and concerts.

◆ The national palace

In 1871, during the Commune, the Thiers government left Paris for Versailles, and sessions of the Assemblée Nationale were held in the Opera. Since 1875, benches installed in the South Wing have been used by the Parliament and the Senate for certain important votes. National Presidential elections took place here from 1879 to 1953, and Parliament also met to vote on every revision to the constitution. In its role as the national palace, Versailles is also used for receptions for important guests such as foreign Presidents.

1. The Royal Family (Jean Nocret)
In this painting of 1670, the Royal Family is depicted as a gathering of the gods. Louis XIV appears as Apollo, with his laurel crown and scepter terminating in a radiant sun. At his knee, the Queen, Marie-Thérèse of Austria, is likened to Juno. The Dauphin is shown as a winged Cupid.

2. The Galerie des Glaces
The walls of this 239 ft (73 m) gallery, built in 1678, are covered with marble and mirrors. In the middle of the ceiling is the young King, painted by Le Brun. De Gaulle started the tradition of having grand state dinners in this gallery for the visit of Khrushchev in 1960.

3. The Royal Chapel
This majestic creation in white stone has a gallery reserved for the Royal Family, princes and dignitaries. The decorations all illustrate parallels between the Old and New Testaments.

4. The Queen's Bedroom
The paneling, lintels, and ceiling medallions are from the Louis XV period, but the furniture and hangings were restored to their original state in 1789, just before Queen Marie-Antoinette left this room forever.

Parc de Versailles and the Trianons

The park at Versailles both extends and complements the Palace, and the two form a coherent whole. The strict geometry of the flowerbeds, the ponds and the Grand Canal reflects the harmoniously ordered architecture of the Palace and echoes its fine perspectives. Decorative features inside the palace and sculptures in the park are designed to glorify the King, the god Apollo, and the sun. Although these embellishments have survivied the test of time, the trees and plants in the park have been less fortunate. Severe gales in 1990 and 1999 caused extensive damage, and though many of the old trees were destroyed, these natural disasters provided the necessary impetus for an ambitious program to restore the park to its original splendor. Once again the gardens of Versailles would be worthy of Le Nôtre, the genius who designed them over three centuries ago.

◆ Louis XIV and Le Nôtre: a passion for gardens

Even before he started to decorate his father's château, Louis XIV hired A Le Nôtre (1623-1700) to design the gardens. The latter was helped in this mammoth task by master of works J-B Colbert, by C Le Brun, who designed numerous statues and fountains, by the architect J-H Mansart, and by the sculptor F Girardon. The work went on for some 40 years. Thousands of men carted countless tons of earth, and thousands of trees were brought in from all over France. Where once there had been woods, pastures and marshes, there were now terraces, grand perspectives, beautifully laid-out paths and borders, little open-air pavilions, places for sharing secrets and places where grand parties could be held. Statues and fountains placed throughout the park added to its charm and grandeur. The gardens were so important to Louis XIV that he insisted on supervising the plans and wanted to be given detailed reports of work in progress. Toward the end of his life, the "greatest king in the world" even wrote a guidebook entitled *A Way of Showing the Gardens at Versailles*.

◆ An ambitious restoration program

The park at Versailles was newly planted once every hundred years (in 1675, in 1775, and in 1875), but was suffering from old age when a violent storm in 1990 blew down more than a thousand trees. This provided an opportunity to take a new look at the gardens and to realize that due to the passage of time, changing fashion and periods of neglect, they now bore little resemblance to Le Nôtre's brilliant design. The subtle landscaping had largely disappeared, and large, unkempt trees blocked the original vistas. It was therefore

decided to replant and restore the park, referring to the plans, drawings and inventories of the period. The whole restoration program, which was given added impetus by a second major storm in 1999, will take a total of some 20 years to complete.

◆ **Opening perspectives and enclosing the groves**

The restoration aims to bring back the contrast between vast, open perspectives and the inticate geometry of the concealed "bosquets" or groves, with their fountains, trelliswork, rock gardens, and marble. Hundreds of chestnut trees, which had grown too tall and bushy, had to be felled and replaced by rows of young trees to open up the Grand Perspective designed by Le Nôtre. From the windows of the palace, there are unimpeded views as far as the Apollo pool and beyond to the end of the Grand Canal. Straight, tree-lined walks increase the impression of depth. The new green carpet of the Allée Royale conceals a service tunnel containing electrical circuits, water pipes, and sound cables. The Encelade grove is once again surrounded by a turf lawn in the form of an amphitheater, with a curtain of trees supported on trellises. Gradually, all the groves are to be restored to their former glory.

◆ **The sculptures**

More than 300 statues, busts, and vases in marble, lead, and bronze decorate the borders, paths, and pools, making the gardens of Versailles a fabulous museum of open-air sculpture. About 50 of these are antiques or copies of originals (or molds taken from them) commissioned from the finest sculptors of the day. The principal theme of the sculptural decorations is inspired by the myth of Apollo, which goes back to Louis XIV's "grand order" of 1674. There are 24 statues and four groups representing the Four Hours of the Day, the Four Seasons, the Four Quarters of the World, the Four Elements, the Four Humors of Man (melancholy, phlegm, choler, and blood), and the Four Poetic Forms (heroic, pastoral, satirical, and lyrical)—in short, everything that is influenced by the course of

the sun. It all amounts to an impressive propaganda program in favor of the Sun King, as well as a marvelous cosmic poem. Other themes for the statues include important figures from Antiquity—Plato, Socrates and Diogenes—and various gods and heroes from mythology, such as Venus, Bacchus, Hercules, and Jupiter. There are also allusions to events in the reign of Louis XIV, especially those concerning war and peace, and warnings to courtiers disguised as allegories, such as the Giant at the Encelade pool who is crushed beneath rocks for having tried to rebel against Jupiter. Finally, fauns, nymphs, and children are scattered everywhere to add a note of fantasy and lightness. As you go from Versailles to Trianon, you leave this world of gods and deified kings

1. The Temple of Cupid
This small temple in white marble was built by Richard Mique in 1778 for Marie-Antoinette. It contains a statue of Cupid by Bouchardon; the original is in the Louvre.

2. The Giant at the Encelade pool
This statue, covered in gold leaf, was made in 1677-8 by Gaspard Marsy, three years after the death of his brother Balthasar. The two made many of the sculptures at Versailles, including the Bacchus pool, *Leto and her Children*, and the statues of *Daybreak* and *Midday*.

3. Apollo pool
The pools are only seen at their finest during the *Grandes Eaux* displays. But supplying water for these causes enormous problems; in Louis XIV's time, the engineers were ordered to whistle to warn of his arrival so the fountains could be turned on.

4. Louis XIV's promenade
Louis XIV was very fond of his gardens, and liked to show off the fine views, the fountains, groves, and statues. He even wrote a sort of guide, *A Way of Showing the Gardens at Versailles*.

5. Pathway of Leto
More than 300 sculptures adorn the gardens at Versailles. Their symbolism almost always echoes that used in the château.

to re-enter the world of man. Even the Grand Trianon, despite its size, appears relatively intimate, not to mention the Petit Trianon and the Queen's hamlet. Like the King's kitchen garden, these are places where kings and queens sought to escape from the weight of their rank and the rituals of etiquette. Here, tired from their trek around the Grande Galerie and the Allée Royale, visitors too can savor their delights.

The Grand Trianon

◆ From Louis XIV to Napoléon

The Grand Trianon has the graceful looks of an Italian palace, with two ground-floor wings joined by a peristyle opening onto the gardens, a flat roof concealed by a balustrade, and pilasters and colonnades in green and pink marble. It was built by Jules Hardouin-Mansart in 1687 for Louis XIV. In 1670, when he undertook the enlargement of Versailles, the King commissioned Le Vau to build him "a house for taking light meals" on the neighboring lands of the Trianon. However, the white and blue faience cladding of this "porcelain Trianon" quickly proved very fragile. So the King had it replaced with a bigger, more solid marble palace, the one you can see today, where he liked to relax and amuse himself with his family away from the constraints of the Court. The furniture dates from Napoléon I, who restored the palace and on occasion stayed there.

◆ Trianon-under-the-Woods: for guests of the Republic

The Grand Trianon's extension wing, known as "Trianon-sous-Bois," has been a residence for heads of state since Charles de Gaulle was President. He preferred it to Versailles, which he thought "excessive."

André Malraux, then Minister of Culture, had Trianon-under-the-Woods restored in 1962. Its two floors and beautiful, paneled rooms have been open to the public since 1999. Recent guests have included Queen Elizabeth II in 1972 and President Boris Yeltsin in 1992.

The Petit Trianon

◆ The influence of Mme de Pompadour

The Petit Trianon was completed in 1678, a masterpiece of linear purity by Jacques-Ange Gabriel. By then Madame de Pompadour, without whom the building would never have existed, had been dead for four years. It was she who had brought the king to Trianon, a place he remembered fondly from his childhood, but which he had neglected on coming to the throne. From 1750, Louis XV went there to indulge his taste for building and his love of botany and agronomy. There he created an experimental garden with heated glasshouses where scientists tried to grow coffee trees, pineapples, and exotic flowers. He also got Jacques-Ange Gabriel to build the New Menagerie, an elegant summer dining room, and the pavilion of the French Garden where he went to classify his dried plants and take a light snack of milk and strawberries during his many walks with Mme de Pompadour.

◆ The dreams of Marie-Antoinette

Louis XVI gave the Petit Trianon to Marie-Antoinete, and she was to give

it much of the distinctive character it still has today. Empress Eugénie, wife of Napoléon III, endeavored to preserve her memory and recover her furniture, which had been dispersed in the Revolution.

More than the château itself, it is the English garden with its *fabriques*, small buildings scattered around the garden, which reveals the tastes of Marie-Antoinette and her time. The radical transformation of the idea of nature, as found in Rousseau, led the aristocrats of the 18th century to reject geometric gardens in the Le Nôtre style and develop a passion for landscaped gardens where rocks and valleys, streams and winding paths, and apparently disordered foliage and flowers conveyed an image of virgin nature. The quest for innocence and a frugal life led to an appreciation of country settings, farms, windmills, and dairies. The desire to bring "beautiful souls" together encouraged them to build temples of love. Marie-Antoinette commissioned the painter Hubert Robert, architect Richard Mique, and gardener Claude Richard to make her an English garden with a theater, a temple of love, a rock pavilion, and her delightful hamlet.

◆ A botanical jewel

Marie-Antoinette dismantled Louis XV's botanical garden, whose collections were transferred to the future Jardin des Plantes. Her garden is still a botanical jewel, with its

varied species, which she had the Navy bring her from North America: tulip trees and junipers from Virginia, ash trees from Carolina, and oaks from Florida. Many of their descendants were still in place when the terrible storm of 1999 struck. Some of the more venerable trees thrown to the ground, such as a Virginia juniper grown from a cutting from a tree dating back to the English Garden's creation, were sold at auction.

Today's great replanting program at Versailles has made it a priority to restore the rural scenes so typical of 18th-century gardens.

1. Petit Trianon
The pure Classical style of the Petit Trianon was influenced by Palladio. It was built for Louis XV by J-A Gabriel in 1763-8.

2. The Orangery
Two gigantic staircases, called the Hundred Steps, lead to the Orangery built by J H-Mansart in 1686. Its hundreds of palms, orange and pomegranate trees are brought into the open once the frosts have passed.

3. Grand Trianon
A loggia connects the palace's two wings and opens onto the garden via a colonnade in pink marble. Built by J H-Mansart for Louis XIV in 1687, the Grand Trianon looks like an Italian palace.

4. *View of the Garden at Versailles* (Robert)
The park at Versailles was freshly planted in 1775. This view, painted in 1774 when the trees were being felled, shows Louis XVI and Marie-Antoinette in the foreground.

5. The King's kitchen garden
Created by Jean-Baptiste de la Quintinie to produce fruit and vegetables for Louis XIV's table, the King's kitchen garden today sells them to the public. The clever gardener managed to transform 22 acres (9 ha) of marshy ground into 29 carefully drained and irrigated gardens, where he defied nature to serve the king strawberries in December and peaches at the beginning of May. Managed today by the École Nationale Supérieure du Paysage, the kitchen garden has 16 plots bordered by pear and apple trees where they grow vegetables such as cabbages, leeks, turnips, artichokes, and spinach.

6. The storm of December, 1999
The storms of 1990 and 1999 caused considerable damage, but were also an opportunity to replant the park as Le Nôtre had designed it. Hundred-year-old trees were sold at auction to friends and patrons of Versailles.

199

PARIS IN DEPTH

Below are details of the main historical, cultural, and tourist sites in the capital.

ARRONDISSEMENTS

1st arrondissement (Right Bank): 450 acres (182.7 ha). In 1999: 16,900 inhabitants; *under 20 years of age:* 14.2%; *over 60:* 19.6%. *Districts:* St-Germain l'Auxerrois, Halles, Palais Royal, Place Vendôme. *Main sites and monuments:* Louvre, Tuileries Garden, Gardens and Arc de Triomphe du Carrousel, Gardens of Palais Royal, Place Vendôme, Garden of Les Halles, Conciergerie, Palais de Justice, Saint-Chapelle.

2nd arrondissement (Right Bank): 245 acres (99.2 ha). In 1999: 19,600 inhabitants; *under 20 years of age:* 14.8%; *over 60:* 15.4%. *Districts:* Gaillon, Vivienne, Mail, Bonne Nouvelle. *Main sites and monuments:* Palais de la Bourse (Stock Exchange), Bibliothèque Nationale (National Library), Richelieu site.

3rd arrondissement (Right Bank): 290 acres (117.1 ha). In 1999: 34,200 inhabitants; *under 20 years of age:* 15.8%; *over 60:* 16.3%. *Districts:* Marais, Arts et Métiers, Enfants Rouges, Archives, St-Avoye. *Main sites and monuments:* Conservatoire des Arts et Métiers (Conservatory of Arts and Crafts), Musée Carnavalet, Musée Picasso, mansions in Rue des Archives.

4th arrondissement (Right Bank): 400 acres (160 ha). In 1999: 30,700 inhabitants; *under 20 years of age:* 13.8%; *over 60:* 21%. *Districts:* Marais, St-Merri, St-Gervais, Arsenal, Notre Dame. *Main sites and monuments:* Notre-Dame Cathedral, Hôtel de Ville (City Hall), Place du Châtelet, Tour St-Jacques, Georges-Pompidou Center, Place des Vosges.

5th arrondissement (Left Bank): 630 acres (254 ha). In 1999: 58,800 inhabitants; *under 20 years of age:* 15.6%; *over 60:* 20.4%. *Districts:* St-Victor, Jardin des Plantes, Val de Grâce, Sorbonne. *Main sites and monuments:* Panthéon, Sorbonne, Hôtel de Cluny, Mosque, Jardin des Plantes (Botanical Garden and museums), Institut du Monde Arabe (Arab World Institute), Val de Grâce.

6th arrondissement (Left Bank): 530 acres (215.4 ha). In 1999: 46,900 inhabitants; *under 20 years of age:* 16.3%; *over 60:* 23.9%. *Districts:* Monnaie, Odéon, Notre-Dame-des-Champs, St-Germain-des-Prés. *Main sites and monuments:* Luxembourg Palace and Garden, Church of St-Germain-des-Prés, Hôtel des Monnaies (the Mint) and Institut de France.

7th arrondissement (Left Bank): 1,010 acres (408.8 ha). In 1999: 57,000 inhabitants; *under 20 years of age:* 16.8%; *over 60:* 24.9%. *Districts:* St-Thomas d'Aquin, Invalides, École Militaire, Gros Caillou. *Main sites and monuments:* Musée d'Orsay, Palais Bourbon (Assemblée Nationale), Hôtel des Invalides, Musée Rodin, Eiffel Tower, Champ de Mars-École Militaire.

8th arrondissement (Right Bank): 960 acres (388.1 ha). In 1999: 39,300 inhabitants; *under 20 years of age:* 19.4%; *over 60:* 20.6%. *Districts:* Champs Élysées, Faubourg du Roule, Madeleine, Europe. *Main sites and monuments:* Place de la Concorde, Grand Palais, Petit Palais, Champs Élysées, Palais de l'Élysée, Madeleine Church, Parc Monceau, St-Alexandre Nevski Cathedral, Arc de Triomphe.

9th arrondissement (Right Bank): 540 acres (217.9 ha). In 1999: 55,800 inhabitants; *under 20 years of age:* 17.1%; *over 60:* 18.4%. *Districts:* St-Georges, Chaussée-d'Antin, Faubourg Montmartre, Rochechouart. *Main sites and monuments:* Opéra-Garnier, Musée Grévin.

10th arrondissement (Right Bank): 710 acres (289.2 ha). In 1999: 89,700 inhabitants; *under 20 years of age:* 19%; *over 60:* 15.2%. *Districts:* St-Vincent de Paul, Porte St-Denis, Porte St-Martin. *Main sites and monuments:* Canal St-Martin, Hôpital St-Louis.

11th arrondissement (Right Bank): 900 acres (366.5 ha). In 1999: 149,200 inhabitants; *under 20 years of age:* 16.8%; *over 60:* 17.2%. *Districts:* Folie Méricourt, St-Ambroise, Roquette, Ste-Marguerite. *Main sites and monuments:* Place de la République, Place de la Bastille, Place de la Nation.

12th arrondissement (Right Bank): 1,575 acres (637.7 ha). In 1999: 136,700 inhabitants; *under 20 years of age:* 17.4%; *over 60:* 20.9%. *Districts:* Bel Air, Picpus, Bercy, Quinze-Vingts. *Main sites and monuments:* Bois de Vincennes, Parc Floral, Musée des Arts d'Afrique et d'Océanie, Parc de Bercy, Opéra-Bastille, Promenade Plantée and Reuilly Garden.

13th arrondissement (Left Bank): 1,765 acres (714.6 ha). In 1999: 171,600 inhabitants; *under 20 years of age:* 19%; *over 60:* 19%. *Districts:* Salpétrière, Gare, Maison Blanche, Croulebarbe. *Main sites and monuments:* Bibliothèque Nationale de France F Mitterrand (National Library), Manufacture des Gobelins.

14th arrondissement (Left Bank): 1,400 acres (562 ha). In 1999: 132,800 inhabitants; *under 20 years of age:* 15.9%; *over 60:* 20.2%. *Districts:* Montparnasse, Parc de Montsouris, Petit Montrouge, Plaisance. *Main sites and monuments:* Catacombs, Parc Montsouris, Atlantique Garden.

15th arrondissement (Left Bank): 2,100 acres (850.2 ha). In 1999: 225,500 inhabitants; *under 20 years of age:* 16.4%; *over 60:* 21.4%. *Districts:* St-Lambert, Necker, Grenelle, Javel. *Main sites and monuments:* Parc Georges Brassens, Parc André Citroën.

16th arrondissement (Right Bank): 1,950 acres (784.6 ha). In 1999: 161,800 inhabitants; *under 20 years of age:* 18.7%; *over 60:* 25.8%. *Districts:* Auteuil, Muette, Porte Dauphine, Chaillot. *Main sites and monuments:* Palais de Chaillot, Trocadéro Gardens, Palais de Tokyo (museum of modern art), Palais Galliera, Bois de Boulogne, Parc de Bagatelle, Zoological Garden, Musée des Arts et Traditions Populaires.

17th arrondissement (Right Bank): 1,400 acres (566.9 ha). In 1999: 161,100 inhabitants; *under 20 years of age:* 18.2%; *over 60:* 20.6%. *Districts:* Ternes, Plaine Monceau, Batignolles, Épinettes. *Main sites and monuments:* Palais des Congrès, Square des Batignolles.

18th arrondissement (Right Bank): 1,480 acres (600.5 ha). In 1999: 184,600 inhabitants; *under 20 years of age:* 18.7%; *over 60:* 20.6%. *Districts:* Grandes Carrières, Clignancourt, Goutte d'Or, Chapelle. *Main sites and monuments:* Sacré-Coeur, Butte Montmartre and Place du Tertre.

19th arrondissement (Right Bank): 1,700 acres (678.7 ha). In 1999: 172,600 inhabitants; *under 20 years of age:* 23.9%; *over 60:* 16.3%. *Districts:* La Villette, Pont de Flandres, Amérique, Combat. *Main sites and monuments:* Cité des Sciences et de l'Industrie (Museum of Science, Technology and

Industry) and Parc de la Villette, Rotonde de la Villette, Parc des Buttes-Chaumont.

20th arrondissement (Right Bank): 1,480 acres (598.4 ha). In 1999: 183,100 inhabitants; *under 20 years of age:* 21%; *over 60:* 17.7%. *Districts:* Belleville, St-Fargeau, Père-Lachaise, Charonne. *Main sites and monuments:* Père-Lachaise Cemetery, Parc de Belleville.

BRIDGES

Passerelle des Arts: Links the Institut (Quai de Conti, 6th) and the Louvre (1st); footbridge ♦ Built between 1982 and 1984 by Louis Arretche to replace an earlier footbridge (1801-04) ♦ Seven steel arches on reinforced concrete pillars ♦ 500 ft (155 m) long, 36 ft (11 m) wide.

Passerelle Debilly: Links Quai Branly (7th) and Avenue de New York (16th) ♦ This footbridge was built in 1900 by Résal, Alby and Lion for the Universal Exhibition; at that time it continued Rue Albert de Mun, and was called the Passerelle de l'Exposition Militaire (Military Exhibition Footbridge). It was moved, and took on its present form in 1906 ♦ Three metal bays ♦ 400 ft (120 m) long, 26 ft (8 m) wide.

Passerelle de Solférino: Links the Musée d'Orsay (7th) to Quai des Tuileries (1st); footbridge ♦ Built between 1997 and 1999 by Marc Mimram on the site of a bridge dating from 1861, which was demolished in 1960 and replaced by a temporary footbridge from 1961 to 1992 ♦ One metal arch; benches and candelabras ♦ 350 ft (106 m) long.

Petit-Pont: Links Rue Saint-Jacques (5th) and Ile de la Cité ♦ This was built between 1852 and 1853 by Michal and Gariel to replace the last of a succession of bridges which have stood here since Antiquity ♦ One masonry arch ♦ 105 ft (32 m) long, 66 ft (20 m) wide.

Pont Alexandre-III: Links Quai d'Orsay (7th) and Cours la Reine (8th), continuing Avenue Winston Churchill ♦ Built between 1897 and 1900 by Resal and Alby for the Universal Exhibition ♦ One metal arch. At either end, monumental pylons bear-

ing gilded bronze statues of Pegasus ♦ In the center, an arrangement of nymphs of the Seine (upstream) and the Neva (downstream); 32 candelabras ♦ 505 ft (154 m) long, 130 ft (40 m) wide.

Pont de l'Alma: Links Place de la Résistance (7th), continuing Avenues Bosquet and Rapp, and Place de l'Alma (8th-16th) ♦ Built between 1970 and 1974 by Cosne, Blanc, Arsac, and Dougnac to replace an earlier bridge (1854-6) ♦ Two metal bays; statue of a Zouave on the pillar on the upstream side ♦ 470 ft (142.50 m) long, 140 ft (42 m) wide.

Pont Amont: Freeway bridge carrying the Périphérique (ring road) between the 12th and 13th *arrondissements* ♦ Built between 1967 and 1969 by Depaquit, Rousselin, Dambre, and Herzog ♦ Four concrete bays ♦ 890 ft (270 m) long, 140 ft (42 m) wide.

Pont de l'Archevêché: Links Quai de l'Archevêché (4th) and Quai de la Tournelle (5th) ♦ This bridge was constructed in 1857 by Pouard, then repaired after an accident in 1911 ♦ Three masonry arches ♦ 220 ft (67.20 m) long, 36 ft (11 m) wide.

Pont d'Arcole: Links Place de l'Hôtel de Ville (4th) and Ile de la Cité (4th) ♦ Built in 1856 by Oudry to replace a footbridge dating from 1828, then reinforced in 1880 and restored between 1994 and 1995 ♦ One metal arch ♦ 260 ft (80 m) long, 66 ft (20 m) wide.

Pont d'Austerlitz: Links Boulevard de l'Hôpital (5th-13th) and Avenue Ledru-Rollin (12th) ♦ Constructed between 1884 and 1885 by Choquet and Guiard to replace a bridge built at the beginning of the 19th century and rebuilt in 1854 ♦ Five masonry arches; pinions bearing the Imperial N, crowned and surrounded by laurels ♦

570 ft (173.80 m) long, 100 ft (30 m) wide.

Pont Aval: Concrete freeway bridge carrying the Périphérique (ring road) between the 15th and 16th *arrondissements* ♦ Built between 1964 and 1968. It is the longest bridge in Paris ♦ 1,025 ft (312.50 m) long, 110 ft (34.60 m) wide.

Pont de Bercy: Links Boulevard de Bercy (12th) and Boulevard Vincent-Auriol (13th) ♦ Built between 1863 and 1864 by Féline-Romany, widened in 1904, then widened again and transformed between 1989 and 1991 ♦ Five masonry arches; the pinions are decorated with garlands sculpted in the form of bull's-eyes ♦ 575 ft (175 m) long, 130 ft (40 m) wide.

Pont de Bir-Hakeim: Links Quai de Grenelle (15th) and Avenue du Président-Kennedy (16th) ♦ Listed in the Supplementary Inventory of Historic Monuments ♦ Two-tier bridge (road on the lower level, Métro line on the upper), built between 1903 and 1905 by Biette, assisted by Thomas and Formigé. Known until 1949 as the Viaduc de Passy, it replaced a metal footbridge built in 1878 ♦ Three plus three metal bays, linked by a masonry structure at the point where it crosses the Ile des Cygnes. Cast-iron mascarons and scallop shells; cast-iron group on the pillars (navigators, blacksmith-riveters); allegorical sculptures on the masonry structure ♦ 780 ft (237 m) long, 81 ft (24.70 m) wide on the lower level, 24 ft (7.30 m) on the upper.

Pont du Carrousel: Links Quai des Tuileries (1st) and Quai Voltaire (7th) ♦ Built between 1935 and 1939 by Malet and Lang to replace the old Saints-Pères bridge continuing the street of the same name, and opened in 1834 ♦ Three reinforced concrete arches 550 ft (168 m) long, 110 ft (33 m) wide.

Pont-au-Change: Links Boulevard du Palais (1st-4th) and Place du Châtelet (1st-4th) ♦ Built between 1859 and 1860 by Lagalisserie and Vaudrey on the site of a bridge that existed before the Romans arrived, and was replaced several times; the 1639-47 version contained houses ♦ Three masonry arches. The pinions are deco-

rated with Napoleon III's N, carved into medallions ♦ 340 ft (103 m) long, 100 ft (30 m) wide.

Pont Charles-de-Gaulle: Links Gare d'Austerlitz (13th) and Gare de Lyon (12th) via Rue Van Gogh ♦ Constructed between 1993 and 1996 by Louis Arretche and Roman Karasinski ♦ Three steel and concrete bays ♦ 680 ft (207.75 m) long, 104 ft (31.60 m) wide.

Pont de la Concorde: Links Quai d'Orsay (7th) and Place de la Concorde (8th) ♦ Listed in the Supplementary Inventory of Historic Monuments in 1975 ♦ Built between 1786 and 1791 by Perronet and widened in 1931, this bridge was known as the Pont Louis XVI, the Pont Révolution, and the Pont National before taking on its current name in 1795 ♦ Five masonry arches ♦ 500 ft (153 m) long, 115 ft (35 m) wide.

Pont-au-Double: Links Ile de la Cité (4th) and Quai de Montebello (5th) ♦ Constructed in 1883 by Bernard and Pérouse to replace the stone bridge built in 1848. In 1634, a bridge was put up in the same place, with a two-story building for the use of patients of the Hôtel-Dieu; it owes its name to the fact that residents had to pay a double denier (two penny) toll to use it ♦ One cast-iron and steel arch ♦ 125 ft (38 m) long, 66 ft (20 m) wide.

Pont du Garigliano: Links Quai André Citroën (15th) and Quai Louis-Blériot (16th), which runs from the Boulevard Exelmans to the Boulevard du Général Martial-Valin ♦ The bridge was built between 1963 and 1966 by Davy and Thénault to replace the Auteuil Viaduct (or Break-of-Day Viaduct), which was built between 1863 and 1865 in place of a ferry crossing ♦ Three metal bays on concrete pillars ♦ 685 ft (209 m) long, 85 ft (26 m) wide.

Pont de Grenelle: Links Quai de Grenelle (15th) and Avenue du Président-Kennedy (16th) ♦ Constructed between 1966 and 1968 by Thénault, Grattesat, and Pilon to replace what was first a wooden bridge built in 1827 and then an 1873 cast-iron bridge ♦ Two main metal bays, linked by a smaller one on the Ile des Cygnes ♦ 720 ft (220 m) long, 100 ft (30 m) wide.

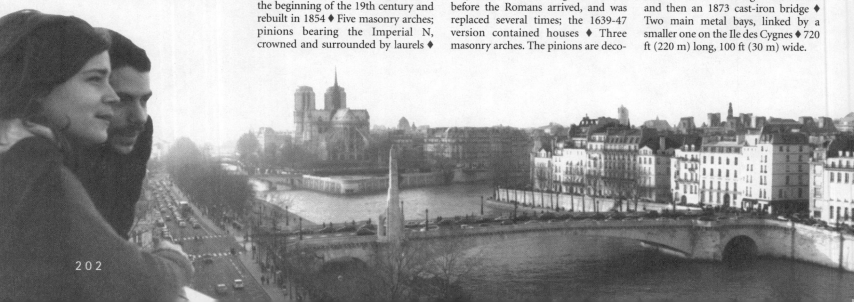

Pont d'Iéna: Links Quai Branly beneath the Eiffel Tower (7th) and Place de Varsovie (16th) ♦ Listed in the Supplementary Inventory of Historic Monuments in 1975 ♦ Built between 1808 and 1814 by Lamendé, and widened in 1937 ♦ Five masonry arches; imperial eagles on the springs between the arches and pillars, four sculptures of warriors (Gallic, Roman, Arab, and Greek) at the ends ♦ 570 ft (155 m) long, 115 ft (35 m) wide.

Pont des Invalides: Links Quai d'Orsay (7th) and Place du Canada, continuing Avenue Franklin D-Roosevelt (8th) ♦ Built between 1854 and 1856 by Lagalisserie and Savarin to mark the Exhibition of 1855 and replace a structure dating from 1829 ♦ Four masonry arches; pillars decorated by allegorical groups and military trophies carved in stone ♦ 500 ft (152 m) long, 59 ft (18 m) wide.

Pont Louis-Philippe: Links Ile Saint Louis and Quai de l'Hôtel de Ville (4th) ♦ This was built between 1861 and 1862 by Féline-Romany and Vaudrey to replace the Pont de la Réforme, which was erected in 1833 and restored in 1848 after a fire ♦ Three masonry arches with bull's-eyes set into them ♦ 330 ft (100 m) long, 50 ft (15.20 m) wide.

Pont Marie: Links Ile Saint-Louis and Quai des Célestins (4th) ♦ This bridge, built between 1614 and 1635 by Christophe Marie, used to be lined by houses which were demolished in 1788; two arches swept away by floods were replaced by a wooden bridge in 1660 and reconstructed between 1667 and 1770; the bridge was restored between 1850 and 1851 ♦ Five masonry arches ♦ 300 ft (92 m) long, 174 ft (22.60 m) wide.

Pont Mirabeau: Links Quai André-Citroën (15th) and Quai Louis-Blériot (16th) ♦ Listed as a historic monument in 1975 ♦ Built between 1893 and 1896 by Résal ♦ Three metal arches; statues on the support posts, escutcheons on the joints of the keystones ♦ 570 ft (173 m) long, 66 ft (20 m) wide.

Pont National: Links Boulevard Poniatowski (12th) and Boulevard Masséna (13th) ♦ Built between 1852 and 1853 by Couche, Petit, Metter, and Gaspard, this bridge was widened between 1936 and 1944 ♦ Five masonry and reinforced concrete arches ♦ 620 ft (188.50 m) long, 112 ft (34 m) wide.

Pont Neuf: Links Rue Dauphine (6th) and Rue du Pont-Neuf (1st) ♦ Listed as a historic monument in 1889 ♦ The bridge was built between 1578 and 1607 by Androuet du Cerceau and Marchand in two sections separated by the tip of the Ile de la Cité; it was then strengthened and regularly restored from the 17th to the 20th century ♦ Seven plus five masonry arches; half-moon turrets on the support posts, mascarons on the cornices; equestrian statue of Henri IV by Jean de Bologne on the platform between the two bridges ♦ 780 ft (238 m) long, 67 ft (20.50 m) wide.

Pont Notre-Dame: Links Ile de la Cité and Rue Saint-Martin (4th) ♦ The bridge was built in 1853 by Gabriel and transformed (metal arch) in 1912 by Dayde. It replaced the succession of structures erected at this very ancient crossing place: the Grand-Pont of Antiquity; in the Middle Ages, the Pont des Planches de Mibray, rebuilt several times from the 16th century on, and lined with houses which were demolished in 1786 ♦ Five metal and masonry arches ♦ 344 ft (105 m) long, 66 ft (20 m) wide.

Pont Royal: Links Rue du Bac (7th) and Quai des Tuileries (1st) ♦ Listed as a historic monument in 1939 ♦ Built between 1685 and 1689, and redesigned in 1852 by Jules Hardouin-Mansart; an early wooden structure, which was destroyed by fire, had been erected to replace a ferry charging a fare to cross the river ♦ Five masonry arches ♦ 426 ft (130 m) long, 54 ft (16.40 m) wide.

Pont Saint-Louis: Links Ile Saint-Louis and Ile de la Cité (4th) ♦ This was built between 1969 and 1970 by Coste and Long-Depaquit to replace seven previous bridges (all destroyed accidentally) on this site ♦ One reinforced concrete arch ♦ 220 ft (67 m) long, 52 ft (16 m) wide.

Pont Saint-Michel: Links Ile de la Cité and Boulevard Saint-Michel (5th) ♦ This was built in 1857 by Lagalisserie and Vaudrey on the site of a bridge erected at the end of the 14th century, then replaced in 1618-24 and lined by houses until 1808 ♦ Three masonry arches; pinions decorated with Napoleon III's N, carved into medallions ♦ 203 ft (62 m) long, 100 ft (30 m) wide.

Pont Sully: Links Quai Saint-Bernard (5th) and Quai des Célestins (4th), in two parts separated by the eastern tip of the Ile Saint-Louis ♦ Built between 1875 and 1876 by Vaudrey and Brosselin to replace two footbridges erected in 1836-7 ♦ Three cast-iron arches plus three cast-iron and masonry arches ♦ Large arm: 520 ft (159 m) long; small arm: 270 ft (82 m) long, 66 ft (20 m) wide.

Pont de Tolbiac: Links Rue Neuve Tolbiac (13th) and Rue Joseph-Kessel (12th) ♦ Constructed between 1879 and 1882 by Bernard and Pérouse ♦ Five masonry arches ♦ 550 ft (168 m) long, 66 ft (20 m) wide.

Pont de la Tournelle: Links Ile Saint-Louis (4th) and Quai de la Tournelle (5th) ♦ Built between 1924 and 1928 by P and L Guidetti to replace two successive bridges, the first of which was destroyed by ice floes in 1637 ♦ Three reinforced concrete arches; statue of Saint Geneviève on the support nearest the Left Bank ♦ 400 ft (122 m) long, 75 ft (23 m) wide.

CABARETS AND MUSIC HALLS

Crazy Horse Saloon: 12, Avenue George V (8th) ♦ Cabaret opened in May, 1951 by Alain Bernardin, in a 250-seat basement room ♦ The show features dances by naked women bathed in colored lights, and enterprising choreography.

Folies-Bergères: 32, Rue Richer (9th) ♦ Music hall with 1700 seats ♦ Built by Plumeret between 1867 and 1869, redesigned by Louis Sari in the 1870s, then restored in 1929 ♦ The foyer, decorated with draperies and candelabras, was originally a garden; it was covered with a glass roof in 1926. The building's Art Deco façade is embellished with a bas-relief of a naked dancer. The interior was designed by Pico ♦ In the early days, there were acrobatic acts, then dance shows, operettas, mime shows, and ballets. Later came performers such as the Isola brothers, illusionists who took over the Folies, Liane de Pougy, La Belle Otéro, Yvette Guilbert, Cléo de Mérode, Mistinguett, and Maurice Chevalier at the start of his career. From 1918, Paul Derval took over the artistic direction with great success, in particular with Josephine Baker. In 1994, Alfredo Arias revived the variety show there with "Fou des Folies."

Lido de Paris: 116 *bis*, Champs-Élysées (8th) ♦ Cabaret with 1,200 seats ♦ The building has a façade shaped like an accordion and was designed in 1932 by J Desbouis; on the second story is the Normandie cinema ♦ The stage juts out into the auditorium, and was built by Franco Bartocino and decorated by Giorgio Vecchia ♦ Dinner shows with the Bluebell Girls, aerial ballets and novelty acts, and dinner dances ♦ The original Lido at 78, Champs-Élysées, known as the "Paris Beach," was designed by E Chaux in 1928. It was both a thermal baths and a combined casino and café-concert. In 1946, the Chirico brothers turned it into a dinner-show venue with variety entertainment, then in 1977 it moved to its current address in order to expand.

Moulin Rouge: 82, Boulevard de Clichy (18th) ♦ Cabaret with 850 seats, surmounted by the sails of the mill that made it famous ♦ It offers lively dinner variety shows which perpetuate the tradition of the French cancan ♦ It was designed in 1889 by J Oller and Ch Zilder, who wanted to copy the famous Moulin de la Galette: they built a completely fake, bright red mill whose sails

were iluminated in the evening; the main attraction was the French cancan. In summer a huge garden was laid out as a café-concert; to one side is a stucco elephant from the Universal Exhibition ♦ The Moulin Rouge had many stars: Yvette Guilbert, La Goulue, and Valentin the Rubber Man. All of these inspired Toulouse-Lautrec, who was a regular patron. At the beginning of the 20th century came the théâtre-concert, in which Mistinguett came to the fore, then cinema in the interwar years; the Moulin only returned to cabaret in the 1960s, when it was restored.

Paradis Latin: 28, Rue du Cardinal Lemoine (5th) ♦ Cabaret with 700 seats ♦ Built by Gustave Eiffel in 1887

and restored between 1973 and 1976 under J Kriegel ♦ The cabaret opened its doors in 1977 with "Paris Paradis," presented by Jean-Marie Rivière, its artistic director. His successors continued to produce variety shows, including a centenary show in 1987 ♦ In the beginning, Napoléon I wanted a theater, the Théâtre Latin, built on this site; it opened in 1803, and had great success after 1830. It was destroyed by fire during the war of 1870-71, then was rebuilt by Eiffel and opened in 1889 as the Paradis Latin, featuring ballets and variety shows. Yvette Guilbert performed there during the Universal Exhibition. Later, in the face of competition from venues in Montmartre, the cabaret closed down and turned into workshops until 1930.

guards shot during the Commune, May 26, 1871.

Bercy: 329, Rue de Charenton (12th) ♦ Area: 1.5 acres (6,100 sq m) ♦ Opened in 1816 and expanded several times. Founded by Gallois de Naives, who built the Bercy wine warehouses, and is buried there (chapel).

Calvaire: 2, Rue du Mont-Cenis (18th) ♦ Area: 0.15 acres (593 sq m) ♦ The oldest cemetery in Paris (the first burials date from the 11th century); closed since 1823, except for the families of those buried there, and only open to the public on November 1-2 ♦ Grave of navigator Louis-Antoine de Bougainville (1729-1811).

Charonne: 119, Place St-Blaise, Rue de Bagnolet (20th) ♦ Area: 1 acre (4,180 sq m) ♦ 654 burial plots ♦ Opened during the Revolution ♦ Graves of actor Pierre Blanchar (1892-1963); writer Robert Brasillach (1909-45); Father Magloire or François Bègue (1837); bones of Federates killed during the Commune.

Grenelle: 174, Rue Saint-Charles (15th) ♦ Area: 1.5 acres (6,375 sq m) ♦ Opened in 1835 ♦ Graves of Léonard Violet who designed the Grenelle district in the 1820s; aviator L Condouret (died 1929).

Montmartre: or Cimetière du Nord, 20, Avenue Rachel (18th) ♦ Area: 26 acres (104,800 sq m); 2,000 burial plots ♦ Opened in 1798 in the abandoned quarries at the foot of Montmartre, which served as a communal grave during the Revolution. Five hundred of the Swiss guards killed at the time of the insurrection of August 10, 1792 were buried there. Temporarily closed, then reopened in 1831 ♦ Graves of writers Théophile Gautier (1811-72), Émile Zola (1840-1902, now in the Panthéon), Stendhal (1783-1842), the son of Alexandre Dumas (1824-95), Alfred de Vigny (1797-1863) and the Goncourt brothers (1822-96; 1830-1870); composers Léo Delibes (1836-91), Offenbach (1819-80), Berlioz (1803-69), and Michel Berger (1942-92); actors and film-makers: Sacha Guitry (1885-1957) and François Truffaut (1932-84).

Montparnasse: 3, Boulevard Edgar-

Quinet (14th) ♦ Area: 46 acres (187,200 sq m) ♦ Former necropolis of the monks of Saint-Jean de Dieu since 1654, it stands on the site of three former farms; the Tour du Moulin (14th-15th century) at the western corner dates from that time. From 1824, it became one of three Paris cemeteries ♦ Burial plots held in perpetuity since 1874 ♦ Graves of sculptor Fréderic-Auguste Bartholdi (1834-1904); poet Charles Baudelaire (1821-67); artists Constantin Brancusi (1876-1957) and Chaïm Soutine (1894-1943); mathematician Henri Poincaré (1854-1912); composer Camille Saint-Saens (1835-1921).

Montrouge: 18, Avenue de la Porte de Montrouge (14th) ♦ Area: 19 acres (75,000 sq m) ♦ Opened in 1820 on land attached to Paris in 1860, it still belongs to Montrouge ♦ Built to replace a first cemetery surrounding the Church of St-Jacques le Majeur de Montrouge, it was extended over land made available when the old fortifications were demolished ♦ Graves of actor Maurice Escande (1892-1973); poet René Crevel (1900-35); writer Albert Simonin (1905-80); painter Nicolas de Staël (1914-55); humorist Coluche (1944-86); scriptwriter Michel Audiard (1920-86).

Passy: 2, Rue du Commandant-Schloesing (16th) ♦ Area: 4 acres (17,060 sq m); 2,615 burial plots held in perpetuity ♦ Opened in 1820 on the site of the former parish cemetery, its entrance was redesigned in 1934 ♦ Graves of writers Tristan Bernard (1866-1947), Jean Giraudoux (1882-1944), and Octave Mirbeau (1848-1917); composers Claude De Debussy (1862-1918) and Gabriel Fauré (1845-1924); painters Édouard Manet (1832-83) and Berthe Morisot (1841-95); actor Fernandel (1903-71); poet Marie Bashkirtseff (1860-84), whose grave is surmounted by an Orthodox chapel.

Père-Lachaise: Boulevard de Ménilmontant (20th) ♦ Area: 110 acres (440,000 sq m); 68,315 burial plots ♦ Former Jesuit property, named for Père de La Chaise, Louis XIV's confessor ♦ The property was bought in 1804 by Prefect of the Seine Nicolas Frochot, who commissioned architect Brongniart to lay out the cemetery. Brongniart razed the buildings to the

CANALS

Canal de l'Ourcq: links La Villette basin to La Ferté-Milon (Aisne), passing through the departments of Seine-St-Denis, Seine-et-Marne, and Oise ♦ Constructed between 1813 and 1821, it was rebuilt and deepened between 1880 and 1883, widened in Paris in 1895, and rebuilt on a much larger scale as far as Pavillons-sous-Bois in 1920 ♦ Length: 68 miles (110 km), 56 miles (90 km) of which is canal, and 6 miles (10 km) is channeled river.

Canal Saint-Denis: links the canals' meeting point (Parc de la Villette) to the Seine in the Saint-Denis commune ♦ Built between 1805 and 1821 (12 locks) and rebuilt between 1890 and

1895 (7 locks, the fourth of which was rebuilt in 1974) ♦ Length: 4 miles (6.6 km).

Canal Saint-Martin: links La Villette basin to the Seine between the Quai Henry-IV and Quai de la Rapée ♦ Built between 1805 and 1825 (9 locks) with tunnels under Rue La Fayette, Boulevard Morland, and Place de la Bastille. Covered over between 1860 and 1862, and in 1906: the first phase of works, over 1 mile (2 km), was along Boulevard Richard-Lenoir; the second phase, along Boulevard Jules-Ferry ♦ Length: 3 miles (4.5 km); includes the Paris-Arsenal boating harbor.

CEMETERIES

Auteuil: 57, Rue Claude-Lorrain (16th) ♦ Area: 1.8 acres (7,172 sq m) ♦ Opened in September, 1800 on land donated by banker Le Coulteux de Canteleu ♦ Graves of engineer Jean-Charles Alphand (1817-91); artists Jean-Baptiste Carpeaux (1827-75), Paul Gavarni (1804-66), and Hubert Robert (1733-1802); composer Charles Gounod (1818-93).

Les Batignolles: 8, Rue Saint-Just

(17th) ♦ Area: 26 acres (104,200 sq m) ♦ Opened in 1833 ♦ Graves of poets Paul Verlaine (1844-96) and André Breton (1896-1966); writer Blaise Cendrars (1887-1961); singer Fedor Chaliapine (1873-1938); painter Édouard Vuillard (1868-1940).

Belleville: 40, Rue du Télégraphe (20th) ♦ Area: 4.5 acres (18,000 sq m) ♦ Opened in 1808 in parkland belonging to the Château de Ménilmontant ♦ Grave of inventor and industrialist Léon Gaumont (1863-1946), who launched the film industry ♦ Pyramid to the memory of 40

ground but preserved the avenues of lime and chestnut trees, giving the green, hilly site its present appearance ◆ Mausoleum of Héloïse and Abélard, Mur des Fédérés (Federates' Wall). Graves of writers Balzac (1799-1850), Gérard de Nerval (1808-55), Alfred de Musset (1810-57), Oscar Wilde (1854-81), Alphonse Daudet (1840-97), Marcel Proust (1871-1922) and Colette (1873-1954); painters Géricault (1791-1824) and Modigliani (1884-1920); actors Sarah Bernhardt (1844-1923), Pierre Brasseur (1905-72) and Simone Signoret (1921-85); musicians Frédéric Chopin (1810-49), Édith Piaf (1915-63) and Jim Morrison (1943-71); spiritualist Allan Kardec (1804-69); Egyptologist Champollion (1790-1832).

Picpus: 35, Rue de Picpus (12th) ◆ Area: 0.75 acres (3,000 sq m) ◆ Opened in 1794 in the garden of a former convent for prisoners executed by the guillotine at Place de la Nation (more than 1,300 in June-July, 1794) ◆ Private cemetery, reserved for descendants of the victims, such as General de La Fayette. Graves of poet André Chénier (1762-94); statesman Victor de Broglie (1785-1870).

Saint-Mandé: Rue du Général-Archinard (12th) ◆ Area: 7 acres (30,000 sq m) ◆ Opened in 1878 on military land beneath the Thiers wall for inhabitants of the commune of Saint-Mandé ◆ Graves of draughtsman Alfred Grévin (1827-92), founder of the waxworks museum, dramatic author Jules Moineaux, father of humorist Courteline (1815-95), composer Alexandre Tansman (1897-1986).

Saint-Vincent: 6, Rue Lucien Gaulard (18th) ◆ Area: 1.5 acres (5,900 sq m) ◆ Opened in 1831 ◆ Graves of writers Marcel Aymé (1902-67) and Roland Dorgelès (1885-1973); painters Maurice Utrillo (1883-1955) and Eugène Boudin (1824-98); composer Arthur Honegger (1892-1955).

Valmy: 102, Avenue de la Porte de Charenton (12th) ◆ Area 5 acres (20,000 sq m) ◆ Opened in 1906 near old fortifications on the edge of the Bois de Vincennes, annexed to Paris in 1919; it has always belonged to Charenton. Monument to the memory of

the gendarmes of Ouvéa (New Caledonia, 1988) and their comrades.

Vaugirard: 320, Rue Lecourbe (15th) ◆ Area: 2.7 acres (15,900 sq m); 2,949 burial plots ◆ Opened in 1798 to replace the old cemetery at the corner of Rue Desnouettes and Rue Vaugirard (1341-1787), and extended several times. Bodies from the Invalides Institution (home for disabled and wounded soldiers) were buried there ◆ Graves of Abbot Groult d'Arcy (died 1843); president Paul Doumer (1857-1932), and three of his sons killed in World War I.

La Villette: 46, Rue d'Hautpoul (19th) ◆ Area: 3.3. acres (13,400 sq m) ◆ Opened in 1828 in the former commune of La Villette (annexed to Paris in 1860), on the site of three cemeteries, two of which date from the 15th and 18th centuries ◆ Graves of naturalist writer Lucien Descaves (1861-1949); sculptor Auguste Heng (1891-1968), one of whose works, *La Pleureuse*, adorns the grave.

CINEMAS

Accatone: 20, Rue Cujas (5th) ◆ Arts cinema; 110 seats. Presents series, festivals, and retrospectives to which directors and artists are invited ◆ The cinema was once a café, Aux Dernières Cartouches, where people practised shooting, then a cabaret, the Gipsy, where Fréhel and Édith Piaf sang. It was converted into a cinema, the Studio Cujas, in 1957, and took on its current name in 1987 ◆ There is an art gallery in the foyer.

Action Christine: 4, Rue Christine (6th) ◆ Arts cinema; 2 screens with 165 and 90 seats, one equipped for 3-D films ◆ Shows repeats of works by great filmmakers and films by young directors ◆ Located in an old building with a listed 17th-century carriage entrance.

Action Écoles: 23, Rue des Écoles (5th) ◆ Arts cinema; 2 screens with 120 and 100 seats. Mainly shows American retrospectives (Marx Brothers, Chaplin, Keaton, Cary Grant, Wilder), and Hitchcock and Fritz Lang films ◆ Opened in 1977 as the Nickel Écoles ◆ A staircase in Carrara marble leads to the basement auditorium.

L'Arlequin: 76, Rue de Rennes (6th) ◆ Arts cinema with 3 screens: 1 with 400 seats and 2 with 100 seats ◆ Shows French and foreign films, and has events such as the Festival d'Automne. Formerly the Lux-Rennes cinema, with a restaurant in the basement, it opened in 1934; from 1949 it became the cabaret La Rose Rouge, where Juliette Gréco made her début. It was bought by Jacques Tati in 1962, renamed L'Arlequin and restored to its original purpose. Between 1978 and 1991, it was

called the Cosmos, and Soviet films were screened there. It was renovated in 1993 and reverted to its present name. In 1998, the small auditoriums were opened in the basement, a former night club ◆ There is a large picture window, a fresco in the foyer representing a Harlequin, monumental stairs leading to the small auditoriums, and a vast reception area.

Balzac: 1, Rue Balzac (8th) ◆ Arts cinema; 3 screens with 400, 160 and 90 seats, renovated in 1993 ◆ The smallest auditorium became a reception room; in the largest, the lighting is from glass stalactites mounted on onyx pillars ◆ Owned by a Russian immigrant, Scholiansky, the Balzac opened in 1935 with *Wedding Night* by King Vidor. It has always had a good reputation; at first it showed American hits, then after the war, great French films. In 1973, it acquired two smaller auditoriums.

Champo: 51, Rue des Écoles (5th) ◆ Arts cinema listed in the Inventory of Historic Monuments; 2 screens with 130 and 120 seats ◆ Shows classic film retrospectives, repeats of art-house films and tributes to contemporary film directors ◆ When the main auditorium, built in 1938, was burnt down, its projection room was reinstalled above the screen, directing the image to a mirror at the back of the room which reflected it onto the screen ◆ Very popular with movie buffs in the Latin Quarter, its films have entertained several generations of students; it was also the cinema of choice for New Wave directors such as Truffaut and Chabrol. The second auditorium

was built in 1956 and called the Actua-Champo.

Cinéma des Cinéastes (Le): 7, Avenue de Clichy (17) ◆ Arts cinema; 3 screens with 315, 90, and 70 seats ◆ Shows recent films, previously unreleased films, retrospectives, and films with a thematic link ◆ Its red, metallic façade opens onto an exhibition gallery in the foyer, designed in stone and metal with frescos; the main Jules-Étienne Marey auditorium is in the Gustave Eiffel style ◆ Formerly the Père Lathuille cabaret, it became the Kursal cabaret in 1906, and the Eden in 1928 before being converted into a cinema in 1932. The Les Mirages auditorium was refurbished in 1937; two small auditoriums were built in 1973; the cinema was renovated in 1991. In 1996, the ARP (Association of Directors and Producers) redeveloped the cinema and gave it its new name.

Cinémathèque Française – Salle Grands Boulevards: 42, Boulevard de Bonne-Nouvelle (10th) ◆ 200 seats ◆ Shows retrospectives, restored old films, experimental films; organizes performances for young people ◆ Its modern frontage opens onto a former cinema, Le Palace, built in 1907, which put on films, concerts, and music-hall. It became L'Amiral in the 1950s, was equipped with a manually operated stage curtain and showed old favorites. In 1975, it was renamed the Brooklyn and specialized in erotic films, then closed in 1993. It was taken over by the Cinémathèque in 1997, when a fire temporarily put the Chaillot site out of commission

Cinémathèque Française – Palais de Chaillot: 7, Avenue Albert-de-Mun (16th) ◆ 290 seats ◆ Shows famous old films. The auditorium is in the east wing of the Palais de Chaillot; after renovation, it kept its walls decorated with engraved shapes and its arcades ◆ The Cinémathèque Française was founded in 1936 by Henri Langlois, Georges Franju and Jean Mitry; it first took over an auditorium in the Champs-Élysées before establishing itself in the Palais de Chaillot in 1966; its aim was to preserve, restore,

and increase awareness of the outstanding films in the history of the cinema ♦ A Cinema Museum was added in 1972.

Les 5 Caumartin: 101, Rue St-Lazare (9th) ♦ Arts cinema; 5 screens with 200, 110, 90, 60, and 40 seats ♦ Shows films in the original language, reruns, and children's films ♦ The main auditorium, Le Cinévog, opened in 1939 on the site of a restaurant; a second auditorium was built in 1966, then four others replacing the first and two last ones in 1971. It was classified as an arts cinema in 1997.

Cinéma Diagonal Europa: 13, Rue Victor-Cousin (5th) ♦ Arts cinema; 270 seats ♦ Shows European films in the original language. One of the oldest cinemas in Paris. The Omnia-Pathé Victor Cousin opened in 1907 on the site of a gymnasium, was renamed the Cinéma du Panthéon in 1930, and showed foreign films in the original language: *Love Parade* by Ernst Lubitsch, with Maurice Chevalier, was shown on opening night. It was renovated in 1998 and became the Diagonal Europa Panthéon.

L'Entrepôt: 7-9, Rue Francis-de-Pressensé (14th) ♦ Arts cinema; 3 screens with 90 seats ♦ Multicultural center with a program of jazz and music concerts, it has a bookshop, a restaurant, and a bar ♦ The former Olympic Entrepôt, designed by Frédéric Mitterrand in 1975, was set up as a meeting place for movie buffs. It became L'Entrepôt in 1987, and widened its cultural policy.

L'Épée de Bois: 100, Rue Mouffetard (5th) ♦ Arts cinema; 2 screens: 75 and 65 seats, dedicated to contemporary filmmakers. ♦ The cinema opened in 1978 on the ground floor and the basement of an apartment building, and took on the name of the avant-garde theater demolished in 1971; it was restored in 1993.

Escurial Panorama: 11, Boulevard de Port-Royal (13th) ♦ Arts cinema; 2 screens with 244 and 85 seats. Shows recent French films, reruns and series,

and children's films; organizes performances for schools, has facilities for societies ♦ The old Royal cinema was built in 1911 in a converted warehouse, then expanded and was modernized in the 1920s. It was renamed the Escurial in 1933, modernized again in 1953 by the film director Jean Gouguet, and in the 1980s when it adopted its current name.

Espace Saint-Michel: 7, Place St-Michel (5th) ♦ Arts cinema; 2 screens: 130 and 100 seats. Shows popular films, works by new directors and filmmakers not widely known in France ♦ The cinema opened in 1912, and at first showed newsreels. It established itself in the Latin Quarter and had great success with *Devil in the Flesh* by Claude Autant-Lara in 1947. Divided into two in 1981, one of its auditoriums was destroyed by fire in 1988. Then it was completely redeveloped (and renamed); it has an area for discussions about films, a bar-restaurant, and a bookshop.

Forum des Images: Porte St-Eustache, Forum des Halles (1st) ♦ 6 screens with 500, 300, 100, 40, 30, and 20 seats ♦ Shows films about Paris and urban culture, classics, little-known films, and themed series; organizes festivals, and meetings with film directors including La Quinzaine des Réalisateurs (Cannes Film Festival directors); access to the audiovisual collection on Paris in the video room (films, short films, documentaries, newsreels, and advertising) ♦ The Forum is located under Les Halles Garden, and opened in 1988 as the Vidéothèque de Paris. Now the Forum des Images, it includes the former Auditorium des Halles and Le Cybertport, a video and Internet reference resource.

Gaumont Cinemas: This is the oldest cinema company, founded in 1895 by Léon Gaumont who built the Gaumont-Palace, the largest cinema of its time, demolished in 1973 ♦ Since the 1920s, the company has mainly concentrated on screening films. Its many cinemas include the Gaumont Ambassade: 50, Avenue des Champs-Élysées (8th), 7 screens (440, 400, 300, 180, 90, 80, and 70 seats); Gaumont Grand Écran Italie: 30, Place d'Italie (13th), 3 screens (650, and 2 with 100 seats); Gaumont Marignan: 27, Avenue des

Champs-Élysées (8th), 6 screens (560, 520, 400, 120, 100, and 70 seats); Gaumont Opéra Premier: 32, Rue Louis-le Grand (2nd), 6 screens (420, 280, 160, 2 with 100, and 80 seats).

Géode: 26, Avenue Corentin-Carriou (11th) ♦ 400 seats ♦ Shows travel and natural history films, and films from fiction ♦ The exterior is covered in a steel shell of polished triangles, which reflect the landscape and the pool around it ♦ The auditorium has a 30-degree rake and a semicircular, 11,000 sq ft (1,000 sq m) screen measuring 85 ft (26 m) in diameter, which plunges the spectator inside the image by means of the *Omnimax* process. This enables a field of 172 degrees to be filmed with a super wide-angle lens, the curvature of the screen compensating for any distortion. Sound and image are controlled by computer ♦ The auditorium opened in 1985 with *Water and Mankind*

Grand Action: 5, Rue des Écoles (5th) ♦ Arts cinema; 2 screens: the Henri Langlois auditorium, 220 seats, and the Henri Ginet, 100 seats ♦ Shows reruns of classic films (new copies), puts on festivals, and invites personalities to introduce films ♦ This former real-tennis court became a café-concert at the end of the 19th century, then a cinema from the beginning of the 20th. In 1950, now known as the Celtic, it began specializing in foreign films in the original language; it was renamed Studio Jean Cocteau in 1972, and decorated with the poet's drawings. It joined the Action group in 1983.

Images d'Ailleurs: 21, Rue de la Clef (5th) ♦ Arts cinema; 2 screens: 150 and 80 seats ♦ Shows African and art-house films from across the world, and retrospectives, organizes meetings and discussions, and caters for societies and schoolchildren ♦ Formerly La Clef, the cinema had 3, later 4 screens, and showed documentaries until it closed in 1981. The Association Images d'Ailleurs revived it in 1990.

Le Latina: 20, Rue du Temple (4th) ♦ Arts cinema; 2 screens with 180 and 60 seats ♦ In 1984, the Cultura Latina association took over the former Le Marais cinema and renamed it ♦ It specializes in Latin-language films (Spanish, French, Italian, Portuguese,

and Romanian) in the original version with subtitles, and meetings with directors and filmmakers ♦ There are temporary exhibitions by Latin artists in the art gallery, and the cinema also houses the Bistrot Latin and a dance hall (Latin music).

Lucernaire Forum: 53, Rue Notre-Dame-des-Champs (6th) ♦ See *Théâtre du Lucernaire*.

Mac Mahon: 5, Avenue Mac Mahon (17th) ♦ Arts cinema; 190 seats ♦ Shows the great classics, puts on tributes and festivals, special programs for children and adults, also previews and press conferences ♦ It opened in 1938, then after the war showed the American films then inspiring film buffs such as Truffaut and Tavernier, the group known as the Mac-Mahonians. The cinema was renovated in 1988.

Majestic Bastille: 4, Boulevard Richard-Lenoir (9th) ♦ Arts cinema; 2 screens with 260 and 100 seats ♦ Shows art-house films, films in the original language, series, and previews; organizes discussions with film crews, performances for schools and societies ♦ It opened in 1934 as the Bastille Palace with a 500-seat auditorium but declined in the 1970s and closed in 1987. Now that the district is being radically transformed, partly because of the new opera house, the cinema was renovated and reopened in 1995 ♦ It has an impressive façade, and a marble and oak interior.

Majestic Passy: 18, Rue de Passy (16th) ♦ Arts cinema, 3 screens with 320, 180, and 150 seats ♦ It has first screenings of popular films, shows art-house films in the original language, also previews, and organizes special evenings ♦ It opened in 1937 as the Royal Passy with a 750-seat auditorium in a brand-new building; it took the name Broadway in 1977 and installed the Speciavision process which gives extra depth to the image. Closed in 1982, it reopened in 1994 ♦ There is a marble staircase in the foyer, which is luxuriously decorated.

Max Linder Panorama: 24, Boulevard Poissonnière (9th) ♦ Arts cinema; 700 seats; auditorium entirely decorated in black, on three levels: orchestra, balcony, and mezzanine ♦ Shows

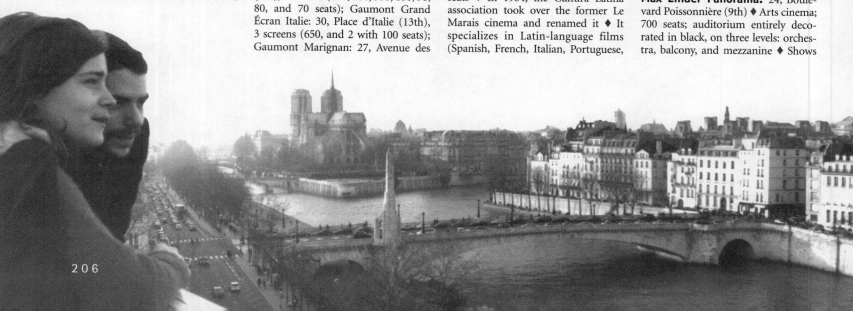

original language movies by French and foreign filmmakers that are not widely seen on the main circuits; organizes film nights and meetings with directors ◆ Linder opened his cinema in 1920 and showed American films there. Various owners later used the auditorium for different functions, then in the 1980s it became a cinema once more, was renovated in 1988 and equipped with a vast panoramic screen, the most modern in Europe at that time.

MK2 cinemas: This company, formed in the 1970s, has a network of multiplexes with some auditoriums for art-house films. The multiplexes were built on the sites of old cinemas and in renovated historic buildings, or newly built in new districts. The cinemas include: MK2 Bastille, the oldest, dating from 1974, 4, Boulevard de Beaumarchais (11th), 4 screens (237, 114, 72, and 45 seats); MK2 Beaubourg, 50, Rue Rambuteau (3rd), 6 screens (185, 120, 105, 65, 50, and 40 seats); MK2 Beaugrenelle, Centre Beaugrenelle, 16, Rue Linois (15th), 6 screens (231, 195, 149, 141, 132, and 85 seats); MK2 Gambetta, 6, Rue Belgrand (20th), in a cinema built by Sauvage in 1929 whose façade has been preserved, 6 screens (556, 246, 179, 121, 78, and 46 seats); MK2 Parnasse, once the Studio de Paris then the Studio Parnasse, 11, Rue Jules Chaplain (6th), 3 screens (160, 80, and 50 seats); MK2 Quai de Seine, 14, Quai de la Seine (19th), in a redeveloped building constructed during the 1889 Universal Exhibition, 6 screens (299, 299, 120, 120, and 2 with 77 seats).

La Pagode: 57 *bis*, Rue de Babylone (7th) ◆ 2 screens with about 180 seats ◆ Shows recent films ◆ This Japanese pavilion has a faïence façade with stained-glass windows, and overlooks a small garden; one auditorium has kept the original Japanese decoration ◆ It was built in 1896 for the director of the Bon Marché department store who gave it to his wife; it reflects the vogue for all things Japanese. Many receptions and parties were held there until 1928 ◆ It was bought in 1931 and turned into a cinema. In 1959, Cocteau staged the première of *Testament d'Orphée* there. Classified as an arts cinema, it is a favorite with movie buffs. Closed in November, 1997, it reopened in November, 2000.

Paramount Opéra: 2, Boulevard des Capucines (9th) ◆ 7 screens, 2 with panoramic screens, with 800, 650, 400, 250, 125, 100, and 95 seats ◆ In 1927, it took over the former Vaudeville theater, built in the 1860s. At that time, it had an auditorium of 2,000 seats with an orchestra, balcony, and mezzanine, a mobile stage for variety shows and a classical orchestra. It was inaugurated by Chang de Schoedsack and Cooper and a show by the Bluebell Girls. In the 1970s, the auditorium was divided into two; three new auditoriums were subsequently opened, and two more at the beginning of the 1980s ◆ The original rotunda façade is surmounted by a cupola and adorned with pilasters and columns with capitals. The foyer is decorated with paneling, and the ceiling with silver-plated motifs; there is a bar for audiences, its walls decorated in carved wood.

Paris Story: 11 *bis*, Rue Scribe (9th) ◆ 190 seats ◆ Shows one multi-image film on a giant three-part screen, with special effects and extracts from video images. The film tells the story of Paris and its way of life, showing its heritage and important events from the foundation of Roman Lutetia to the Grande Arche. First set up in 1991 by Ch Ruty, at 78 *bis*, Boulevard des Batignolles as the Paristoric, it moved to the Opéra district in 1995.

Quartier Latin: 9, Rue Champollion (5th) ◆ Arts cinema; 2 screens with 100 and 70 seats ◆ Shows European films and little-known movies from Africa, Asia, and the Middle East, and puts on festivals and repeats ◆ This former bar of the Théâtre des Noctambules was first a cabaret, featuring Y. Guilbert, Théodore Botrel, Noël-Noël, and Raymond Souplex, then in 1951 a theater, the Quartier Latin. A cinema opened there in 1956; the second auditorium was built in 1984. It was renamed the Utopia Champollion the following year, then the Utopia, before reverting to its first name.

Racine: 6, Rue de l'École de Médecine (6th) ◆ Arts cinema, 275 seats ◆ Has first screenings of new art-house films, shows little-known foreign films, repeats, and children's programs ◆ It opened in 1965 in a former surgical instruments store; at first an arts cinema, it later specialized in horror films.

It was known as the 14 Juillet Racine, then the Racine-Odéon; it belongs to the Ciné-Classic group.

Reflet Médicis: 3-7, Rue Champollion (5th) ◆ Arts cinema; 3 screens with 175, 170, and 130 seats ◆ Shows retrospectives, repertory films, and first screenings of art-house films; puts on festivals and themed evenings ◆ In 1939, it opened as the Théâtre des Noctambules, the theater of Jean Vilar, Gérard Philippe, and Maria Casarès. The auditorium was converted into a cinema in 1956. Later it joined up with its neighbors: the Studio Logos, opened in 1963 and specializing in art-house films, and the Studio Médicis, dedicated to Louis Jouvet. Now they all bear the same name ◆ To the left of the screen, a stained-glass window is a reminder of its theatrical past. It also has a cinema bookshop.

Le République: 18, Faubourg du Temple (11th) ◆ Arts cinema; 290 seats ◆ Has first screenings of art-house films and films in the original language, and shows series and retrospectives; organizes discussions and shows for children ◆ This very old cinema opened in 1911 on the site of the Cirque Olympique. It was converted into a concert hall at the beginning of the 1920s, restored to its original purpose in 1930 and named the Templia. Classified as an arts cinema in 1969, it was completely refurbished and decorated in a modern style, and inaugurated in the presence of film historian H Langlois; it was then called the Action République. Subsequently, it became the Républic Cinéma, the Réflet Républic (annexed to the Cinémathèque in the 1990s), and then the République.

Rex: 1, Boulevard Poissonnière (2nd) ◆ 7 screens including Le Grand Rex, classified as a historic monument with 2,800 seats; other auditoriums with 100 to 500 seats ◆ Shows popular films; organizes special events (the Night of the Césars film awards ceremony), a fantasy film festival, and an aquatic show at Christmas ◆ Together with the Gaumont-Palace, this was one of the great cinemas of the inter-war years ◆ Built of reinforced concrete, it was inaugurated in December, 1932, when the people of Paris had their first glimpse of its vast façade and ornate

entrance. The interior was in Oriental style with flowers and palm trees, and the basement contained various services (bar-restaurant, hair salons, cloakrooms, first aid, kennels, and a nursery). The auditorium had 5,000 seats (orchestra, balcony, and mezzanine) with space for 60 musicians; an 80 ft (24 m) wide stage and a high ceiling decorated with stars. On opening night, there was dancing by the Rex Girls and other acts before the screening of *The Three Musketeers* by H Diamant-Berger ◆ The cinema had several owners, including the Gaumont company; it became the German soldiers' cinema during the Occupation, then was requisitioned to house prisoners of war. Later, it reverted to its old repertoire with great success, showing *Pinocchio*, *Les Casse-Pieds*, *La Chartreuse de Parme*, and *Joan of Arc*; but the special events disappeared, apart from the aquatic show, the Féerie des Eaux, devised in the 1950s. Three new underground auditoriums were built in the basement in 1974, and four others ten years later.

Saint-André-des-Arts: 30, Rue St-André-des-Arts (6th) ◆ Arts cinema; 3 screens including the Saint-André-des-Arts bis, 12, Rue Gît-le-Cœur: 180, 150, and 190 seats ◆ Art-house and popular films ◆ Founded in 1971 by R Diamantis who opened 2 auditoriums in a 17th-century building, replacing a former cardboard business, and opened with *The Salamander*, by A Tanner; in 1979, he added the Gît-le-Coeur cinema to them.

Saint-Germain-des-Prés: 22, Rue Guillaume-Apollinaire (6th) ◆ Arts cinema; 280 seats ◆ The auditorium is dedicated to G de Beauregard, a New Wave producer ◆ Formerly the Bilboquet (1969), it became the Olympic Saint-Germain in 1979, then the Saint-Germain-des-Près in 1985; it was in danger of disappearing in 1992 (to be taken over by the restaurant next door), but was saved thanks to local petitions and the support of the city of Paris. It was completely renovated in 1999.

Saint-Lambert: 6, Rue Péclet (15th)

♦ Arts cinema; 3 screens with 189, 99, and 75 seats ♦ Program changes daily, with more than 25 films a week, and screenings for children in school holidays ♦ A cinema with 300 seats was built in 1935 in a 1930s building, replacing a functions room. The balcony was turned into a second auditorium in 1986, and another added in the basement in 1992 ♦ The entrance and the main auditorium are in Art Deco style.

Les 7 Parnassiens: 98, Boulevard du Montparnasse (14th) ♦ Arts cinema; 7 screens: 260, 245, 120, 70, 55, 45, and 30 seats ♦ It opened in 1978, showing films in the original language. Renovated in 1995, the complex has a large foyer at the end of a shopping arcade, Les Parnassiens, which also opens onto Rue Delambre. Shows art-house films, popular films, African films, and programs for children.

Studio Galande: 42, Rue Galande (5th) ♦ Arts cinema; 92 seats ♦ Opened in 1973, it screens about twenty films a week, and every Friday and Saturday evening shows the musical comedy *Rocky Horror Picture Show*; fans call out the lines, spray each other with water, and throw rice. Programs for children.

Les Trois Luxembourg: 67, Rue Monsieur-le-Prince (6th) ♦ Arts cinema; 3 auditoriums: 130, 110, and 80 seats ♦ First multi-screen complex, opened in 1966 and renovated in 1986. Façade decorated with modern sculpture representing the world of the cinema. It shows films reflecting art-house trends and retrospectives.

UGC cinemas: In 1971, independent owners formed a company out of this network, which started after the war. Its remit was to show a quota of French and foreign films of cultural and artistic interest to the State, and a quota of films subsidized by the State. It manages well-established cinemas and multiplexes including the UGC Champs-Élysées: 65, Champs-Élysées (8th), Prestige auditorium (450 seats); UGC George V:

146, Avenue des Champs-Élysées (8th), 11 screens with one Prestige auditorium (420, 400, 170, 130 seats, and 7 screens with 80 to 100 seats); UGC Normandie (which owes its name to the famous luxury liner): 116, Avenue des Champs-Élysées (8th), 4 screens with one Prestige auditorium (865, 280, 250, and 150 seats); UGC Ciné Cité Bercy: 2, Cour St-Émilion (12th), 18 screens (4,500 seats); UGC Ciné Cité les Halles: Place de la Rotonde, Forum des Halles (1st), 19 screens (3,250 seats).

Studio des Ursulines: 10, Rue des Ursulines (5th) ♦ Arts cinema. 130 seats ♦ Shows new films and retrospectives of old films ♦ The cinema opened at the beginning of the 20th century, and was taken over in 1926 by Armand Tallier, founder of the avant-garde Art et Essai movement. He established an avant-garde cinema, the Studio des Ursulines, which owes its name to a former convent on the site, destroyed in the 18th century ♦ The first program consisted of a short pre-war film, *Mimosa la dernière grisette*, an avant-garde film, *Entr'acte*, by René Clair, and a previously unreleased film, *Joyless Street* by Pabst. Later memorable events included the première of *The Shellfish and the Clergyman* by Germaine Dulac, based on a screenplay by Antonin Artaud, at which the Surrealists staged a riot, and successes such as *The Blue Angel* by von Sternberg which ran for more than a year ♦ In 1998, the *Studio des Ursulines* was taken over by the Association of Film Directors and Producers, and continues as an arts cinema.

Studio 28: 10, Rue Tholozé (18th) ♦ Arts cinema. 170 seats ♦ Shows recent films, repertory films, children's films, and shorts. The screening of *Napoléon* by Abel Gance in 1928 gave the cinema an avant-garde reputation. In 1930, Buñuel's *L'Âge d'Or*, combined with an exhibition of paintings by the Surrealists (Dali, Max Ernst, Miro, Man Ray, etc), caused a scandal: the auditorium and exhibition were wrecked, and the film was banned. Subsequently, the cinema passed through various owners while mainly showing great American comedies. After World War II, it was taken over by G Roulleau and sponsored by J Cocteau and A Gance, and showed

Napoléon again as a sound film; it was then classified as an arts cinema ♦ Its foyer was decorated by Alexandre Trauner, and has a plaque to Cocteau, who designed its wall lights.

CONCERT HALLS AND OPERA HOUSES

Auditorium des Halles: Forum des Halles, Porte St-Eustache (1st) ♦ 580 seats ♦ Built at the beginning of the 1980s, as part of the second phase of the Forum des Halles building development created by Cl Vasconi and G Pancréac'h ♦ Musical concerts.

Auditorium du Louvre: Pyramide du Louvre and Galeries du Carrousel (1st) ♦ 450 seats ♦ Built at the same time as the Pyramide du Louvre (Louvre Pyramid), and opened in 1989 ♦ Concerts, retrospectives of music on film ("Classics in Images"), films and television shows, combined with lectures and discussion days on cultural themes.

Auditorium Saint-Germain des Prés: 4, Rue Félibien (6th) ♦ 355 seats ♦ Located in the building that Clément Cacoub converted in the 1990s on the site of the old Saint Germain market; this had been built in 1817 to replace the fair of the same name, which fell out of use shortly before the Revolution ♦ Jazz concerts, musical and comedy shows, children's shows.

Châtelet: see Théâtre musical de Paris.

Cité de la Musique: Parc de la Villette (19th) ♦ Elliptically shaped, movable auditorium with 800 to 1,200 seats ♦ It is located in a conch-shaped building which also contains the Musée de la Musique, designed by Christian de PorzamParc at the end of the 1980s ♦ Concerts of classical, contemporary, and traditional music.

Olympia: 28, Boulevard des Capucines (9th) ♦ 2,000 seats. This was reconstructed in 1997 in identical form to the redesined version of 1956, but it is 130 ft (40 m) deeper than the earlier building, and uses more modern technical methods. The billiard room has been listed as a historic monument ♦ The Olympia was built at the begin-

ning of the 1890s by Nevinans and Jandelle. At first it was a music hall, opened by Oller, its creator, with La Goulue and Loïe Fuller; acrobatic acts and American vaudeville shows were put on there, and there were performances by singers such as Yvonne Printemps, Georgius, Fréhel, Damia, and Lucienne Boyer. It was turned into a cinema, then taken over by Bruno Coquatrix who opened it in 1954 with Lucienne Delyle and Aimé Barelli, converted it and directed it until 1979 ♦ The most famous artists have sung there: Édith Piaf, Trenet, Brassens, Brel, Halliday, Sardou, and Bécaud, and groups such as the Rolling Stones. Many singers still perform there.

Opéra Comique: (Salle Favart) Place Boïeldieu (2nd) ♦ National opera, with 1,300 seats ♦ The building was constructed by the architect Louis Bernier in the 1890s, to replace the one which was destroyed by fire in 1887 (400 victims). The façade is decorated with columns, caryatids, medallions, and niches with statues ♦ An earlier theater was built on a plot belonging to the Duc de Choiseul (known at the time as the Place des Italiens, after which it was named for a while). It opened in 1783 with the Opéra-Comique company, directed by Favart and featuring, among others, Madame Favart, Madame Dugazon and the tenor Trial. It burned down for the first time in 1838, and was rebuilt ♦ The *Damnation of Faust* by Berlioz, works by Victor Massé, Ambroise Thomas, Meyerber, Léo Delibes, Bizet (including *Carmen, Manon*, and *Lakmé*), and *Pelleas et Mélisande* by Gustave Charpentier were performed there ♦ Directors: Carvalho, A Carré, and J Savary.

Opéra de Paris-Bastille: 120, Rue de Lyon (12th) ♦ A national theater with three auditoriums: main theater, 2,700 seats; amphitheater, 450 seats; studio, 230 seats ♦ Built by Carlos Ott between 1984 and 1989, on the site of

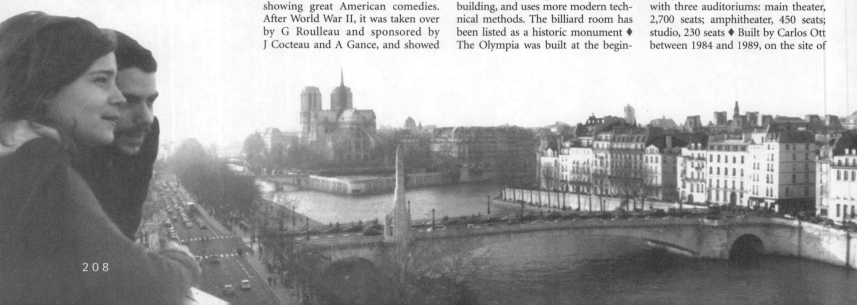

the old Gare de la Bastille ♦ Semi-cylindrical glass and stone façade. In the main theater, granite walls and wooden seats covered in black velvet, glass canopy ceiling, huge stage surrounded by moving platforms for rapid scene changes, movable orchestra pit, midnight blue curtain by Cy Twombly. There are buildings in which all the skills needed for productions are brought together, and where scenery can be built and stored ♦ The aim in building the theater was to create a great, modern, people's opera house that could put on a large number of productions. It opened on July 13, 1989 with a pleiad of famous artists in a Bob Wilson production, and was officially opened in March, 1990 with *Les Troyens* by Berlioz ♦ Director: H Gall.

Opéra de Paris-Palais Garnier:
Place de l'Opéra (9th) ♦ National theater with 971 seats ♦ A huge, composite building, constructed between 1862 and 1875 by Charles Garnier in the luxurious, baroque style that was sought after by the brilliant society of the Second Empire. The choice of an open site that would highlight the building was made after the assassination attempt on Orsini in front of the old Opéra in Rue Le Peletier. Restoration work was done in 1936, the 1960s, and in 1994-96 ♦ Façade with loggia, decorated with columns; statues, groups carved in stone, busts of composers and librettists, flat-topped dome over the auditorium ♦ Inside, the majestic main staircase, public foyer sumptuously decorated with allegorical paintings, red and gold auditorium with ceiling painted by Chagall in 1964 (decoration inspired by operas and ballets); the stage is equipped with a large amount of machinery ♦ Since its creation the Opéra-Garnier has put on operas and ballets, and featured famous performers such as Callas, Nureyev, and Béjart ♦ Directors: M Lehmann, G Auric, R Liebermann, B Lefort, and H Gall.

Salle Cortot:
114 *bis*, Rue Cardinet (17th) ♦ 400 seats ♦ Constructed in concrete by Auguste Perret in 1928, in the outbuildings of a Neo-Renaissance mansion built by Cochet in 1882. Alfred Cortot and Auguste Mangeot founded the École Normale de Musique there in 1919 ♦ Stage in the

form of a shell, wood-paneled walls and ceiling ♦ Classical music concerts.

Salle Gaveau:
45, Rue La Boétie (8th) ♦ 1,000-seat auditorium with stalls and two circles ♦ It was created in the building of the Gaveau piano firm, built in reinforced cement between 1906 and 1907 by J Hernant, and renovated at the end of the 20th century ♦ Classical-style façade with stone cladding; decoration on the walls of the auditorium in staff, plaster, and gray and gold wood; organ case by Mutin-Cavaillé-Coll ♦ Classical music concerts.

Salle Pleyel:
252, Rue du Faubourg Saint-Honoré (8th) ♦ Three auditoriums: main hall, 2,300 seats; Salle Chopin, 470 seats; Salle Debussy, 100 seats ♦ This was created by the Pleyel family of piano makers in the building constructed for them in 1927 by Auburtin, Granet, and Mathon. In 1961 it was modified, then in 1981 it was renovated and modernized for acoustic purposes by Guillomot and Metzer, and in 1995 Christian de Portzamparc redesigned it again, including the entrance hall ♦ A reinforced concrete and brick construction whose façade lets in light through nine large bay windows ♦ The Orchestre de Paris (Paris Orchestra) gives its concerts here.

Théâtre du Châtelet - Théâtre Musical de Paris:
Place du Châtelet (4th) ♦ Municipal theater with 2,000 seats ♦ Commissioned by Haussmann and built between 1861 and 1862 by Gabriel Davioud, it was intended as a venue for spectacular popular performances ♦ The building is in the Neoclassical style; its arcaded façade, dominated by four allegorical statues, is inspired by the Italian Renaissance. Inside, it has a semicircular auditorium in the Italian style; columns and arcades decorated with paintings ♦ At first it was known as the Théâtre Impérial du Châtelet, before assuming its current name; it was renovated several times: in 1962, 1979 (when it was taken over by the City and became the Théâtre Musical de Paris), 1989 (the columns were removed from the auditorium and a new curtain was created by Gérard Garouste), and finally in 1998-9 ♦ The theater has put on performances by Diaghilev's Ballets

Russes, Nijinski, the singer Caruso and Mahler (his Second Symphony); it had great successes with *Around the World in Eighty Days, Michel Strogoff*, and many operettas in which Luis Mariano triumphed. The Colonne concerts were put on here from 1874 ♦ Today the theater is used for opera, classical music, and dance ♦ Directors: M Lehmann and J-P Brossmann.

Zénith:
Parc de la Villette (19th) ♦ Adjustable auditorium with about 6,000 seats ♦ This vast marquee was built on a temporary basis in 1984, by Philippe Chaix and Jean-Paul Morel. The building intended to replace it never got beyond the planning stage. The Zénith has become part of the La Villette landscape as a popular music venue ♦ It consists of a metal structure, covered with a double membrane of PVC-coated canvas, and contains a concrete tower inherited from the old abattoirs. The red aircraft on top has become its emblem ♦ Used for variety shows and rock concerts.

COVERED ARCADES

Galerie Colbert:
Between 6, Rue des Petits-Champs and 4, Rue Vivienne (2nd) ♦ Listed in the Supplementary Inventory of Historic Monuments ♦ This elegant arcade, laid out in a right-angle, was built in 1826 by Billaud and identically reboutiqued in the 1980s: imitation marble columns with Corinthian capitals under the arcades, decorative friezes and motifs, lighting by wall lamps. At the right-angle turn there is a rotunda 50 ft (15 m) in diameter, with a statue in the center ♦ A company of speculators, Adam and Co, decided to build the arcade in competition with the Galerie Vivienne, with which it now communicates; they then rented it to luxury boutiques. The arcade was closed owing to its dilapidated condition, then in 1974 its buildings adjoining Rue Vivienne were acquired by the Bibliothèque Nationale (National Library), which had to demolish some of them before reconstructing the arcade ♦ Today not a single boutique is open any more, except the café at the entrance to Rue des Petits-Champs, which is restored in 1900s style, and the Colbert boutique which sells the publications of the Bibliothèque Nationale ♦ 270 ft (83 m) long, 16 ft (5 m) wide.

Galerie de la Madeleine:
Between 9, Place de la Madeleine and 30, Rue Boissy-d'Anglas (8th) ♦ Fairly wide arcade built in 1845 by Théodore Charpentier ♦ Caryatids on either side, rich décor, glass roof supported by flying buttresses ♦ The Place de la Madeleine entrance is next to the Lucas Carton restaurant, decorated by E Gounevitch between 1904 and 1905; the entrance on Rue Boissy-d'Anglas

is paneled in dark green ♦ There are several boutiques in the arcade: clothes, flowers, ornaments, and crafts ♦ 175 ft (53 m) long, 13 ft (4 m) wide.

Galerie Véro-Dodat:
Between Rue Jean-Jacques-Rousseau and Rue du Bouloi (1st) ♦ Listed in the Supplementary Inventory of Historic Monuments ♦ It was opened in 1826 by two butchers, Véro and Dodat, who had made their fortunes under the Restoration. It soon became a short-cut from the Les Halles district to the Palais-Royal, and was lit by gas from very early on ♦ Façade on Rue du Bouloi decorated by two male figures ♦ Black and white paving, Neoclassical décor, palm leaf frieze beneath the top of the walls, ceiling of glass panes alternating with paintings ♦ In the 19th century, prints were sold here by Aubert, who was editor of *La Caricature* and *Le Charivari*, and a friend of poet Gérard de Nerval. When new streets were built in the area, fewer people used the arcade ♦ The boutiques with their windows framed by copper-lined arcades have an old-fashioned charm: ornaments, fabrics, old books, musical instruments, a restaurant and brasserie ♦ 260 ft (80 m) long, 13 ft (4 m) wide.

Galerie Vivienne:
Between 4, Rue des Petits-Champs and 6, Rue Vivienne (2nd) with an opening onto Rue de la Banque ♦ Listed in the Inventory of Historic Monuments ♦ This elegant, right-angled arcade was built in 1823 by the architect J Delannoy for a lawyer

called Marchoux who had bought the neighboring buildings. It was very successful from the start, partly thanks to the proximity of the Palais-Royal. In 1832, a Cosmorama was introduced: this used magnifying mirrors to show three-dimensional landscapes. The adventurer Vidocq was a famous resident. The number of people visiting the arcade plummeted at the end of the 19th century, however. Marchoux's daughter bequea-thed it to the Institut de France, which still owns it today ♦ It is made up of several sections linked by covered arcades and steps. The entrance on Rue des Petits-Champs was reconstructed in 1844; the porch is decorated with caryatids ♦ After this come the large rectangular hall, a small rotunda, and the main gallery, which has a mosaic floor and is lined with arcades, decorated with staff between the boutiques (above which there are second-story apartments) and covered with a glass roof supported by transversal wooden flying buttresses; another rectangular hall leads into the narrower arcade which opens onto Rue Vivienne ♦ Today the arcade is very popular; there are various boutiques with wood-covered fronts: bookstore, ready-to-wear clothes, brasserie, tearoom, artificial flowers, toys, ornaments, and wine store ♦ 580 ft (176 m) long, 10 ft (3 m) wide at the narrowest point.

Passage Brady: Between 43, Faubourg St-Martin and 46, Faubourg St-Denis (10th) ♦ Opened in 1828 by a businessman called Brady to house numerous boutiques and second-story apartments ♦ Its size was reduced when the Boulevard Sébastopol was built in 1854, and its rotunda in the central area has disappeared, but the light fittings under the glass roof have been preserved. The extension on the other side of the boulevard is not covered ♦ It has received little maintenance, and is now occupied exclusively by Indian and Pakistani boutiques, which have moved in gradually since the 1970s: restaurants, hairdressers, grocery and craft stores ♦ 710 ft (216 m) long, 11 ft (3.50 m) wide.

Passage du Caire: Between 2, Place du Caire and 237, Faubourg St-Denis (2nd); other entrances at 44 and 16, Rue du Caire and 33, Rue d'Alexandrie ♦ The earliest covered arcade apart from the Palais-Royal gallery. It was designed by the architect Trételle, built in 1797 and opened in 1798 as part of a vast development program; it was named in commemoration of Bonaparte's entrance into Cairo during the Egyptian campaign ♦ The roof consists of large panes of plain glass, and as a result the arcade is very light. Conical rotundas mark the intersection of the three main branches: Passage du Caire, Passage Ste-Foy, and Passage St-Denis, which can be reached through five entrances ♦ The building containing the Place du Caire entrance is decorated with three heads of the goddess Hathor, above which runs a frieze of Egyptian-style figures and chariots; the windows on the upper stories form trefoil arcades ♦ Today the stores have lost their wood covering, and are occupied exclusively by garment wholesalers and suppliers for ready-to-wear boutiques; these have replaced the old lithographic printing studios ♦ 1,180 ft (360 m) long, 9 ft (2.60 m) wide at the narrowest point.

Passage Choiseul: Runs between 40, Rue des Petits-Champs and 23, Rue Saint-Augustin (2nd) ♦ Built in 1827 by F Mazois and A Tavernier as part of a huge property development carried out by the Mallet and Co Bank, this arcade was an extension of Rue de Choiseul; a second branch was opened in 1829, on Rue Sainte-Anne. A number of homes were demolished as a result, except for a part of the Hôtel de Gesvres, whose façade forms part of the entrance on the Rue Saint-Augustin side. It was immediately successful, thanks to its position between the Grands Boulevards and the Palais-Royal. M Comte's children's theater moved in; later the arcade was taken over by Offenbach; Lehmann rebuilt it in 1857, and it became the Bouffes-Parisiens, which still has a door opening onto the arcade. No 23 was the bookstore of A Lemerre, the publisher of the Parnassians (Sully Prudhomme, Coppée, Leconte de Lisle, and Heredia); Verlaine published his first poems there in 1864, and Anatole France

worked there for ten years. Céline lived at No 64, then at No 67; this is the setting for the Passage des Bérésinas in *Mort à crédit*. With the arrival of the couturier Kenzo in the 1970s, the arcade became fashionable again ♦ The arcades incorporate the mezzanine, above which there is a second story under the glass roof, and a third one above it; in the arcades are boutiques with wood-covered fronts ♦ Nowadays the arcade is very busy; staff from the neighboring banks and offices shop in its numerous boutiques: clothes, costume jewellery, toys and gifts, drawing and painting equipment, printing and copying, secondhand books, and fast food restaurants and cafés at either end ♦ 620 ft (190 m) long, 16 ft (3.90 m) wide.

Passage du Grand-Cerf: Between 10, Rue Dussoubs and 145, Rue St-Denis (2nd) ♦ Listed in the Inventory of Historic Monuments ♦ Built around 1835 in the Neoclassical style, and restored identically between 1989 and 1990, the arcade is named after the Hôtellerie du Grand Cerf (Great Stag Inn), which moved to this site before the Revolution and was sold in 1812; some of the buildings around its courtyard were preserved. It was also the terminus for the stagecoaches of the East of France Messageries Royales (Royal mailcoach service), which went into decline with the creation of the Paris railway stations. The number of people using the arcade fell dramatically, after which it was bequeathed to the Assistance publique (Health and Social Security Services) in 1862, then abandoned and closed down owing to its dilapidated condition. It has now been bought by a company which has restored it ♦ This very light arcade is the highest in Paris (nearly 40 ft/ 12 m). It has a glass roof with a metal frame; under this there are two stories of apartments which have been completely rebuilt, and above it is a further story and loft. The arcades are decorated with coffer ceilings; cornice mouldings run along above the wood-covered boutique fronts ♦ Art galleries, boutiques selling antiques, African art, ornaments, gifts, costume jewellery, and ready-to-wear clothes ♦ 380 ft (117 m) long, 10 ft (3 m) wide.

Passage du Havre: Between 69, Rue Caumartin and 109, Rue Saint-Lazare (9th) ♦ Built by Bartaumieux in 1845, and opened in 1846; demolished when the Éole Métro was built, then reconstructed by Macary, but in a modernized form ♦ A rotunda was added to the original L-shaped arcade at the junction of the first two arms, and a new branch opening onto Rue du Havre. The two levels are linked by escalators ♦ Located between the Grands Magasins and the Gare Saint-Lazare, it still attracts many shoppers and has a large number of boutiques ♦ About 475 ft (145 m) long, 12 ft (3.65 m) wide at the narrowest point.

Passage de l'Industrie: Between 27, Boulevard de Strasbourg and 42, Faubourg Saint-Denis (10th) ♦ When the arcade opened in 1827, it was lined with boutiques and studios; the section on the other side of the boulevard, running toward Faubourg St-Martin, became the Rue Gustave Goublier in 1936 ♦ The arcade is not covered, apart from a small vaulted area under the building ♦ Today it is mainly occupied by stores selling hairdressers' accessories ♦ 354 ft (108 m) long, 26 ft (8 m) wide.

Passage Jouffroy: Between 10, Boulevard Montmartre and 9, Rue de la Grange-Batelière (9th) ♦ Built between 1845 and 1846, it was opened in 1847 and immediately made a name for itself. The basement of a fabric boutique was occupied successively by the Bal Montmartre (Montmartre Dance Hall), a puppet theater, a shadow show theater, a café-concert, and Le Petit Casino, which remained there until the 1950s. It is still in vogue and very busy ♦ On the Rue de la Grange-Batelière side, it forms an L-shape. The iron and cast-iron structure of the frame gives it a light, airy quality, which is accentuated by a sumptuous glass roof. Wood is used only for decoration: framing, beading, and skirting boards ♦ Many boutiques have an upper story: bookstore, second-hand booksellers, postcards and cinema posters, prints, crafts, stones and jewellery; Oriental shop, home decoration boutiques, tearoom-caterer, fast food, Hôtel Chopin, and the display window of the neighboring Musée Grévin ♦ 460 ft (140 m) long, 14 ft (4.20 m) wide.

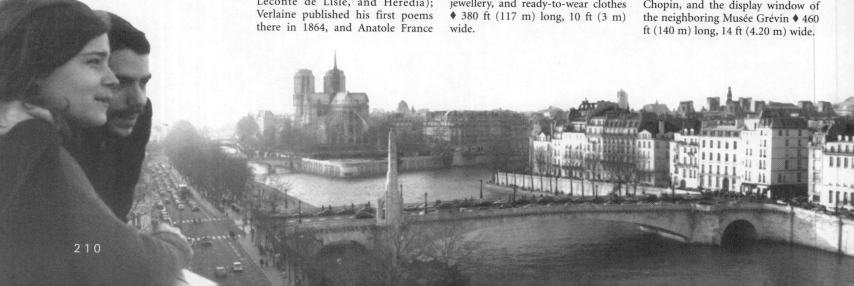

Passage des Panoramas: Between 10, Rue Saint-Marc and 11, Boulevard Montmartre (2nd) ♦ Opened in 1800, this was one of the first covered arcades in Paris. It ran between two rotundas in which long trompe-l'œil pictures were projected on to the walls with the spectator at the center. These panoramas (hence its name) were put on until 1831. With its luxury boutiques and proximity to the Théâtre des Variétés, which was much visited by artists, the arcade became a Mecca of Parisian life under the Restoration. In 1817, it was the first thoroughfare in Paris to be equipped with gas lighting. Other branches were opened up in 1834: the Galeries de la Bourse, Feydeau, Montmartre, Saint-Marc, and Les Variétés (the theater has a door opening onto it) ♦ A busy arcade lined with boutiques and an upper story under the glass roof; the Stern printing and engraving firm, with its wood-paneled décor, stamps and clothes stores, cafés, and fast food ♦ 435 ft (133 m) long, 10 ft (3.20 m) wide.

Passage du Ponceau: Between 119, Boulevard Sébastopol and 212, Rue St-Denis (2nd) ♦ A high, narrow arcade near the Passage du Caire. There are two upper stories; only the boutiques near Boulevard Sébastopol (and a few pieces of decoration) remain of the old arcade. The glass roof has been replaced by a vaulted plastic ceiling ♦ Mainly ready-to-wear clothes and fast food ♦ 300 ft (92 m) long, 8 ft (2.50 m) wide.

Passage des Princes: Between 5 bis, Boulevard des Italiens and 97, Rue de Richelieu (2nd) ♦ Opened in 1860 by the banker J Mirès on the site of a residential hotel, the Hôtel des Princes, this was the last covered arcade to be built in Paris. The AGF insurance company bought it and commissioned architects A Georgel and Mrowiec to restore it (1995) ♦ The original entrance on Rue de Richelieu, with its columns and coffered ceiling, was reconstructed; a second entrance was built. The glass roof is supported by a beautiful metal frame; on the Boulevard des Italiens side, the rotunda is topped by a colored glass dome dating from the 1930s ♦ There are no longer any boutiques in the arcade ♦ 260 ft (80 m) long, 11 ft (3 m) wide.

Passage Puteaux: Between Rue de l'Arcade and Rue Pasquier (8th) ♦ Opened in 1839, this fairly short arcade was called the Passage Pasquier for a while, before taking on the name of its developer. From the start it was less successful than had been expected; this was because the railroad station for trains to St-Germain-en-Laye, although originally planned for the Rue Tronchet area, was in the end built in the Europe district ♦ The arcade still has its six bays, decorated with moldings, under a glass roof with a metal frame; it opens onto Rue Pasquier, under a freestone building; the Rue de l'Arcade entrance is framed by Corinthian pilasters ♦ Only a small number of businesses ♦ 95 ft (29 m) long, 9 ft (2.80 m) wide.

Passage Vendôme: Between 16, Rue Béranger and 3, Place de la République (3rd) ♦ Built in 1827 on part of the land belonging to the Filles du Sauveur convent, this arcade then ran from Boulevard du Temple to the Carreau du Temple market ♦ When the Place de la République was developed in 1869, part of the glass roof was changed, and at the same time the façade on Boulevard du Temple was removed ♦ The arcade used to house about 40 boutiques; nowadays it is very quiet ♦ 200 ft (60 m) long, 13 ft (4 m) wide.

Passage Verdeau: Between 31 bis, Rue du Faubourg Montmartre and 6, Rue de la Grange-Batelière (9th) ♦ This arcade was opened in 1846 as an extension to the Passage Jouffroy, and named after one of the members of the company sponsoring both sites. After a period of decline, it is now popular again with collectors thanks to the reopening of the neighboring Hôtel Drouot auction rooms in 1980 ♦ A light-filled arcade in the Neoclassical style, with entrances framed by Corinthian pilasters and a high, fish-bone glass roof ♦ Numerous boutiques selling secondhand books and comic books, postcards, prints, paintings, and bric-à-brac, not to mention fast-food outlets and a tea-room ♦ 250 ft (75 m) long, 12 ft (3.75 m) wide.

DEPARTMENT STORES

Bazar de l'Hôtel de Ville (BHV): 52-64, Rue de Rivoli (4th) ♦ Store built at the beginning of the 20th century: clothes, fashion accessories, perfumes, toys, bookshop, and especially known for household equipment ♦ Its founder, Xavier Ruel, a stallkeeper, rented a store called Le Bazar Napoléon at the corner of Rue de Rivoli and Rue des Archives in 1856. As it expanded, Ruel gradually bought up the whole block. In 1912-13, the store was completely refurbished, except for the Rue de Rivoli façade: several basement levels were developed, elevators installed, and display windows instaled ♦ The iron-framed rotunda by Roy makes the store visible from a distance.

Bon Marché (Le): 22, Rue de Sèvres (7th) ♦ Store built in the late 19th century and early 20th century: clothes, fashion accessories, perfumes, furniture, interior design, toys, groceries, caterers ♦ In 1852, a former department manager from Petit St-Thomas, Aristide Boucicaut, went into partnership with Videau and opened a store at the corner of Rue du Bac ♦ Boucicaut became sole proprietor, and put up a new building on the site of the former Hospice des Petites-Maisons. A Laplanche was the first architect, between 1869 and 1872, followed by Ch Boileau. The latter commissioned G Eiffel to build the steel skeleton. The high glass roofs and the wrought-iron balustrade around the second story are in the style of the original interior decoration ♦ Zola described the store in Au Bonheur des Dames ♦ Around 1910, a new store was built on the other side of Rue du Bac. It served as a military hospital at the beginning of World War I, was destroyed by fire in 1915, and rebuilt in 1923. Its Art Deco decoration was removed in 1975, when the store was redesigned as a supermarket ♦ The interiors of the two establishments were regularly modernized during the 20th century.

Carrousel du Louvre: 99, Rue de Rivoli (1st) ♦ Modern shopping arcade built by Ieoh Ming Pei as part of the Grand Louvre scheme in 1993 ♦ It runs beneath the Place du Carrousel, is lit by an upside-down glass and steel pyramid, and houses boutiques in keeping with the museum: a vast bookstore, others selling objets d'art and interior design, the Studio-Théâtre, rooms for conferences and exhibitions, and restaurants.

Forum des Halles: Rue Pierre-Lescot (1st) ♦ A modern shopping and cultural center, the Forum's boutiques sell gifts, interior design, leisure items, household equipment, and clothes; there are restaurants, a swimming pool, a gymnasium, cinemas, and L'Auditorium des Halles ♦ It was built in 1979 to plans by Cl Vasconi and G Pancréa'ch on the site of the former Les Halles market (demolished in 1969) and the Châtelet-les-Halles RER station, to which it has direct access. Four shopping levels with tiered windows surround an open square, decorated with a sculpture by Julio Serva, *Pygmalion*. At ground level, glass and steel buildings (J Willerval) border the Jardin des Halles (Cl and Fr–X Lalanne). On Level 3, a long gallery containing the larger stores and cinemas leads to the Place Carrée.

Galeries Lafayette: 40, Boulevard Haussmann (9th) ♦ Department store built in the early 20th century: clothes, fashion accessories, perfumes, furniture, interior design, bookshop, toys, etc. Founded by Ferdinand Chanut for Alphonse Kahn and Théophile Bader, the store was built by Georges Chedanne (1906-07), then extended towards Rue de Mogador (1910-12), in order to enlarge their fancy goods store, opened in 1895 on the corner of Rue Lafayette and Boulevard Haussmann ♦ One of the two large original halls has survived: surrounded by arches and surmounted by a vast, steel-framed glass cupola, it opens onto the surrounding stories; the second hall was demolished in 1926 when the store was modernized. The Art Nouveau wrought-iron balustrades and the remains of the façade on Chaussée d'Antin date from the Belle Époque. But the vast central staircase has been demolished. From 1932-36, P Partout built new façades. The roof terrace was

removed in order to add two further stories.

Printemps (Au):
64, Boulevard Haussmann (9th) ♦ Today's department store dates from the late 19th century and the early 20th century: clothes, fashion accessories, perfumes, furniture, interior design, bookshop, toys, etc ♦ The first building was constructed in 1883 by Paul Sédille, replacing the store founded by Jules Jaluzot, destroyed by fire two years earlier. On the stone façade, statues by H Chapu represent the Four Seasons; on the corners, four highly decorated lantern domes are topped by Carrier-Belleuse sculptures. It was very luxurious for its day, the first department store lit by electricity ♦ René Binet renovated it in 1905, then built a new store between 1907 and 1908. The latter, similar to the first, had seven stories, decorated with Art Nouveau wrought iron; the octagonal great hall was covered by a glass cupola. On the outside, however, the corner towers were larger. This building was destroyed by fire in 1921, and rebuilt exactly by Wybo, who was able to renovate the original glass cupola.

Samaritaine :
75, Rue de Rivoli (1st) ♦ Department store in Art Deco style: it caters for everything, including a food hall, and a well-known home decoration department. In 1870, Ernest Cognacq opened his store and called it La Samaritaine after the pump installed under one of the arches of the Pont Neuf in the time of Henri IV. He developed the store with Louise Jay, whom he later married ♦ It was rebuilt by Frantz Jourdain in 1905 with two basement stories, a metal frame and an exuberant, colorful decorative style using carved wood, iron spiral scrolls around the store sign, mosaics, and ornamental copper plaques. Some of the interior's features were lost during subsequent design changes ♦ In the 1920s, the store was extended toward the Quai du Louvre and a monumental iron-framed façade was built with stone cladding, designed by Jourdain and Sauvage. It had a central glass roof, and at the top a terrace providing one of the most beautiful views over central Paris. Today, it houses a restaurant, the Tout Paris. Between Rue Boucher and Rue Rivoli, a new building was constructed in the same style.

Trois Quartiers (Les):
23, Boulevard de la Madeleine (1st) ♦ Luxury shopping center: clothes, perfumes, interior design, jewelry, sports goods, etc. Above the three shopping levels are offices. The new complex replaced the Trois Quartiers department store, built around 1930 by Faure-Dujarric, with an iron structure and stone cladding in the style of the era. It was rebuilt between 1988 and 1991 by J-J Ory on the lines of the previous building with polished stone and glass criss-crossed by steel. The rounded shape of the Duphot-Madeleine corner gives the building a ship-like appearance. The interior, designed by J M Wilmotte, features polished metal, white marble, sanded glass, and a great deal of light ♦ The new design united and completely transformed the various buildings in the Rue Duphot and Boulevard de la Madeleine which one of the successors of the Gallois-Gignoux, the store's founders, had bought up in the late 19th and early 20th centuries. In 1829, the Gallois-Gignoux had opened a store at 21, Boulevard de la Madeleine, calling it Les Trois Quartiers after a successful play which ran at the Théâtre Français in the year of their marriage, 1827.

HOSPITALS

Bichat - Claude-Bernard:
46, Rue Henri-Huchard (18th) ♦ General hospital resulting from the merger of two institutions ♦ The first, the Hôpital Bichat, moved into a former tax collectors' building in 1882, after part of the Hôtel-Dieu was demolished (rebuilt between 1928 and 1940). Since 1988, it has occupied a modern tower begun in the late 1970s. The second, the Hôpital Claude-Bernard, is in the former Bichat premises and treats various contagious diseases there. It opened in 1884 for patients convalescing from cholera, but was then in the Aubervilliers commune.

Boucicaut:
78, Rue de la Convention (15th) ♦ Hospital built between 1894 and 1897 by the Legros (father and son). It was designed with separate wards, something new at the time: the main courtyard was thus surrounded by small buildings linked by gardens. The Health and Social Security Services built it in accordance with the wishes of Madame Boucicaut, who had bequeathed part of her fortune to it on her death. The hospital was finally closed in 2000; its departments were transferred to the Hôpital Européen Georges-Pompidou.

Broca:
54-56, Rue Pascal (13th) ♦ Modern institution specializing in the care of the elderly. Rebuilt between 1979 and 1982, it is part of the Broca-La-Rochefoucault group with a hospital in the 14th *arrondissement*. Paul Broca was a great neurologist and founder of anthropology in France ♦ The Hôpital Broca was established in 1892 and redeveloped between 1896 and 1898. It replaced the former Hôpital de Lourcines for women suffering from venereal diseases, established since 1836 in the former Cordelières convent founded by Marguerite de Provence in 1284. It stands next to a park laid out around the remains of the convent church.

Broussais:
96, Rue Didot (14th) ♦ Hospital founded in 1885 and rebuilt from 1928. It replaced the wards built in less than three months in 1883 to care for the victims of a cholera epidemic in the Hôpital des Mariniers ♦ Verlaine was a patient and wrote some of his poems there ♦ It was enlarged several times and finally closed in 2000; its departments were transferred to the Hôpital Européen Georges-Pompidou.

Cochin:
27, Rue du Faubourg Saint-Jacques (14th) ♦ Hospital group with buildings of diverse origin, built between the 17th and 20th centuries. The Cochin general hospital was founded by Abbot Jacques-Denis Cochin, priest of St-Jacques du Haut-Pas, and built between 1780 and 1782 to plans by Viel. It was called the Hospice St-Jacques du Haut-Pas, then the Hôpital du Sud, before adopting its founder's name ♦ In 1904, the Hôpital Ricord, which treated venereal diseases, was attached to it. It was established at 111, Boulevard de Port-Royal in a former house for Capuchin novitiates ♦ Another section of the Hôpital Cochin came from the Abbey of Port-Royal, built between 1636 and 1660 in the former Hôtel de Clagny. Its remains include the chapel, restored in 1952, the nuns' chancel, the chapter room, three of the arcades in the cloister, part of the Guémenée ward, and three staircases with balustrades ♦ After the expulsion of the nuns (replaced by nuns of the Order of the Visitation, who were themselves dispersed during the Revolution), the institution became a prison known as Port-Libre. Then, in 1796, it was allocated to the Breast-Feeding unit, and in 1814 to the Maternity unit; the opening of the Boulevard de Port-Royal altered its boundaries ♦ In the 1880s, the hospital was extended and a delivery clinic (the Baudeloque) was built in the gardens of the Maternity wing and opened in 1890. Since then, modern buildings have been added to the complex, which is associated with the Hôpital Saint-Vincent-de Paul.

Européen Georges-Pompidou:
20, Rue Leblanc (15th) ♦ General hospital built between 1995 and 2000 and opened in December, 2000. It consists of nine main building complexes, linked to one another. Good use is made of natural light; the façade is built of concrete and white varnished aluminum, with pearl gray granite, glass, and wood for the interior. The building opens onto the city on three sides: to the east and west toward the outer boulevards and public transport; to the north onto the Parc André-Citroën ♦ Within the complex is a pedestrianized hospital road, covered by a monumental glass roof ♦ This ultramodern university hospital unites the departments of the former Boucicaut, Broussais, and Laënnec Hospitals and the Rothschild Orthopaedic Service, which moved there in the second half of 2000. It is equipped with modern, innovative facilities and offers comfortable surroundings for the sick. This state-of-the-art hospital has highly specialized medical departments and research projects (cancer research, cardiovascular conditions). A considerable area is reserved for recreational activities: relaxation room, sports hall, crèche, cafeteria, newspaper and gift shop.

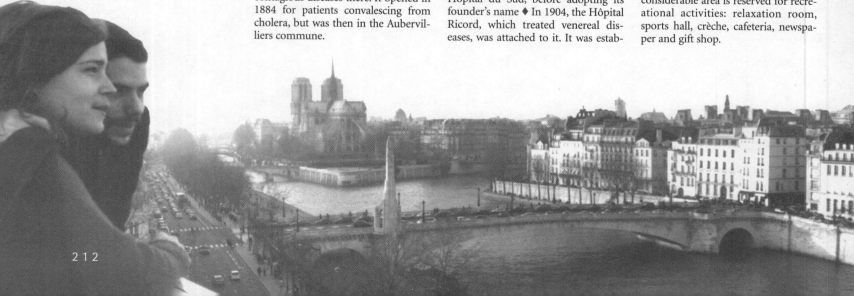

Fernand Widal: 200, Rue du Faubourg Saint-Denis (10th) ♦ Hospital established in a former municipal nursing home built by Théodore Labrouste in 1858 ♦ The monumental buildings are arranged symmetrically around two courtyards, on either side of a central road connecting the entrance to a modern building on the site of the former chapel ♦ In 1653, Saint Vincent de Paul founded a nursing home in the present Faubourg Saint-Martin. It moved to the Faubourg St-Denis, then after the opening of the Boulevard Magenta relocated to its current site ♦ It was not until 1959 that the hospital adopted the name of one of its eminent doctors, famous for his serological diagnosis of typhoid fever; his statue stands in front of the main courtyard ♦ The hospital is attached to the Hôpital Lariboisière, and specializes in gerontology, psychiatry, physiotherapy and, above all, toxicology; it houses the Poisons Center.

Hôtel Dieu: 1, Place du Parvis Notre-Dame (4th) ♦ The present Hôtel-Dieu buildings were built between 1865 and 1877 by Stanislas Diet and Jacques Gilbert: a Classical-style façade overlooks the forecourt; there is a vast interior courtyard lined with arches on two levels and a chapel in the Neo-Renaissance style ♦ The hospital replaced the former Hôtel-Dieu built in the 12th century at the same time as Notre-Dame. Enlarged several times, it replaced a charitable institution founded in the 7th century which had buildings on both banks of the Seine. The former hospital was razed to the ground during works carried out by Haussmann; it stood partly on the square now occupied by the statue of Charlemagne.

Institut Curie: 8, Rue Louis-Thuillier (5th) ♦ The Institute combines three establishments. The first, the modern, concrete Claudius-Regault hospital, was opened in 1991 with some of the most advanced radiotherapy equipment in Europe ♦ The second, a private hospital, made of steel and glass, was built in 1965 at 26, Rue d'Ulm ♦ The third, the former hospital at 12, Rue Lhomond, built in red brick, dates from 1936. It became an important center for molecular biology in 1995, and is dedicated to research ♦

The Institute owes its name to Marie Curie, who specialized in the field of radioactivity, was twice a Nobel prize winner, and founded the Institut du Radium. The hospital specializes in cancer research and has a paediatric service.

Laënnec: 42, Rue de Sèvres (7th) ♦ Hospital built between 1635 and 1649 to plans by Gamard, with 18th-century additions ♦ The façade is Classical in style. The brick and stone buildings comprise two stories and attics with dormers set in them. The two main blocks are cruciform and attached to the arms of the chapel transept. The courtyard entrance has a triangular pediment surmounted by a lantern and a spire. Eight courtyards separate the various wings, including the Cour La Rochefoucauld with its tiled roofs, and the partly restored Cour Gamard, which dates fron the 17th century ♦ The hospital's benefactors included Cardinal La Rochefoucauld; it was first intended for the terminally ill (its original name was the Hôpital des Incurables). Closed in 1869, it reopened in 1874 as the Hôpital Temporaire, and adopted the name Laënnec in 1878. It was finally closed in 2000: its departments were transferred to the Hôpital Européen Georges-Pompidou.

Lariboisière: 2, Rue Ambroise-Paré (10th) ♦ Institution belonging to the Lariboisière-Fernand-Widal group ♦ It was built between 1846 and 1852 under the direction of P Gautier in an area with a rising population following a terrible cholera epidemic. Called the Hôpital du Nord, it was later named after Élisa Roy, Comtesse de Lariboisière who, on her death, left a considerable legacy for its completion. The buildings are divided up into separate wards, linked by glass-covered walkways on both sides of a central courtyard (this was the first hospital in France to be built with wards). At the rear of the courtyard is a chapel, its façade adorned with Doric and Ionic columns, and statues of Faith, Hope, and Charity; inside, a marble monument by Ch Marochetti is dedicated to the Comtesse de Lariboisière. In the rest of the hospital, the sculptures are by Noël-Jules Girard, a pupil of David d'Angers ♦ In the 20th century, new rooms and buildings were constructed as well as a three-storey technology

block beneath the courtyard and a helicopter platform ♦ The main activities are mobility aids, digestive pathology, cardiology, and obstetric gynaecology; there is a center for the head and neck, and the sensory organs.

Necker-Enfants Malades: 149, Rue de Sèvres (15th) ♦ General hospital with a mixed group of buildings constructed at different periods ♦ The complex is designed with wards, and in 1926 combined the former Hôpital Necker and the Hôpital des Enfants Malades (for sick children). The first was founded in 1778 in a former convent by Suzanne Necker, wife of Louis XVI's minister, then rebuilt in the 19th century; the second was established in 1802 at the former Enfant Jésus hospital-orphanage, and was the first paediatric establishment in the world; it was enlarged in 1939 and 1958. This is where Laënnec made his most important discoveries ♦ In 1968, the hospital expanded considerably when the teaching hospital was built by A Wogenscky in Rue de Vaugirard (coloured hall, interior design by Luis Ferto and R Wog, and a sculpture by Martha Pan). More redevelopments were carried out in the 1980s and 1990s.

La Pitié-Salpêtrière: 47, Boulevard de l'Hôpital (13th) ♦ The Hôpital de la Salpêtrière was built in the 17th and 18th centuries on the orders of Louis XIV, and has been enlarged several times; it is the largest hospital in Paris. The monumental entrance under an archway is fronted by a statue of Pinel, an 18th-century doctor, and opens onto a wide courtyard lined with flowerbeds. Facing it is the three-arched façade of the Saint-Louis chapel with its octagonal dome built by L Bruant between 1657 and 1677; the four naves are arranged in the form of a Greek cross and separated by four chapels. Bossuet and Bourdaloue preached there; today it caters for several religions and exhibitions are regularly held there ♦ The Mazarin division, in the left part of the hospital, was built in the second half of the 17th century, first to plans by Le Vau, then by A Duval, Le Muet, and L Bruant; it houses the La Force building, a former prison. To the right is the Lassay division, built in the 1750s and funded by the Marquise de Lassay, and other

buildings constructed by Boffrand, Payen, and Viel. Further buildings were added later. The Hôpital de la Pitié stood on the site of the Paris Mosque; it was rebuilt in the southern part of the hospital grounds between 1905 and 1910, then expanded with the addition of several buildings between the wars, and again in the 1970s and 1990s when it was attached to La Salpêtrière. A new cardiology center was built on Boulevard Vincent Auriol from 2000 ♦ The Louis XIV general hospital stood in the grounds of the former Grand Arsenal, where gunpowder was made; its name comes from the saltpeter used in the process. Too many poor people were living in the streets, and the king decided to build the hospital in 1656 to house some of them. In 1684, he added a women's prison, La Force, for prostitutes and convicted women; one of these women served as the model for the novel *Manon Lascaut* by Abbé Prévost; the courtyard surrounded by the prison buildings today bears his name. The massacres of September, 1792 took place at La Salpêtrière. In 1796, the hospital was assigned to the mentally ill, and managed by pioneers such as Pinel, who adapted the treatment of the most severely disturbed patients, and Charcot, the first holder of a clinical chair for the treatment of nervous diseases.

Les Quinze-Vingts: 26-28, Rue de Charenton (12th) ♦ Hospital specializing in ophthalmology. The buildings date from different periods, the oldest from the late 17th century: these are the Chapel of Saint-Louis, renovated in 1962, which has 19th-century pictures; the principal's lodgings; the left wing of the former hospital; and the monumental front door, surmounted by a triangular pediment ♦ The building has a long history. Between 1699 and 1705, on the orders of Louis XIV, R de Cotte and J Beausire built U-shaped barracks, on land planted with vegetables and fruit trees, for the King's Musketeers, disbanded in 1775. The buildings were then turned into stores before Cardinal de Rohan, grand almoner of France, bought them and built a new hospice; in 1785, as gover-

nor of the Institut des Quinze-Vingts, he transferred it to this site. Formerly in Rue St-Honoré, it had been founded in 1254 by Saint Louis to accommodate 300 crusaders who returned blind from their expedition. The Institut was called the House of the Blind during the Revolution, and was temporarily part of the Institution for Blind Young People; later it became a hospice where an ophthalmological clinic was opened in the 1880s ◆ In 1959, many of the former buildings were demolished to expand the hospital.

Robert-Debré: 48, Boulevard Sérurier (19th) ◆ Children's hospital with maternity unit. Built between 1984 and 1988 by P Riboulet, it was dedicated to Professor Robert Debré who devoted his life to paediatrics ◆ The curving white façade has receding terraced stories, and is decorated with mosaics; a large gallery runs through the whole complex. It has a crèche, day nursery, restaurant, shops, interior gardens (by Liliane Tribel), and terraces.

Saint-Antoine: 184, Rue du Faubourg Saint-Antoine (12th) ◆ General hospital established in 1795-96 in the grounds of the former Royal Abbey of Saint-Antoine, founded in 1198 and rebuilt in 1767 by Lenoir ◆ Some of these buildings remain, including the façade surmounted by a triangular pediment. Two wings were added in 1796 and 1802, and another was redeveloped. Other modifications and new buildings followed: two wards and a maternity unit in the second half of the 19th century; then others throughout the 20th century ◆ The first teaching hospital in Paris was established there in 1965, and was housed with other new departments in nine- and ten-storey buildings (1965-70). Some other departments were enlarged at the same time: gastroenterology, radiology, haematology, and cancer research, and a casualty department.

Saint-Joseph: 185, Rue Raymond-Losserand (14th) ◆ Hospital built from the late 19th century to World War I; it became an institute in 1977, and was renovated and modernized from 2000, with new buildings surrounded by gar-

dens ◆ A small hospital was built in September, 1884, then brick wards with tiled roofs were added up to 1914 ◆ It opened a school for nurses in 1924 and was attached to the Broussais-Hôtel-Dieu teaching hospital in 1969. A college for nursing auxiliaries opened there in 1971.

Saint-Louis: 1, Avenue Claude-Vellefaux (10th) ◆ Hospital built between 1607 and 1611 by Cl Vellefaux and enlarged in the late 20th century. It was built following a decision by Henri IV at the end of the Plague epidemics in the late 16th century and in 1606; at that time, it stood outside the city walls and was dedicated to Saint Louis, who died of the Plague in 1270 ◆ The old hospital is a Classical stone and brick construction, forming a vast quadrilateral. In the center, the buildings are bordered by an old covered way with outer wards at rightangles at each corner, topped by high attics with dormers and surrounding a square inner courtyard. The hospital was abandoned after the epidemics, then requisitioned several times, and finally reopened after a fire at the Hôtel-Dieu in 1773. In the 19th century, it was modernized, and new rooms and buildings were added. Restored since then, it is dedicated to teaching and research ◆ In the 1980s, a new hospital was built by Badani and Roux-Dorlut to the north of the historic buildings; the first phase was finished in 1984, the second in 1989. The façades of the buildings have a maximum of four stories, and echo the style of the old ones; some departments are in the basement, separated by patios and covered by a paved garden; these were decorated with M Blondel, D De Rougeont, and R Gratalup with fountains, street lights, etc ◆ The hospital was formerly general, and now specializes in dermatology, haematology, and cancer research.

Saint-Vincent de Paul: 82, Avenue Denfert-Rochereau (14th) ◆ Hospital specializing in maternity, gynaecology, and children's diseases ◆ The present buildings largely date back to 1861 ◆ It was established in the former Hospice de Maternité, which became the Hospice des Enfants-Trouvés in 1814, on the site of the Institution de l'Oratoire, built in 1655; the chapel survives. From 1838, a kind of turnstile was built in the wall to Rue d'Enfer, which enabled

mothers in distress to abandon their baby anonymously. At that time, there was a building for asses, whose milk was given to the children.

Sainte-Anne: 1, Rue Cabanis (14th) ◆ Psychiatric hospital ◆ It was mainly built in the second half of the 19th century with materials taken from buildings and churches destroyed to make way for the wide thoroughfares of the Haussmann plan. Some more recent buildings face Rue d'Alésia. On one side of a long avenue lined with trees are two rows of six wards for patients, surrounded by administrative buildings; on the other side are the admission buildings. It stands in a 32 acre (13 ha) park with several statues mostly dating from the early 20th century; it also has a museum and a considerable library ◆ The hospital tradition of this site is very old: the Sanitat St-Marcel was established there in the 15th century, and the Maison de Santé de Marguerite de Provence in the 18th century; Anne of Austria had a hospital built there (poorly patronized, it was turned into a farm). Napoléon III built a psychiatric institution there, and commissioned Haussmann to build it;

he in turn gave the job to Quesnel ◆ New buildings were constructed in 1869 to provided a center for the first chair of psychiatry in France; then a surgical ward was added between 1899 and 1900 by E Perronne.

Tenon: 4, Rue de la Chine (20th) ◆ General hospital built between 1870 and 1878 by M-E Billon ◆ Tenon was a surgeon and doctor who developed treatments for work-induced complaints, and advocated a plan to reform hospitals ◆ The hospital was gradually enlarged and modernized: a new ward was built on Avenue Gambetta (1880-1920); electricity was installed, laboratories set up, specialist departments established from 1930, and a new radiology department opened in 1961. From 1963, the older buildings were renovated and new ones built: specialist technical departments opened (kidney dialysis, scanning center, radiotherapy, and computerization). The new building, Gabriel, was opened in 1994 ◆ At that time, this was the first Health and Social Security hospital to employ secular nurses. A Béclère developed fluoroscopy there, preparing the way for tuberculosis screening.

LIBRARIES AND MULTIMEDIA COLLECTIONS

Arsenal: 1, Rue de Sully (4th) ◆ The Bibliothèque de l'Arsenal is open to Masters level academics, and researchers ◆ It specializes in history and literature, and is attached to the Bibliothèque Nationale de France – the National Library ◆ It is located in a building constructed between 1718 and 1745 by Boffrand, after a fire wrecked the residence of the Grand Master of the Artillery, built at the end of the 16th century for the statesman Sully ◆ The new residence was allocated to René d'Argenson, Marquis de Paulmy, a member of the French Academy. From 1757, he gathered together a large encyclopedic collection of books, prints, maps, and plans, subsequently enlarged by various acquisitions. In 1797, the library became the National Public Library. The writer Charles Nodier was responsible for it from 1824-44; he invited writers and artists there (Mus-

set, Hugo, Dumas, and Vigny) ◆ The apartments, decorated for the wife of Marshal de la Meilleraye, and the music room are listed as historic monuments, and have been preserved. Around 1920, the library joined the Union of National Libraries in Paris; in 1934, it was attached to the Bibliothèque Nationale and formed one of its departments from 1977. The Arts and Entertainment department is due to move to Rue de Richelieu from 2005 ◆ The library contains 1,000,000 volumes, 100,000 prints, 14,000 manuscripts, 3,000 maps and plans, about 1,000 musical works, and 11,460 periodicals. It holds specialist collections on the theater, the Saint-Simon movement, Huysmans, Georges Pérec, and the Bastille archives It also has an exhibition area.

Forney: 1, Rue du Figuier (4th) ◆ The Bibliothèque Forney is a lending

library, open to all ♦ It specializes in the fine arts, applied arts, technology, and crafts. The library is located in the Hôtel de Sens, built between 1475 and 1519 at the instigation of Tristan de Salazar to replace the residence belonging to the Archbishops of Sens. ♦ The building is both medieval (ogival arches, turrets with narrow loopholes) and early Renaissance (main staircase in the keep, gardens), and has ornamental 20th-century additions (gargoyles) ♦ The City of Paris bought this mansion in 1911 and had it restored at the end of the 1920s ♦ The library was founded by the industrialist Samuel Forney, who wanted to improve the situation of craft trades at the end of the 19th century; originally at 11, Rue Titon (2nd), it moved to the Hôtel de Sens in 1961 ♦ It has 200,000 books, 2,200 periodicals, 40,000 exhibition catalogues, 5,000 old posters, 10,000 modern posters, samples of wallpapers and fabrics, 1,000,000 postcards, more than 2,000 files of slides on crafts, thousands of photographic reproductions, and albums of engravings.

French National Library (BNF) – Rue de Richelieu site: 58, Rue de Richelieu (2th) ♦ The Bibliothèque Nationale de France is open to researchers ♦ This former royal library was built up from the time of Charles V, and particularly from the time of Louis XI ♦ It was housed in two buildings on Rue Vivienne, built by F Mansart in 1645 and belonging to the Colbert family; in the 18th century it expanded into the Hôtel de Nevers. Between 1724 and 1735, architect Robert de Cotte added two galleries surrounding the main courtyard ♦ In the middle of the 19th century, new buildings were constructed on Rue de Richelieu and Rue des Petits-Champs as well as the main Reading Room (steel structure and natural lighting from above through nine cupolas). Inaugurated in 1868, this room was designed by Labrouste, and decorated with gilding and paintings by Desgoffes ♦ Today, since the transfer of printed matter and periodicals to the François-Mitterrand site, this library looks after specialist collections (manuscripts, prints and photographs, maps, plans, coins and medals): it has more than 800,000 maps and plans, 12,000,000 prints and photographs, more than 200,000

manuscripts and wood engravings, more than 500,000 coins and medals, and about 1,500,000 musical pieces and collections.

French National Library (BNF) – Tolbiac site: Quai François Mauriac (13th) ♦ The new Bibliothèque Nationale de France is divided into two levels: the upper stories, open to anyone over 16, and the garden level, reserved for researchers ♦ This is a modern encylopedic library, built between 1990 and 1995 by D Perrault ♦ It is rectangular in shape and consists of four glass towers, 260 ft (80 m) high, which symbolize open books and stand at the corners of the library area, linked to the lower stories in the base or platform. Between the towers, a vast wooden esplanade contains a garden planted with trees ♦ The interior decoration features polished metal and wood. In the hall is the *Waterlilies* tapestry by Roy Lichtenstein, woven at the Aubusson factory; in the West Hall is a sculpture in polished aluminium by Louise Bourgeois; at the end of the garden level reading rooms there are compositions by J-P Bertrand, G Garouste, M Raysse, and Cl Viallat ♦ The upper stories contain more than 300,000 volumes and 2,300 periodicals; the audiovisual room has 10,000 CDs, 3,000 films, 170,000 digitized images, about 100 multimedia CD-ROMS, and 1,000 music scores. The garden level has about 13 million documents from the Rue de Richelieu site (books, rare books, microfilms, microfiches, CD-ROMS, and digitized collections), of which 380,000 volumes and 4,700 periodicals are freely available; there is Internet access ♦ The library is a copyright library, and organizes exhibitions.

History Library of the City of Paris: 24, Rue Pavée (4th) ♦ The Bibliothèque Historique de la Ville de Paris is open to all members of the public. It covers the history of Paris and the Ile de France ♦ It is housed in the Hôtel de Lamoignon, the former Hôtel d'Angoulême, built between 1594 and 1598 by Diane de France, Duchesse d'Angoulême. In the courtyard, the large main building is flanked by side wings, decorated with Corinthian pilasters and high dormer windows with triangular pediments. The painted beams in the Reading

Room are typical of the lavishly decorated interiors of their period ♦ In 1688, the Lamoignon family settled there; then, in 1751, Antoine Moriau, the king's state prosecutor, set up his library there, dedicated to the history of Paris, which he later bequeathed to the City ♦ Occupied by various businesses and workshops after the Revolution, the building was bought by the City of Paris in 1928. Since 1969, it has housed the present library, founded in 1871 after the library in the Hôtel de Ville was set on fire during the Commune ♦ It has 1,000,000 volumes, 50,000 periodicals, 14,000 plans, 502 atlases, 35,000 old photographs, about 100,000 sets of documents on current affairs, and 15,000 manuscripts (topography, archaeology, Revolution, and theater), and various literary collections (Sand, Flaubert, Boileau, and Voltaire).

Mazarine: 2, Quai de Conti (6th) ♦ The Bibliothèque Mazarine is open to all members of the public, subject to seats being available (140) ♦ It is an encyclopedic library, especially strong on history ♦ It is located at the Institut de France, built by Le Vau in the second half of the 17th century at the instigation of Cardinal Mazarin ♦ The Reading Room is decorated with paneling from the Cardinal's library (which used to be in the former residence of President Tubeuf, in Rue de Richelieu); the antiques, busts, and objets d'art formerly belonged to him; the chandeliers are by Boulle and Caffiéri ♦ The first library to open to the public on certain days, it was restored between 1968 and 1974 ♦ The main collection consists of the Cardinal's collections to which others have been added over the centuries: there are collections on Catalan, Germanic, and Scandinavian cultures, on Pascal and Jansenism, travel journals, and geography ♦ The library has 500,000 volumes (180 from the 16th and 17th centuries) of which more than 30,000 are freely available, 2,600 periodicals, 2,370 volumes of early printed books, 4,639 manuscripts, and prints (including portraits and views of towns).

Médiathèque at La Villette: Cité des Sciences et de l'Industrie, 30, Avenue Corentin-Cariou (19th) ♦ The Médiathèque de La Villette is open to all members of the public ♦ This is a

modern multimedia library, dedicated to science and technology, industry and crafts, and is part of the Cité des Sciences; it consists of multimedia collections and facilities for children. Built in the 1980s in the Parc de la Villette, it has three levels ♦ The documents, some of which can be taken out on loan, are directly accessible: they include books on open shelves, audiovisuals on more than 170 consoles, and educational software packages on 40 IT stations ♦ There are film shows and meetings with personalities in the Paul Painlevé Room; the Louis-Braille Room is for the partially sighted, and there is a room for topical scientific and technical matters (written documents, video, and sound). The Médiathèque has more than 280,000 volumes, of which nearly 202,000 are in the contemporary collection, 2,130 periodicals, 1,248 CD-ROMS, 1,300 educational software packages, 3,500 audiovisual documents, and Internet access.

Pompidou Center Information Library: Place Georges-Pompidou (4th) ♦ The Bibliothèque Publique d'Information du Centre Georges Pompidou is open to all members of the public, with facilities for the blind and partially sighted ♦ The library is on three levels; it contains directly accessible documents: books on open shelves, 400 microfilm readers, and sound and audiovisual documents ♦ This modern multimedia encyclopedic library was built during the 1970s at the Georges-Pompidou Center; it was inaugurated in 1977 and entirely renovated between 1998 and 2000 ♦ It has 350,000 volumes, more than 2,300 periodicals, 6,000 maps and plans, press files on cultural and social current affairs; 2,000 music scores, 10,000 CDs and 300 music videodiscs; 2,700 spoken audio documents, 2,200 documentary and animated films, 200 educational software packages, 1,200 learning documents for 135 languages, 200 reference and multimedia CD-ROMS, and Internet access; there are 16 stations for viewing television from across the world.

Sainte-Geneviève: 10, Place du Pan-

théon (5th) ♦ The Bibliothèque Sainte-Geneviève is open to any person over 18 ♦ This encyclopedic library houses one of the oldest collections in Paris ♦ The building was constructed between 1844 and 1850 by H Labrouste on the site of the former Collège Montaigu. Its stone façade, decorated with a garland of stylized foliage, is Neoclassical in style; the names of 810 illustrious people are engraved on it; it has 42 large windows to light the Reading Room ♦ There are two rows of pillars in the vestibule, where the walls are decorated with trees from every country by A Desgoffes ♦ Inside the building, the metal framework of iron and cast iron (one of the first) is left visible in the Reading Room, which consists of two naves; the stylized joists are separated by slender cast-iron columns ♦ The library took over the books and manuscripts of the former Abbey of Ste-Geneviève; in 1932, J Doucet, a bibliophile, left a large collection of 19th-century works to it. The Bibliothèque Nordique in Rue Valette, which is associated with the library, was founded in 1868, and has a rich collection of literature from northern Europe. The Bibliothèque Sainte-Geneviève has about 2,000,000 documents (including 12,000 periodicals) of which 16,000 books, 280 periodicals and CD-ROMS are freely available; in the reserve collection are manuscripts, early printed books, and about 120,000 volumes from the 16th to the 19th centuries; the Bibliothèque Nordique has 160,000 volumes and 3,460 periodicals.

Municipal Libraries: In addition to the libraries described above, the City of Paris has 26 municipal lending libraries (*Bibliothèques municipales*).

MARKETS

ART
Marché de la Création: Boulevard Edgar-Quinet (14th) ♦ Sundays ♦ Artists sell their works on the median strip.

BIRDS
Marché aux Oiseaux: Place Louis-Lépine (4th) ♦ Sundays ♦ Sells not only birds but also domestic animals and fish, plus all petfood and other requisites. Established at the same time as the flower market in Place Louis-Lépine.

BOOKS
Marché du Livre Ancien et d'Occasion: Parc Georges-Brassens, Rue Brancion (15th) ♦ All day Saturdays and Sundays ♦ Established in the Baltard pavilions in the former horse market, built between 1904 and 1907.

CLOTHES
Carreau du Temple: Corner of Rue Eugène Spuller and Rue Dupetit-Thouars (3rd) ♦ Every morning, except Mondays ♦ This very old clothes market owes its name to the Templars' enclosure, located on this site in the Middle Ages. A wooden rotunda and four wooden pavilions were built there in the late 18th and early 19th centuries, replaced in 1863 by iron and cast-iron buildings by Jules de Méridol. Some of the pavilions survive; they have been restored and were listed as historic monuments in 1981. The first Paris Fair took place there in 1904.

FLEA MARKETS
Marché aux Puces de Montreuil: Avenue de la Porte-de-Montreuil (20th) ♦ Saturdays, Sundays, and Mondays ♦ Mainly a secondhand clothes and goods market, which gradually became established at the Porte-de-Montreuil. From the 17th century, the old-clothesmen were driven away from the center of Paris toward the outskirts; some of them started this market.

Marché aux Puces de la Porte-de-Vanves: Avenue de la Porte-de-Vanves (14th) ♦ Saturdays and Sundays ♦ Market selling old papers for collectors, secondhand goods; artists' square, established in the 1920s.

Marché aux Puces de Saint-Ouen: Avenue de la Porte-de-Clignancourt (18th) ♦ Saturdays, Sundays, and Mondays ♦ Secondhand goods, furniture, books, trinkets, pictures, and secondhand clothes. About 3,000 stallholders and unauthorized peddlers spread across various markets: Vernaison, Biron, Jules-Vallès, Paul-Bert, Malik, and Serpette.

FLOWERS
Marché aux Fleurs: Place Louis-Lépine and Quai de Corse (4th) ♦ Daily, except Sundays ♦ The market, created by Imperial decree in 1808, was inaugurated in 1809. Three rows of stalls with about forty florists, and others on the riverside road.

Marché aux Fleurs: Place de la Madeleine (8th) ♦ Every day, except Mondays ♦ Small market established since 1832.

Marché aux Fleurs: Place des Ternes (17th) ♦ Daily, except Mondays ♦ Small market set up near the entrance to an Art Nouveau Métro station, designed by Hector Guimard.

GENERAL
Marché d'Aligre: Place d'Aligre (12th) ♦ Daily, except Mondays ♦ Food, clothing, and secondhand goods are here available. From the 17th century onward, a market was established here for the benefit of the market gardeners from St-Mandé and Nogent, then for the butchers. A new market which is called Marché Beauvau, was built in the late 18th century over a much larger area, after the demolition of a town house and the opening of five new streets. It was extended again 'in the mid-19th century; later, the open-air market expanded.

OLD PAPERS
Marché aux Vieux Papiers: Avenue de Paris, Saint-Mandé ♦ Wednesdays.

SCRAP METAL
Marché à la Ferraille: Rue J-H Fabre (18th) ♦ Saturdays, Sundays, and Mondays ♦ Scrap metal market on both sides of the street, on the north side of the Bvd Périphérique (ring road).

STAMPS
Marché aux Timbres: Cours Marigny (8th) ♦ Thursdays, Saturdays, Sundays, and holidays ♦ Rare stamps and collections of stamps from across the world; the market is on the corner of Avenue Marigny and Avenue Gabriel.

In addition to these specialist markets, Paris also has about 75 food markets including 13 covered markets and 3 open-air markets.

MONUMENTS AND SITES

Arab Institute: 1 Rue des Fossés-Saint-Bernard (5th) ♦ The Institut du Monde Arabe was built in 1987 by J Nouvel, P Soria, G Lézènes, and Architecture Studio on the initiative of France and 20 Arab countries, to improve exchanges between Western and Arab cultures ♦ The tall glass and steel building consists of two parts, separated by a narrow arcade opening onto a patio; this follows the shape of the bend in the riverside road. The north façade, overlooking the river, has a glazed steel structure built on horizontal lines. The south façade, also glazed, is covered with 240 aluminum panels and thousands of apertures which open and close as the intensity of the light changes ♦ The Institute has a museum, temporary exhibition rooms, a library, a documentation center, a meetings room, and a bookshop.

Arc de Triomphe: Place Charles-de-Gaulle (8th, 16th, 17th) ♦ Commissioned by Napoléon I to celebrate the Republican and Imperial victories ♦ Building was begun by Chalgrin in 1806, but work was interrupted by the fall of the Emperor and not resumed until 1823; it was completed in 1836. The four pillars are decorated with bas-reliefs depicting the Revolution and the Empire: on the Champs-Élysées side, *The Marseillaise* by Rude, which illustrates the departure of the army in 1792, is balanced on the other side by *The Triumph of 1810* by J-P Cortot ♦ At the top of the building, a small museum describes its history. Above it, the terrace providess extensive views over Paris.

Arc de Triomphe du Carrousel: Place du Carrousel (1st) ♦ Built by Percier and Fontaine between 1806

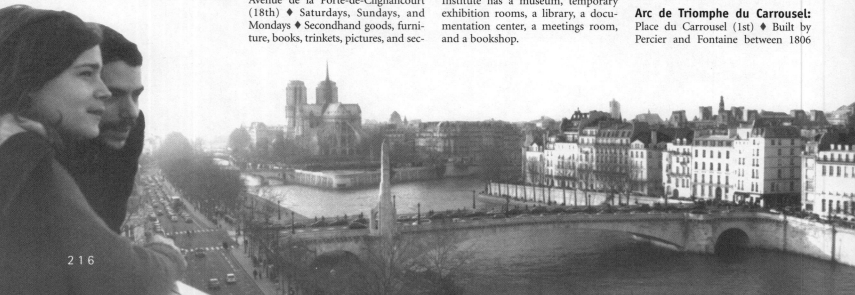

and 1808 to commemorate the victories won by the Napoleonic armies in 1805 ♦ It was inspired by the Arch of Septimius Severus in Rome ♦ Statues of soldiers from the Grande Armée stand on the eight marble Corinthian columns framing the three arches; basreliefs celebrate the 1805 campaign. On top is a quadriga, a chariot and horses led by an allegorical statue of the Restoration, set between statues of Victory and Peace; this was executed by Bosio in 1828, replacing the horses of Saint-Mark's, which were returned to Venice ♦ The arch takes its name from the *carrousel* (tournament) that Louis XIV held there on June 5-7, 1662 to mark the birth of the Grand Dauphin.

Arènes de Lutèce: 49, Rue Monge and Rue de Navarre (5th) ♦ The remains, bordered by grassy areas, of the amphitheater and its terraces built at the end of the 1st century, preserved and restored in the square of the same name ♦ The site of the arena is still visible, despite the buildings in Rue Monge which partly cover it. Today, it is a public garden, used by *pétanque* players and school children; shows are performed there in the summer months ♦ In Roman times, the Arènes was a large amphitheater on the eastern edge of Lutetia (Paris), seating 15,000 spectators for gladiatorial contests, musical concerts, and dance and acrobatic shows; it was destroyed in the 3rd century. A Convent of English nuns and nuns of the Order of the Visitation moved there in the 17th century, but the remains of the convent were only discovered during building work around Rue Monge, where the Bus Company had acquired land. Most of the Arènes was sold off in lots, and Victor Hugo and V Duray had to intervene to safeguard what had survived of the amphitheater when the remains of the convent were demolished.

Assemblée Nationale: see Palais Bourbon.

Beaubourg: see Pompidou Center.

Bourse: 4 Place de la Bourse (2nd) ♦ The Stock Exchange, built by Napoléon I on the site of the Convent of the Filles de Saint-Thomas, confiscated during the Revolution. Begun by A Brongniart in 1808, it was completed by E Labarre in 1826. The Neoclassical building is surrounded by a peristyle of Corinthian columns. The west and east façades are fronted by flights of steps, surrounded by allegorical statues: *Trade* by A Dumont, *Justice* by F-J Duret, *Agriculture* by Ch-É Seurre, and *Industry* by J Pradier. In the early 20th century, two wings were added by J-B Clavel at the north and south ends of the building, which was originally rectangular ♦ Inside, the main dealing room is 82 ft (25 m) high, its ceiling lit by a central glass roof and decorated with allegorical grisaille paintings by Ch Meynier and A Abel de Pujol; above them are galleries. Dealing on the floor stopped in 1987; these operations now take place in the computer room in the basement. On the second story, the meeting room (until 1865 the Tribunal de Commerce) is adorned with Corinthian pilasters and grisaille paintings.

Champ de Mars: see École Militaire.

Conciergerie: 1, Quai de l'Horloge (1st) ♦ The remains of the Royal Palace of the Capetians. The name refers to the time when the king, on leaving it, entrusted it to the concierge (who at that time had considerable responsibility and far-reaching powers) ♦ Along its river front are four slate-roofed towers, which have been restored; from west to east, these are: the Tour Bonbec, crowned with ramparts, which dates from Saint Louis; the twin towers of Argent and César, built in the early 14th century under Philip the Fair; the Tour de l'Horloge (clock tower), built in 1350 by John the Good. In the 16th century, Henry III had the first clock replaced with one that still survives today; its face, decorated with fleur-de-lis on a blue background, was sculpted by Germain Pilon. The Neoclassical buildings between the towers date from the 19th century ♦ Inside, the medieval rooms were built under Philip the Fair and John the Good in the 14th century: the guard room has two naves with ogival arches; the huge men-at-arms room, measuring 210 ft (63 m) by 90 ft (27 m), has four naves with nine spans and pillars with capitals decorated with foliage, and was formerly the lower level of the Great Hall where the king welcomed his guests (now attached to the Palais de Justice); the Rue de Paris, associated with the executioner, occupies the last span of the men-at-arms room, but is separated from it; finally, there are the kitchens with their ogival arches and large fireplaces ♦ The other buildings, including the so-called Chapel of the Girondins, are known as the prison quarters; they were renovated after a fire in 1776, and in the 19th century. This was one of the focal points of the Revolution; as early as the 15th century, it was used as a prison to relieve the one at the Châtelet. On the ground floor, Marie-Antoinette's cell has been reconstructed; on the second story are various rooms, including the one in which the Revolutionary Court was held; these were restored in 1989 for the Bicentenary of the Revolution. Various objects and documents date from that period ♦ Famous prisoners before the Revolution included: Enguerrand de Marigny, former chamberlain to Philip the Fair, Ravaillac, the Marquise de Brinvilliers, and Damiens; during the Revolution, besides Marie-Antoinette, there were Madame Élisabeth, Madame du Barry, Madame Roland, André Chénier, Lavoisier, Robespierre, and Fouquier-Tinville; later, Cadoudal, Maréchal Ney, and Ravachol.

École Militaire-Champ de Mars: 1, Place Joffre (7th) ♦ Built by J-A Gabriel between 1768 and 1773 ♦ The impressive façade is in the Classical style, and overlooks the Champ de Mars. It has a portico with eight Corinthian columns supporting a pediment and a quadrangular dome (clock by Lepeautre); the two low wings which flank it were added by Brongniart ♦ Inside, the chapel, built between 1768 and 1773, stands in the main courtyard, which is entered via two porticos with Doric columns and leads to the drill court, surrounded by the buildings of the military academy ♦ The École Militaire was founded to train 500 officer-cadets with no private means; one of them was Napoleon Bonaparte. Today, it is a center for military academies and defense studies ♦ In front of it, on the Champ de Mars side, is an equestrian statue of Marshal Joffre, sculpted in 1939 by Maxime Réal del Sarte ♦ The Champ de Mars, redesigned around 1765, was the training ground of the École Militaire; since then, it has become a huge garden planted with trees, with views of Chaillot hill beyond the Eiffel Tower. It was the setting for the Federation's celebrations in 1794, and hosted the first Industrial Exhibition in 1798 before becoming a racecourse, later replaced by the one at Longchamp. Then, between 1908 and 1928, it became a park, bordered by fine apartment buildings.

Expiatory Chapel: Square Louis XVI, 29, Rue Pasquier (8th) ♦ The Chapelle Expiatoire was built in memory of Louis XVI and Queen Marie-Antoinette by Louis XVIII to plans by P Fontaine between 1816 and 1826, on the site of the Madeleine Cemetery, where the king and queen had been buried with more than 1,000 other victims of the Revolution ♦ The entrance leads to a hall flanked by symbolic graves, with the chapel beyond. The Neoclassical building is shaped like a Greek cross, covered by a cupola; a sculpted pediment is supported by four Doric columns. Inside is a coffered ceiling with rosettes; on each side is a sculpted group: *Louis XVI Supported by an Angel* by Bosio and *Marie-Antoinette Kneeling at the Foot of Religion* by Cortot, below which is an inscription about the monarchs. In the crypt is a marble altar over the place where Louis XVI's body was found ♦ A royalist, Descloseaux, who lived in a house adjoining the cemetery and had located the site of the royal burials, bought some of the lots when it was closed and sold off in 1794. In January, 1815, Louis XVIII had the remains of the sovereigns exhumed, and solemnly transported to the Basilica of Saint-Denis, at the same time as the foundation stone of the monument was laid.

Grande Arche de la Défense: (Courbevoie) ♦ Monument built between 1985 and 1989 by the Danish architect Johann Otto von Spreckelsen, and completed by Paul Andreu; the foundation stone was laid by President Mitterrand in 1985 ♦ Steps lead up to the great hollow cube, its sides measuring about 360 ft (110 m); it has a concrete structure and a façade of white Carrara marble and glass. In the center of the monument is a white, sail-like structure with portholes, held by a network of cables; it is decorative and functional, serving as a shelter and

windbreak. Beside it, external elevators rise up to the roof, where there are vast panoramic views; the Foundation for Human Rights has its headquarters there, and the building also houses the Ministry of Supplies and the offices of several large companies ♦ The Grande Arche marks the western end of the city's historic east-west axis.

Hôtel de Ville: Place de l'Hôtel de Ville (4th) ♦ City Hall. The present building dates from 1874-82 and was built by Théodore Ballu and Pierre Deperthes on the site of the old building, destroyed by fire in 1871 ♦ It is a Neo-Renaissance structure, almost identical to its predecessor, originally ordered by François I and designed by Dominenico da Cortona (known as Le Boccador). It contains a Salon des Tapisseries (tapestries), a crafts gallery, a large function room (164 ft (50 m) long, 39 ft (12 m) wide, and 43 ft (13 m) high), a Salon des Arcades, and other rooms decorated by Puvis de Chavanes, J-P Laurens, and Georges Bertrand.

Hôtel des Monnaies: see Coins Museum.

Institut de France: 23, Quai de Conti (6th) ♦ Building constructed by Le Vau, on the site of the Tour de Nesle between 1662 and 1670. The semicircular façade is dominated by the former chapel and flanked by two square buildings (one of them houses the Mazarine Library). Behind, the buildings are arranged around the courtyard ♦ In the hall is the mausolum of Mazarin, made of marble, stone, and bronze by Coysevox. The cupola of the former chapel is today used for the formal receptions and annual meetings of the five academies of the Institute. The building was erected in accordance with the wishes of Mazarin, who had bequeathed to the kingdom a considerable sum of money for its construction, as well as his library, which is one of the richest collections in the world. The Quatre-Nations College (or Collège Mazarin) was looked after by monks; it was dedicated to the education of young people coming from the recently conquered provinces. After

serving as a prison under the Revolution, in 1805 it became the seat of the Institut de France, set up in 1795 when it was located in the Louvre.

Invalides: Esplanade des Invalides (7th) ♦ The Hôtel des Invalides, founded by Louis XIV for elderly and wounded soldiers (hence the name), was built between 1671 and the early 18th century ♦ The buildings are arranged symmetrically on either side of the main courtyard and the churches. The entrance on the esplanade leads to a garden with a display of 17th- and 18th-century bronze cannons. The splendid Classical façade is 640 ft (195 m) long, and was designed by Libéral Bruant. Ionic pilasters frame the great portal, topped by an equestrian statue of Louis XIV set between figures representing Justice and Prudence by G Coustou (1733); the king's face was remodeled by Cartelier in 1815. The main courtyard is flanked all round by arcades on two levels, interrupted by four central pavilions with sculpted triangular pediments. The Church of St-Louis-des-Invalides, or the Soldiers' Church, was built there between 1679 and 1710 by J Hardouin-Mansart, based on Bruant's plans; it contains the tombs of many marshals and admirals of the Empire, and war leaders from 1914-18 and 1940-45 (including Franchet d'Esperey, Leclerc, Giraud, and Juin). The church is linked by a covered way to the Dôme Church (1677-90). Designed in the shape of a Greek cross, it was also built by J Hardouin-Mansart: its façade has a portico of superimposed Doric and Corinthian columns; the dome is the most elegant and the tallest in Paris ♦ The buildings house the Hôpital des Invalides and three museums: the Army Museum, the Museum of Relief Models, and the Museum of the Order of the Liberation (see Museums).

July Column: Place de la Bastille (4th, 11th, 12th) ♦ The Colonne de Juillet is a bronze column commemorating the Revolution of July, 1830. It was built between 1833 and 1840 and set up in the Place de la Bastille by Louis-Philippe; it was restored in 1989 ♦ This column replaced the elephant fountain project, planned by Napoléon I ♦ It is 150 ft (47 m) high, and has an impressive Corinthian capital; it is sur-

mounted by the *Spirit of Liberty* by A Dumont. The names of the victims of the 1830 Revolution are inscribed on its shaft, and those of the 1848 Revolution on the base. The base is made of white marble and is circular in shape; it supports a square plinth, decorated with a series of symbolic bronze medallions and a lion on the west side ♦ Inside, a staircase leads to the upper gallery.

Louvre: Palais du Louvre, Quai du Louvre (1st) ♦ Formerly a fortress, built by Philippe-Auguste, dating from the late 12th century, the palace has undergone many redevelopments to suit the needs of successive monarchs. Charles V built a residence there. François I razed the fortress to the ground (now only the foundations survive), and had a palace built in the Italian Renaissance style by Lescot (the Lescot wing to the west of the Cour Carrée). Cathérine de Médicis and Henry IV added galleries along the Seine which linked with the Palais des Tuileries, built for Cathérine de Médicis by Philibert Delorme and Bullant. Louis XIII enlarged Henri IV's Cour Carrée with the Pavillon de l'Horloge, built by Le Mercier. Louis XIV had the Cour Carrée completed by Le Vau and Cl Perrault, then the Tuileries; he was responsible for the great colonnade and the Pavillon de Marsan (rebuilt, like the Pavillon de Flore, after the Tuileries was set on fire in 1871). The palace was not completed until the 19th century, when the Pavillon de Rohan was built by Louis XVIII, and other buildings were added by Napoléon I and during the Second Empire. The Tuileries Palace disappeared, destroyed by fire in 1871 ♦ In the 1980s, the appearance of the Cour Napoléon was changed with the addition of a glass pyramid, 70 ft (21.65 m) high, on a square base measuring 113 ft (34.50 m); it is supported by stainless steel tubes and cables, and rises above the museum's underground reception rooms. See also Louvre Museum.

Louvre des Antiquaires: 2, Place du Palais-Royal (1st) ♦ Freestone building, flanked by arcades on two sides, built in 1854 by Percier and Fontaine, and housing more than 200 art and antique stores on three levels ♦ Its style of architecture was in keeping with the buildings beside the Tuileries. A luxury

hotel, the Grand Hôtel du Louvre, formerly stood there, with boutiques in the arcades. The boutiques were very successful, and were replaced, from 1860, by the Grands Magasins du Louvre, founded by Alfred Chauchard, while the hotel was rebuilt nearby. This elegant department store closed in 1972.

Madeleine: see Church of Sainte-Marie-Madeleine.

Obelisk, Place de la Concorde: Place de la Concorde (8th) ♦ This is a pink granite monolith, 75 ft (23 m) high, presented to King Louis-Philippe by the Pasha of Egypt, Mehemet-Ali, in 1831, and erected in October, 1836 ♦ This Rameses II obelisk (13th century BC), came from Luxor, and is carved with hieroglyphs celebrating the deeds of the Pharaoh; the story of its journey to Paris, which took more than two years, is recorded on the granite pedestal.

Palais Bourbon: Place du Palais-Bourbon and Quai d'Orsay (7th) ♦ Built in the 18th century, at the same time as the Hôtel de Lassay, and redeveloped during the Revolution and in the 19th century to house the Assemblée Nationale. On the Place du Palais-Bourbon side, the portal is framed by Corinthian columns, and leads to the main courtyard which has buildings dating from the late 18th century. The Seine façade was added by Poyet under the First Empire; it was inspired by ancient temples; Cortot sculpted the pediment in 1842. Next door is the Hôtel de Lassay, which under Louis-Philippe became the President of the National Assembly's residence, and was raised by one story and connected by a gallery to the palace; it has large arched windows overlooking the river, and has kept its 18th- century decorative style ♦ Inside the Palais Bourbon are: the Sessions Room, built in 1795 by J-P Gisors and E-C Leconte, and redesigned between 1829 and 1832, decorated with marble Ionic columns with gilded bronze capitals, sculptures by Pradier and Rude, and paintings by Delacroix and Vernet; the Antechamber, with a ceiling painted by Horace Vernet; the Salon Casimir-Périer, with Corinthian columns supporting a coffered ceiling; and the Library, decorated by Delacroix ♦ The first palace

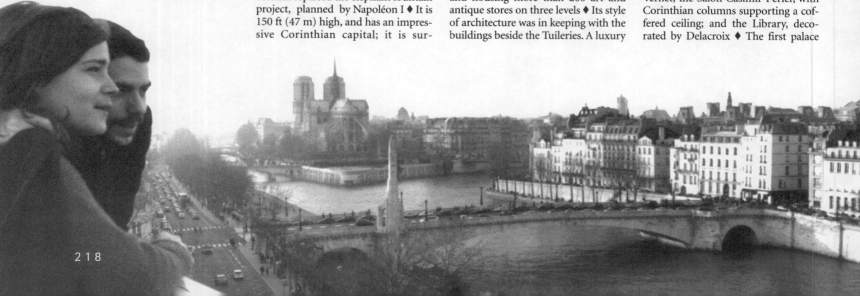

was built from 1722 by Giardini, then Lassurance, for Louise-Françoise de Bourbon, daughter of Louis XIV and Madame de Montespan; at that time, its gardens ran down to the Seine. The residence of the Marquis de Lassay was built next door at the same time. It was declared national property, and was given to the Conseil des Cinq-Cents in 1795 and redesigned: function rooms were transformed, the semicircular Salle de l'Assemblée was built, and a new block with a Corinthian portico added to the main courtyard; it then housed the Assemblée Nationale, the French Parliament. Under the Empire, the Hôtel de Lassay was made the residence of the President of the Assemblée, then reverted to the Duc du Bourbon during the Restoration; later the Duc d'Aumale sold it back to the Assemblée Nastionale.

Palais de Chaillot: Place du Trocadéro (16th) ♦ This monumental group of buildings, inspired by the Classical period, was built by G Davioud for the Universal Exhibition in 1878, then transformed by J Carlu, L-H Boileau, and L Azéma for the 1937 Exhibition ♦ They removed the impressive central body and its two towers, replacing it with the present square and extending the wings with long curving structures containing new galleries. The façades are lined by pilasters ♦ The palace is surrounded by 25 acres (10 ha) of gardens, running down to the Seine and decorated with statues. In the center is a long, rectangular pool, with spectacular fountains and statues ♦ The Palais de Chaillot houses the Maritime Museum, the Museum of Mankind, the Museum of French Monuments, the Henri-Langlois Cinema Museum, the Cinémathèque, and the Théâtre National de Chaillot.

Palais des Congrès: 2, Place de la Porte Maillot (17th) ♦ Built between 1971 and 1974 to plans by G Billet, S Maloletenkov, and H Guiboud, on waste ground formerly occupied by the Luna-Park fairground, which opened in 1909 and was demolished in 1948. This building, originally trapezoid in shape, was rebuilt and enlarged by Christian de Portzamparc in the 1990s. It has an impressive, sloping façade overlooking the square, with five stories and two basements ♦ It houses a

large amphitheater with more than 3,700 seats, designed for shows and concerts, surrounded by luxury boutiques on two levels; in addition, it has several other theaters, meeting and conference rooms, and offices. It is connected to the Hôtel Concorde-Lafayette, located in the high neighboring tower; its shopping galleries bustle with activity.

Palais de l'Élysée : 55, Rue du Faubourg Saint-Honoré (8th) ♦ The Élysée Palace was built between 1718 and 1720 as a residence for Louis de la Tour d'Auvergne, Comte d'Évreux; it has been the residence of the Head of State since 1873 ♦ It has preserved its original appearance despite many alterations carried out by its occupants: the Marquise de Pompadour, who decorated and furnished it; the financier Baujon, who commissioned the architect Boulée to turn it into a real palace; Murat, who had to renovate it because it had been converted into apartments (where the de Vigny family lived), and stores (the Salon Murat and the stairs leading down to the hall survive). Napoléon I then took it over and began to renovate it (at that time it was called the Élysée Napoléon); he signed his abdication there after the Hundred Days. In 1816, the palace was renovated and given to the Duchesse de Berry, who added an orangery. It became national property in 1848, and was given to Prince Louis Napoléon Bonaparte who had extensive works carried out there by Lacroix, replacing the adjoining residences with new buildings and opening the Rue de l'Élysée; he gave some glittering receptions there before leaving it for the Tuileries, after which his guests stayed there. The palace was given its present function under the Third Republic; new additions included a ballroom, a winter garden, and an impressive functions room, ordered by scientist Sadi Carnot in anticipation of the 1889 Universal Exhibition.

Palais de Justice : 4, Boulevard du Palais (1st) ♦ The entrance to the Palais de Justice leads to the Cour du Mai (the clerks of the Courts of Justice planted a tree there on May 1, hence the name). This was the seat of Parliament in the Middle Ages, then the High Court of Justice. The buildings were redesigned many times, particu-

larly in the 19th century by J-L Duc and É T Dommey, during the reigns of Louis-Philippe and Napoléon III. They had already been rebuilt in 1785 by Desmaisons, Couture, and Antoine after a fire in 1776; the ornamental railings were installed in 1787 ♦ The façade on Boulevard du Palais, with its portico and Doric columns, surmounted by allegorical statues, is reached by a broad flight of steps. The impressive western façade on Rue Harlay was rebuilt under Haussmann by J-L Duc ♦ Inside, to the right of the gallery, is the Waiting Hall, the former Grand'Salle of the medieval palace. It was rebuilt for the first time in 1622 after a fire, then again by Duc and Dumet after a fire during the Commune in 1871, in the spirit of the former room. The same was done to the Chambre Dorée adjacent to it, formerly the apartment of Saint Louis. The Revolutionary Court sat in this room during the Terror.

Palais de Tokyo: 11, Avenue du Président-Wilson (16th) ♦ Concrete building in Neoclassical style, designed by J-Cl Dondel, A Aubert, P Viard, and M Dastugue for the 1937 Universal Exhibition as a site for museums. The two wings of the building are connected by square pillars on the avenue side, and on the Seine front by a colonnade overlooking a pool decorated with statues. The two façades are clad in stone blocks and decorated with sculptures ♦ The east wing houses the Museum of Modern Art of the City of Paris. The palace replaced the military stores building, constructed in 1836 in the former workshops of La Savonnerie, the royal carpet factory, which was transferred to Les Gobelins in 1826.

Panthéon: Place du Panthéon (5th) ♦ Built between 1758 and 1790 by Soufflot, then Rondelet, the Panthéon is a last resting place for the "Great Men" of France. It was designed in Neoclassical style, combining a Gothic structure with Greek architecture, and built in the form of a Greek cross. It is surmounted by a dome, supported by a colonnade. A bas-relief by David d'Angers (1831) decorates the pediment of the peristyle with its Corinthian columns ♦ Inside are monumental Corinthian columns, and many paintings, including those by

Puvis de Chavannes on the life of Sainte Geneviève, and a reconstruction of Foucault's pendulum experiment. The crypt contains several galleries for the tombs: 76 people have been buried or transferred there, including 26 with national honours: the most famous are Victor Hugo in 1885, Émile Zola in 1906, Monet in 1964, and, more recently, Marie and Pierre Curie in 1995, and Malraux in 1996 ♦ Originally, the Panthéon was built to replace the Church of Sainte-Geneviève. It was rebuilt under the Revolution by Quatremère de Quincy and turned into a temple dedicated to great men; it retains this function today despite serving in between for short periods as a place of worship. Length: 360 ft (110 m); width: 270 ft (82 m); height of the dome: 273 ft (83 m).

Pompidou Center: Place Georges-Pompidou (4th) ♦ The Centre National d'Art et de Culture Georges-Pompidou, also known as the Centre Beaubourg, was built by Renzo Piano and Richard Rogers, based on an idea by President Pompidou, and was inaugurated in February, 1977; it was restored between 1998 and 2000 by Renzo Piano ♦ It is a five-story modern glass and steel building. The escalators are housed inside a transparent tube on the outside of the building, along with service pipes painted according to their function. The esplanade is lively, and on the south side is the mechanical fountain by Niki de Saint-Phalle and Jean Tinguely, inaugurated in 1983 ♦ The Center houses the Information Library (see Libraries), the National Museum of Modern Art (see Museums), the IRCAM Center for Experimental Music, two cinema screens, a bookshop, and a restaurant with a rooftop terrace; the Center organizes shows and exhibitions ♦ 5.9 million visitors (1997).

Sainte-Chapelle: see Église de la Sainte-Chapelle

Sewers: Corner of Quai d'Orsay and the Pont de l'Alma (7th) ♦ The sewer (*égout*) system installed under the Second Empire by Belgrand extended over 370 miles (600 km), at the time of his

death in 1878; today, it is a 1,240 miles (2,000 km) network of main and feeder tunnels and pipes. An exhibition room documents the history of the system and its various collecting and emptying methods.

Sorbonne: Place de la Sorbonne (5th) ♦ The Sorbonne was built around Lemercier's 17th-century chapel, which houses Richelieu's tomb; the other buildings date from 1881 to 1901, and were designed in the Clasical style by H-P Nérot. Two series of superimposed columns adorn the front of the chapel, which is decorated with 19th-century statues and surmounted by a dome; it forms one of the sides of the Place de la Sorbonne ♦ On the Rue des Écoles, a majestic façade contains the main entrance to the University, decorated with allegorical statues; this leads to a vast hall and the main lecture theater, decorated with the *Bois Sacré des Arts et des Sciences* by Puvis de Chavannes ♦ The main courtyard is flanked on the east side by the library, built above several lecture theaters; on the south side by a raised square in front of the chapel, with statues of Hugo and Pasteur; on the north side by a gallery of arcades above which is an old restored sundial ♦ The Collège de Sorbonne was founded by Robert de Sorbon who acquired the first house in 1254, followed by others reaching as far as the present-day Rue Champollion, thanks to Louis IX's support. In the 17th century, Richelieu decided to rebuild it: the old buildings were demolished and the new Sorbonne constructed between 1627 and 1629; a new chapel was built from 1635, the only surviving element from that period. Under the Third Republic, the Sorbonne had again become too small, and was rebuilt, this time to coincide with a new national plan for higher education.

Thermes de Cluny: 6, Place Paul Painlevé (5th) ♦ Remains of the thermal baths of Lutetia, built in about the year 200. They contained various rooms and interior courtyards; the *frigidarium* (cold room) has been preserved. It is now associated with the

Musée de Cluny. See also Museum of the Middle Ages.

Eiffel Tower: Champ de Mars (7th) ♦ The Tour Eiffel was built by Gustave Eiffel (plans by Nouguier and Koechlin, assisted by Sauvestre) between 1887 and 1889 for the Universal Exhibition ♦ Surmounted by a network of television aerials since 1957, it is 984 ft (300 m) high. The four main pillars meet at the second upper platform, reached by steps and elevators. The tower was thoroughly restored for its Centenary ♦ An audiovisual museum tells its history; there are restaurants and a brasserie for visitors. On the top level, G Eiffel's office has been reconstructed ♦ The building was fiercely criticized, and nearly destroyed when its concession expired in 1909, but it was saved by its potential as a wireless telegraphy mast. It has become the symbol of Paris. 6.4 million visitors (1999).

Tour St-Jacques: Square de la Tour Saint-Jacques (4th) ♦ Built between 1508 and 1522 by Jean de Felin and restored by Ballu and Chenillon in 1853 ♦ The tower was designed in Flamboyant Gothic style with high narrow windows, and decorated with sculptures. At the top is a statue of Saint Jacques Le Majeur, surrounded by his symbols: the eagle, the lion, and the ox; on the ground floor is a statue of Pascal, who is said to have carried out his experiments on atmospheric pressure there ♦ The tower is the last remnant of the Church of Saint-Jacques-de-la-Boucherie (parish church for the butchers' guild); it was a departure point for Santiago de Compostela in the Middle Ages, and was demolished during the Revolution. Since 1891, it has served as a meteorological station; it is now also a center for the control of air pollution.

Val-de-Grâce: see Church of Val de Grâce.

Vendôme Column: Place Vendôme (1st) ♦ The Colonne Vendôme was built in 1810 on the model of Trajan's Column in Rome; it stands on the same pedestal which bore the equestrian statue of Louis XIV before the Revolution ♦ It is 144 ft (44 m) high; bronze bas-reliefs describing the Austerlitz campaign unfurl upward in

a spiral. On top is a statue of Napoléon I as a Roman emperor by A Dumont, carved in the reign of Napoléon III ♦ Chaudet had sculpted an earlier statue, but this was removed in 1814, and melted down to make the statue of Henry IV on the Pont Neuf; at first, it was replaced by a white flag, then,

successively, by a large fleur-de-lis, a statue of the "Little Corporal" by Seurre (in 1833), and finally the statue by Dumont, which was pulled down during the Commune along with the column, on the orders of Courbet. Both column and statue were restored at Courbet's expense in 1875.

MUSEUMS

Advertising (Musée de la Publicité): 107, Rue de Rivoli (1st) ♦ This used to be known as the Poster Museum and was located in Rue de Paradis. It took on its current name in 1981, and has belonged to the Union of Applied Arts since 1990; it now occupies the same building as the Museum of Applied Arts at the Louvre ♦ A new display of its collections was produced by Jean Nouvel at the end of the 1990s ♦ The collection is composed of large donations (Pochet in 1901, Braun in 1941), and posters supplied by agencies, advertisers, and graphic designers: 50,000 old posters (pre-1949) and 50,000 modern posters; films, and objects used in advertising.

African and Oceanian Art (Musée National des Arts d'Afrique et d'Océanie): 283, Avenue Daumesnil (12th) ♦ The building was constructed between 1928 and 1931 for the Colonial Exhibition of 1931, and was intended to house the Museum of the Colonies ♦ The façade is decorated with a large bas-relief illustrating the contribution made by the former colonies ♦ From 1935 to 1960 it was called the Museum of France Overseas ♦ Rich collection of the art and technology of black Africa (statues, masks, and objects in ivory and bronze), North Africa (jewelry, pottery, furniture, and carpets), and the countries of Oceania (painted barks from Australia and sculptures from Melanesia) ♦ Tropical aquarium and terrarium with crocodiles and tortoises.

Applied Arts (Musée des Arts Décoratifs): 107, Rue de Rivoli (1st) ♦ Since 1905 the museum has been housed in the Napoléon wing of the Louvre, which was built by Percier and Fontaine under the First Empire, the southern part being completed under

the Third Republic; it was renovated from 1985 to 1990 and from 1993 to 2001 ♦ On the Classical-style façade, niches containing statues of famous figures of the Empire period alternate with windows, which are arched on the first story and rectangular on the second ♦ Collections of crockery, glass, gold plate, enamel work, furniture, tapestries, paintings, and sculpture from the Middle Ages to the 20th century.

Arab World (Musée de l'Institut du Monde Arabe): 1, Rue des Fossés Saint-Bernard (5th) ♦ This museum devoted to Arab-Muslim civilization forms part of the Institute's modern building, which was built between 1981 and 1987 on the initiative of France and 19 Arab countries, and is an interpretation in glass and aluminum of the architectural style of Arab-Islamic civilization ♦ More than 300 pieces, from Antiquity to the 20th century, are displayed on three levels: objects in ceramic, metal, wood, textile, ivory, glass; carpet art; graphic arts, sculpture and paintings; collection of astrolabes. Temporary exhibitions.

Army (Musée de l'Armée): Hôtel des Invalides (7th) ♦ A museum of military history, housed in the Hôtel des Invalides, which was built for Louis XIV in the 17th century by Libéral Bruant ♦ Collections containing more than 500,000 pieces (arms, armour, uniforms, small-scale models, paintings), recording the military art and history of France and the world; outstanding items include the Dauphin's armor, armor from the 16th century, the chimera collection in the Henri IV room, helmets and armor in the Oriental Room ♦

Museum of Relief Models (Musée des Plans-reliefs): more than 100

models of fortified towns from the 17th to the 19th centuries.

Arsenal (Pavillon de l'Arsenal):
21, Boulevard Morland (4th) ♦ Opened in 1988, this museum presents the planning and architecture of Paris, with a permanent exhibit, The City and its Projects ♦ Up-to-date model of Paris, documents, slides, and videodisk showing the stages of the capital's construction: city wall built by Philippe-Auguste, origins of the Grands Boulevards, walls built by the Farmers-General, Haussmann's Paris, city limits defined by Thiers, Paris and its region ♦ Information and Documentation Center.

Balzac's House (Maison de Balzac):
47, Rue Raynouard (16th) ♦ This house and garden in the former village of Passy was Balzac's home from 1840 to 1847. In the 18th century, the house was an outbuilding of a private mansion which has since disappeared. At the beginning of the 20th century it was turned into a private museum, then in 1949 became the property of the City of Paris, before reopening to the public in 1960; the layout of the collections was redesigned in 1987 ♦ Manuscripts, original editions, illustrations, a bust, and personal belongings of the author (portraits, coffee-pot, turquoise-studded cane); temporary exhibitions, and library.

Bourdelle (Musée Bourdelle):
16, Rue Antoine Bourdelle (15th) ♦ The museum is devoted to the memory of the sculptor Bourdelle and his works, and its layout centers around the studio that he occupied from 1885; since opening in 1949 it has been enlarged several times, and was reorganized in 1992 by Christian de Portzamparc ♦ Works by Bourdelle, his studio and apartment, bronzes in the garden; the sculptures include *Heracles the Archer, Dance, Monument to General Alvear*, and décor for the Théâtre des Champs-Elysées.

Carnavalet (Musée Carnavalet):
23, Rue de Sévigné (3rd) ♦ A museum devoted to the history of Paris and located in the Hôtel Carnavalet (Renaissance and 17th century) ♦ The mansion was built from 1548 by Nicolas Dupuis for Jacques des Ligneris, the

President of the Chamber of Inquiries at the Paris Parliament; it was then acquired in 1578 by Françoise de Kernevenoy, whose name has remained with the building in the altered form of Carnavalet. It was enlarged and modernized in the mid-17th century by François Mansart for the financier Boislève, and was then owned by Madame de Sévigné from 1677 to 1696. The building changed hands several times before being bought by the City of Paris in 1866 to house its collections; the museum was opened in 1880 and extended to include the neighbouring Hôtel Le Peletier de Saint-Fargeau, which was renovated at the beginning of the 20th century ♦ About 500,000 pieces are displayed in 140 rooms, covering the prehistory and history of Paris from Antiquity to the present day: archaeological objects, documents, models, sculptures, paintings, prints, and furniture; the collections include some neolithic dug-out canoes discovered in Bercy in 1991, the 17th-century Grand Chamber from the Hôtel La Rivière, furniture and decorative objects from Parisian residences at the time of Louis XV, a Second Empire ceremonial cradle, and paintings by Corot: *Pont Saint-Michel* and *Quai des Orfèvres*.

Catacombs (Catacombes):
Place Denfert-Rochereau (14th) ♦ Ossuary laid out in abandoned underground pits. Bones were transferred here between 1786 and 1814 from the Cimetière des Innocents, then from other discontinued Parisian cemeteries; the bones include those of victims of the Revolution; five to six million bodies are deposited here ♦ Historic rooms, late 19th-century sculpture, a monument commemorating the foundation of the Catacombs, galleries containing the piles of bones, with skulls and tibias forming ornamental crosses; among the interesting features are the Samaritaine fountain, and the Sacellum and Passion crypts.

Cernuschi (Musée Cernuschi):
7, Avenue Velasquez (8th) ♦ A museum devoted to the art of the Far East. It was set up in the home of Henri Cernuschi, after he bequeathed the building to the City of Paris in 1893 along with his collections, which were subsequently expanded; the museum opened in 1898 ♦ Buddhist statues; classical Chi-

nese art: bronzes, pottery, porcelain, statuettes, paintings, in particular a 5th-century seated Bodhisattva, and horses and grooms (Tang period).

Chemin du Montparnasse:
21, Avenue du Maine (15th) ♦ At the far end of an avenue lined with studios and greenery, an artist's studio and "artists' canteen" have been turned into a community museum which was opened in 1998 ♦ Paintings from the interwar years until today (including Foujita), a film telling the history of the area, and temporary exhibitions.

Cognacq-Jay (Musée Cognacq-Jay):
8, Rue Elzévir (3rd) ♦ A museum devoted to the 18th century; founded by Ernest Cognacq and Louise Jay, it was originally located in the Boulevard des Capucines from 1931 to 1988, then moved to the Hôtel de Donon, built in 1575 for a Controller-General of the King's Buildings ♦ Rooms decorated with old wood paneling ♦ 18th-century works of art: drawings by Watteau, paintings by Boucher, Chardin, Fragonard, Greuze, and Canaletto, pastels by Quentin de la Tour, furniture, Dresden china, and precious objects from the Age of the Enlightenment.

Coins (Musée de la Monnaie):
11, Quai de Conti (6th) ♦ The former Hôtel de la Monnaie is a Neoclassical building, constructed for Louis XV between 1771 and 1776 by the architect Jacques-Denis Antoine, and used for the manufacture of coins until 1973 ♦ exhibition of 2,000 coins and 450 medals and tokens (taken from the 30,000 coins and 75,000 medals and tokens that the museum possesses), sculptures, paintings, and prints relating the history of France; collection of medals by Pierre-Jean David-d'Angers; display of manufacturing techniques and their evolution ♦ Gift shop.

Dalí (Espace Montmartre-Dali):
11, Rue Poulbot (18th) ♦ Founded in 1993, this museum has a collection of more than 300 sculptures and lithographs by the Surrealist Dali, including the *Spatial Elephant* and the *Comical Dreams of Pantagruel*.

Dapper (Musée Dapper):
35 *bis*, Rue Paul-Valéry (16th) ♦ A museum

devoted to African civilization. It was opened in 1986 in a residential apartment building dating from 1910, then in 2000 it was renovated and expanded ♦ It belongs to the Dapper Foundation (named after the 17th-century Dutch humanist), created in 1983 in Amsterdam with the aim of promulgating and conserving African heritage ♦ African works of art are shown at an annual exhibit; library and bookshop.

Delacroix (Musée National Eugène-Delacroix):
6, Place Furstemberg (6th) ♦ Founded in 1952 in the house where Delacroix lived from 1857 to 1863, and renovated at the beginning of the 1990s ♦ Delacroix's apartment and garden studio; paintings and lithographs; objects belonging to the painter.

Discovery (Palais de la Découverte):
Avenue Franklin-Roosevelt (8th) ♦ The museum was created on the initiative of scientists, including Jean Perrin, and located in the Grand Palais, which was built to mark the World Fair of 1937 ♦ Its aim is to bring science within reach of everyone, in a stimulating way and using as much experimentation as possible ♦ Images, models, videos, interactive displays, hands-on experiments, and experiments with commentary by the demonstrators. All of these are used to present the various disciplines: mathematics, physics, chemistry, Earth sciences, and astronomy (with the planetarium which was rebuilt in 1979).

Dolls (Musée de la Poupée):
Impasse Berthaud (3rd) ♦ Opened in 1995 in an old house entered through a small paved courtyard ♦ Display of more than 300 dolls, from 1850 to the present day, with their accessories, furniture, and miniature toys ♦ Temporary exhibitions, specialist shop, and dolls' hospital.

Fairground Art (Musée des Arts Forains):
53, Avenue des Terroirs-de-France (12th) ♦ Located in the last remaining Bercy wine warehouses, which have been restored by J-P Wilmotte ♦ Fairground art from the

end of the 19th century to 1950: shooting ranges, carrousels, side-shows, and mechanical musical instruments (group visits only).

Fans (Musée de l'Éventail):
2, Boulevard de Strasbourg (10th) ♦ The museum was created in 1993 by A Hoguet, a maker and restorer of fans, in the workshops of the Hoguet company, which are located in the upper stories of a 19th-century block ♦ Room fitted out in 1893 by the fan-makers Lepault and Deberghe: original décor and furniture, blue fabric wall coverings with fleurs-de-lys embroidered in gold thread ♦ Collection of fans from the 17th century to the present day, in various materials including ivory and tortoiseshell, bird of paradise and ostrich feathers ♦ Workshop where fans are made and restored, and gift shop.

Fashion and Textiles (Musée de la Mode et du Textile):
107, Rue de Rivoli (1st) ♦ The museum was opened in 1997 in the Napoléon wing of the Louvre, next to the Applied Arts Museum ♦ It houses the collections of the Central Union of Applied Art and the French Union of the Art of Costume (tens of thousands of costumes, accessories, and pieces of fabric since the 15th century), and displays its collections by theme; these change every six months or so.

French Monuments (Musée National des Monuments Français):
Palais de Chaillot, Place du Trocadéro (16th) ♦ The museum is located in the east wing of the Palais de Chaillot, built for the Universal Exhibition of 1937. In the form of casts, models, and reproductions, it presents a panorama of French monumental sculpture from the Middle Ages to the 19th century ♦ It is currently being restructured and renovated to form part of an Architecture and Heritage Zone ♦ Founded at the instigation of Viollet-le-Duc in 1879, when it was known as the Museum of Comparative Sculpture, it was opened to the public in 1882 in the old Palais du Trocadéro.

Galliera (Musée Galliera):
10, Avenue Pierre-1er-de Serbie (16th) ♦ This museum of Fashion and Costume has been located since 1977 in the Palais Galliera, built between 1878 and 1888 for the duchess of the same name ♦ The palace is inspired by the Italian Renaissance; its façade on the Avenue du Président Wilson is composed of three large arcades, adorned with statues representing Painting, Sculpture, and Architecture ♦ Collection of 70,000 pieces: costumes from the 18th and 19th centuries, couturiers' creations, jewellery, hats, canes, umbrellas, parasols, shoes, fans, and gloves ♦ Workshops and lectures.

Grand Palais (Musée du Grand Palais):
3, Avenue du Général Eisenhower (8th) ♦ The building was constructed by H Deglane, L Louvet, and A Thomas between 1897 and 1900, to replace the Palais de l'Industrie for the Universal Exhibition of 1900 ♦ Great hall surmounted by a vast central dome; façades in the Classical style, consisting of an iron frame covered with stone; decorative columns and statues; on the corners, chariots drawn by four horses by G Récipon; in front of the northern façade, a pond adorned with statues representing the Seine and its tributaries by R Larche (1900) ♦ Temporary art exhibitions.

Grévin (Musée Grévin):
10, Boulevard Montmartre (9th) ♦ This wax museum was founded in 1882 by Arthur Meyer and the caricaturist Alfred Grévin in a building constructed by Eugene Esnault-Pelterie ♦ 450 life-size wax figures, some historical and some contemporary, are displayed in appropriate settings; there is a Palace of Mirages and a magic show.

Guimet (Musée National des Arts Asiatiques Guimet):
19, Place d'Iéna (16th) ♦ Founded in 1889 in a building commissioned by the industrialist Émile Guimet to house his collection of Asian art, and built between 1885 and 1888; it became a national museum in 1929, acquired new collections in 1945, then was renovated in 1983 and from 1996 to 2000 ♦ More than 45,000 pieces from all over Asia, from Pakistan to Japan and South-East Asia: Khmer sculptures, Tibetan paintings, bronzes and ceramics from China, Korean and Japanese jewelry, bronzes from Java, black and gold lac-

quered furniture from Thailand, and Chinese jade and ivory carvings ♦ The annexe, the Hôtel Heidelbach, a Neoclassical building surrounded by a Japanese garden, was renovated in 1993: galleries of the Buddhist Pantheon of Japan and China (paintings and sculptures).

Health and Social Security (Musée de l'Assistance Publique):
47, Quai de la Tournelle (9th) ♦ Opened in 1934, and located in the former Hôtel Martin. Dating from 1630 and attributed to Mansart, this became the mansion of Madame de Miramion, a wealthy widow who founded a community of the Holy Family ♦ Collections of paintings, sculptures, crockery, baby's bottles, and medical and surgical equipment (including Dupuytren's instrument case and Laënnec's stethoscope), showing how hospitals evolved from the foundation of the Hôtel-Dieu in the 7th century to the present day. The collections are organized around themes: the church and hospitals; foundlings; hospital care for the destitute from alms-giving to modern charities; the hospital as a health facility.

Victor Hugo's House (Maison de Victor Hugo):
6, Place des Vosges (4th) ♦ Museum founded in 1902 in the former Hôtel de Rohan-Guéménée (or Hôtel de Lavardin), which was built in the 17th century; Victor Hugo lived there from 1832 to 1848 ♦ Apartment furnished and decorated with objects brought from the author's other residences; portraits and busts of the poet; on the second story, a display of drawings by Victor Hugo (the museum owns 600 of them), and temporary exhibitions.

Hunting and Nature (Musée de la Chasse et de la Nature):
60, Rue des Archives (3rd) ♦ Located in the Hôtel Guénégaud des Brosses, built between 1651 and 1655 by François Mansart for J-Fr Guénégaud, Sieur des Brosses, who commissioned it to replace two medieval houses. After that it changed hands several times, and was nearly destroyed before being bought by the City of Paris in 1960; restored and refitted thanks to F Sommer and his wife, collectors who moved their Hunting and Nature foundation into the building in 1967 ♦

Animal trophies, stuffed animals from the five continents (including a lion, an elephant, and an ostrich); collection of objects related to hunting (pikes, knives, guns, and crossbows); drawings and paintings of hunting scenes; and vases and plates with hunting scene decorations.

Jacquemart-André (Musée Jacquemart-André):
158, Boulevard Haussmann (8th) ♦ The museum is located in a Second Empire mansion, built in 1869 by the architect Parent for Édouard André and Nélie Jacquemart ♦ Décor and furnishings of a wealthy 19th-century home with winter garden; "Italian museum": collections of paintings and sculpture from the Italian Renaissance; the Flemish masters and the 18th-century French School ♦ Bookshop, gift shop, and café.

Jeu de Paume:
Place de la Concorde (1st) ♦ A museum of modern art in a former real-tennis court, built in 1861 by Napoléon III as part of the plan for the Tuileries Garden ♦ Since the beginning of the 20th century it has been devoted to art exhibitions; in 1986 its Impressionist collections were transferred to the Musée d'Orsay. Its interior was then redesigned by the architect Antoine Stinco to house contemporary works; the new museum opened in June, 1991.

Judaism (Musée d'Art et d'Histoire du Judaïsme):
71, Rue du Temple (3rd) ♦ Created in 1986 in the Hôtel de Saint-Aignan, which was built for the Comte d'Avaux in 1650 by the architect Pierre Le Muet, and in 1668 became the property of the Duc de Saint-Aignan. It was bought in 1962 by the City of Paris in 1962, then restored ♦ Religious objets d'art, manuscripts, documents concerning the art and history of Judaism, mainly in France. Paintings by artists including Chagall, Modigliani, and Soutine ♦ Bookshop, cultural activities, auditorium, and café.

Leclerc and the Liberation of Paris (Mémorial du Maréchal Leclerc de Hautecloque et de la Libération de Paris) – Musée Jean-Moulin:
23, Allée de la Deuxième-DB, Jardin Atlantique (15th) ♦ Museums of contemporary history

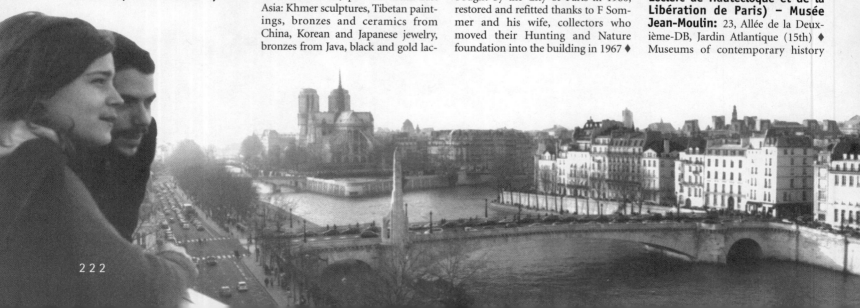

opened in 1994 ♦ Archives, objects, documents, photographs, audiovisual material, uniforms, all relating to the Liberation of Paris, Marshal Leclerc, and Resistance leader Jean Moulin.

Legion of Honor (Musée de la Légion d'Honneur):
2, Rue de Bellechasse (7th) ♦ This historical museum was opened in 1925, and is located in the Hôtel de Salm, which was built in 1788 for the Prince of Salm-Kyrbourg, then in 1804 became the seat of the Legion of Honor; it was restored after being set on fire by the Commune in 1871 ♦ Collection of objects, paintings and documents about the orders of knighthood and nobility under the Ancien Régime, the history of the Order of the Legion of Honor, and religious and foreign orders.

Louvre (Musée du Louvre):
Cour Napoléon (1st) ♦ Art museum located in the Palais du Louvre . In 1793 it was opened by the Convention in the Grande Galerie, then in the Salon Carré and the Galerie Apollon, to house works from Versailles, and then a number of masterpieces brought from countries conquered by Napoleon, which for the most part were soon restored to their owners. Under the Restoration its collections were enriched by more works (including the Venus de Milo), and new rooms were opened (the Museum of Greek and Egyptian Antiquities). In 1848, the museum became the property of the State, and accumulated many works through donations, purchases and legacies: ancient statues, major canvasses, objets d'art ♦ In 1981, the Grand Louvre project began; the layout was completely transformed: it was able to expand by taking over the Richelieu wing, formerly occupied by the Ministry of Finance; a new reception area was created in the Cour Napoléon, surmounted by a glass pyramid designed by Pei Ieoh Ming ♦ Various departments: Oriental, Egyptian, Greek, Etruscan and Roman Antiquities; Sculpture; Objets d'art; Paintings of the French, Italian, Spanish, English, and Northern Schools; the Medieval Louvre.

Maillol (Musée Maillol):
59-61, Rue de Grenelle (7th) ♦ Created in 1996 thanks to the Dina Verny Foundation

set up by the sculptor's model ♦ The building used to house the old Recollet Convent; the façade is embellished by the Four Seasons Fountain, made in 1739 by Edme Bouchardon; Alfred de Musset lived there from 1824 to 1839 ♦ Main works by the sculptor himself, paintings and drawings by prestigious artists: Gauguin, Bonnard, Dufy, Matisse, Kandinsky, Ingres, Foujita, Valadon, and Picasso. Temporary exhibitions.

Mankind (Musée de l'Homme):
Palais de Chaillot, Place du Trocadéro (16th) ♦ Located in the Palais de Chaillot, which was built for the Universal Exhibition of 1937 by Carlu, Boileau, and Azéma, this museum is the heir to the old Trocadéro Museum of Ethnography and the anthropological gallery of the Museum of Natural History to which it belongs ♦ In the vast entrance hall, where temporary exhibits take place, an Indian totem-pole rises to a height of 52 ft (16 m). Everything related to mankind is brought together here in one place: anthropology; paleontology; prehistory (the stages of the human adventure are illustrated by reconstructed figures); ethnology (arts and objects of the world are shown in galleries devoted to black and white Africa, the Near East, the peoples of the Arctic, Asia, Oceania and America). There is a music exhibit displaying 400 instruments, including a prehistoric lithophone from Vietnam, formed from ten stones of different lengths, and a 19th-century Javanese gamelan (an orchestra of percussion instruments) ♦ Bookshop.

Maritime (Musée de la Marine):
Palais de Chaillot, Place du Trocadéro (16th) ♦ A museum of the history of navigation, located in the west wing of the Palais de Chaillot, built for the Universal Exhibition of 1937 by architects Jacques Carlu, Hippolyte Boileau, and Léon Azéma on the site of the old Palais du Trocadéro ♦ It contains the collections of the first Maritime Museum, founded in December, 1827 and opened in the Louvre ♦ Collection of models of boats, a series of paintings of French ports by Joseph Vernet, a collection of lenses by Augustin Fresnel, various objects; films about the history of liners and steamships.

Marmottan (Musée Marmottan):
2, Rue Louis-Boilly (16th) ♦ Created in 1934 in a mansion bought in 1882 from the Duchesse de Valmy by Jules Marmottan, who heightened and converted it to accommodate his collections. His son gave it to the Institut de France in 1932 ♦ To house the Impressionists, rooms were built in the basement in 1971 by Carlu, then restored in 1989 ♦ Rhenish Primitives, Flemish tapestries, stained-glass windows, collection of Impressionist paintings, including Monet's *Impressions au Soleil Levant* and *Le Pont de l'Europe à la Gare Saint-Lazare*.

Middle Ages-Cluny Thermal Baths (Musée National du Moyen Âge-Thermes de Cluny):
6, Place Paul Painlevé (5th) ♦ The flamboyant mansion of the Abbots of Cluny, built at the end of the 15th century by Jacques d'Amboise, stands next to the remains of the thermal baths, constructed in the second to third centuries, whose *frigidarium* has been conserved. The State bought the whole site in 1843 and turned it into a museum, which opened in 1844 and became a national museum at the beginning of the 20th century ♦ Thematic exhibits illustrating daily life and artistic activity in the Middle Ages: many tapestries including the *Lady with the Unicorn*, fabrics, furnishings, stained-glass windows, gold plate, enamel work, jewelry, and various objects; sculptures, including numerous capitals, and in particular the statue-columns from Notre-Dame, and the heads of the kings of Judah which were knocked down in 1793 and rediscovered in 1977 during building work in Rue de la Chaussée-d'Antin.

Modern Art (City of Paris) (Musée d'Art Moderne de la Ville de Paris):
11, Avenue du Président–Wilson (16th) ♦ Located in the east wing of the Palais de Tokyo, which was built by Dondel, Aubert, Viard, and Dastugue for the Universal Exhibition of 1937, the museum opened in 1961 ♦ Collections illustrating the great movements in modern European art, from the beginning of the 20th century to the present day: Fauvism, Cubism, Dadaism, the Paris Surrealist school, abstract art, New Realism; paintings by Derain, Vlaminck, Picasso, Braque, Gris, Soutine, Modigliani, Delaunay, Dufy, and

Matisse. The works on display include Raoul Dufy's *The Fairy Electricity*; Chagall's *The Dream; The Paris Dance* and *Pastoral* by Matisse, and Derain's *Figures Seated on the Grass*.

Modern Art (National) (Musée National d'Art Moderne):
Centre Georges-Pompidou, Rue St-Martin (4th) ♦ This museum contains the collections of the former Museum of Modern Art, founded in 1937, and the National Center for Contemporary Art, opened in 1967. It is located in the museum opened in 1977 in the Georges-Pompidou Center, and renovated between 1997 and 2000 by Renzo Piano ♦ Works by artists representing all the great movements of the 20th century: Fauvism (Derain, Marquet, and Matisse), Cubism (Braque and Picasso), Dada, abstract art (Kandinsky, Mondrian, and Klee), Surrealism (De Chirico, Dali, and Miró), American painting (Pollock and Rothko) and contemporary art (Tinguely, Warhol, Arman, Niki de Saint-Phalle, César, and Vasarely).

Montmartre (Musée de Montmartre):
12, Rue Cortot (18th) ♦ A museum devoted to the history of the Montmartre district, and located in a former family mansion called the Manoir de Rosimond, which dates from the 17th century and belonged to Claude de la Rose, known as Rosimond, who was an actor in Molière's company; others who lived here were Renoir, Émile Bernard, Suzanne Valadon, Utrillo, and Léon Bloy ♦ Documents, photographs, paintings, drawings, posters, and objects recalling the history of the area; reconstruction of the Café de l'Abreuvoir, and Gustave Charpentier's study; Émile Bernard room.

Moreau (Musée Gustave-Moreau):
14, Rue de la Rochefoucauld (9th) ♦ This museum, conceived and designed by Gustave Moreau to exhibit his work, is located in his family home, which was extended between 1895 and 1896 ♦ Paintings, drawings, watercolors by the artist; apartment on the second story, studio on the third and fourth stories.

Moulin: see Leclerc.

Music (Musée de la Musique): Parc de la Villette, 221, Avenue Jean-Jaurès (19th) ◆ Set up by Hammoutène in the Cité de la Musique, created by architect Christian de Portzamparc in 1991 ◆ About 900 instruments (of the 4,000 or so in the museum's collections) are displayed on an audio-visual journey providing a panorama of the history of music from the 17th to the 21st centuries; paintings, sculptures, and models.

Natural History (Musée National d'Histoire Naturelle): 57, Rue Cuvier (5th) ◆ The Museum of Natural History was instituted by the Convention in 1793 ◆ From the Jardin Royal created in 1635 under Louis XIII, it inherited medicinal plants and also its buildings. The oldest, on Rue Cuvier, date back to the 17th and 18th centuries. Other buildings were added later: new greenhouses made of cast-iron, iron and glass (1834-1836); the Gallery of Mineralogy and Geology, with pediments adorned by sculptures by Pradier (1841); the Zoology building (1889), now completely restored and turned into the Great Gallery of Evolution by P Chemetov and B Huidobro (scenography by R Allio), which opened in 1994; the Galleries of Anatomy and Palaeontology (1896), then Botany (1935) ◆ In the Great Gallery there is a succession of stuffed animals and display cabinets illustrating the diversity of the living world and the place of man in evolution; the Gallery of Palaeontology has a collection of fossils, including a mammoth and dinosaurs; thousands of rocks and minerals, including a collection of giant crystals, are displayed in the Gallery of Mineralogy; 1,500 specimens of insects in the Gallery of Entomology ◆ Temporary exhibitions are held in the various galleries.

Nissim-de-Camondo (Musée Nissim-de-Camondo): 63, Rue Monceau (8th) ◆ The museum is in a mansion built in 1863 and rebuilt in 1911 in the style of the 18th century; in 1935 the house and its collections of 18th-century art were bequeathed by the Comte de Camondo to the Central Union of Applied Arts; the museum is named after his son, who was killed in aerial combat in World War I ◆ Furniture by fine cabinetmakers, 18th-century wood paneling, carpets from the Savonnerie, tapestries from Beauvais and Aubusson, gold plate, porcelain, objets d'art, prints, and paintings.

Notre-Dame Archaeological Crypt (Crypte Archéologique Notre-Dame): 1, Place du Parvis de Notre-Dame (4th) ◆ Archaeological museum set up following the excavations carried out between 1965 and 1972 to build an underground car park ◆ Roman remains, discovered in the 19th century: walls of Gallo-Roman rooms heated by hypocaust, cellars of houses in the old Rue Neuve-Notre-Dame, foundations of more recent buildings, etc.

Orangery (Musée de l'Orangerie): Terrasse du Jardin des Tuileries, Place de la Concorde (8th) ◆ The 330 ft (100 m) long building was constructed in 1852 by A Bourgeois at the far end of the terrace beside the water, to provide shelter for the orange trees that adorned the Tuileries in summer. The narrow façades are framed by columns and surmounted by a triangular sculpted pediment ◆ The museum has housed Monet's Water Lilies since 1927, and the Walter-Guillaume collection since 1984; more recently, works by other artists were added: Cézanne, Renoir, Le Douanier Rousseau, and Picasso ◆ Currently being renovated until 2002.

Order of the Liberation (Musée de l'Ordre de la Libération): 51 *bis*, Rue de Latour-Maubourg (7th) ◆ A museum of modern history, founded after World War II. It is located in a house built in 1747 to plans by Robert de Cotte ◆ Documents, relics, drawings, and various souvenirs recall the great moments of the Resistance, the deportation camps, and everything relating to the Companions of the Liberation; manuscripts by General de Gaulle.

D'Orsay (Musée d'Orsay): 1, Rue Bellechasse (7th) ◆ This museum is devoted to the fine art of the 19th century, and is located in the former Orléans Rail Station, designed by Victor Laloux and built at the end of the 19th century for the Universal Exhibition ◆ The original building, with its iron and metal framework and monumental stone façade, was converted into a museum and opened in 1986; the interior was designed by Gae Aulenti ◆ Sculpture, paintings, architecture, and applied arts are presented chronologically. Works include *The Spring* by Ingres; *Fourteen-year-old Dancer* by Degas; Millet's *Evening Angelus*; Courbet's *A Burial at Ornans*; and paintings by Gauguin, Manet, Cézanne, and Caillebotte ◆ 2.3 million visitors (1997).

Petit Palais (Musée du Petit Palais): Avenue Winston-Churchill (8th) ◆ Built by Ch Girault for the 1900 World Fair, the Classical-style trapezoid stone building surrounds a semicircular courtyard. Main features are the domed hall and richly-decorated galleries, façades bordered by colonnades, and a portal with a semicircular arch ◆ The building houses the City of Paris Museum of Fine Art, based on the 19th-century Dutuit and Tuck collections: furniture, objets d'art, prints, drawings, and paintings from Antiquity to the 19th century; Roger Cabal donation: icons from the 15th to 17th centuries.

Photography (Maison Européenne de la Photographie): 82, Rue François-Miron (4th) ◆ A museum of contemporary art, opened in 1996 in the Hôtel Hénault de Cantobre, which was built at the beginning of the 18th century; this was restored and enlarged by architects Yves Lion and Alan Levitt, preserving one balcony and a staircase with wrought-iron banisters ◆ More than 12,000 photographic works produced since 1958, and thematic or monographic exhibitions ◆ Studios, video library, auditorium, and library.

Picasso (Musée Picasso): 5, Rue de Thorigny (3rd) ◆ Opened in 1985, and located in the former Hôtel Salé, built in 1656 by Jean Bouillier, known as Jean de Bourges; it was redesigned in the 18th century, then restored between 1974 and 1984; the interior layout was designed by Roland Simounet; the former garden has been restored ◆ Works by Picasso, some donated by Jacqueline Picasso, others acquired more recently: paintings, sculptures, pottery, prints, and drawings, presented by period and by theme.

Popular Arts and Traditions (Musée National des Arts et Traditions Populaires): 6, Avenue du Mahatma-Gandhi (16th) ◆ The building was constructed by Jean Dubuisson between 1960 and 1968, and consists of a horizontal space dominated by a tower which contains temporary exhibits, an auditorium, and offices; the glass doors have wooden handles designed by Marta Pan ◆ The museum houses the old Museum of Ethnography from the Trocadéro ◆ Large collections of objects from the preindustrial era, from various regions of France; displays concerning man's relationship with his environment, his technical methods, customs, and beliefs.

Postal Service (Musée de la Poste): 34, Boulevard de Vaugirard (15th) ◆ Built by architect A Chatelin in 1957 ◆ The museum was founded in Rue Saint-Romain (6th) in 1942, on the initiative of E Vaillé, the librarian of the Post Office Ministry, who assembled a major collection in the first half of the 20th century ◆ It has about 15 rooms in which the history of the postal service is presented through posters, almanacs, calendars, uniforms, various objects (folding scales, postboxes, seals, and engravings); methods of transport, airmail, the role of the Post Office in the 1870-71 war (air balloons, pigeon post), the role of postmen; there is also a display of furnishings: an Art Deco ticket-office window, presses, a 1930 recording and franking machine, and a reconstructed line-engraving workshop.

Radio (Musée de Radio-France): 116, Avenue Président-Kennedy (16th) ◆ The museum was set up in 1966 in the Maison de Radio-France, built between 1955 and 1962 by H Bernard ◆ Objects, photographs, advertisements, and radio and television sets showing the evolution of the transmission of information; reconstruction of a 1935 television studio.

Rodin (Musée Rodin): 77, Rue de Varenne (7th) ◆ This has been located since 1919 in the Hôtel Biron, built by J Aubert in 1728 for Abraham Peyrenc de Moras who sold it to the Duc de

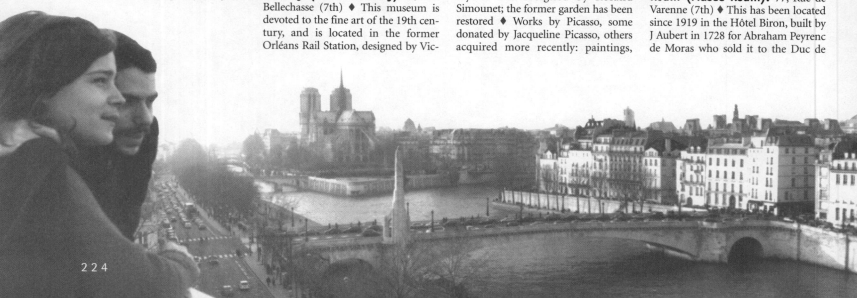

Biron ♦ Isadora Duncan, Cocteau, and Matisse lived here, then Rodin, who donated his collections to the State ♦ Works by the sculptor include *The Thinker, The Burghers of Calais* (in the garden), *The Kiss, The Bronze Age,* and *The Hand of God*; drawings, and photographs of Rodin's work.

Romantic Period (Musée de la Vie Romantique): 16, Rue Chaptal (9th)

♦ Former private house built in the Restoration style, where the painter Ary Scheffer lived from 1830 to 1858 ♦ Works by Ary Scheffer, refurnished studio, mementos of George Sand (paintings, jewelry, and manuscripts); temporary exhibitions.

Science and Industry (Cité des Sciences et de l'Industrie): 30, Avenue Corentin-Cariou (19th)

♦ A museum of science and technology, created in a building constructed between 1969 and 1973 to house the saleroom of the abattoirs at La Villette. After the closure of the abattoirs it was turned into a museum, designed by the architect Adrien Fainsilber and opened in 1986 ♦ It has several departments: Explora, a permanent exhibition about the Earth and the Universe, life, matter and communication, using multimedia and computers; the Planetarium; Technocité, a survey of technology; the Job Zone (Cité des Métiers); the giant aquarium; the Children's Zone (Cité des Enfants) with three exhibition areas for different age groups; and the Louis Lumière cinema (documentary films).

Technology (Musée National des Techniques): 292, Rue Saint-Martin (3rd)

♦ Located on the site of the old Priory of Saint-Martin-des-Champs, which was founded in the 11th century; the restored chevet of the priory's church forms the entrance to the museum, which occupies buildings from the 18th century by Antoine and from the 19th by L Vaudoyer. The museum was opened in 1802 and enlarged in 1836; it has been renovated several times (in 1958, 1978, and the 1990s) ♦ Collections of objects illustrating the history of transport, scientific instruments, materials used in engineering and communications, including Cugnot's road steamer (1770), Clément Ader's aircraft (1897), marine chronometers, old clocks, robots, microscopes, and the Lumière brothers' first camera.

Zadkine (Musée Zadkine): 100 *bis*, Rue d'Assas (6th)

♦ Located in the former studio of the sculptor Zadkine, who occupied it from 1982 to 1967 ♦ Stone and wood sculptures in the museum's rooms and in the garden; works include *Woman with Fan, The Priestesses of Bacchus, Prometheus,* and a model of the *Destroyed City*.

PARKS AND GARDENS

Bois de Boulogne: Western Paris, between the Porte d'Auteuil and the Porte Maillot (16th)

♦ 2,090 acres (846 ha) ♦ A remnant of the old Rouvray Forest (planted with durmast oaks) which in the Middle Ages covered the whole of north-west Paris ♦ The Bois owes its name to a church, no longer in existence, which was built by Philip the Fair to commemorate his pilgrimage to Notre-Dame de Boulogne-sur-Mer ♦ It was devastated during the Revolution and the invasions of 1814-15, then replanted and redesigned by Alphand, Davioud, and Barillet-Deschamps under Napoléon III. He donated it to the City of Paris, on condition it was developed as a public park. The Bois became a fashionable spot, attracting high society and becoming famous in the Belle Époque ♦ More than 400,000 trees; lakes, rivers, and waterfalls; roads, avenues, paths, and bridle paths ♦ The Bagatelle and Pré-Catelan parks, Auteuil and Longchamp racecourses, Racing Club de France, a zoological garden (Jardin d'Acclimatation), the National Museum of Popular Arts and Traditions, the Upper (Supérieur) and Lower (Inférieur) Lakes (well stocked with fish and water birds).

Bois de Vincennes: To the east of Paris, between the Porte Dorée and the Porte de Charenton (12th)

♦ 2,450 acres (995 ha) ♦ This was the royal hunting forest in the Middle Ages ♦ Under Louis XV it was completely replanted and had straight avenues driven through it. Then under Napoléon I it was partly cleared and used by him as a parade ground, before being turned into a landscaped park by Alphand under Napoléon III, who donated it to the City of Paris: exotic trees, ornamental lakes, waterfalls, bridle paths, and footpaths. The Colonial Exhibition of 1931 was held there ♦ Lakes Daumesnil, de Gravelle, and des Minimes, a floral park, adventure playground, zoological gardens, Vincennes racecourse, arboretum, George Ville (or Paris) farm, du Breuil School of Horticulture, International Buddhist Institute, and Cartoucherie de Vincennes theaters.

Champ de Mars: Quai Branly, Avenue de la Motte-Piquet (7th)

♦ 60 acres (24 ha) ♦ Former parade ground for the École Militaire ♦ Opened to the public in 1780, it became a rallying point for national demonstrations during the Revolution, then a racecourse, and one of the sites for the Universal Exhibitions. In 1908 it was turned into a landscaped garden by Jean-Camille Formigé ♦ Large lawns, clipped yews on each side, laid out in the English style, and a view from the Ecole Militaire to the Eiffel Tower. Hundred-year-old trees (a Byzantine hazel tree, a pterocarya), statues, lakes, ponds, and grottos.

Jardin Atlantique: Gare Montparnasse, Place des Cinq-Martyrs-du-Lycée-Buffon (15th-14th)

♦ 8 acres (3 ha) ♦ Garden built on a platform above the TGV lines at the Gare Montparnasse, laid out in 1994 by landscape gardeners François Brun and Michel Pena to symbolize the ocean ♦ Large lawn, small theme gardens dotted with water features; nearly 500 trees (red and pedunculated oaks, and American and Oriental plane trees), 5,000 shrubs and several tens of thousands of perennials and grasses; central fountain; decorations suggesting the ocean. Adventure playground for small children, five tennis courts, table tennis tables and fitness area, all bordered by a long pergola wound around with climbing plants.

Jardin d'Acclimatation (Zoological Gardens) - Exploradrome: Carrefour des Sablons, Bois de Boulogne (16th)

♦ 49 acres (20 ha) ♦ Park for children ♦ It was designed in 1860 by Davioud and Barillet-Deschamps, on the initiative of the Imperial Society for Zoological Gardens, to house animals and plants newly introduced to France ♦ During the Siege of Paris, the animals were eaten and the dovecote was used for sending mail. The tower was rebuilt in 1875 by Ch-J Simonet ♦ The aviary and the stables date from that time, and have been converted ♦ Wild animals (birds, bears, deer, and monkeys) and a small farm for domestic animals, created in 1977. Distorting mirrors, Punch and Judy show, adventure playgrounds, Enchanted River, mini racing circuit, miniature train, and a Green Museum which was set up in 1975 by archeologists to help children discover the arts. The Exploradrome opened in December, 1998 as a center for learning about science and multimedia: exhibitions, activities (optical illusions, creation of a tornado, and rolling square wheels), introduction to multimedia, and workshops for children.

Jardin de l'Arsenal: Boulevard de la Bastille (12th)

♦ 2,5 acres (1 ha) ♦ Terraced garden, running from the Bastille to the Pont Morland along the east bank of the Arsenal harbor where there are gulls and mallards. Riverside walk lined by maple trees; many roses, clematis, honeysuckle, and springtime bulbs. Bronze statue by Henri Arnold, *Young Woman Crouching*.

Jardin Catherine-Labouré: 33, Rue de Babylone (6th)

♦ 2 acres (0.7 ha) ♦ Former garden of the Convent of the Compagnie des Filles de la Charité ♦ Orchard, currant bushes and hazel hedges, kitchen garden; lawns, avenue lined with linden trees, arbor covered with vines ♦ Green workshops for children.

Jardin des Enfants aux Halles: 105, Rue Rambuteau (1st)

♦ Garden for children, designed by F-X and Cl Lalanne at the end of the 1980s ♦ Six play "worlds": the tropical forest, the soft world (pools full of ping-pong balls), the world of geometry and sound (musical steps), the volcanic world, the mysterious island (reached by a slide), and the lost city and its labyrinth.

Jardin des Halles: Rue Berger, Rue Rambuteau (1st) ♦ 11 acres (4 ha) ♦ Platform garden on the former site of Les Halles, above the Forum, completed in 1988 ♦ 600 trees, thousands of shrubs; arcades and arbors covered with climbing plants (clematis, Virginia creeper, jasmine, and wisteria); large tropical greenhouse surrounded by clumps of flowers; 11 fountains, and a children's garden.

Jardin des Plantes: Place Valhubert, Rue Buffon (5th) ♦ Botanical gardens, 58 acres (24 ha) ♦ It was founded in 1635 at the instigation of Héroard and Guy de la Brosse, doctors to Louis XIII, and opened in 1640. In the 18th century, it was managed by Buffon, assisted by the botanist Jussieu and the naturalist Daubenton; in 1793 it became a museum of natural history ♦ Flower beds throughout, bordered by double rows of clipped plane trees; rose garden planted in 1990; garden of irises and perennials created in 1964; garden of the Ecole de Botanique (School of Botany); alpine garden (more than 2,000 mountain plants); maze with a belvedere, covered with Mediterranean plants; large greenhouses containing several thousand species of plants, including tropical greenhouses open to the public. All around are buildings used for research and exhibits: mineralogy, botany, palaeontolgy, evolution, and the menagerie ♦ Some very old trees: a false acacia (1636), a cedar of Lebanon (1734), and a Japanese sophora (1747), planted by Jussieu.

Jardin des Serres d'Auteuil: 3, Avenue de la Porte d'Auteuil (16th) ♦ 12 acres (5 ha) ♦ Horticultural garden designed by Jean-Camille Forgé ♦ It was created between 1895 and 1898 on the site of a flower garden with greenhouses laid out in 1761 for Louis XV. Some of its acreage was lost when the Auteuil freeway junction was built in 1969 ♦ There is a vast flowerbed in front of the steps leading to the terrace; numerous shrubs and more than 260 trees: bare palms, Montpellier maple, yellowwood, Chinese parasol, caramel tree, and platycarya; fountain

by Jules Calou; iron and glass greenhouses, built in the 19th century, used for growing palm trees, azaleas, succulents, ficus and tropical plants (papayas, banana trees, Egyptian blue lotus, orchids, bromeliads, various begonias, and giant water lilies) ♦ Offices of the Department of Paris Parks, Gardens and Green Spaces.

Jardin des Tuileries: Place de la Concorde (1st) ♦ Created around the Tuileries Palace at the end of the 16th century, redesigned by Le Nôtre in 1664 ♦ More than 20 different species including laricio pine, white mulberry, and Judas tree; round pond in the middle of the Grand Carré, octagonal pond and hemispherical area sloping up to the Place de la Concorde.

Jardin du Carrousel: Place du Carrousel (1st) ♦ 69 acres (28 ha) with the Tuileries Garden ♦ Designed at the end of the 19th century on the site of the Tuileries Palace, which was burned down in 1871; redesigned in 1994 by Jacques Wirtz and reconstructed as a platform garden above the galleries of the Louvre ♦ Linden trees and yews around the Carroussel arch; hedges leading down to the garden.

Jardin du Luxembourg: Boulevard Saint-Michel (6th) ♦ 55 acres (22 ha) ♦ Created in 1617, it owes its name to the Duc de Piney-Luxembourg, the owner of the estate which was bought by Marie de Médicis ♦ Chestnut trees and paulownias; open space around the octagonal pond, designed by Le Nôtre; Médicis fountain decorated with sculptures, built in 1630; formal garden in front of the Palais du Luxembourg, English-style garden to the south; orangery containing oleander trees, palm trees, camphor trees, and pomegranate trees; tennis courts, puppet theater, apiary, and orchard.

Jardin Médiéval: Corner of Boulevards St-Michel and Saint-Germain (5th) ♦ 1.2 acres (0.5 ha) ♦ Garden inspired by the Middle Ages, created in 2000 as an extension to the Musée de Cluny ♦ Theme areas: Unicorn Forest, kitchen garden, medicinal garden; courtyard (meadow dotted with flowers), decorated with a fountain with silver reeds; garden of love, celestial garden, two clearings including one for children (games inspired by the ani-

mals of the *Lady with the Unicorn*) ♦ The Carpet of a Thousand Flowers leads to Square Paul-Painlevé.

Jardin Sainte-Périne: Rue Mirabeau, Avenue de Versailles (16th) ♦ 7 acres (3 ha) ♦ This garden has been open to the public since 1977 ♦ It used to be the park of the Sainte-Périne Institution, which moved in the 1860s to a stately home that had belonged to the canons of Saint Genevieve and was sold during the Revolution ♦ English-style garden with a lawn adorned by clumps of flowers; numerous trees: plane, maple, linden, chestnut, sophora, a paper mulberry, and persimmon.

Jardin Villemin: Avenue de Verdun, Rue des Recollets (10th) ♦ 4 acres (1.6 ha) ♦ Formerly the garden of the Villemin Hospital, it opened in 1977 ♦ Exotic species, soap tree, paper mulberry, corkscrew hazel, and pyramidal hornbeam ♦ An extension to the Canal Saint-Martin was created in 2001.

Jardins des Champs-Élysées: Cours la Reine, Avenue Matignon, Avenue Franklin D Roosevelt (8th) ♦ 34 acres (14 ha) ♦ A promenade with a view of the Tuileries, designed by Le Nôtre for the king from 1667. It was restored between 1830 and 1840 by Hittorff, who put in the lighting and fountains and built the present-day Restaurant Ledoyen and the Pavillon Laurens ♦ English-style gardens, redesigned in 1859 by Alphand next to where the Grand and Petit Palais were built for the 1900 Universal Exhibition.

Jardins du Palais-Royal: Place Colette (1st) ♦ Gardens of the old Palais-Royal, originally designed by Le Nôtre ♦ The central fountain is framed by two long lawns bordered by two double rows of clipped linden-trees ♦ Sandpits and a play area for children have been laid out in the northern part of the gardens, which are surrounded on three sides by buildings constructed at the beginning of the 1780s for the Duc d'Orléans, known as Philippe Égalité; Colette, Cocteau, Christian Bérard, and Mireille lived there. The regular façades contain arcades with restaurants and boutiques dealing in objets d'art. To the south is a double row of colonnades, built under the Restoration, then a courtyard and two

ponds decorated by the turning steel balls of Pol Bury's *Two Fountains for the Palais-Royal* (1985). Beyond this, the Cour d'Honneur (Court of Honour) is lined by Buren's truncated columns (1985-6).

Jardins du Trocadéro: Avenue de New York, Place du Trocadéro-et-du-11-Novembre (16th) ♦ 23 acres (9 ha) ♦ Created by R Ladat for the Universal Exhibition of 1937, on the site of gardens laid out by Alphand for the 1878 Exhibition ♦ Two English-style gardens on either side of the Palais de Chaillot; various trees (pedunculated oak, paulownias, Byzantine hazels, pterocaryas, and a young sequoia donated in 1989 by "the American people"); a small artificial river, in the center, facing the Seine; the Warsaw fountains with their powerful jets, by architects Paul Maître and Roger Expert; numerous statues ♦ The underground aquarium in the northeastern part is due to open in 2001.

Parc André-Citroën: Quai André-Citroën, Rue Saint-Charles (15th) ♦ 34 acres (14 ha) ♦ This garden, opened in 1992, was designed by architects Patrick Berger, Jean-François Jodry and Jean-Paul Viguier, and landscape gardeners Gilles Clément and Alain Provost ♦ In the center is a large lawn stretching down to the Seine, bordered on one side by a canal and on the other by two greenhouses framing a water peristyle on a stone square; "serial" gardens (gold, silver, blue, and red), a garden with fallowland flora, a black garden, and a white garden.

Parc de Bagatelle: Allée de Longchamp, the road from Sèvres to Neuilly in the Bois de Boulogne (16th) ♦ 60 acres (24 ha) ♦ The park of the Château de Bagatelle, created by Thomas Blaikie after the château was built (1775) ♦ In the center, an English-style landscaped garden with ornamental lakes (including one with water lilies), waterfalls, grottos, rocks, and a belvedere; to the north, conifers and an oak forest. Small formal garden and its collections: irises, clematis; rose garden (laid out in 1906) including more than 1,300 varieties.

Parc de Belleville: Rue des Couronnes, Rue Julien-Lacroix (20th) ♦ 11 acres (4 ha) ♦ Garden opened in

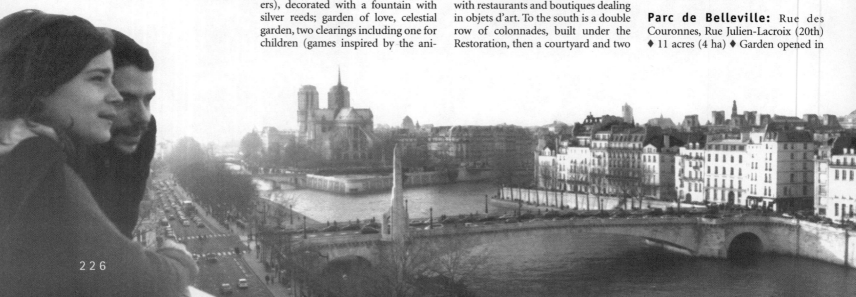

1988 in an area restored and designed by architect François Debulois and landscape gardener Paul Brichet ♦ The sloping terrain of the Belleville hill is laid out with steps and winding paths. Around a central main path marked by ponds, fountains, and waterfalls, there are two lawns, flowerbeds, many shrubs, and a large variety of trees (sophoras, catalpas, linden trees, Virginia tulip trees, yews, apple trees and flowering pear trees) ♦ Open-air theater, play areas, and a wooden village for children.

Parc de Bercy: Rues Paul-Belmondo, Joseph-Kessel, François-Truffaut (12th) ♦ 33 acres (13 ha) ♦ Designed by architects Marylène Ferrand, Jean-Pierre Feugas, Bernard Leroy, and Bernard Huet, and landscape gardeners Yann Lecaisne and Philippe Raguin. The park opened in stages, starting in 1997 ♦ It is located on the site of a wine warehouse on an old estate that was broken up in the middle of the 19th century ♦ There are three areas: the Grande Prairie (Great Grass Area), bordered by conical oaks, is a succession of lawns, dotted with trees and pavillions, and linked by steps to the main terrace, which is planted with linden trees and runs alongside the Seine; the parterres, which are nine cultivated plots (kitchen garden, orchard, vine arbors, rose garden, maze, and scented garden), and the House of Gardening; the densely planted romantic garden is designed around a canal and ponds, linked to the parterres by footbridges, and planted with Corsican pines, silver birches and weeping willows (exhibits in the Lake House). Fountain, sculptures, and stone arches.

Parc de la Butte du Chapeau-Rouge: Boulevard d'Algérie, Avenue Debidour (19th) ♦ 12 acres (5 ha) ♦ Built on a gypsum hill and opened in 1939, this park was decorated by Léon Azéma with fountains, waterfalls, steps and shelters ♦ Central lawn, tulip trees, weeping sophora, Bohemian olive tree, clumps of rose bushes and perennials, and a rockery.

Parc des Buttes-Chaumont: Rue Botzaris, Rue Manin (19th) ♦ 61 acres (25 ha) ♦ Created by Alphand, Davioud, and Barillet-Deschamps between 1864 and 1867 ♦ Laid out over former gypsum quarries on what was known at the time as Bald Mountain; later it became a public garbage dump ♦ Now it is a steeply undulating park with promontories and grottos. Numerous birds nest in the trees, some of which are over 100 years old (chestnut, plane, and sophora); the lake has various species of fish and water birds; on its island, linked to the garden by two bridges, is the Temple of Sibyl; waterfall.

Parc de Choisy: 128-160, Avenue de Choisy, Rue Charles-Moureu (13th) ♦ 11 acres (4 ha) ♦ Created in 1937 by Édouard Crevel near the Dental Institute ♦ The park is framed by two English-style gardens. Lawn, pond bordered by clumps of flowers, avenues lined by chestnut trees, gingko bilobas, weeping beeches, sophoras, and linden trees ♦ Sculpture by Richard Serra, and areas laid out for games.

Parc Floral de Paris: Route de la Pyramide, Bois de Vincennes (12th) ♦ 76 acres (31 ha) ♦ Botanical garden designed in 1969 by Daniel Collin for the International Flower Show, on an area left free by the army after World War II ♦ Several sectors: valley of flowers (annuals); Four Seasons garden (perennials); water garden; pine forest; collections of houseplants, medicinal plants, bonsais, and cacti ♦ Sculptures and mobiles by various artists; exhibition hall.

Parc Georges-Brassens: Rue des Morillons (15th) ♦ 19 acres (7 ha) ♦ This park was completed in 1983 on the site of the old Vaugirard abattoirs (1895-1974) ♦ Before that it was a market garden, which in turn had replaced a vineyard ♦ Rose garden, scented garden crisscrossed by numerous paths, central pond; decoration: two bronze bulls, a bust of Brassens, and a donkey pulling a cart.

Parc Monceau: Boulevard de Courcelles (8th) ♦ 20 acres (8 ha) ♦ Designed by Alphand, Davioud, and Barillet-Deschamps in 1862 ♦ A previous garden had been laid out there by Carmontelle, around a folly built by the Duc de Chartres (the future Philippe Égalité) in 1778. It was enlarged and reworked in 1793 by Thomas Blaikie, then bought by the City of Paris in 1860 ♦ Four monumental gates; Corinthian columns and statues; Italian-style bridge, grotto, oval pond by Carmontelle (goldfish, carp, and ducks) embellished by an island with a large weeping willow; undulating lawns; tall trees: sycamore maple, Oriental plane, gingko biloba, purple maple, and fig.

Parc Montsouris: Boulevard Jourdan, Avenue Reille (14th) ♦ 38 acres (15 ha) ♦ Designed by Alphand between 1875 and 1878 ♦ English-style garden: vast lawns, clumps of trees, a lake overlooked by a gingko biloba; waterfall and grotto ♦ Railway lines run through it which are hidden in sunken cuttings lined by trees.

Parc de la Villette: Avenue Corentin-Cariou, Boulevard Macdonald (19th) ♦ 86 acres (35 ha) ♦ Designed by Bernard Tschumi as a 21st-century park, adjoining the Cité des Sciences et de l'Industrie ♦ Grassed play areas, theme gardens (bamboo, mirrors, and mist), cubic red buildings or "follies," each with a function (information, restaurant, children's workshops, and viewpoint); activity areas: Great Hall, Zénith, and Cité de la Musique.

Promenade Péreire: Boulevard Péreire (17th) ♦ 4 acres (1.4 ha) ♦ Platform garden, opened to the public in 1989 ♦ Seven enclosed gardens: lawns and perennial plants bordered by willow-leaf pear trees, clipped laurels and shrubs; landscape sculptures by Boris Lejeune.

Promenade Plantée: Planted walkway running from the Bastille (corner of Avenues Daumesnil and Ledru-Rollin to the Bois de Vincennes, 12th) with several entrances ♦ 16 acres (6.5 ha): 3 miles (4.5 km) long; 30-100 ft (9-30 m) wide ♦ Laid out from 1988 on the old rail track that used to link the Bastille with La Varenne-St-Maur: it runs along the Viaduc des Arts, a bridge built above the Jardin de Reuilly, then a path at street level, and finally a passageway under the Périphérique (ring road), before reaching the Bois de Vincennes ♦ Hedges of shrubs, rose bushes, linden trees, flowering cherry trees, and maples; vine arbors, pergolas, and theme gardens on the Reuilly terraces; ponds and a grotto.

Square de la Roquette: Rue de la Roquette, Rue Servan (11th) ♦ 5 acres (2 ha) ♦ A garden created in 1977 on the site of the Petite Roquette prison, which was demolished in 1974 ♦ Landscaped garden: numerous trees and shrubs, beds of perennial plants, undulating terrain with winding paths, steps, and a wide footbridge between Rue Servan and Rue Merlin.

Square des Batignolles: Place Charles-Fillon (17th) ♦ 4 acres (1.6 ha) ♦ Designed by Alphand in 1862 ♦ English-style garden: tall trees, rockery, stream flowing into an ornamental lake with carp, goldfish, and mallard ducks.

Square du Temple: Rue du Temple, Rue de Bretagne (3rd) ♦ 2 acres (0.8 ha) ♦ Garden designed by Alphand in 1857 and laid out on the site of the Grand Prior of the Temple Enclosure, which was razed to the ground in 1853 ♦ Purple plum, linden, weeping ash, and Caucasian pterocaryas; ornamental lake bordered by hollyhocks in summer; grotto, waterfall, and pavilions.

Square Jean-XXIII: Quai de l'Archevêché, rue du Cloître-Notre-Dame (4th) ♦ 3 acres (1 ha) ♦ The first public park in Paris, created in 1844 by Prefect Rambuteau, and enlarged in 1911 ♦ This was the site of the Archbishop's Palace, which was destroyed in 1831 ♦ Linden trees, Japanese wild cherry, apple blossom, Siberian elm, Byzantian hazel, laburnum, and tamarisk.

Square René-Le Gall: Rue Croulebarbe, 43, Rue Corvisart (13th) ♦ 8 acres (3 ha) ♦ Opened in 1938 and laid out by Jean-Charles Moreux on the site of kitchen gardens previously cultivated by workers from the Gobelins factory on the bank of the Bièvre ♦ Densely planted with well-trimmed hedges and copses; summerhouses covered with climbing plants; Renaissance garden; and huge play area. Steps decorated with sculptures composed of pebbles, flints, and shells.

Square Sarah-Bernhardt: Rue de Lagny (20th) ♦ 3 acres (1.2 ha) ♦ Neo-

classical-style garden created in 1936 ♦ Lawn surrounded by pterocaryas, yews clipped into cones, and numerous species of trees, flowerbeds, play area, obelisk, and open-air theater.

WORSHIP

BASILICAS

Notre-Dame des Victoires: Place des Petits-Pères (2nd) ♦ Catholic faith ♦ Built in several stages between 1629 (foundation stone laid by Louis XIII) and 1740, based on plans by P Le Muet ♦ This former church of the Monastery of the Augustins Déchaussés (Les Petits Pères) is Jesuit in style. Its two-story façade, with Ionic and Corinthian columns, is surmounted by a triangular pediment bearing the arms of France. A single arcaded nave with side chapels. The richly-decorated interior contains paneling and a collection of paintings by C Van Loo in the chancel; Lully's tomb with a bust by Collignon ♦ The church was established as a basilica by Pius XI in 1927; it is a place of pilgrimage, with many ex-voto tablets.

Sacré-Coeur: 37, Rue du Chevalier de la Barre (18th) ♦ Catholic faith ♦ Built by Abadie from 1875 and completed in 1910 by Lucien Magne, this building in the Romanesque-Byzantine style was inspired by the Church of St-Front at Périgueux ♦ It is 420 ft (129 m) high, and dominates the landscape. The dome is 272 ft (83 m) high, and its 275 ft (84 m) bell tower houses la Savoyarde, the largest bell in the world. The porch is decorated with statues and the bronze doors with bas-reliefs. Inside, a mosaic by Luc-Olivier Merson covers the vault of the chancel; the great statue of the Sacred Heart, by Bénet, is made of solid silver ♦ The basilica was built as a place of pilgrimage because of a vow made during the 1870 War. The choice of site made by the Archbishop of Paris, Monseigneur Guibert, required the acquisition of land and the approval of the Assemblée Nationale (1873). The nature of the terrain meant that 83 pits, 125 ft (38 m) deep, had to be dug and filled with cement, in order to support the building. Length of the basilica: 280 ft (85 m); width: 115 ft (35 m); height: 275 ft (84 m). 5 million visitors in 1997.

Ste Jeanne d'Arc: 18, Rue de la Chapelle (18th) ♦ Catholic faith ♦ The building of the basilica was in response to a vow made by the Archbishop of Paris after the Battle of the Marne. The architect Georges Gosson undertook the first phase of works between 1932 and 1935: the heavy façade in the manner of a medieval fortress, and the first span of the nave covered by a cupola, are typical of his style. After building was interrupted, the church was completed in 1960 with a rectangular concrete nave by Pierre Isnard. The stained-glass windows are signed by Léon Zack. The basilica is next to St-Denis de la Chapelle, with which it is associated.

CATHEDRALS

Notre-Dame: Place du Parvis Notre-Dame (4th) ♦ Catholic faith ♦ Gothic cathedral built in the 12th and 13th centuries, partially redeveloped in the 18th century and restored in the 19th century ♦ The main part of the building is Gothic: 12th-century chancel and transept, nave, façade with its two towers, and 13th-century chapels; the transept façades were rebuilt around 1250 in alignment with the chapels, and lighter and more elegant single-span flying buttresses have replaced the first ones ♦ Inside, a double aisle runs alongside the nave on both sides and a double ambulatory skirts round the chancel; part of the chancel's cloister survives, dating from the 14th century. In the early 18th century, new decoration for the chancel was carried out by Robert de Cotte, on the orders of Louis XIV, to fulfil the vow made by Louis XIII who placed the kingdom under the protection of the Virgin in 1638; only the stalls remain, the *Pietà* by Coustou and the statues of Louis XIII and Louis XIV. In the late 18th century, some alterations were made to the building (removal of the pier in the central portal, replacement of some stained-glass windows with plain windows), before the statues and the spire were destroyed and the tombs desecrated during the Revolution, and the cathedral was plundered in 1831 ♦ Restoration was carried out in the late 19th century by Lassus and Viollet-le-Duc who made some additions (such as grotesque animal figures). In the 20th century, the treasure house was renovated and some pictures and sculptures were brought back; the façade is now regularly whitewashed ♦ Notre-Dame was the scene of many important events: in 1239, the Crown of Thorns brought back from Constantinople was placed there by Saint-Louis while Sainte-Chapelle was being built; in 1302, the solemn opening of the first States General took place there under Philip the Fair; in 1430, the coronation of Henry VI, king of England and France; in 1455, a service to begin the rehabilitation of Joan of Arc; in 1447, the Te Deum was sung after Charles VII had reconquered his kingdom; in 1572, the marriage of Marguerite de Valois and Henri de Navarre, the future Henri IV, who, as he was still a Huguenot, had to wait outside until the end of the ceremony before he could enter; in the reign of Louis XIV, the Te Deum was sung after each military victory; in 1793, the cathedral became the Temple of Reason; in 1804, the coronation of Napoléon I; in 1853, the marriage of Napoléon III and Eugénie de Montijo; on November 17, 1918, the Te Deum was sung to celebrate victory; on August 26, 1944, the victory Te Deum was sung in the presence of General de Gaulle ♦ Length: 430 ft (130 m); width: 115 ft (35 m); height of the towers: 225 ft (69 m) ♦ 12 million visitors a year.

St-Alexander Nevsky: 12, Rue Daru (8th) ♦ Orthodox faith ♦ Russian building, listed as a historic monument, built between 1859 and 1861 by Kouzmine and Strohm to replace an early 19th-century chapel, which had become too small ♦ The plan is in the form of a Greek cross. The impressive central spire is surrounded by four smaller spires, built above the corners of the arms of the cross. The narthex with trefoil arches is covered by a dome and a small gilded cupola. Below, the tympanum is decorated with a Christ Pantocrator ♦ The interior decorations, like those of the iconostasis, were entrusted to 19th-century Russian artists including Alexander Iegorovich Beidemann. The crypt, where church services are held in French, was redecorated between 1955 and 1956 ♦ Length: 112 ft (34 m); width: 92 ft (28 m); height: 157 ft (48 m).

St-Stéphane: 7, Rue Georges-Bizet (16th) ♦ Orthodox faith ♦ Greek church built by Émile Vaudremer between 1890 and 1895 at the request of a wealthy Greek sponsor ♦ It is built in the form of a Greek cross, surmounted by a cupola ♦ Painted ceiling, frescos by Charles Lameire, and iconostasis by Ludwig Thiersch.

CHAPEL

Notre-Dame de la Compassion: 2, Boulevard d'Aurelle-de-Paladines (17th) ♦ Catholic faith ♦ Building in the form of a Latin cross decorated with arches and columns, constructed in 1842 in memory of Ferdinand d'Orléans, Louis-Philippe's eldest son, who died in an accident ♦ The royal chapel, which was moved when the Palais des Congrès was built (it was originally located at 25, Boulevard Pershing, where the accident took place), is now located next to the church, designed by Conzet. The mausoleum and *The Descent from the Cross* were sculpted by H de Triqueti to designs by Ary Scheffer; the stained-glass windows were made in the factory at Sèvres from drawings by Ingres.

CHURCHES

Assomption: 263 *bis*, Rue St-Honoré (1st) ♦ Catholic faith ♦ Church built between 1670 and 1676 on the circular plan of Romanesque Baroque churches. The rotunda, 79 ft (24 m) in diameter, is decorated with a fresco by Ch de la Fosse and covered by a massive dome ♦ Inside are Corinthian pilasters and 17th- and 18th-century paintings. This chapel of a convent, destroyed in the 19th century, was closed during the Revolution and restored to the faith under the patronage of Sainte-Madeleine before reverting to its original name in 1842. Since 1851, it has been the church for the Polish community in Paris.

Madeleine: see Sainte-Marie-Madeleine.

Notre-Dame d'Auteuil: Place d'Auteuil (16th) ♦ Catholic faith ♦ Church in the Romanesque-Byzantine tradition, built between 1877 and 1892 by

Vaudremer at the instigation of Abbot Lamazou to replace the old church in the village of Auteuil, which dated from the medieval era ♦ The bell tower, surmounted by a lantern, is made of stone; the façade is decorated with a tympanum and a statue of the Virgin by H-Ch Maniglier ♦ The interior is designed like a basilica and contains the *Our Lady of Sorrow*, sculpted by Carpeaux (1870) and the tomb of Monseigneur Lamazou; the works of art belonging to the former church are preserved in the crypt ♦ A cemetery once stood on the site of the present-day Place d'Auteuil, in the center of which is an obelisk in gray porphyry, placed on the tomb of the Chevalier d'Aguesseau around 1760 and restored in 1802.

Notre-Dame de Bercy: Place Lachambaudie (12th) ♦ Catholic faith ♦ Dating from 1826, it was burnt down during the Commune, then rebuilt in 1873 by Antoine-Jules Hénard. It contains some remarkable pictures including *La Résurrection de la Fille de Jaïre* by Charles de Lafosse.

Notre-Dame des Blancs Manteaux: 12, Rue des Blancs-Manteaux (4th) ♦ Catholic faith ♦ Church built between 1685 and 1690 to plans by Dom Antoine de Machy ♦ Its façade dates from the early 18th century. The triangular pediment, supported on Doric and Ionic pilasters, came from the former Church of St Éloi des Barnabites, destroyed when the Boulevard du Palais was opened. Inside, the barrel vault was altered by Baltard in the 19th century. The Chapel of Ste-Geneviève (which Baltard constructed in 1844) houses a collection of early 17th-century paintings of scenes from the Old Testament; in the right aisle is *The Adoration of the Shepherds* by J-M Bralle; the Baroque pulpit dates from 1749, and is decorated with marquetry panels inlaid with ivory and pewter ♦ In 1258, a monastery was founded on this site by the mendicant friars of the order of St Augustine (also called the Blancs-Manteaux — the White Coats — because of their robes); when their order was dissolved, they left their name to their successors, the hermit friars of Saint Guillaume (Guillemites). They received the body of Louis d'Orléans, who was assassinated on the orders of John the Fearless. In

the 17th century, the Benedictines of the St-Maur congregation, who had settled in the rebuilt monastery, made it into a renowned intellectual centre.

Notre-Dame de Bonne-Nouvelle: 25 *bis*, Rue de la Lune (2nd) ♦ Catholic faith ♦ Built by H Godde between 1824 and 1830 on the site of a shrine dating from the 17th century, whose tower has been preserved ♦ The church is designed like a basilica; Doric columns support a barrel vault; the chancel is decorated with a painted trompe-l'oeil frieze. The church contains many paintings including *La Bienheureuse Isabelle de France* by Ph de Champaigne.

Notre-Dame de la Croix: 2 *bis*, Rue Julien-Lacroix (20th) ♦ Catholic faith ♦ Church in Neo-Romanesque style built between 1860 and 1869 by Héret. It is approached by monumental steps; it has a 256 ft (78 m) bell tower. The framework is partly in metal (vaulted joists and ribs); the organ is by Cavaillé-Coll ♦ A chapel was built in the hamlet of Ménilmontant under the Restoration, its name recalling the oratory of Ste-Croix-de-la-Bretonnerie. After the district was annexed to Paris, Haussmann had this large church built at the request of the inhabitants.

Notre-Dame de Lorette: 1, Rue Fléchier (9th arr) ♦ Catholic faith ♦ Built between 1823 and 1836 by Hippolyte Lebas to serve the district of la Nouvelle Athènes, which was being developed ♦ The statues of Faith, Hope, and Charity surmount the façade which has a Corinthian portico and sculpted pediment (*Homage to the Virgin* by Leboeuf-Nanteuil). The richly decorated interior contains many paintings, including those from the Chapelle des Baptêmes (Adolphe Roger, 1840) and the Chapelle de la Vierge (V Orsel and A Périn, 1864), and works by E Devéria, A Vinchon, A Hesse, A Périn, and Picot; the statue of John the Baptist was designed by Lebas and executed by Duret. The door of the cell where Abbot Sabatier was confined during the Commune is still visible ♦ The name *lorettes* was given to the elegant courtesans of the district in the middle of the 19th century.

Notre-Dame du Travail: 59, Rue Vercingétorix (14th) ♦ Catholic faith ♦

Modern-style church, built between 1899 and 1901 by J Astruc ♦ A characteristic feature is the metal used for columns, arches, and supports; it has a wooden ceiling and stone walls; the basic plan is Romanesque. Materials from the Industry Pavilion, built for the 1855 Universal Exhibition and demolished in 1899, were reused in the church ♦ The bell, brought back from Sebastopol as a Crimean War trophy, was given to the parish by Napoléon III ♦ Built on the initiative of Abbot Soulange-Bodin for the humble inhabitants of the district, most of whom worked in factories and workshops.

Réformée du Marais: (formerly the Temple Sainte-Marie): 17, Rue St-Antoine (4th) ♦ Protestant faith ♦ The Reformed Church of the Marais was built in the Classical style between 1632 and 1634 by Villedo to plans by François Mansart, and was restored in the 19th century ♦ It has a dome and two oval chapels, a porch with a round arch and a convex roof. The interior décor is Baroque ♦ It was the chapel of the convent of La Visitation Ste-Marie, established in the Marais in 1621; St-Vincent-de-Paul was the Superior until 1660; the Marquis de Sévigné and Superintendent Fouquet were buried there. The convent was demolished during the Revolution and the church turned into a political club ♦ In 1803, it was handed over to the Protestant faith.

St-Ambroise: 71 *bis*, Boulevard Voltaire (11th) ♦ Catholic faith ♦ Built in 1866 by Th Ballu in a medieval style combining Romanesque and Gothic. The façade is flanked by two square towers topped by an octagonal spire surrounded by pinnacles. The porch has three round arches, flanked by columns, is surmounted by a gallery with a row of small arches, a gable with a central rose window and a triangular pediment ♦ Inside, the Chapels of Saint Augustin and Saint Ambroise are decorated with paintings of events in their lives ♦ This site was occupied from the 17th century by the Order of the Annonciades; a first chapel was replaced by the Church of Notre-Dame de Protection (1654-57), renamed St-Ambroise after the estate was sold in the late 18th century. The present church replaced it, after the Boulevard Voltaire was opened and the

district transformed by Haussmann.

St-Augustin: 46, Boulevard Malesherbes (8th) ♦ Catholic faith ♦ Church inspired by Byzantine architecture, built between 1860 and 1871 by V Baltard on the site of a temporary wooden church, dating from 1850 ♦ The cast-iron and iron structure is surmounted by a monumental 200 ft (60 m) dome, topped by a lantern with ornamental apertures. The site dictated the shape of the building, widening as it recedes from the façade, which is entirely taken up by a large sculpted porch with three arches, decorated with statues. Inside is a bronze statue of Joseph; the transept is decorated with paintings by Bouguereau.

St-Christophe de Javel: 28 Rue de la Convention (15th) ♦ Catholic faith ♦ Built between 1926 and 1934 on the site of a church dating from 1898, which had become too small ♦ It was built with reinforced concrete to a Classical plan by Ch Besnard. The façade is made of brick; its cement pediment has ornamental apertures and is decorated with a monumental statue of Saint Christopher (P Vigoureux); inside are large frescos by J Martin-Ferrières and stained-glass windows by H-M Magne.

St-Denis de la Chapelle: 76, Rue de la Chapelle (18th) ♦ Catholic faith ♦ The 18th-century façade has a statue of Joan of Arc; the nave dates from the early 13th century (remains of the former church); the rest was built in the late 16th and 17th centuries, after the Wars of Religion; the whole building has been restored many times ♦ Joan of Arc meditated there in September, 1429 before advancing on Paris.

St-Denis du St-Sacrement: 68 *bis*, Rue de Turenne (3rd) ♦ Catholic faith ♦ Church built between 1826 and 1835 by Godde, who was commissioned by the City after it had bought the former Benedictine Monastery of St-Sacrement; the order was dissolved during the Revolution ♦ The peristyle with Ionic columns on the façade is surmounted by a pediment sculpted by J-J Feuchères (1844); the porch is

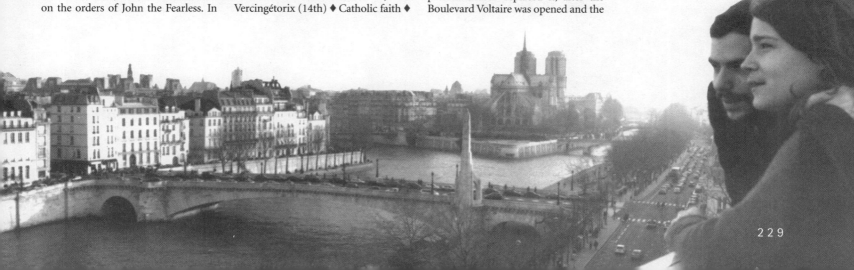

decorated with statues. Many paintings and sculptures (works by J-D Court, F-E Picot, H Decaisne, J Debay, J-J Perraud, and J Thomas) in the chancel and the chapels, in particular *La Déposition de Croix* by Delacroix (1843) and *Le Père Eternel, Jésus-Christ et la Vierge, and Saint Denis Prêchant dans les Gaules* (on the chancel cupola) by A de Pujol (1838).

Saint-Esprit: 7, Rue Cannebière (12th) ♦ Catholic faith ♦ Built in 1931 by P Tournon. Concrete building, with external brick cladding, inspired by Santa-Sophia: the great central cupola is surrounded by smaller, flattened cupolas. It has a vast crypt ♦ The church's interior decoration comprises paintings in the apse executed under the direction of Maurice Denis: *The Way of the Cross* by G Desvallières, mosaics by M Imbs, and enamel work by Gaudin.

St-Étienne du Mont: 1, Place Ste-Geneviève (5th) ♦ Catholic faith ♦ The architecture is a blend of Flamboyant Gothic and Classical and Renaissance décor; it was built between 1492 and 1626, and partly restored in the 19th century ♦ The tall façade is on three levels, each one set back from the preceding level, and was built between 1610 and 1622. In the center is a rose window and there is a second, smaller rose window above it in the triangular gable. The statues and the bas-reliefs were remade in the 19th century. The slender tower is surmounted by a lantern and a small turret ♦ The interior is decorated in Flamboyant style. Its most famous element is the Renaissance rood screen, unique to Paris, built by Antoine Beaucorps between 1521 and 1545; its flat, latticed arch, 30 ft (9 m) across, terminates in two spiral staircases; the sculpted stone gallery is half the height of the nave. The splendid organ dates from the 17th century; the pulpit is Baroque in style. The paintings in the chapels are mainly from the 17th century. In the Chapel of Sainte-Geneviève is a 19th-century gilded copper casket containing a fragment of the saint's original tomb, discovered in 1802 ♦ The church replaced an earlier building that had become

too small; it was constructed in about 1220 above a crypt, which had previously served as a church. Begun in the late Middle Ages, the church was built next to the Abbey of Ste-Geneviève, which was demolished in 1807. Building took a long time, and it was not until 1610 that Queen Margot laid the foundation stone of the façade. Racine and Pascal were buried there. The church became the Temple of Filial Piety during the Revolution. In 1794 and 1795, the bodies of Mirabeau and Marat, expelled from the Panthéon, were placed in the small cemetery, which was then behind the chevet. On January 3, 1857, the Archbishop of Paris, Monseigneur Sibour, was stabbed there by a banned priest.

St-Eugène: 4 *bis*, Rue Ste-Cécile (9th) ♦ Catholic faith ♦ Built between 1854 and 1855 by Lusson and Boileau, this church is typical of the Haussmann period; it was assigned to Saint Eugène, in honor of Empress Eugénie. It is Neo-Gothic in style. For the first time in Paris, iron and cast iron were used for the columns, the arches, and the gallery (polychrome) ♦ Painted stained-glass windows.

St-Eustache: 2, Rue du Jour (1st) ♦ Catholic faith ♦ Built between 1532 and 1637 on the site of a small 13th-century church, formerly dedicated to Sainte Agnès ♦ This Gothic building followed the plan of Notre-Dame; its decoration is partly Renaissance (façade of the transept) and partly Classical (entrance façade, built in the 18th century). It was restored by Baltard after a fire in 1840 ♦ The 17th-century stained-glass windows were designed by Philippe de Champaigne. The interior houses Colbert's tomb and the Chapelle des Charcutiers (butchers), restored by J M Armleder (paintings in the lower part) ♦ Berlioz directed his Te Deum there for the first time ♦ Length: 290 ft (88 m); width: 141 ft (43 m); nave height: 110 ft (33.46 m).

St-Germain l'Auxerrois: 2, Place du Louvre (1st) ♦ Catholic faith ♦ Church in Flamboyant Gothic style, dating partly from the 13th century (chancel and apse) and partly from the 15th century (Flamboyant porch by J Gaussel), altered in the 18th century and restored between 1838 and 1855 by

V Baltard and J-B Lassus ♦ The Neo-Gothic bell tower by Ballus contains a carillon ♦ Inside: a late 17th-century churchwardens' pew, designed by Le Brun; altarpieces from the 16th century; aisle chapels decorated with works of art; the tombs of many artists, such as Boucher, Chardin, Van Loo, Coypel, Coysevox, Soufflot, and the poet Malherbe ♦ On this site, a chapel dating back to the Merovingians was burnt down by the Normans; a church was built there in the 11th century, then rebuilt in the 13th century; it became the parish church of the kings of France when they resided at the Louvre. Warning of the Saint-Bartholomew Massacre was sounded by the matins bell. The church was closed during the Revolution and plundered during a riot in 1831.

St-Germain-de-Charonne: 4, Place St-Blaise (20th) ♦ Catholic faith ♦ This small village church was built in the 15th century and restored several times in the 18th and 19th centuries. It has kept its parish cemetery ♦ Inside, the 18th-century painting of Saint Germain blessing Sainte Geneviève and modern stained-glass windows by Adeline Hébert-Stevens, Pauline Peugnez, and Paul Bondy ♦ This was the church of the winegrowing commune of Charonne, annexed to Paris in 1859; previous churches were built there on the site of an oratory which commemorated the meeting of Saint Germain and the future Sainte Geneviève.

St-Germain des Prés: 3, Place St-Germain-des-Prés (6th) ♦ Catholic faith ♦ Church partly Romanesque (tower, nave, and transept), partly Early Gothic (chancel, ambulatory and its chapels), built in the 11th and 12th centuries, altered in the 17th century (vault) and restored in the 19th century ♦ It is named after Saint Germain, Bishop of Paris ♦ Paintings in the nave and chancel (1845-61) by H Flandrin; polychrome décor by A Denuelle; tomb of Olivier and Louis Castellan by sculptor Girardon; memorial to Jean-Casimir of Poland by the Marsy brothers ♦ Only a few artefacts survive from the former church of the Benedictine Abbey of St-Germain (founded in the 6th century and dedicated to Saint Vincent). After its destruction by the Normans, the church was rebuilt from

the 11th century with three towers, and dedicated by Pope Alexander III in 1163. Its wooden vault was replaced in the 17th century by a vault in the Gothic style. At the same time, the monastery, its cloister and the Lady Chapel were sacrificed when the Rue de l'Abbaye was opened. Damaged during the Revolution, the church was repaired and restored (1819-23) under the direction of the architect Godde; the transept's two towers were leveled and the axial chapel rebuilt. The fourth level of the tower was rebuilt by Baltard; the original capitals, which were replaced, are preserved in the Musée de Cluny.

St-Gervais-St-Protais: 2, Rue François-Miron (4th) ♦ Catholic faith ♦ Church in the Late Gothic style, built between 1494 and 1657 ♦ The Classical façade (the first in Paris) was built under Louis XIII between 1616 and 1621 with three superimposed series of double columns: Doric, then Ionic, and Corinthian above. Carved wooden portal ♦ The Flamboyant double flying buttresses of the chancel rest against the abutments, decorated with pinnacles and gargoyles in the form of fantastic animals. The stained-glass windows date from the 16th century to the early 17th century, and the carved chancel stalls from the 16th century. The Chapelle Dorée (1628) is decorated with painted panels set into the woodwork. Stone organ loft; works of art in the various chapels ♦ It is possibly the oldest parish church on the Right Bank: a basilica was dedicated to two saints in the 6th century. The marriage of the Marquise de Sévigné was celebrated there in 1644; the painter Philippe de Champaigne and Chancellor Le Tellier, father of statesman Louvois (for whom Bossuet delivered the funeral oration), were buried there. More recently, on Good Friday, 1918, a bombardment caused more than 200 casualties there. The organ was played by the Couperin family from 1656-1826.

St-Honoré d'Eylau: 9, Place Victor-Hugo (16th) ♦ Catholic faith ♦ Built in 1855 by E Debressene and enlarged in 1884, the church houses two famous paintings: *The Adoration of the Shepherds* by Tintoretto and *The Nativity of the Virgin* by J Restout (1774). An annexe, the New Church of

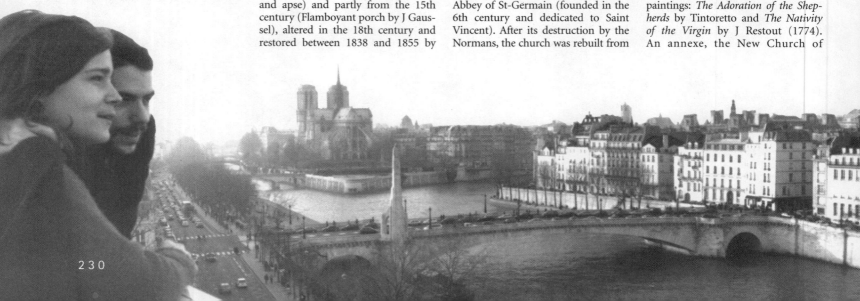

St-Honoré-d'Eylau, was built in 1897 on the site of a chapel at 66 *bis*, Rue Raymond-Poincaré: Neo-Romanesque façade in red brick, cast-iron Neo-Gothic interior, redesigned in 1974 by A Le Donné; Stations of the Cross by J Aubert.

St-Jacques du Haut-Pas: 252 *bis*, Rue St-Jacques (5th) ♦ Catholic faith ♦ Building constructed between 1630 and 1684 by D Gittard ♦ The façade is decorated with four columns supporting an entablature and a triangular pediment. The tower is square ♦ Inside, an oval cupola above the second span; Gothic chancel. The Lady chapel was built by L Bruant and decorated by A Glaize (1868); the side chapels house *The Annunciation* by the Le Nain brothers and *The Contrition of Saint Peter* by J Restout ♦ This chapel of a former charitable benefice, which provided aid for pilgrims to Santiago de Compostela, was founded in the 13th century. It became a parish church, and was rebuilt in the 17th century. The foundation stone was laid by Gaston d'Orléans in 1630. Building was interrupted, then resumed in 1675 thanks to the Duchesse de Longueville. The Duchess's heart was placed there on her death; the Abbot of St-Cyran, Port-Royal's spiritual adviser (who converted many to Jansenism) and the astronomer J-D Cassini were buried there.

St-Jean-Baptiste de Belleville: 139, Rue de Belleville (19th) ♦ Catholic faith ♦ Church in the Neo-Gothic style, with two spires measuring 220 ft (67 m), built between 1854 and 1859 by Lassus and Truchy ♦ It replaced the former church built in 1635 on the site of a 16th-century chapel.

St-Jean Bosco: 7, Rue Alexandre-Dumas (20th) ♦ Catholic faith ♦ Church built of reinforced concrete between 1933 and 1937 by Rotter for the Salesian Fathers ♦ A characteristic feature of the building are its accentuated vertical lines. The décor consists mainly of the mosaics by Maumejéan and the stained-glass windows by Bessac and Gaudin. A reliquary holds the relics of Dom Bosco, founder of the Société des Prêtres de St-François-de-Sales (Salesians).

St-Joseph des Carmes: 70, Rue de Vaugirard (6th) ♦ Catholic faith ♦ Built between 1613 and 1620 for the Monastery of the Carmelites. The façade, with its Classical pediment, surmounted by an Italian-style dome (the second of its kind built in Paris), is Jesuit in style ♦ Inside, the chancel, the transept, and the chapels contain 17th-century paintings, a marble Virgin and Child inspired by Bernini, and the memorial to Monseigneur Affre. Bartholet Flamaël's *Elijah Raised onto an Iron Chariot* adorns the cupola (Elijah being considered the founder of the Carmelites). In the crypt, an ossuary for the victims of the Revolution, tombs of F Ozanam (one of the founders of the Conférence de St-Vincent de Paul), and Monseigneur Baudrillart (former rector of the Institut Catholique) ♦ In the monastery garden, 115 refractory priests were massacred in September, 1792; the monastery then became a prison where Alexandre and Joséphine de Beauharnais, and Madame Tallien were incarcerated. The buildings were bought for a community of nuns, and later housed the School for Higher Ecclesiastical Studies, where Lacordaire and F Ozanam taught. They were taken over by the Institut Catholique.

St-Julien le Pauvre: 1 Rue St-Julien-le-Pauvre (5th) ♦ Catholic faith ♦ Former Merovingian basilica, rebuilt between 1165 and the mid-13th century, restored in the 17th and late 19th centuries. Nave with barrel vault (no transept) and 17th-century arcades; 13th- and 16th-century capitals with plant designs; iconostasis enclosing the apse; Romanesque chancel and apsidal chapels; 17th-century wrought-iron lectern; Virgin and Child made of wood (16th-17th century) ♦ The monks of the Abbey of Longpont who occupied it in the 12th century, turned it into a priory for several centuries, a meeting place for University gatherings. Plundered in 1524, then gradually abandoned, it was not restored until after the priory was transferred to the Hôtel-Dieu by Cardinal Mazarin. It was used as a warehouse between the Revolution and 1826, and was later returned to the Hôtel-Dieu, then restored in 1889 and handed over to the Greek Melchite religion.

St-Laurent: 68 *bis*, Boulevard de Strasbourg (10th) ♦ Catholic faith ♦ Flamboyant church, built in the 15th century (on the site of a Merovingian basilica, then a Romanesque church), enlarged in the 16th and 17th centuries (nave and transept vault) and altered in the 19th century ♦ The Neo-Gothic façade (Classical portal by Lepeautre dating from 1621) was rebuilt between 1863 and 1867 when the Boulevard de Strasbourg was opened. The tower, which is for the most part original, was raised and surmounted by a lantern in the 18th century; the spire dates from the 19th century ♦ A remarkable feature of the interior are the 5 ft (1.50 m) carved keystones dating from the mid-17th century. The chancel was decorated by Lepeautre in the 17th century in the Corinthian style. The stained-glass windows, dating from the 1930s and 1950s, are by P Gaudin, except for three designed by Galimard in the 19th century. The 18th-century Lady Chapel (vault painted with an Assumption, and 1899 statue in Carrara marble); the organ dates from 1682.

St-Leu-St-Gilles: 92, Rue St-Denis (1st) ♦ Catholic faith ♦ Constructed from 1319 to replace a chapel, built by the Abbey of Saint-Magloire, which had become too small. The façade with two small slate-roofed towers was restored in the reigns of Louis XV and Louis-Philippe (reconstruction of the north tower). The nave is 14th century, the chancel early 17th century. The church was considerably altered by V Baltard (chevet and side chapels) when the Boulevard de Sébastopol was opened ♦ Inside, a carved group depicting *Sainte Anne et la Vierge Enfant* by J Bullant, and an 18th-century painted panel of the *Miracle de la Rue aux Ours; Pélerins d'Emmaüs* by J Restou.

St-Louis-en-l'Ile: 19 *bis*, Rue St-Louis-en-l'Ile (4th) ♦ Catholic faith ♦ Built between 1664 and 1725 by architects Le Vau, Le Duc, and J Doucet ♦ The entrance portal is made of carved oak; it is surmounted by an openwork tower, remade in 1765. A clock hangs like a sign over the entrance ♦ Inside, the décor is richly Baroque with carved motifs and gilding; many paintings ♦ The church replaced a small chapel in the former Ile aux Vaches. Abbot Bossuet was its priest from 1864 to

1888; he left a collection of original paintings and beautiful old ornaments.

St-Martin des Champs: 36, Rue Albert-Thomas (10th) ♦ Catholic faith ♦ Formerly the Church of St-Martin-des-Marais, built in 1854 in timber and stone to cater for the growing population, and inaugurated in 1856. The simple façade, with a semicircular tympanum, has an oeil-de-boeuf with a Greek cross. The bell tower was added by Vaudry in 1933. Inside, paintings and Stations of the Cross by Villé (1889-90); organ by Cavaillé Coll; in the marriage sacristy, busts of Abbot Bruyère, the church's founder, and Henri Chapu. Frédérick Lemaître's funeral was held there in January 1876.

St-Médard: 141, Rue Mouffetard (5th) ♦ Catholic faith ♦ Built between the 15th and 18th centuries on the foundations of a 13th-century church. The Flamboyant façade and portal were redesigned in the 18th century; the 15th-century tower was raised in the 16th century ♦ Inside, the nave is Gothic in style; the chancel, completed in the 17th century, was modernized in the next century in Classical style. The 17th- and 18th-century paintings include *Les Vendeurs Chassés du Temple* by Ch Natoire, *Le Christ Mort* by the School of Ph De Champaigne, and *Saint-Joseph et L'Enfant Jésus* by Zurbaran ♦ The Church of the Bourg de St-Médard, probably of Merovingian origin, is attributed to the 12th century; it was attached to the abbey of Ste-Geneviève up to the Revolution. At the end of December, 1561, during the Wars of Religion, a riot took place: exasperated by the bells which drowned their pastor's voice, the Protestants took refuge in a nearby house, and provoked a confrontation with the church's congregation. The Miracles of the Convulsionists took place there from 1727 to 1732. These cures had taken place on the tomb of Deacon Pâris, in the cemetery. These waves of collective hysteria led to the churchyard being closed.

St-Merri: 78, Rue St-Martin (4th) ♦ Catholic faith ♦ Church in the Flamboyant Gothic style, built between

1510 and 1552 ♦ The sculpted façade is very ornate; its statues were remade in 1842 ♦ Flamboyant interior (vault of the transept). The chancel was redecorated in 1752 by the Slodtz brothers; the Communion chapel was added by Boffrand in 1744, on the site of the charnel houses. The organ case is by master-joiner Germain Pilon; the chapel walls (with a Ste-Marie the Egyptian) were painted in the 19th century ♦ Around 700, there was an oratory on the site; Saint Merri was buried there. A church was built and dedicated to Saint Peter and Saint Merri, then to Saint Merri alone, and was turned over to the canons of Notre-Dame. It was rebuilt around 1200, then again in the 16th century to cater for the growing population. The rood screen, which enclosed the canons' chancel, was removed in the 18th century. The church was a victim of the Revolution and 19th-century rebellions, but it was protected during the Commune when it was used as a hospital for the National Guard.

St-Nicolas des Champs: 254, Rue St-Martin (3rd) ♦ Catholic faith ♦ This Late Gothic church was built in the 15th century, altered in the 16th, 17th and 18th centuries, and restored in the 19th century. It has a 15th-century façade and tower, and a Renaissance portal surmounted by a Flamboyant arch; long nave with ogival vault, partly in the Flamboyant style; monumental, marble high altar; chapels decorated with paintings from the 16th to the 19th centuries (including N Coypel, S Vouet, and L Bonnat). The organ, which was made in the late 16th century, was enlarged and redesigned ♦ A first chapel was built in the enclosure of the Priory of St-Martin des Champs. It became a parish church in the 12th century, was rebuilt between 1420 and 1480 and then enlarged, with alterations to part of the nave, the side aisles, the apsidal chapel, the south portal, and the top of the tower. It became the Temple of Marriage and Fidelity during the Revolution, then was returned to the faith and restored in the first half of the 19th century. Guillaume Budé, Théophile de Viau, and Madeleine de

Scudéry were buried there, and Talma was baptized there.

St-Nicolas du Chardonnet: 23, Rue des Bernadins (5th) ♦ Catholic faith ♦ The church was built between 1656 and the mid-18th century ♦ The façade took on its final shape in 1934 ♦ The Classical interior is in the Jesuit style, decorated with pictures by Restout, Coypel, Le Lorrain, Lagrenée, Le Brun, and Corot (*Baptism of Christ*). The memorial to Charles Le Brun (benefactor of the parish) and his wife, sculpted by Coysevox, is next to the memorial to the painter's mother, made to designs by Le Brun ♦ Originally, a chapel was built on this site, in an enclosure planted with thistles, used for combing woolen cloth; the church was dedicated to Saint Nicholas, patron saint of boatmen. In 1977, Monseigneur Ducobourget chose this parish for his community of fundamentalist Catholics.

St-Pierre de Chaillot: 33, Avenue Marceau (16th) ♦ Catholic faith ♦ A robust building in the Neo-Byzantine style, constructed in concrete between 1933 and 1938 by Émile Bois ♦ The massive façade is decorated with a large tympanum, sculpted by H Bouchard and representing the life of Saint Peter ♦ The octagonal bell tower recalls the Romanesque towers in the Limousin region. The interior was designed in the shape of a Greek cross with a central section surmounted by a dome and a lantern 213 ft (65 m) high. At the entrance to the chancel, a large fresco by Nicolas Unterseller symbolizes the Catholic Church; the stained-glass windows are by the Mauméjean brothers, and there are sculptures by Bouchard ♦ There was a chapel on this site dating from the 11th century; it was enlarged in 1679 after the village of Chaillot had been built as a suburb of Paris. From the late 19th century, the growth of the district required a larger building.

St-Pierre de Montmartre: 2, Rue du Mont-Cenis (18th) ♦ Catholic faith ♦ One of the oldest churches in Paris. The 18th-century façade has bronze doors by Tommaso Gismondi, added in 1980. Most of the interior dates from the 15th and 16th centuries, and the massive chancel vault goes back to 1147, the date of the church's consecra-

tion (built on a former shrine) ♦ Various archaeological remains: marble pillars from a former Roman temple on the Butte, and a 12th-century capital. Tombstones: Adélaïde de Savoie, founder of the abbey of Montmartre, and Catherine de La Rochefoucault.

St-Pierre de Montrouge: Place Victor-et-Hélène-Basch (14th) ♦ Catholic faith ♦ Church built between 1863 and 1870, after Petit-Montrouge was joined to Paris, in a blend of Romanesque, Byzantine, and Italian styles ♦ The elegant porch is surmounted by a tower 190 ft (58 m) high, with a spire and a lantern at the top. The interior is like a basilica with a wooden vault. The tower served as a watch tower during the Siege of Paris, and the nave as a refuge during the Commune for the wounded of 1871.

St-Roch: 296, Rue St-Honoré (1st) ♦ Catholic faith ♦ One of the largest churches in Paris, built from 1653 (Louis XIV laid the foundation stone) and consecrated in 1740, after works were interrupted on several occasions. Classical architecture, remarkable paintings and sculptures, including *The Assumption* by J-B Pierre (in the cupola of the Lady chapel), restored in 1992; the *Nativity* group by M Anguier, *Christ in the Garden of Olives* by E Falconet, *Saint Denis Preaching* by J Vien, and *The Miracle of the Burning Bush* by G-F Doyen ♦ The Chapel of Ste-Suzanne stood on this site, built in the 16th century, and was annexed to the first Church of St-Roch. The present church witnessed the baptism of Molière's son (whose godfather was the king) and the funerals of Chérubini and Musset. Corneille, Le Nôtre, Diderot, and Mignard were buried there. On the steps of this church, Bonaparte suppressed the Royalist rebellion against the Convention in October, 1895.

St-Serge: 93, Rue de Crimeé (19th) ♦ Orthodox faith ♦ Russian church which looks like a chalet, on the slopes of the Buttes-Chaumont ♦ The Orthodox Church acquired this building in the 1920s; it was built between 1858 and 1865, and was originally a Protestant temple, used by the German Lutheran community in Paris. It was then redeveloped between 1925 and 1927: the porch and exterior staircases

were added in decorated wood; the tower followed in the 1950s ♦ The richly decorated and painted interior is by Staletzky; the iconostasis is in the traditional style with a Christ in Majesty in the center of it, surrounded by symbols of the Evangelists ♦ The Institute of Theology, associated with the church, was opened in 1925. This Russian-speaking parish church is noted for its a capella chants in Slavonic languages.

St-Séverin: 1, Rue des Prêtres-St-Séverin (5th) ♦ Catholic faith ♦ Building in the Flamboyant Gothic style (except for the tower, which is older), begun in the middle of the 13th century (tower and first three spans of the nave), and finished in the 15th century (chancel, back of the nave, and spire) and early 16th century (side chapels). The façade dates from the 13th century, including the portal which originates from the former Church of St-Pierre-aux-Boeufs on the Ile de la Cité, demolished in 1837. The lantern contains one of the oldest bells in Paris (1412) ♦ Inside is a Flamboyant pillar with spiral ribs, in the center of the double ambulatory; Flamboyant chancel with Classical décor based on drawings by Le Brun; stained glass in the high windows of the chancel and nave (dating from the 14th and 16th centuries) and in the ambulatory (J Bazaine, 1966); chapels decorated with paintings from between 1838 and 1863; organ by Dupré and Fichon (1745) ♦ Originally, the Séverin oratory stood on this site, then a chapel destroyed by the Normans in the 9th century and rebuilt in the 10th century; the Fourth Crusade was advocated there around 1180. The chapel was replaced by the present church, which dates from the 13th century; a fire around 1448 meant that one third of the church had to be rebuilt.

St-Sulpice: Place St-Sulpice (6th) ♦ Catholic faith ♦ Church in the Classical style (one of the largest in Paris), built in the 17th and 18th centuries in several stages by various architects: Gamard, Le Vau, Gittard, Oppenordt, and Servandoni. The 18th-century façade is flanked by two towers; originally, a triangular pediment separated them, but it was destroyed by lightening after it was built. Double portal with Doric columns, below, and Ionic

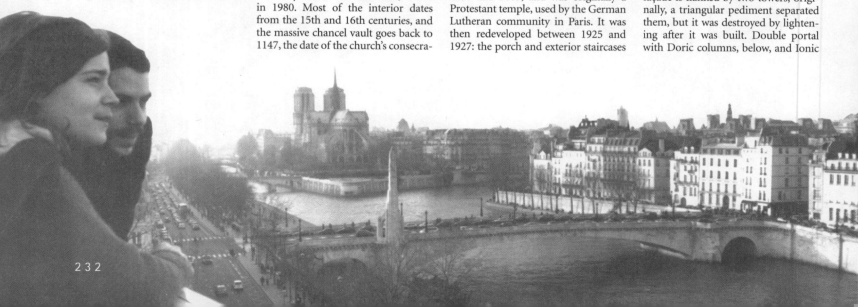

above ◆ Inside, a nave lined with Corinthian pilasters with capitals, and a barrel vault; a monumental organ (designed by Chalgrin, 1776); the transept has a flattened cupola; in the chancel, statues by Bouchardon and his pupils. The chapels of the ambulatory and the aisles are decorated with mural paintings dating from the 19th century and stained-glass windows from the late 17th century; the cupola dedicated to the Virgin was painted by F Lemoyne (1731); on the walls are pictures by Van Loo. The aisle chapel on the right is decorated with frescos by Delacroix ◆ This building replaced a small 13th-century parish church, dedicated to Saint Sulpice (Bishop of Bourges) and founded by the Abbey of St-Germain-des-Prés; the church was enlarged several times, and all that remains of the early building are a few walls in the crypt. As the local population grew, it was decided to rebuild, and works were begun in 1646; Anne of Austria laid the foundation stone. But the works, slowed down by the Fronde and then interrupted for 40 years for want of funds, lasted for more than a century.

St-Thomas d'Aquin:
Place St-Thomas d'Aquin (7th) ◆ Catholic faith ◆ This former chapel of the Dominican novices (dating from 1631) was rebuilt between 1682 and 1688 by P Bullet, then from 1722; the façade, in the Jesuit style, was finished in 1770 by Brother Claude, with doors by Ch Butteux. Inside, the monks' chancel was built behind the main chancel (now the Chapel of St-Louis), whose vault is painted with a *Transfiguration* by F. Lemoyne (1724); above the high altar is a Christ in Majesty in gilded bronze ◆ During the Revolution, the church was turned into a meeting room for the Jacobin club, then into the Temple of Peace. The monastery buildings served as an armory, then as the Artillery Museum before the Army Museum took it over; today, these buildings still belong to the Army.

St-Vincent de Paul:
Place Franz-Liszt (10th) ◆ Catholic faith ◆ Church built between 1824 and 1844 by J-B Lepère and Hittorff, when the St-Lazare priory lands were divided into lots. In front of the church are steps and two horseshoe-shaped side ramps;

the façade is flanked by two towers 177 ft (54 m) high, connected by a balustrade and decorated with statues of Saint Peter and Saint Paul. The pediment, sculpted by Ch Leboeuf-Nanteil, illustrates the glorification of Saint Vincent de Paul. The portico has two rows of Ionic columns; large bronze doors by François Calla, based on a drawing by Farochon, depict the apostles ◆ The interior was designed like a basilica. The nave, covered by a coffered painted ceiling, is separated from the aisles by rows of Ionic columns supporting the Corinthian columns of the galleries; on the frieze, on both sides of the nave, are paintings by Hippolyte Flandrin (1848-53) of saints and doctors of the Church. There is a bronze *Calvary* by F Rude; the Lady chapel was painted by Bouguereau, with a statue of the *Virgin Presenting the Infant Jesus* by Carrier-Belleux; on the apsidal vault is Picot's *Christ in Majesty*; stained-glass windows by Marshal de Metz and Bontemps.

Ste-Anne de la Maison Blanche:
186, Rue de Tolbiac (13th) ◆ Catholic faith ◆ Huge church in the Romanesque-Byzantine style, built by Bobin between 1894 and 1912. Tall façade with two towers, vast pendentive cupola, barrel vault, and round arches. Monumental altar; large collection of stained-glass windows, and mosaic decorations by Mauméjean (1937-8).

Sainte-Chapelle:
4, Boulevard du Palais (1st) ◆ Large Gothic chapel built between 1241 and 1248, and restored in the mid-19th century by F Duban and J-B Lassus, then E Boeswillwald. The elegant nave is dominated by a spire, rebuilt several times (the last time in 1857) ◆ The Sainte-Chapelle is on two levels. The upper level was the high chapel, a royal shrine containing relics. Its walls consist mainly of remarkable stained-glass windows, two thirds of which are original; they are flanked by elegant pillars with finely sculpted capitals. The lower level was for people of lesser rank. The vaults, supported by colored columns, are decorated with a starry sky; the floor is inlaid with tombstones ◆ The Sainte-Chapelle was built in the former palace by Saint Louis to house Christ's Crown of Thorns, and a fragment of the real

Cross brought back from the Holy Land.

St-Clotilde:
23 *bis*, Rue Las-Cases (7th) ◆ Catholic faith ◆ Built by F Gau and T Ballu between 1846 and 1856, in imitation of a Gothic cathedral. Sculpted façade, with a rose window and two spires ◆ Inside, paintings by Bouguereau and Leneveu, Stations of the Cross sculpted by Pradier, organ by Cavaillé-Coll; César Franck was the incumbent from 1858-90.

Ste-Élisabeth:
195, Rue du Temple (3rd) ◆ Catholic faith ◆ Church built between 1628 and 1645 by M Villedo, altered in the 19th century (right aisle, chancel, and far end of the nave) ◆ The façade has a curvilinear pediment, decorated with 19th-century statues, in the Classical style ◆ In the chancel, *The Apotheosis of Saint Elisabeth*, painted by Jean Alaux; at the back of the chancel is a large collection of carved wooden panels of Flemish origin (17th century); at the back of the high altar is a 17th-century *Pietà* carved in wood; organ by Suret (1853) ◆ Before the Revolution, Ste-Élisabeth-de-Hongrie was the church of a convent of Franciscan nuns, founded in 1614 with the support of Louis XIII and Marie de Médicis, who laid its foundation stone in 1628. When it became a parish church, the architect Godde added an aisle to it and designed the semicircular chevet (1829).

Ste-Marguerite:
36, Rue St-Bernard (11th) ◆ Catholic faith ◆ Small church built in 1625, enlarged several times in the 17th century, then around 1760 by Victor Louis who built the Chapel of Souls in Purgatory. The gables of the transept are decorated with 18th-century bas-reliefs ◆ Inside, works by J Restout, B Féret, L Galloche, Lagrenée, and Briard, and in the chevet the white marble memorial to Catherine Duchemin, Girardon's wife, carried out by his pupils. The most remarkable element, unique of its kind in Paris, is the Chapel of Souls in Purgatory, entirely decorated with a trompe-l'oeil by the Italian painter Paolo-Antonio Brunetti (false columns, statues, and bas-reliefs), and a painting by Briard in the middle of it ◆ Ste-Marguerite was first attached to the parish of St-Paul, then it became independent in 1712. Not much remains from the cemetery,

closed in 1806, except for a cross marking the grave of a ten-year-old child, buried in June, 1795, who for a long time was thought to be Louis XVII.

Ste-Marie des Batignolles:
63, Rue Legendre (17th) ◆ Catholic faith ◆ Church of the former village of Batignolles, built in the Neoclassical style from 1826 to 1828 by A Molinos, and enlarged in 1834 and 1851 by E Lequeux. It was designed like a basilica, which was a feature of Restoration church building. It has a pediment supported by four columns, and a bell tower above the porch. Inside, the chancel is decorated with paneling and the back of the altar is painted with a Virgin surrounded by cherubs and clouds; 17th-century Christ carved in painted wood, and a polychrome bas-relief of the Black Madonna.

Sainte-Marie-Madeleine:
Place de la Madeleine (8th) ◆ Catholic faith ◆ Church built in the 18th and 19th centuries in the shape of a Greek temple with Corinthian columns. The pediment by Ph-H Lemaire depicts the Last Judgment ◆ Inside, a single nave lit by three cupolas and divided into three spans by columns; many sculptures by Rude, Pradier, F Duret, A Bary, A de Pujol, and Ch-E Seurre ◆ Begun from 1764 by Contant d'Ivry, then Couture; works were interrupted during the Revolution and resumed by Vignon under Napoléon I. The emperor wanted to make the building into a temple glorifying the French Armies. Louis XVIII ordered it to be a parish church; the works, under the direction of J Huvé, were not finished until 1842, when it was dedicated by Louis-Philippe ◆ Length: 354 ft (108 m); width 140 ft (43 m); height: 100 ft (30 m).

Trinité:
Place d'Estienne-d'Orves (9th) ◆ Catholic faith ◆ Church from the Haussmann period, built between 1861 and 1867 by Th Ballu in the style of religious buildings of the Second Empire, with a décor loosely inspired by the Italian Renaissance ◆ The façade has three arches surmounted by a central rose window; above, the tower is square at the base, becomes hexagonal,

and terminates with a lantern and cupola; it is decorated with many statues depicting the Apostles and the cardinal virtues. In front of the church are three fountains with allegorical statues of Faith, Hope, and Charity ♦ Inside, the monumental chancel is flanked by green stucco columns; the pillars of the nave are decorated with figures of the Apostles; paintings by F Jobbé-Duval, F Barrias, and E Delaunay; organ by Cavaillé-Coll (1869), played by Olivier Messiaen for 61 years ♦ Length: 30 ft (9 m); width: 112 ft (34 m); height: 100 ft (30 m).

Val-de-Grâce: 1, Place Alphonse-Laverand (5th) ♦ Baroque church, inspired by the Gesù Church in Rome, built between 1645 and 1665 by Lemercier. The façade has a double series of superimposed columns and two triangular pediments. The dome, by P Le Muet and G Le Duc, is one of the highest in Paris (134 ft/41 m); it is supported by 16 pilasters ♦ Inside is a cupola painted by Mignard; allegorical sculptures by M Auguier on the pendentives, and bas-reliefs on the arches in the chapels; there is a canopy inspired by Bernini's in St Peter's, Rome ♦ The Chapel of Saint-Louis leads to the 17th-century cloister ♦ The church was built following the vow made by Anne of Austria to build a church if she had a son; it belonged to the Benedictine Convent of Val de Grâce. Closed down in 1790, the convent was turned into a military hospital, the predecessorer of the present Hôpital du Val-de-Grâce.

MOSQUES

Mosquée de Paris: 2, Place du Puits-de-l'Ermite (5th) ♦ Muslim faith ♦ Mosque built between 1922 and 1926 in the Hispanic-Moorish style by Ch Heubès, R Fournez, and M Mantout, and renovated in 1992; it is the largest mosque in Europe (80,700 sq ft/7,500 sq m) ♦ It was built of reinforced concrete and clad with decorative materials (green tiles, earthenware, mosaics, and wrought iron) from North Africa. The complex has a 110 ft (33 m) high minaret and several buildings devoted to the various activities of the mosque and the Muslim Institute: the building

dedicated to worship; the patio decorated with mosaics; the prayer room with marble columns; the cupola decorated with cedar wood, and magnificent carpets (dedicated to religious activity); the lecture theater with a carved and painted wooden ceiling, and bronze and openwork chandeliers; the library with its wealth of books dedicated to teaching Arabic and introducting Islamic civilization (it organizes cultural activities). Added to these are a registry office (marriages) and commercial activities: Turkish bath, restaurant, and cafeteria ♦ The mosque commemorates the 100,000 Muslims who died for France in World War I, and was inaugurated by the President of the Republic, G Doumergue, and the Sultan of Morocco, Moulay Youssef.

Mosquée Adda'wa: 39, Rue de Tanger (19th) ♦ Muslim faith ♦ Mosque built in 1979 in a former warehouse; it has a vast prayer room and is being redeveloped ♦ It followed a small prayer room, opened at 15, Rue de Belleville (19th) in the early 1960s, then a mosque set up temporarily in part of the Church of Ménilmontant (a notable example of Christian-Muslim co-operation). Since 1995, the recreational center in Rue Tanger has organized seminars for intercultural and inter-religious meetings. Its leaders have planned a major architectural project, aimed at turning the present building into a real mosque.

PROTESTANT CHURCHES

Billettes: 24, Rue des Archives (4th) ♦ Protestant faith ♦ The Temple des Billettes was built between 1755 and 1758 by Brother Claude, a Dominican architect ♦ The façade has a very severe aspect with pilasters surmounted by a triangular pediment and a bell tower; nave with four spans, with aisles and galleries; circular chancel; in the sacristy, paintings by J C Loth: *The Good Samaritan* and *Curing the Blind Man of Jericho* (17th century). At the north end, the cloister survives, dating from about 1427, partly restored in the late 19th century ♦ At the instigation of Philip the Fair, the church replaced a convent chapel, occupied since 1299 by the Sisters of Mercy of the Charité Notre-Dame. In the 17th century, Reformed Carmelites replaced them. The church was rebuilt in the late 14th

century, and again by the Carmelites. It was handed over to the Lutherans in 1812. Concerts are regularly held there.

Étoile: 54, Avenue de la Grande-Armée (17th) ♦ Protestant faith ♦ Neo-Gothic building constructed in 1874 by Swedish architect W Hansen on land acquired in 1868 by Pastor Bersier. The façade has a large central porch and two minor porches, surmounted by a circular window; above, an ogival window and a rose window flanked by pilasters, and two small spires ♦ Inside, a large circular window in the apse illuminates the nave; the stained-glass windows are decorated with Christian symbols ♦ A first chapel was built there by Lebert in 1868, at No 45 in the same avenue.

Oratoire: 145, Rue St-Honoré (1st) ♦ Protestant faith ♦ Former church built between 1621 and 1630 for the congregation of the Priests of the Oratory, founded by Cardinal de Bérulle, and handed over to the Reformed Church by Napoléon I in 1811 ♦ Classical architecture, 18th-century façade on two stories; monument of Admiral de Coligny in the chevet (1889) ♦ Inside, a single nave with side chapels and arcades with Corinthian pilasters ♦ Sermons by Bossuet, Bourdaloue, and Massillon were given there; the funerals of Richelieu, Louis XIII, Anne of Austria, and Rameau were held there; also in this church, Talleyrand dedicated the first constitutional bishops.

Pentemont: 106, Rue de Grenelle (7th) ♦ Protestant faith ♦ Former church, built between 1747 and 1756, redeveloped by Baltard and given to the French Reformed church in 1844 ♦ Plan adapted from the Greek cross; small portal with Ionic columns and curved pediment; semicircular window above the portal; cupola above the rotunda, depressed brick vault above the chancel, pilasters with finely wrought Ionic capitals in the transept ♦ This was formerly the Convent of the Word Incarnate, taken over in 1672 by the Bernadines of Pentemont, a congregation from the diocese of Beauvais. The Abbess had it rebuilt and the site was visited by the Dauphin in 1753. The convent was popular in the 18th century with young girls from the nobility, and was a house of retreat for

impoverished genteel ladies. Joséphine de Beauharnais stayed there for over a year in 1782.

Saint-Esprit: 5, Rue Roquépine (8th) ♦ Protestant faith ♦ Temple built by Th Ballu and V Baltard between 1863 and 1865 on land given by the city. The building is rectangular with canted corners; a small bell tower rises above the long façade with Ionic columns. Nave with galleries, covered by a glass roof; decorative sculptures; organ by Cavaillé-Coll ♦ The 30th General Synod of the Reformed Church took place there in 1872, followed by the 31st after the separation of Church and State.

Sainte-Marie: see (Churches) Réformée du Marais.

SYNAGOGUES

Notre-Dame de Nazareth: 15, Rue Notre-Dame de Nazareth (3rd) ♦ Jewish faith ♦ Built in 1851-2 by Alexandre Thierry on the site of another synagogue which was in danger of collapse ♦ It is Romanesque-Byzantine in style, and became a model for other synagogues ♦ The entrance is via three delicately sculpted arcades leading to a patio; the central arcade has pilasters and small columns; a rose window illuminates the broad recessed pediment ♦ Inside is a double gallery; the upper story is lined with arches, supported by cast-iron columns and others which mark the boundary of the nave and aisles; a decorative frieze unites the various elements ♦ In the early part of the 19th century, a first synagogue opened in Rue du Temple. The present building suffered considerable damage during bombing raids in October, 1941.

Rue Pavée: 10, Rue Pavée (4th) ♦ Jewish faith (Ashkenazi) ♦ Art Nouveau building made of concrete, built by H Guimard in 1913 for the considerable Russian-Polish community in the district. The narrow site influenced its architecture; the façade's vertical lines are emphasized by the tall pilasters, and alleviated by windows on four stories; the curved gable encloses the Tables of the Law. The stylized décor of the porch is inspired by plant forms ♦ Inside: paneling, pillars, and wrought iron are handled in a typical Art Nouveau manner.

Synagogue des Tournelles:
21 *bis*, Rue des Tournelles (4th) ♦ Jewish faith (Sephardic) ♦ Built by M E Varcollier between 1872 and 1876. The Romanesque façade has two two levels of double arches with pilasters, surmounted by a semicircular pediment with a rose window, crowned by the Tables of the Law ♦ The interior was designed by G Eiffel, and the steel framework was built by the Forges et Ateliers de Normandie. Along the sides are two stories of galleries, made of exposed iron and cast iron, lined with arcades supported by columns with fluted pillars; above, in the form of a frieze, is the text of the Hebrew law. A large stained-glass window overlooks the Place des Vosges ♦ The synagogue replaced the one in Place des Vosges, built from 1867 in a former mansion which became the town hall of the 4th *arrondissement*, and was burnt down during the Commune ♦ Length: 148 ft (45 m); width: 72 ft (22 m); height: 69 ft (21 m).

Victoire: 44, Rue de la Victoire (9th) ♦ Jewish faith (Ashkenazi); Egyptian and Tunisian oratories ♦ The Romanesque-Byzantine building was constructed by A Aldrophe between 1865 and 1874, and restored in 1966-7; it is the largest synagogue in France ♦ Its high façade overlooks an interior courtyard; it consists of three arches and five large windows with rose windows in the upper part; on the semcircular gable is a stele bearing the Tables of the Law ♦ The interior porch is decorated with four columns in green stucco. The aisles are surmounted by galleries with arcades separated by marble columns with capitals, supported by square pillars; they surround the vast nave. Beneath the ceiling is a second gallery lined with small columns; at the back of the building are two superimposed galleries. The semicircular sanctuary is lit by rose windows symbolizing the 12 tribes of Israel; its portico is richly decorated; the Scrolls of the Law are kept in a display area decorated in the Romanesque style. The stained-glass windows are by Lusson, Lefèvre, and Oudinot ♦ The synagogue was built on the site of a former mansion occupied by Louis Bonaparte and his wife, Hortense, in 1802. It suffered considerable damage when a bomb exploded in 1941. Length: 144 ft (44 m); width: 92 ft (28 m); height: 93 ft (28.40 m).

RAILROAD STATIONS

Gare d'Austerlitz: 55, Quai d'Austerlitz (13th) ♦ Serves the southern suburbs; the Bordeaux-Hendaye, Vierzon-Montluçon, and Limoges-Toulouse lines; Spain and Portugal ♦ Traffic: main lines, 7,899,000 passengers (1999); suburban, 8,500,000 (1997) ♦ The present station was built between 1862 and 1869 by Renaud and redesigned several times. The external stone façade stands between Boulevard de l'Hôpital and Quai d'Austerlitz; it is Classical in style, and decorated with two sculptures representing Art and Science, which overlook Place Valhubert; some of these buildings are being renovated ♦ In the Departures Hall, parallel with the Seine, a clock overhangs the main façade. Beneath the arms of Orleans and Paris, statues of Agriculture and Industry flank massive openings, separated by Ionic pilasters ♦ On the walls on either side are the names and arms of the cities which the station originally served. The façade opens onto the Departures Hall; the great steel Central Hall (920 ft/280 m) is currently being renovated (2000-2002) ♦ The first station was the Jardin des Plantes "pier" on the Paris-Orléans line, built by Callet and opened in 1843. During the Siege of 1870, the size of the Central Hall made it a good place to manufacture air balloons ♦ The underground suburban station was built in 1969.

Gare de l'Est: Place du 11 Novembre 1918 (10th) ♦ Serves the eastern suburbs; the Reims-Sedan-Longwy, Metz-Forbach, Nancy-Strasbourg, and Troyes-Mulhouse-Bâle lines; Luxembourg, Germany, Switzerland, Central and Eastern Europe ♦ Traffic: main lines, 10,503,000 passengers (1999); suburban, 9,750,000 (2000) ♦ Built between 1847 and 1849 by F Duquesney, the Strasbourg "pier" was enlarged in 1854 and renamed the Gare de l'Est. This was redeveloped in 1900, and doubled in size between 1928 and 1931. The façade consists of two symmetrical parts. The left-hand block was the first; its two-storey buildings flank the Entrance Hall, which has a semicircular opening and is surmounted by a statue representing Strasbourg by J-H Lemaire; above the monumental clock are allegorical statues of the Rivers Seine and Rhine by J Brian. The matching right-hand block was built by Bernaut in 1931, and decorated with a statue symbolizing Verdun and, above the clock, two female figures by Varenne representing the Rivers Marne and Meuse. The arcade running along the façade is decorated with carved capitals and 32 coats of arms of cities served by the Paris-Strasbourg line ♦ In the station forecourt, there is a modern fountain by Michèle Blondel; an inscription recalls the Saint-Laurent fair, which was held there ♦ The hall on the left of the station is for main line traffic, and consists of two stories beneath Classical arcades; a composition by Albert Herter (1926) commemorates the departure of conscripts to the Front in 1914. The hall on the right is for suburban traffic, and was built in 1930s style with ticket offices and boutiques; it occasionally stages exhibitions and craft fairs.

Gare de Lyon: Place Louis-Armand (12th) ♦ Serves the south-eastern suburbs; the south-east of France with lines to Dijon-Besançon, Mâcon, Lyons, Valence and the Alps (Évian, Annecy, Chambéry, St-Gervais, Bourg-St-Maurice, Modane, Grenoble, and Briançon), Nîmes-Montpellier-Perpignan, and Avignon-Marseilles-Toulon-Nice; Switzerland and Italy ♦ Traffic: main lines, 28,393,000 passengers (1999); suburban 19,500,000 (1998) ♦ The present station was built by N Toudoire in 1899, expanded in 1927 and redeveloped several times. It has preserved its Neo-Classical façade and its 220 ft (67 m) clock tower with four faces, their big hands measuring 13 ft (4 m). On the second storey is the Train Bleu restaurant, a former buffet inaugurated by President Loubet in 1901 and listed as a historic monument; it has kept its Belle Époque decoration and murals representing the cities served by the old Paris-Lyons-Mediterranean Company, which ran the line ♦ The first station was built on this site between 1847 and 1852 by A Cendrier, and was regarded as the best designed station in the world ♦ The Express-Orient train, which became the Orient-Express service to Constantinople, was inaugurated in 1883; the Train Bleu, the luxurious Paris-Vintimille train, was inaugurated in 1922 ♦ For the 1900 Universal Exhibition, the Paris-Lyons-Mediterranean Company decided to rebuild the station ♦ It was enlarged, then redesigned in 1950 when the Paris-Marseilles line was electrified. In 1960, track was added for the first RER rapid transit line, from St-Germain-en-Laye to Boissy-St-Léger; then in 1980, the suburban station was built underground, and connected to the RATP network (Paris public transport system). Later, the station was adapted to take the high-speed TGV service, inaugurated in September, 1981.

Gare Montparnasse: Place Raoul-Dautry (15th) ♦ Serves the western suburbs; Brittany (Rennes-St-Brieuc-Brest and Vannes), the Le Mans-Nantes, Poitiers-La Rochelle, and Bordeaux-Hendaye and Toulouse lines; Spain and Portugal ♦ Traffic: main lines, 24,662,000 passengers (1999); suburban, 9,500,000 (1999) ♦ This very modern station was built between 1958 and 1970 by E Baudoin, U Cassan, L de Hoyn de Marien, and J Saubat, as part of the Maine-Montparnasse redevelopment scheme, which completely reshaped the district ♦ The large U-shaped glass and steel façade of the building, whose wings house offices and premises of the PTT (French post office and telephone service), reveals the building's three levels, linked by escalators. The top level contains the Passenger Hall, with its monumental abstract *Architectonic Integrations* (1971) by Vasarely on the side walls. The intermediate level houses the vast hall reserved for ticket offices and ticket machines; the floor is decorated with mosaic arabesques symbolizing travel. On the bottom level is a shopping arcade, the Chapel of St-Bernard (1969) and RATP facilities. The platforms built for high-speed TGV trains were covered with a stone platform supporting the Atlantique Garden ♦ The first station was built in Place de Rennes (now Place du 18 Juin

1940), between 1849 and 1852, on the site of the Maine "pier," the terminus of the Paris-Sèvres-Versailles line. In 1895, there was a spectacular accident: the locomotive of a train from Granville ran out of control and burst through the front of the building ♦ To deal with the fast-rising rush-hour traffic, two outer stations were built in 1927 and 1937 to take the main-line trains, while the original station handled the suburban lines. It was there that General Leclerc accepted the surrender of the German forces on April 25, 1944. The old station was demolished in 1965.

Gare du Nord: 18, Rue de Dunkerque (10th) ♦ Serves the northern suburbs; the Beauvais-Le-Tréport, Boulogne-Calais, Arras-Dunkirk, Arras-Lille, Maubeuge-Jeumont, and Laon-Hirson lines; Brussels, Amsterdam, Berlin, London, and Stockholm ♦ Traffic: main lines, 21,833,000 passengers (1999); suburban 50,000,000 (1998) ♦ The station was built between 1861 and 1864 by Hittorff, and expanded in 1899 and 1976 ♦ The monumental façade, flanked by two wings and decorated with pilasters with Ionic capitals, is 590 ft (180 m) wide. It is lit through large glass roofs, set above the central arcade and the two side arcades, and supported by a steel structure and cast-iron pillars with Corinthian capitals. On the top, statues by Cavelier and Gumery represent Paris (center) and foreign cities served by the station. At street level are Doric columns with capitals, surmounted by statues representing the main cities in the north of France ♦ The station replaced the North "pier," inaugurated in 1846, the terminus for the Belgian frontier, which soon proved inadequate. From there, on December 12, 1851, Victor Hugo left for exile in Belgium in disguise. Under the Second Empire, the

Compagnie du Nord launched its "series" of trains designed to attract different social classes to rail travel. In 1899, further building was necessary. From 1926, the Golden Arrow, running from Paris to Calais, connected in England with another luxury train which ran to and from London ♦ In 1976, an underground suburban station was built, connecting with the Métro; in the 1990s, alterations were made to take the new high-speed train lines: TGV Nord-Europe, Eurostar (Paris-London), and Thalys (Paris-Brussels-Cologne-Amsterdam).

Gare Saint-Lazare: Rue Saint-Lazare (8th) ♦ Serves the western suburbs and Normandy. Traffic: main lines, 9,883,000 passengers (1999); suburban, 35,000,000 (1998) ♦ The present buildings were constructed by Just Lisch between 1886 and 1889: the broad Classical-style façade joins the two forecourts in Rue de Rome and Rue du Havre. Large windows link it to the Hôtel Terminus (now the Concorde St-Lazare). The front part of the station consists mainly of a large reception hall and waiting room. Modern sculptures by Arman decorate the forecourts. The station's history is closely allied to that of the city's regional rail network. The ever-increasing numbers of passengers meant that a new building had to be constructed along Rue St-Lazare to replace the "pier" (in Place de l'Europe) of the Paris-St-Germain line, inaugurated in 1837 by Queen Marie-Amélie. The Rue du Havre and the Rue de Rome were built at that time, and a tunnel under Place de l'Europe. As passenger numbers continued to grow, the station was first enlarged with a wing on the Rue de Rome and was completely rebuilt at the end of the 1880s. This station was a great source of inspiration for the painter Claude Monet.

SPORT AND RACING

Aquaboulevard: 4, Rue Louis-Armand (15th) ♦ Devoted to sports and leisure activities. Fifteen acre (6 ha) water park inaugurated in 1989; it has a five-storey building designed by

A Ghinlamila and R Hendricks. Large pool and beach area, with a giant artificial whale; children's paddling pool, pools of various shapes, waterfalls, water cannon, wave machines, slides, and jacuzzi; sports halls (tennis, squash, and gymnastics).

Hippodrome d'Auteuil: Bois de

Boulogne (16th) ♦ Racetrack opened in 1873 by the Steeple-chase Society (originally established at Longchamp), which acquired a concession on this part of the Bois de Boulogne between Auteuil and the lakes ♦ 89 acres (36 ha) ♦ The Grand Steeplechase of Paris, which started in 1874, is its most spectacular race; this elegant social event takes place in May.

Hippodrome de Longchamp: Bois de Boulogne (16th) ♦ Racetrack for flat racing, built by the Society for Encouraging Improvements in Horse Racing, and inaugurated in 1857 ♦ 143 acres (58 ha) ♦ The biggest annual races are the Grand Prix de Paris, established in 1863, which takes place on the last Sunday in June, and the Prix de l'Arc de Triomphe, on the first Sunday in October (since 1920). The Abbey of Longchamp stood to the north of the racecourse and was demolished in 1795; some of its ancillary buildings remain, occupied by the International Center for Childhood.

Hippodrome de Vincennes: 2, Route de la Ferme, Bois de Vincennes (12th) ♦ Created in 1863, with grandstands by Davioud, flanking a central pavilion reserved for the Emperor; renovated in 1980 by Ph Monin and Th Mostini ♦ 124 acres (50 ha) ♦ Its track is particularly well-suited to trotting races.

Palais des Sports: 1, Place de la Porte de Versailles (15th) ♦ Stadium with 6,000 seats, built between 1959 and 1960 by P Dufau and V Pajardis de Larivière to replace the Vel'd'Hiv (velodrome) in Rue Nélaton. It is covered by a cupola, made out of diamond-shaped aluminum tiles, which rests on concrete porticos. Originally dedicated to sporting events, the Palais des Sports still holds boxing matches, but today mainly stages large shows: ballets by Béjart, Roland Petit, and Nureyev (who triumphed there), the Bolshoi Ballet, productions by Robert Hossein, and singers.

Palais Omnisports de Bercy: 8, Boulevard de Bercy (12th) ♦ Building constructed in the north-west part of the former Bercy warehouses by Michel Andrault, Pierre Parat, Aydin Guvan, and Jean Prouvé. It is shaped like a truncated pyramid on an octago-

nal plan, and is supported by a metal frame supported by four concrete shafts; above its sloping outer walls, covered with turf, are the glass façades which light the interior. This large stadium has flexible seating arrangements (8,500 to 17,500), and can host 24 different sports, as well as cultural and artistic events. It has staged the French Tennis Open, and hosted tours by Michel Sardou and Johnny Halliday, as well as *Aïda* by Verdi (1984); in early 2001, there was another Verdi performance to mark the centenary of the composer's death.

Parc des Princes: 24, Rue du Commandant-Guilbaud (16th) ♦ The largest stadium in Paris, designed for soccer and rugby, rebuilt between 1968 and 1972 by Roger Taillibert over the *Périphérique* (ring road). It is oval in shape; the two terrace levels and the roof are supported by external buttresses made out of prestressed concrete, which obviates the need for pillars. Redeveloped and modernized in two stages between 1999 and 2002, it has a 50,000-seat capacity. Many soccer matches and several Five Nations rugby matches have taken place there. In addition to sports, it also welcomed the Pope for a religious gathering of young people in 1980; Johnny Halliday for his 50th birthday celebrations, and the Rolling Stones.

Racing Club de France: Chemin de la Croix-Catelan, Bois de Boulogne (16th) ♦ Set up in 1882 by students at the Lycée Condorcet (who held running races in the Bois de Boulogne), the club became the Racing Club de France in 1885, and acquired the Croix-Catelan concession in 1886 ♦ It held the Olympic Games there in 1900 ♦ Today, its members have nearly 50 tennis courts, volleyball courts, swimming pools, a decathlon track, a grass track, and a physical training ground.

Stade Charlety: 99, Boulevard Kellermann (13th) ♦ New building by H and B Gaudin which opened in 1994, replacing a first stadium built in 1938, which had become too small ♦ The concrete and steel structure is decorated with marble, granite, and stainless steel; four tilted 130 ft (40 m) masts support the floodlights ♦ Mainly intended for athletics and rugby, it has a 20,000-seat capacity, a sports hall in

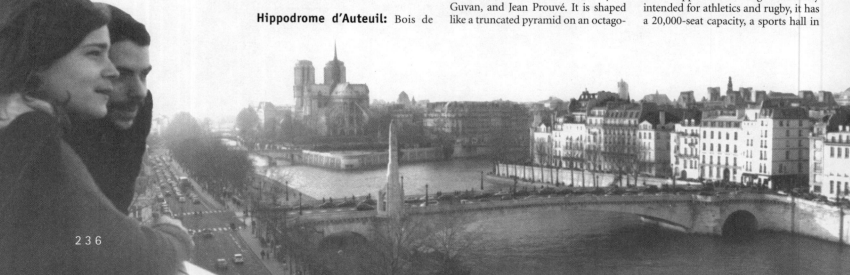

Avenue Coubertin, and is headquarters to the National Olympic Advisory Board ♦ This was the first place in Paris to be liberated in August, 1944. Michel Jazy beat the 5,000-meter European record there in 1965, and Eunice Barber set a new French long jump record there in 1999.

Stade de France: 360, Avenue des Prés, Saint-Denis ♦ Stadium designed by architects Macary, Zublena, Regembal, and Costantini, built from 1995 and inaugurated in January, 1998. Designed to accommodate major sports events, shows, and concerts, it can accommodate 80,000 spectators for soccer and rugby matches, 75,000 for athletics meetings and the Olympic games, and between 600,000 and 1,000,000 people for shows. The soccer World Cup was played there in 1998 and the Six Nations tournament matches were held there in 2001; Johnny Halliday performed there in 1999.

Stade Roland-Garros: Avenue de la Porte-d'Auteuil (16th) ♦ Tennis stadium inaugurated in 1928, extended and modernized in the late 1980s. It is named after the aviator who successfully completed the first crossing of the Mediterranean in 1913 and was killed in aerial combat in 1918. The French Open takes place there.

THEATERS

Abbesses: 31, Rue des Abbesses (18th) ♦ The Théâtre des Abbesses is a municipal theater with 400 seats ♦ An annex of the Théâtre de la Ville, built by Charles Vandehove and opened in 1996 with Cocteau's *The Unjustly Suspected Wife* ♦ Entered through a small passageway and an interior courtyard; red Neoclassical façade bearing inscriptions by D Barry, peristyle with white columns; curtain by Olivier Debré ♦ Director: Gérard Violette.

Antoine: 14, Boulevard de Strasbourg (10th) ♦ The Théâtre Antoine is a member of the Association of Private Theaters; 875 seats ♦ The building, dates from 1880 ♦ It used to house the Théâtre des Menus-Plaisirs (variety, vaudeville, operettas) where André Antoine performed with his Théâtre Libre (Free Theater) from 1891 on. It was not until 1897 that he became the theater's director and gave it his name. Simone Berriau succeeded him from 1943 to 1984; she had the auditorium restored and put on Sartre, Camus, Cocteau, and boulevard theater, notably with Jacqueline Maillan ♦ Directors have included: A Antoine, F Gémier, S Berriau, H Bossis, and D Dares.

Atelier: 1, Place Charles-Dullin (18th) ♦ The Théâtre de l'Atelier is a member of the Association of Private Theaters; 565 seats; listed façade ♦ Built by the architect Haudebourd in 1822; its Neo-Classical façade is decorated with masks and heads ♦ It was founded in 1922 by Charles Dullin in the old Théâtre de Montmartre, created by J-J Seveste. The theater was also used as a school of drama. Plays by Cocteau, Achard, Salacrou, J Romains (*Volpone*, which was a great hit), F Marceau, and Anouilh were created there ♦ Directors have included: Ch Dullin, A Barsacq, and P Franck.

Athénée: 4, Square de l'Opéra Louis-Jouvet (2nd) ♦ The Théâtre de l'Athénée-Louis Jouvet is a listed theater with two auditoriums: Louis Jouvet, 565 seats; Christian Bérard, 86 seats ♦ The building was constructed in 1893; interior fittings in the rococo style ♦ The theater was erected in the outbuildings of the former Eden-Théâtre, dating from 1883; the auditorium was vast and sumptuously decorated to resemble an Indian palace. It was known as the Athénée-Comique before taking on its current name in 1899. Plays by Giraudoux, and *Knock* by Jules Romains were produced there ♦ Directors have included: A Deval, Jouvet, J Mercure, and P Bergé, who had the little Christian Bérard Theater built in 1977.

Bastille: 76, Rue de la Roquette (11th) ♦ 200 seats (downstairs) and 150 seats (upstairs) ♦ The Théâtre de la Bastille dates from the 1920s ♦ Once a local cinema known as the Cyrano, it became the Théâtre Oblique around 1970, then in 1982 the Théâtre de la Bastille ♦ Directors have included: J-Cl Fall and J-M Hordet.

Bouffes du Nord: 37 *bis*, Boulevard de la Chapelle (10th) ♦ 500 seats ♦ The building dates from 1876 ♦ Known for many years as the Théâtre Molière, the Théâtre des Bouffes du Nord put on many light comedies in the interwar years, then fell out of use for a long time. It was Peter Brook who revived it as an avant-garde venue with experimental theater and innovative techniques; he produced *Ubu aux Bouffes*, *The Mahabharata*, and *The Cherry Orchard* there ♦ Directors have included: M Rozau, S Lissner, and P Brook.

Bouffes Parisiens: 4, Rue Monsigny (2nd) ♦ The Théâtre des Bouffes Parisiens is a member of the Association of Private Theaters: 668 seats ♦ The building dates from 1827 ♦ Once the Théâtre des Jeunes Acteurs (Young Actors' Theater), where children gave interlude performances between the comic numbers, it became the Salle Choiseul in 1846 (after there was a ban on putting children under 15 on stage), then took on its current name in 1855; the theater, which at that time was directed by Offenbach, was enlarged and decorated ♦ Operettas were frequently produced there: *Ba Ta Clan* (Halévey and Offenbach), *La Belle Hélène*, *Phi-Phi*, and *Dédé* (with Maurice Chevalier), and *Three Waltzes* ♦ Directors have included: Nicky Nancel and J-Cl Brialy.

Cartoucherie: Route du Champ-de-Manœuvre (12th) ♦ The Théâtres de la Cartoucherie have five auditoriums: Théâtre du Soleil (Sun Theater), Théâtre de l'Épée de Bois (Wooden Sword Theater), Théâtre de la Tempête (Tempest Theater), Atelier du Chaudron (Cauldron Studio), and Théâtre de l'Aquarium (Aquarium Theater) ♦ The earliest buildings date from the end of the 19th century ♦ Ariane Mnouchkine, the director of the Théâtre du Soleil, moved into the abandoned sheds of the Vincennes parade ground, fitted them out with her company, and opened the theater in 1970. Other companies joined her, including the Théâtre de l'Épée de Bois in 1968, to create avant-garde theater in the various auditoriums, which were renovated in 1978 by J Nouvel and G Seigneur.

Comédie Caumartin: 25, Rue Caumartin (9th) ♦ Member of the Association of Private Theaters; 380 seats ♦ Formerly the Comédie Royale, founded in 1901, the theater took on its current name in 1923; it was renovated in 1952 after a long closure, then took in the Jacques Fabbri Company ♦ It puts on boulevard theater; one great hit was *Boeing-Boeing* by M Camoletti ♦ Directors have included: R Rocher and D Petitdidier.

Comédie-Française-Salle Richelieu: Place Colette (1st) ♦ National theater with 896 seats ♦ The theater was built between 1786 and 1790 by Victor Louis, altered in 1822 and 1863, then restored after a serious fire in 1900. Since 1970 it has once again been reorganized and modernized ♦ Its façade is lined with columns and decorated with medallions showing Corneille, Molière, Racine, Hugo, and others. Inside, an Italian-style auditorium in red and gold tones; numerous statues, including *Voltaire Seated* by Houdon, *Talma* by David d'Angers, *Tragedy*, and *Comedy*; gallery of busts, ceiling by Albert Besnard (1913), and curtain by Olivier Debré (1987) ♦ In 1791 the theater was taken over by the Comédie-Française company, which played Corneille, Racine, and Molière there: notable actors were Talma, Mlle Mars, and Mlle George ♦ The permanent company of the Comédiens-Français mainly performs the classical repertoire ♦ The Français also uses the Vieux-Colombier, and the Studio-Théâtre (136 seats), which was created by architect Michel Sené in the Carrousel du Louvre; it was opened in 1996, and is mainly used for new productions ♦ Directors have included: J-F Mahérault, A Housset (known as Houssaye), J Copeau, J Le Poulain, A Vitez, J Lassalle, J-P Miquel, and M Bozonnet.

Chaillot: 1, Place du Trocadéro (16th) ♦ The Théâtre de Chaillot is a national theater; two auditoriums: Salle Jean Vilar, 1,000 seats; Salle Gémier, 430 seats ♦ It is located in the Palais de Chaillot. The old palace, built for the Exhibition of 1878, had a huge central auditorium in which the Théâtre National Populaire (TNP) was

founded in 1920; it was destroyed, then rebuilt at basement level by the Niemans brothers. Many artists decorated both the theater and the foyers, entrances, and marble-covered staircases: 22 painters, including Jaulmes, Vuillard, Bonnard, and Dufy, and 13 sculptors, including Bourdele, Cazaubon, Belmondo, and Louis Muller ♦ Between 1951 and 1963, the main auditorium witnessed the brilliant theatrical venture of the TNP (founded by Firmin Gémier); this was where Jean Vilar created his spare productions, and actors such as Gérard Philipe, Jeanne Moreau, Georges Wilson, and Philippe Noire won renown. The theater was rebuilt at the beginning of the 1970s and took on its current name, while the TNP was transferred to Villeurbanne. In 1966 the little Gémier Theater was created to put on experimental theater ♦ Directors have included: Firmin Gémier (first theater), J Vilar, G Wilson, A Vitez, and J Savary.

Champs-Élysées: 15, Avenue Montagne (8th) ♦ The Théâtre des Champs-Élysées has three auditoriums: Grand Théâtre, 1,901 seats; Comédie des Champs-Élysées, 621 seats; Studio des Champs-Élysées, 249 seats ♦ The theater is a monumental concrete structure, built by the Perret brothers and opened in 1913. It was the most modern and beautiful theater of the time ♦ The theater was intended for opera and dance, and decorated by Maurice Denis; curtain by Ker Xavier Roussel. Performers have included Richard Strauss, Toscanini, Paderewski, Pavlova, Chaliapine, the Diaghilev ballets, and the Revue Nègre, and conductors such as Munch, Solti, and Karajan ♦ The Comédie, decorated by Édouard Vuillard, was directed by Louis Jouvet from 1922 to 1934; plays by Pirandello (with S Pitoëff), Shaw, J Romains (*Knock*), Giraudoux, Achard, Cocteau, Anouilh, M Aymé, and Yasmina Reza were produced there ♦ The Studio was opened in 1923 as an experimental theater, and run for a few years by Gaston Baty and his actors, including Marguerite Jamois.

Colline: 15, Rue Malte-Brun (20th) ♦

The Théâtre de la Colline is a national theater with two auditoriums: main theater – Salle Maria Casarès, 750 seats; little theater, 200 movable seats ♦ Built by architects Fabre and Perottet between 1985 and 1988, on the site of the old TEP (Théâtre de l'Est Parisien) which in turn replaced a cinema ♦ Glass façade ♦ Devoted to contemporary theater ♦ Directors have included: J Lavelli and A Françon.

Daunou: 7, Rue Daunou (2nd) ♦ The Théâtre Daunou is a member of the Association of Private Theaters; 448 seats ♦ Built in 1921 by Bluysen on the site of a hotel ♦ Founded by Jane Renouardt, it opened with *A Hell of a Little Blonde* by A Birabeau and P Wolff, followed by the smash hit, *Shut your Mouth*, by M Yvain and Y Mirande. Pierre Brasseur was discovered there in *The Dazzled Heart* by Descaves, and Louis de Funès in R Dhéry's *The Beautiful Moustache*. After the theater was renovated in 1977, Michel Roux played here many times, and J-L Cochet revived plays by Guitry ♦ Directors have included: R Sancelme and his wife, and Denise Petitdidier.

Déjazet: 41, Boulevard du Temple (3rd) ♦ The Théâtre Déjazet is the only surviving building from the "Boulevard of Crime"; it is an old real-tennis court, built in 1778. The ceiling of the auditorium and the roof of the stage are painted with frescoes recalling the Boulevard of Crime ♦ The real-tennis court became a bathing establishment at the time of the Revolution, and was then turned into a variety theater known as the Folies Meyer, then the Folies Nouvelles, where Offenbach made his début in 1855. It owes its name to the actress Virginie Déjazet, who bought it in 1859 and appointed her son as director. Victorien Sardou triumphed there in 1860. The theater then changed hands, and specialized in vaudeville at the end of the 19th century: *The Shooting Range* and *My Sister's Child* by Mouézy-Éon. After being used for a while as a cinema, the building became a theater again in the 1980s.

Édouard VII-Sacha Guitry: 10, Place Édouard-VII (9th) ♦ The Théâtre Édouard VII-Sacha Guitry is a member of the Association of Private Theaters; 400 seats ♦ The theater was

founded in 1916 by Alphonse Franck, in an auditorium built as a cinema between 1912 and 1914 by the English architect Sprague. Closed since May, 1999 ♦ The operetta *Phi-Phi* was a hit there before Sacha Guitry put on his plays, including *Mozart* and *Désiré*, some of which featured Lucien Guitry, who also acted in classical plays. The theater was used as a cinema again during the 1930s ♦ Directors have included: A Franck and L Vartet.

Est Parisien: 159, Avenue Gambetta (20th) ♦ 400 seats ♦ Fitted out in 1983 in a rehearsal room, previously a parking lot, restored by the Perset Studio ♦ The Théâtre de l'Est Parisien was first located, from 1962, in a former cinema in Rue Malte-Brun; this auditorium was reconstructed in the 1980s, then occupied by the Théâtre de la Colline ♦ Classical and contemporary repertoire ♦ Director: Guy Rétoré.

Fontaine: 10, Rue Fontaine (9th) ♦ The Théâtre Fontaine is a member of the Association of Private Theaters; 627 seats ♦ The building dates from 1947 ♦ Founded by A Puglia and J Richard in a former dance hall in 1951 ♦ For many years it put on comic theater; Desproges and Sylvie Joly performed there; *The Clan of Widows* ran there for a long time ♦ Director: D Deschamps.

Gaîté Montparnasse: 26, Rue de la Gaîté (14th) ♦ The Théâtre de la Gaîté Montparnasse is a member of the Association of Private Theaters; 411 seats ♦ This elliptically-shaped building dates from 1868 ♦ At first it was a café-concert, then a mime show theater, where Colette performed in 1913; it became the Georgius Studio d'Art Comique, then a music hall. The auditorium was transformed in 1945 by Dullin's pupil Agnès Capri, who put on Jean-Pierre Grenier and Olivier Hussemot (*La Parade* and *Orion the Killer*) ♦ Directors have included: A Capri, Chr and T Tsingos, M Fagadeau, L-M Colla, and C Mahéo.

Gymnase-Marie Bell: 38, Boulevard de Bonne-Nouvelle (10th) ♦ The Théâtre du Gymnase-Marie Bell is a member of the Association of Private Theaters; 783 seats ♦ Built in 1820 on the site of the Bonne-Nouvelle cemetery ♦ Façade with large arcaded bay

windows on two levels; auditorium in the Italian style ceiling decorated with an allegorical painting of the Four Seasons ♦ Originally called the Théâtre du Gymnase Dramatique, it became known for some years as the Théâtre de Madame, patronized by the Duchesse de Berry. Mesdemoiselles Rachel, Déjazet, and Léontine Fay made their débuts here, and plays were produced by Dumas the Younger, Émile Augier, Eugène Scribe, Jules Sandeau, and Sardou. The theater was renovated in 1880 and took on its current name in 1958. It had numerous successes: *The Ironmaster* by Georges Ohnet, *The Lord's Vines* by R de Flers and F de Croisset, plays by H Bernstein, Cocteau's *Les Parents Terribles*, *Good Soup* (featuring Marie Bell) by F Marceau, plays by J Genêt, F Sagan, and one-man shows (Coluche, G Bedos, T Le Luron, and the mime artist Marceau) ♦ Directors have included: Poirson, H Bernstein, Marie Bell, and J Bertin.

Hébertot: 78 *bis*, Boulevard des Batignolles (17th) ♦ The Théâtre Hébertot is a member of the Association of Private Theaters; 637 seats ♦ Built in 1838 by the architect Lequeux ♦ The old Théâtre de Batignolles became the Théâtre des Arts after its renovation at the beginning of the 20th century, before taking on its current name in 1940. Many famous actors have perfomed there: Dullin, J Copeau, Georges and Ludmilla Pitoëff, and Jean-Laurent Cochet and his company; Cocteau put on *Orpheus* and *The Infernal Machine*, and Gérard Philipe was discovered in Giraudoux's *Sodom and Gomorrha* and *Caligula* by Camus ♦ Directors have included: Seveste, R d'Humières, J Hébertot, the Valère-Desailly Company, and F Ascot.

Huchette: 23, Rue de la Huchette (5th) ♦ The Théâtre de la Huchette is a member of the Association of Private Theaters; 100 seats ♦ Opened in 1948 by Marcel Pinard and Georges Vitaly. Since 1957 it has been presenting Ionesco's *The Bald Prima Donna* and *The Lesson*, played in turn by a group of actors ♦ Directors have included: J Legré.

La Bruyère: 5, Rue La Bruyère (9th) ♦ The Théâtre La Bruyère is a member of the Association of Private Theaters;

330 seats ♦ Opened in 1943 ♦ From 1944, Jean Vilar applied his ideas about drama here in *Don Juan*, then Robert Dhéry created his *Branquignols*. Later, authors such as Dino Buzzati and Vaclav Havel were discovered there, and Laurent Terzieff produced American plays ♦ Directors have included: G Vitaly and S Meldegg.

Lucernaire: 53, Rue Notre-Dame-des-Champs (6th) ♦ The Théâtre du Lucernaire is a National Center for Art and Experimentation; two auditoriums of 120 seats: the Théâtre Noir and the Théâtre Rouge ♦ In 1965 the Théâtre du Lucernaire was founded in the Impasse Odessa (14th), opening with Laurent Terzieff. In 1980 it added a café-theater, an exhibition room, a restaurant, and a bar; in 1984 it was awarded the title of National Center for Art and Experimentation ♦ Numerous new productions and performances of classic plays; several shows every evening ♦ Directors have included: Chr Le Guillochet and L Berthommé. See also under Cinemas.

Madeleine: 19, Rue de Surène (8th) ♦ The Théâtre de la Madeleine is a member of the Association of Private Theaters; 728 seats ♦ It opened in 1924 with the musical comedy *Manon Fille Galante*, featuring André Brûlé and Jeanne Marnac, and was later mainly devoted to Sacha Guitry until the war years (*The New Testament, Désiré*, and *Don't Listen to the Ladies*). Danielle Darrieux made her theatrical début here, and Elvire Popesco triumphed in *La Mamma* by André Roussin ♦ Directors have included: R Trébor and A Brûlé, B-L Deutsch, J Desailly, and S Valère.

Marigny: Carré Marigny (8th) ♦ The Théâtre Marigny is a member of the Association of Private Theaters; two auditoriums: Main Theater, 1,000 seats; Popesco Theater, 300 seats ♦ Built by Hittorff in 1855 ♦ This theater was called the Bouffes-Parisiens, since it was twinned with the one in the Passage Choiseul; Offenbach produced comic operas and operettas there. It was turned into a panorama, built by Charles Garnier in 1883, then back into a theater in 1896; variety shows and ballets, then music hall were performed in this richly decorated auditorium. In 1925 it was renovated once

again, and took on the name Théâtre Marigny under the direction of Léon Volterra; after World War II it took in the Renaud-Barrault company, then the Grenier-Hussenot company. It was renovated at the instigation of Elvire Popesco in 1965 ♦ Directors have included: A Deval, L and S Volterra, E Popesco, and H de Mallet.

Mathurins: 36, Rue des Mathurins (8th) ♦ The Théâtre des Mathurins is a member of the Association of Private Theaters; two auditoriums: 392 and 84 seats ♦ Built by Siclis, it opened in 1900 with a play by Tristan Bernard in which Marguerite Deval performed. Between the wars, the Pitoëff company put on many plays here, including Ibsen's *The Doll's House* with Ludmilla Pitoëff ♦ Directors have included: S Pitoëff, J Marchat, M Herrand, and L Vartet.

Michodière: 4 *bis*, Rue de la Michodière (2nd) ♦ The Théâtre de la Michodière is a member of the Association of Private Theaters; 700 seats ♦ Built in 1925 by Bluysen and Bailly; bas-relief by Henro Navarre above the stage curtain ♦ Performers and directors: Gustave Quinson, Victor Boucher, Yvonne Printemps, Pierre Fresnay, François Périer, and Jacques Crépineau, whose productions included works by E Bourdet and A Roussin, and plays adapted from English: *Just Out, Fric-Frac* (with Arletty and Michel Simon), *The Ostrich Eggs, Bobosse, Gog and Magog*, and *Mixed Doubles*.

Mogador: 26, Rue Mogador (9th) ♦ The Théâtre Mogador is a member of the Association of Private Theaters; 1,800 seats ♦ Built in 1919 by Bertie Crewe ♦ Formerly the Palace Théâtre, it took on its current name in 1920, and put on mainly operettas: *Imperial Violets, Vienna Dances and Sings*, and *Naples with the Kiss of Fire*. After its renovation in 1981 by René Decaux, it reopened in 1983 as a venue for plays and musical comedies ♦ Directors have included: Sir A Butt, Cora Laparcerie, J Hébertot, and H Varna.

Montparnasse: 31, Rue de la Gaîté (14th) ♦ The Théâtre du Montparnasse is a member of the Association of Private Theaters; 700 seats ♦ The theater was founded in 1819, then rebuilt twice, the last time being in 1886; it was

restored in the 1990s, but still has an old café which has kept its late 19th-century appearance. Plays of every kind have been produced there. Frédérick Lemaître and Marie Dorval made their débuts in this theater; Gaston Baty, who was the director from 1930 to 1942, put on plays including *Les Caprices de Marianne* (Marivaux), *Macbeth* (Shakespeare), and *The Threepenny Opera* (Brecht). Directors have included: Sevestre, G Baty, and M Jamois; currently Myriam de Colombi.

Musical de Paris: see (Concert Halls) Théâtre du Châtelet.

Nouveautés: 24, Boulevard Poissonnière (9th) ♦ The Théâtre des Nouveautés is a member of the Association of Private Theaters; 585 seats ♦ Built in 1920 by A Thiers (decoration by Alice Courtois) ♦ Founded in 1878 by Brasseur, this vaudeville theater was at first located on Place de la Bourse, then at 28, Boulevard des Italiens; Feydeau was the accredited playwright. After being destroyed in 1911 when the Rue des Italiens was opened, it moved to its present address. It put on operettas and Rip's variety shows; a great hit in the 1950s was *The Little Hut* by A Roussin, with Suzanne Flon; it then featured a succession of comedians: D Cowl, J Lefebvre, and R Lamoureux ♦ Director: D Moreau-Chantegris.

Odéon-Europe: 1, Place Paul-Claudel (6th) ♦ The Théâtre de l'Odéon-Théâtre de l'Europe is a national theater with 340 seats ♦ Built between 1778 and 1783 by M-J Peyre and Ch De Wailly, then rebuilt in identical form after fires in 1799 and 1818 ♦ The façade is in the ancient Greek style; Italian-style auditorium, ceiling by A Masson (1965) ♦ Originally called the Théâtre-Français, because it was intended to house the Comédie-Française. Under the direction of Giorgio Strehler from 1983 to 1990, it was known as the Théâtre de l'Europe, after which it took on its current name ♦ In the 1780s, *The Marriage of Figaro* by Beaumarchais, and *Charles IX or the School of Kings* by Marie-Joseph Chénier, caused a scandal there, and played to packed houses. In the 19th century, the theater put on both the classical repertoire and plays by Naturalist and Romantic playwrights, notably *Marion Delorme* and *Ruy Blas*

♦ In its early days, famous actors won renown here: Talma, Mlle George, Marie Dorval, and Bocage. Foreign companies were frequently invited ♦ Directors (often performers) have included: Harel and Porel in the 19th century, Antoien, J-L Barrault, P Dux, J Toja, A Vitez, and G Lavaudant.

Œuvre: 55, Rue de Clichy (Cité Monthiers, 9th) ♦ The Théâtre de l'Œuvre is a member of the Association of Private Theaters; 400 seats ♦ Built in 1892, then renovated in 1995 ♦ Lugné-Poë founded an avant-garde theater here, known as the Maison de l'Œuvre, where he put on A Jarry's *Ubu Roi* and discovered authors such as Sarment, Crommelynck, Achard, Sal-acrou, and Anouilh; Jouvet, Dullin, Pitoëff, and Barsacq performed there; Jean Marais came to fame in *The Knights of the Round Table* by Cocteau. Later, plays by English authors were produced, featuring mainly G Wilson and J Dufilho ♦ Directors have included: Lugné-Poë, P Franck, G Hébert, and G Wilson.

Palais-Royal: 38, Rue Montpensier (1st) ♦ The Théâtre du Palais-Royal is a member of the Association of Private Theaters; 746 seats ♦ Built in 1783 by Victor Louis ♦ Once a puppet theater and then the Théâtre du Beaujolais, it was bought in 1788 by Mlle de Montansier, who immediately extended it, then opened very successfully with Mlle Mars in 1790. In 1830 the actor Dormeuil had it renovated; it was restored again by Sédille and decorated by Boyard in 1880. Mme Déjazet and Mme Hortense Schneider performed there; it put on a succession of comedies: many plays by Eugène Labiche (*The Italian Straw Hat* was a great hit), *La Vie Parisienne* by Meilhac and Halévy, then Feydeau's *The Gentleman is Hunting* and *The Turkey*, and others by M Hennequin, Y Mirande, F Dorin, and J Poiret (*La Cage aux Folles*). In 1965, M Rouzières founded the Palais-Royal Encounters there with Mme Dussane ♦ Directors have included: Mlle Montansier, Dormeuil, G Delcroix, G Quinson, J de Létraz, and J-M Rouzière.

Poche-Montparnasse: 75, Boule-

vard du Montparnasse (6th) ♦ The Théâtre de Poche-Montparnasse is a member of the Association of Private Theaters; two auditoriums ♦ The first theater was opened in 1943 and extended in 1958; the second, in the basement, in 1984 ♦ Jean Vilar made his début here with *Césaire* by J Schlumberger and *Thunder in the Air* by A Strindberg; plays by Audiberti, Brecht, Ionesco, and Roland Dubillard have been produced there ♦ Directors have included: Marcel Oger, Renée Delmas, and Étienne Bierry.

Porte Saint-Martin: 16, Boulevard St-Martin (10th) ♦ The Théâtre de la Porte Saint-Martin is a member of the Association of Private Theaters; 1,100 seats ♦ Built in 1781 by the architect Lenoir ♦ It originally housed the Opéra-Royal company, after a fire at the Opéra, then the author-actor Dumaniant took it over in 1802. It was closed for a while, then used for acrobatic acts and mime (Théâtre de Jeux Gymniques), and finally restored and reopened in 1814. Marie Dorval made her début here and Frédérick Lemaître appeared there. Alexandre Dumas triumphed with *Henri III and his Court* and *La Tour de Nesle*; Victor Hugo with *Marion Delorme* and *Lucrèce Borgia*; the theater had more successes under the Third Republic: *The Two Orphans*, *Cyrano de Bergerac*, and *Napoléon IV*, and later with *Hair* ♦ Directors have included: Dumaniant, Saint-Romain, Ch J Harel, Max Régnier, and H and B Régnier.

Renaissance: 20, Boulevard St-Martin (10th) ♦ The Théâtre de la Renaissance is a member of the Association of Private Theaters; 707 seats ♦ The theater was built in 1872 by the architect Lalande ♦ Sculpted façade by Carrier-Belleuse. Italian-style auditorium ♦ Main successes: Musset's *Lorenzaccio*, *La Parisienne* by H Becque, Rostand's *La Samaritaine*, *La Châtelaine* by A Capus, *La Célestine* and *Les Séquestrés d'Altona* by Sartre ♦ Directors have included: Sarah Bernhardt from 1893 to 1899, F Gémier, L Guitry, and Niels Arestrup.

Rond-Point: 2 *bis*, Avenue Franklin-Roosevelt (8th) ♦ The Théâtre du Rond-Point has two auditoriums: Renault-Barrault, 760 seats; Jean Vauthier, 170 seats ♦ Circular building constructed by Daviuod in 1855; the interior was remodeled at the beginning of the 1990s ♦ The theater is located in the former Palais de Glace (Ice Palace), which contained a Panorama under Napoléon III; it was opened in 1981 ♦ Directors have included: J-L Barrault and M Maréchal.

St-Georges: 51, Rue St-Georges (9th) ♦ The Théâtre St-Georges is a member of the Association of Private Theaters, 492 seats ♦ The building dates from 1907. Its sober trompe-l'œil façade is brightly lit in the evening before the shows ♦ Productions: *Mademoiselle* by Jacques Deval, Montherlant's *Nobody's Son*, *Patate* by Marcel Achard, *Tchao* by Marc-Gilbert Sauvageon with Pierre Brasseur, plays by Maria Pacôme, and Anouilh's *The Goldfish* were produced there ♦ Directors have included: F Delahalle and M-F Mignal.

Silvia Monfort: 106, Rue Brancion (15th) ♦ The Théâtre Silvia Monfort is a municipal theater with 415 seats ♦ Built from 1990 by Claude Parent ♦ Building in the form of a metal pyramid ♦ Founded at the initiative of the City of Paris, and opened in January, 1992 ♦ Initially, Silvia Monfort had started a marquee theater in the former abattoirs at Vaugirard. She put on the French première of *Zarathustra*, and numerous classic plays: *Bajazet*, *Iphigénie*, and *Britannicus*, and Aeschylus's *The Persians* ♦ Director: R Santon.

Soleil: see Cartoucherie.

Théâtre-Français: see Comédie-Française.

Tristan Bernard: 64, Rue du Rocher (8th) ♦ The Théâtre Tristan Bernard is a member of the Association of Private Theaters; 400 seats ♦ Once the hall of a private school for Belgian girls, this became the Théâtre Tristan Bernard when he became its director at the beginning of the 1930 ♦ Its great successes have been: *Frenzy* by Peyret-Chapius, *The Third Witness* by D Nohain and, more recently, *André le Magnifique* ♦ Directors have included: T Bernard, Ch de Rochefort, M Grant, D Nohain, and E Saiovici.

Variétés: 7, Boulevard Montmartre (2nd) ♦ The Théâtre des Variétés is a listed theater, and a member of the Association of Private Theaters; 920 seats ♦ Built in 1807, in the style of a Greek temple ♦ Around 1830 it was a meeting place for artists and writers ♦ Frédérick Lemaître put on the first production of *Kean* by Alexandre Dumas there; *La Vie de Bohême* was first performed in 1849; comic opera triumphed there thanks to Offenbach (*La Belle Hélène*, *Bluebeard*, and *La Grande Duchesse* with Hortense Schneider); at the end of the 19th century, the repertoire consisted mainly of variety shows and comic plays by R de Flers and G de Caillavet; today the type of plays known as "boulevard theater" are put on there ♦ Directors have included: H Cogniard, E Bertrand, F Samuel, and J-P Belmondo.

Vieux-Colombier: 21, Rue du Vieux-Colombier (6th) ♦ 300 seats ♦ The Théâtre du Vieux-Colombier is a national theater belonging to the Comédie-Française, which performs its contemporary repertoire there ♦ Founded in 1913 by Jacques Copeau in the former hall of the Athénée-Saint-Germain, it was bought by the State in 1986; it reopened in 1993 ♦ Others apart from Copeau who won renown there were Jouvet, Vilar (*Murder in the Cathedral*), the Jacques Fabbri Company, and Roger Planchon. Plays by Molière, Claudel, Shakespeare, Sartre (first production of *Huis Clos*), Schiller, Adamov, and Audiberti were performed there.

Ville-Sarah Bernhardt: Place du Châtelet (4th) ♦ The Théâtre de la Ville-Sarah Bernhardt is a municipal theater with 1,000 seats ♦ Built and opened in 1862 ♦ It still has its original arcaded façade, which hides the modern, reinforced concrete interior; movable stage ♦ The Théâtre Lyrique (as it was called when it was founded) became the Théâtre des Nations in 1879, then was handed over to Sarah Bernhardt, who created the Aiglon there and stayed until her death in 1923; in 1957 it once again became known as the Théâtre des Nations, before taking on its current name in 1968, when the interior was entirely rebuilt. It is now given over to modern plays ♦ Some of the plays performed here have been: *La Dame aux Camélias*, *Athalie* (Sarah Bernhardt), *Those Ladies in Green Hats*, and *The Flies* ♦ Directors have included: S Bernhardt, Charles Dullin, Jean Mercure, and Gérard Violette.

Zoos

Ménagerie du Jardin des Plantes: 57, Rue Cuvier (5th) ♦ This is one of the oldest zoological gardens in the world ♦ The 14 acre (5.5 ha) park houses a large number of animals in 19th- and early 20th-century buildings: ♦ The zoo was officially founded in December, 1794. The collection was built around animals requisitioned from fairgrounds and the menageries of Versailles and the Duc d'Orléans. Napoléon I commissioned its earliest buildings, including the bear pit, which was started in 1805. ♦ In the 1980s, new animal houses were constructed, and major renovations carried out.

Parc Zoologique de Vincennes: 153, Avenue de St-Maurice (12th) ♦ This zoo belongs to the National Museum of Natural History ♦ The triangular, 37 acre (15 ha) park is laid out around Lac Daumesnil, in an area containing much greenery and other lakes; it has a collection of about 1,200 animals, which enjoy semi-freedom ♦ Its foundation dates from the presentation of a zoological park to the Colonial Exhibition of 1931 ♦ The cages and office premises are hidden by imitation rocks made from wire mesh and reinforced concrete; in the center are ponds and islands; there are three belvederes. The animals are cut off by ditches, which give visitors a better view. At the northern entrance, a large rock is occupied mainly by mountain animals; it also contains water tanks ♦ The zoo had to be closed in 1982 because had become dilapidated; it was restored, then reopened in the mid-1990s ♦ Its mission is to study and conserve animals; endangered species are bred there, then returned to nature; 100 giraffes have been born at the zoo since it opened ♦ Workshops for children.

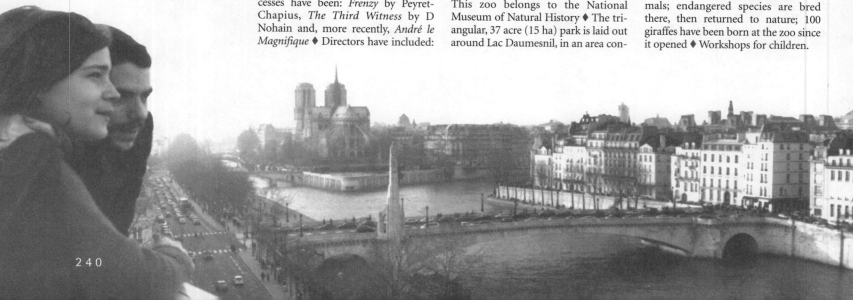

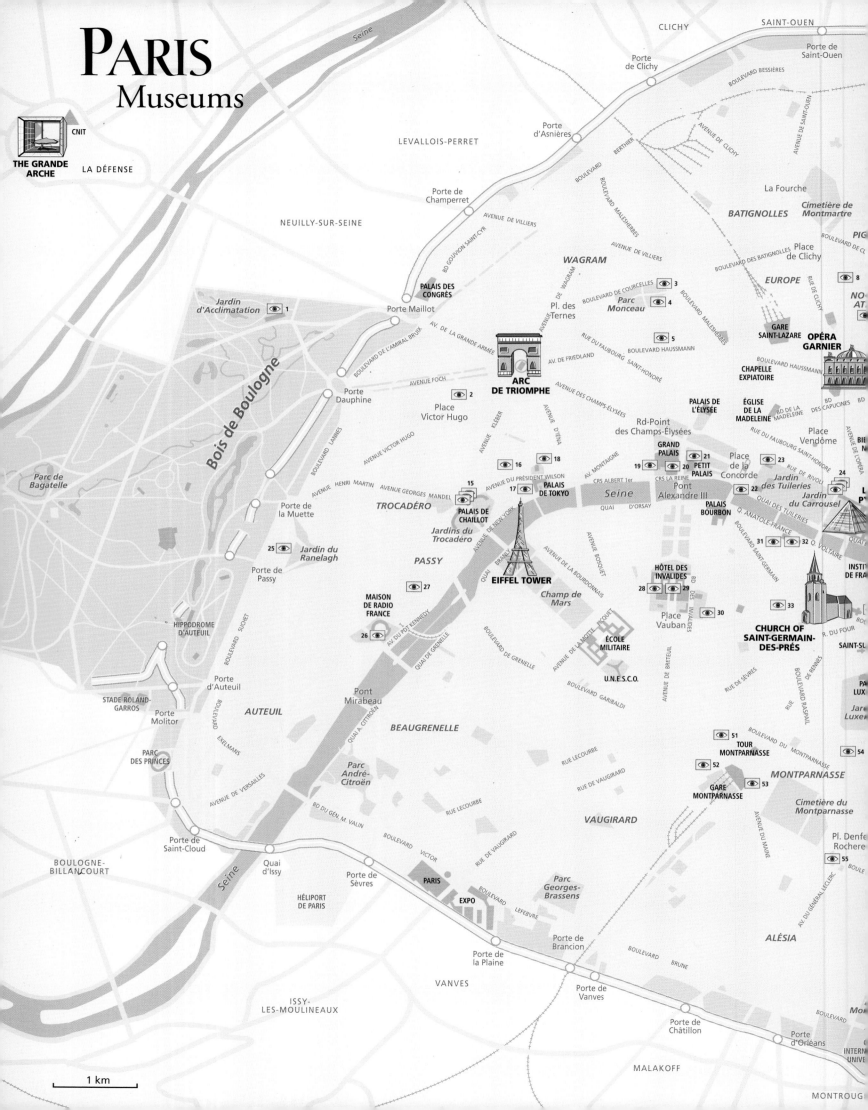

Paris
Museums

THE GRANDE ARCHE CNIT

LA DÉFENSE

SAINT-OUEN

CLICHY

Porte de Saint-Ouen

Porte de Clichy

LEVALLOIS-PERRET

Porte d'Asnières

AVENUE DE SAINT-OUEN

AVENUE DE CLICHY

La Fourche

BATIGNOLLES

Cimetière de Montmartre

PIG

NEUILLY-SUR-SEINE

Porte de Champerret

AVENUE DE VILLIERS

BD GOUVION SAINT-CYR

AVENUE DE VILLIERS

WAGRAM

BOULEVARD MALESHERBES

BOULEVARD DES BATIGNOLLES

Place de Clichy

EUROPE

RUE DE CLICHY

BOULEVARD DE CL

👁 8

NO AT

PALAIS DES CONGRÈS

Porte Maillot

AV. DE LA GRANDE ARMÉE

AVENUE DE WAGRAM

Pl. des Ternes

BOULEVARD DE COURCELLES

Parc Monceau

👁 3

👁 4

BOULEVARD MALESHERBES

GARE SAINT-LAZARE

OPÉRA GARNIER

Jardin d'Acclimatation 👁 1

RUE DU FAUBOURG SAINT-HONORÉ

BOULEVARD HAUSSMANN

👁 5

BOULEVARD HAUSSMANN

CHAPELLE EXPIATOIRE

Bois de Boulogne

Porte Dauphine

AVENUE FOCH

ARC DE TRIOMPHE

AV. DE FRIEDLAND

AVENUE DES CHAMPS-ÉLYSÉES

PALAIS DE L'ÉLYSÉE

ÉGLISE DE LA MADELEINE

BD DE LA MADELEINE

BD DES CAPUCINES

BD

👁 2

Place Victor Hugo

AVENUE KLÉBER

AVENUE D'IÉNA

Rd-Point des Champs-Élysées

RUE DU FAUBOURG SAINT-HONORÉ

Place Vendôme

AVENUE DE L'OPÉRA

BIE N

BOULEVARD LANNES

AVENUE VICTOR HUGO

👁 16

👁 18

AV. MONTAIGNE

GRAND PALAIS

👁 21

PETIT PALAIS

👁 23

RUE DE RIVOLI

👁 24

L P

Porte de la Muette

AVENUE HENRI MARTIN

AVENUE GEORGES MANDEL

AVENUE DU PRÉSIDENT WILSON

👁 17

PALAIS DE TOKYO

Seine

19 👁

👁 20

Place de la Concorde

Jardin des Tuileries

👁 22

Jardin du Carrousel

TROCADÉRO

15

PALAIS DE CHAILLOT

Pont Alexandre III

CRS ALBERT 1er

CRS LA REINE

BOULEVARD SAINT-GERMAIN

Q. ANATOLE-FRANCE

QUAI DES TUILERIES

👁 31 👁 32 Q. VOLTAIRE

QUA

Jardins du Trocadéro

QUAI D'ORSAY

PALAIS BOURBON

INSTI DE FRA

Jardin du Ranelagh

👁 25

PASSY

AVENUE DE NEW-YORK

BRANLY

EIFFEL TOWER

AVENUE DE LA BOURDONNAIS

BD DES INVALIDES

HÔTEL DES INVALIDES

👁 28 👁 29

👁 33

CHURCH OF SAINT-GERMAIN-DES-PRÉS

Porte de Passy

👁 27

Champ de Mars

AVENUE DE LA MOTTE-PICQUET

Place Vauban

👁 30

R. DU FOUR

SAINT-S

HIPPODROME D'AUTEUIL

BOULEVARD SUCHET

MAISON DE RADIO FRANCE

AV. DU PDT KENNEDY

AVENUE BOSQUET

ÉCOLE MILITAIRE

AVENUE DE BRETEUIL

RUE DE SÈVRES

BOULEVARD RASPAIL

PA LUX

👁 26

QUAI DE GRENELLE

U.N.E.S.C.O.

Jar Luxe

Parc de Bagatelle

Parc de Bagatelle

BOULEVARD EXELMANS

Pont Mirabeau

BOULEVARD DE GRENELLE

BOULEVARD GARIBALDI

RUE DE VAUGIRARD

BOULEVARD DU MONTPARNASSE

👁 51

👁 54

STADE ROLAND-GARROS

Porte d'Auteuil

Porte Molitor

AUTEUIL

BEAUGRENELLE

QUAI A. CITROËN

RUE LECOURBE

TOUR MONTPARNASSE

👁 52

MONTPARNASSE

PARC DES PRINCES

Parc André-Citroën

RUE LECOURBE

RUE DE VAUGIRARD

GARE MONTPARNASSE

👁 53

AVENUE DE VERSAILLES

BD DU GÉN. M. VALIN

RUE DE VAUGIRARD

VAUGIRARD

AVENUE DU MAINE

Cimetière du Montparnasse

Porte de Saint-Cloud

Quai d'Issy

Porte de Sèvres

PARIS

BOULEVARD VICTOR

Parc Georges-Brassens

Pl. Denfer Rochere

👁 55

BOULE

BOULOGNE-BILLANCOURT

HÉLIPORT DE PARIS

Porte de Brancion

AV. DU GÉNÉRAL LECLERC

ALÉSIA

ISSY-LES-MOULINEAUX

EXPO

BOULEVARD LEFEBVRE

Porte de la Plaine

VANVES

Porte de Vanves

BOULEVARD BRUNE

Mo

Porte de Châtillon

INTERM UNIV

Porte d'Orléans

1 km

MALAKOFF

MONTROUG

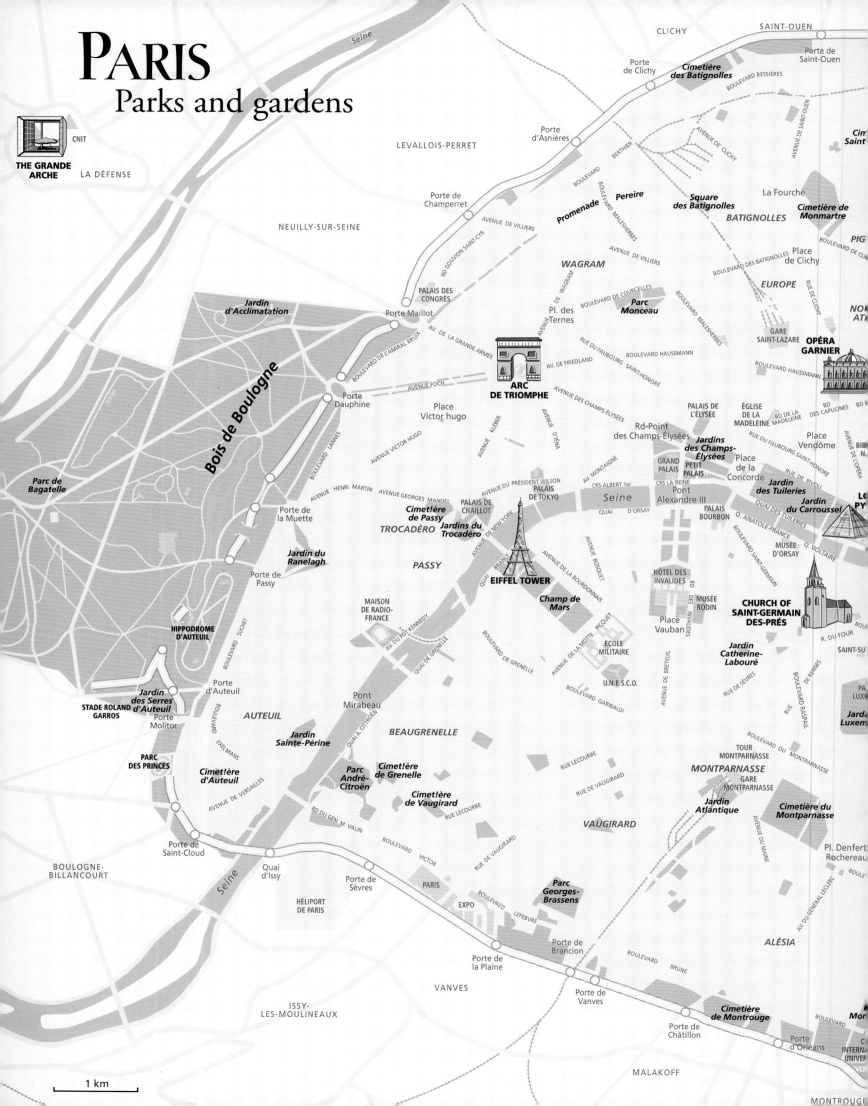

PARIS
Parks and gardens

CNIT

THE GRANDE ARCHE   LA DÉFENSE

SAINT-OUEN

CLICHY

Seine

Porte de Clichy

Porte de Saint-Ouen

Cimetière des Batignolles

BOULEVARD BESSIÈRES

AVENUE DE SAINT-OUEN

Porte d'Asnières

LEVALLOIS-PERRET

Porte de Champerret

NEUILLY-SUR-SEINE

BOULEVARD

AVENUE DE VILLIERS

BD GOUVION SAINT-CYR

BERTHIER

AVENUE DE CLICHY

Porte Maillot

PALAIS DES CONGRÈS

Promenade Pereire

BOULEVARD MALESHERBES

La Fourche

Square des Batignolles

Cimetière de Monmartre

BOULEVARD DE CLI

PIG

AT

Jardin d'Acclimatation

AVENUE DE VILLIERS

WAGRAM

AVENUE DE WAGRAM

Pl. des Ternes

BOULEVARD DE COURCELLES

Parc Monceau

BOULEVARD MALESHERBES

GARE SAINT-LAZARE

Place de Clichy

EUROPE

RUE DE CLICHY

OPÉRA GARNIER

NOU ATI

AV. DE LA GRANDE ARMÉE

ARC DE TRIOMPHE

AVENUE FOCH

Porte Dauphine

BOULEVARD DE L'AMIRAL BRUIX

AV. DE FRIEDLAND

RUE DU FAUBOURG SAINT-HONORÉ

BOULEVARD HAUSSMANN

AV. DES CHAMPS-ÉLYSÉES

BOULEVARD HAUSSMANN

BD DES CAPUCINES

BD DE LA MADELEINE

RUE DE L'OPÉRA

BIB NA

Bois de Boulogne

Place Victor hugo

AVENUE KLEBER

AVENUE D'IÉNA

PALAIS DE L'ÉLYSÉE

Rd-Point des Champs-Élysées

Jardins des Champs-Élysées

ÉGLISE DE LA MADELEINE

Place Vendôme

Place de la Concorde

RUE DE RIVOLI

Parc de Bagatelle

BOULEVARD LANNES

AVENUE VICTOR HUGO

AVENUE HENRI MARTIN

AVENUE GEORGES MANDEL

AV. MONTAIGNE

GRAND PALAIS

PETIT PALAIS

Jardin des Tuileries

Jardin du Carrousel

LO PY

Porte de la Muette

AVENUE DU PRÉSIDENT WILSON

PALAIS DE CHAILLOT

PALAIS DE TOKYO

AV. CRS ALBERT 1er

CRS LA REINE

Seine

QUAI D'ORSAY

Pont Alexandre III

QUAI DES TUILERIES

MUSÉE D'ORSAY

Q. VOLTAIRE

Cimetière de Passy

TROCADÉRO

Jardins du Trocadéro

PALAIS BOURBON

Q. ANATOLE-FRANCE

Q. VOLTAIRE

Jardin du Ranelagh

Porte de Passy

PASSY

AVENUE DE NEW YORK

QUAI BRANLY

EIFFEL TOWER

AVENUE DE LA BOURDONNAIS

AVENUE BOSQUET

HÔTEL DES INVALIDES

BD DES INVALIDES

MUSÉE RODIN

BOULEVARD SAINT-GERMAIN

CHURCH OF SAINT-GERMAIN DES-PRÉS

HIPPODROME D'AUTEUIL

BOULEVARD SUCHET

MAISON DE RADIO-FRANCE

Champ de Mars

AVENUE DE LA MOTTE PICQUET

ÉCOLE MILITAIRE

Place Vauban

AVENUE DE BRETEUIL

Jardin Catherine-Labouré

R. DU FOUR

SAINT-SU

Jardin des Serres d'Auteuil

STADE ROLAND GARROS

Porte d'Auteuil

Porte Molitor

AV. DU PDT KENNEDY

QUAI DE GRENELLE

BOULEVARD DE GRENELLE

U.N.E.S.C.O.

BOULEVARD GARIBALDI

RUE DE SÈVRES

BOULEVARD RASPAIL

RUE DE RENNES

PA LUX

Jard Luxem

PARC DES PRINCES

AUTEUIL

BOULEVARD EXELMANS

Pont Mirabeau

QUAI A. CITROËN

Jardin Sainte-Périne

BEAUGRENELLE

RUE LECOURBE

RUE DE VAUGIRARD

BOULEVARD DU MONTPARNASSE

TOUR MONTPARNASSE

MONTPARNASSE

Cimetière d'Auteuil

AVENUE DE VERSAILLES

Parc André-Citroën

Cimetière de Grenelle

Cimetière de Vaugirard

RUE LECOURBE

GARE MONTPARNASSE

Jardin Atlantique

Cimetière du Montparnasse

AVENUE DU MAINE

BD DU GÉN. M. VALIN

BOULEVARD VICTOR

RUE DE VAUGIRARD

VAUGIRARD

Pl. Denfert Rocherea

Porte de Saint-Cloud

BOULOGNE-BILLANCOURT

Quai d'Issy

Seine

Porte de Sèvres

HÉLIPORT DE PARIS

PARIS

EXPO

BOULEVARD LEFEBVRE

Parc Georges-Brassens

ALÉSIA

BOULEVARD BRUNE

AV. DU GÉNÉRAL LECLERC

Mor

Porte de Brancion

Porte de la Plaine

VANVES

Porte de Vanves

Porte de Châtillon

Cimetière de Montrouge

BOULEVARD

INTERN UNIVE

ISSY-LES-MOULINEAUX

Porte d'Orléans

MALAKOFF

MONTROUGE

1 km

PARIS
Places of entertainment

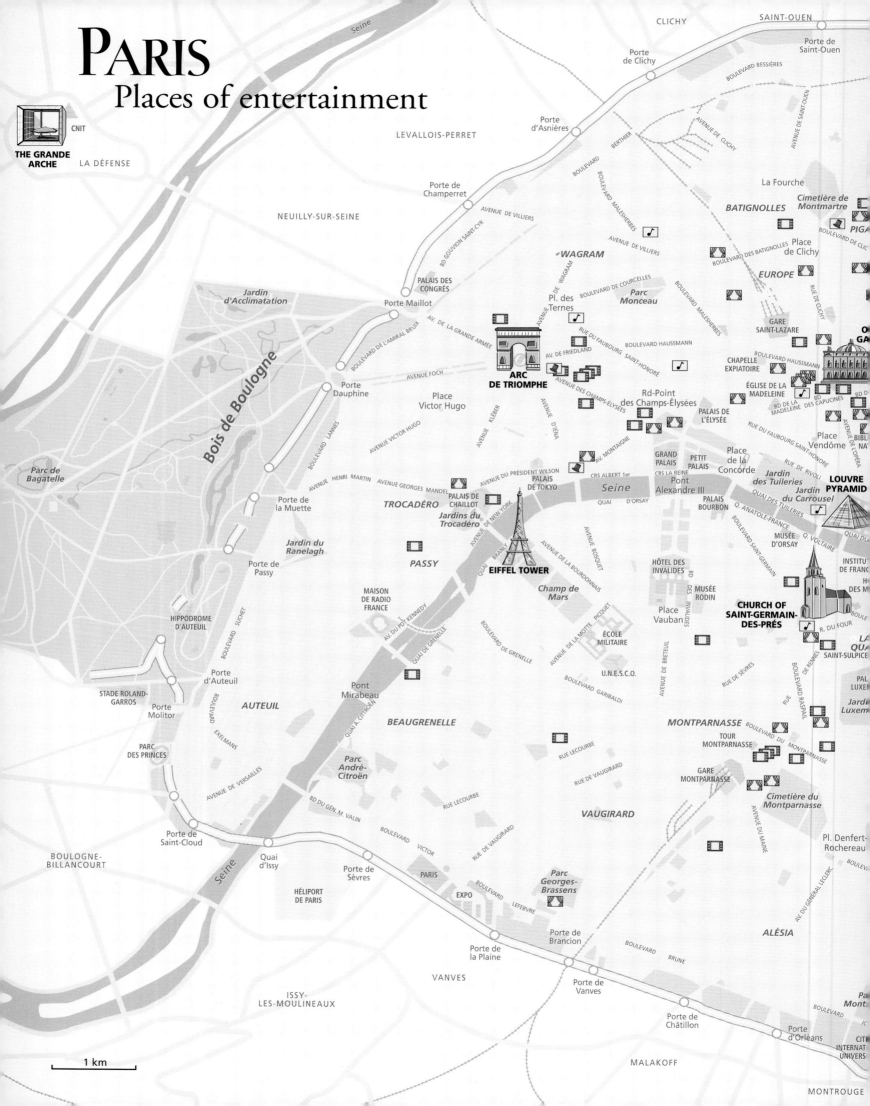

THE GRANDE ARCHE — CNIT — LA DÉFENSE

LA DÉFENSE

SAINT-OUEN

CLICHY

Porte de Saint-Ouen

Porte de Clichy

BOULEVARD BESSIÈRES

Porte d'Asnières

LEVALLOIS-PERRET

AVENUE DE SAINT-OUEN

La Fourche

BATIGNOLLES

Cimetière de Montmartre

PIGA

Porte de Champerret

NEUILLY-SUR-SEINE

AVENUE DE VILLIERS

BD GOUVION SAINT-CYR

AVENUE DE VILLIERS

WAGRAM

BOULEVARD MALESHERBES

BOULEVARD DES BATIGNOLLES

Place de Clichy

BOULEVARD DE CLIC

EUROPE

Jardin d'Acclimatation

PALAIS DES CONGRÈS

Porte Maillot

AVENUE DE LA GRANDE ARMÉE

AVENUE DE WAGRAM

Pl. des Ternes

BOULEVARD DE COURCELLES

Parc Monceau

BOULEVARD MALESHERBES

GARE SAINT-LAZARE

RUE DE CLICHY

O GA

ARC DE TRIOMPHE

RUE DU FAUBOURG SAINT-HONORÉ

AV. DE FRIEDLAND

BOULEVARD HAUSSMANN

CHAPELLE EXPIATOIRE

BOULEVARD HAUSSMANN

BOULEVARD DE L'AMIRAL BRUIX

AVENUE FOCH

Porte Dauphine

AV. DES CHAMPS-ÉLYSÉES

ÉGLISE DE LA MADELEINE

BD DE LA MADELEINE DES CAPUCINES

BD D

Bois de Boulogne

BOULEVARD LANNES

Place Victor Hugo

AVENUE KLÉBER

AVENUE D'IÉNA

Rd-Point des Champs-Élysées

PALAIS DE L'ÉLYSÉE

RUE DU FAUBOURG SAINT-HONORÉ

Place Vendôme

BIBL NA

AVENUE DE L'OPÉRA

LOUVRE PYRAMID

Parc de Bagatelle

AVENUE VICTOR HUGO

AVENUE HENRI MARTIN

AVENUE GEORGES MANDEL

AVENUE DU PRÉSIDENT WILSON

AV. MONTAIGNE

GRAND PALAIS

PETIT PALAIS

Place de la Concorde

Jardin des Tuileries

RUE DE RIVOLI

Porte de la Muette

TROCADÉRO

PALAIS DE CHAILLOT

PALAIS DE TOKYO

CRS ALBERT 1er

CRS LA REINE

Pont Alexandre III

Jardin du Carrousel

Q. ANATOLE-FRANCE

MUSÉE D'ORSAY

Jardin du Ranelagh

Jardins du Trocadéro

AVENUE DE NEW YORK

Seine

QUAI D'ORSAY

PALAIS BOURBON

BOULEVARD SAINT-GERMAIN

Q. VOLTAIRE

QUAI DU

Porte de Passy

PASSY

QUAI BRANLY

EIFFEL TOWER

AVENUE DE LA BOURDONNAIS

HÔTEL DES INVALIDES

MUSÉE RODIN

INSTITUT DE FRANC

HÔ DES M

MAISON DE RADIO FRANCE

AV. DU PDT KENNEDY

Champ de Mars

AVENUE BOSQUET

BD DES INVALIDES

CHURCH OF SAINT-GERMAIN-DES-PRÉS

R. DU FOUR

LA QUA SAINT-SULPICE

HIPPODROME D'AUTEUIL

BOULEVARD SUCHET

Place Vauban

AVENUE DE LA MOTTE-PICQUET

ÉCOLE MILITAIRE

RUE DE RENNES

BOULEVARD RASPAIL

PAL LUXEM

Jard Luxem

Porte d'Auteuil

QUAI DE GRENELLE

BOULEVARD DE GRENELLE

AVENUE DE BRETEUIL

RUE DE SÈVRES

STADE ROLAND-GARROS

Porte Molitor

AUTEUIL

BOULEVARD EXELMANS

Pont Mirabeau

BEAUGRENELLE

U.N.E.S.C.O.

BOULEVARD GARIBALDI

MONTPARNASSE

BOULEVARD DU MONTPARNASSE

PARC DES PRINCES

QUAI A. CITROËN

RUE LECOURBE

TOUR MONTPARNASSE

BOULEVARD DU MONTPARNASSE

Porte de Saint-Cloud

AVENUE DE VERSAILLES

Parc André-Citroën

RUE LECOURBE

RUE DE VAUGIRARD

GARE MONTPARNASSE

AVENUE DU MAINE

Cimetière du Montparnasse

BD DU GÉN. M. VALIN

RUE DE VAUGIRARD

VAUGIRARD

BOULOGNE-BILLANCOURT

Quai d'Issy

Porte de Sèvres

PARIS

BOULEVARD VICTOR

RUE DE VAUGIRARD

Pl. Denfert-Rochereau

BOULEV

HÉLIPORT DE PARIS

EXPO

BOULEVARD LEFEBVRE

Parc Georges-Brassens

AVENUE DU GÉNÉRAL LECLERC

ALÉSIA

Porte de Brancion

BOULEVARD BRUNE

Pa Mont

Porte de la Plaine

BOULEVARD

VANVES

ISSY-LES-MOULINEAUX

Seine

Porte de Vanves

Porte de Châtillon

Porte d'Orléans

CIT INTERNAT UNIVERS

MALAKOFF

MONTROUGE

1 km

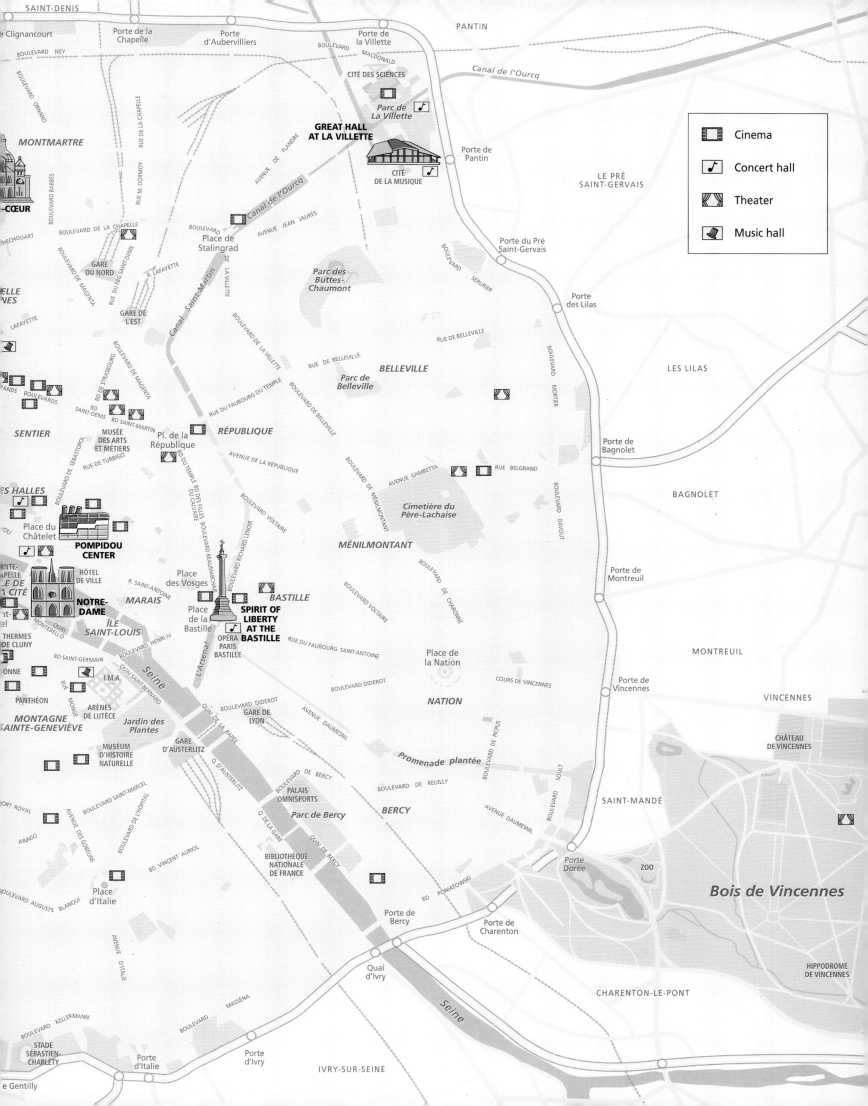

IN THE HEART OF THE CITY

IN THE STREETS OF PARIS

ROOFS

For a long time, attics were where the poorest accommodation was to be found, but now they are highly prized for their spectacular views of the city. After the first roof terraces appeared at the beginning of the 20th century, almost all the apartment buildings in Paris acquired roofs covered in zinc.

Roofs and roofing

The ubiquitous zinc cladding on the rooftops of Paris is a fairly recent phenomenon which began in the 19th century. At that time, the population was constantly growing, and the need for housing was crucial. Residential properties were built with the principal aim of accommodating a large number of people at the lowest possible cost. Zinc, being easy to lay, cheap, and weather-resistant, was the ideal material.

In ancient times, roofs made of tiles in the Italian style were the most common, for example those at the Baths of Cluny (now the Museum of the Middle Ages). In Medieval times, some roofs were covered in shingles, while grander buildings, such as churches, were covered in slate. Only a few buildings were protected by lead, such as as the Sainte-Chapelle and Notre-Dame.

In the 17th and 18th centuries, slate was used for palaces, mansions, and religious buildings. Many apartment buildings in Paris had red tiles. Mansard roofs appeared around the middle of the 16th century, and this style was used for many buildings. In 1551, Pierre Lescot used them at the Louvre. They are named for François Mansart, who often used them in his buildings.

Shivering in a garret

Up to the end of the 19th century, rooms in the garrets or attics were too cold in winter and too hot in summer, and were used by domestic servants and the poorest people. They were known as "maids' rooms." In his *Mysteries of Paris* (1842-3), Eugène Sue compared the various stories of buildings with the social positions of their occupants. The second story was for the middle-class businessman, the third was for the moneylender, the fourth for the working man and his family, while the *grisette*, the typical working-class girl, lived alone in the attic. Emile Zola described life on the top story in *Pot-Bouille* (1882), with its "icy cold coming through the zinc on the roof. It was bare, clean, with that sickly smell you get in poor people's lodgings."

Elevators were invented in about 1870, and in 1905 there was a complete turnaround when their use became widespread. The plans of a mansion on Quai d'Auteuil show how the social distribution had been turned completely upside down. The staff lived on the lower stories while the luxurious apartments were at the top of the building.

Roof terraces and hanging gardens

The taste of Parisians for rooftop living is a new phenomenon, deriving from technological and architectural innovations of the late 19th century, which were then developed in the 20th century. Chief of these were the elevator and the roof terrace.

One of the first roof terraces was built in 1908 for the Crédit Lyonnais bank (No 6, Rue Ménars, 2nd *arrondissement*). This was a 7,500 sq ft (700 sq m) hanging garden for the exclusive use of women employees. In 1927, another breakthrough came when Le

1. View down over rooftops
Zinc roofs have been part of the Paris scene since the second half of the 19th century. Inexpensive and weatherproof, zinc was used to cover the attics of residential properties. Even today, it is still widely in use.

2. Mansard roofs
Mansard roofs were introduced in 1551 by Pierre Lescot at the Louvre, and proved widely successful.

In the Haussmann period, they were an integral part of the city's large apartment buildings.

3. *The Delivery Men* (Jean Girault)
In this 1961 film, Francis Blanche and Danny Cowl play two delivery men who work at La Samaritaine, and happily scale the rooftops in the course of their rounds.

4. Panoramic view of Paris with the dome of the Panthéon
From a landscape filled with rooftops, certain great buildings stand out, like the dome of the Panthéon shown here, and provide landmarks for people scanning the Paris skyline.

Corbusier published his *Five Points Toward a New Architecture*. There he described a new type of elevation which placed great value on the roof terrace. Architects were quick to follow his lead, as can be seen in the Rue Mallet-Stevens in the 16th arrondissement, which has five mansions dating from 1927-9.

Exceptional views

Discovering Paris from the rooftops is not a new idea. In the 17th century, authors such as Saint-Maurice and Germain Brice noted good, accessible places where the whole of the city could be viewed.

Today, many buildings provide such views. The main department stores have roof terraces, and some, such as La Samaritaine, provide an orientation map. A restaurant, the Toupary, has unrestricted views and is similarly equipped.

Rooftops are also used for scientific activities, including several observatories. The largest is the Paris Observatory, built in the 17th century, which in the 19th century was rivaled by the one in the old École Polytechnique, Rue Descartes.

by them. Georges Caillebote, the painter and great patron of the arts, painted them several times. In 1930, René Clair filmed *Sous les Toits de Paris*, with its opening shot sweeping across the roofs of the city before going down to the street. In *Un Monde sans Pitié*, made in 1989, director Eric Rochaut had his characters crossing from one roof to the next.

More recently, roofs have been used for new museums. For example, the roof of the Grande Arche at La Défense is a work of contemporary sculptor Jean-Pierre Raynaud.

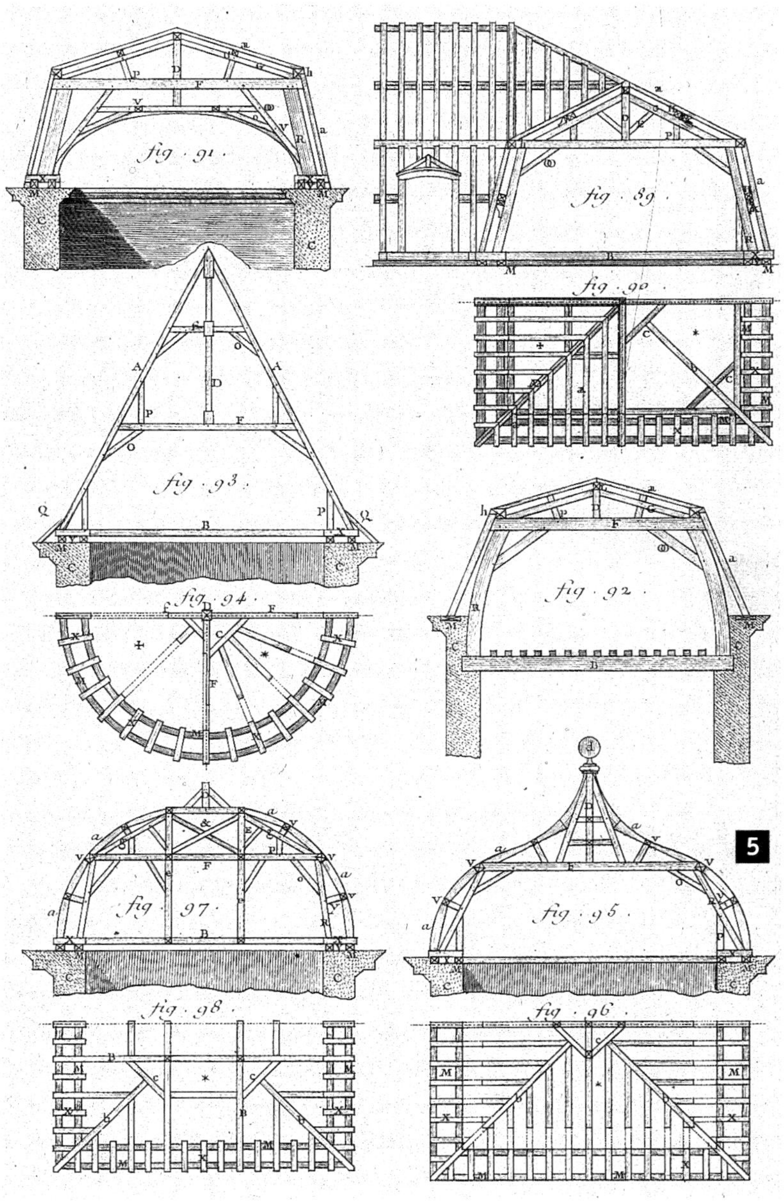

Inspiring artists

Rooftops are always fascinating because they are such an unknown aspect of the city. Many artists have been inspired

fig. 91.
fig. 89.
fig. 90.
fig. 93.
fig. 94.
fig. 92.
fig. 97.
fig. 95.
fig. 98.
fig. 96.

5. Plate from the *Encyclopédie*
This plate from Diderot's *Encyclopédie* shows the great diversity of roof types in the 18th century.

6. Roof in red tiles
It is unusual to find roofs covered with red tiles in Paris. Tiles are mainly used for individual houses and small apartment buildings.

7. Roof-terrace
Roof-terraces have been very fashionable since they appeared in Paris in the late 1920s, after Le Corbusier had advocated them.

1. Medieval houses
Like these examples at Nos 11 and 13, Rue François Miron, in the Marais, houses in the Middle Ages were made of wood; stone was reserved for the most opulent buildings.

2. Hôtel de Sens
Built between 1474 and 1507 by the Bishop of Sens, this mansion combines defensive features taken from Medieval castles and a few modest Renaissance decorations confined to some of the windows.

3. Place des Vosges
This square was designed under Henri IV and opened in 1611 on the occasion of Louis XIII's betrothal. The 36 mansions surrounding the square were built of brick and stone in a style popular at the beginning of the 17th century. The stone was used for the structure and the brick as infill.

HOUSES, MANSIONS, AND APARTMENT BUILDINGS

In the course of time, the city's stock of private houses has been the main element in its growth and development. Although the earliest types are no longer in existence, those which have survived provide a historical overview of the entire city, its inhabitants, and their way of life. These houses, apartments, and mansions form the framework of the Parisian landscape.

The oldest houses: 15th-16th centuries

In the Middle Ages, the size of the streets and houses was influenced by the presence of ramparts enclosing the city. The winding alleyways were just wide enough for the pedestrians and teams of animals that used them. The lack of space dictated the size of the dwellings, which were tall and narrow to save space on the ground.

The houses at Nos 11 and 13, Rue François Miron, in the Marais, are typical late-Medieval dwellings, with half-timbered façades and gabled roofs. There were stores at street level, and living quarters in the upper, overhanging stories.

Fires were constantly destroying these wooden houses. To overcome this scourge, visible beams and overhanging stories were forbidden in the 16th century, and the façades were coated with plaster. Gables tended to produce leaks in the walls, so they disappeared and were replaced by roofs with ridges parallel to the street.

Birth of the mansion: 15th-16th centuries

In the Middle Ages, the term *hôtel particulier* (mansion) was used to describe the town house of the king, lord, or prelate. The Hôtels de Sens and de Cluny are the oldest aristocratic dwellings in the capital. Located at No 1, Rue du Figuier and No 6, Place Paul Painlevé respectively, they now house the Forney Library and the National Museum of the Middle Ages. Although basically derived from the Medieval château, they contain many new features. For example, the Hôtel de Cluny, built at the end of the 15th century, consists of a dwelling standing between a courtyard and a garden. This form of layout was to prove very popular, and was adopted for several mansions built in the Marais at the end of the 16th century, like the Hôtel de Donon (today the Musée Cognacq-Jay) at No 8, Rue Elzévir.

Brick and stone at the beginning of the 17th century

Henri IV was the driving force behind an unprecedented program of building works: squares, bridges, hospitals, and markets were built to modernize

5. Hôtel de Sully
The Hôtel de Sully was built in the reign of Louis XIII, probably by Baptiste Androuet du Cerceau. The original plan (1625) was for a façade in brick and stone, but this was abandoned. This is a typical mansion set between a courtyard and a garden. The entrance courtyard is richly decorated, announcing the wealth and social rank of the owner.

4. Vaulted staircase at the Hôtel de Mayenne
The Hôtel de Mayenne was built in 1606, when brick and stone were widely used. The stone was used for the building's framework, the pillars and vaults, while brick was used for the non-load bearing parts.

the capital. The houses of the nobility were now built in a new style, using brick and stone. Stone was used for the structure of the building, the window frames, and corners, as can be seen in the Place Dauphine (on the Ile de la Cité, between the Palais de Justice and Pont Neuf) and Place Royale (now Place des Vosges). They represented a new concept in house-building, in which space and light played essential roles. Brick and stone continued to be used for the mansions of the Louis XIII period, then quickly went out of fashion.

Evolution of the classic mansion

At the end of the 17th century, after a slow process of evolution, the mansions' principal characteristics became fixed. They were designed to suit the aristocratic way of life, responding to their owners' need to entertain guests away from the noise and bustle of the city. The main building usually stood between a courtyard and a garden, as at the Hôtel de Sully, No 62, Rue Saint-Antoine. The courtyard led to the street, and was where all visitors entered and left. Behind the house, the garden was a more private space, the preserve of the master of the house and his guests. In the most opulent types, there was a second courtyard, known as the servants' yard, next to the kitchens and outbuildings, where the servants could do their work without disturbing their master.

Mansions adapt to their location: 18th century

While the traditional type, built "between courtyard and garden," was the most widely adopted mansion form until the end of the 18th century, their layout could nevertheless be modified to suit the land they stood on. On the Ile Saint-Louis, the residential part of many mansions was built next to the quayside and looked out on the Seine. In the 18th century, the Marais went out of fashion and was supplanted by Saint-Germain. In this new suburb, the mansions mostly followed the edicts of the 17th century, though the decorative style was sometimes different. At the Hôtel Matignon (No 57, Rue de Varenne), today the Prime Minister's residence, the sober façades are very sparsely decorated. The splendors of these houses are displayed not on the external walls but in the interior decoration (Hôtel de Soubise, No 60, Rue des Francs-Bourgeois, now the National Archives).

Middle-class houses and apartments: 17th and 18th centuries

Houses with narrow fronts covered in plaster were built throughout the 17th

6. Cross-section of a mansion
Mansions in the 17th and 18th centuries had rectangular or square rooms, laid out in a similar way on the ground floor and second story. This simple pattern concealed some complex social arrangements, the rooms being divided into a number of separate apartments for the master and lady of the house. The building usually had three stories and a mansard roof (much used by the architect Mansart).

1

2

1. Rue de Lille
In the Regency period after the reign of Louis XIV, the court returned to Paris from Versailles. Many mansions were built, particularly in the Faubourg Saint-Germain. While the façades were fairly modest, the portals were decorated in an even more spectacular style than in the previous period.

and 18th centuries. You can see them in the central districts, in Les Halles, and particularly around the Fontaine des Innocents. Near these houses, beside the street, are luxury apartment buildings made of freestone for the wealthy middle class. The ground floor is usually occupied by one or two stores. The apartments are on the upper stories, with one part of the building often reserved for rented accommodation. External decoration is often limited to the carriage entrances and the ironwork.

First rented apartment buildings

At the end of the 17th century, the multi-occupant apartment building made its appearance in Les Halles, at Nos 2-12, Rue de la Ferronnerie. In the second half of the 18th century, apartment blocks expanded, becoming more popular than private houses.

The novelty of the multi-occupant building lay in having independent dwellings ranged above each other on separate stories.

Before this time, renting was confined to private housing, and was an arrangement between the owner and the tenant.

At No 54, Rue de Seine and No 137, Rue Vieille du Temple, the façades typically copied the style of the more opulent apartment buildings: freestone was used, there was a decorated carriage entrance, a mezzanine floor, and stores occupied the ground floor.

The Industrial Revolution and the rise of rental blocks

The Industrial Revolution played a crucial role in the spread of rental blocks. Now these buildings became a form of financial investment. Under the reign of Louis-Philippe, new streets such as the Rue Rambuteau were built. Following the style of the Rue du Pont Louis-Philippe, they were lined with apartment buildings. The advent of new materials led to new methods of construction. Glass technology became more advanced, and windows were made larger, reducing the amount of blank wall. Similarly, the use of cast iron meant that long balconies could be built. Owners tried to give their façades an appearance that matched the rents they charged.

4. Apartment building, Haussmann period
These blocks were built to precise specifications and were very successful. Above the rusticated ground floor, the upper stories were topped by attic apartments and encircled by balconies.

5. Cross section of an apartment building
This typical 19th-century building has stores at street level, with apartments for wealthy occupants on the next two or three stories, and others for the less well-off on the upper stories.

4

2. Façade (19th century)
Rules brought in by Haussmann forced owners and builders to build their façades on similar lines. Balconies, cornices, and roofs had to conform with their neighbors.

3. Apartment building, No 28, Place Saint-Georges
Built in 1841, this apartment house was occupied by the famous Marquise de la Païva, and stands in the Saint-Georges district, which was then fashionable. Its Neo-Renaissance façade is typical of its period.

In this way, some blocks were left fairly plain while others were more richly decorated.

Haussmann's apartment buildings

As soon as he came to the throne, Napoléon III encouraged Haussmann to modernize the capital and improve housing standards. To reduce epidemics, they pulled down the old districts where poor families were crammed together in appalling sanitary conditions. In their place, broad avenues such as the Rue de Rennes and the Boulevards Saint-Michel and Magenta were built and lined with apartment buildings. Haussmann imposed draconian conditions on the construction of these blocks: façades the same height and made of freestone, no overhangs, sparse decoration, and stylistic unity. The popularization of the elevator in the 1860s changed the stories' desirability. Where the second story had once been the most sought-after, now people wanted to live at the top of the building. Betwen 1852 and 1870, more than 100,000 apartment blocks, built in a similar style, completely changed the city's appearance.

Mansions in the Second Empire

Many middle-class people became very rich in the Second Empire. In the Faubourg Saint-Germain and the areas around the Champs-Elysées and Place de l'Étoile, majestic mansions were built. The word mansion was no longer used to refer to houses of the nobility but to a particular architectural type. Unlike the façades of Haussmann's apartment buildings, the mansions were lavishly decorated, borrowing from many historic styles. On the Champs-Elysées, the Neo-Renaissance

6. Hôtel Menier, Avenue Van Dyck
Mansions in the Second Empire kept to the "house between courtyard and garden" layout, and took their decorative style from the past, in contrast to the plain apartment buildings being built at the same time.

7. Cité des Fleurs
This green enclave was designed in 1847, at a time when Parisians were beginning to move to the outer suburbs. Lined with houses of varied design, it has scarcely changed since it was built.

mansion of Mme de Païva, built in 1856, was one of the most splendid examples of its day.

The working-class house
Many working-class people living in the city center were driven out by Haussmann's schemes and emigrated to the outer districts. They moved into hovels where hygiene was nonexistent. Napoléon III, aware of the humanitarian measures adopted in England and Germany, released funds to build housing for workers. In 1849, the Cité Napoléon, at No 58, Rue de Rochechouart, offered clean lodgings for workers with shared cooking and washing facilities. This experiment was repeated in several working-class districts, both in houses and apartments.

Façades become more lavish
At the end of the 19th century and the beginning of the 20th, changes to highway regulations revolutionized the appearance of apartment buildings. The law of 1884 authorized larger projecting elements on façades, which led to the appearance of bow windows and corner domes. The new regulations encouraged a new flowering of ornamental sculpture, using eclectic and Art Nouveau forms. Guimard's Castel Béranger at No 14, Rue La Fontaine and Lavirotte's apartment building at No 29, Avenue Rapp are the best-known examples. In 1902, a further law allowed buildings to have three more stories, up to a maximum of eight.

Technical improvements
Meanwhile, advances in construction techniques ushered in new types of apartment building. These improved structures used reinforced concrete, iron, and glass, and had much larger windows. Glass walls in the façade brought extra light to the studio workshops in Rue Réamur (2nd and 3rd *arrondissements*), and also led to the creation of a new type of building, the purpose-built artist's studio. Many studios and studio houses were built in Montparnasse, such as the Ozenfant house designed by Le Corbusier at No 53, Avenue Reille, and the block at No 31, Rue Campagne Première, built by Arfindson in 1911.

Social housing: late 19th century
Social housing was introduced under Napoléon III and developed with the help of private finance. At the end of the 19th century, philanthropic and humanitarian associations raised the money for affordable housing in working-class districts. These were mostly confined to the outskirts of the capital, and consisted of blocks that

4. Rue Réaumur
Built in the Second Empire, Rue Réaumur was extended from Rue Saint-Denis to the Bourse between 1895 and 1905. The surrounding land was mainly acquired by garment manufacturers. The street's commercial identity was quickly established and is evident in the façades of the buildings. These combine stone, iron, and glass, building materials that typified the Industrial period and were especially suited to buildings used by the garment industry. Iron was given particular emphasis at No 124, Rue Réaumur, attributed to Georges Chédanne, which was originally occupied by fabric makers. For its period (1903), it was a highly innovative structure, designed around an iron skeleton. The use of large panes of glass admitted a great deal of light into the workshops.

1. Place Etienne-Pernet
At the beginning of the Third Republic, the architecture of apartment blocks moved away from the rigid Haussmann style. An ornamental sculptural style was becoming popular, prompting the design of more adventurous façades.

2. Castel Béranger, No 16, Rue La Fontaine
The balconies of Castel Béranger, built by Hector Guimard in 1897, display fantastic shapes typical of Art Nouveau.

3. Boulevard Soult
This chain of boulevards named for Napoléon's marshals reveals another aspect of the city. The brick used for these multi-story buildings gives them an identity and aesthetic quality which can be found in many buildings in the outer districts.

conformed to the hygiene standards of the day. The apartments were better equipped than their predecessors, each having their own kitchen with running water, gas, and toilet facilities. At the same time, individual houses were built in terraces along simple streets. These usually had a small front garden, were one or two stories high and made of brick. Many were built in the 19th and 20th *arrondissements*, especially around Rue de la Mouzaïa, and today are much sought after by well-to-do people who value their quiet location and green surroundings.

Multistory blocks on the outskirts
Between 1910 and 1920, overpopulation proved disastrous for the health of many families. The private associations could

5. Artists' studios, No 65, Rue la Fontaine
The use of ceramic on façades appeared from the middle of the 19th century and was widespread until the middle of the 20th. Ceramic was flexible and lent itself to all kinds of designs. In 1926, archi-tect Sauvage used simple white ceramic panels on his artists' studios (16th *arrondissement*).

6. Multistory blocks in the outer districts
These multistory apartments were built from the 1920s on the site of the Thiers city wall, to provide clean, hygienic housing for the less well-off. They formed a unified mass like a belt surrounding almost the whole of the city. The blocks conformed to a well-established type, divided into groups set around open courtyards and green spaces. Their concrete frame was covered with bricks, giving them a specific character.

not cope with this alone, and the City of Paris decided to become involved in the building of social housing. In 1922, the wall put up by Thiers was demolished to build multistory blocks and a green belt. Over the next decade, huge buildings went up all around the capital. These were made of brick and were laid out around spacious, grassy courtyards.

Interwar period
After World War I, while the rate of apartment building slowed, a small number of architects were inspired by the Modernist movement to look for new solutions. The architects Elkouken, Patout, Sauvage, and Roux-Spitz were active in the movement, each developing his own individual style.

Modern apartments from the "Glorious Thirties"
Following World War II, a housing crisis shook France, and the capital in particular. In some districts, the housing stock was dilapidated and living conditions were very bad. From the 1960s to the mid-1970s, these condemned buildings were gradually demolished and replaced by large high-rise blocks. These borrowed from interwar theories of town planning and were built side by side on enormous pedestrian platforms. At the same time, the increasing development of service industries spurred the

building of new office blocks. For more than 15 years, huge housing and office towers were built. Those in the 13th *arrondissement* between Place de l'Italie and Porte d'Ivry were especially massive, as were those in the 15th, in the development known as the Front de Seine. The business district at La Défense to the west of the city, almost entirely devoted to office blocks and towers, was also built in the 1960s.

20th-century apartments
Towards the end of the 1970s, while the condemned blocks and the city's industrial wasteland had been gradually

4. Place de Séoul
In Montparnasse in the 1980s, architect Bofill designed a great urban complex organized around three open spaces. The original style of the Place de Séoul contains references to Antiquity, and stands next to the Place de Catalogne. It is lined with façades in smoked glass, which rise in monumental columns.

converted to new residential areas, it was the way these districts were renovated that really made the difference. The height of new buildings was now more tightly regulated, and the new apartment buildings fitted more harmoniously into the existing scheme of things.
In 1979, architects Christian de Portzamparc and Georgia Benamo together showed the way forward with their building on the Rue des Hautes-Formes in the 13th *arrondissement*.
In the 1980s, more and more older buildings were included in the large-scale renovation projects. The renovations in

1. Apartment building, No 100, Boulevard de Belleville
This block, built in 1989 by Frédéric Borel, offers a new interpretation of the rules in force. The central space is set back and designed around a courtyard opening onto the street, providing a breathing space on the boulevard.

2 Les Hautes-Formes
In 1979, Portzamparc and Benamo built the Hautes-Formes complex, one of the first to break with the massive buildings of previous decades. This group of buildings was designed for an uneven landscape, and reintroduced a more human scale.

3. Front de Seine
The Front de Seine was built in the 1960s according to the ideas of the Modern movement, separating the functions of traffic, living, and working. Cars were relegated below ground and the complex was given both mass and height.

the Bercy district, on the site of the former wine warehouses, were typical of this new trend. In 2000, the architects Simon, Galiano, and Tenot won a major prize for their group of sixteen houses, the Ilot des Amandiers in the heart of the 20th *arrondissement*. Their architectural achievement was to integrate a completely new housing scheme into an existing street, one of the steepest in Paris.

5. Apartment building, Nos 132-134, Rue des Pyrénées
While building regulations in the late 1970s were strict about building lines, they did allow façades to be other than straight. In 1994, Michel Bourdeau designed this apartment building with a façade consisting of two huge, curved, prefabricated concrete sections, set at a slant and finished in color.

6. Apartment buildings, Rue Balard
This block was built in 1986 by architect Zubléna. It has undulating façades that break with the surrounding buildings. At the same time, it fits well into its urban environment with a ceramic cladding that echoes the style of the neighboring building.

THE COVERED ARCADES

About 30 of the 240 covered arcades around at the beginning of the 19th century survived Haussmann's building schemes. Today there are no more than 20 of these passages. While some have been restored to give Parisians a taste of bygone days, other more humble ones, though just as picturesque, are slipping into decline.

Birth of the arcades

The first arcades appeared at the end of the 18th century, when the middle classes were beginning to prosper in business and Paris was rife with property speculators. The middle classes bought land cheaply and opened covered arcades. These were all on the Right Bank, the capital's economic center, while the Left Bank, with its universities, remained the educational center it had been since the Middle Ages. Luxury stores, confectioners, and tea rooms opened there, like the confectioner Milletot in Passage des Panoramas. Although the total number of arcades peaked at 240, their viability was precarious, and depended heavily on the whims of fashion.

A new place to walk

The arcades allowed people to stop and look around. Although enclosed by the city, they were free from the bustle of the streets, and, unlike many streets in Paris, were lit and heated, and protected people from being hit by a carriage or sprayed with mud. In his *New Portrait of Paris*, Louis-Sébastien Mercier observed: "In a city made for luxury and wandering about, where it was unpleasant if not dangerous to venture into the street, the crowds were forced to find places where they could stop in front of store windows without having to worry about being jostled or suffering an accident. This was the reason for ... the increase in covered arcades."

The first arcades

The wooden galleries around the Palais-Royal garden, built in 1786 and demolished in 1829, were the forerunners of the arcades. They were inspired by architectural arcades and covered markets; they were also perhaps influenced by the Arab souks which the French had discovered thanks to Bonaparte's Egyptian campaign. While the first arcades were covered by a wooden framework, this was soon replaced by more modern materials. Glass and iron were widely adopted, making the frameworks both stronger and lighter.

Luxurious arcades between Palais-Royal and the Stock Exchange

Galerie Véro-Dodat

Two astute butchers, Véro and Dodat, whose business had made them very comfortably off, had the idea in 1826 of building an arcade opening onto Rue du Bouloi, in the 1st *arrondissement*, just opposite the Messageries Générales, a mail depot. The print-dealer Aubert, who exhibited Daumier, and the actress Rachel moved into the

5. Cross-section of an arcade
This entrance to an arcade, with a pediment, columns, and an Antique decorative style, reflects the architectural features that were fashionable in 1830-40.

6. Passage Choiseul
It was completed in 1827. Owned by the bankers Mallet, it was built on the site of the mansion of Marquis de Gesvres, governor of Paris in 1703, who made it the most famous haunt in Paris. It has an entrance to the Théâtre des Bouffes Parisiens, as Offenbach renamed the theater when he bought it in 1855.

1. Galerie Véro-Dodat
The front of Robert Capia's boutique, specializing in antique dolls, is a combination of dark wood and brass.

2. Bookstore in Galerie Vivienne
The booksellers Siroux have been in the arcade for decades, and their stalls stock a range of old and modern books.

3. Galerie Vivienne
This arcade, completed in 1826, has an impressive, harmonious structure, emphasized by its columns and capitals.

4. Galerie Colbert
The Galerie Colbert opened to the public in 1826, and was remade in 1985. Kermel, author of *Les Passages de Paris 1831-1834*, thought its rotunda was particularly attractive.

Galérie Véro-Dodat, which was equipped with the first public gaslights. With its black and white marble paving, and glass roof interleaved with painted panels, it looks like a long and opulent vestibule. Today Robert Capia, the famous antique doll collector, and Franco Maria Ricci, the Milanese publisher whose magazine bears his name, have premises there.

Galerie Vivienne

This arcade was built in 1823 and has three entrances in Rue des Petits-Champs, Rue de la Banque, and Rue Vivienne. It was designed by architect François Delannoy, winner of the Grand Prix de Rome and very keen on the Greco-Roman style, which he used here. There are storefronts separated by broad pilasters, a glass roof resting on triangular pediments, and vaulted arches. At No 13 is the staircase of the mansion where Vidocq lived, a former convict who became a brigadier of police. A tea room, and stores selling floral bouquets and old books await the casual visitor.

Galerie Colbert

This 1826 arcade belongs to the Bibliothèque Nationale and was, with Galerie Vivienne, one of the most refined built in the period 1825-30, with marble half-columns supporting the arcade and giving it a very elegant appearance. It leads to the garden of Palais-Royal via the narrow Passage des Deux Pavillons. Its plaster and wood fell into decay, and the arcade was demolished, then rebuilt faithfully by Louis Blanchet in 1985. He restored the Pompeian paintings in the rotunda to their original colors. The arcade now contains the Charles-Cros Museum of Sound.

Passage Choiseul

This arcade was designed by architects Mazois and Tavernier and opened in 1827. It has two entrances, one on Rue des Petits-Champs, the other on Rue Saint-Augustin. It has strong links with French poetry, particularly the Parnassians (Sully Prudhomme, François Coppée, Leconte de Lisle, and José Maria de Heredia) who came here to see their publisher, Alphonse Lemerre. Verlaine mentioned it in *Dédicaces*: "The Passages Choiseul with their scents of times past, oranges, rare parchments, and glove-sellers!"

Arcades on the Grands Boulevards

At the beginning of the 19th century, the Grands Boulevards were taken over by wealthy people of leisure, who liked to be seen and went regularly to the theaters on Boulevard Montmartre and Boulevard des Italiens.

Passage des Panoramas

Zola draws on this arcade in *Nana*: "She loved the Passage des Panoramas. From her youth she still had a passion for the glitter of things from Paris, fake jewels, gilded zinc, and cardboard masquerading as leather." Many of its boutiques were famed throughout the city, and kept it fashionable until the Second Empire: chocolates at Marquis, Jean-Marie Farina's "genuine Eau de Cologne," gloves at

1. Passage Jouffroy
This arcade next to the Musée Grévin was the first in Paris to be equipped with heating, which made it a great success. People dashed in from the freezing streets to warm themselves over the hot-air vents, and were sometimes very reluctant to move on.

2. Passage du Grand Cerf
Completely renovated in 1994, this arcade is the highest in the city, its glass roof 39 ft (12 m) above the pavement. It was built on the site of the Grand Cerf tavern, departure point for the Royal Mail coach service to eastern France.

3. Passage des Deux Pavillons
This arcade in the 1st *arrondissement* links Palais-Royal and Place des Petits-Pères.

4, 5. Passage du Caire
The entrance in Place du Caire is decorated with a frieze of figures above reliefs of the goddess Hathor, and reflects the craze for all things Egyptian in the reign of Napoléon Bonaparte. The old lithographers' and packaging workshops in its three covered avenues have been replaced by clothing wholesalers.

A la Lampe Merveilleuse, and Cidevant, the young men's outfitters. It owed its name to two rotundas by the entrance on Boulevard Montmartre, from where people could see immense panoramic views. An engraver has been in the Passage since 1840. This is a very striking store, the carved woodwork a blend of Renaissance and Napoléon III styles.

Passage Jouffroy

Passage Jouffroy was built in 1846 between Boulevard Montmartre and Rue de la Grange-Batelière in the latest materials, with a ceiling and framework in cast iron. It came to fame in 1882, when the popular waxworks, the Musée Grévin, opened there.
Today its neighbors include antiquarian and movie bookstores, an Arab pâtisserie, and a small hotel.

Passage Verdeau

Continuing the line of Passage Jouffroy, this arcade opened in 1846 and is more secluded than its neighbor. The entrance is at No 6, Rue de la Grange-Batelière.
Antique dealers, bookstores, and cafés share its charmingly musty atmosphere.

Passage des Princes

Passage des Princes opened at No 5, Boulevard des Italiens in 1860, and runs through to Rue de Richelieu. This is the last of the large Parisian *passages* and the only one dating from the Second Empire. Further arcades were not built after 1840 as such shopping areas became less fashionable when the department stores started to appear, attracting more and more customers. The Passage des Princes has a glass roof with a double pitch, and was fully renovated in 1995.

Exotic arcades, the old and the new

Passage du Caire

This is the longest and also one of the oldest arcades in the city. Its main arm links Rue Saint-Denis and Place du Caire in the 2nd *arrondissement*.
It was constructed at the same time as the square and street of the same name, on the site of the Filles-Dieu convent, and at that time was partly paved with tombstones from the nuns' graves. The arcade was built in 1799, its name commemorating Napoleon Bonaparte's Egyptian campaign of the previous year. Not everyone liked it, however: Amédée de Kermel wrote in *Le Livre des Cent et Un* (1831): "It has neither the richness of Egypt, nor its smells, nor the grandeur of its buildings ... Cairo in this backwater! It's an outrage, a treble outrage!" The arcade is in the heart of the Sentier, the garment district, and is currently occupied by ready-to-wear wholesalers.

Passage Brady

Passage Brady was built in 1828 between Rue du Faubourg Saint-Denis and Rue du Faubourg Saint-Martin. Today, like the nearby Passage du

Prado, it is filled with Indian and Pakistani restaurants and stores selling ethnic craftwork, saris, and a huge selection choice of spices and exotic products.

Other arcades near Rue Saint-Denis

Passage du Bourg l'Abbé

This arcade opened in 1828 at No 120, Rue Saint-Denis. Its best entrance is at No 3, Rue de Palestro, where the gate is framed by two caryatids standing on columns, the work of Aimé Millet. They are allegories of Business and Industry, and are surrounded by an anchor, a wheel, and an anvil.

Passage du Grand Cerf

This arcade built in about 1835 runs between No 145, Rue Saint-Denis and No 10, Rue Dussoubs. Over the main entrance are the arms of Paris. It is 128 yd (117 m) long and covered by an impressive glass roof 39 ft (12 m) high, making it the highest arcade in Paris and the best lit. There are two fully glazed wooden stories and a third attic story. Aerial bridges punctuate its length.

In the 1980s, it was threatened with demolition, but in 1994 it was restored and today contains art galleries, fashion boutiques, a tea room, and several antique dealers.

Passage du Havre, close to the railroad

If there had been no railroad to the west of France, and therefore no Gare Saint-Lazare, it is unlikely that this arcade would have been built in 1848. It has two arms branching out from a rotunda, and was first opened as the Passage du Chantier de Tivoli, a reference to the nearby Tivoli amusement park, which used to lie slightly to the north in Rue de l'Europe. Being close to the station kept the arcade permanently busy.

The Passage du Havre was demolished in the 1990s because of work on the Eole subway line. Later rebuilt by architect Macary, it is filled with fashion boutiques.

6. Boutiques in Passage Jouffroy
The specialist traders in this attractive two-legged arcade sell a wide range of exotic goods, from Oriental ivories to old toys and puppets, gifts for mothers and brides, chocolates and pastries, art books, and movie books.

7. Passage des Princes
The Passage des Princes was designed by Mirès and opened in 1860. At that time it stood opposite the Passage de l'Opéra, which was demolished in 1925.

FOUNTAINS

Paris has more fountains than there are days in the year: almost 400 in all, about a hundred of which have appeared since the 1980s. Whether in the form of gushing springs, cascades, drinking fountains, or quiet ponds, they have become a basic part of city planning, a delight to both eye and ear. However, in the days before all this was technically possible, the fountains of Paris rarely gave out more than a thin dribble of water, which was mainly used for drinking and domestic purposes.

A precious commodity

Water is essential to life, and for a long time it was seen as something sacred. When Paris was Lutetia, the fountains were placed under the protection of Greek or Roman gods. In medieval Paris, the saints took over this role. In the Renaissance, when people drew their models from Antiquity, the fountains were decorated with aquatic gods. Even so, whether they were embellished by figures from mythology or Christianity, the oldest fountains in Paris were usually just small utilitarian structures that people went to for the water they needed that day. Everyone drank there, both people and animals. Water sellers did a roaring trade, their importance symbolized by the arms of Paris on the seal of their guild. Water was in short supply and valuable. Paris remained desperately short of it until the beginning of the 19th century, when the development of fountains had a great social impact.

A thin trickle

Under the Ancien Régime, the city's only water supply came from the Seine, from three ancient aqueducts, and wells that were often polluted or dry. Until 1782, only the Samaritaine pump and those at Pont Notre-Dame were allowed to draw water from the Seine. It was far too little for a capital city. Even then, some of this water (from the Arcueil aqueduct and all the Samaritaine's supply) was reserved for the king, his palaces, and gardens. Most of the public fountains were only small stone containers backing on to buildings and fitted with a reservoir which gave out a thin trickle of water. Even the biggest had few bowls or basins, for fear of wastage. Using water for other than utilitarian purposes was a criminal offence. And while architects often dreamed of "engines to raise water," the most animated thing about their fountains was the sculptures.

Fountains surviving from this period include the Mannerist-style Fontaine des Haudriettes (1765, on the corner of Rue des Archives) and the Fontaine de Jarente (1783, Impasse de la Poissonnerie). There were three exceptional fountains. Two were for public use: the Fontaine des Innocents and the Fontaine des Quatre-Saisons. The third, the Médicis fountain, was in the Queen's garden at the Luxembourg Palace.

Fontaine des Innocents: a Renaissance celebration

In 1549, festive decorations were put up for the arrival in Paris of King Henri II. To mark the occasion, sculptor Jean Goujon built the Fontaine des Innocents, the first really monumental fountain in Paris. Far from the usual little stone container, this was a vast three-sided loggia with one alcove facing Rue Saint-Denis, and the other two on Rue aux Fers (the present Rue Berger). Watery bas-reliefs of undulating nymphs, sea monsters, and

1. Fontaine du Pot-de-Fer

This street-corner fountain was one of 15 which Louis XIV had built for Paris. It was designed by architect M Noblet, and was probably modified in the 18th century. In 1673, the city had about 50 fountains, which on average supplied people with 6 pt (4 l) of water a day.

2. Stone and water as sculpture

Not until the 19th century did public fountains take on a purely decorative role.

3. Fontaine de l'Observatoire

This 1874 fountain is one of the most beautiful in Paris. The sea horses, sculpted by E Frémiet, a pupil of Rude, are full of life and movement.

4. Fontaine Louvois

Completed in 1839 by L Visconti and J B Klagman, this fountain is an example of the tiered design which was common in the 19th century.

tritons covered its surfaces in carvings of great imagination and fluidity. However, like all the fountains of its day, the water itself had no part in the decorations, but was simply for the use of local people who drew it off via small lion-headed taps in the base.

In 1787, this masterpiece of French sculpture was threatened with demolition, but in the end was saved. It was moved, its shape altered, and completed in the Second Empire by the sculptor Pajou, who added bas-reliefs to its fourth side and a nymph to the third. Today, the Fontaine des Innocents stands near Les Halles, and since the beginning of the 19th century has had water streaming down its sides.

Fontaine des Quatre-Saisons

The Four Seasons Fountain, or the Fontaine de Grenelle (from the street where it stands), was built in 1739-45 by the royal sculptor Edme Bouchardon (1698-1762). It was exceptionally large for its time – 95 ft (29 m) wide and 38 ft (11.6 m) high – and decorated with unusual splendor. In the center, the City of Paris is seated "as though at the entrance to a temple." At the feet of this figure, river gods representing the Seine and the Marne seem to be paying homage to it. Four statues and four bas-reliefs depict the Seasons. In the pediment are the arms of France. However, like all the Paris fountains of its period, this magnificent edifice provided only a few trickles of water for domestic use. Even before it was built, Voltaire was on the warpath: "I have no doubt that Bouchardon can make a fine piece of architecture out of this fountain; but what is a fountain if it only has

5, 6. Fontaine Médicis

Built for Marie de Médicis around 1630, this fountain is modeled on Italian grottos. Its niches were decorated with "teardrops of water" and contained a basin and fountain in the middle. In 1864, it was moved to the end of a long narrow pool designed by Gisors. He added statues to the niches including this group sculpted by Ottin, which shows Polyphemus mad with grief at the sight of Galatea, the sea nymph he loves, in the arms of Acis.

7. Fontaine Saint-Sulpice

This fountain facing the Church of Saint-Sulpice was completed by L Visconti in 1848, and pays tribute to four great preachers of the 17th century: Bossuet, Fénelon, Fléchier, and Massillon.

1. Fontaine des Mers
Hittorff was commissioned in 1833 to decorate the Place de la Concorde, and ordered a dozen famous sculptors to produce these two fountains. The Fountain of the Seas and the Fountain of the Rivers stand on either side of the obelisk, praising France's prosperity and alluding also to the Seine and the Navy Ministry at each end of the square.

2. Fountain in the Parc André Citroën
Children love this fountain with its rows of 120 intermittently spurting jets. It was designed in 1992 by A Provost and J-P Viguier.

3. Fontaine du Canyone Austrate
In this fountain at Bercy, designed in 1988, sculptor G Singer has created a hollowed-out landscape, inspired by American canyons, in which water pours down in cascades.

two taps for water-carriers to fill their buckets?" He added: "Fountains should be built in public places, and every fine monument should be visible from all sides." Not until the following century were his wishes fulfilled.

More and more water

When he was First Consul, Bonaparte wanted to know how to "do something great and useful for Paris." "Give it water," was Prefect Chaptal's reply. Soon after this, in 1802, a law was passed to divert the River Ourcq. In 1824, the Canal de l'Ourcq came into use. Thanks to technical progress and the successful channeling of water from distant sources via aqueducts and canals, the city's water supply was considerably enlarged in the 19th century. As the network of pipes was built up to carry water directly into the houses, the fountains gradually lost their utilitarian function and took on a symbolic and decorative role.

Fountains commemorating Napoléon I

In a decree of 1806, Napoléon I ordered the building of 15 new fountains. In all, nearly 30 were built during his reign, mostly between 1806 and 1812 by architect Bralle. And though the plan to build a fountain at the Bastille in the shape of an elephant was finally abandoned, this was the period when the first fountains with jets of water

and basins made their appearance, most notably in Place des Vosges. Commemorative fountains also came in. These were put up in the middle of squares to commemorate the Grande Armée and their Napoleonic campaigns. The Palm Fountain in Place du Châtelet is a typical example. Here the jets of water were less important than the names of the Emperor's victorious battles carved on the column, the figure of Victory on top of it, and the palm-leaf capital recalling the Egyptian campaign (1798). Also from this period is the Fontaine du Fellah (Rue de Sèvres), which with its eagle and Egyptian style clearly refers to the Napoleonic era; and the Fontaine de Mars (Rue Saint-Dominique) which links the god of war (Mars) and the goddess of health (Hygeia), an allusion to the nearby military hospital.

Monumental fountains dedicated to famous people

Most of the big sculpted fountains in Paris today were built in the 19th century, especially during the July Monarchy (1830-40) and the Second Empire. It was not enough for them to be purely decorative, however. There had to be a reason for them. So it was that a new generation of monumental fountains was built, located on sites and decorated with sculptures that linked them to a famous person. The fountain dedicated to the naturalist Georges Cuvier

(1840-46) shows Natural History surrounded by animals and is located beside the Jardin des Plantes. Near the Comédie Française is the Molière Fountain (1841-44), decorated with allegories of Comedy and Serious Theater. The fountain in Place Saint-Sulpice (1843-48) honors the religious eloquence of four preachers: Bossuet, Fénelon, Fléchier, and Massillon.

4. Wallace Fountain
These fountains, presented to the City of Paris in 1872 by Sir Richard Wallace, were for passers-by to drink from. Later, the drinking cups were removed for reasons of public health. In the year 2000, a program was launched to build new drinking fountains of a new design.

5. Fontaine Stravinsky
This playful, colorful fountain, located near the Pompidou Center, was designed in 1983 by sculptors Jean Tinguely and Niki de Saint-Phalle. Its 16 figures, including Life, Love, G Clef, Snake, Clown's Hat, and Death, are a tribute to the composer Igor Stravinsky, whose inspired music borrowed from all kinds of serious and popular works.

Fountains in major developments

Decorative fountains also figured in many of the great urban schemes. One of the most spectacular is the Fountain of the Seas and the Fountain of the Rivers (1836-40), part of the major plan to design Place de la Concorde, which Hittorff was commissioned to carry out in 1833. He also designed the four Champs Elysées Fountains

(1840) and the ornamental basin at the Rond-Point to improve the sweeping perspective between the Arc de Triomphe and the Tuileries. The Fontaine Saint-Michel (1858-60), which was built during Baron Haussmann's rebuilding program, is a grandiose polychrome creation mixing bronze, green, and red marble, and yellow stone. The Observatory Fountain (1867-1874), including compelling sculptures by Carpeaux and Frémiet, is an integral part of the scheme for a broad avenue between the Luxembourg Garden and the Observatory, which the architect Davioud built from 1866.

In all the fountains of this period, except for those at Concorde and the Observatory, the emphasis was on architecture and sculpture, with the actual fountains playing a secondary role.

Spectacular fountains

Water cascades down the terraces of Parc de Belleville, spreads out in a glassy expanse in front of the Cité des Sciences de la Villette, rises in tall columns on the main courtyard at La Défense and around the Pyramid in the Louvre, spouts forth in rhythmic bursts at the Stravinsky Fountain in Beaubourg, and spurts upward in a random, playful manner in the Parc André Citroën. Once Paris had acquired a plentiful supply of water, it became the primary element in the design of new fountains.

The Universal Exhibitions in the late 19th and early 20th centuries gave a great spur to the development of fountains, many of which used the new wonders of electric light to create special effects. There were also some more permanent creations, such as the pools and

fountains at Trocadéro (1937) which extended over 6 acres (2.5 ha). These included ornamental pools flowing into one another; oblique jets 160 ft (50 m) long propeled by a kind of hydraulic cannon; and banks of water columns, sprays, and cascades.

Fountains on the increase

Fountains were used to embellish about a hundred new squares built between 1925 and 1940. Two outstanding examples from this period are the fountains at Porte de Saint-Cloud (1936, sculpted by Paul Landowski) and, in honor of the great composer, the Debussy Fountain (1932, the work of Jan and Joël Martel).

Then in the 1980s came a real boom in the number of fountains built. One of the reasons for this was the government's new environmental policy, by which all new public building schemes were obliged to spend 1% of the construction costs on decoration. This made it much easier to finance new fountains. Not only architects and landscape designers, but also famous sculptors were invited to design fountains. Among them were François-Xavier Lalaine (the rows of fountains in Place de l'Hôtel de Ville, 1983) and Pol Bury (the floating metal balls at Palais-Royal, 1985). There were painters too, such as Yaacov Agam (the fountains combined with 86 colored mosaics on the esplanade at La

Défense, 1977) and the architect/composer Bernhard Leitner with his "sound cylinders" in Parc de la Villette, 1987). Fountains were now seen as essential ingredients in the design of public places, in much the same way as plants and trees. They came in all sizes, from the helix in the gardens at Les Halles, measuring only 21 sq ft (2 sq m), to the fountain in Kellermann Park, which is 2,340 sq yd (1,960 sq m). Rather more subtle is the strangely erupted pavement of *l'Embacle* in Saint-Germain-des-Prés, while the Stravinsky Fountain by the Pompidou Center makes its impact with movement and bold colors.

Drinking fountains

In 1872, Sir Richard Wallace, a wealthy Englishman who had been living in Paris for a long time, presented the City with 50 drinking fountains. Originally designed by Charles-Auguste Lebourg, there are now about 80 of them, the City having built others at its own expense. Although the water from these fountains is drinkable, the metal cups that used to be chained to them have been removed for reasons of public health. For the year 2000, the city decided to build some new drinking fountains. The chosen design is very sober, 5.3 ft (1.63 m) tall, and was selected for its "modernity and beauty of line." Some are already in use, for example in Place Saint-Michel.

STREETS AND AVENUES

Paris inherited a rectilinear network of streets from ancient Lutetia. From the Middle Ages, every era added new districts to this core, with streets that became increasingly straight and broad. Then, in the Second Empire, Haussmann drove his new boulevards and avenues through the center to relieve congestion in the city and restore fluidity.

Difficult to date

In 52 BC, no sooner had the Romans conquered the main settlement of the Parisii tribe than the small town of Ile de la Cité sprang up around a main cross-street. When Lutetia expanded on the Left Bank, the new city was organized around a main axis, the cardo, leading to the road to Orléans and following the line of present-day Rue Saint-Jacques. The streets of Paris are difficult to date. There are streets dating back to ancient times, such as Rue Saint-Jacques, but its width has varied over time, its roadway is higher, and most of the houses along it were built between the 18th and 20th centuries. Some avenues laid out in the 17th or 18th century, like the Avenue de Saxe or the Champs-Elysées, had no houses on them until the end of the 19th century. It is unclear whether streets should be dated from when they were first marked out, or from the time houses were built beside them. The city's streets are also difficult to categorize. Many were urbanized over a period of time, others were part of a housing scheme, while still others were built through an existing urban structure.

The old pathways

In general, the streets which were gradually built up are the oldest in the city and are mainly to be found in the center. These are the old Medieval ways, like the Rue de Buci which led from a gate in Philippe-Auguste's city wall to the Abbey of Saint-Germain-des-Prés, or old roads which have become incorporated in the city, such as the Rue du Faubourg Saint-Antoine and Rue Mouffetard. Some streets, especially the Medieval ones, contain natural features and older buildings. The streets which developed from pathways often have a winding shape following the local contours, such as the Rue Berbier du Mets in the 13th *Arrondissement*. Some streets follow the counterscarp of the old city walls, such as Rue Mazarine, Rue de l'Ancienne-Comédie, and Rue Monsieur-le-Prince. Others are part of a network converging on the old city gates, like Rue du Cherche-Midi, Rue

1. Rue des Barres
This Medieval street, nestling between the Church of Saint-Gervais and the Seine, escaped the 19th-century building programs. In this kind of street you can still find the last surviving houses from the 15th and 16th centuries.

2. Rue du Petit-Musc
This road was built in the Middle Ages just outside Philippe-Auguste's wall, and was then urbanized between the 16th and 18th centuries, when the houses along it were built.

3. Near Sacré-Coeur
The old streets of Mont-martre village were brought into the city's urban plan from 1860, but some have kept their old rural character.

4. Rue Saint-Dominique
This old suburban road was urbanized in the 18th and 19th centuries, and has become a shopping street like other old streets incorporated into a new district.

5. Avenues Foch and de la Grande Armée
These avenues were urbanized in the 19th century. Both converge on Place de l'Étoile, designed at the end of the 17th century.

Streets in housing estates

These streets mostly date from more recent times and are located on the outskirts of Paris. However, some developments within the city walls also had streets, such as Rue Beautreillis and Rue Charles V, built on the site of the old Hôtel Saint-Pol (13th century), and the Rue de l'Odéon, Rue Crébillon, and Rue Casimir-Delavigne built on the site of the old Hôtel de Condé in the 18th century. The streets built through an existing townscape were part of modernization schemes and are, by definition, relatively modern and central. Many of them were built by Prefect Haussmann in the Second Empire, such as the Boulevards de Sébastopol, du Palais, and Saint-Michel. The Rue Dauphine, however, dates from 1608, and Rue Bonaparte and Rue de Seine are from the beginning of the 19th century.

Streets such as these travel in a straight line through an entire district to link one landmark with another. For example, the Avenue de l'Opéra opened the way from Palais-Royal to the Opéra-Garnier, while the Rue de Rennes linked the Gare Montparnasse to Saint-Germain-des-Prés.

6. Turgot's map, mid-18th century
This detail of Turgot's map shows the Luxembourg and Odéon district before the Théâtre de l'Odéon was built and the housing development laid out, and before the Boulevard Saint-Germain was constructed in the Second Empire. The size of the gardens shows how open the area still was.

7. Building the Boulevard Sébastopol
When this boulevard was made in the Second Empire, many houses had to be demolished between Rue Saint-Denis and Rue Saint-Martin.

Building lines

From the First Empire, a building line was laid down for almost all the streets in Paris. However, it was only applied to reconstructions, and many streets only share a common line along part of their length, like the Rue des Francs-Bourgeois. Architectural harmony also varies a great deal, depending on the origins and history of the streets concerned.

Old streets which were gradually absorbed by the city often reveal signs of their history in their buildings. Houses on estates are of a more consistent design. This is true of the Rue de l'Odéon and the Rue Caumartin, built at the end of the 18th century. In the course of time, new buildings bring further contrasts. Thus the streets belonging to Medieval developments are today often lined with houses from the 17th and 18th centuries, such as the Rue Pastourelle in the "Temple New Town."

The new streets built under the Second Empire are also lined with similar-looking buildings This is especially true of Haussmann's boulevards.

From shopping streets to residential avenues

The history and typology of streets have a bearing on their present use. Most of the shopping streets are old, narrow streets laid out in the Middle Ages, such as Rue Mouffetard, Rue de Buci, and Vieille du Temple. There are some exceptions, however, such as Rue Rambuteau, which was driven through a Medieval district in about 1840, or Rue Violet, which was built through a planned development around 1830. On the whole, streets on estates have remained residential or contain just a few specialist stores, like Rue de la Paix, which opened at the beginning of the 19th century and specializes in luxury goods. The broad avenues, built relatively recently to provide main streets for the new districts, have remained strictly residential. Examples are Avenue Foch, built in the Second Empire, and Avenue Henri-Martin, from the end of the 19th century.

Contemporary streets

Between 1960 and 1970, town planning in Paris was influenced by the so-called Modern Movement, which was against streets, because they were old-fashioned, having been built to cater for cars and pedestrians. This was the time when urban freeways came into being, for example along the banks of the Seine (Front de Seine) and at Maine-Montparnasse, and pedestrian-only or pedestrianized streets (Rue Saint-Denis and Rue Saint-Séverin). Since the 1990s, however, streets have reasserted their position as multi-functional, sociable places. The new districts are built with roads suitable for both traffic and pedestrians, for example in the new development areas at Bercy and Tolbiac.

SQUARES

Squares, even more so than streets, give cities an image. The squares of Paris reflect the diversity of its districts and the richness of its history, from the splendid Place Vendôme, originally the setting for a statue of the Sun King, to the small, "villagey" Place du Tertre and Place de la Contrescarpe, or the Place de l'Étoile where avenues radiate from a triumphal arch dedicated to the glory of the Empire, and the Place de Catalogne, the image of a 20th century seeking to renew its bonds with the past.

The evolution of squares

Squares are generally easier to date than streets, even if the buildings surrounding them are replaced in the course of time by others of different periods. Squares are mostly built from the wish to reclaim some valuable open space in a densely built city. Unlike streets, which are needed for getting about, squares are a luxury and involve a voluntary act of sacrifice. In a sense, the story of town planning can be seen as the gradual process of public spaces occupying more and more of the city. For a long time, there were hardly any squares in Paris, as was true of most other cities. In the Middle Ages, the Place de Grève, in front of the Hôtel de Ville, and the forecourt of Notre-Dame were really quite small. A few squares began to appear from the 17th century, often at the request of of Henri IV, who built the first royal square, now the Place des Vosges. In the 18th century, people dreamt up new squares dedicated to Louis XV or Louis XVI, but apart from the present Place de la Concorde, most of these projects were shelved. In the 19th century, especially under Prefect Haussmann's influence,

squares were seen as something the city needed, to help the traffic, for public health (squares are open spaces where fresh air can circulate), and to show off old and new buildings. Like all the cities in France, Paris provided itself with the legal and financial means to expropriate property to build new squares, not to mention the lands taken over in the name of National Property after the Revolution. When new districts were being built in a well-to-do area, they were all given their own square. The 19th century was certainly the great age of the square, and large numbers were built.

Types of square

There are two main types of square, the "planned" and the "acquired." The former are squares for which space was earmarked when a new district was being built, and the latter are squares acquired by expropriating and demolishing existing buildings on the site. In general, planned squares are immediately surrounded by buildings, as happened with the royal squares in the 17th century. There are exceptions, however, such as the circus at Étoile, now

the Place Charles-de-Gaulle. It was laid out as an esplanade by royal decree in 1768, but the decision to surround it with mansions was only taken under the Second Empire, in 1854. It is nevertheless rare for planned squares to be built up gradually. Acquired squares may be completed both gradually and by so-called "direct" means. A square is said to be directly acquired when its form has been planned and drawn out from the beginning, even if its completion only happens in stages. This was the

case with Place Saint-Sulpice, which was designed and partly built in the 18th century, then completed at the beginning of the 19th century. On the other hand, when the idea to enlarge a square develops gradually, in the course of time, this is said to be a gradual acquisition. For example, between the medieval forecourt of Notre-Dame and the present square, built in the Second Empire, there was a square about halfway between the two in size, which was impeded by a mid-18th century building fac-

1. Place Louis-XV
For reasons of space, the city's final royal square, now Place de la Concorde, was opened in 1763 on the edge of the city, on the axis leading from the Louvre to the Place de l'Étoile.

2. Place des Vosges
This square was built at the beginning of the 17th century at the instigation of Henri IV. It is one of the first royal squares, and is surrounded by identical houses.

3. Place Furstenberg
Place Furstenberg was built after the Revolution on the site of a courtyard belonging to the Abbey of Saint-Germain-des-Prés. It has retained its original, almost private atmosphere.

4. Place St Sulpice
This square was built to open the space in front of the 17th-century Church of Saint-Sulpice. A Jesuit seminary had to be moved to make way for it. The fountain dates from 1844.

ing the church that was demolished in the 19th century.

Acquired squares are generally located in the middle of Paris since, by definition, the space for them has to be cleared of existing buildings. Planned squares tend to be on the outskirts, in the new districts, and assume the existence of open spaces.

As well as these two major types, there are all kinds of individual cases. For example, the Place du Tertre in Montmartre, or the Place de Passy in the 16th *arrondissement* are both former village squares which have been incorporated into the city. Place Saint-Germain-des-Prés and nearby Place Furstenberg both occupy open spaces on former private property, namely the entrance and stables courtyards of the Abbey of Saint-Germain-des-Prés. Some squares stand in spaces left over when streets are widened. Place Henri-Mondor, at the Carrefour de l'Odéon, stands on the site of the old roads that disappeared when the Boulevard Saint-Germain was built.

The shapes of squares
The shape of a square gives it its character, and is often determined by its future use, and whether it will form a road junction or stand on its own. "Squares" are not always square: they may be circular to ease traffic congestion; semi-circular, like the Place du Panthéon designed by architect Soufflot; or elongated like the Place de l'Admiral Coligny facing the Louvre colonnade, which opens up this façade. Square-shaped squares confine traffic to their edges, as at the Place des Vosges and Place Vendôme, at least until the latter was opened up by the Rue de la Paix and Rue de Castiglione at the beginning of the 19th century.

The shape of other squares is dictated by the building at their center, for example the Place de la Madeleine. Others have a rather loose shape, which to some extent makes it less obvious that they are built around a centerpiece; this is the case at Place de la Bastille and Place Denfert-Rochereau. Many other squares do not have a regular shape, having been laid out as part of a road widening scheme or to form a crossroads. This need not impair their potential charm, as Place des Abbesses and Place de la Contrescarpe convincingly prove.

Some squares rank as monuments in their own right, usually because the buildings around them are all similar. The royal squares are built in this style, for example Place des Vosges, with its rows of mansions and facing pair of royal pavilions, or Place Vendôme and Place des Victoires with their façades set between pilasters. Sometimes the square is laid out before its principal building has been completed. In Place de l'Opéra, the buildings around the square were designed by Rohault de Fleury even before Garnier had won the competition in 1860 to build the Opéra.

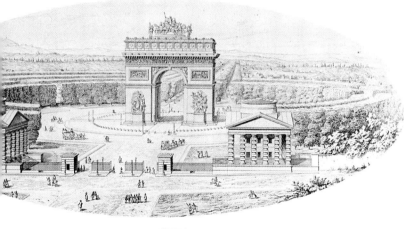

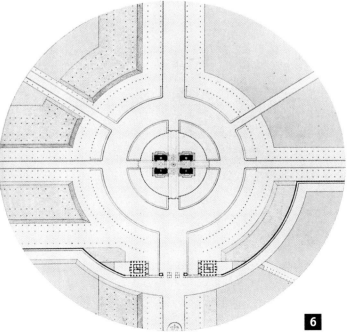

5. Place Vendôme
At the end of the 17th century, this square was built to provide a setting for a royal statue and to help the developers make a profit from the surrounding lots. With its uniform mansions surrounding the square, it is typical of property developments at that time. Under the Empire, the square was decorated with a column, and the Rue de la Paix was built, connecting it to the Grands Boulevards.

6. View and map of Place de l'Étoile
This view and map were drawn from an engraving from about 1835. The Place de l'Étoile began as a simple circus closing the axis from the Louvre via the Champs-Elysées, later extended to the Seine. It features on the line of the enclosing wall of the Farmers-General, and two pavilions were built there by architect C-N Ledoux on the eve of the Revolution. In 1806, Napoléon chose the center of the circus for his Arc de Triomphe, dedicated to the Grande Armée and designed by Chalgrin.

The royal squares

The city's first two royal squares were the work of Henri IV, the real founder of urban development in Paris. In 1605-9, the king commissioned architects Androuet du Cerceau and Métezeau to build the Place Royale (now Place des Vosges) on land belonging to the Hôtel des Tournelles. This was the first large, regularly shaped square in Paris, with identical houses and façades supported on arcades. It was initially used for royal celebrations; then a square garden was built in the middle in the 19th century.

Place Dauphine, completed in 1607 on the site of the garden of the Palais de la Cité, is triangular in shape to match the pointed tip of the Ile de la Cité. Like all the royal squares, its houses had to be identical to form a worthy setting for the statue of the king. This, however, did not prevent the houses from being modified by later occupants.

Two more royal squares were built in Louis XIV's reign: the Place des Victoires in 1679 and Place des Conquêtes (now Place Vendôme) in 1686-99, both of which were designed by J Hardouin-Mansart and inserted into sites which already had buildings on them. The final royal square, Place Louis XV (now Place de la Concorde), was designed by J-A Gabriel and completed between 1755 and 1768, and is the only one to have been built on the edge of

the city, on open land belonging to the king. It forms a kind of esplanade at the entrance to the capital on the road from Versailles, and is on the same axis as the Champs-Elysées, a broad avenue designed by Le Nôtre at the end of the 17th century. It opens onto both the Tuileries and the Seine, and for its time was a completely new concept in urban design. It broke with the usual closed plan of royal squares, opening up spectacular views and linking with the natural environment of the gardens and the river.

Squares in urban developments

From the middle of the 18th century to the middle of the 19th, a large number of landed properties were parcelled out in lots for private housing. Attractive squares were often added to make the lots more attractive to buyers. The Place de l'Odéon was one such, dating from the end of the Ancien Régime. This was part of the development on the site of the old Hôtel de Condé in 1779-83. It is semi-circular in shape, and faces the Théâtre de l'Odéon built by De Wailly and Peyre, and was surrounded by identical buildings; newly built streets radiated from it to the rest of the development. At that time, some squares built as part of housing developments also contained a market. This was the case with the Place d'Aligre, built in 1776-80 by architect N-S Lenoir.

The resumption of property developments under the Restoration gave rise to many small squares in the city. Often they were tucked away in the center of the plot, like Place François I, near Avenue Montaigne, or Place Saint-Georges in the 9th *arrondissement*, built in 1823-4 by architect A Constantin. Some squares were so enclosed that they were almost hidden, like the tiny Square de la Cité Trévise, also in the 9th.

Squares from the Haussmann period

The network of streets and boulevards opened up by Haussmann in the Second Empire brought the construction of several new squares. Most were at junctions where several boulevards came together. For example, the Place de la République leads to the Grands Boulevards and to the Boulevards Magenta and Voltaire, and

the Avenue de la République. A junction may also consist of a simple crossroads marked by a monument. For Place Saint-Michel, the architect G Davioud designed the Fontaine Saint-Michel and the surrounding buildings in 1858, while for Place Malesherbes, V Baltard designed the Church of Saint-Augustin in 1860.

Monumental squares connected to a great building are fairly uncommon. The Place de l'Hôtel de Ville and the forecourt of Notre-Dame are there to open up the space in front of the building, as are the Place Dupleix and Place Léon-Blum, the latter in front of the town hall of the 11th *arrondissement*. The most developed square is the Place du Châtelet with its two symmetrical theaters and fountain dedicated to the Empire. But its buildings are still fairly restrained, and Haussmann wanted the open

1. Place du Théâtre de l'Europe

This was built at the end of the 18th century in front of the Théâtre de l'Odéon, as part of the development of the old Hôtel de Condé. It is semicircular in shape, and the streets of the new district fan out from it.

2. Place de l'Abbé-Henocque

At the beginning of the 20th century, this part of the 13th *arrondissement* was being laid out, and the circus provided a centerpiece for the surrounding development. It was planted with trees from the beginning, and has recently been renovated.

3. Place de Catalogne

Built by Ricardo Bofill, this development is surrounded by massive buildings. It is one of the few "squares" to be built in Paris in the second half of the 20th century, when the 14th *arrondissement* was being modernized. Its circular shape has been widely used over the centuries.

space to be on a modest scale. Also from this period are squares laid out at the old gates in the wall of the Farmers-General: Place Pigalle, Place de Clichy, and Place d'Italie.

New squares

As happened with streets, so squares were also viewed unfavorably by the "modern" town planners. In the new districts built in 1960-70, there are no streets or squares, only pedestrian zones. Many old squares were spoiled at that time. The Place des Fêtes, near the Buttes-Chaumont, was broken up (it has since been restored), and the surfaces of the Place Dauphine and Place Vendôme were raised for underground parking lots. Then squares, and streets too, came back into fashion in the 1980s. New ones were built, though very few in number because they were seen as a risky exercise. The massive Neoclassical buildings surrounding a circular basin in the Place de Catalogne, behind the Gare Montparnasse, designed by the Catalan architect R Bofill, had clear associations with the past. At La Villette, architect B Huel integrated C N Ledoux's rotunda of 1784 into the renovated Place Stalingrad, a triangular space bordered by two grassy mounds. Most of today's projects are concerned with the renovation of existing squares, such as the Place de l'Hôtel de Ville, which has been pedestrianized and embellished with fountains by F X Lalanne; and the little Place A Laveran, facing Val-de-Grâce, which now also has fountains that have become very popular.

For proof of how difficult it is to design a square today, we need look no further than the Place de la Sorbonne, which is continually being dismantled and reworked.

4. Place du Tertre

This square in Montmartre has no specific shape and the buildings around it have no special pattern, but its proximity to Sacré-Coeur and the popularity of the district for tourists have made it a great attraction.

5. Place de la Nation

Along with Étoile, this is one of the squares built under Louis XIV to provide an entrance to Paris.
Two columns designed by C N Ledoux in 1788 survive from the old customs barrier.

6. Porte Maillot

This square stands at the end of the Avenue de la Grande Armée, on the axis joining the Louvre to La Défense, where the outer boulevards converge. The central part became a public garden in the 20th century.

LIGHTING AND ILLUMINATIONS

The Eiffel Tower sparkles, the outlines of bridges are thrown into relief by bluish or bronze lights, statues are illuminated, and the streets are well-lit. For centuries, however, the streets were plunged into total darkness at nightfall, their only light coming from the moon. Not until the 16th century did early forms of public lighting begin to appear.

The city in darkness

In the Middle Ages, the city seemed a safe place during the day, protected by stout walls. At night, however, people were terrified when the narrow streets were plunged into darkness. Medieval people dreaded the night, seeing it as a hellish place made for robbers and murderers, for demons and ghosts.

Protective measures

Various measures were undertaken to increase public safety. Some were aimed at expelling people considered "undesirable." In 1351, for example, King Jean the Good ordered all those on the fringes of society to be expelled. Other measures had a similar aim but were less brutal. One consisted of ringing a curfew at Notre-Dame at seven or eight in the evening, according to the time of year. After that, patrols commanded by the knight of the watch roamed the streets, on foot and on horseback, to make sure that no one disturbed the peace.

"Walking lights"

Despite these measures, some lights continued to shine in the night. In fact, anyone going into the street after curfew had to carry a lighted torch.

Candles could also be used, the object being to show that your intentions were honorable, rather than to see or be seen.

In addition to torches, there were also lanterns carried by sentries appointed by leading citizens to guard property.

At the end of the 16th century, torch-carriers went to the wealthy districts to persuade people going home from a dinner or a ball to let them light the way with their bright torches.

Lighting the city

The first steps

In 1318, Philippe V had the first permanent light installed at Châtelet gate. After that, however, the city was rarely lit up except on special occasions, such as the arrival of an important visitor. The idea of street lights made little progress. In 1516, in his *Utopia*, Thomas More described his ideal city, but said nothing about lighting it at night.

In Paris, however, something was about to be done. In 1524, people were asked to place a lantern in their windows. In 1558, after this measure had failed, Parliament ordered lanterns to be placed on every street corner. Later these were hung on poles or hoisted on pulleys attached to buildings. This was the start of modern public lighting.

Important advances

Real progress was not made until the reign of Louis XIV

5. The lantern carrier
Until the end of the 19th century, lantern carriers were constantly on the move in the dark streets, looking for customers to guide in exchange for a few coins.

6. Street lamps
In Paris, oil lamps were used from 1757. When gas lighting came in at the beginning of the 19th century, street lights became widespread. They were made of cast iron and many were decorated with plant motifs.

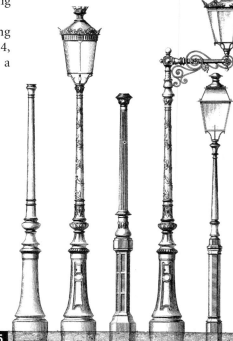

1. Hittorff lamp
In the 1830s, architect Hittorff was commissioned to lay out the Place de la Concorde and designed these splendid cast iron candelabra, which are still there today.

2. Les Invalides
Since the 1970s, the City of Paris has expanded its policy of illuminating buildings. This is the golden dome of the Invalides, completed in 1706.

3. Place de la Concorde
Behind the obelisk in Place de la Concorde is the Madeleine Church. From the top of the hill of Montmartre, the illuminated Church of Sacré-Coeur beams down over the Right Bank.

4. In front of the BNF
On the forecourt of the French National Library, architect Perrault incorporated these sleek spotlights into his architectural scheme.

(1643-1715). In 1667, the capital had 6,500 lanterns. The first improvements in street lighting came from scientific and technical discoveries rather than from more lanterns. In 1757, for example, the first oil streetlights, which were both practical and economical, were put up in Rue Dauphine and later throughout the city. They replaced some "8,000 lanterns lit by badly positioned candles which the wind blew out, and which gave out only a pale,

flickering, uncertain light cut by dangerous moving shadows," as L S Mercier described them in the *Tableau de Paris*.

At the beginning of the 19th century, the advent of gas lighting marked a new era. It was launched in the Passage des Panoramas, which in the 1820s was one of the most popular places in Paris. France was a little behind England, which had immediately taken up this invention, made by Frenchman P Lebon in 1799. However, by

the end of the 1840s, Paris had 13,770 gas lamps. The final leap to modern times came with the arrival of electric streetlights in 1920. In 1990, the city had more than 70,000.

Aesthetic concerns

As street lighting became more efficient, people started thinking more about its appearance. Influential architects working on installing or redesigning the lighting of streets, squares, and bridges were particularly concerned with their positioning and with integrating streetlights into their urban setting. When J Hittorff was commissioned in 1833 to lay out the Place de la Concorde, he himself designed the splendid cast-iron candelabra which still adorn the square. Similarly, architect V Baltard designed the streetlamps on Pont Neuf.

A variety of uses

In the 19th and 20th centuries, gas lighting appeared more and more on the public highways, and also in places of leisure such as cafés and billiard halls. Gas was more practical and economical than candles, and encouraged the city's developing night life.

As electricity came in, light was put to new uses. It was used not only to light places, but also to create nocturnal landmarks. This completely changed the visual environment of people living in Paris. One very good and effective example is the yel-

low "M" in a circle put up in the 1950s to indicate Métro entrances. From the 1920s, moreover, the city witnessed the arrival of brilliant, colored, and – most beguiling of all – winking lights.

Paris, "City of Light"

Since the end of the 1970s, the City of Paris has commissioned many new projects to illuminate the city and its heritage. Today, more than 150 monuments are totally or partly illuminated. The illumination of the bridges, river banks and quaysides on the Ile de la Cité shows off the historic heart of Paris. The framework of the Eiffel Tower is studded with thousands of bulbs which, every evening, can be seen from more than 12 miles (20 km) away. Painters and sculptors are also asked to design colored lighting schemes for various buildings; in 2000, they included Fabrice Hybert at the Arc de Triomphe and Sarkis at the Panthéon. Merely to mention the illuminations in the Champs-Elysées is enough to evoke Paris in the minds of foreigners. Lighting schemes such as these have become one of the city's great attractions.

7. Hector Guimard's lanterns
Guimard's famous Art Nouveau Métro entrances were thought most unusual when he designed them at the beginning of the 20th century. Some carry lanterns, such as this one at Bastille, more to announce their presence than to provide light.

8. Contemporary lighting
In the capital's new districts, contemporary streetlights are designed to harmonize with their surroundings.

1. Saint-Germain-des-Prés
Dominated by its 11th-century bell tower, the oldest in Paris, the church has a portal with 12th-century statues and a 17th-century porch.

2. St Julien-le-Pauvre
The nave of this small church built from the 12th century has four bays and no transept. The style is Gothic with some Romanesque elements. Since 1889, the church has been the Melchite (Greek Catholic) church, with a liturgy prescribed by Saint John Chrysostom.

CHURCHES, TEMPLES, SYNAGOGUES AND MOSQUES

In Paris, as in the rest of France, the Catholic faith is the most widely represented, with Notre-Dame-de-Paris and Sainte-Chapelle the jewels among its many Gothic churches. Over the centuries, more and more churches have been built, and the city's religious architecture embraces many other faiths as well: Protestant, Orthodox, Muslim, Jewish, and Buddhist.

Saint-Germain-des-Prés: the senior member

The oldest existing church dates from the Merovingian period. In 543, Childebert, son of Clovis, took the advice of Saint Germain, future Bishop of Paris, and had a basilica built to house remains of the Holy Cross. Several Merovingian kings were buried there after Childebert. In the 8th century, the building became an abbey belonging to the Order of Saint Benedict. The abbey owned vast arable lands (extending over the whole of today's 6th and 7th *arrondissements*) and was a great intellectual powerhouse.

Dawn of the Gothic period

From the year 1000, the city expanded, spilling outward from the Ile de la Cité to which it had withdrawn during the Viking invasions of the 9th century. Half-timbered houses, churches, and colleges were built along the banks of the Seine, amongst vineyards and fields. In the 12th century, a new architectural style was introduced, the Gothic, which seemed to defy the laws of gravity. The Church was the biggest

landowner, and began an ambitious church-building program which included Saint-Martin-des-Champs (3rd *arrondissement*) and Saint-Pierre-de-Montmartre (18th *arrondissement*) which featured ogival vaults for the first time. The most famous Gothic churches stand in the city's historic center, in the Latin Quarter and on the Ile de la Cité.

Saint-Julien-le-Pauvre

Just by the Seine, in the 5th *arrondissement*, is the Church of Saint-Julien-le-Pauvre. It stands on the site of a 6th-century church and refuge for pilgrims on their way to Santiago de Compostela. Building began in the 12th century. Traces of the Romanesque style are evident in the Gothic apses, which are supported by heavy buttresses. The building has been restored several times over the centuries, and in the 17th century its façade was redesigned.

Notre-Dame-de-Paris: the seat of spiritual power

In 1163, Bishop Maurice de Sully started the construction of the city's largest religious build-

ing on the site of a 6th-century Carolingian basilica. Rock was dug from the nearby limestone hills and transported by boat to the huge building site. It took almost a century to complete the bulk of the work, then another hundred years to finish and decorate the building. The rose windows lighting the nave were an unprecedented size, measuring 43 ft (13 m) in diameter. In the 19th century, Viollet-le-Duc undertook the

cathedral's restoration, and added its spire.

Sainte Chapelle

This church is taller and lighter than Notre-Dame. It was commissioned by Saint Louis (who consecrated it in 1248) to house Christ's Crown of Thorns. Walls were reduced to thin pillars supporting huge stained-glass windows that illustrate more than a thousand religious scenes. These and the fine inte-

6. Twisted columns at Saint-Séverin
The Church of Saint-Séverin is a fine illustration of Flamboyant Gothic art. The double ambulatory, a very rare feature in Paris and the Ile-de-France, was built between 1489 and 1494, and has palm tree vaults supported by twisted columns.

7. Sainte Chapelle
The building has two chapels. In the upper one, the slender pillars supporting the vault also frame the stained glass windows, which take up the whole of the space between the external buttresses.

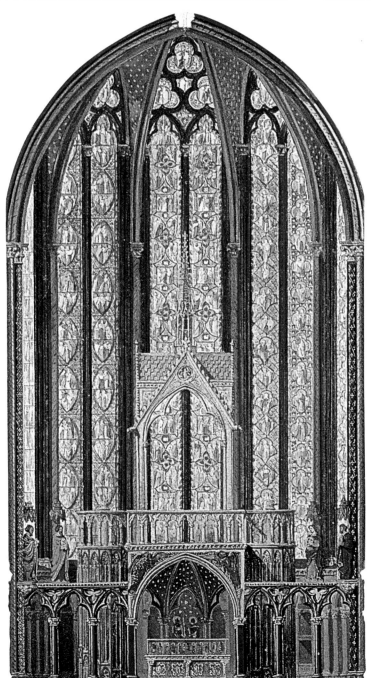

3. Notre-Dame
The flying buttresses behind the choir have a span of 50 ft (15 m) and were a great architectural achievement in their day. They were built by Jean Ravy, master of works from 1318 to 1344.

4. Saint-Paul Saint-Louis
Completed in 1641 (the name Saint-Paul was added in 1802), this is the only Jesuit church in Paris. Modeled on the Gesù Church in Rome – at the time it had the largest dome in Paris.

5. Saint-Gervais-Saint-Protais
On July 24, 1616, Louis XIII laid the foundation stone of the classical façade of the Church of Saint-Gervais-Saint-Protais, with its superimposition of the three Classical orders.

rior decorations make Sainte-Chapelle a masterpiece of Gothic architecture.

Flamboyant art in Paris
New churches were built in the 15th century as the city expanded: Saint-Germain-l'Auxerrois (1st *arrondissement*), Saint-Nicolas-des-Champs (3rd), Saint-Merri (4th), Saint-Médard and Saint-Séverin (5th), Saint-Laurent (10th), and Saint-Germain-de-Charonne (20th). These churches were not as tall as the earlier Gothic churches, but were very elegant with subtly thought-out decorations. At Saint-Séverin, twisted columns encircle the double ambulatory, and Saint-Germain-l'Auxerrois has an exceptional porch by Jean Gaussel.

Magnificent Renaissance buildings
In 1528, François I decided to make the Louvre his residence, and built new churches for the capital. Saint-Eustache in Les Halles was begun in 1532. Its nave with five vaults and its side chapels echo those of Notre-Dame. Although basically a Gothic building, its decoration

was inspired by the Renaissance. Cardinal Richelieu was baptized and Louis XIV made his first communion there; today it stages many concerts. Saint-Gervais-Saint-Protais (4th *arrondissement*) was built between 1494 and 1657. The interior is Late Gothic, but the façade incorporates the three Classic orders – Doric, Ionic, and Corinthian. The parish is run by the Monastic and Lay Brothers of Jerusalem, whose liturgy is derived from the Eastern Church. Saint-Etienne-du-Mont (5th *arrondissement*) is best known for its roodscreen of 1540, the only one to have been preserved. Its stone lacework is extremely elegant, and was inspired by the Italian Renaissance. The church houses a casket with fragments from the sarcophagus of Sainte Geneviève, the patron saint of Paris.

The Golden Age of Classicism
Under Louis XIII and Louis XIV, the capital was remade in a Classical image. Domes were widely used, and the Italian Baroque style now appeared. Façades were given regular orders of columns surmounted

1. Saint-Etienne-du-Mont

The façade, built between 1610 and 1620, blends Classical elements with the Gothic fabric. The foundation stone was laid by Marguerite de Valois, first wife of Henri IV, in 1610. After the façade was damaged in the Revolution, the church was restored by architect Baltard from 1861 to 1868.

2. Saint Roch

The altar of the Lady Chapel with its Nativity group, sculpted in 1655 by Michel Anguier, comes from the Church of Val-de-Grâce, where it was replaced by a copy. The lighting and the theatrical staging are Baroque in tone.

3. Val-de-Grâce

The Classical façade of the Church of Val-de-Grâce is surmounted by a dome designed by Pierre Le Muet and Gabriel Le Duc, which recalls the dome of Saint Peter's, Rome.

4. The Panthéon

The Panthéon was built on the plan of a Greek cross designed by Soufflot. Begun in 1764, it is 360 ft (110 m) long, 270 ft (82 m) wide, and surmounted by a dome which is 270 ft (82 m) high to the top of the lantern. In 1791, the building was transformed by the Revolutionary government into a pantheon to "receive the ashes of the great men of French liberty."

5. Église de la Trinité

The Trinité church was built in 1861-7 by T Ballu, in a Neo-Renaissance style. It is linked to the square in front by a balustrade and two flights of steps. Three fountains are surmounted by allegorical statues representing Faith, Hope, and Charity.

by a pediment, as at Saint-Roch and the Sorbonne Chapel, built at the beginning of the 17th century in the style of the Gesù Church in Rome.

Val-de-Grâce

The Val-de-Grâce is one of the best-preserved architectural complexes in Paris. The church is located in the Faubourg Saint-Jacques, where many monasteries and convents had already been built. It was founded in 1645 as an act of thanks by Anne of Austria, when she at last became a mother after 21 years of waiting. Her son, Louis XIV, laid the foundation stone when he was seven years old. The building is mainly influenced by the Roman Baroque style, with a dome decorated by sculptures and a canopy like the one made by Bernini for Saint Peter's, in Rome.

Saint-Louis-des-Invalides

Louis XIV wanted to impose his own sense of grandeur on Paris. The city was transformed with broad perspectives and buildings glorifying the army. He commissioned J-H Mansart to design the Hôtel Royal des Invalides to house his wounded soldiers. In 1676, 6,000 invalids moved into the building. Mansart also designed the Church of Saint-Louis-des-Invalides, which was dedicated to the soldiers, and the Dôme des Invalides. The Classical

cupola was completely regilded in the 1990s.

Return to Antiquity

In the 18th century, Paris joined the Classical revival that was taking over in Europe. Religious architecture adopted the Neoclassical style, which lasted into the Empire.

Church of Saint-Sulpice

This church was begun in 1646 in a Greco-Roman style, but was not completed until the following century. Servandoni was commissioned to design the façade, which has a two-story colonnade. The Chapelle des Saints-Anges was decorated by Delacroix and the sculptor Pigalle.

The Panthéon

In 1744, Louis XV was very sick and decided that, if he recovered, he would build a monument to Sainte Geneviève. When he was cured, the king commissioned plans from Soufflot, asking him to blend "the lightness of Gothic buildings with the purity of Greek architecture." However, there was a danger the building would collapse, and the plans had to be revised. This was undertaken by Rondelet, who took over on his master's death in 1780.

The Madeleine

The Madeleine was originally designed as a Temple of Glory, dedicated to the soldiers of the Grande Armée, then was redes-

ignated as a Catholic church in 1813 on Napoléon's orders. It was not completed and opened until 1842, under Louis-Philippe. Many of the city's celebrities are buried there.

Mixed styles of the 19th century

After a furious bout of destruction in the Revolution, the Concordat of 1801, which delivered ownership of the churches to the local communes, led to a policy of church building which lasted throughout the 19th century. Under the Restoration and

6, 7. Church of Notre-Dame-du-Travail
This church, built in 1892-1902 in Rue Guilleminot by Jules Astruc, has a fairly classical exterior, with its long nave, two side aisles, and freestone and brick construction.
The interior of the church has an iron framework, which was very new at the time.

8. Notre-Dame-de-l'Arche-d'Alliance
This is one of the city's most recent churches, a concrete, glass, and metal addition to a district in the throes of regeneration.

the Second Empire, architects looked back to past models and borrowed from the Byzantine, Romanesque, and Gothic styles. Churches in the old center of Paris included Saint-Augustin (8th *arrondissement*), Trinité (9th), and Saint-François-Xavier (7th), while Sainte-Clothilde (7th), Notre-Dame-de-Lorette (9th), and Saint-Vincent-de-Paul were built around the new boulevards. Other churches were built in the inner suburbs, which have since become part of the city, for example Notre-Dame-de-Bercy (12th *arrondissement*), Notre-Dame-de-la-Gare (13th), and Sainte-Marie-des-Batignolles (17th). In 1876, the basilica of Sacré-Coeur was begun in a Romanesque-Byzantine style.

The advent of iron

Architects began using metal in their buildings from 1850. The first church with an all-metal interior was Saint-Eugène-Sainte-Cécile, Rue du Conservatoire (9th *arrondissement*), inaugurated in 1855 by Empress Eugénie. Narrow cast-iron pillars support the Neo-Gothic vaults. In 1902, architect Jules Astruc left the internal iron framework bare at Notre-Dame-du-Travail ("a universal sanctuary for workers").

Churches of the 20th century

Ever since the Church separated from the State in 1905, churches have been funded privately. However, the number of religious buildings never ceased to grow, because the population was continually on the increase. In 1914, it passed three million.

Very eclectic styles

New churches built in the first half of the 20th century continued to borrow freely from the past. The Neo-Rom-anesque style was used at Saint-Lambert-de-Vaugirard (15th *arrondisse-ment*) and at Notre-Dame-de-la-Croix (20th), the Gothic at Saint-Christophe-de-Javel and Saint-Antoine-de-Padoue (both 15th *arrondissement*), and the Romanesque-Byzantine at Saint-Pierre-de-Chaillot (16th *arrondissement*) and Saint-Ferdinand-des-Ternes (17th). At Sainte-Odile, Porte de Champerret, whose 235 ft (72 m) bell tower is the tallest in Paris, reinforced concrete was used for the first time, covered in pink brick.

Notre-Dame-de-l'Arche-d'Alliance

Inaugurated in 1998, this church on Rue d'Alleray (15th *arrondissement*) is basically a brown cube resting on 12 pillars and enclosed in a metal net. The baptistery is located beneath the church, but is visible through the transparent flooring. Two churches were inaugurated in 2000: Saint-Luc, Rue de l'Ourcq (19th *arrondissement*) and Saint-François-de-Molitor (16th).

Protestant churches

In 1801, when Napoléon I re-established freedom of worship, the first Protestant churches moved into former Catholic buildings. Only in the second half of the 19th century were the first Protestant churches built.

Buildings transferred to the Protestant faith

The Temple de la Visitation, Rue Saint-Antoine (4th *arrondissement*), a Classical-style

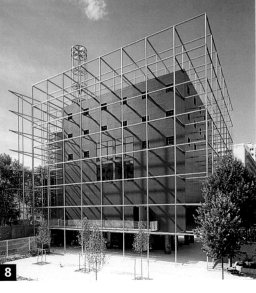

1. Temple de l'Oratoire
The Royal Chapel of the Oratory was originally designed as a Catholic church, founded in 1616 and built by Métezeau to plans by Le Mercier. It was famous for its preaching, and the Court came to hear Malebranche, Bossuet, and Bourdaloue. One of its ceilings was painted by Simon Vouet. It was transferred to the Protestants in 1811.

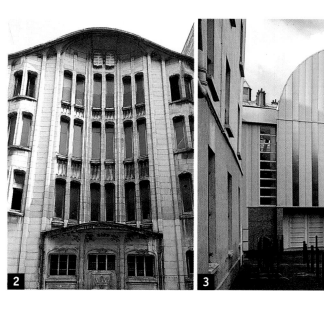

round church built between 1632 and 1634 by F Mansart, was originally designed for the Filles de Visitation Sainte-Marie. In 1803, it was handed over to the French Reformed Church. Les Billettes, Rue des Archives (4th *arrondissement*) was a convent from 1290, before a church was built there at the end of the 15th century and replaced by another in 1755-8. A fine Medieval cloister, the only one in Paris, has survived. The Église des Billettes was transferred to the Lutherans in 1812. The Oratory, Rue Saint-Roch (1st *arrondissement*), was given to the Reformed Church in 1811 by Napoléon I. It was originally a chapel, founded in 1616 by the Mother House of the Oratorians, on the site of the Hôtel de Gabrielle d'Estrées.

New Protestant churches

In Rue Roquépine (7th *arrondissement*), the architect Baltard built the Temple du Saint-Esprit (1863-5). The Reformed Church of the Annunciation, Rue Cortambert (16th) was built at the end of the 19th century, and at that time too the Protestant community in Belleville acquired the Temple de Paris-Belleville, Rue Julien-Lacroix (20th).

Orthodox churches

Russia and France formed friendly relationships in the 19th century. Liberal-minded and revolutionary Russians found refuge in France, and were joined after the Bolshevik Revolution by White Russians. They mostly settled in the 8th, 15th, and 16th *arrondissements*. Their best-known churches include the Cathedral of Saint Alexander Nevsky, Rue Daru (8th *arrondissement*), one of the most popular meeting places of the Russian community. It was built in 1861 in a Neo-Byzantine style by the architects of Saint Petersburg, and is crowned by golden onion domes. Other, more secluded places of worship are also worth discovering. At the end of a courtyard at No 91, Rue Lecourbe, a wooden chalet surmounted by a blue onion dome houses the Church of Saint-Séraphin-de-Sarov. Other Orthodox communities have their own churches, for example the Greeks at Saint-Etienne, Rue

Georges-Bizet, and the Rumanians at the Eglise des Saints-Archanges, near Place Maubert-Mutualité.

The synagogues

After 1850, many Ashkenazi Jews from Poland settled in the Marais, and needed new places of worship. Alexandre Thierry built the synagogue in Rue Notre-Dame-de-Nazareth in 1851. In Rue des Tournelles, another building, with an interior designed by Gustave Eiffel, was inaugurated in 1876. In Rue Pavée, the synagogue built by Hector Guimard in 1913 has a façade with four windowed stories.

Today, the synagogue in Rue des Tournelles has become Sephardic, and backs onto the Ashkenazi synagogue in Place des Vosges, in the old Hôtel de Louis Barbier de la Rivière. The Great Synagogue in Rue de la Victoire (2nd *arrondissement*)

5. Orthodox church in Rue Daru
The Church of Saint-Alexander-Nevsky, Rue Daru (8th *arrondissement*) is the most famous Russian Orthodox church in Paris. The architecture is Byzantine, and much like Santa Sophia in style. The interior decoration is especially fine, with mosaics, paintings, and icons. The building was financed by the Orthodox communities in France, and was inaugurated in 1861.

2. Synagogue in Rue Pavée
The Agoudas Hakehilos in Rue Pavée, in the Marais, was designed by Hector Guimard in 1913. Its freestone façade is very restrained.

3. New Synagogue (19th *arrondissement*)
The first synagogues opened in the Marais, then new ones were built in eastern Paris, in the 19th and 20th *arrondissements*, where there are also Jewish schools and crèches.

4. Buddhist Institute at Vincennes
The Kagyu Dzong Tibetan temple was built in 1983 at the Buddhist Center near the Great Pagoda in the Bois de Vincennes. It was consecrated by the venerable Kalou Rimpoche, and each year is visited by lamas representing different concepts of Buddhism, who give lessons and organize meditation sessions.

has two oratories, Tunisian and Egyptian. A further 30 synagogues have opened in the 19th and 20th *arrondissements*.

The mosques
The Paris Mosque is the most famous Muslim place of worship in the city. In 1920, the French government decided to build it in memory of the 100,000 Muslims who died in World War I, to provide a place for 20,000 Parisians to worship. It was designed by Fournez, Heubès, and Mantout in a Hispanic-Moorish style and was inaugurated in 1926. Many other places of prayer have appeared since, particularly in north-eastern Paris where most of the Muslim community live.

The wooden Tibetan temple at Vincennes
Buddhism only reached Paris in the 1950s, imported by refugees from southeast Asia. In addition to the many private and public places of worship in the 13th *arrondissement*, such as the Altar of the Buddhist Cult, which opened in 1985 in Rue du Disque, there is also the Kagyu Dzong Tibetan temple at the Buddhist Center in the Bois de Vincennes; it was built in 1983 under the supervision of the Buddhist Master, Kalou Rimpoche.

6, 7. The Paris Mosque
The Paris Mosque was built between 1922 and 1926 by architects Fournez, Heubès, and Mantout, and is surmounted by a 110 ft (33 m) minaret. It represents the religious aspect of the Muslim Institute and has a cultural dimension, which includes teaching, and also offers a tea room, a hammam, and a boutique. The courtyard was inspired by the Alhambra at Grenada, and has a large basin in the middle. Verses from the Koran decorate the mosaic friezes on the walls. The prayer room is decorated with cedar panels.

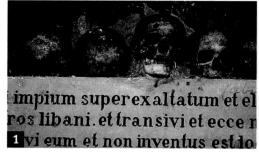

impium super exaltatum et el
ros libani. et transivi et ecce r
1 vi eum et non inventus est lo

1. The Catacombs
Between 1786 and 1814, bones from the Cimetière des Innocents were stored in the Catacombs. During the Revolution, Danton and Robespierre were probably buried there, along with many other people.

2. Père-Lachaise
This is the largest and most visited of the Paris cemeteries. In summer, people come to see its statues and walk beneath its hundred-year-old trees. It was laid out by A Brongniart, who is buried there.

CEMETERIES

Before the Revolution, people were buried all over the city in small cemeteries, churches, and the graveyards beside them. When Paris expanded in the 18th century, huge necropolises were built outside the city walls. This was the period when Père Lachaise, Montparnasse Cemetery, and Montmartre Cemetery were laid out. A few older, more secluded burial grounds have survived, some of which date from times of great civic unrest and bloodshed.

The city with 19 cemeteries

Paris has 19 cemeteries. The most distant, like Thiais, Saint-Ouen, and Bagneux, are in the suburbs. Others, such as Valmy (12th *arrondissement*) and Gentilly (13th *arrondissement*), became municipal cemeteries in the early 20th century.

Death in Paris before the Revolution

Cemeteries, churches, and parish graveyards

The first cemeteries in Paris date from the Gallo-Roman period, and were very small. The Cemetery of the Innocents was 8,600 sq yd (7,200 sq m) in area; Saint-Séverin was 1,075 sq yd (900 sq m); and most were no more than 120 sq yd (100 sq m) – much less than present-day cemeteries which cover several acres.

Up to the French Revolution, Paris had 52 parish graveyards. Many other people were buried in the churches, and in monasteries and convents. Burial consisted of adding a body to the existing pile in a communal ditch.

Cimetière des Innocents

This cemetery was located in the space between Rue Saint-Denis, Rue aux Fers (now Rue Berger), Rue de la Ferronnerie, and Rue de la Lingerie, and for 800 years was the biggest cemetery in Paris. At least two million Parisians were buried there. It was probably opened in the 10th century, and then, defying all the rules of public health, included within Philippe-Auguste's city wall from 1186. For centuries, people asked for it to be closed. The smell was appalling, and the dangers of infection were far too high.

Finally, in 1780, after a communal ditch collapsed, tipping hundreds of decomposing corpses into the cellars of nearby houses, it was shut down.

The Catacombs

Once this and the other cemeteries within the city walls had been closed, followed by the banning of any further burials in churches, the authorities had to find somewhere to put the millions of skeletons they were left with. They chose some former quarries at La Tombe-Issoire. There, an enclosure of nearly 13,000 sq yd (11,000 sq m) was laid out, and, beginning in 1786, the skeletons were transferred

3. Tombs in Père Lachaise
From 1800 to 1830, tombs were inspired by Antique forms (pyramids, obelisks, columns, steles, and sarcophaguses). In the second half of the 19th century, chapels became more popular.

4. Crematorium at Père Lachaise
Cremation was allowed in France from 1887. The city of Paris commissioned architect Formigé to develop several crematoriums. This one has a Byzantine appearance with alternating layers of gray and white stone.

there in an operation lasting 15 months. Every night, carts piled high with their macabre load rumbled aross Paris. The Catacombs are open to the public, and contain six million skeletons of people buried over a period of 1,500 years.

Huge necropolises at the gates of Paris

As the city expanded, and more and more rich people were demanding burial plots, the need for new cemeteries became urgent. They were laicized in 1791, and administrative power was transferred to the local communes.

Père Lachaise, a hill in the country

Père Lachaise, in the north-east of Paris, covers 110 acres (44 ha) planted with 5,300 trees. Before it became a cemetery, it was called the Bishop's Field, having belonged to the Bishop of Paris in the Middle Ages, and was covered with vines and fruit trees. At the end of the 14th century, it was acquired by Régnault de Wandenne, who built a folly there (commemorated by Rue de la Folie-Regnault in the 11th *arrondissement*). Then, in the 17th century, the hill passed to the Jesuits, one of whom was Père de la Chaize, confessor to Louis XIV, whence its present name.

A slow start

In 1804, Count Frochot, Prefect of the Seine, bought this green and spacious land on the orders of Napoléon I. Brongniart was commissioned to convert it into a cemetery. However, the so-called East Cemetery met with little public enthusiasm. In 1805, only 15 people were buried there, and no more than 19 the following year. To attract more burials, the supposed remains of Abelard and Héloïse were transferred there with great pomp and ceremony in 1817, along with those of Molière and La Fontaine. This sparked the necessary demand (33,000 people by 1830). In fact, Père Lachaise was such a success that it was extended six times between 1824 and 1850 to reach its present size. Since then, the cemetery has been in constant demand.

A resting place dedicated to artists and warriors

The many artists buried there include Pissarro, Géricault, Gustave Doré, Ingres, Daumier, Corot, Daubigny, Marie Laurencin, Max Ernst, Delacroix, Jacques-Louis David, Flandrin, and Seurat. Among the writers are Molière, La Fontaine, Balzac, Jules Romains, Colette, Musset, Alphonse Daudet, Paul Eluard, Oscar Wilde, Marcel Proust, Apollinaire, and Georges Pérec. There is no shortage of musicians; for example, Bellini, Rossini, Poulenc, and Chopin; or singers – Edith Piaf, Mouloudji, and Jim Morrison, whose tomb has become a place of pilgrimage – and actors, including Yves Montand, Pierre Brasseur, Elvire Popesco, and Sylvia Monfort.

Napoléon I, who was the driving force behind the cemetery, wished to be buried at Père Lachaise, and most of his marshals are in fact buried there, many in impressive mausoleums.

Montparnasse Cemetery

The cemetery for southern Paris opened in 1824. At that time, the

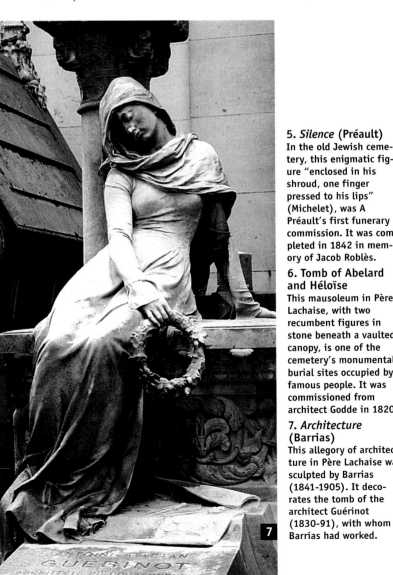

5. *Silence* (Préault)
In the old Jewish cemetery, this enigmatic figure "enclosed in his shroud, one finger pressed to his lips" (Michelet), was A Préault's first funerary commission. It was completed in 1842 in memory of Jacob Roblès.

6. Tomb of Abelard and Héloïse
This mausoleum in Père Lachaise, with two recumbent figures in stone beneath a vaulted canopy, is one of the cemetery's monumental burial sites occupied by famous people. It was commissioned from architect Godde in 1820.

7. *Architecture* (Barrias)
This allegory of architecture in Père Lachaise was sculpted by Barrias (1841-1905). It decorates the tomb of the architect Guérinot (1830-91), with whom Barrias had worked.

hill called Mont Parnasse was outside the city limits. Originally it was used by market gardeners, and in the 17th century the monks of Saint-Jean-de-Dieu buried their dead in the Hôpital de la Charité. Inside the present cemetery, the Charité windmill still survives, though without its sails. In the 18th century, the students of the Collège de Clermont (now the Louis-le-Grand) moved there. Today the Rue Emile Blanchard divides the 44 acre (18 ha) cemetery into two parts. The northern entrance leads to Brancusi's *Kiss*, which was the Rumanian sculptor's way of celebrating the double suicide of two friends.

Famous artists and writers

Among the artists who chose Montparnasse Cemetery as their last resting place are the sculptors Jean-Antoine Houdon, François Rude, Jules Dalou, Henri Laurens, and Zadkine (whose studio was in Rue d'Asselas); also the history painter François Girard, and the Cubist André Lhote. Littré, who wrote the famous Littré dictionary, is in the Third Division; the publisher Pierre Larousse is in the 14th, and Louis Hachette in the 15th. Famous writers include Guy de Maupassant, Baudelaire (whose tomb bears his portrait), Théodore de Banville, Léon-Paul Fargue, Robert Desnos, Jean-Paul Sartre, and Marguerite Duras. Of the more recent burials, the best known is probably Serge Gainsbourg.

Montmartre Cemetery

This cemetery was laid out in 1798 on the site of an old abandoned quarry. At first called the Field of Rest, then the North Cemetery, it was closed in 1806 for want of space, then enlarged and reopened in 1831. Today it covers 25 acres (10 ha). Writers buried there include Stendhal, Heine, Théophile Gautier, and Alfred de Vigny, alongside the composer Berlioz, and film directors Sacha Guitry and François Truffaut. Among the painters are Fragonard, Greuze (whose tomb is decorated with the statue *Young Girl with Broken Pitcher*), and Degas, who spent his life tirelessly prowling the nearby Boulevard de Clichy, where he had his studio.

Secluded cemeteries

Picpus Cemetery

This small private cemetery is in the former community of the Canonesses of Saint-Augustin. It houses the remains of the 1,306 victims of the guillotine put up in June, 1794, on Place du Trône-Renversé (now called Place de la Nation).

They include the aristocrats Alexandre de Beauharnais, first husband of Empress Joséphine; Prince Victor de Broglie; Madame de Montmorency-Laval, the last Abbess of Montmartre; the poet André

5. Statue of Kamienski
This statue in Montmartre Cemetery depicts a Polish soldier in the Foreign Legion, who died under fire at Magenta in 1859. His last words were: "I die calm, Polish, and Christian. Farewell dreams, illusions, and conceits."

6. In Montparnasse Cemetery
The sculptor Charles René de Saint-Marceaux (1845-1915) created this marble recumbent figure in Montparnasse Cemetery.

1. Funeral of Edith Piaf
In 1963, thousands of the singer's admirers accompanied her coffin to Père Lachaise. She is buried not far from the poet Gérard de Nerval and the painter Eugène Delacroix.

2. Tomb of Serge Gainsbourg
In Montparnasse Cemetery, the tomb of Gainsbourg, legendary author of many famous songs, who died in 1991, is covered with flowers, soft toys, and poems.

3. Montmartre Cemetery
Among the original tombs in this cemetery in northern Paris is the undated one of Anatole, the "rural policeman of the free commune of Old Montmartre."

4. Sculpture of Victor Brauner
Brauner and his wife are buried in Montmartre Cemetery. The Rumanian sculptor (1903-66) himself designed this very serene, hieratic, double-headed portrait in marble.

Chénier; and many ordinary people.

In 1803, after the cemetery had been abandoned, it was bought by the victims' families, and now only their descendants may be buried there.

Here too is the tomb of General de La Fayette, husband of Marie-Adrienne de Noailles, whose family was decimated; since 1934, it has been decorated with an American flag.

Cimetière du Calvaire

Cimetière du Calvaire is the most secluded cemetery in Paris. It lies huddled around the Church of Saint-Pierre-de-Montmartre, and is open only two days a year, November 1 and 2. It is also the oldest, dating from the 11th century. It is reserved for the descendants of the 80 families buried in its 700 sq yd (600 sq m) confines.

These include the actress Camille, mistress of Frederick the Great of Prussia and Casanova, and Louis-Antoine de Bougainville, "the first Frenchman to sail round the world, 1729-1811," as his epitaph declares.

Saint-Vincent Cemetery

This cemetery was opened in 1831 to take over from the Calvaire, which was full. It overlooks the Lapin-Agile cabaret and the Montmartre vineyard. Local lovers are buried there, alongside writers Marcel Aymé and Roland Dorgelès, the painter Maurice Utrillo, and the caricaturist Alexandre Steinlen. Also there is the actor Harry Baur, best known in the role of Jean Valjean, the hero of Victor Hugo's *Les Misérables*, who was tortured to death by the Germans in 1943.

The rural Charonne Cemetery

In the shadow of the Romanesque Church of Saint-Germain-de-Charonne, more than 650 tombs cluster in a space of 5,000 sq yd (4,200 sq m). Charonne Cemetery was opened in the Revolution, and enlarged several times since. It contains the skeletons of the Federalists of 1871, who were buried in a makeshift ditch. Also here are the two sons of André Malraux, who were killed in the same car accident with their mother, Josette Malraux-Clotis. Another occupant is the house painter François Bègue, known as Magliore, a winelover who passed himself off as Robespierre's secretary; his bronze statue faces the entrance.

The unseen dead

Many burial sites in Paris have been built over. Beside the Church of Saint-Séverin (5th *arrondissement*), the Gothic buildings in the little square were erected in the 15th century over a charnel-house where remains from the communal ditch for suicides were placed. In Square Louis XVI, Rue Pasquier (8th *arrondissement*), on the site of an expiatory chapel, hundreds of Swiss Guards were buried after the Tuileries Massacre of 1792, along with the 1,500 people guillotined in Place de la Concorde (then Place de la Révolution). Beneath the July Column, in the middle of Place de la Bastille, are two cellars which contained the remains of some 300 victims of the Revolutions of 1830 and 1848.

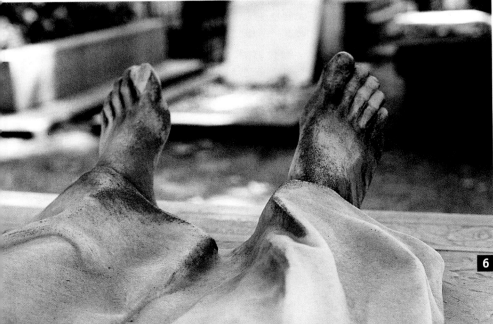

7. Charonne Cemetery
This cemetery beside Saint-Germain-de-Charonne, the old communal church at Charonne, was absorbed into the city in 1859. The writer R Brasillach, who was accused of collaborating and shot in 1945, is buried there.

1. F. Bienvenüe
F Bienvenüe (1852-1936) was the man who built the Métro. Graduating from the École Polytechnique, the Breton engineer worked for the City of Paris from 1886.

2. Place Saint Michel
Watertight chambers had to be sunk so the Métro could cross the Seine.

3. Cars in 1900
The first Métro cars were made of wood.

THE MÉTRO

This subway system first appeared at the beginning of the 20th century, when the population of Paris was growing rapidly, and since then has kept pace with the city's continuous expansion. It runs mostly underground, today more deeply than ever, and in a hundred years its network has formed a giant spider's web extending far beyond the inner city. The Métro is quick, efficient, with frequent trains on 14 lines, and makes its own contribution to the city's life and culture.

Relieving traffic congestion

At the beginning of the 20th century, the broad avenues built by Haussmann were no longer able to keep the traffic flowing. With a population of three million, the city was developing fast, and the streets were overcrowded with horse-drawn vehicles, carriages, buses, and electric streetcars. What was needed was a means of transport that did not travel at street level. Serious thought had been given to this since the 1870s. Most engineers envisioned an aerial rail system some 20 ft (7 m) above ground. One even dreamed up a viaduct following the course of the Seine.

While people in Paris worked on crazy projects, elsewhere they were building. The first subway, 3.7 miles (6 km) long, opened in London in 1863; there was an aerial railroad in New York by 1868, and one in Chicago by 1892. In Continental Europe, the first city to acquire a subway was Budapest, in 1896.

Digging the tunnels

Paris was getting ready for the 1900 Universal Exhibition. The authorities were aware of the large number of visitors there would be, and decided they must act. In addition, the City of Paris and the State wanted to see a network connecting the different main line stations.

Fulgence Bienvenüe, head of the city's Bridges and Highways department, was asked to make a pilot study for an electric underground railroad. Work began immediately, backed by a law of March 30, 1898. Bienvenüe had barely two years to build the Métro. Despite the difficulties involved – moving sewers and pipework, and drilling into the rock – he met his target.

Dynamic results

After 17 months of uninterrupted labor by 2,000 construction workers, mostly working in the open or a short distance beneath the surface road network, Line 1, running 6 miles (10 km) from Porte de Vincennes to Porte Maillot, and calling at the Exhibition site, was opened to the public on July 14, 1900. It had 16 stations, and a total journey time of 30 minutes. By January, 1901, the Métro had already carried four million passengers. Line 2, from Porte Dauphine to Nation via a northern loop, was begun in December, 1900, and completed in April, 1903. It ran partly above street level, like Line 6, its southern counterpart. From now on, construction continued at a frantic pace.

Technical wizardry

In 1908, digging Line 4 (Porte de Clignancourt to Porte d'Orléans) posed a great technical challenge: the line had to pass under both arms of the Seine at Ile de la Cité.

The engineer Fülgence Bienvenüe opted for a system of

watertight chambers, which were floated into position and then lowered onto the river bed. In the small, compressed-air "work area," a 6 ft (1.8 m) compartment in the lower part of the chambers, workers dug and drilled, passing the rubble out through chimneys and bringing the chambers down to the required depth of 50 ft (15 m) beneath the Seine. These chambers were then linked up to others dug below ground on the Ile de la Cité and Place Saint-Michel, which contained the two stations with their platforms and twin lines of tracks.

Extending the network

Before World War I, the Paris Metropolitan Railroad Company (CMP) was running ten lines and had carried a total of half a billion passengers. Before 1939, two lines were added to the original ones, which had themselves been extended, some beyond the city limits like the 3-mile (5-km) stretch from Gare du Nord to Eglise de Pantin (Line 5). In World War II, the Métro proved very valuable. Some stations were used as shelters, and, in the absence of

4. Porte Dauphine station
This cast-iron and glass entrance was completed by H Guimard in 1900. Only this and the one at Abbesses have been preserved.

5. Guimard's ornamental style
Guimard's curved shapes are typical of Art Nouveau, with their plant and animal forms featuring birds, dragonflies, etc.

6. Austerlitz viaduct
This metal bridge was built especially for the Métro between 1902 and 1904. The decoration is by Formigé, who designed the Métro's superstructures.

buses and taxis at street level, the volume of traffic increased considerably. The passenger total passed the billion mark in 1941, and reached 1.6 billion in 1946. In 1948, the CMP was charged with collaborating in the war; their Métro concession was withdrawn, and transferred to the RATP (Paris City Transport Authority).

Linking the Métro and RER

In the 1960s, the ever-increasing growth of the suburbs made new extensions necessary. In 1965, plans were drawn up to connect the future new towns of Evry, Cergy-Pontoise, and Saint-Quentin-en-Yvelines to the city network. In Paris itself, deep-level stations were built, and in 1969 the RER (Regional Express Network) opened Line A, and then gradually linked up the whole of the Ile-de-France with the city center.

Constant technological innovations

In 1900, the first motor units had rigid axles and looked like streetcars, as no one had yet devised any other shape for them. At first they drew wooden passenger cars, which were soon replaced by others with a metal

body. From 1908, trains were powered by Sprague-Thomson electric motors at front and back. In the 1950s, the first articulated trains appeared, then in 1956, on Line 11, new, quieter trains appeared with pneumatic wheels. In 1967, the lines were equipped with centralized control rooms and trains that could run on autopilot. In 1998, the Météor (Rapid East-West Métro) came into service on Line 14 with fully automatic trains.

The story of the stations

Named for famous and unknown people

Many stations have well-known names. Montparnasse-Bienvenüe commemorates the man who built the Métro, and several are named for politicians (Gambetta, Félix Faure, Garibaldi, and Jaurès) and writers (Alexandre Dumas, Anatole France, Victor Hugo, Voltaire, and Zola). Military people are well represented, particularly Napoléon I's marshals (Cambronne, Duroc, Exelmans, Hoche, and Kléber, for example). Among the scientists are Jussieu, Parmentier, Lamarck, Monge, and Pierre Curie

7. Works near Saint-Lazare station
The building of this new transport system meant disemboweling the city, which paralyzed the traffic for many months.

8. Tunnels on the North-South line
The first north-south line (Porte de Clignancourt to Porte d'Orléans) was particularly difficult to build, as it involved crossing the Seine and not getting in the way of the private railroad companies.

1. Palais-Royal station
This entrance to Palais-Royal station in Place Colette is now the "Kiosk for Night Owls" (2000), designed by J-M Othoniel. It is made of glass beads and aluminum.

2. Europe station
Since 2000, video screens set in the walls show documentaries of daily life in Europe's major cities.

(though not Marie, his no less famous wife). In fact, only one station is named for a woman: Louise Michel, the revolutionary Socialist. Among the unknown people are Corentin Celton, Corentin Cariou, and Jacques Bonsergent, who were taken hostage and shot during World War II.

Stations recalling a bygone Paris

The old village of Glacière ("ice-house"—Line 6) owes its name to the Bièvre, a tributary of the Seine, now filled in, which contained a series of pools. When these froze in winter, people went out from Paris to skate on them. The ice was also collected and kept in large stone wells for the benefit of the local inhabitants in summer. Poissonnière ("fish-trader"—Line 7) and Marcadet-Poissonniers (Lines 4 and 12) are on the route used for bringing sea fish from the North to market at Les Halles. They were brought in by mule until the Gare du Nord opened. Rue du Bac (Line 12) is a reminder of the old flat-bottomed ferry ("*bac*" in French) used in the 16th century to bring blocks of stone across the Seine to build the Château des Tuileries.

Hidden stations

Down beneath the city are several stations to which access has been closed off. At Arsenal they made cannons, weapons, and gunpowder for the defence of Paris. Today, the station buildings house a library. The Champ de Mars, in front of the École

Militaire, was used for maneuvers from 1770 to 1789. It hosted the Universal Exhibitions of 1867, 1878, 1889, 1900, and 1937, and Eiffel built his Tower there in 1889. Croix Rouge takes its name from the crossroads where, in 1514, Guillaume Briçonnet, Abbot of Saint-Germain-des-Prés, had a large, red-painted cross erected. It was

removed in 1650. These stations were shut on September 2, 1939. Champ de Mars-Tour Eiffel is now an RER station.

The Métro in the City

New shapes for a new means of transport

In 1900, Hector Guimard was commissioned to design the

Métro entrances. He opted for glass walls and a canopy framed in cast iron, a light, inexpensive, and flexible material which he forged in shapes representing plant forms, dragonflies, and butterflies. His Art Nouveau style drew both admiration and scorn. Today, only two entrances have been preserved, those at Abbesses and Porte

Dauphine stations. In 2000, Guimard was succeeded by Jean-Michel Othoniel, who designed the unusual *Noctambules* (Night Owls) entrance in Place Colette (1st *arrondissement*).

Stations with a theme

In 1967, André Malraux, then Minister of Culture, initiated a policy of theming stations to link them with their location. Ever since he turned the station at Louvre-Rivoli into a "museum of Antiquity," this idea has continued to develop. Varenne, near the Rodin Museum, contains reproductions of the artist's principal sculptures. In other stations, montages of documents establish the link with what lies above. These include the storming of the fortress and the march to Versailles at Bastille; the Museum of Natural History at Jussieu; the Palace of Discovery at Champs-Elysées-Clémenceau, and, since 1989, ceramic tiles proclaiming the Declaration of Human Rights at Concorde station.

The Métro as cultural space

In 1974, the RATP decided to create special events "in the form of temporary exhibitions or whatever form might be appropriate." Auber station has staged various events, including its Musicians' Week in 1977 for the "Métro, Molto, Allegro" campaign, at which 100 musicians gave 200 concerts. Since then, the policy has been expanded, for example with poetry on station walls and in the trains, photographic competitions, and ballets, while musicians of every kind have performed in the Métro. Anniversaries have given rise to various special events. Nine stations held symbolic celebrations for the centenary of the Métro and the advent of Year 2000: health was the theme at Pasteur, national heritage at Tuileries, and the cinema at Bonne-Nouvelle. Since March, 2000, as a way of giving station walls a new look, the RATP has been asking well-known people to contribute their comments on paintings in the Louvre.

3. Louvre-Rivoli station
In this station on Line 1, you can see copies of the most famous works in the Louvre's collections.

4. Bercy station (12th *arrondissement*)
In the New East of Paris, this station is very close to the Ministry of Finance, seen here in the background.

5. Météor
The station platforms on the Météor line have indirect lighting to show up the whole of the underground space.

6. Pont de Bir-Hakeim
In 1902, a competition was organized to design a two-level bridge carrying road traffic on the lower level and the Métro above.
Louis Biette was the architect of the winning design.

7. Saint-Germain-des-Prés station
Nine stations were selected to mark the centenary of the Métro with special installations. Saint-Germain-des-Prés has celebrated literature since May, 2000.

STATICONS

Six mainline stations connect the capital to its suburbs and the rest of the country. Most were built when rail transport first came in, and since then have expanded to meet the demands of passengers and new generations of trains.

The first stations

With the introduction of railroads from 1837, Paris blossomed with mainline stations, those modern "cathedrals of humanity," as Théophile Gautier called them. Paris lies at the hub of a centralized State, and the planning and location of these stations brought an enormous new network into being, its arms extending in every direction. Today its six mainline stations are: Gare Saint-Lazare, Gare du Nord, Gare de l'Est, Gare de Lyon, Gare d'Austerlitz, and Gare Montparnasse.

Piers and private companies

The first buildings designed for the railroad were not called stations but "piers," a word borrowed from the language of harbors, with "routes" (for tracks) and "quays" (for platforms). Not until the second generation of buildings was the term *gare* (station) finally adopted. When the network was being built, the State financed the infrastructure, and parceled out the tracks to private companies under agreed conditions of use and rates of payment. The companies ran into ever-increasing losses, and in 1937

were bought up by the State and nationalized to form the SNCF (French National Railroad Company).

Gare Saint-Lazare: mainly for the suburbs

In 1837, the Paris-Saint-Germain railroad came into being, the first passenger line in France. The original, temporary "pier" was up by Place de l'Europe, in north-western Paris, and was the terminus for the lines from Saint-Germain and Versailles, each of which had two platforms and two tracks. It was redesigned from 1851 for the Western Company, then

grew in size, nibbling away at the surrounding area. In 1870-80, the Gare Saint-Lazare became a favorite subject with the Impressionists, who used the bridge at Place de l'Europe as a vantage point for observing the trains and the vast iron halls. In 1889, the station took on its present appearance. The Western Company's architect, Juste Lisch, designed huge buildings with façades influenced by 17th-century Classicism and windows typical of the 19th century. These formed a single façade between two

courtyards, the Cour de Rome and the Cour du Havre. From 1925, the station served the western suburbs with the new Standard electric motor and trailer trains. In 1933, the first double-decker cars were built, remaining in service until 1984. Today, this is the busiest station in Paris, with 1,400 trains and 460,000 passengers a day.

"Châteaux in the wind"

This was poet Jacques Réda's description of the Gare du Nord and the Gare de l'Est, which he used for the title of a book in

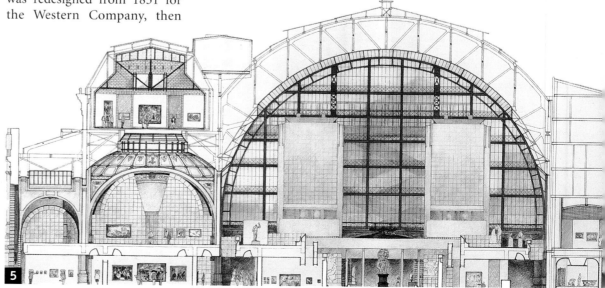

1. Front of Gare du Nord
On the right of the façade of the Gare du Nord, built from 1861 by Hittorff, are statues representing the cities of London and Vienna.

2. Platforms at Gare du Nord
The central hall is very elegant with a main span of 115 ft (35 m) supported by two rows of cast-iron columns and two side vaults of 56 ft (17 m) resting on cast-iron consoles. It has 18 tracks, plus those for the Eurostar and Thalys trains.

3. Suburban train at the Gare Saint Lazare
More than 115 million passengers per year, of whom 95% come from the suburbs, take their train to this station which, by the end of the 20th century, had become one of the largest suburban stations in Europe.

4. Gare d'Austerlitz
The façade of the Gare d'Austerlitz was rebuilt in 1865-68 by Pierre-Louis Renaud, the architect of the Compagnie d'Orléans, who was a shareholder in the project.

1987. The two stations have a similar plan, and are in fact wide open to great networks of tracks.

Gare du Nord: the station for Europe

In 1861, Baron de Rothschild, president of the Northern Company, commissioned Jacques Hittorff, a French architect born in Germany, to build a station linking Paris with the Belgian border. Hittorff set out to design a building big enough to handle a traffic flow that would never stop growing. His huge metal-framed windows were one of the most innovative designs of the day, as was his skeleton of iron and cast iron. The freestone façade is like a triumphal arch in praise of the railroad company: 525 ft (160 m) wide and punctuated by pilasters with two corner pavilions. The roof is crowned with pairs of statues representing the great cities of northern France and Europe, including Lille, London, Brussels, Amsterdam, and Vienna.

Europe at the gates of Paris

The Golden Arrow was a luxury train designed in 1926 with individual armchairs and waiter service. It ran from Paris to London in seven hours, including the ferry between Calais and Dover; this service was discontinued after World War II. In 1994, the station hall was renovated for the Eurostar service which travels via the Channel tunnel to London in three hours. The Thalys, the latest high-speed trains, complete 18 return trips a day between Paris and Brussels.

Gare de l'Est

The so-called Strasbourg "pier," on the site of the old Saint-Laurent market, is now the left wing of the present building. It was built in 1847-50 by Duquesney: a single vaulted hall with five tracks. This was soon found to be inadequate. As passenger numbers grew, from two million a year in 1877 to 12 million by 1911, the station was periodically enlarged. Then, in 1924-31, the architect Descubes built a right wing to match the left, and between them a freestone centerpiece with a great semicircular window. This gave the Gare de l'Est its massive present-day appearance. On top of the right wing, the statue of the city of Verdun balances the one of Strasbourg on the original building.

From dream to nightmare

The legendary Orient Express was launched in 1883. Known

5. Cross-section of Gare d'Orsay
This station was commissioned from Victor Laloux in 1898. The passenger hall is made of iron and is 130 ft (40 m) wide.

6. Gare du Nord
The station was substantially altered for the Eurostar service. Bare stone and polished metal were chosen for the mezzanine level.

7. Eurostar train
Eurostar trains make several return trips a day between Paris and London.

1. Gare de l'Est
This station was begun in 1847. The façade has two wings and a hemispherical rose window beneath a pediment. The wing with the statue of the city of Strasbourg is the original one. The wing added in 1931 is surmounted by the statue of Verdun.

2. Gare de Lyon
A bell tower with a four-faced clock rises above the front of Gare de Lyon, built by M Toudoire from 1895. The station was last modified in the 1990s.

as "the train of kings and the king of trains," it took wealthy travelers to Istanbul via Munich, Vienna, and Bucharest. It stopped running in 1977 but was later revived as the Nostalgia Orient Express, a private service. The Gare de l'Est was also the station of no return: hanging in the station is a large painting by Herter (1926) depicting soldiers leaving for the front in World War I.

In the south-east of Paris

Gare de Lyon: the station for the Côte d'Azur

In view of the upcoming Universal Exhibition of 1900, architect Marius Toudoire was commissioned in 1895 by the PLM Company (Paris-Lyons-Mediterranean) to build a station on the site of the old Lyon "pier," which served two areas already popular with tourists, the Alps and the Côte d'Azur. It was built in freestone with a bell tower containing a clock with four faces. The façade is decorated with statues of Paris and Marseilles, and allegories of Navigation, Steam, Engineering, and Electricity exalt the industrial age in the form of languorous nudes. The centenary of the PLM in 1907 gave rise to some very special celebrations at the station. The composer Massenet wrote a special piece entitled *The PLM March*. The famous gourmet restaurant Le Train Bleu, with its Belle Epoque murals, is named after a luxury train which carried the rich and famous to the Mediterranean. In 1981, the South-East TGV (high-speed train) ran for the first time from the Gare de Lyon. Ten years later, the station was thoroughly modernized in keeping with the regeneration of eastern Paris. It was enlarged on the north-east side, with apartment buildings being demolished to make way for a huge parking lot. The Gare de Lyon also has a large suburban section, including RER Line A, which opened in 1977.

Gare d'Austerlitz: looking for a future

The first trains from the Gare d'Austerlitz went to Orléans, then to the whole of south-west France. The station was built in eastern Paris in 1850, and very soon was overflowing. It was rebuilt for the first time in 1862 by Polonceau, who designed the iron-framed windows, then restructured in 1924 with longer platforms. Its façade on the Seine side has always been very narrow, from lack of space. In 1967, the Paris-Bordeaux Etendard and the Paris-Toulouse Capitole, both running at 125 mph (200 km/h), made it the most modern station in Paris. That did not last long, however. In 1990, the Gare Montparnasse acquired the Antlantique high-speed train, and traffic decreased considerably. Apart from its suburban traffic via the RER Line C, Austerlitz only handles long-distance trains to central France, Spain, and Portugal.

Gare Montparnasse: facing the Atlantic

The first railroad station in this southern district of Paris opened in 1852. At that time, it was opposite Rue de Rennes, on the site of the present shopping center.

On October 22, 1895, there was a spectacular accident when a locomotive smashed right through the front of the

3. Le Train Bleu
The Gare de Lyon's famous restaurant was opened with great ceremony by President Loubet in 1901, and was classified as a historic monument in 1972. Many celebrities have eaten there, from Sarah Bernhardt to Louise de Vilmorin.

4. The Little Belt
Weeds have invaded these tracks belonging to a vanished age, when the Little Belt railroad ran around the capital until 1934.

building. It was also here that General von Choltitz signed the German surrender in 1944. After various modifications, the station was finally demolished in 1965.

The new building went up in 1974, and was again redesigned in 1990 by architects Baudouin, Cassan, de Marien, Lopez, and Saubot, incorporating the Gare Vaugirard with a second hall spanning the tracks.

The glass, steel, and concrete Gare Montparnasse is the only 20th-century mainline station in Paris, serving the west of France with TGV Atlantique high-speed trains. The Atlantique Garden, built on a concrete base above the railroad tracks, adds a welcome expanse of greenery to this part of Paris.

New uses for old buildings

Gare d'Orsay: a successful conversion

In 1897, the Orléans Railroad Company bought some land facing the Seine from the State in order to build a station for trains to Nantes, Bordeaux, and Toulouse. The Gare d'Orsay was designed by Victor Laloux, and opened in 1900. However, it was never big enough, and was abandoned in 1939, being subsequently used for various purposes. After being threatened with demolition, it was saved in 1978. Its conversion into a museum has meant it could be preserved in its original size. The façade still bears the initials P-O (Paris-Orléans).

The Little Belt

All around Paris there are rusty tracks recalling one of the city's most picturesque railroads, the *Petite Ceinture* or «Little Belt». It opened in the middle of the 19th century and was a great success. However, with the advent of the Métro and the automobile, it gradually lost its usefulness. The passenger service was stopped in 1934 and replaced by the PC, a circular bus route. Today, the railroad compagny organizes open days so that people can take a trip back through time. The Golden Arrow bar/restaurant (20th *arrondissement*) has opened in one of the old stations on the Little Belt.

Gare de la Bastille and Viaduc des Arts

The little Gare de la Bastille was knocked down in the 1980s. It opened in 1859 to link Paris with Mulhouse, thus relieving the Gare de Strasbourg (later the Gare de l'Est). But instead of being a mainline station, its trains only ran to Verneuil-l'Etang in the suburbs, which stood on the Paris-Mulhouse line. The station was eventually replaced by the Opéra-Bastille in 1981.

Only the viaduct survives, and here a public garden called the Promenade Plantée has been laid out, beneath which varous arts and crafts studios have taken over the space under the arches.

5. Gare Montparnasse
The new Gare Montparnasse is very modern (1990) and stands on a different site from the first station, built in 1852.

6. Accident on October 22, 1895
On that day, the Granville Express smashed through the front of the station and fell into the street, killing a stall owner.

7. Off on vacation
In July, 1936, thanks to the advent of paid vacations, thousands of French people set off by train with their families.

1. Parc de Bagatelle
This park in the Bois de Boulogne was laid out round a château built in 1777 for the Comte d'Artois, and designed in the Anglo-Chinese style by T Blaikie. It was redesigned in the 19th century, and bought by the City of Paris in 1905.

2. The Allée Royale
The present appearance of the Bois de Vincennes is mainly due to a design scheme completed under the Second Empire, modeled on English-style gardens. The magnificent Allée Royale is rather more in the French style.

PARKS AND GARDENS

The city's parks and gardens provide an essential breathing space, contributing to the ecological balance and making Paris a beautiful place to live. Many are decorated with wonderful sculptures of every period. Although at one time Paris had few large parks within the city limits, today it has a fine range of interesting and unusual public gardens.

Woods: the lungs of Paris

In Ancient times and in the Middle Ages, Paris had very few gardens. The city was very tightly packed within its surrounding walls, and beyond lay open countryside. Forests surrounded Lutetia and the later Merovingian city. The two nearest ones later became the Bois de Boulogne and the Bois de Vincennes, today the city's principal green spaces.

Royal forests

The Bois de Boulogne is a piece of the Forêt de Rouvray, which covered the north-west of Paris and the nearby hills. It was given its present name in the 15th century. The first paths were made there in the reign of Louis XI. Under Henri IV, 15,000 mulberries were planted, and then Louis XIV built wide, straight rides for hunting with hounds. The Bois de Vincennes was also prized for its stocks of deer and wild boar, and became the hunting ground of the kings of France, which to some extent limited forest clearance. Louis XI planted a large quantity of oaks, as did Louis XV, and had

grand avenues built on the axis of the Château. The forest was then opened to the public.

Palaces in the forest

Soon, these two large woods acquired buildings. The Abbey of Longchamp, founded in the Bois de Boulogne in the 12th century, became a world-famous place of pilgrimage. The Château de Madrid, built under François I, was one of the wonders of Renaissance architecture; it was destroyed in the

19th century. Of all the buildings that stood there in the 18th century, only the Bagatelle has survived: a delightful Neoclassical "folly," hastily built in two months in 1775 by François-Joseph Bélanger for the Comte d'Artois, the future Charles X. In the Bois de Vincennes, Charles V added the fortified section of the Château, originally built by Philippe-Auguste. The Château de Vincennes is today one of the most remarkable examples of medieval

architecture in the Ile-de-France; it was enlarged from 1652 by Louis Le Vau.

Making the modern woodlands

The two woods took on their present appearance under the Second Empire. Napoléon III, in conjunction with Haussmann, Prefect of Paris, commissioned Jean-Charles Alphand to design them, assisted by the horticulturalist Pierre Barillet-Deschamps and architect Gabriel Davioud. The aim was

5. Bois de Vincennes
Between the Porte Dorée and Joinville-le-Pont, the 2,450 acres (995 ha) of the Bois de Vincennes display a great variety of scenery and activities.

6. Bois de Boulogne
Like the Bois de Vincennes, this park also benefited from landscaping carried out under Haussmann. It caters not only for walkers, but also for cyclists and horseriders, who have their own circuits of, respectively, 9 miles (15 km) and 15 miles (25 km).

3. Lake in the Bois de Vincennes
Lac Daumesnil and Lac des Minimes are the two largest in the Bois de Vincennes. Their curving shapes provide magificent views of the wooded areas.

4. Temple de Reuilly
Designed by architect Gabriel Davioud, the Temple de Reuilly stands at the tip of the island of the same name in Lac Daumesnil. The island is connected by a bridge to the Ile de Bercy. The

Classical architecture of the Temple follows a model frequently employed in English parks in the 18th century.

to domesticate the woods and make them into a useful resource for all Parisians. The Bois de Boulogne became an English-style park, crossed by a network of roads and winding paths; two lakes connected by a cascade were built, with three streams flowing from them, and 400,000 trees were planted. The success of this enterprise was soon reflected in the Bois de Vincennes, which also acquired two large expanses of water: the Lac des Minimes and Lac Daumesnil, each with islands planted with rare trees. On the Ile de Reuilly, Davioud built a small Antique-style temple, identical to the Temple of Sybil in the Buttes-Chaumont.

Multi-functional spaces

Today, a very mixed assortment of people use the two parks. Some go there for the peace and quiet, and others to take part in one of the many activities on offer. The nocturnal scene in the Bois de Boulogne has certainly damaged its reputation. However, for daytime visitors there are two racetracks, a zoological garden, the rose gardens in the Parc de Bagatelle, and the

restaurants of the Pré-Catalan. Both parks have plenty of sports facilities too. In 1931, the Bois de Vincennes hosted the colonial Exhibition, and some of its buildings are still there. The former Cameroon and Togo pavilion first became the Museum of the Timber Industry, and from 1977 has been a Buddhist temple. Like most green spaces in Paris, the two parks suffered badly in the storm of December 26, 1999. Whole areas of woodland were destroyed, and have had to be replanted, which will take several decades.

The major parks and gardens

The gift of royalty: Tuileries, Luxembourg, Palais-Royal, and Monceau

The main historic gardens were built at the same time as the royal residences. They were inseparable from these ceremonial palaces, and were for the exclusive use of the sovereign. Today they are independent of the building for which they provide a setting, and are among the best-loved green spaces in the capital.

1. The Carrousel
The Carrousel Garden was laid out in 1871 after the destruction of the Tuileries Palace, and was redesigned by J Wirtz as part of the Grand Louvre project.

5. Beehives in the Luxembourg Garden
The beekeeping school in the Luxembourg Garden is supplied with flowers from a nearby orchard with 701 apple and pear trees.

The Tuileries:
a masterpiece by Le Nôtre

The Palais des Tuileries, ordered by Catherine de Médicis, was the first major development in the realm of parks and gardens. The palace, built to the west of the Louvre from 1564, was provided with a magnificent, enclosed, Medieval-style garden. In the 17th century, the great gardener André Le Nôtre turned it into a Classical park, with broad avenues opening the perspective to the west, the future Champs-Elysées. The garden is flanked by two terraces on the north and south sides, and divided into three parts: the Octagon, from Place de la Concorde to the octagonal pool; the Grand Couvert, the tree-covered central area; and the Grand Carrée, formed by borders surrounding the round pond and the "private gardens" of Napoléon III. The Tuileries were usually restricted to the Court, but were open to the wealthier citizens on Sundays. The ordinary public were only admitted on one day a year, Saint Louis's Day (August 25). The palace was burnt down during the Commune in 1871, and was succeeded by the Carrousel Garden, where Napoléon I had built a triumphal arch. It was recently renovated in the spirit of the 17th century, like the Tuileries. It is the most famous garden in Paris, and today has cafés, restaurants, museums (the redesigned Orangerie and Jeu de Paume), and from time to time a fairground.

Luxembourg:
in the Italian style

The Jardin du Luxembourg came about when Marie de Médicis commissioned Salomon de Brosse to build her a palace and gardens to remind her of the Pitti Palace and Boboli Gardens in Florence. The palace is now the seat of the Sénat (Upper House) and opens onto a 20-acre (8-ha) park. On part of the land formerly belonging to a Carthusian monastery (acquired in 1617), 2,000 elms were planted and large borders laid out; the fountains were supplied from the recently-built Arcueil aqueduct. The wonderful Fontaine Médicis, inspired by Italian-style grottos, and later the large central pond by Le Nôtre, where people sail their model boats, were added. This French-style garden has been redesigned several times, and was extended to the south from 1810 by the gardens of the Avenue de l'Observatoire. A pleasant orchard and a beekeeping school (opened in 1856 and rebuilt in 1991) stand on the far south-west side of the garden. The Luxembourg Garden is in the center of Paris, close to the Latin Quarter, and also has tennis courts and a puppet theater. It is mainly used by students, and is one of their favorite places to meet.

Palais-Royal:
the enclosed garden

Palais-Royal is not like the city's other gardens. It was built in 1624 by Desgots for Cardinal Richelieu, and was then the largest garden in Paris. Later, it became the only public garden to be entirely surrounded by buildings: the palace to the south (today the seat of the Council of State, the Constitutional Council, and the Ministry of Culture), and identical, exclusive apartment buildings, built by Victor Louis for the Duc d'Orléans from 1781. In the 18th century it was a mecca for loose living, where Diderot liked to wander beneath the avenues of lime trees and meditate, on the vagaries of his day. Here too, Camille Desmoulins harangued the crowd on July 12, 1789, two days before the storming of the Bastille. The Palais-Royal

3. Parc Monceau
This park is a subtle blend of the Anglo-Chinese garden laid out in the 18th century by Carmontelle, and the new designs directed by J-C-A Alphand under the Second Empire, making it one of the most fascinating parks in Paris.

4. Buttes-Chaumont
Laid out in one piece on the site of the old America quarries, this park has a unique appearance. Its rocky promontory, grottos, and two bridges make a strong contrast with the green of the trees and the waters of the lake.

remains one of the most pleasant gardens in Paris, and has recently acquired new benches designed by Jean-Michel Wilmotte.

Monceau: the Anglo-Chinese park

Louis-Philippe d'Orléans, Duc de Chartres, had this park laid out. It was designed in 1778. Its north entrance has a rotunda by Claude-Nicolas Ledoux which was originally a customs barrier

in the wall of the Farmers-General. Until 1860, this marked the limits of the city. The park was designed by Carmontelle in the fashionable Anglo-Chinese style. At that time it had a Chinese gate, a marble temple, an island of flowers, a windmill, an Egyptian pyramid, and a minaret. The park was bought up by the City in 1870, and some of it was sold for development. The remaining 20 acres

(8 ha) were redesigned by Alphand, and were surrounded by luxurious mansions. Alphand sought to preserve the romantic charm of the old park, and kept some of the architectural pieces. He nevertheless created a park typical of its era, with hills and a cascade, an Italian-style bridge, and the marvelous entrance gates. The park was finally replanted with purple maples, sycamores, Oriental plane trees, and fig trees.

The Haussmann period: Buttes-Chaumont and Montsouris

The Second Empire was an important period in the devel-

opment of the city's parks and gardens. For the first time, large green spaces were designed and integrated into the city's urban planning scheme. The Buttes-Chaumont (1867) and Parc Montsouris (1878) were laid out on land that was difficult to build on because of its old gypsum and limestone quarries, and provided places to walk and relax for two rapidly growing districts. Measuring 62 acres (25 ha) and 40 acres (16 ha) respectively, they are the two largest parks in Paris. Under the direction of Jean-Charles Alphand, they were designed and built by landscape gardener Barillet-

5. The Tuileries
This first major garden in Paris (1564) has a fine collection of sculptures. Today, Maillol's famous nudes are joined by works by Coustou, Rodin, and Giacometti.

6. The Luxembourg Garden
The Luxembourg Garden was created in 1617 by Marie de Médicis and has since been substantially altered. Chalgrin extended it to the Obser-

vatory, then Haussmann's new streets and the growing city cut off its south-eastern section. The "Luco" is still, however, one of the city's great gardens, along with the Tuileries.

1. Parc Montsouris
This park in the 14th *arrondissement* is the southern equivalent of the Buttes-Chaumont, and was also built over old quarries; but its views are more restful, and on the south side continue over the park of the Cité Universitaire.

2. Kellermann Park
This park by J Grébier, the famous designer of private gardens and urban promenades, is typical of garden design in the 1930s. It stands on the site of Thiers's fortified wall, which surrounded Paris until 1919.

3. Parc André-Citroën
Together with the Parc de la Villette, this park represents a new generation of gardens. Neither English nor French, it mixes several types of landscaping with large lawns, glasshouses, and themed or activity gardens.

4. Parc de Bercy
Built on the site of the old barrel stores at Bercy, this park is more of a classic garden; it has kept its old plane trees, maples, and chestnuts.

Deschamps, architect Davioud, and engineer Belgrand in a style owing much to English parks. There were lawns, lakes, wild gardens, rocks, small bridges set in rockeries, and large suspension bridges providing viewpoints, all in a hilly setting with a few surprise elements tucked away, and magnificent views across Paris. Unusually, the Buttes-Chaumont and Montsouris are both crossed by railtracks: the now disused Little Belt line, and the RER Line B.

Parks from the interwar years

Not many parks were built in the open space created when the Thiers fortifications were demolished, beginning in 1919.

Architects and politicians wanted to design a Green Belt, an immense park running around the whole city. Instead, large numbers of apartment blocks were built there, leaving only a small amount of space for a few squares. Two real parks did come out of this scheme, however. The buildings of the Cité Universitaire, dating from the 1920s, are in a fine setting, with huge lawns on the south side. The Parc Kellermann (1937-50) at the Porte d'Italie is very different, having been much more rigorously designed by Jacques Gréber. It runs along the hillside and over the old bed of the River Bièvre, and includes a French garden, a landscaped

5. Butte du Chapeau-Rouge
This is probably the most beautiful of the 1930s gardens. It was laid out by architect L Azéma, who designed a wonder- ful panorama looking toward the plain of Romainville.

6. Buttes-Chaumont
Once they have reached the Temple of Sybil, visi- tors are at the top of the Buttes-Chaumont, and can admire the whole urban landscape, from the Pleyel Tower to Sacré-Coeur, and the Orgues de Flandre.

park, an artificial river, and a large fountain. Similar in spirit is the Square de la Butte-du-Chapeau-Rouge, laid out in 1939 at Porte du Pré-Saint-Gervais, which despite its name is the size of a park.

New parks: Georges-Brassens, La Villette, Bercy, and Citroën

There were no further park-building programs until 1974. Then, however, the Vaugirard abattoirs closed, and the Parc Georges-Brassens was laid out on the site, paving the way for a new generation of green spaces. This park retains some elements from its industrial past (bronze bulls at the entrance, and the bell tower from the auction hall) along with a pool, pathways, beehives, and a scent garden. In recent years, the Paris landscape has generally benefited from the decline of industrial activities: on the sites of the abattoirs at La Villette, the Citroën factories, and the wine warehouses at Bercy, three new parks have enabled the city at least partly to make up for the delay in providing green spaces. These new parks are quite different in concept, showing a wide range of approaches to the art of garden design. Bercy has a certain Classicism and makes good use of its old trees, while La Villette comes across as a prototype for an urban park, using both plants and man-made installations to good effect. The Parc André-Citroën is also very innovative, with a huge lawn, fountains, and glasshouses beside wonderful themed gardens and an "activity garden," created by landscape designer Gilles Clément.

Promenades and squares

The promenades

The first promenades in Paris were an extension to the Tuileries. The Cours-la-Reine, a large planted avenue running beside the Seine to the present Place de l'Alma, was opened by Catherine de Médicis in 1617. Fifty years later, André Le Nôtre was commissioned to design the Grand-Cours, which became the Champs-Elysées, its name coming from Greek mythology. This promenade was later converted by Alphand into the English-style gardens you see today. Another famous promenade was the Grands Boulevards, running from the Bastille to the Madeleine on top of the ramparts surrounding the city, which were planted from 1680. The Second Empire was also a good period, with most of the broad streets built by Haussmann being planted with trees. The Boulevard Richard-Lenoir, which covers part of the Canal Saint-Martin, was one of the most remarkable achievements of this period, providing a total of 15 squares, which then gradually disappeared; the whole boulevard was completely renovated in 1996.

7. Parc André-Citroën
The three parks built at the beginning of the 1990s (La Villette, Bercy, and André-Citroën) mark a turning point in the history of town planning in Paris. After 30 years of inactivity, the City and the State got together to provide the city with large open spaces for leisure and culture. However, the creation of these gardens perpetuated the old practice of building them in unprofitable places such as former industrial sites. Unlike London, Paris has long thought of these places as a luxury.

1. Parc de Belleville
This 11-acre (4.5-ha) park opened in 1988 and overlooks the whole of Paris, rising up the steep slope of Belleville Hill between Rue Piat and Rue Bisson.

2. Champs-Élysées
These gardens designed by Le Nôtre as an extension to the Tuileries now flank part of the world's most famous avenue. The gardens were redesigned by Alphand in 1859 in the English style then fashionable, after some of the theaters and panoramas had been demolished.

The first private squares

One of the first private squares in Paris was the Cité de Trévise (1841), a green space modeled on the English square, surrounded by apartment buildings and reserved for their occupants. This fashion led to the Square d'Orléans, a speculative development located in the center of an enclave off Rue Taitbout. It was modified by Alphand to suit the Parisian way of life, and became one of the key elements in Haussmann's town planning: children's games were catered for, but it was forbidden to lie on the grass, and semi-tropical plants were also introduced. Some 20 of these squares were laid out during the Second Empire, both in the center (Tour Saint-Jacques) and further out (Montholon, Batignolles, etc).

A new kind of garden: the 1930s

In the 20th century, garden design took on an architectural character. The squares of the 1930s were often laid out on the sites of old gasworks (Squares Saint-Lambert and Parc de Choisy), and equipped with bandstands, shelters, and fountains. One of the most beautiful of these is the Square René-le-Gall, designed by Jean-Charles Moreux on the old gardens of workers at the Gobelins tapestry works; it follows the course of the River Bièvre and is divided into three parts (a children's playground, a wood, and a Renaissance-style garden), and has an outstanding collection of rock figures featuring heads of men and birds by Maurice Garnier.

A new policy for parks and gardens

As part of a new urban policy, a large number of green spaces have been created in the last 20 years. In addition to the large parks, promenades are also undergoing a great revival. The Promenade Plantée is the best known, a green avenue running almost 3 miles (4.5 km) from Place de la Bastille to the Bois de Vincennes, partly on the Avenue Daumesnil viaduct and partly on the old tracks of the Little Belt railroad. The new squares also reveal changes in garden design. The Jardin Atlantique sits on a concrete platform over the tracks of Gare Montparnasse; there is the nature garden next to Père-Lachaise, and the Square Héloïse-et-Abelard with its Garden of the Five Senses. Today, nothing seems impossible.

Botanical gardens

Jardin des Plantes

The "Royal Garden of Medicinal Plants," built by Guy de La Brosse, physician to Louis XIII, was the first garden in Paris to be open to the public. This important scientific center (linked to such names as Buf-

5. Promenade Plantée
This green promenade, completed in 2001, crosses the very varied landscape of eastern Paris, its route taking it past the Square Hector-Malot and through the Reuilly Gardens.

6, 7. Jardin des Plantes
This splendid park was the first botanical garden in Europe, and with its complex of museums and scientific institutes is worth several visits. Not far from the Cedar of Lebanon planted by Bernard de Jussieu in 1734 is the labyrinth, designed by Edme Verniquet.

3. Arsenal basin
This final stretch of the Canal Saint-Martin, just before it reaches the Seine, was the first to be redesigned with gardens and a promenade. In 1983, it was redesignated as the the city's official boating marina.

4. Glasshouses at Auteuil
These glasshouses were built in 1898 to grow plants for the city's parks and gardens. The glasshouses at Rungis are now larger, but these still play an important role.

fon, Jussieu, and Daubenton) became the National Museum of Natural History, and is today prized by plant lovers as well as by walkers and joggers. The flower garden, set between avenues of plane trees, is con-stantly the focus of attention: in May, the cherry trees in flower give it a unique beauty. The Botanical School and the Great Labyrinth are musts for enthusiasts. Similarly, the Ménagerie will delight animal lovers; the Jardin des Plantes is also an important ornithological site.

The glasshouses at Auteuil and the Parc Floral
Despite the glasshouses which appeared at Rungis in 1968, there is still a lot of horticultural activity at the glasshouses of Auteuil, designed by Jean-Camille Formigé in 1898. Each year, 100,000 plants leave these splendid iron and glass structures to decorate municipal buildings. They are also worth visiting for the pleasant French garden in which the glasshouses stand. In the Bois de Vincennes, the Parc Floral opened in 1969. It has a Valley of Flowers, a Garden of the Four Seasons, and themed gardens. Since 1998, these gardens, along with the École Du Breuil, which trains gardeners, and the Parc de Bagatelle, have formed the "Botanical Garden of France and French-speaking Countries."

BRIDGES

The city's 37 bridges were built as Paris expanded, providing important crossing points which helped the capital to develop in a relatively balanced way on both banks. All the way through central Paris, from Charenton in the east to Billancourt in the west, these bridges span the Seine at regular intervals. The materials from which they were made – variously wood, stone, cast iron, and concrete – reflect the periods to which they belong.

The first bridges

The Roman bridges consisted of a wooden platform resting on stone piles, and replaced the Gallic ones that were made wholly of wood. In the 1st century AD, Lutetia had two bridges: the Petit Pont and the Grand Pont. The Petit Pont joined the Left Bank to the Ile de la Cité in line with Rue Saint-Jacques, and the Grand Pont continued this line to Rue Saint-Martin on the Right Bank. For more than a thousand years, they suffered regularly from floods and fires but were always rebuilt. These were the only bridges in Paris until the end of the 13th century.

Pont-au-Change

In 1141, the Grand Pont was destroyed after another flood, and was moved to the west and renamed the Pont-au-Change. Louis VII granted a charter stipulating that money could be changed at this place and that the moneychangers should pay 20 sous a year to have a stall there. From 1304, Philip the Fair allowed goldsmiths to set up businesses there. Nearly a century later, in 1402, birdsellers were also allowed to trade, following an act by Charles VI, provided their cages did not impede passers-by. The Pont-au-Change was destroyed by fire in 1621, and rebuilt in stone. In 1858-9, Haussmann's building schemes led to a new version, 340 ft (103 m) long with three elliptical stone arches.

Stone bridges topped with houses

The original Grand Pont was replaced by Pont Notre-Dame, which went through several wooden versions, all of which collapsed, until a stone bridge was completed in 1514. The bridge then had 68 brick and stone houses on it, all identical and numbered, to be rented as stores and dwellings; these were all owned by the City. This was a very lively bridge, the busiest in Paris, crossed by royal processions and kings making ceremonial entrances. The Pont Notre-Dame has been rebuilt several times. The present structure was opened in 1919 by R Poincaré, President of the Republic, and consists of one 200 ft (60 m) metal arch and two side arches in stone. It stands slightly downstream from the old Grand Pont.

Houses, stores, and watermills

With its neat rows of houses, the Pont Notre-Dame became the model for other existing bridges and new ones being built. The Petit Pont, Pont Saint-Michel, and Pont Marie (1614-35) were also given houses. On the Pont-au-Double (1634), the Hôtel-Dieu (general hospital) obtained permission from François I to put up a two-story building for sick patients. The prevailing theory was, the heavier the bridge, the more solid it was. Stores usually occupied the ground floor. Bridges continued to have houses on them until the 18th century.

Grain mills and water pumps were attached to the pillars of bridges and drew their power from the Seine. The most famous of these was the Samaritaine pump, made in 1665, which supplied the center of Paris with water. The name was later used for the department stores founded by Ernest Cognacq, the first of which opened in 1869 in Rue du Pont-Neuf.

Pont-Neuf

The Pont-Neuf is the most popular and frequently depicted bridge in Paris. It was built to connect the Abbey of Saint-Germain-des-Prés with the Louvre. The foundation stone was laid

on May 31, 1578, by Henri III in the presence of his mother Catherine de Médicis and his wife Louise de Lorraine. However, because of the Wars of Religion, work was not completed until 1607, in the reign of Henri IV. It is 780 ft (238 m) long, 65 ft (20 m) wide, and divided into two parts with seven arches on the main arm of the Seine (of which six today are depressed, basket arches) and five on the short arm. It was built with sidewalks, which were new at that time. This was the first bridge not to have houses

on it, and it quickly became a popular place to walk, and the home of a picturesque market.

From Louis XIV to Louis XVI

Pont Royal

The building of the Pont Royal began in 1685, commissioned from Jules Hardouin-Mansart and wholly financed by Louis XIV. It was built to connect the Louvre and the Boulevard Saint-Germain. This stone bridge succeeded an old wooden one, destroyed by fire and then by a devastating flood. It has five

1. The bargees' water tournament
The bargees held their tournament between the Pont Notre-Dame and the Pont-au-Change. The houses on these bridges were the only ones in Paris to be numbered. These identical dwellings, two or three stories high, were made of wood and formed streets across the Seine. Each had a box-like structure projecting over

the river for drawing water and waste disposal.

2. Pont-au-Change
This bridge is named for the moneychangers. King Louis VII allowed them to set up there in 1141. It was rebuilt in 1858-9, and is stamped with the "N" of Napoléon III.

3. Pont Royal
The Pont Royal was built by Gabriel to plans by

Jules Hardouin-Mansart, and has kept its original appearance. It has been a historic monument since 1939.

4. Pont de la Concorde
The Pont de la Concorde connects the Assemblée National and the Place de la Concorde. It was originally called the Pont Louis XVI and later the Pont de la Révolution.

arches, is 425 ft (130 m) long, and is one of the finest examples of the Classical style.

Pont de la Concorde

The Pont de la Concorde (1786-91) was designed by Jean-Rodolphe Perronnet, architect to Louis XVI and head of Bridges and Highways. This

masterpiece of stonework is 502 ft (153 m) long, with five depressed arches. It was enlarged in 1931 with two sections, one on either side of the bridge, carried on independent pillars.

Napoléon I and technical innovations

Pont des Arts

This bridge between the Institut de France and the Louvre was built in 1802-4, and used metal for the first time. Its light, cast-iron arches support a horizontal platform. After being damaged several times by barges, the bridge was demolished in 1980 and relaced by a copy in steel, with bigger arches. This is a pedestrian footbridge, and is very popular with Parisians. Concerts and exhibitions are held there, like the one organized in 1999 in honor of the African sculptor Ousmane Sow.

Pont d'Austerlitz

The Pont d'Austerlitz was built in 1806 and consists of five cast-

5. Pont Neuf
This was the first bridge in Paris not to have houses. It was begun in 1578 and completed in 1607. It has 381 *mascarons*, grotesque masks decorating the cornices, some of which have had to be replaced over the years; hemispherical turrets crown each of the pillars. In the 1980s, an old-fashioned fair was held there, and in 1985 it was wrapped for several weeks by the artist Christo.

iron arches resting on metal cushions. At the time it was at the cutting edge of technology.

Pont d'Iéna

The Pont d'Iéna was begun in 1807, facing the École Militaire, its name celebrating one of the Grande Armée's victories. It reveals the advances made in stonework techniques; its tympanums are decorated with Imperial eagles.

Suspension bridges

Suspension bridges first appeared under the Restoration and in the reign of Louis-Philippe.

Pont de Grenelle

The Pont de Grenelle (1825-1827) was the first suspension bridge. It was completely rebuilt in 1966.

Pont d'Arcole

Built to connect the Hôtel de Ville and the Ile de la Cité, and to deal with the growth in road traffic during the 19th century, the Pont d'Arcole was originally called the Passerelle de Grève when it was completed in 1828. It is one of the oldest iron bridges in all of France. Architect Cadiat designed a metal structure with a single depressed arch and a span totalling 260 ft (80 m).

In August, 1944, during the Liberation of Paris, the French 2nd Armored Division crossed the bridge to reach the Hôtel de Ville.

From the Alma to Pont Mirabeau

Pont de l'Alma

This bridge was built during the Second Empire at the time of the Crimean War, when Napoléon III was keen to pay tribute to his soldiers. Four colossal statues, each 20 ft (6 m) high, represent members of the army, including a *zouave*, which is used to measure flood levels.

Pont Mirabeau

This three-arched metal bridge was begun in 1896, its granite pillars decorated with marine gods, and owes its reputation as much to the poet Apollinaire as to its slender form. Apollinaire used the image of the Seine flowing beneath the bridge as the setting for a meditation about the joys and sorrows of love.

Pont Alexandre III

The Pont Alexandre III was built for the Universal Exhibition of 1900, and is named for

the Tsar. His son Nicholas II laid the foundation stone in 1896, consolidating the friendship between France and Russia. The bridge is made wholly of metal, with one arch depressed to the limits to protect the view of the Invalides. At each corner are monumental pillars 58 ft (17 m) high crowned by a gilded bronze Pegasus, while the center of the bridge has statues in beaten copper representing the nymphs of the Seine and the Neva, Saint Petersburg's river. Elaborate bronze lamps complete the design.

The viaducts and the Métro

In 1900, the advent of the Métro changed the lives of Parisians. For its architects, one of the main concerns was to make it span the Seine.

Pont de Bir-Hakeim

The Pont de Passy opened after the Universal Exhibition. It is now called the Pont de Bir-Hakeim to commemorate the French victory in Libya in 1942. It has two levels, with a road bridge on the lower level and the Métro lines running above it.

Viaduc d'Austerlitz

This viaduct in the east of the city is solely for the Métro, and was a great technical achievement. It was built in 1903-4 with a single span of 460 ft (140 m), the longest span of any bridge in Paris.

New bridges

Pont Charles-de-Gaulle

Work on this bridge connecting Bercy and the Gare d'Austerlitz

4. Zouave on Pont de l'Alma
In the 1970s, when the original Napoléon III-period bridge was being replaced by one better suited to road traffic, the *zouave* was the only statue to be preserved. It was used to measure floods on the Seine. In 1910, it was covered up to the chin.

1. Pont d'Iéna
This bridge was completed in the reign of Napoléon I, and was nearly destroyed by the Prussians in 1815 because it reminded them of their many battles with the Emperor. Louis XVIII had to intervene firmly to stop them.

2. Pont d'Austerliz
Built under the Empire, cracks quickly appeared in its structure. In 1854 it was declared dangerous and was rebuilt. In 1884, its width was doubled to 98 ft (30 m) to cope with the traffic.

It is decorated with sculptures of weapons.

3. Pont Alexandre III
This bridge joins the Invalides and Avenue Winston Churchill, and has sparkled with light since its gilded bronze Pegasus figures were restored in 1991. It is made completely of metal, and was built in 1898-1900 by architects Réal and d'Alby.

began in 1993. The architects L Arretche and R Karasinski designed a horizontal girder bridge, 680 ft (207 m) long with an upper platform in concrete. Its metal roadway, in the form of an aircraft wing, gives it an aerodynamic shape.

Solférino Footbridge

This graceful 350 ft (106 m) steel footbridge connects the Musée d'Orsay and the Tuileries Gardens. It has a single metal arch and was completed in 1999.

Bridges of the future

The city is continually evolving, and there are plans to built a footbridge in easten Paris to connect the French National Library and the Parc de Bercy. Some bridges have been pedestrianized and their lighting improved to show off their architectural details. At night, the view along the river sparkles with light.

5. Pont des Arts
This First Empire bridge was effectively for pedestrians only with its shrubs, flowers, and benches. Like the other bridges in Paris, people had to pay a toll. Its name comes from the old name for the Louvre, the Palais des Arts.

6. Pont Charles-de-Gaulle
This resolutely contemporary work is part of the spectacular development of south-eastern Paris, which has included the French National Library and the new Parc de Bercy. The bridge was designed to relieve the Pont d'Austerlitz downstream, the busiest in Paris. Its lighting was designed to show off its design.

LIVING IN PARIS

THE SEINE

The Seine gave Paris its landscape, economy, and history. It provided the city with a communications route which for a long time was central to most of its activities. It has also had its wayward moments, which have taken a great deal of effort and hard work to overcome. Today, the Seine has become one of the city's major attractions, enjoyed both by tourists and Parisians, who never tire of walking beside it.

The city on the river

The Seine is 480 miles (776 km) long and flows from the Langres plateau to the sea. The Gauls worshipped its source as a goddess. It has several large tributaries and a network of canals, providing communications and trading links which have shaped the city's identity. Paris was founded and developed at a point where roads converged, and the river could be crossed without great difficulty using a fairly large island (the Ile de la Cité), which in turn provided a natural defensive position.

Conquering the Seine

The bed of the Seine is fairly level, making it easy to navigate. However, its banks were muddy in many places, which is how the Marais, or marsh, district acquired its name. Gradually, bankside roads were built and the ground level raised over the centuries by several feet, which brought stability to the districts beside the river. As this process went on, rooms at street level in medieval times were converted into cellars. There were dangerous times too. When the river was at its lowest in summer, the

pollutants and domestic refuse poured into it turned the Seine into a cesspit. Public health schemes in the 19th century, together with the reduction of trading activities on the river, improved the quality of the water. On the other hand, between autumn and spring there were often disastrous floods, which tore down many bridges. As recently as January, 1910, many districts found

themselves under water, and the Métro was also flooded. Photographs of that time record the extraordinary sight of Parisians going down the Avenue Montaigne in boats. The construction of barrages upstream has since helped the authorities to control the river more effectively.

Extremely cold spells have also had a dramatic effect. During the winter of 1709-10, while

people could cross the frozen Seine in a coach, thousands died of starvation because food supplies could not be brought in by river.

Supplying Paris with water

Although there were wells, springs that could be tapped, and the Roman aqueduct at Arceuil which Louis XIII restored to use, these were never enough to supply the city's daily

5. Apple market, Port de l'Hôtel-de-Ville, 1920
Paris relied for a long time on the Seine for its food supplies. Harbors and markets crowded the banks, providing food, fuel, and building materials. From the 19th century, these suppliers gradually left the river and moved up to La Villette on the new canal network.

1. Front de Seine
This district downriver from the Eiffel Tower was built around 1970, and is one of the first examples of the new building schemes on the banks of the Seine.

2. Ile de la Cité
Paris grew up around this island from Gallo-Roman times, and it has kept its original name.

3. Booksellers on Quai de Montebello
The booksellers are very much part of the riverside scene in the center of Paris, and still attract customers in search of engravings or rare books.

4. Bercy
The new Ministry of Finance at Bercy was designed by architect Chemetov and spans the Quai de la Rapée. From there, the Assembiée Nationale can be reached quickly by boat.

needs. Despite the health risks involved, people drew most of their water from the Seine. Pumps were set up to improve distribution. One of them was placed on the Pont-Neuf in 1605 to supply the Louvre Palace, and remained in service until 1813. It was called the Samaritaine, and was decorated with a statue of the woman of Samaria who, according to the Gospels, offered water to Jesus. The name is preserved today in the nearby department stores called the Samaritaine.

From the end of the 18th century, the Perrier brothers designed and installed steam-driven pumps on the Quai d'Orsay and at Chaillot. The building of the Canal de l'Ourcq during the Empire, then the harnessing of other rivers feeding vast reservoirs at Ménilmontant and Montsouris, were the main responses to the water problem in the 19th century.

The old river trades

Merchants and their products

Two old dugout canoes 6,000 years old were discovered during excavations at Bercy, and indicate that fishing was then an important activity. In the Gallo-Roman era, the boatmen of Paris controlled water transport on the Seine, forming a sort of ruling body which provided the city with public monuments such as the Altar to Jupiter in the Cité, and the thermal baths at the Hôtel de Cluny. The river

6. Relaxing by the river
Once the sun starts shining in spring, the banks of the Seine (shown here is a riverside road on the Ile Saint-Louis) fill up with lovers, walkers, and groups of visitors looking for a quiet spot, away from the bustle of the center.

7. Dog clipper on the quayside, 1920
Many trades flourished on the bank of the river, some of them unusual, like this dog clipper, others essential, like the washerwomen. Gradually they were all banned for public health reasons.

traders grew increasingly prosperous in the Middle Ages. The guild of river traders was one of the core elements in the urban elite; its members, headed by the Merchant Provost, founded the city's municipal institutions. The boat from the badge of this guild still features on the city's coat of arms, accompanied by the famous motto: *Fluctuat nec mergitur* (It sails and does not sink).

For a long time, Paris received most of its food supplies by river. Not only did this busy trade make the merchants wealthy, it provided work for large numbers of clerks, laborers, boatmen, and retailers. Various specialist harbors or docking places were set up along the banks of the river. The Port en Grève, by the Hôtel de Ville, was the busiest of them all, while one of the islands, the Ile Louviers, housed a number of timber yards before it was joined to the Right Bank to form the Quai Henri IV.

Craftsmen and washerwomen

During the Middle Ages, all kinds of trades and activities started up along the river. Its water powered the wheels of numerous mills, and filled the vats of the dyers and tanners. The discharges and smells emitted by the tanners upset people living nearby and polluted the river, forcing them eventually to move to the River Bièvre. This was bad for the beavers living there, for whom the river was named. Nor did it do much to

1. On the bank at Quai Saint-Bernard
On the Left Bank, opposite the Ile Saint-Louis, the Saint-Bernard harbor which used to serve the wine market, has been turned into a Museum of Open Air Sculpture.

2. Arsenal basin
Formerly a ditch in the city's fortifications, the Arsenal basin links the Canal Saint-Martin to the Seine. It has recently become a very popular marina.

3. Quai de la Rapée
The warehouses at Port de la Rapée have been redeveloped to provide an esplanade, the heavy barges giving way to restaurants by the river and on boats.

clean the Seine in Paris, as the Bièvre flowed into it upstream of the city, near the present Gare d'Austerlitz, and also supplied a small stream along the line of today's Rue de Bièvre.

The laundry business was also as polluting as it was necessary, giving laborious paid work to a large population of washerwomen. The better-off ones paid for a place on the laundry boats, and the others worked from the river banks. It is difficult now to imagine the crowded banks, the steam from the laundry vats, the chatter of the washerwomen, and the dust rising from the ashes they used as a washing powder, not to mention the lines of washing hung out to dry. The whiteness they achieved with all that labor was by no means perfect. In the 18th century, very wealthy Parisians sent their washing off to the country, or even to London and Holland. In the following century, the process was to some extent mechanized, and new public health laws gradually limited this trade by the river, although the last laundry boat did not close until 1937.

Bathing places

People using the river to wash or bathe in could not afford to

be too modest or over-concerned about hygiene aspects; they also had to suffer the taunts of the washerwomen, never the most discreet of commentators.

Bathing establishments developed in the second half of the 18th century, using water filtered from the river which was then heated and supplied to individual bathtubs. One of these, opened by Deligny in 1785, near today's Pont de la Concorde, introduced a new feature, a pool for everyone with changing rooms and diving boards; they also gave swimming lessons. Bathing in the river was finally banned on grounds of indecency in 1800; the Deligny swimming pool, which was closed for restoration in 1993, sank shortly afterward, while it was being restored.

Building the riverside roads

Building along the river banks began in 1312 when Philip the Fair commanded the Merchant Provost to improve trading conditions by building up the Left Bank around the present Quai des Grands Augustins. On the Right Bank, the same was soon done at the Quai de la Mégisserie and the Quai des Célestins. In about 1530, François I, fol-

lowed by Henri IV at the beginning of the 17th century, filled in the gap between these two roads. On the Ile de la Cité, harbor facilities were less important, and the first bankside road (Quai de l'Horloge) was not built until the 1580s, followed by the Quai des Orfèvres (around 1600).

In the 19th century, the quaysides were rebuilt on two levels (upper quay and bankside road) and extended to help link Paris

4. Docks at La Villette
In the 19th century, before railroad and highway transport were developed, these docks between the Canal Saint-Martin and the Canal de l'Ourcq were the main goods harbor in Paris.

5. Canal Saint-Martin
With its many locks and swing bridges, the Canal Saint-Martin is now mainly used for boat trips.

with a number of nearby villages. The last great upheaval was in the 1960s, aimed at speeding the flow of road traffic with better roads beside the river. This approach has since been discontinued.

The Seine in the Industrial Age

From boats to barges

From the Middle Ages, the Seine became increasingly filled up with hazardous obstacles in the form of bridges, mills, and pumps. Flat-bottomed boats rigged with one or two sails were pulled along by horses, or by men known as haulers. Then a mechanical drive was invented, the aquamotor. This consisted of a fixed boat with paddle wheels driven by the current which operated a winch.

At the beginning of the 19th century, steam boats gradually took over from the old boats and, in the Industrial Age, river transport was considerably improved, reaching its height around 1900. Then there were trains of barges on the river, such as those used to transport the enormous amount of building materials needed during construction of the first Paris Métro line.

The canals

The river had become difficult to navigate. It was too narrow and not deep enough, and so, at the beginning of the 19th century, a network of three canals was built to link the Seine upstream from the Ile Saint-Louis to the Lower Seine via the Arsenal basin and northern Paris. These were the Canal Saint-Martin (2.8 miles/4.5 km long), the Canal Saint-Denis (0.6 miles/ 1 km), and the Canal de l'Ourcq (just over 1 mile/ 2 km). Harbor facilities were improved by extending the wine market on Quai Saint-Bernard and building large warehouses near the present Arsenal basin. However, river transport was increasingly concentrated on the docks at La Villette. During the 20th century, competition from the railroad and road transport brought about a decline in the river trade.

6. Rue de Lyon in the great flood of 1910
In January, 1910, the Seine suffered one of its biggest floods on record. Many streets could only be reached by boat and part of the Métro network was under water.

7. Piscine Deligny
This vast barge anchored at Quai Anatole-France was for a long time a very popular swimming pool. It was the last surviving pool on the Seine, then accidentally sank after it had closed for restoration in 1993.

1. On the way to Bercy
These traditional barges still carry materials up and down the river, and make a sharp contrast with the new buildings at the Gare de Lyon business district.

2. Floating concert near the Pont des Arts
Music nights on boats are becoming increasingly popular with lovers of jazz, rock, and reggae. Most of them are at Quai de Montebello and Quai de la Gare.

The attractions of the Seine

From "water coaches" to the bateaux-mouches

In the 18th century, there was a "water coach" service on the Seine, the boats being drawn by horses. In 1825, a steamboat traveled three times a day from Paris to Saint-Cloud in the western suburbs. A major change took place in 1867 when the City of Paris commissioned Plasson to set up a new water transport service.

The Paris Waterbus Company was formed, with river boats (*bateaux-mouches*) running through Paris and a suburban service to Charenton and Suresnes. In 1886, it merged with two other companies, giving it a total fleet of 105 boats operating a 25 mile (40 km) service with 47 stopping places, and carrying some 25 million passengers a year. It was eventually put out of business in 1934 by competition from the Métro and road transport. Today, the river is mostly given over to tourism, with several boat companies offering river trips. The five million passengers they carry each year make the Port of Paris the largest center in the world for water tourism. Since 1997, a company has revived the old waterbus service.

Canal Saint-Martin

This is the best known of the city's canals, and crosses five *arrondissements*. Now boat cruises provide enjoyable and picturesque views of the districts it passes. Beside it on the Quai de Jemappes is the Hôtel du Nord, the setting for the famous film of the same name, made in 1938. The canal is crossed by many footbridges, its banks are planted with trees and shrubs, and at night it is illuminated. In the Haussmann period (1865) it was covered over from the Quai de Valmy to the present Paris-Arsenal boating harbor, which was opened in 1983 near the Bastille.

A stroll by the river

Despite the picturesque and historic nature of the riverside booksellers, whose stalls by the parapets are an essential part of the city's image, many Parisians had begun to avoid the river because it was polluted and its bankside roads were too full of traffic. At the end of the 20th century, major changes have encouraged walkers to return to the Seine. Now you can walk along the banks for about 6 miles (10 km), and there are new footbridges, such as the Passerelle Debilly, for crossing from one side to the other. In addition, on some Sundays, riverside roads normally open to traffic are limited to pedestrians, cyclists, and roller-bladers. As you walk along by the river, the view changes between the city center, with all its famous historic buildings, and the newer districts where contemporary and sometimes controversial buildings now stand close to the river. Like the view, the people also change. In summer, sunbathers lie out beneath the Tuileries and the Louvre, and fashionably dressed people are in the cafés, restaurants, and discos on barges at the Quai de la Tournelle and the Quai François-Mauriac. Some evenings you can see people dancing the tango beside the river at Quai Saint-Bernard.

3. Salsa beside the river
You can also find salsa and tango dancers by the river, to the delight of passers-by who come upon them by chance.

4. Life on the water
Some people have opted for a more unconventional life on old barges moored below the bankside roads.

Living on the water

Some people who love the river decide to live on it, usually in barges. Moored to the river bank, these barges have a very bohemian atmosphere. The community spirit needs to be strong: if one barge is moored outside another, and the one on the inside wants to move, then everyone has to work together for twenty minutes to complete the maneuver. But the daily life of the 150 floating homes in Paris is not just a matter of mutual co-operation. Life by the river bank is noisy and regularly punctuated by backwash from other boats, and the official moorings, which people pay the City to use, are not sheltered from the nightly procession of tourist boats. This is why most of them seek the calmer surroundings of the Arsenal basin.

The Seine and the arts

Poets and singers are forever producing verses and songs about the Seine, just as writers have always written about it, but it is not merely a simple backdrop. The Seine has always been a serious source of inspiration for many artists.

The Seine in painting

The English painter William Turner (d 1851) was one of the first. In the course of his life, he made a kind of topographical inventory of all its outlines and curves, both in Paris and elsewhere. After him, Impressionists such as Renoir, Sisley, and Caillebotte immortalized the river in the decade 1867-77. Monet's sunrise painting of 1873, *Impression, Soleil Levant*, gave the Impressonist movement its name, and depicts a view of the Seine. On its banks, at the town of Chatou, Derain and Vlaminck developed Fauvism.

The Seine in opera

In 1916, Giacomo Puccini set the Seine to music in his fluid and impressionistic one-act opera, *Il Tabarro* (The Greatcoat). The Seine and its dense mists provide the framework for the action, though Puccini's chief aim was to capture what the river meant to the people who used it. Michele, a boatman, and Giorgetta are a couple devastated by the loss of their baby. The resolution of their torment is violent and fatal for Luigi, the docker who loves Giorgetta. Michele kills him and hides him under his long coat, which symbolizes the river: "We all wear a greatcoat where sometimes we conceal joy, and sometimes grief."

5. *Paris, le quai des Grands-Augustins* (Marquet)
Albert Marquet (1875-1947) moved from Impressionism to Fauvism, and in 1898 worked with Matisse in the Luxembourg Garden and on the banks of the Seine. He continued to paint Paris, often directly from his studio on Quai Saint-Michel, and later from another on Quai des Grands-Augustins.

6. Pont des Arts
This famous footbridge downstream from the Ile de la Cité is a favorite spot for artists to set up their easels and paint views of the Cité and the riverside.

7. Music Festival
Each year, on June 21, the Music Festival takes to the streets and squares of Paris, and also to the riverside for concerts and dances.

The Seine on film

Jean Vigo's *L'Atalante* (1934) portrays the hard and wretched life of boatmen. Jean (played by Jean Dasté) is a boatman who marries Juliette (Dita Parlo) and takes her on board his barge, *L'Atalante*. Helped by Old Jules (Michel Simon), Jean sails slowly along the Seine and the canals of northern France. One day, Juliette is tempted by the big city, but the men of *L'Atalante* rescue her from her false illusions.

1. Underground chapel
This well-preserved chapel in Rue Pierre-Nicole is believed to date from the Early Christian period.

2. Beneath Rue de Poissy
Underground rooms have been used since Ancient times for Christian worship.

3. The Catacombs (15th *arrondissement*)
This sculpture from the Catacombs shows Mahón, the prison in Minorca where the artist had been held.

BENEATH THE CITY

Beneath the capital, much goes on that is not widely known but is essential for the smooth running of the city. At a depth of between 16 ft (5 m) and 115 ft (35 m) are hundreds of miles of passages forming a vast labyrinth. These are the remains of the Ancient and Medieval quarries which ran through the subsoil of several arrondissements. Another network belongs to the 1,300 miles (2,100 km) of sewer pipes which provide an essential service for the city's 2 million inhabitants.

Quarries and catacombs

The Gallo-Roman and Medieval quarries

In the Gallo-Roman period, the subsoil of Lutetia was quarried for stone to build the thermal baths of Cluny, as well as forums and arenas. This process continued throughout the Middle Ages. In the 12th century, the quarries all lay beneath the Left Bank. The first were located beneath the present Odéon and Luxembourg districts. When these were worked out, the quarry owners abandoned them for sites further south. This went on for several centuries until they had explored sites all over the present 5th, 6th, 13th, 14th, 15th, and 16th *arrondissements*.

Maintaining the quarries

In the 18th century, these cavernous holes formed an underground network which was incapable of supporting the weight of the buildings on the surface.
In 1774, the authorities, mindful of the risks of collapse, set up the General Inspectorate of Quarries.

Organizing the Catacombs

On May 21, 1765, a law was passed banning human burials within the walled city, and paved the way for the Catacombs. In order to check the epidemics which were decimating the population, the law ordered the closure of cemeteries inside the walls, and the transfer of their skeletons to the disused quarries. In 1786, the first skeletons from the Cimetière des Innocents, near Les Halles, were transferred to the new Catacombs. The transfers continued until 1788, then were resumed from 1842 to 1860. In the end, the remains of more than 5 million Parisians, taken from some 17 cemeteries and 145 religious communities, were moved in this way.

The modern Catacombs

The present layout of the Catacombs dates from the 19th century. In 1806, Héricart de Thury, Inspector General of Quarries, redesigned the Catacombs so they would be fit for visitors. He sealed off the ossuary to isolate it from the rest of the network and secure it against trespassers. The skeletons were laid out in galleries, together with quotations from the Bible, and from poets and philosophers.

Smugglers and cave-dwellers

From the beginning, the old quarries were used by various groups. Up to the 18th century, thieves and smugglers sought refuge there. In the 19th century, their cool, damp atmosphere attracted new occupants. Vats of beer were stored in them, and the famous Paris mushroom was grown there. Today, the old quarries are used by a new breed of cave-dwellers who hold illegal parties and concerts there.

Shelters and bunkers

The city's network of old quarries and underground galleries extends much further than just the Catacombs. During World War II, they were often used as air raid shelters. Their great potential did not escape the notice of the German forces occupying Paris. Beneath strategic locations such as railroad stations, they set up a number of secret command posts and connecting bunkers.

Nuclear shelters

In the Cold War, the defensive possibilities of these underground areas were re-examined. In 1959, the nuclear threat led to the first nuclear shelter being built, beneath the Marché Saint-Honoré. Since then, others have been built beneath the Place de l'Italie and the Maison de la Radio.

The sewers

Paris without sewers

Until the 14th century, Paris had only a rudimentary system of household waste disposal.

4. Mushroom bed
Brewers made use of the old quarries as beer cellars, and mushroom growers used them to produce the famous Paris mushroom.

5. Sewer tunnel
Water from the main pipes flows into exit tunnels more than 13 ft (4 m) wide which carry it to the treatment plants.

Trash and waste liquids were poured out on the streets and piled up in huge cesspits which became a major source of epidemics. Despite laws being passed to improve standards of hygiene, the capital was devastated by plague in 1348.

The invention of sewers

In the reign of Charles V, Hugues Aubriot, Provost of Paris, had the central channels carrying waste along the streets arched over to form tunnels. This method was used until the 18th century, but was not adopted everywhere. At the end of the 18th century, at the instigation of Police Chief Nicolas de Reynie, all the streets were cobbled and sewage tunnels were used everywhere. However, in a few years the system became blocked up and was no longer adequate.

The first underground sewers

At the beginning of the 19th century, Paris had only 15 miles (25 km) of sewers. The City's Inspector of Works, Bruneseau, decided to modernize the network and extend it by 7 miles (12 km). Two cholera epidemics persuaded the authorities to improve the system further, and in 1842 the first underground tunnels were completed; these ran for 60 miles (100 km) beneath the city.

Improving public health

In the Second Empire, Prefect Haussmann commissioned engineer Belgrand to build a coordinated water and sewage system for the whole of Paris. This included the disposal of waste water and rainwater, and resulted in the modern network which is still used today.

The modern sewers

Four different kinds of tunnel are used for drainage. The basic underground sewage tunnels are no more than 33 ft (10 m) wide. The secondary and main tunnels are located under the principal streets. Finally, an enormous tunnel carries the waste beyond the city limits. At first, sewage was poured into the Seine, but now it is piped to sewage farms for treatment.

There are also storm drains, which prevent floods during a rainstorm by drawing off the excess water to the Seine.
The sewers also house pipes carrying drinking water and telephone cables.

Cleaning procedures

The sewers need regular maintenance to function properly. Millions of cubic feet of water travel through the tunnels, leaving large amounts of sediment behind. To remove these, the sewer workers insert a large wooden ball in the pipes, which pushes out some of the deposit; this is then treated in a special plant. This is followed by a cleaning out process. Mobile barriers in the pipes work like floodgates holding back a river. Water is let in through an opening in the lower part of the dam, and drives out the remaining waste.

The rat population

The sewer worker's job has changed little since Haussmann's day. The men use the same tools and have to follow basic safety rules. Each day, they encounter large numbers of rats. It is thought that there are three times as many rats living underground as there are humans on the surface.

6. Cleaning out in a sluice boat
Today, the sewer workers use mobile sluice systems to shift the sediment toward the treatment area.

7. A Paris street in 1872
In the 19th century, the sewage sytem was co-ordinated by Belgrand. Nearly all the pipes carrying drinking water passed through the sewers.

1. The bird market
On Quai de la Mégisserie, between the Samaritaine department store and Châtelet, are hundreds of cage birds, as well as kittens, puppies, and tortoises.

2. The flower market
The flower market in Place Louis Lépine, next to the Police Headquarters, is held every day of the week except Sunday.

MARKETS AND SMALL TRADERS

Markets bring life to the streets of Paris and its "hundred villages." They have their regulars, who know where each stall is to be found. The small traders keep us in touch with the old values of craftsmanship and meticulous work.

The markets of Paris

The city has 85 markets, 73 of which are for food (60 open-air and 13 covered) and 12 are specialist markets for stamps, leather products and clothing, birds, handicrafts, and books, plus three flower markets and four flea markets.

Les Champeaux: before Les Halles

Stalls and markets have been around in Paris since at least the 5th century, when the Palu or Palud, the city's first market, opened near the Petit Pont. A few centuries later, in 1136, Louis VI opened a new market, Les Champeaux, which later became Les Halles. People came there from Brussels and Amsterdam to do business. Cloth-makers, weavers, and second-hand clothes dealers all paid a special fee to trade there. Streets in the area recall their various trades: Rue de la Lingerie, Rue de la Chanvrerie (hemp producers), and Rue de la Grande Friperie (second-hand clothes).

Les Halles: a wholesale market in the middle of Paris

In 1183, Philippe-Auguste ordered two large buildings, Les Halles, to be erected on the site of Les Champeaux. This huge market grew steadily over the centuries. In 1851, architect Baltard was commissioned to build two vast and spacious iron halls, full of air and light. These halls were demolished in the 1970s and the wholesale market was transferred to Rungis in the Paris suburbs. Since then, a shopping center, the Forum des Halles, has taken its place.

Saint-Germain Fair

In 1482, the local market in Saint-Germain-des-Prés was authorized by Louis XI to become a fair. Stalls, taverns, and sideshows competed to serve a cosmopolitan population; ordinary people and the nobility mixed freely. Its 140 stalls were destroyed by fire in 1762 and were replaced in 1813 by a new covered market on the orders of Napoléon I. In the 1980s, local protesters saved the building from total destruction, and since 1998 it has been a shopping center.

Food markets today

These make up the great majority of the city's markets: 73 out of 85. They bring a great deal of life to their neighborhoods, and each one has its regulars.

Picturesque covered markets

The 13 covered markets are among the oldest in Paris; some of them are in halls of the Baltard type. The Enfant-Rouges market, Rue de Bretagne (3rd) is one such; it was approved by letters patent in 1616. The Europe market, Rue Corvetto (8th) is the smallest of the city's covered markets. The daily Aligre market (12th) is 300 years old and has very competitive prices. It is held in a market hall dating from 1840, and is much used by foreigners living nearby. The fish market is held at the weekend in Rue Castagnary (15th); a lighthouse stands at the entrance. At Passy's very lively covered market (16th), each stall has a different type of roof, made of thatch, slate, or wood.

Open-air markets

Each district has its own market. The one in Rue Montorgueil (1st) is very busy and pleasantly old-fashioned, a

6. Strong man from Les Halles
"These strong, robust men work in Paris and elsewhere carrying loads of goods and merchandise for a certain mutually and politely agreed sum. They are also called carriers, porters, strong men, shovel boys, wheelers, pennymen, etc." **(Universal Dictionary of Trades)**

7. Marché d'Aligre
The hall is for food-sellers, while out on the square are secondhand dealers, and others selling exotic goods, secondhand clothes, and flowers. On Sunday, a brass band plays old favorites.

3. Saint-Pierre market
Around Place Saint-Pierre (18th) in Lower Montmartre, this market sells a colorful jumble of fabrics at bargain prices.

4. Rue Lepic
At Montmartre, from Place Blanche to the Rue des Abbesses, the picturesque Rue Lepic stages a food market from Tuesday to Sunday.

5. Boulevard de Belleville
This market is held on Tuesday and Friday mornings. It sells huge amounts of fruit and vegetables, and is also a good place for shoes.

reminder of the days when the Normandy fish merchants passed through it on their way to Les Halles with their fish and shellfish. In the picturesque Rue Mouffetard (5th), the colorful pyramids of fruit and vegetables line the cobblestones of the narrow, sloping street, one of the oldest in Paris. In Rue de Seine, in the Latin Quarter, the displays spill over into the roadway. Rue Cler (7th) is wider, and lined with splendid and very varied displays designed to make everything look especially attractive; on Sundays, a brass band adds yet more color to the scene. The market in Rue Daguerre (14th) is pedestrianized to encourage browsing. Rue de Lévis (17th) is very lively, with food stalls next to stores selling fabrics and dry

goods. There are also three organic markets, in Boulevard Raspail (6th), Place Brancusi (14th), and Boulevard des Batignolles (17th).

Flower and bird markets
There are still three flower markets in Paris: at Ternes, Madeleine, and Ile de la Cité. The largest is at Place Louis-Lépine, Ile de la Cité. It operates all year, except Sundays, when a bird market takes over. There are 36 stalls selling exotic shrubs, cacti, fruit trees, bonsai, and flowers sold in pots and by the bunch. In 1793, a wardress from the Conciergerie came to buy carnations and tuberoses to brighten the cell where Marie-Anoinette was imprisoned. The Quai de la Mégisserie is the special preserve of seed mer-

8. The Paris Fair, 1904
The first Paris Fair was held in March, 1904 at the Carreau du Temple, in a huge iron and glass hall which Haussmann had built in 1860. There were 486 exhibitors. The following year, the Fair moved to the Grand Palais, and then was staged at various other venues in the capital. In 1925, it found a permanent home at the Parc des Expositions, Porte de Versailles (15th).

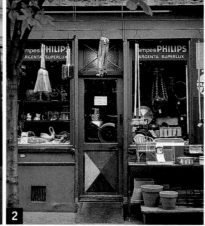

chants and birdsellers. Here the air is filled with strange shrieks and smells, and you can buy budgerigars, turtledoves, canaries, mynah birds, and peacocks kept in cages next to fish, dogs, rabbits, mice, and tortoises.

Flea markets

The markets at Saint-Ouen, Montreuil, and Vanves are open three days a week on Saturday, Sunday, and Monday, and continue the tradition of the old ragmen. Their stalls stand on the same patches of wasteland. In the interwar years it was the intellectuals, particularly the Surrealists, who made flea markets fashionable. They sell furniture, antiques, pictures, secondhand clothes, as well as records, trinkets, silverware, and so on, from some 3,000 stalls and boutiques. Their customers include Parisians, provincials, and visitors from abroad. The Aligre market in Place d'Aligre also sells second-hand objects and clothes.

Clothes, stamps, and old books

At Carreau du Temple (3rd), open every morning, you can buy a whole outfit for next to nothing. The iron and glass halls were built in 1863, replacing the old wooden halls of 1808. In the Middle Ages, the predecessors of these merchants sold their secondhand clothes from pitches on the ground. In the streets nearby, they specialize in leatherware.
Collectors of stamps, postcards,

and telephone cards gather every Thursday, Saturday, and Sunday at the Carré Marigny (8th), near the Rond-Point des Champs-Elysées, doing deals sometimes worth thousands of francs. Beneath the glass roofs beside the Parc Georges-Brassens (15th) is a weekend market for old and second-hand books which attracts bibliophiles searching for rare and out-of-print books as well as bargains. Even more unusual is the "creative market", held every Sunday on Boulevard Edgar Quinet (14th), which sells objets d'art.

The small traders

"The people we call small traders are nearly all foreigners. The Savoyards work with wood; people from the Auvergne are nearly all water carriers; those

from the Limousin are masons; most of the men from Lyons are porters and sedan chair carriers; the Normans are stonecutters, pavers, balers, china repairers, and rabbit-skin merchants; the Gascons are wigmakers and medics; those from Lorraine are itinerant cobblers, tilers, and roof repairers." That was how Louis-Sébastien Mercier described the capital's small traders in his *Tableau de Paris* (1781-9). The water carriers delivered their precious liquid from the Seine to the upper

stories of their clients' houses. The porters were the equivalent of removal men, and carried the furniture and the entire contents of houses on their backs. The men from the Auvergne were also traditionally charcoal burners, a distinct community which did not mix with other people. They remained remote for several centuries.

North of the Seine

Since the Middle Ages, the butchers – who at that time had a reputation for cruelty – and

1. Exotic goods store
To leave Paris, you need only wander round Belleville, the Goutte d'Or district, the Passage Brady, or the Marais to find hundreds of these exotic stores.

2. Hardware store
These charming survivors of a slowly vanishing age sell an amazing array of unexpected goods and gadgets.

3. Kitchen utensils
All the restaurateurs know they have to go to Les Halles to stock up with new, gleaming equipment for their kitchens.

4. Booksellers
The booksellers have been on the river banks since the beginning of the 17th century, and are a legend in their own right.

5. Percussion instrument maker
Instrument makers have stores in certain specific streets, such as the Rue de Rome, just west of the Gare Saint-Lazare.

the skinners from the Saint-Jacques-de-la-Boucherie district (today near the Châtelet), polluted the Seine with their waste, as did the tanners, tawers, and furriers on the Quai de Gesvres and the Quai de la Mégisserie. Later, Louis XIV banned them from using the river and sent them to the banks of the Bièvre, where they stayed until the river was covered over in 1912.

At the end of the 16th century, the washerwomen and laundresses gathered around the Pont Neuf to "beat the river." They put so much effort into their work that they were accused of wearing out the washing from rubbing it too hard. In the middle of the 19th century, there were laundry boats moored along the Seine. The last one, at Quai du Bourbon, on the Ile Saint-Louis, remained there until 1942.

Craftsmen old and new

Carpenters and furniture makers

The furniture makers settled in the Faubourg Saint-Antoine more than seven centuries ago. Louis XI granted permission for the abbesses from the Royal Cistercian Abbey (founded in 1198, on the site of the Hôpital Saint-Antoine) to let various traders settle on their land, so freeing them from the constraints of the guilds. Later, Louis XIV motivated these craftsmen still further by allowing them to copy pieces from the royal workshops. The many yards and alleyways leading off the Faubourg are still filled with woodcarvers, cabinetmakers, bronzesmiths, inlayers, gilders, clothmakers, upholsterers, and wallpaper makers.

The booksellers

The booksellers appeared beside the Seine as soon as the Pont-Neuf was completed in 1607, but were regularly driven away by royal edicts. In 1891 they were finally allowed to leave their book boxes permanently in place instead of taking them away each evening. The boxes had to conform to a specific size and color. In line with the concession granted them by the City of Paris, they are also required to trade from one precise spot. They work outdoors in all weathers, "and are so worn by the air, the rain, frosts, fogs, and bright sunshine that they end up looking like statues on cathedrals" (Anatole France). Today, rather less poetically, you could also add "and by the ravages of pollution."

Musical instruments and lead soldiers

The stringed instrument and bow makers trained at the Mirecourt National School in Lorraine, chose to settle in the Rue de Rome (9th), where you can also buy all sorts of music scores. The reason for this was the proximity of the Conservatory of Music, which has been in Rue de Madrid since 1911. Lead soldiers are to be found at one end of the arcades in Palais-Royal, beside the premises of the oldest heraldic engraver in Paris.

Glass and porcelain

The Rue de Paradis (10th) sparkles with crystal, porcelain, and pottery of every shape and size. The big manufacturers from the Vosges and Limoges all have stores and showrooms there. The House of Baccarat has opened its own museum, and in the Cité des Arts de la Table you can see all kinds of contemporary glass and porcelain.

The Sentier: the garment district

The Sentier district stands between Boulevard Poissonnière, Boulevard de Bonne-Nouvelle, and Rue Réaumur. It has been a traditional trading district since the Middle Ages, when sellers of woven goods first settled there. In the 15th century, embroidery, lace, and wool and silk fabrics were sold there. The Sentier is still the center of the garment district, handling anything from large rolls of wholesale fabric material to the finest of trimmings. In its cluttered streets, hundreds of garments hung on portable metal racks are pushed directly from the workshops hidden away in the courtyards to the prosperous wholesalers with street frontage.

6. The Bièvre
The River Bièvre has been covered over since 1912. It flowed into Paris at the Poterne des Peupliers and joined the Seine near the Pont d'Austerlitz. Tanneries, taweries, and dye works lined its banks, causing dreadful pollution.

7. The coppersmith
Coppersmiths are a vanished trade, but used to make pots and pans, also fountains, finely carved bathtubs, and warming pans in repoussé copper.

8. Old bakery
In the Marais, around Rue des Francs-Bourgeois and Rue des Rosiers, hairdressers have taken over the old bakeries.

ANTIQUE AND SECOND-HAND DEALERS

Since the 1970s, as the districts and special centers selling antiques have expanded, along with the syndicates selling art objects, Paris has become an international center visited by collectors from all over the world. There is something here to suit every taste and pocket.

Le Louvre des Antiquaires

The Louvre des Antiquaires is located between Palais-Royal and the Louvre Palace in a building by Percier and Fontaine dating from 1850. It formerly housed the Grands Magasins du Louvre and the 700-room Grand Hôtel du Louvre. The interior was completely redesigned and reopened in October, 1978. It has luxurious boutiques on three levels and a large exhibition room on the second story, and made an immediate impression on wealthy collectors. Its 250 dealers offer a diverse range of objets d'art, furniture, drawings and paintings from every period, as well as walking sticks, fans, dolls, clocks, watches, and even antique locks.

Saint-Paul Village

The small stores in this part of the Marais (4th) stand on old medieval streets: the Rue des Jardins-Saint-Paul, Rue Saint-Paul, and Rue de l'Ave-Maria. The Saint-Paul Village has a pedestrian zone, some 60 fairly reasonably priced second-hand and antique dealers, and craft studios hidden away in medieval cellars. Four times a year, the dealers take over the streets for a grand open-air display – a good chance to discover a 19th-century ceramic piece, an old curio, or a 1930s lamp.

Le Carré Rive Gauche

Le Carré Rive Gauche is a must for people interested in antique objets d'art. Located in the aristocratic part of Saint-Germain (7th), it dates from May, 1977, when the antique dealers of Rue de Beaune had the idea of forming an association of dealers from the Quai Voltaire, Rue des Saints-Pères, Rue de l'Université, and Rue du Bac, the four streets making up a perfect square. Its membership grew rapidly, from 40 at the outset to 120 in the 1980s. Each year in May, they hold a five-day open week, the Cinq Jours de l'Objet Extraordinaire, when anyone can go into the boutiques and slightly intimidating galleries of the Carré Rive Gauche to find rare and unusual antiques.

Swiss Village

The name of this antiques center in the 15th *arrondissement* comes from the village of Swiss chalets built there for the Universal Exhibition of 1900. It stands at No 78, Avenue de Suffren and No 52, Avenue de la Motte-Piquet. The site was completely renovated in 1968, and now contains 120 boutiques specializing in a mixture of Neoclassical statues, Chinese and Japanese furniture, antique silver, African sculpture, lace, and old books.

The flea markets

In the 19th century, ragmen sold all kinds of things near the old *fortifs*, the fortified wall surrounding Paris, which was built in 1844. After the wall was demolished from 1920, markets set up there, expanded, and started to include antiques in their range of goods.

The Saint-Ouen flea market, near Porte de Clignancourt (18th), is by far the largest. It has about ten specialist markets dealing in, for example, the Napoléon III period (Marché Biron), the 1900s (Marché des Rosiers), assorted antiques (Marché Paul-Bert), second-hand goods (Marché Jules-Vallès), and secondhand clothes (Marché Malik).

The flea markets at Porte de Vanves and Montreuil are held

1. Village Saint-Paul
Four times a year, antique hunters in search of unusual pieces invade the alleyways behind the Church of Saint-Paul-Saint-Louis (4th).

2, 3. The Carré Rive Gauche
This center is located in four streets forming a perfect square, and has more boutiques than any other antique district in the world.

4. Viaduc des Arts
Beneath the Promenade Plantée near the Bastille are the studio-boutiques of some 50 craft workers.

on Avenue Georges-Lafenestre (15th) and beside the Périphérique at Montreuil respectively. They trade in second-hand goods and clothes, and you can still find unusual things for a reasonable price.

Viaduc des Arts

The Viaduc des Arts is geared to contemporary objects and craftwork. It was started in the 1990s, when City Hall decided to renovate the arches supporting the old railroad between Bastille and Varennes-Saint-Hilaire, to the south-east of Paris.

The arches of the old "Paris viaduct" in the 12th *arrondissement*, between Nos 9 and 129, Avenue Daumesnil, are made of pink brick, freestone, and light wood, with large windows, and house 45 craft workers. In their studio-boutiques, they make and exhibit a wide range of applied art: stringed instru-ments, embroidery, furniture, gold objects, upholstery, jewelry, gilded leather, weaving, and engraved and sculpted stonework and ceramics.

5. Marché Biron
The Marché Biron is a specialist market within the Saint-Ouen flea market, and deals in the Napoléon III period. Every week, from Saturday to Monday, the 1,300 dealers here attract thousands of visitors.

6. Louvre des Antiquaires
This slightly intimidating place has a large exhibition room and boutiques on three levels occupying 108,000 sq ft (10,000 sq m), and deals in all kinds of expensive antiques.

7. Flea market at Montreuil
Visitors to this market can happily elbow their way to the front and haggle. It is one of the few flea markets to have kept the carefree spirit of the old markets.

1. Rue Ramponeau
In Belleville, people of all religions live together and community relations are good. This district embodies the spirit of cosmopolitan Paris.

2. Mouna Coiff
Immigrants have created new trades, like these Afro hairdressers of which there are dozens in the 18th *arrondissement* around Barbès-Rochechouart.

EXOTIC TRADITIONS

In multicultural Paris, you can sample all kinds of exotic lifestyles: dance the salsa in a Cuban club near the Odéon; celebrate Saint Patrick's Day in an Irish pub by the Opéra; watch the Chinese New Year procession in the 13th, or the one to the Hindu god Ganesh in the 18th; enjoy a kosher meal in a Jewish restaurant in the Marais, or celebrate Easter in the Russian Orthodox Cathedral in Rue Daru.

City of many cultures

Paris owes much of its present cultural wealth to the successive waves of immigrants who helped to shape it and ensure its vitality. The most significant of these include the Jews from Central Europe who came in the Middle Ages and in the 19th century; French provincials coming to seek their fortune in the capital; North Africans and African Jews who came to France in the colonial period or after it; political exiles of many nationalities – Russians, Spaniards, Latin Americans, and Kurds; Asian political refugees who came in the last decades of the 20th century – not to mention all those foreigners who decided to live in Paris because they love it.

Apart from the many Parisians of foreign origin who have taken French citizenship, in 1990 16% of the the city's population were from other countries. Some of these adopted Parisians live all over the city, like the Italians, Spanish, and Latin Americans. Others live in particular districts where they can keep their traditions alive. These "mini-continents" are often themselves divided into a diffuse pattern of enclaves and cultures.

African Paris

The Algerians, Moroccans, and Tunisians who came to work in Paris around 1950-60 settled in the most deprived districts in the city, from the Goutte d'Or to Ménilmontant, later moving on as further waves of immigrants arrived or renovation programs forced them out. The renovation of the Goutte d'Or (18th) has spared only the area round Barbès-Rochechouart, where the sidewalks are crammed with gamblers and stalls overflowing from stores such as Tati. Beneath the elevated Métro is a market where the smells of fresh mint and spices for *couscous* hang in the air. Further north, toward Rue des Poissonniers and Château-Rouge Métro station, the district took on a Black African character between 1975 and 1990. The market in Rue Dejean sells bananas, yams, spices, and fish. In the streets nearby, small stores sell a mixture of everything: cassettes, Afro-Caribbean cosmetics, perfume burners, live birds, multicolored fabrics, and *jellabas* from the Ivory Coast and Senegal. On Fridays, the prayer mats are put out on the sidewalks in front of the local mosques, which are too small to accommodate everybody.

The Far East in Paris

Some 45,000 Parisians came from Cambodia, China, Vietnam, and Laos from the end of the 1950s; most became natu-

3. Dejean market
All Africa meets here in this highly exotic market in the 18th *arrondissement* near Château-Rouge. There are people from the Congo Democratic Republic, the Ivory Coast, Mali, and Algeria and the North African countries.

4. Russian rhythm
Russians arrived in Paris after the October Revolution. Their descendants have opened several restaurants where you can find borscht flavored with vodka. They also have several churches, including the Saint-Alexis Cathedral, Rue Daru, in the 8th *arrondissement*.

ralized French citizens. The first arrivals settled in the Arts-et-Métiers district (3rd), and many started up wholesale jewelry businesses. From 1975, large numbers of refugees moved into the tower blocks in the south of the 13th, turning the "Choisy triangle" into a sort of Chinatown. Here, signs are covered with ideograms; supermarkets such as the Tang brothers' store overflow with rice and exotic fruits; restaurants are guarded by stone lions and dragons to drive evil spirits away; there are temples with buddhas seated on thrones, where you can also consult the oracle or play chess. Since 1984, the Chinese New Year has been celebrated with a parade decked out with dragons and other ritual figures which move to the sound of tambourines and cymbals. Each year, this event attracts more and more Parisians.

At the end of the 1970s, other Chinese districts were established near Rue Marx-Dormoy (18th) and in larger numbers in Belleville (19th and 20th).

Indian Paris

Since the end of the 1970s, the new waves of immigrants have mostly consisted of Turks, Kurds, Pakistanis, Indians, and Sri Lankans working in the garment workshops in the Sentier and the Temple.

The Indians and Pakistanis have turned the Passage Brady, the upper part of Rue du Faubourg-Saint-Denis, and Rue Louis-Blanc (10th) into small corners of Colombo, Islamabad, and Pondicherry. Everywhere, small stores emit spicy smells and the sound of exotic music, and others sell colorful saris, shiny jewels, garlands of flowers, and turbans. Every year, since 1985, the Hindus parade the elephant-headed god Ganesh in the streets of the 18th *arrondissement* where their temples are located.

5. Fabric store
It is no problem to make a *jellaba* in Paris. The fabrics sold in this store are all colors of the rainbow, just like the ones they sell in Ouagadougou, capital of Burkina Faso.

6. Avenue d'Ivry
Chinese and Vietnamese restaurants in the Avenue d'Ivry, in the 13th *arrondissement*, now face stiff competition from others in Belleville (19th and 20th), which has become the city's second Chinatown.

7. Faubourg Saint-Denis
In the upper part of Rue du Faubourg-Saint-Denis, in the La Chapelle district (18th), near the Gare du Nord, large numbers of Indian and Pakistani stores have recently opened.

THE LUXURY TRADE

The way the various districts of Paris have developed is closely linked to the story of French fashion, which for several centuries has drawn inspiration from the city's streets, squares, and gardens. Even today, the opening of a new boutique excites passion and curiosity, bringing life to a sleepy districts, or a forgotten street. Fashion can take over a place and transform it, adding a new dimension to a city which has long been in thrall to the pleasures of luxury.

Around the Louvre Palace

The areas of Paris that specialize in fashion have been grouped around the Louvre Palace and the Tuileries Garden since the Renaissance. In the early days, the local craftsmen and storekeepers were encouraged by their royal clients to learn how to make fine clothes and accessories. Initially, these were bought by the aristocracy, then by the wealthy middle classes, and more recently by an international clientele looking for quality products with a history and reputation behind them.

Palais-Royal

Today, the gardens of the Palais-Royal and their 18th-century arcades continue to attract fashion designers and decorators. The fronts of the boutiques and their interior design are wholly traditional, and contain an echo of the extraordinary Neoclassical fashions that were launched during the Directoire. Didier Ludot, an antique dealer, has three boutiques here with a unique collection of haute couture clothes from the earliest times to the present day.

From Place Vendôme to Faubourg Saint-Honoré

The oldest fashion houses still in business are located between Place Vendôme and Rue du Faubourg-Saint-Honoré. They date from the 19th century, when much of the city was being modernized and improved, and was attracting tourists from overseas who had heard about French luxury goods and the style and taste of Parisian women.

In 1857, a young Englishman called Charles Frederick Worth moved into the Rue de la Paix near the Palais des Tuileries where the Imperial court was living. He founded the haute couture business: each season, he presented collections of dresses modeled by parading mannequins to his wealthy clients. After they had made their choice, the garments were made to measure, exclusively for them. Like artistic masterpieces, they bore the name of the couturier. Their ostentatious style glorified the beauty and social standing of the women who wore them. Haute couture became the flagship of French fashion, and its success led to the founding of many new companies.

Today, some 20 houses maintain this tradition, even though few women buy their extremely expensive creations. The couturiers present a dream image which can then be imitated by the more affordable ready-to-wear companies.

Lanvin, Chanel, and Lacroix

Some of the older houses have survived and are still in the same district. In Rue du Faubourg-Saint-Honoré, near Rue Royale, the famous House of Jeanne Lanvin is still as splendid as ever. In a smaller street, close to Place Vendôme, one of the most celebrated fashion houses keeps up a tradition inherited from Worth. The House of Chanel, founded in Rue Cambon in 1919, remains eternally fresh while safeguarding hallowed French traditions. Each season, gowns, perfumes, accessories, and cosmetics are created in the style developed

5. Chaumette
Furs made their appearance in Paris fashion houses at the end of the 19th century.

6. Romy Schneider
Often, foreign clients embody the image of the Parisienne very successfully, like Romy Schneider, who was adopted by Chanel.

7. Christian Lacroix
The dream gowns of Christian Lacroix are all part of the legendary image of Parisian luxury.

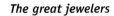

1. Yves Saint-Laurent
Since the 1950s, the elegant creations of Yves Saint-Laurent have personified a look that is both classic and modern, reflecting the taste of women in Paris. His workshops reveal his commitment to old-fashioned craftsmanship and skills.

2. Christian Dior
The House of Dior is proud of its image, and its Avenue Montaigne store is decorated in a style dating from its founder's times. Dior is an ambassador for Parisian taste, and its gray and white stucco windows can be found abroad in other great cities.

3, 4. Avenue Montaigne
Avenue Montaigne has been dedicated to the luxury trade for more than a century, its large show windows displaying an array of luxury items. Today, the old French firms such as Nina Ricci, Dior, and Vuitton live side by side with the great Italian designers.

by the firm's founder. The business adapted to all the major fashion changes of the 20th century. Its style is simple, practical, and modern, both for the Chanel suit and the little black dress which revolutionized women's wardrobes in the 1920s and have remained essential items ever since.

Christian Lacroix opened his house in 1986 in Rue du Faubourg-Saint-Honoré, close to Pierre Cardin, the famous couturier of the 1960s. Although he is one of the youngest French couturiers, he has revived a tradion for craftsmanship which many designers had let go. His fabrics, embroidery, lace, macramé work, and other decorative elements recall the fine workmanship of gowns from the past. These salons and their privileged clients, their excellent workshops, and the special atmosphere to be found in such places follow the traditions of the 19th-century fashion houses.

The great jewelers

The great jewelers of Paris settled in Place Vendôme. The precious jewels made by Boucheron, Chaumet, and Van Cleef and Arpels reveal a French influence that is linked to the creativity of French couturiers. The cut of the stones and the way the precious metals are crafted are very much in line with innovations in the fashion business.

The House of Cartier was founded in 1847, and in the Belle Epoque moved to the Rue de la Paix. Here the jeweler built his reputation, acquiring a faithful clientele and international fame. He became jeweler to fifteen royal courts in Europe, and was sought after by business people and demimondaines. His secret was to adapt his creations to the tastes of the day by means of constant technical innovation. Cartier first made his name with jewels bearing animal motifs, then at the end of the 19th century he became famous for his wristwatches; a century later, the company won new fame with its cigarette lighters for men.

Perfumes

Located between Rue Saint-Honoré and Place Vendôme is the House of Guerlain, founded in 1828 and one of the oldest businesses still trading in Paris. The history of this company

1. Chanel N°5
Coco Chanel was the first couturier to link her name to a perfume. In the 1920s, Chanel No 5 epitomized the liberated, active, modern Parisienne.

2. Van Cleef & Arpels
The House of Van Cleef, founded in 1906, perpetuates the idea of inaccessible luxury.

3. Ring by Boucheron
The House of Boucheron was founded in 1858, and supplied Indian and Persian princes.

and its 321 perfumes is closely tied to the development of the fashion business. Mitsouko (1919) is a reminder of Puccini's opera *Madame Butterfly*, while Vol de Nuit evokes the aviator-writer Saint-Exupéry and flying in the 1930s. Fine perfume first made its name in Paris in the 18th and 19th centuries. Perfumers and scientists collaborated in the development of new processes which added to the city's reputation. At the beginning of the 20th century, Paul Poiret and Gabrielle Chanel created the first fashion perfumes and this influenced the thinking of the perfumers. Since then, the fashion houses all produce a collection of scents adapted to the tastes of the day.

Fashion accessories

Since the Renaissance, there have always been accessories to go with fashionable clothes. Many craftsmen specialized in making "fashion objects," using their special techniques and skills. Shoemakers, leather workers, milliners, and glovemakers were some of the many trades which helped to launch high fashion. They took premises from the Sentier district, which has specialized in garment manufacture since the 19th century, to the Rue du Faubourg-Saint-Honoré. In this field, the House of Hermes has been one of the leaders since 1837. Its store is very British in style, and reveals the company's origins as a maker of horses'

harnesses. Since the 1920s, Hermes has sold accessories, clothes, and household and travel items made by techniques rooted in the art of saddlemaking. Now one of the main luxury businesses in Paris, it makes its leather goods in its own workshops and so retains its name for craftsmanship. The milliner Philippe Model, and the shoemakers Christian Louboutin and Michel Perry also contribute to the international reputation of accessories designed and made in Paris.

Young designers of the 1980s

In the 1980s, the young designer Jean-Paul Gaultier moved to the Galerie Vivienne, an old shopping arcade which had been forgotten, but was on the fringes of the fashion district. His style shows the creativeness and freedom of the Paris couturiers. He brings opposing elements together. His woman flirts with men's styles, while his Western fashions include Oriental influences, and he revisits the past to blend it with contemporary features in a style that is both poetic and committed. His success has led to the development of a new fashion district between Palais-Royal and Place des Victoires. Here are many famous foreign designers including the Japanese firms Kenzo, Yohji Yamamoto, and Comme des Garçons, whose avant-garde creations have influenced the course of French fashion.

A new luxury district: the Golden Triangle

After World War I, many luxury firms in Paris were attracted to a new district built during the Haussman era. They settled between Avenue Montaigne, Avenue Georges-V, and the Champs-Elysées, near the luxury hôtels. The Neoclassical buildings lining these vast shady avenues offered great scope for building magnificent show windows, and the district was soon nicknamed the Golden Triangle.

From Poiret to Dior

The couturier Paul Poiret was one of the first to leave the Rue de la Paix and move close to the Champs-Elysées; that was in 1909. He was the innovative designer who liberated women from the corset and revolutionized Paris fashion with his more functional garments, attracting a young, emancipated clientele of actresses and American women. Later, Madeleine Vionnet and Nina Ricci transferred their operations to the Avenue Montaigne. Today in this district, various foreign houses,

6. Diamond and rubies by Van Cleef & Arpels
This company developed a classically based floral style which it has adhered to for many years. In the interwar years, this jeweler was also well known for its exotic jewels revealing Chinese and Japanese influences.

particularly Italian ones (Prada, Dolce e Gabanna, and Valentino) live alongside great French names such as Givenchy, Courrèges, Yves Saint-Laurent, and Celine.

At the corner of Rue François I and Avenue Montaigne, the House of Dior has assured the fame of the Golden Triangle for more than 50 years. American journalists called his postwar style the New Look. To foreign observers, his narrow-cut gowns with rounded shoulders epitomized Parisian elegance. Yves Saint-Laurent and Gianfranco Ferre continued the spirit of Dior, emulating his flair and refinement. Dior's windows, as always, are decorated with stucco and 18th-century furni-

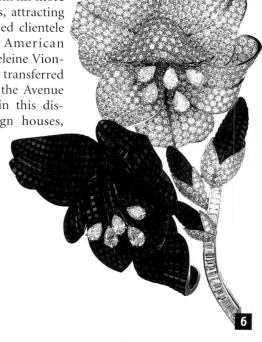

ture, and now feature the dream gowns created in the House's workshops by John Galliano.

Louis Vuitton

Louis Vuitton, the famous accessories house, reigns supreme in the Champs-Elysées. The company has been producing its own handbags and baggage since 1854. Vuitton himself was famous for inventing the first flat valises for railroad travel, and the monogrammed waterproof material he used. These valises made Louis Vuitton a legendary brand, used by stars and royalty on their visits to Paris.

Saint-Germain

The Left Bank developed slowly as a fashion center. The Deux-Magots, at the beginning of the 19th century, was one of the first famous stores in the Saint-Germain district. They sold a wide range of fabrics at set prices, an innovation at the time, and also bonnets, gloves, shawls, and ready-made garments – the

4. Gaultier
Designer Jean-Paul Gaultier could only be from Paris! His world and his commitment have created a style of enormous flexibility.

5. Trunk by Vuitton
Accessories are essential to haute couture. Since the 19th century, Parisians have bought their trunks and valises from the House of Vuitton. In its workshops Vuitton continues the craft traditions of the trunkmakers.

beginning of the ready-to-wear business. The district developed under the patronage of the nobility who moved there under the Empire and, after the torments of the Revolution, revived the Rues du Bac, Saint-Dominique, and de Sèvres, which were then taken over by stores selling garments and novelties. In 1869, Bon Marché set up as a competitor to department stores on the Right Bank such as Au Printemps and

7. The milliner, 1925
Milliners have almost disappeared today, but haute couture continues to use hats in its parades, enabling designers such as Marie Mercier to carry on working.

8. On the catwalk at Lacroix
Each season, Paris is visited by buyers and the international press for the haute couture and ready-to-wear fashion shows which keep Paris at the leading edge of fashion design.

Galeries Lafayette, which catered for a large and varied clientele on the more heavily populated Right Bank.

Saint-Germain-des-Prés had its big moment of fame after World War II when it became the district favored by disaffected young people. Jazz-lovers became converts to Existentialism and moved into the old boulevard. Not until the 1960s, however, did the ready-to-wear boutiques of the young avant-garde designers come to rank in importance with the antique dealers and gallery owners of the Rue Bonaparte.

Yves Saint-Laurent and ready-to-wear

Yves Saint-Laurent opened his own fashion house in 1963 in Avenue Georges-V. However, three years later he chose Place Saint-Sulpice for his first ready-to-wear store. This was more reasonably priced than haute couture, and for it he designed a style for the modern, liberated woman. His trouser suits, safari

outfits, and three-quarter length coats influenced by professional clothing were some of his solutions in the quest for a new kind of womenswear. Since then, his designs have brought a fresh elegance and a modern, comfortable, and functional look to the Paris scene. The YSL brand is one of the best ambassadors of French taste and Parisian luxury throughout the world.

Sonia Rykiel

The designer Sonia Rykiel was also drawn to the bohemian and intellectual atmosphere of the boulevard. In 1968, she launched her collection of practical and affordable knitted gowns, sweaters and trousers, and made black her dominant color. The success of this creative and bold designer, like that of Chanel, demonstrates the role that women have played in Paris fashion.

Paris and fashion are always evolving. At the end of the 20th century, fashion has joined the move to new districts. The Marais and its famous museums have attracted new fashion designers who have opened their boutques next to art galleries, tea rooms, and interior design stores. In this network of medieval streets, artists like Issey Miyake and Azzedine Alaia have developed a more intimate style. While the luxury trade has helped to make Paris famous, the city continues to renew itself with artists of all nationalities adding to its more tolerant and multi-faceted look.

CAFÉS, RESTAURANTS, AND HÔTELS

*Paris has an infinite variety of cafés, from the simplest to the most sophisticated, used by regulars
and passers-by. Paris is the capital of good food, and you can eat well in a vast range of brasseries,
neighborhood bistros, wine bars, and gourmet restaurants. Similarly, the hotels range from palatial five-star
establishments to small, charming hotels.*

The cafés: a Parisian institution

Coffeehouses started in the 17th century when coffee came to the European continent, and were quickly very successful. The most famous is Le Procope, Rue de l'Ancienne Comédie, founded by an Italian, Francisco Procopio dei Coltelli in 1686, where literary people gathered. The comfort to be found in some places, along with the quality of the drinks they served, and their general exoticism, bore no comparison to the smoky bars and cabarets used by ordinary people. In 1723, Paris had 380 cafés, almost all of them on the busier Right Bank. The fashionable cafés – the Caveau, Café de Chartres (the future Café Véfour), and the Café Valois – were in the Palais-Royal district, where revolutionary clubs met and discussed their ideas. In 1789, Camille Desmoulins harangued the crowd at the Café Foy.

Meeting places for high society

In the 19th century, a leisured crowd of wealthy bourgeois and aristocrats met in the cafés of the Grands Boulevards: the Café Riche, Café Anglais, and Chez Tortoni on Boulevard des Italiens, and the Café de la Paix by the Opéra. People discussed politics in these places, and painters, sculptors, and writers enjoyed passionate arguments. Then café-gardens began to open. The Café de la Régence, a sumptuous establishment in Rue Saint-Honoré, was for chess players; at the Café Frascati, Rue de Richelieu – located in the courtyard of a mansion built by Brogniart – Parisians gathered to eat ice creams.

In these luxurious cafés, special attention was paid to the decorations, using mirrors, crystal ceiling lights, marble tables, and stucco and gilded ornaments to create a refined atmosphere. An American journalist, Donald Grant Mitchell, stayed in Paris in 1847 and wrote this description: "The Parisian takes his chocolate there and his newspaper, his small cup of coffee and his cigar, his mistress, and his ice cream. The provincial takes his lunch and his *National* there, his absinth, and his wife ... In Paris, they live their lives in public; for a Frenchman, the café is what the Stock Exchange is in a strictly commercial society."

Bistros

The cafés of Paris are also bistros, the name coming from the time the Cossacks were in Paris in 1814, and were forbidden to enter bars selling alcohol. The bolder ones did risk it sometimes, however, urging their comrades with the words "Bistro! Quick!" Bistros are convivial places, and have had their regulars ever since. Finan-cial people and businessmen gather around the Bourse, politicians near the Assemblée Nationale, students near their colleges, sports fans at the Café aux Sports or L'Olympique, immigrants at the Petit Kabyle or A la Ville d'Oran, and artists and writers in Saint-Germain-

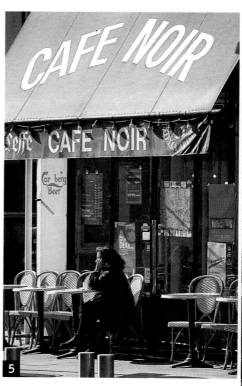

1. Coffee time
All over the city, cafés open till all hours give people the chance of a break, and a place to meet someone.

2. The "zincs"
Standing at a zinc bar is part of life in Paris. In the older-style cafés, people tell each other their latest news, and analyze the scandals of the day.

3. The George V
Located on Avenue Georges-V (8th), this elegant brasserie-restaurant has views of the Arc de Triomphe.

4. Angélina
At Angélina's tea room in Rue de Rivoli, time seems to have stood still. Hot chocolate lovers wait to be served on dark-red velours chairs amid the outmoded but much loved 1900s décor.

des-Prés or Montparnasse. In the 1950s, before the arrival of television, sodas and Coca-Cola, as well as pinball machines, were an essential part of café life.

Themed cafés today
There are philosophical cafés and literary cafés, and also cyber cafés. In the 1990s, themed cafés began to open in Paris. The Café Orbital, Rue de Médicis (6th) was the first to make the Internet available to the public. The Web Bar, Rue de Picardie (3rd), located in an old jewelry workshop designed by the Eiffel studio, has an area of 4,300 sq ft (400 sq m). Web browsers also use the Cybercafé Latino, Rue de l'École Polytechnique (5th) and AOL@Vivendi Café, Rue de Tilsitt (8th), which occupies the 16,150 sq ft (1,500 sq m) space of the former Boutique Danoise.

Music cafés are also very popular. La Jungle, Rue d'Argout (2nd), in an old prostitutes' hôtel, offers salsa and reggae; the Café du Trésor, in the street of the same name in the middle of the Marais, changes its program every day of the week.

Museum cafés and decorative cafés
Cafés flourish around or inside museums. Opposite the Louvre Pyramid, the terrace of the Café Marly is a meeting place for models and ministers. At the Musée d'Orsay, the Café des Hauteurs is located beneath fine ironwork and a wonderful clock. In the Musée de l'Homme, at Trocadéro, the Totem has one of the most impressive views of Paris. One of the cafés noted for its décor is Café Charbon, Rue Oberkampf (11th), in an old café-theater whose vast size, decorated oak panels, and frescos recall the Belle Epoque. The Café Antoine, Rue La-Fontaine (16th) has remained the same since it was built in 1911, with painted panels, a pewter bar, and moldings to remind customers that this whole enclave was designed by Hector Guimard, one of the finest exponents of Art Nouveau.

Tea rooms
At Angélina, Rue de Rivoli, in the old Maison Rumpelmayer, the 1900s décor is as splendid as ever. There you can try a smooth hot chocolate, accompanied if you wish by pastries with Crème Chantilly and chestnut purée. Beneath the glass roof of the Galerie Vivienne (2nd), A Priori Thé serves brunch every weekend. In the shadow of the Church of Saint-Séverin (5th), The Tea Caddy has tinted windows and old paneling, and offers English-style pastries. Some newcomers include T for 2 Café, which opened in 2000 in the Cour Saint-Emilion, an old barrel store in Bercy, once famous for its wines.

From La Tour d'Argent to Nouvelle Cuisine
Restaurants, like cafés, arrived in Paris around 1765. The Revolution speeded the process by

5. The Café Noir
This café in Rue Montmartre is mainly decorated in red, and offers more than just drinks from its tiled bar. It is a popular music café, and in the evening has DJs, funk, and techno for its young, trendy customers.

6. Café de la Paix, 1900
Middle-class customers on the terrace of the Café de la Paix in the Belle Epoque. In *The Pleasures of Paris* (1867), A Delveau described a "varied and generally distinguished

clientele. Literary people hardly ever go there, and the tarts never."

7. Web Bar
The Web Bar cybercafé in Rue de Picardie (3rd) runs training courses on the Internet. You can also eat there.

making the cooks of deposed noble families open their own establishments.

By 1803, Grimod de la Reynière, the famous food critic, could write that Paris was "definitely the best place in the universe for eating well." Today there are old and very famous restaurants, such as La Tour d'Argent, where guests eat their duck in blood sauce in a room overlooking Notre-Dame and the Ile de la Cité. It was originally an inn, which opened in the reign of Henri II in 1592. Four centuries later, many great names of Nouvelle Cuisine such as Joel Robuchon, Guy Savoy, Michel Rostang, Le Divellec, Lucas Carton, and H Faugeron have their own restaurants in Paris.

Brasseries: an import from Alsace

Brasseries are an important part of the Paris culinary scene, and date from 1870 when Alsace-Lorraine was annexed by the Prussians, and Alsatians had to move to the capital and teach it to drink beer.

Some of them have kept their traditional décor, which became established between 1880 and 1930. You can find it at Bofinger, Rue de Bastille, a Belle Epoque brasserie specializing in sauerkraut dishes.

Lipp, in Boulevard Saint-Germain, was founded in 1900 by Marcelin Cazes from the Auvergne, and is an institution, like Maxim's, in Rue Royale. Others to note are Chez Flo, Cour des Petites-Ecuries (10th),

La Coupole, Le Dôme, and Le Sélect in Montparnasse, Le Boeuf sur le Toit near Champs-Elysées, and Le Vaudeville, Rue Vivienne, which has kept its 1930s style with its moldings and bar.

Bistros and small restaurants

The bistros are more modest places. Chez Julien, an old local eating-place in Rue du Faubourg-Saint-Denis, has kept its Art Nouveau décor with glass and enameled panels designed by Trézel. At Chartier, Rue du Faubourg-Montmartre, they have been serving cheap meals for generations in a Belle Epoque setting in the middle of a very picturesque and noisy

setting. It has a partner, the Bouillon Racine in the Latin Quarter.

Bistros where people go for coffee are an essential element in the gastronomic scene. With their imitation leather banquettes and zinc bar tops, they offer a basic menu. Examples include Aux Charpentiers, Rue Mabillon (6th) in the old premises of a carpenters' guild; the Bistrot du Curé, Boulevard Clichy (9th); Les Zygomates, Rue de Capri (12th), an old butcher's store which has become one of the most famous places in the district; and Chez Paul, Rue de la Butte-aux-Cailles (13th), which serves a beef stew and braised tripe.

Regional and ethnic restaurants

There are also many restaurants serving regional dishes, for example Au Petit Bougnat, Rue Léopold-Bellan (2nd), which is very typical of the Corrèze; the Brasseries Alsaciennes; Au Bascou, in Rue Réaumur, where they serve piperade and squid in its own ink like in the Basque country; and Le Guilvinec (12th), whose name evokes the salty tang of Brittany. All the countries of the world seem to be represented nowadays. There are chic Japanese restaurants in the 2nd *arrondissement*, more popular Chinese ones in the 13th; in the 18th the cuisine is North African; while in Rue de

5. Café de la Paix
The Café de la Paix in Place de l'Opéra is part of the Grand Hôtel, built during the Second Empire. This vast period-style café is a popular meeting place after the theater.

6. The Ritz
The Ritz in Place Vendôme is one of the most famous hôtels in Paris. It was founded in 1898 by César Ritz and has kept its late 18th-century-style décor. Its bar is also a landmark.

7. The Royal Monceau
The Hôtel Royal Monceau in Avenue Hoche was a house of retreat for nuns until the 1920s. It was bought in 1924, and converted into a luxury hôtel.

1. Place des Vosges
Many cafés have opened beneath the arcades in Place des Vosges (4th). In good weather, Parisians and tourists enjoy the special atmosphere of these terraces.

2. Bateau Lavoir
This picturesque café in Montmartre was once the artists' studio where, among others, Picasso, Juan Gris, Van Dongen, and G Braque lived, as well as poets such as Apollinaire and Francis Carco.

3. Café de Paris
In 1867, in *The Pleasures of Paris*, A Delveau described how "people lunched in the morning, and had supper about midnight – and, my goodness, what an extraordinary crowd they were!"

4. Hôtel du Brabant
Paris has a vast choice of hôtels in every category. Small, charming hôtels are seen as typically Parisian, and are particularly sought after.

Belleville (19th) you find Caribbean, Indian, African, and Chinese restaurants.

New trends

Since the 1990s, wine bars have also been fashionable, for example Le Verre Volé, Rue de Lancry; Jacques Mellac, Rue Léon Frot (11th), where the owner harvests and produces his own wine; and Au Clown-Bar, Rue Amelot (11th), with its murals of clowns. In 2000, new homemade soup bars opened, such as Spécial Comptoir, Rue Oberkampf, and the Bar à Soupes, Rue de Charonne.

From small to luxury hotels

Paris has an abundance of hôtels in every category.

Charming hotels

In Place de la Sorbonne, the Select Hôtel, with its old stone and massive beams, is a good base for the Latin Quarter. In Rue du Cardinal-Lemoine, the Hôtel des Grandes Écoles, located in Pascal's old home, is a country house in the middle of the capital. The Relais Christine, between Odéon and Saint-Germain-des-Prés, is more luxurious. Breakfast is served in medieval cellars, and a courtyard garden adds to its charm. The Hôtel de l'Abbaye, Rue Cassette, brings a breath of the country to the heart of Saint-Germain-des-Prés with its birdsong and open fire in the Lounge.

The Atelier Montparnasse, Rue Vavin, seems to living in 1930, while the Hôtel Prima-Lepic, Rue Lepic, at the top of Montmartre, has a rural atmosphere and a winter garden. Also in Montmartre, the Terrass Hôtel in Rue Joseph de Maistre has a terrace courtyard overlooking the whole of Paris.

Luxury hotels

The Crillon in Place de la Concorde, built in the 18th century by J A Gabriel, has 163 guest rooms for the world's "top people." Some of its lounges, the Salons des Aigles, des Batailles, and the Marie-Antoinette, are classified historic monuments, as is the interior courtyard. The bar counter in the Piano Bar was made of broken glass by the sculptor César. The reputation of the Ritz, in Place Vendôme, where Hemingway stayed, is assured. The Grand Hôtel, Rue Scribe (2nd), was opened by Empress Eugénie in 1862. The Opéra Lounge, with its 48 statues of musicians, is one of the most impressive reception rooms in the city. The Bristol, Rue du Faubourg-Saint-Honoré, is an 18th-century house. Its 13,000 sq ft (1,200 sq m) gardens are the largest hotel gardens in the capital. On the 7th story, a swimming pool looks out on the rooftops of Paris.

1. Madame Geoffrin's salon
In the 18th century, the salon of Madame Geoffrin (1699-1777) in Rue Saint-Honoré, on the Right Bank, was popular with writers and artists. There they held many lively debates about the *Encyclopédie*.

2. Balzac's house
In this small house on the hill in Passy, Balzac wrote *La Rabouilleuse*, *La Cousine Bette*, *Le Cousin Pons*, and corrected his *Comédie Humaine*.

THE WRITERS' CITY

From François Villon to Balzac and Proust, many writers established strong links with Paris.
There is something about this city of seedy districts and bright lights, cheap restaurants, and luxury mansions
which has attracted foreign intellectuals from all over the world, and which they have written about in
a host of famous novels.

Epitaphe dudit Villon

François Villon and the Latin Quarter

Paris in the time of Villon, the "accursed poet," consisted of the Latin Quarter and the Ile de la Cité. Born in 1431 and originally named François de Montcorbier or François Des Loges, Villon was brought up by the chaplain of the monastery of Saint-Benoît, Rue des Écoles. From his little room, he could hear the Sorbonne bell ringing nearby. But he preferred the streets and taverns such as La Mule, just opposite the monastery, or, across the Petit-Pont in the Ile de la Cité, the Trou Perrette, Rue de la Juiverie, and the Grosse Margot, near the cloister of Notre-Dame. Sometimes he went to Les Halles, to the Cabaret des Trumelières, one of the most infamous places in Paris.

The fashion for salons

Literary salons flourished in the 17th and 18th centuries, and played an important part in the circulation of ideas. In 1650, hostesses received their guests lying in bed, while their visitors sat in the *ruelle*, the space between the bed and the wall. The most famous of these salons was the Hôtel de Rambouillet, located where the Louvre Pyramid now stands. Malherbe, Scarron, Vaugelas, and the young Corneille were regular visitors. In the following century, hostesses moved from their bed to a table, which everyone sat around to exchange witticisms. Fontenelle and Marivaux went to the salon of Madame de Tencin, Rue Neuve-Saint-Honoré. From 1750, the Encyclopedists, including Voltaire, Diderot, and d'Alembert, met at Madame Geoffrin's in Rue Saint-Honoré on the Right Bank, and on the Left Bank they went to Madame du Deffand and her niece Julie d'Espinasse in Rue Saint-Dominique.

Victor Hugo's house-cum-museum

In 1832, Victor Hugo moved into the third story of the former Hôtel de Rohan-Guéménée at No 6, Place des Vosges. For 16 years, before his exile to Guernsey, he wrote most of *Les Misérables* and his major dramas *Ruy Blas* and *Les Chants du Crépuscule* there. In Place des Vosges, he saw his daughter Léopoldine married, and received his friends Sainte-Beuve, Dumas, Vigny, Lamartine, and Balzac. The house became a museum in 1902, and now displays photographs, books, and personal possessions reflecting the author's life, as well as his drawings, of which there are more than 3,000.

5. Villon's epitaph
This poem, also known as *The Ballad of the Hanged Men*, was written by François Villon after he had been condemned to be hanged and strangled for theft in 1463. The poet had made the Latin Quarter his favorite haunt, dividing his time between brawling in the streets and studying at the University.

6. Balzac's study
Here you can see the table where the writer sat and corrected several volumes of *La Comédie Humaine*. Next to it, the living room recalls the presence of Madame Hanska, one of his mistresses, whom he married shortly before his death in 1850.

3. Hugo's study
Victor Hugo lived in the former Hôtel Rohan-Guéménée, Place des Vosges, from 1832 to 1848. There he wrote *Les Chants du Crépuscule*, *Les Rayons et les Ombres*, *Les Voix Intérieures*, and a large part of *Les Misérables*.

4. Verlaine
The poet Verlaine often went to the cafés on Boulevard Saint-Michel, and Le Procope in Saint-Germain-des-Prés.

In the footsteps of Balzac and Zola

Balzac's Paris

The house of the author of the *Comédie Humaine* stands between No 47, Rue Raynouard and Rue Berton, in the 16th *arrondissement*. There, in his "shack in Passy," the writer took refuge in 1840 to hide from his creditors. To gain admittance to the house, visitors had to know the password "I am bringing the lace from Belgium" or "The plum season has arrived." The house was turned into a museum in 1960. In 1845, Balzac published his *History and Physiology of the Boulevards of Paris*. There he paid tribute to the Grands Boulevards, which provided him with much of his inspiration. He himself dreamed of making a fortune on the Boulevard Montmartre, opening a large café where George Sand would be the cashier and Théophile Gautier a waiter. This project never got off the ground, however.

Zola and his on-the-spot research methods

Zola was born in Paris, and with his Rougon-Macquart series sought to paint a huge picture of the society of his day. Armed with notebooks for jotting down the slightest observation, he roamed popular districts such as the Goutte d'Or. In *L'Assommoir*, his heroes Coupeau and Lantier know all the cheap eating-places in the Butte Montmartre – as they well might, since Zola had tried them all. Then he turned to the Nouvelle Athènes district, where a police report of 1891 noted that "he goes with prostitutes not to have relations with them, but to collect their thoughts and memories, no doubt so he could write about them."

The Hôtel de Lauzun and men of letters

This mansion on the Ile Saint-Louis was built by Louis Le Vau in 1656. In 1842, it was bought by the bibliophile Jérôme Pichon, who decided to rent rooms to writers. Théophile Gautier lived there for a while in 1848, and Baudelaire wrote most of his *Fleurs du Mal* in a room on the fourth story. Later, the Austrian poet Rainer Maria Rilke moved in there while he was working as secretary to the sculptor Rodin.

The Goncourt brothers

The Goncourt brothers wanted to live in a quiet neighborhood, and in 1868 they moved into a house with a garden at No 53 (now 67), Boulevard de Montmorency, in the village of Auteuil. After Jules died in 1870, Edmond was visited every Sunday afternoon by friends such as Zola, Daudet, Maupassant, and Gautier. When he died in 1896, he bequeathed the funds to set up a literary society which would award an annual prize to a writer. The Académie

7. L'Assommoir
"At the Poissonnière barrier, the crowd continued to trudge along in the cold of the morning. You could make out the locksmiths in their blue smocks, the masons in their white overalls, the painters in their thick coats, under which they wore a long smock. From a distance, they had a dusty kind of anonymity, a neutral color marked with patches of faded blue and dirty gray. Every so often, one of these workers stopped to light his pipe, while the others around him, unsmiling, kept on walking." (Emile Zola, *L'Assommoir*)

1

1. Restaurant Drouant
In this restaurant in Place Gaillon, near the old National Library, the members of the Goncourt jury, the most prestigious literary prize, met in November to choose the best work of the year.

2. Hotel at 13, Rue des Beaux-Arts
In this hôtel, formerly the Hôtel d'Alsace, Oscar Wilde died in 1900. Jorge Luis Borges always stayed there on his visits to Paris.

2

Goncourt was founded, its first members including Huysmans and Octave Mirbeau. The Goncourt house was bought by the City of Paris and given back to the Académie Goncourt, which awarded its first prize in 1903.

Marcel Proust

Marcel Proust was born at Auteuil in 1871 and spent his childhood at No 9, Boulevard Malesherbes. As a young man he met Marie Benardski in the gardens of the Champs-Elysées; later he wrote about her as Gilberte Swann. When his parents died, Proust moved to No 102, Boulevard Haussmann. In the last years of his life, the Ritz, which he had been going to for more than 20 years, became a kind of second home for him. "What amuses me are the gatherings that anyone can go to, which are like firework displays. At the Ritz, no one bothers me and I feel at home," he noted. In his suite, which can be visited today, he received Paul Morand, Jean Cocteau, and Madame de Chevigné, one of the models for his Duchesse de Guermantes. The Musée Carnavalet has a reconstruction of one of the author's rooms.

Robert Desnos and the Saint-Merri district

"At the corner of Rues Saint-Martin and de la Verrerie/A feather floated across the pavement/With old papers chased by the wind/A bird sang in the Square des Innocents/Another

5

6

5. Les Tuileries
High society enjoyed walking in the leafy Tuileries, as did the young Marcel Proust in the company of his governess.

6. Colette on her balcony in Palais-Royal
"It's all a show to me here, especially the children. Many of them are charming, and most are extraordinarily agile. The lanky ones run faster than the well-built ones." (*Le Fanal bleu*)

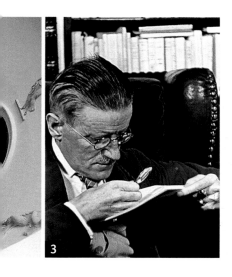

3. James Joyce
By staying in Paris for 20 years, and perhaps had these lines by Mercier in mind: "Paris is the homeland of a literary man, his only home-land." (*Le Tableau de Paris*)

4. Pont de Tolbiac
The gloomy, desolate Pont de Tolbiac has inspired many writers, from Léo Malet and his detective Nestor Burma to Patrick Modiano, who loves the most unlikely settings.

replied from the Tour Saint-Jacques/There was a long cry in Rue Saint-Bon/And a strange darkness crept over Paris." ("*Portes Battantes*")

The poet Robert Desnos spent his early years in Rue Saint-Martin, before moving in 1913 to No 9, Rue de Rivoli. In 1944, shortly before he was arrested, he wrote about the district around the Church of Saint-Merri.

Colette at Palais-Royal

Colette came from Burgundy, and discovered Paris at the age of 20. She then left it only for brief periods. She had an apartment overlooking the gardens of Palais-Royal, at No 9, Rue de Beaujolais, from 1938 until her death in 1954. There she wrote, among other works, *Paris à ma Fenêtre*, which described Paris in the Occupation.

Writers in the streets of Paris

Many authors have written affectionately about Paris, each in his or her own way, including Apollinaire, Aragon, and Léon-Paul Fargue. Apollinaire wrote *Strolling by the River* (1918), and Aragon brought out *Paris Peasant* (1926), which guided readers through the covered arcades and the Grands Boulevards. Fargue, in *The Walker in Paris*, described Belleville and Ménilmontant. Among the thriller writers, Léo Malet sent his detective Nestor Burma into the seedier districts, while Simenon invented Inspector Maigret, a very realistic character who lived in Boulevard Richard-Lenoir and hunted killers in every part of the city.

After World War II, Sartre and Beauvoir preferred sitting in the cafés of Saint-Germain-des-Prés to walking, and were joined by many of the city's intellectuals.

Foreign exiles in Paris

Many writers have come to Paris from elsewhere in Europe and America, and decided to settle there.

Adam Mickievicz and the Polish Romantics

Mickievicz is the most famous Polish poet, and led the Romantic movement in his country. He lived in Paris from 1830 to 1844, and a museum was dedicated to him in 1903 at No 6, Quai d'Orléans in the 4th *arrondissement*. It contains the richest collection about Poland outside the country itself, with books, paintings, maps, and many objects associated with Frédéric Chopin, including his death mask.

From Joyce to Hemingway and Henry Miller

James Joyce left Ireland for Paris in 1920. He stayed for 20 years, winning literary recognition there with *Ulysses* and *Finnegan's Wake*. Hemingway also discovered Paris in the 1920s, at the same time as Scott Fitzgerald and John Dos Passos. While living at No 113, Notre-Dame-des-Champs, he wrote *A Moveable Feast* about Paris. Whenever he received a royalty payment from the United States, he put it to good use in the Ritz Bar. Henry Miller lived with his companion Anaïs Nin at the Villa Seurat, near Parc Montsouris, then moved to Pigalle to write *Quiet Days in Clichy*. All these writers went to Shakespeare & Co, the famous bookshop by the river, opposite Notre-Dame, which is still a favorite with booklovers today.

Writers' Paris today

In *Living is My Business* (1978), Georges Pérec, who died prematurely in 1982, described the secret life of an apartment building in the Plaine Monceau. Daniel Pennac set his police stories' Monsieur Malaussène in Belleville, an area he knows well. Patrick Modiano, a tireless explorer of the streets of Paris, sends his characters off at random on journeys which result in them laying claim to some particular area. His is a ghostly Paris, in which life on the fringes plays an important part: in arcades, warehouses, and the outer boulevards.

7. Sartre and Beauvoir at Saint-Germain-des-Prés
Jean-Paul Sartre and Simone de Beauvoir were so well-known in this Left Bank district that people started calling the Church of Saint-Germain-des-Prés "Sartre Cathedral." Sartre was a regular at the Café de Flore and the Café des Deux Magots, and in autumn 1945 launched his magazine *Les Temps Modernes*. At that time, Saint-Germain-des-Prés was a place where people went to enjoy themselves. At the Tabou and the Club Saint-Germain, Sartre and Beauvoir met Boris Vian, a jazz buff, who often joined the band on trumpet, and Juliette Gréco, the famous singer.

1. Paul Fort at the Closerie des Lilas, 1920
The poet Paul Fort (1872-1960) chose the Closerie des Lilas to meet people such as F Carco, G Apollinaire, and C Vidrac.

2. The Select, 1926
The Select could well call itself the "American Bar" as it was here that the American intelligentsia got together. Among them were Hemingway, the Paris-born Anaïs Nin, and Henry Miller.

ARTISTS' CAFÉS

As long ago as the late 18th century, literary people, painters, and sculptors took to meeting in the warmth of a café. At the Procope, the Encyclopedists held lively discussions. Later, the Impressionists settled in the brasseries of the Batignolles district and in Place Pigalle. Then the artists moved down to Montparnasse and Saint-Germain, where people still talk about them at La Coupole, the Flore, and the Deux-Magots. Today, "cafés philo," where people go for a philosophical debate, are very popular.

5. Le Procope
Le Procope attracted all kinds of people over the centuries, from actors at the Comédie Française to politicians and writers. They included Molière, Racine, Rousseau, and Beaumarchais, who celebrated the first night of his *Marriage of Figaro* there; Danton, who lived nearby, and Marat, who had a printing works in the district, plotted the Revolution there, and were succeeded by romantics such as Sainte-Beuve, Hugo, and Musset.

Le Procope: the city's first café

The oldest café in Paris is Le Procope, opened in 1636 by a Sicilian, Procopio dei Coltelli, in Rue des Fossés-Saint-Germain, now Rue de l'Ancienne-Comédie. In 1689, when the Comédie Française moved there, it became a meeting-place for artists and, soon after, the main center of literary life. In *Le Café ou l'Ecossaise*, Voltaire used the café's décor as the setting for a discussion beween himself, Grimm, d'Alembert, and Marmontel, in which they "agreed on two or three points, and argued about two or three thousand others where they did not see eye to eye." The Procope remained popular for many years, later with Romantic writers such as Musset, Gautier, and Hugo, then Verlaine and Oscar Wilde. Today it is a restaurant.

Montmartre and the Impressionists

The Café Guerbois, at No 9, Avenue de Clichy, has been demolished, but around 1863 it was discovered by Manet. Every Friday before dinner, the painter met his friends in the front room, people such as Renoir, Degas, Sisley, Pissaro, Monet, Emile Zola, and Nadar, the photographer. The back room was for billiards, and opened onto a small courtyard garden. The Batignolles group, who later became the Impressionists, talked about the new theories of painting, including painting in the open air and the use of color. Zola used this café in his writings, but renamed it the Café Baudequin, and the art critic Duranty set it in a novel called *The Double Life of Louis Seguin* under the name Café Barbois, "always full of unusual and interesting people."

La Nouvelle Athènes, Place Pigalle

After the war of 1870, the Nouvelles Athènes on the corner of Place Pigalle and Boulevard Pigalle became a popular meeting place, especially because its terrace on the square could be enclosed in winter. The Impressionists moved over there, having tired of the noise of the billiards players at the Guerbois. Some new people joined their group: Forain and Raffaelli, who painted ordinary people, and Zandomeneghi, who was sympathetic to Impressionism. The old originals still went

6. At the Deux Magots
This café is in the district where the Surrealists gathered. Jean Giraudoux went there to have breakfast, and François Mauriac for his evening apéritif. In the 1960s, New Wave actors filmed there. Here we see Bernadette Laffont, Gérard Blain, Jean-Claude Brialy, and director Claude Chabrol.

3. La Coupole
This old wood and coal warehouse was opened in 1927 by René Lafon. Its clients included Aragon, Colette, and Picasso. It is now a restaurant.

4. Les Deux Magots
Set in the middle of Saint-Germain-des-Prés, its décor has not changed since 1914, when the former antiques store was converted into a café.

there, but, wrote the painter Caillebotte to his friend Pissarro, who had left Paris for a more affordable life in the suburbs, "Degas has upset things for us. It is a pity he has such a poor character. He spends his time holding forth in the Nouvelle Athènes and wherever else he goes."

The golden age of Montparnasse

From the beginning of the 20th century, the artists left Montmartre for the Montparnasse district. The Closerie des Lilas, at the end of Boulevard Montparnasse, was made famous by the poet Paul Fort, who adopted it in 1903 and never left. Every Tuesday, he met his friends Jean Moréas, Jules Laforgue, and Jules Romains. Later, Léautaud and André Gide started going there. Painters and sculptors met there too, including Picasso, Fernand Léger, Jacques Villon,

Brancusi, Albert Gleizes, and Le Fauconnier. Elsa Triolet and the writer Aragon met there. In the 1980s, the writers Philippe Sollers and Jean-Edern Hallier, and the psychoanalyst Jacques Lacan, were also regulars.

Carrefour Vavin

The owner of La Rotonde, a man from the Auvergne called Victor Libion, bought the café in 1911. He liked artists, and soon people from all over Europe were going there. Some had come down from Montmartre, like Picasso, Juan Gris, Modigliani and Georges Braque, and others had recently moved to Paris. They included the sculptor Lipchitz, and the painters André Lhote and Moise Kisling. Among the writers were Jean Giraudoux, Francis Carco, Léon-Paul Fargue, and Apollinaire.

Other cafés in Montparnasse

After World War I, the artists stayed on at La Rotonde, but intruders and hangers-on eventually drove them away to the

Dôme, on the other side of Boulevard Montparnasse. La Coupole, designed by architect Le Boucq, opened in 1927. On opening night, the guests included Kisling, Vlaminck, Foujita, Jean Cocteau, and Blaise Cendrars. The sculptor Calder and the Surrealist Man Ray also adopted it, while some Americans, including Henry Miller and Hemingway, favored Le Select.

Saint-Germain-des-Prés: Café Flore

As Jean-Paul Sartre wrote: "Many people, from Charles Maurras to Apollinaire, from the Surrealists to the Existentialists, were seeking a way to achieve freedom." At the Flore, in 1898, Maurras founded the extreme right-wing movement Action Française, and in 1917, Apollinaire started up the magazine *Les Soirées de Paris* at the café. But it was not just a literary café: the painter Derain, and the sculptors Giacometti and Zadkine were also regular customers.

Café des Deux Magots

Opposite the Church of Saint-Germain-des-Prés, the Deux Magots, founded in 1891, became a favorite resort in the interwar years for writers such as Alfred Jarry, James Joyce, Stefan Zweig, and Robert Musil. Around 1945, Jean-Paul Sartre and Simone de Beauvoir left the Flore, where people came to stare at them, and settled down to work in the Deux Magots.

Across the road, the Brasserie Lipp, which Marcellin Cazes from the Aveyron region bought in 1920, soon became very popular. Colette, André Gide, and Hemingway, who saluted it in his book *A Moveable Feast*, were regulars, soon joined by Max Ernst, Giorgio de Chirico, and Giacometti.

The fashion for "cafés philo"

At the end of the 20th century, teachers and philosophy enthusiasts had the idea of getting a number of people to meet and debate a chosen topic in the field of philosophy. The craze started at the Café des Phares, Place de la Bastille, then caught on all over the capital at, for example, Le Cavalier Bleu, Rue Saint-Martin, Le Relais des Arts, Rue Monge, and Le Sofa, Rue Saint-Sabin.

There are still plenty of literary cafés: Les Marronniers in the 4th *arrondissement*, and La Maroquinerie in the 20th organize readings, poetry evenings, and meetings with authors.

7. Café des Phares
Marc Sautet, a doctor of philosophy, decided to start philiosophical discussions on a wide range of subjects at the Café des Phares, Place de la Bastille. The first "café-philo" was born, and others soon followed.

ARTISTS' HOUSES AND STUDIOS

Paris is the capital of the arts, and many artists have come to live and work there, leaving their mark on the city.
They worked in studios at the Louvre and in mansions in the Nouvelle Athènes district, in wooden huts in
Montmartre and Montparnasse, and in impressive villa–studios dating from the 1920s.
Today, Paris continues its association with the fine arts, providing light–filled studios
for a new generation.

Studios at the Louvre

In 1594, when Henri IV became king, he decided to resume the building work at the Louvre, which had been interrupted in 1572 by the Wars of Religion. While the riverside Galerie du Bord de l'Eau was being built, he ordered the ground floor to be set aside for artists working on Crown assignments. To have lodgings at the Louvre meant both official recognition and guaranteed material security, as the king himself supervised the upkeep of the premises. This tradition was maintained by his successors. In the reign of Louis XIII, one of the most famous artists living there was the painter Simon Vouet.

Distinguished guests

When Louis XIV left the Louvre Palace for Versailles, the Court vacated a large number of rooms, which were immediately occupied. The sculptors Coysevox, Le Hongre, and Girardon moved in, with Girardon taking a studio on the Cour de Reine, where he kept all his collections. Others taking studios included the cabinetmakers Boulle and Oppernordt, painters such as Coypel, goldsmiths, and tapestry-makers. In the 18th century, the sculptor Pajou was at No 9, Rue des Orties-du-Louvre (parallel with the Seine beside the Galerie du Bord de l'Eau); the painter Hubert Robert was at No 10, and Chardin at No 11. Some artists lived at the Louvre with their whole family, for example Fragonard, who stayed there for forty years. Under Napoléon I, David, the official painter, had several rooms in the Colonnade wing: his own studio, the one where his pupils worked, and a third where he painted large-scale works such as *The Rape of the Sabine Women*.

From the Louvre to the Sorbonne

In 1806, Napoléon I decided to make the Louvre a museum in order to exhibit the royal collections and those he had amassed in the course of his campaigns. The hundreds of artists then living there were asked to leave in return for an annual pension. Some found new quarters at the Sorbonne, where the Emperor had some fifty rooms reserved for them. In 1821, however, these premises were sold to the University, which brought the era of official studios to an end.

The 9th *arrondissement*: the painters' and sculptors' district

After 1830, many artists settled in the Nouvelle-Athènes and Saint-Georges area, where a speculative property development was built between Rue Blanche, Rue Saint-Lazare, Rue de la Tour-des-Dames, and Rue de La-Rochefoucauld. Mansions and residential properties with provision for studios became available. The history painter Delaroche moved into No 58, Rue Saint-Lazare. At No 11, Rue de Navarin, Hébert built himself a huge house with a studio on the fifth story. From 1845 to 1857, Delacroix lived at No 54,

1. The Louvre
In the Ancien Régime, the king allowed artists to have studios in the Palais du Louvre.

2. Musée Delacroix
Delacroix's last studio house is now a museum.

3, 4. Studios
In northern Paris, there are still many studios like these in the Rue de Garneron (18th, left) and in Rue Aumont-Thiéville (17th, right).

Rue Notre-Dame-de-Lorette, while Géricault and Chassériau also settled in the area, moving house several times.

From studio to museum

Some of these studio houses have survived destruction and change of use. At the end of a lane near Nouvelle Athènes is the studio house of Ari Scheffer, where the Dutch painter lived from 1830 and held Friday soirées for guests such as Delacroix, Liszt, Chopin, and George Sand. Today, it houses George Sand's collections, among others, and has become the Museum of Romantic Life. Nearby, at No 14, Rue de La-Rochefoucauld, is the mansion of Gustave Moreau, the Symbolist master, which he bequeathed to the State on his death and where he had had enormous studios. Today it is a museum, filled with the artist's paintings and drawings.

From Right Bank to Left

In 1857, the painter Eugène Delacroix, who had been living in Nouvelle Athènes, crossed the Seine to be closer to the Chapelle des Saints-Anges at the Church of Saint-Sulpice, where he was working. He chose the delightful Place de Furstenberg, close to the Church of Saint-Germain-des-Prés. In his journal he noted, "The view of my garden and the cheerful nature of my studio give me constant pleasure." His studio house has been turned into a national museum with the help of the Friends of Delacroix, and holds regular exhibitions.

Rodin and the Hôtel Biron

In 1908, after working in a number of studios, including the Dépôt des Marbres at No 182, Rue de l'Université, and the Folie Neubourg, near the Boulevard d'Italie, Rodin moved into the Hôtel Biron in Rue de Varenne, a fine 18th-century building. There he had the space he needed to carry out his monumental works. However, in 1912, an order threatened him with eviction. He decided to leave all his works and his collections to the State, provided they were exhibited at the Hôtel Biron. In return, he was allowed to stay in the house for rest of his life. Now, in the rooms and

5. Musée G. Moreau
This temple of Symbolism in the 9th is located in the mansion where the artist had his studio. Here many of his paintings and drawings are on show.

6. Maillol in his studio
Maillol was from the Languedoc, but arrived in Paris when he was very young. Dina Vierny, his model and companion, organized the creation of the Musée Maillol at Rue de Grenelle (7th) in a fine mansion.

7. École des Beaux-Arts
The buildings at the École des Beaux-Arts in Rue Bonaparte date from the 17th century to the 19th.

1. Place du Tertre
On the Butte Montmartre, painters sell naive and realist pictures to the thousands of tourists and visitors. They can also do a portrait in just a few minutes.

2. Modigliani at the Dôme
The Dôme in Montparnasse, along with La Coupole and La Rotonde, was a favorite with artists after World War I. Modigliani's studio was nearby in Cité Falguière.

garden of the Hôtel Biron, visitors can trace the artist's career through the bronze and marble works on show.

Where famous sculptors lived

The studio houses of Bourdelle and Zadkine have survived the development fever which seized Montparnasse at the end of the 1960s, and form islands of greenery among the modern apartment buildings. At No 18, Rue Antoine-Bourdelle, the sculptor's monumental works overflow into the garden, filling the porticos and terraces as well as his studio, which has been preserved in its original condition. Bourdelle came to Paris from Montauban, and discovered this place soon after his arrival: "A magnificent house with a very quiet entrance, and a room 16 ft (5 m) by 20 ft (6 m) and 20 ft (6 m) high, with windows 10 ft (3 m) high and 16 ft (5 m) wide." Ossip Zadkine lived at the "Assas Folly," at No 100 *bis*, Rue d'Assas, a more secluded place but full of atmosphere, which has been converted into a museum. In this little house, the Russian sculptor completed most of his life's work between 1928 and 1967, when he died.

Brancusi's studio at the Pompidou Center

The Rumanian sculptor Brancusi arrived in Paris in 1904, and 12 years later moved into No 8, Impasse Ronsin in the 15th *arrondissement*. He stayed there until his death in 1957, surrounded by famous neighbors such as Max Ernst, Niki de Saint-Phalle, and Jean Tinguely. In 1956, he bequeathed all his works to the State, and when the Impasse Ronsin was demolished in the 1970s, his studio was moved and reassembled by the National Museum of Modern Art, in accordance with the artist's wishes. The studio's new home was designed by architect Renzo Piano on the esplanade at Beaubourg, where the artist's extraordinarily refined creations can now be viewed.

5. Chagall at the Beehive
From 1910, the Russian painter lived at the Beehive, Passage Dantzig (15th), next to Soutine, Léger, and Modigliani. They worked in the rotunda which Chagall is here pointing out.

6. Contemporary studio
In 2000, new studio apartments in glass and aluminum were built in the New East, between the Gare de Lyon and Bercy.

7. Avenue Junot
The poet Tristan Tzara built his house at No 15, Avenue Junot (18th); more artists' studios followed at Nos 22, 24, and 26.

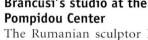

3. Musée Zadkine
In *The Mallet and the Chisel*, Zadkine wrote: "Dr Merlin, who I often saw at the Café de la Rotonde, told me there was a house for rent at No 100, Rue d'Assas ... It was marvelous: a garden and a house to live in and a large studio for work."

4. La Cité Fleurie
The 30 half-timbered houses of the Cité Fleurie still stand on Boulevard Arago. Rodin, Maillol, and Gauguin all lived there.

Wooden studios in Boulevard Arago

At No 65, Boulevard Arago, near the Santé prison, two wooden buildings stand in a garden planted with acacias and wistaria. They are divided into 29 studio apartments, built using materials from the Universal Exhibition of 1878. Many famous artists lived there, including Gauguin, Modigliani, the painter Jean-Paul Laurens, and the sculptors Rodin and Maillol, who shared an apartment with a foundry. In 1934, a library was set up at No 18 to provide access to German works banned by the Nazis.

The Cité almost disappeared in 1971, then was classified in 1976. Today, painters, engravers, and sculptors still have studios there.

A new life for the Bateau Lavoir

The legendary Bateau Lavoir stands on a hill in Montmartre, which at the dawn of the 20th century was one of the leading places for art and artists. The wooden building was originally designed as a craft workshop, then in 1889 was divided into ten studios, each one double the normal room height and with north-facing windows. The rents were very low, but so was the level of comfort: there was no water, no gas or electricity. Among the painters who lived there were Van Dongen, Modigliani, Juan Gris, and Picasso, who painted his *Demoiselles d'Avignon* there.

In 1970, the Bateau Lavoir was destroyed in a fire. It was rebuilt three years later by the City of Paris and continues to house studios, even though concrete has replaced the original wood.

Still going: the Beehive

In Passage de Dantzig, near the Parc Georges-Brassens, the Beehive still hums with activity. This former wine pavilion from the Universal Exhibition of 1900 was rebuilt there in 1902 by Alfred Boucher, the official sculptor, to provide studios for young artists. Its name comes from its honeycomb design. It was cheap, and soon attracted artists such as Zadkine, Soutine, Fernand Léger, Laurens, Archipenko, and Brancusi. The ground floor is for sculptors, and the second story for painters.

Space and light: studios in the interwar years

In the interwar years of the 20th century, a good number of studio-villas were built on spare, unadorned lines and with much emphasis on light. Many of them were in the lanes around the Parc Montsouris, in the 14th *arrondissement*. At No 53, Avenue Reille is the studio house built by Le Corbusier in 1923; at No 50, Avenue René-Coty is the tall studio designed by J-J Lemordant, which dates from 1929. At Nos 3, 5, and 7, Rue Gaugnet are three studios where well-known artists such as Nicolas de Staël and Hans Hartung lived. Not far away is the Villa Seurat, which was occupied by Soutine and Dali. In the 1930s, the École des Beaux-Arts built a huge building at No 1, Rue Jacques-Callot in the 6th *arrondissement*. Windows run the full length of the five-story façade, bringing light to the whole of the interior.

Contemporary studios

Today, Paris still welcomes artists, even though the number of studios being built is less than before. The Cité Internationale des Arts at No 18, Rue de l'Hôtel-de-Ville, on the edge of the Marais, is the result of a combined scheme developed by the State, the City of Paris, and foreign organizations. It was built in 1965, and contains 270 studio apartments, two-thirds of which are for painters, sculptors, photographers, and engravers from abroad. In the Citroën development complex, 38 studios were built in 1995 by architect Michel Kagan.

1. Théâtre Français
The Théâtre Français (now the Comédie Française) was built in 1786-90 by Victor Louis and has been restored several times, particularly after a fire in 1900 and in 1973-4 when it was suffering from wear and tear.

2. Théâtre de la Ville
Located on Place du Châtelet, this is the old Théâtre Lyrique. It was built in 1862 by Davioud and taken over by Sarah Bernhardt in 1898.

THEATERS, CONCERT HALLS, AND CINEMAS

Paris is the city of pleasure, with more places of entertainment on offer than ever before. More than 200 theaters and café-theaters, huge concert halls, art and experimental cinemas and brand-new multiplexes offer a wonderfully varied choice of places to go.

Theaters

The real-tennis courts: the first theaters

In the Middle Ages, the fore-courts of churches such as Notre-Dame Cathedral were used to stage mystery plays. Later, real-tennis courts were also used for theatrical performances. The Hôtel de Bourgogne in Rue Mauconseil, built in 1548 in the Les Halles district, became the capital's principal theater in the 17th century. Others followed, such as the Hôtel Guénégaud. At ground level, the spectators stood in what we now call the stalls, and at the back was the amphitheater or "circus," with seating on benches. In 1641, Richelieu built a private theater, the Palais Cardinal (later the Palais-Royal). In 1671, Louis XIV followed his example in the Tuileries with the Salle des Machines, where the Comédiens Français played; this troupe was directed by the playwright Molière.

The Age of Enlightenment

In the 18th century, the theaters left the palaces and real-tennis courts for completely separate buildings, which became a forum for the new ideas of the age. The Théâtre Français (later the Odéon) was one such. Designed by Peyre and de Wailly from 1767 and ressembling a Greek temple with columns and pediments, and steps up to the entrance, it was built on a huge square. Next to the Palais-Royal, Victor Louis built another Théâtre Français (later the Comédie Française) between 1786 and 1790. This has been restored several times over the years.

Italian-style auditoriums

The so-called Italian-style auditorium first appeared in the 18th century. Most were semicircular in shape, with several levels (dress circle, balcony, and gallery) partly divided into boxes. People could use their boxes as they pleased. The enormous center light was always kept on, the audience wishing to be seen as well as watch the play. As in apartment buildings, the higher up the spectators went, the further down the social scale they were. Astutely placed staircases ensured that the different social classes did not have to mix. The stage was now separated from the auditorium and all the audience had seats.

The "Boulevard of Crime"

In 1764, the Boulevard du Temple, in eastern Paris, was lined with trees. Here Nicolet built the first canvas booth, amusing passers-by with a repertoire of acrobats, puppet shows, and performing animals. In 1791, a decree gave "every citizen the right to build a theater and put on plays of every kind." Many theaters were built over the next century: the Funambules, the Folies-Dramatiques, the Théâtre Historique, owned by A Dumas, and the Cirque Olympique. However, in 1862 orders were given to demolish the "Boulevard of Crime" (so called because of the melodramas performed there). One of its buildings escaped destruc-

5. *The Theater in the 18th century* (wash drawing by Claude Gillot)
Seen here are famous characters from the *commedia dell'arte*, which was introduced to European theaters at the beginning of the 17th century.

6. Théâtre des Variétés
In his novel *Nana*, Zola described this theater's large auditorium where "tall jets of gas lit the great crystal chandelier with a blaze of pink and yellow flames."

7. Théâtre de la Huchette
This theater has presented two plays by Ionesco (*The Bald Prima Donna* and *The Lesson*), since 1957.

3. Théâtre des Champs-Elysées
This theater was built in concrete in 1911-13 by the Perret brothers. On its façade are reliefs by the sculptor Bourdelle.

4. The TEP
The TEP (Théâtre de l'Est Parisien) was founded by Guy Rétoré in 1963, and is a prime example of a theater located outside the city center in a working-class district. It was replaced by the Théâtre National de la Colline.

tion: the Théâtre Libertaire de Paris, which is still active.

Boulevard theaters on the Right Bank

In the 19th century, most of the theaters were in the central area of the Right Bank. Many are still there today, including the Gymnase, Palais-Royal, Porte Saint-Martin, Théâtre Antoine, the Athénée, Bouffes-Parisiens, and the Théâtre Marigny. The Théâtre des Variétés, in Boulevard Montmartre, built in 1807, has kept its name and its façade.

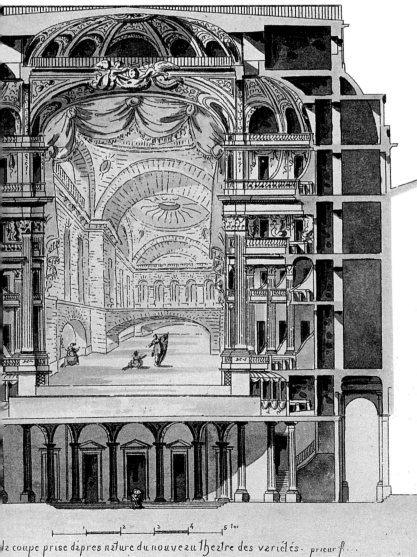

la coupe prise d'après nature du nouveau Theatre des variétés. prieur f...

Its most brilliant period was in the 1860s, with Offenbach. Zola described it in his novel *Nana*. The Théâtre de la Ville was built in 1862. Sarah Bernhardt hired it and made it her theater from 1898 to 1922. On the Left Bank, the only area to offer theatrical entertainment is the Rue de la Gaîté, which is lined with cafés, cabarets, and theaters, including the Gaîté Montparnasse and the Théâtre Montparnasse.

Simplified architecture of the 20th century

Around the Champs-Elysées, new theaters appeared at the beginning of the 20th century: the Théâtre des Mathurins (1900); the Théâtre des Champs-Elysées with its simplified lines, designed by the Perret brothers in 1913; the Théâtre de la Madeleine in Rue de Suresnes, which opened in 1924 and was closely associated with Sacha Guitry until after World War II. Further south, in the new Palais de Chaillot, the Niermans brothers designed a huge auditorium in 1937 with vestibules, galleries, and foyers surfaced with marble and polished stone. There, after World War II, Jean Vilar led the adventurous Théâtre National Populaire.

Fringe theaters

At the Cartoucherie de Vincennes (the old ammunition works in the 12th *arrondissement*), Ariane Mnouchkine started a new kind of theater in 1968, in which the actors and audience all take part in the same story. The Bouffes du Nord (10th) has been preserved as it was in 1876; in 1974, the British director Peter Brook and his company took over the theater. The Carré Sylvia Montfort (15th) was a canvas marquee before it was replaced by a building in the shape of a metal pyramid. From 1985 to 1988, the architects Fabre and Perrottet built the Théâtre National de la Colline in the east of the city with a glass façade, a 770-seater circular auditorium, and a small theater for more experimental works.

Café-theaters

In the 1960s, café-theaters began to appear. The pioneers included the Royal in Montparnasse, the Vieille Grille in the Latin Quarter, and the Fanal in Les Halles. The Café de la Gare, which has featured entertainers such as Coluche, Lhermitte, Josianne Balasko, Michel Blanc, Miou-Miou, and Gérard Jugnot under the leadership of Romain Bouteille, is now in the old Auberge de l'Aigle d'Or, Rue du Temple, which Apollinaire was particularly fond of.

Concert halls

The Théâtre de Châtelet, in Place du Châtelet, has seating

1. Salle Pleyel
The Salle Pleyel concert hall was built by Marcel Aubertin in 1924 in Rue du Faubourg-Saint-Honoré after extensive acoustic trials by the physicist Gustave Lyon.

2. The Rex
The Rex on Boulevard Poissonnière was conceived by producer Jacques Haïk. It has an Art Deco façade and was modeled on luxurious American movie houses.

3. Paramount Opéra
The Paramount Opéra opened in 1951, and is one of five cinema complexes on the Boulevard des Italiens.

4. Gaumont Grand Écran
This cinema in Place de l'Italie has three projection rooms; the largest has 652 seats.

5. UGC Ciné-Cité Bercy
As part of the regeneration of eastern Paris, the 12th *arrondissement* now boasts a new complex with 18 theaters.

for 2,003 people. It was built in 1862 by Gabriel Davioud. Its repertoire covers 20th-century music, operas, and concerts designed around one composer. The Salle Gaveau, Rue de la Boétie (8th), was built in 1907 and was listed as a historic monument in 1992. The Théâtre des Champs-Elysées puts on operas, recitals, chamber music, and dance. The Salle Pleyel, one of the most famous classical concert halls in the city, in Rue du Faubourg-Saint-Honoré (8th), was founded in 1927. The Cité de la Musique in La Villette, designed by Christian de Portzamparc in 1995, has a modular concert hall.

The Salle Favart (1890) and the Opéra-Bastille (1984-9) present music and opera. The Opéra-Garnier, a showpiece from the Second Empire, is today devoted to dance.

The variety theaters include the Olympia, Boulevard des Capucines, which opened in 1893 and has kept its original façade, though it has been moved a few yards, but the Bobino in Rue de la Gaîeté has been completely demolished. The Zénith, the Palais Omnisports de Bercy, and the Palais des Congrès are much larger and are now the main venues for popular concerts.

Cinemas

The first movie houses

The first cinema show, by the Lumière brothers, took place in Paris at the Salon Indien of the Grand Café, near the Opéra, in 1895. The earliest films were shown in café-concerts, and later were featured on variety bills. Then, in the 1920s, the first movie houses appeared. Before World War II, Paris had about 200 cinemas, which increased to 400 in 1950.

Legendary cinemas of the interwar years

The Max Linder cinema in Boulevard Poissonnière was opened by the famous comedy actor after World War I, but in more recent times was threatened with closure. It was completely renovated and equipped with an excellent sound system, and since 1987 has shown an original repertoire of films. The Grand Rex, also in Boulevard Poissonnière, was designed by the Americans A Bluysen and J Eberson in the style of lavish US movie houses, and opened in 1932; it was listed as a historic monument in 1981. The première of *Cleopatra* was held there, and there too R Benzi conducted his first symphony orchestra at the age of eight. The walls of the vast 21,500 sq ft (2,000 sq m) auditorium were decorated like a Spanish-Moorish city by M Dufresne, and illuminated by special projectors. The screen is 60 ft (18 m) wide and 30 ft (8.5 m) high. During the Christmas season, there are fountains on display.

Art and experimental cinemas

In 1928, Studio 28 in Rue Tholozé (18th) was one of the first avant-garde cinemas in Paris. It was located in a late 19th-century theater and, in 1930, gave the first showing of Buñuel's highly controversial *L'Age d'Or*. The lighting in the auditorium was designed by Jean Cocteau.

In Rue de Babylone in the 7th is La Pagode, a Chinese-style pavilion with a ceramic façade. It was built in 1896 by A Marcel. Recently restored, it reopened in 2000. The Mac-Mahon (17th), where director François Truffaut discovered his passion for American films, is where the great American classics are shown.

Avant-garde cinemas reached their peak in the 1960s. In the Latin Quarter, small cinemas suddenly blossomed in the Rue Champollion, Rue de la Harpe, Rue Saint-Séverin, Rue de l'Ecole-de-Médecine, and Rue Cujas (Le Champo, Studio des Ursulines, Action Christine, and Action Ecoles). They are still there today, showing recent and classic films in their original languages.

6. At the Winter Circus
All kinds of shows appear at the Cirque d'Hiver, designed by Hittorff in 1852: musical comedies, concerts, avant-garde theater, and puppet shows.

7. Gala night at the Opéra-Garnier
An evening dress affair at the Opéra-Garnier in the days when people went there to see world-famous singers – before this role was taken over by the Opéra-Bastille.

The first multiplexes

In 1967, a new concept was born when, in Rue Monsieur-le-Prince, the Trois Luxembourg cinema opened. This was the first multiplex in Paris, with three cinemas on three different levels, each showing a different program of films. The concept quickly spread. In 1968, the Marignan-Concorde, in the Champs-Elysées, built two cinemas, one with 500 seats, the other with 1,200. Each chair had an ashtray, as smoking was then still allowed in theaters. Everything was designed for the audience's comfort: there was a vast foyer with posters and photographs, a bar, comfortable chairs, and plenty of legroom. Soon, three other cinemas opened in the Champs-Elysées: the Terminal Foch, the Publicis Matignon, and the Gaumont Champs-Elysées. The Normandie was converted on similar lines.

Multiscreen cinemas were also built in shopping centers: in the Forum des Halles, in Montparnasse, and Beaugrenelle (15th); there was the Ciné-Havre in the 9th, and the Paramount Maillot in the 17th.

Cinema in Paris today

In 2001, Paris had 373 screens in 94 cinemas. While some of the avant-garde cinemas only just survive, the multiplexes are continually growing, for example the Gaumont Parnasse (14th) and the UGC Ciné-Cité Bercy (12th) which have 12 and 18 screens respectively, along with bars, fast-food outlets, and play areas.

The distribution of cinemas has also changed. Those in the smart districts have gone. Eastern Paris had the highest number of cinemas in the 1950s, but now has hardly any, despite initiatives such as the MK2 in Quai de Seine (19th), where the adjoining café and restaurant have brought new life to the district.

Special cinemas and 3-D movies

In 1936, the movie buff Henri Langlois founded the Cinémathèque Française, which still shows movies organized around a theme. The Pompidou Center regularly shows art movies or rare films from around the world. The Forum des Images in the Forum des Halles has an archive of films about Paris. The Géode, at the Cité de la Villette, has an 11,000 sq ft (1,000 sq m) semi-circular screen, and is a favorite with 3-D movie fans.

8. Le Champo
François Truffaut was particularly fond of Le Champo, which opened in 1938 and in the 1960s became one of the Latin Quarter's best-known avant-garde cinemas.

9. Studio 28
In Rue Tholozé in Montmartre, Studio 28 opened in 1928 with Abel Gance's *Napoléon*. In 1930, Buñuel's *L'Age d'Or* shocked many who saw it, and the film was banned until 1981.

In the front hall is a quotation by Jean Cocteau: "This cinema for masterpieces, a masterpiece among cinemas."

PARIS BY NIGHT

*Venice had its canals, and London its dark alleyways, but Paris had Haussmann and gaslight.
Its broad, brightly lit avenues stimulated a great passion for night life in the Second Empire. Paris, already the
cultural capital of Europe, now led the field in nighttime entertainments. The concept of "Paris by Night"
was born. In recent years, modern technology has added further sparkle to the City of Light.*

Wild dance halls

The joyful period of the Belle Epoque was already being felt in the popular and fashionable dance halls in the first half of the 19th century. Théophile Gautier spoke of "wild dance halls" when describing the exploits of his contemporaries in popular places such as the Bal Bullier in Montparnasse and the Bal de l'Opéra, where men and women let themselves go and danced polkas, mazurkas, quadrilles, and romping gallopades.

The mad frenzy of the cancan

A new and strange dance appeared and became popular: the cancan. Maupassant described it in *La Femme de Paul*: "Women with splayed thighs shrouded by skirts, leapt about and revealed their underwear. They swung their legs above their heads with surprising ease, swayed their bellies, waggled their backsides, and shook their breasts, while from them spread a powerful smell of female sweat. The men crouched like toads and urged them on with obscene gestures ..."

Cabarets and cafés-concerts

Later, when Maupassant's civil servant took his wife to the theater three times each winter, Zola's worker took his girlfriend or wife every Saturday to one of the noisy dance halls which were opening all over the city. At the cabaret, or café-concert, wine and absinth led to a bout of wild dancing, and helped him to forget his troubles, his financial problems, his kids, and the rigors of daily life.

At the Moulin Rouge

The end of the century was the heyday of the big dance halls like the Moulin Rouge, at the foot of the Butte Montmartre, whose the most successful attraction was the "naturalist quadrille," the future French cancan.

The world of Montmartre symbolized the whole era, and was immortalized by Toulouse-Lautrec who painted the star performers: dancers like La Goulue, Nini Pattes-en-l'air, La Môme Fromage, and Jane Avril, and other performers from the Moulin Rouge such as Valentin the Rubber Man.

During the Belle Epoque, the golden age of the dance hall reached its height with the "wild" dance halls of the suburbs, the "Apache" dancers, and the Auvergne dance halls lit by oil lamps, and also the more fashionable dance halls where diamonds glittered beneath the ceiling lights.

The jazz revolution

The reputation of Paris as a city of pleasure did not slacken after World War I. "Negro music" was spreading from America, and soon conquered the hearts and legs of a young generation anxious to forget the trenches and have a good time. The Moulin Rouge had by now become a music hall, and here Mistinguett and Maurice Chevalier led the dance under the slogan "Life is not for worrying." Josephine Baker waggled her belt hung with bananas and launched the Charleston.

At the popular venues, people danced to the accordeon in *bals musette* in Montparnasse, the Latin Quarter, and at the Bastille, where, at the Balajo, the fashion was for sambas, rumbas, the java, and, above all, the tango with its suggestive poses and fiery Latin passion.

1. The Moulin Rouge
La Goulue, Jane Avril, and Valentin the Rubber Man have gone, but the sails of the Moulin Rouge, the first great music hall, still turn at the foot of the Butte Montmartre.

2. The Lido
The Lido, with its lights, sequins, and feathers, is faithful to its old formula, but its revues are still a great attraction for foreign visitors to the city.

3. The Cigale
In Boulevard Roche-chouart, the Cigale is one of the top places in Paris for rock concerts and jazz.

**4. *La Clownesse*
(Toulouse lautrec)**
In this blend of Japanese print and Impressionist painting, the female clown Cha-U-Kao is captured fixing her costume.

5. The Queen
This popular gay night club in Champs-Elysées is a disco, open from midnight until dawn. Each night of the week, the style of music changes.

Existentialist nights

After World War II, there was an abrupt change of style. In Saint-Germain-des-Prés, a cellar 50 ft (15 m) by 25 ft (8 m) was the magnet for young people. At the Tabou, they danced – and philosophized too. The "troglodytes of Saint-Germain-des-Prés" brought life to the district, which once more became the meeting place for intellectuals. The most successful cellars were the Vieux Colombier, where Claude Luter on trumpet played New Orleans blues, the Club Saint-Germain, and the Caveau de la Huchette, where they danced bebop, while on the Right Bank there was Sidney Bechet's Slow Club. It was the age of swing, bebop, slow blues, and jive, followed by cha-cha and the twist.

Paris by night in 2000

The major revues like the Lido, the Crazy Horse, the Moulin Rouge, and the Folies Bergère contin-ued to prosper around Pigalle and the Champs-Elysées, but the pleasures of Paris night life are to be found elsewhere.

The Champs-Elysées area is today popular with Americans who love the local galleries, cafés, and the chic and flashy boutiques. They go to the Chesterfield Café to take in its blues and country music, and to the Buddha Bar and the Barfly which play easy-listening music. The pubs, especially the Irish ones, have been very fashionable for 20 years. There is Kitty O'Shea near the Opéra, and Corcoran's and The Quiet Man in Les Halles.

Bars have taken over from the cafés of the Grands Boulevards. They are often cosy, small places, and currently those in the Bastille are the most popular. Their names (Barrio Latino, Havanita Café, and Boca Chica) show the attraction of Latin America, and Cuba in particular, with its rum and salsa. People dance to tropical music at the Java, the Corail, and the Chapelle des Lombards, and at the Étoiles near the Gare de l'Est. Another "must try" is the nightclub scene at, for example, Les Bains, the Queen, the Gibus, the Rex Club, the Folies Pigalle, the Privilège, the Casbah, and the Locomotive.

The *ginguettes*, or open-air dance halls, are also coming back in an updated form. Some are on barges, like the Guingette Pirate, near the new National Library, which plays a mixture of old and new sounds. Nearby, the Batofar is for techno-lovers. Square Tino-Rossi is open to anyone who wants to dance.

6. The Tabou in 1950
After World War II, night life moved to the Left Bank. Juliette Greco and Boris Vian were the stars of the cellars of Saint-Germain-des-Prés, especially the Tabou.

7. The Bal Mabille
The wild "cancan" started at the Bal Mabille around the middle of the 19th century. This later developed into the French cancan which was all the rage in the Belle Epoque.

8. The Barrio Latino
The latest fashion in nightlife is a warm atmosphere, tapas and tequila, all of which they can supply at the Barrio Latino in the Bastille.

INDEX

Page numbers in **bold** refer to main entries, those in *italics* to captions.

Index

Index

Index

356

Photo credits

Key: r = right; l = left; t = top; b = bottom; c = center; tr = top right; tl = top left; br = bottom right; bl = bottom left; cr = center right; cl = center left

10 1 Photothèque des musées de la Ville de Paris – **10, 11** 2 Archives Larbor – **11** 3 Droits Réservés – **12** 1 Archives Larbor – **12** 2 Archives Larbor – **13** 3 Archives Larbor – **14** 1 Archives Larbor – **14, 15** 2 Photothèque des musées de la Ville de Paris – **15** 3 Archives Larbor – **16** 1 Giraudon – **16, 17** 2 Photothèque des musées de la Ville de Paris – **17** 3 Giraudon – **18** 1 Archives Larbor – **18** 2 RMN – **18** 3 Archives Larbor/BDIC – **19** 4 Archipress – **22** 1 Mazin Rosine – 2 F. Eustache/Archipress – 3 Mazin Rosine – 4 Mazin Rosine – **22, 23** Air Images/Ph. Guignard – **22, 23** b Mazin Rosine – **23** 1 L. Bœgly/Archipress – **24, 25** Air Images/Ph. Guignard – **26** l 1 Mazin Rosine – 2 K. Poulsen/Rapho – **26, 27** 3 Mazin Rosine – **27** r 2 Mazin Rosine – l 1 Roger Viollet – **28** 2 Mazin Rosine – 3 Mazin Rosine – **28, 29** 3 Belzeau/Rapho – **29** 2 Archives Larbor – **30** 1 Mazin Rosine – 2 Mazin Rosine – **30, 31** 3 C. Rive/Côté Vues – **31** 2 Mazin Rosine – 3 F. Eustache/Archipress – **32** 1 Mazin Rosine – 2 Roger Viollet – **32, 33** 3 D. Staquet/Côté Vues – **33** 2 Texier Simon – 4 Texier Simon – 5 W. Louvet/Côté Vues – **34** 1 Archives Larbor – 2 F. Eustache/Archipress – 3 Archives Larbor – **35** 1 Mazin Rosine – 2 D. Taulin-Hommel/Scope – **36** 1 and 2 F. Eustache/Archipress – 4 Mazin Rosine – **36, 37** 3 Mazin Rosine – **37** 3 RMN – 5 C. Goupi/Côté Vues – **38** 1 M. Guillard/Scope – 2 C. Goupi/Côté Vues – 3 De Visme/Sipa Press – **39** 4 Mazin Rosine – 5 M. Guillard/Scope – 6 Mazin Rosine – **40** 1 Ch. Gesquière/Scope – 2 C. Goupi/Côté Vues – 3 Archipress – **41** 4 C. Goupil/Côté Vues – 5 O. Martin/Archipress – **42, 43** Air Image/Ph. Guignard – **42** br Mazin Rosine – b l F. Eustache/Archipress – tr F. Eustache/Archipress – t l F. Eustache/Archipress – **44** 1 and 2 Mazin Rosine – bl Archives Larbor – **45** 3 Archives Larbor – 4 J. C. Martel/Archipress – **46** 1 and 2 F. Eustache/Archipress – 3 N. Hautemanière/Scope – **47** 4 Galeron/Scope – tr 5 Keystone – **48** 1 and 3 F. Eustache/Archipress – 2 S. Matthews/Scope – **49** 4 F. Eustache/Archipress – 5 F. Eustache/Archipress – **50** 1 Archives Larbor – 3 Mazin Rosine – **50, 51** 2 Mazin Rosine – **51** 4 M. Hauber/Archipress – 5 Mazin Rosine – **52** 1 Jausserand Pascale – 2 N. Hautemanière/Scope – 3 Mazin Rosine – **53** 4 Jausserand Pascale – 5 Mazin Rosine – 6 Mazin Rosine – **54** 1 Roger Viollet – 2 F. Eustache/Archipress – **55** 3 F. Eustache/Archipress – 4 F. Eustache/Archipress – 5 F. De Visme/Sipa Press – **56, 57** Air Images/Ph. Guignard – **56** bl Archipress/L. Bœgly – t Mazin Rosine – c Mazin Rosine – cl RMN © ADAGP 2001 – **58** 1 Sipa Press – 2 Mazin Rosine – **58, 59** 3 F. Eustache/Archipress – 4 Mazin Rosine – **58** c B. Rieger/Archipress – **59** 5 Archipress – **60** 1 RMN – 2 RMN © Picasso Administration 2001 – **60, 61** 3 RMN © Succession H. Matisse 2001 – **61** 4 RMN © ADAGP 2001 – 5 RMN © ADAGP 2001 – 6 RMN © ADAGP 2001 – **62** 1 RMN © ADAGP 2001 – 2 RMN © ADAGP 2001 – **63** 3 M. Denance/Archipress – 4 RMN © ADAGP 2001 – 5 M. Denance/Archipress – **64** 1 Keystone – **64, 65** 2 C. Bowman/Scope – 3 L. Bœgly/Archipress – **65** 4 F. Eustache/Archipress – 5 Mazin Rosine – **66** 1 L. Bœgly/Archipress – 2 Giraudon – 3 L. Bœgly/Archipress – **66, 67** 4 F. Eustache/Archipress – 5 Giraudon – **67** 6 Texier Simon – **68** 1 and 2 D. Beck/Côté Vues – **68, 69** 3 Mazin Rosine – 4 F. Eustache/Archipress – **69** 5 L. Bœgly/Archipress – **70** 1 F. Eustache/Archipress – 2 F. Eustache/Archipress – 3 Mazin Rosine – **71** 4 Archipress – 5 Archipress – 6 L. Bœgly/Archipress – **72** t Mazin Rosine – cl RMN – **73, 74** Air Images/Ph. Guignard – **73** bl Mazin Rosine – c Mazin Rosine – **74** 1 Sipa Press – 2 Mazin Rosine – **74, 75** 3 Mazin Rosine – **75** 4 Mazin Rosine – **76** 1 Mazin Rosine – 2 RMN – 3 Mazin Rosine – tl A. Altwein/DPA/AFP – **77** 4 Mazin Rosine – 5 Texier Simon – **78** 1 RMN – 2 RMN – 3 RMN – **78, 79** 4 RMN – 5 RMN – **80** 1 Archives Larbor – 2 RMN – **80, 81** 3 RMN – **81** 4 RMN – 5 RMN – **82** 1 RMN – 2 RMN – 4 RMN – 3 RMN – **83** 5 RMN – 6 RMN – **84** 1 P. Antoine/Côté Vues – 2 P. Antoine/Côté Vues – 3 F. Eustache/Archipress – **85** 4 Mazin Rosine – 5 Keystone – **85** 6 A. Goustard/Archipress – **86** 1 Roger Viollet – 2 Mazin Rosine – 3 Jourdain/Archipress – **86, 87** 4 P. Antoine/Côté Vues – 5 Mazin Rosine – **87** 6 Archives Larbor – **88** 1 Mazin Rosine – 2 Mazin Rosine – 3 Mazin Rosine © ADAGP 2001 – **89** 4 L. Bœgly/Archipress – 5 Mazin Rosine – **90** 1 Mazin Rosine – 2 Archives Larbor – 3 P. Lemaotre/Archipress – **90, 91** 4 Mazin Rosine – **91** 5 Pitamitz/Sipa Press – **92, 93** Air Images/Ph. Guignard – **92** r Mazin Rosine – l RMN – t Mazin Rosine – **94** 1 Mazin Rosine – 2 S. Rasmussen/Côté Vues – 3 Mazin Rosine – **94, 95** 4 Delagarde/Moatti/Sipa – **95** 5 F. Eustache/Archipress – **96** 1 Bernand – **96, 97** A. Goustard/Archipress – **96** tl Archives Larbor – **97** 3 Roger Viollet – 4 Mazin Rosine – 5 RMN – **98** 1 F. X. Bouchart/Archipress – 2 Archives Larbor – **98, 99** 3 RMN © ADAGP 2001 – 4 P. Antoine/Côté Vues – **99** 5 F. Eustache/Archipress – **100** 1 Keystone – 2 Afp – **100, 101** 3 F. Eustache/Archipress – **101** 4 L. Bœgly/Archipress – 5 J.C. Martel/Archipress – **102** 1 Mazin Rosine – 2 AFP – 3 Dœrr Jean-Christophe – **103** 4 Mazin Rosine – 5 Mazin Rosine – 6 D. Beck/Côté Vues – **104** 1 Mazin Rosine – 2 L. Bœgly/Archipress – 3 J. Guillard/Scope – 4 J. Maurice/Archipress – **104, 105** 5 A. Boulat/Sipa Press – **105** 6 AFP – **106, 107** Air Images/Ph. Guignard – **106** br F. Eustache/Archipress – bl Texier Simon – tr J. Grenier/Scope – tl L. Bœgly/archipress – c R. César/Archipress – **108** 1 Mazin Rosine – 2 RMN – **109** 3 B. Rajau/Côté Vues – 4 Roger Viollet – **110** 1 Roger Viollet – 2 RMN – **110, 111** 3 L. Bœgly/Archipress – **110** tl RMN – **111** 4 Haley/Sipa Press – 5 B. Rajau/Côté Vues – **112** 1 F. Eustache/Archipress – 2 AFP – **112, 113** 3 Texier Simon – 4 Mazin Rosine – **113** 5 F. Eustache/Archipress – 6 Mazin Rosine – **114** 1 Roger Viollet – 2 J. Grenier/Scope – 3 F. Eustache/Archipress – **115** 4 F. Eustache/Archipress – 5 RMN – **116** 1 Mazin Rosine – 2 Photothèque des musées de la Ville de Paris © ADAGP 2001 – **117** 3 Texier Simon – 4 Archives Larbor – **118** 1 F. Eustache/Archipress – 2 R. César/Archipress – **118, 119** 3 De Visme/Sipa Press – **119** 4 Roger Viollet – 5 RMN – 6 F. Eustache/Archipress – **120** 1 F. Eustache/Archipress – 2 L'illustration/Keystone – 3 F. Eustache/Archipress – **121** 4 F. Eustache/Archipress – 5 RMN – **122** 1 RMN – 2 Archives Larbor – 3 RMN © ADAGP 2001 – **123** 4 RMN – 5 RMN – **124, 125** Air Images/Ph. Guignard – **124** bl Mazin Rosine – r Mazin Rosine – t L. Bœgly/Archipress – cl Mazin Rosine – **126** 1 Chenot/Sipa Press – 2 Mazin Rosine – **126, 127** 3 Mazin Rosine – **127** 4 L. Bœgly/Archipress – **128** 1 A. Boulat/Sipa Press – 2 Mazin Rosine – 3 Sipa Press – **129** 4 J. Witt/Sipa Press – 5 F. Eustache/Archipress – **130** 1 Sipa Press – 2 Mazin Rosine – **130, 131** 3 F. Eustache/Archipress – **131** 4 F. Eustache/Archipress – 5 Manez and Favret/Archipress – **132** 1 H. Hughes/Côté Vues – 2 Mazin Rosine – **132, 133** 3 A. Lorgnier/Côté Vues – **133** 4 Mazin Rosine – 5 G. Fessy/Archipress – **134** 1 L. Bœgly/Archipress – 2 Archives Larbor – **134, 135** Roger Viollet – **135** 4 L. Bœgly/Archipress – 5 J. Guillard/Scope – 6 Mazin Rosine – **136, 137** Air Images/Ph. Guignard – **136** br Alfred/Sipa Press – bl Ginies/Sipa Press – t Mazin Rosine – **138** 1 Mazin Rosine – 2 Ginies/Sipa Press – **138, 139** 3 E. Maurice/Pix – **140** 1 Mazin Rosine – **140, 141** 2 Roger Viollet – **140** tl Roger Viollet – **141** 3 Keystone – 4 Dœrr Jean-Christophe – **142** 1 Ginies/Sipa Press – 2 Keystone – **143** 3 Mazin Rosine – 4 J. M. Delage/Sipa Press – **144** 1 J. M. Delage/Sipa Press – 2 Dupont/Sipa Press – **145** 3 Archives Larbor – 4 Archives Larbor – **146** 1 Mazin Rosine – 2 F. Eustache/Archipress – 3 Ganeron/Scope – **147** 4 L. Bœgly/Archipress – 5 Texier Simon – **148** 1 Mazin Rosine – 2 Mazin Rosine – **149** 3 F. Eustache/Archipress – 4 Mazin Rosine – **150** 1 F. Eustache/Archipress – 2 F. Eustache/Archipress – **151** 3 Keystone – 4 Texier Simon – 5 O. Martin Gambier/Archipress – **152, 153** Air Images/Ph. Guignard – **152** b Mazin Rosine – t Mazin Rosine – tr F. Eustache/Archipress – cr Mazin Rosine – cl N. Hautemanière/Scope – **154** 1 Mazin Rosine – **154, 155** 2 Mazin Rosine – **155** 3 Texier Simon – 4 Alfred/Sipa Press – **156** 1 Archives Larbor – 2 Archives Larbor – tl Archives Larbor – **157** 3 Keystone – 4 Photothèque des musées de la Ville de Paris – **158** 1 M. Denance/Archipress – 2 F. Eustache/Archipress – 3 F. Eustache/Archipress – **159** 4 Mazin Rosine – 5 Dœrr Jean-Christophe – **160** 1 Keystone – 2 L. Bœgly/Archipress – **160, 161** 3 N. Hautemanière/Scope – **161** 4 Mazin Rosine – **162** 1 Mazin Rosine – **162, 163** 2 Keystone – 163 3 F. Eustache/Archipress – **163** 4 R. César/Archipress – 5 N. Hautemanière/Scope – **164** 1 O. Martin Gambier/Archipress – 2 M. Denance/Archipress – **165** 3 M. Denance/Archipress – 4 Mazin Rosine – **166** 1 Keystone – **166, 167** 3 Mazin Rosine – 2 Texier Simon – **167** 4 Afp – 5 F. Eustache/Archipress – **168** 1 Mazin Rosine – 2 Mazin Rosine – **168, 169** 3 M. Denance/Archipress – **169** 4 Archives Larbor – 5 S. Bersout/Archipress – **170, 171** Air Images/Ph. Guignard – **170** bl Mazin Rosine – r Mazin Rosine – t A. Legrain/Photothèque de l'établissement public du Parc et de la Grande Halle de la Villette – tl Texier Simon – cl L. Bœgly/Archipress – **172** 1 Mazin Rosine – 2 Keystone – 3 Mazin Rosine – **172, 173** 4 Mazin Rosine – 5 Texier Simon – **174** 1 De Visme/Sipa Press – 2 Dœrr Jean-Christophe – 3 F. Eustache/Archipress – **174, 175** 4 F. X. Bouchart/Archipress – **175** 5 S. Rasmussen/Côté Vues – **176** 1 Archipress – 2 A. Venturi/Côté Vues – **176, 177** 3 Texier Simon – **177** 4 F. Eustache/Archipress – 5 Archipress – 6 Mazin Rosine – **178** 1 L. Bœgly/Archipress – 2 L. Bœgly/Archipress – 3 Jausserand Pascale – **179** 4 Jausserand Pascale – 5 Dœrr Jean-Christophe – **180** 1 Mazin Rosine – 2 Mazin Rosine – **180, 181** 3 Schwartz/Sipa Press – **181** 4 Mazin Rosine – 5 Archives Larbor – 6 Mazin Rosine – **182** 1 Mazin Rosine – **182, 183** 2 L. Goustard/Archipress – **182, 183** 3 F. Eustache/Archipress – **183** 4 Jausserand Pascale – 5 Jausserand Pascale – 6 Jausserand Pascale – **184, 185** Air Images/Ph. Guignard – **184** b C. Goupi/Côté Vues – t F. Eustache/Archipress/2001 Johan Otto Von Spreckelsen – **186** 1 L. Bœgly/Archipress – 2 F. Eustache/Archipress © Johann Otto Von Spreckelsen 2001 – **186, 187** 3 Alfred/Sipa Press – **187** S. Rasmussen/Sipa Press – **188** 1 Roger Viollet – 2 C. Goupi/Côté Vues – **188, 189** 3 L. Bœgly/Archipress – **189** 4 C. Goupi/Côté Vues – 5 F. Eustache/Archipress © ADAGP 2001 – 6 F. Eustache/Archipress – **190, 191** Air Images/Ph. Guignard – **190** b Mazin Rosine – t Mazin Rosine – **192** 1 Mazin Rosine – 2 Mazin Rosine – **192, 193** 3 Mazin Rosine – **193** 4 Mazin Rosine – **194** 1 RMN – **194, 195** 2 Mazin Rosine – **194** t Archives Larbor – **195** 3 Mazin Rosine – 4 Mazin Rosine – **196** 1 Mazin Rosine – 2 P. Lemaitre/Archipress – **196, 197** 3 Mazin Rosine – **197** 4 RMN – 5 Mazin Rosine – **198** 1 Mazin Rosine – **198, 199** 2 F. X. Bouchart/Archipress – **199** 3 Mazin Rosine – 4 Archives Larbor – 5 P. Lemaitre/Archipress – 6 AFP – **200** Air Images/Ph. Guignard – **201** Gardin Nanon – **241** Air Images/Ph. Guignard – **248** Archives Larbor – 1 N. Hautemanière/Scope – 2 Pitomitz/Sipa Press – 3 De Visme/Sipa Press – 4 Mazin Rosine – **248, 249** Archives Larbor – **249** 1 Mazin Rosine – 2 Mazin Rosine – 3 V. Prado/Côté Vues – **250** F. Eustache/Archipress – **250, 251** Roger Viollet – **252** 1 Chamussy/Sipa Press – 2 Ginies/Sipa Press – 4 F. Eustache/Archipress – **253** 3 Christophe L. – 5 Kharbine/Tapabor – 6 Burlet/Sipa Press – 7 J. C. Martel/Archipress – **254** 1 Mazin Rosine – 2 Mazin Rosine – 5 Mazin Rosine – **255** 3 De Visme/Sipa Press – 4 Mazin Rosine – 6 Photothèque des musées de la Ville de Paris – **256** 1 Mazin Rosine – 2 J. C. Martel/Archipress – 4 F. Eustache/Archipress – 5 Archives Larbor – **257** 3 Mazin Rosine – 6 F. Eustache/Archipress – 7 F. Eustache/Archipress – **258** 1 J. C. Martel/Archipress – 2 Texier Simon – 4 F. Eustache/Archipress – **259** 3 Texier Simon – 5 M. Denance/Archipress – 6 Ph. Guignard/Images Diffusion – **260** 1 A. Goustard/Archipress – 2 Archipress – 4 N. Hautemanière/Scope – **261** 3 Mazin Rosine – 5 M. Denance/Archipress – 6 S. Couturier/Archipress – **262** 1 N. Hautemanière/Scope – 2 Pitamitz/Sipa Press – 5 Bibliothèque Forney – 6 Roger Viollet – **263** 3 J. C. Martel/Archipress – 4 Archipress – **264** 1 F. Eustache/Archipress – 2 F. Eustache/Archipress – 6 Giniès/Sipa Press – **265** 3 F. Eustache/Archipress – 4 Mazin Rosine – 5 Mazin Rosine – 7 S. Bersout/Archipress – **266** 1 Mazin Rosine – 2 Mazin Rosine – 3 Mazin Rosine – 5 Mazin Rosine – **267** 4 Mazin Rosine – 6 Bibliothèque Forney – 7 Mazin Rosine – **268** 1 C. Goupil/Côté Vues – 2 Mazin Rosine – 4 Roger Viollet – **269** 3 Mazin Rosine – 5 De Visme/Sipa Press – **270** 1 N. Hautemanière/Scope – 2 L. Maisant/Côté Vues – 3 Galeron/Scope – 4 C. Mazières/Côté Vues – 6 Archives Larbor – **271** 5 Mazin Rosine – 7 Archives Larbor – **272** 1 RMN – 2 Mazin Rosine – 5 F. Eustache/Archipress – **273** 3 F. Eustache/Archipress – 4 L. Maisant/Côté Vues – 6 Archives Larbor – **274** 1 F. Eustache/Archipress – 2 B. Galeron/Scope – 4 Mazin Rosine – **275** 3 Air Images/Ph. Guignard – 5 Air Images/Ph. Guignard – 6 F. Eustache/Archipress – **276** 1 Mazin Rosine – 2 C. Goupil/Côté Vues – 3 Mazin Rosine – 5 RMN – 6 Bibliothèque Forney – **277** 4 F. Eustache/Archipress – 7 Mazin Rosine – 8 F. Eustache/Archipress – **278** 1 Mazin Rosine – 2 Mazin Rosine – 3 Mazin Rosine – 6 Mazin Rosine – **279** 4 J. C. Martel/Archipress – 5 Mazin Rosine – 7 Centre des Monuments Nationaux – **280** 1 Mazin Rosine – 2 Dœrr Jean-Christophe – 6 F. Eustache/Archipress – 7 R. César/Archipress – **281** 3 Mazin Rosine – 4 Mazin Rosine – 5 F. Eustache/Archipress – 7 S. Camboulive/Archipress – **282** 1 L. Leguyader/Côté Vues – 2 F. Eustache/Archipress – 3 F. Eustache/Archipress – 5 Jausserand Pascale – **283** 4 S. Bersout/Archipress – 6 L. Bœgly/Archipress – 7 O. Martin Gambier/Archipress – **284** 1 M. Hauber/Archipress – 2 Mazin Rosine – 5 Viallefont-Haas Myriam – 6 RMN – **285** 3 Texier Simon – 4 RMN – 7 Viallefont-Haas Myriam – **286** 1 Roger Viollet – 2 S. Bersout/Archipress – 5 Viallefont-Haas Myriam – **287** 3 Mazin Rosine – 4 Mazin Rosine – 6 Viallefont-Haas Myriam – 7 Mazin Rosine – **288** 1 Marguerite/Ratp – 2 Roger Viollet – 3 Barinet/Ratp – 7 Ratp – 8 Roger Viollet – **289** 4 Mazin Rosine – 5 Mazin Rosine – 6 Mazin Rosine – 7 Minoli/Ratp – **290** 1 Texier Simon – 2 Dumax/Ratp – 6 Texier Simon – **291** 3 A. M. Collet/Ratp – 4 B. Chabrol/Ratp – 5 J. F. Mauboussin/Ratp – 7 J. F. Mauboussin/Ratp – **292** 1 F. Eustache/Archipress – 2 F. Eustache/Archipress – 5 RMN – **293** 3 AFP – 4 Texier Simon – 6 M. Denance/Archipress – 7 F. Eustache/Archipress – **294** 1 Mazin Rosine – 2 C. Mazières/Côté Vues – 5 A. Goustard/AFP – 6 Roger Viollet – **295** 3 O. Martin/Archipress – 4 Texier Simon – 7 Rue des Archives – **296** 1 Mazin Rosine – 2 Texier Simon – 5 Mazin Rosine – **297** 3 Mazin Rosine – 4 Mazin Rosine – 6 Spikermeier/Sipa Press – **298** 2 Mazin Rosine – 3 F. Eustache/Archipress – **299** 3 Mazin Rosine – 4 F. Eustache/Archipress – 5 M. Hauber/Archipress – 6 P. Schwarz/Sipa Press – **300** 1 J. Guillard/Scope – 2 Dœrr Jean-Christophe – 5 Mazin Rosine – 6 L. Bœgly/Archipress – **301** 3 F. Bouchart/Archipress – 4 Mazin Rosine – 7 Air Images/Ph. Guignard – **302** 1 N. Hautemanière/Scope – 2 Mazin Rosine – 5 Air Images/Ph. Guignard – **302** 6 Centre des Monuments Nationaux – **303** 3 Mazin Rosine – 4 Mazin Rosine – 7 Spikermeier/Sipa Press – **304** 1 Photothèque des musées de la Ville de Paris – 2 Mazin Rosine – **304, 305** 3 Mazin Rosine – **305** 3 Mazin Rosine – 4 Mazin Rosine – **306** 1 Mazin Rosine – 2 Mazin Rosine – 4 Mazin Rosine – **306, 307** 5 Mazin Rosine – **307** 5 Mazin Rosine – 6 Mazin Rosine – **308** V. Prado/Côté Vues – **308, 309** Roger Viollet – **310** 1 Mazin Rosine – 2 Mazin Rosine – 5 Archives Larbor – **311** 3 Mazin Rosine – 4 Mazin Rosine – 6 Mazin Rosine – 7 Archives Larbor – **312** 1 Mazin Rosine – 2 Mazin Rosine – 6 Archives Larbor – **313** 4 Mazin Rosine – 5 Mazin Rosine – 7 Roger Viollet – tl 3 Mazin Rosine – **314** 1 Mazin Rosine – 2 Mazin Rosine – 5 Archives Larbor – 6 De Visme/Sipa Press – **315** 3 Mazin Rosine – 4 Mazin Rosine – 7 AFP – **316** 1 Zinhioglu/Sipa Press – 2 Sipa Press – 3 M. Haubert/Archipress – 6 Archives Larbor – **317** 4 Service Général des Carrières de Paris – 5 Compagnie Générale des Eaux – 7 Archives Larbor – **318** 1 N. Hautemanière/Scope – 2 M. Denance/Archipress – 6 Archives Larbor – **319** 3 Mazin Rosine – 4 J. C. Martel/Archipress – 5 N. Hautemanière/Scope – 7 F. Eustache/Archipress – 8 Archives Larbor – **320** 1 N. Hautemanière/Scope – 2 Jausserand Pascale – 3 Mazin Rosine – 6 Dœrr Jean-Christophe – 7 Centre des Monuments Nationaux – **321** 4 N. Hautemanière/Scope – 5 V. Prado/Côté Vues – 8 Mazin Rosine – **322** 1 Mazin Rosine – 2 Jausserand Pascale – 5 J. Grenier/Scope – **323** 3 Mazin Rosine – 4 C. Goupi/Côté Vues – 6 Jausserand Pascale – 7 S. Bersout/Archipress – **324** 1 Coret/Sipa Press – 2 Pelletier Florence – **325** 3 Mazin Rosine – 4 J. M. Delage/Sipa Press – 6 Mazin Rosine – 7 Mazin Rosine – **326** 1 Sipa Press – 2 B. Simmons/Sipa Press – 5 Droits Réservés – **327** 3 A. Sel/Sipa Press – 4 A. Sel/Sipa Press – 6 G. Botti/Stills – 7 Barthelemy/Sipa Press – **328** 1 Chanel – 2 Pitanitz/Sipa Press – 3 Boucheron – 6 Van Cleef and Arpels – **329** 4 Boisière/Sipa Press – 5 L. Vuitton – 7 Roger Viollet – 8 Afp – **330** 1 N. Hautemanière/Scope – 2 V. Prado/Côté Vues – 3 Sipa Press – 5 N. Hautemanière/Scope – 6 Roger Viollet – **331** 4 J. Grenier/Scope – 7 V. Prado/Côté Vues – **332** 1 J. Grenier/Scope – 2 Pelletier Florence – 3 P. Gould/Scope – 5 Bouchart/Archipress – **333** 4 Gardin Nanon – 6 M. Gambier/Archipress – 7 Jausserand Pascale – **334** 1 RMN – 2 J. C. Gesquière/Scope – 5 Archives Larbor – 6 Archives Larbor – **335** 3 Photothèque des musées de la Ville de Paris – 4 Roger Viollet – 7 Archives Larbor – **336** 1 AFP – 2 V. Prado/Côté Vues – 5 Roger Viollet – 6 Dazy Renè – **337** 3 Freund Gisèle/Archives Larbor – 4 F. Eustache/Archipress – 7 Rue des Archives – **338** 1 Roger Viollet – 2 Roger Viollet – 5 BNF/Archives Larbor – 6 Roger Viollet – **339** 3 Mazin Rosine – 4 I. Eshragi/Scope – 7 Mazin Rosine – **340** 1 Mazin Rosine – 2 Arnaudet/RMN – 5 RMN – **341** 3, 4 Mazin Rosine – 6 Brassai Gilberte/Archives Larbor – 7 F. Eustache/Archipress – **342** 1 Mazin Rosine – 2 Roger Viollet – 3 Photothèque des musées de la Ville de Paris – 6 Mazin Rosine – **343** 3 D. Martin Gambier/Archipress – 4 Mazin Rosine – 7 F. Eustache/Archipress – **344** 1 S. Bersout/Archipress – 2 Mazin Rosine – 5 RMN – **345** 3 Mazin Rosine – 4 Dœrr Jean-Christophe – 6 Giraudon – 7 J. C. Gesquière/Scope – **346** 1 Bernand – 2 Nebinger/Sipa Press – 6 Niko/Sipa Press – **347** 3 Nebinger/Sipa Press – 4 Nebinger/Sipa Press – 5 Meigneux/Sipa Press – 7 Sipa Press – 8 Pelletier Florence – 9 Pelletier Florence – **348** 1 Gayet/Sipa Press – 2 Lido de Paris – 6 Rue des Archives – **349** 3 Texier Simon – 4 RMN – 5 Le Carpentier/Sipa Press – 7 Archives Larbor – 8 J. Maurice/Archipress.

Photogravure Art Nord, Aire-sur-la-Lys – Impression Grafica Editoriale Printing, Bologne.
Dépôt légal : septembre 2001 – Imprimé en Italie – 585012/01
10081864(I) 7(CSBTS 150) 585012 septembre 2001